Alberto Giacometti: Toward the Ultimate Figure

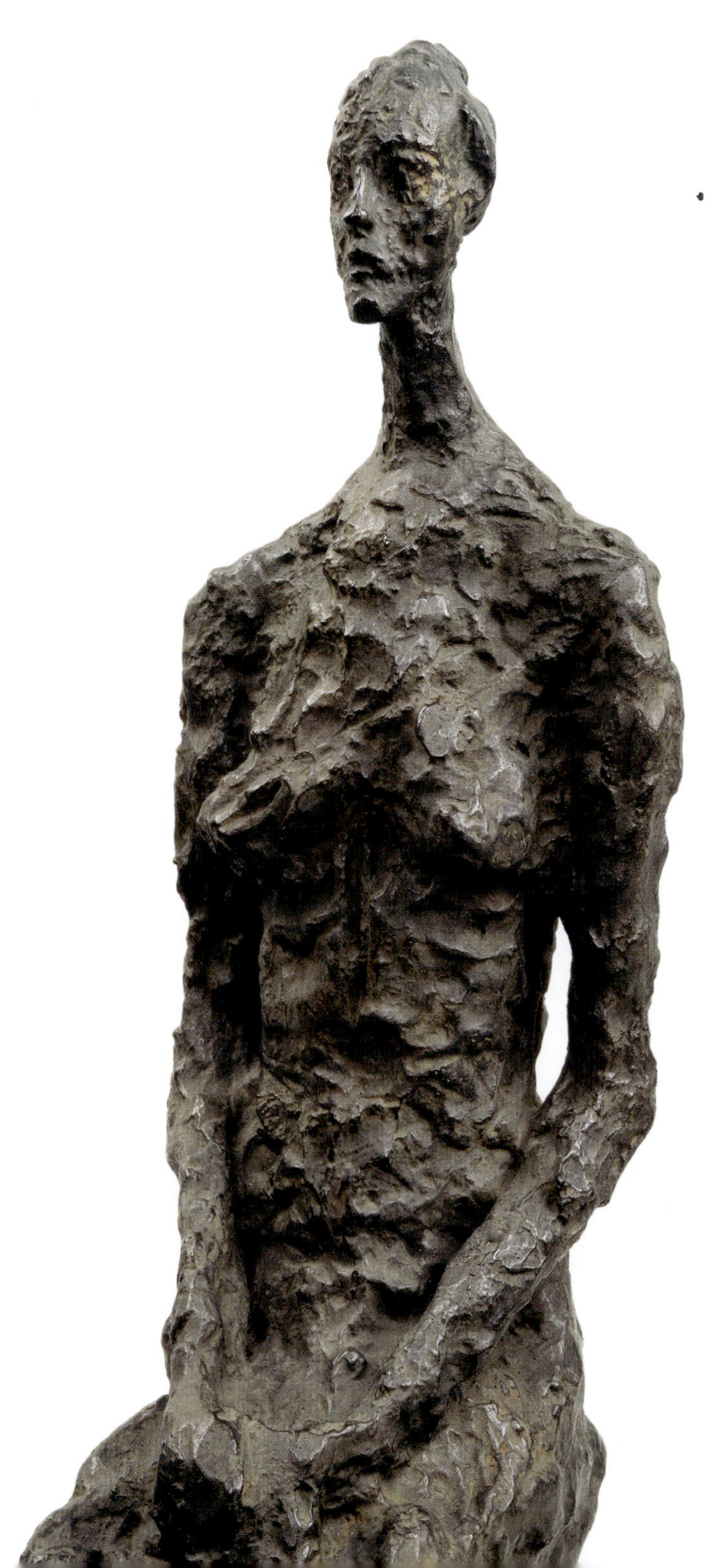

ALBERTO GIACOMETTI

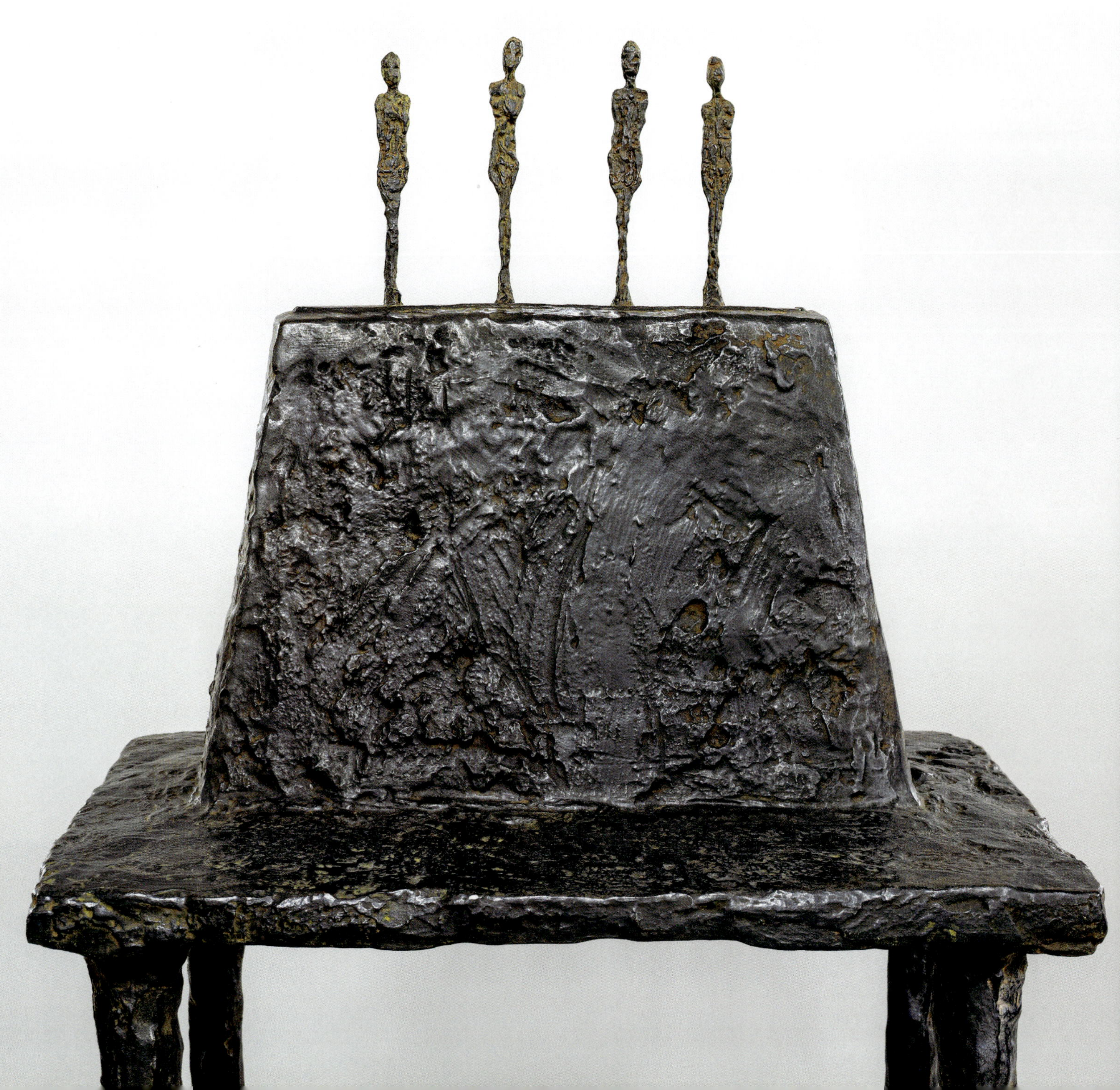

TOWARD THE ULTIMATE FIGURE

Edited by

Émilie Bouvard

Essays by

Serena Bucalo-Mussely

Hugo Daniel

Ann Dumas

Catherine Grenier

Catharina Manchanda

Romain Perrin

William H. Robinson

William Keyse Rudolph

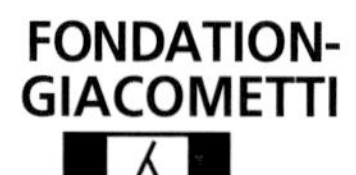

THE CLEVELAND MUSEUM OF ART

DISTRIBUTED BY YALE UNIVERSITY PRESS, NEW HAVEN AND LONDON

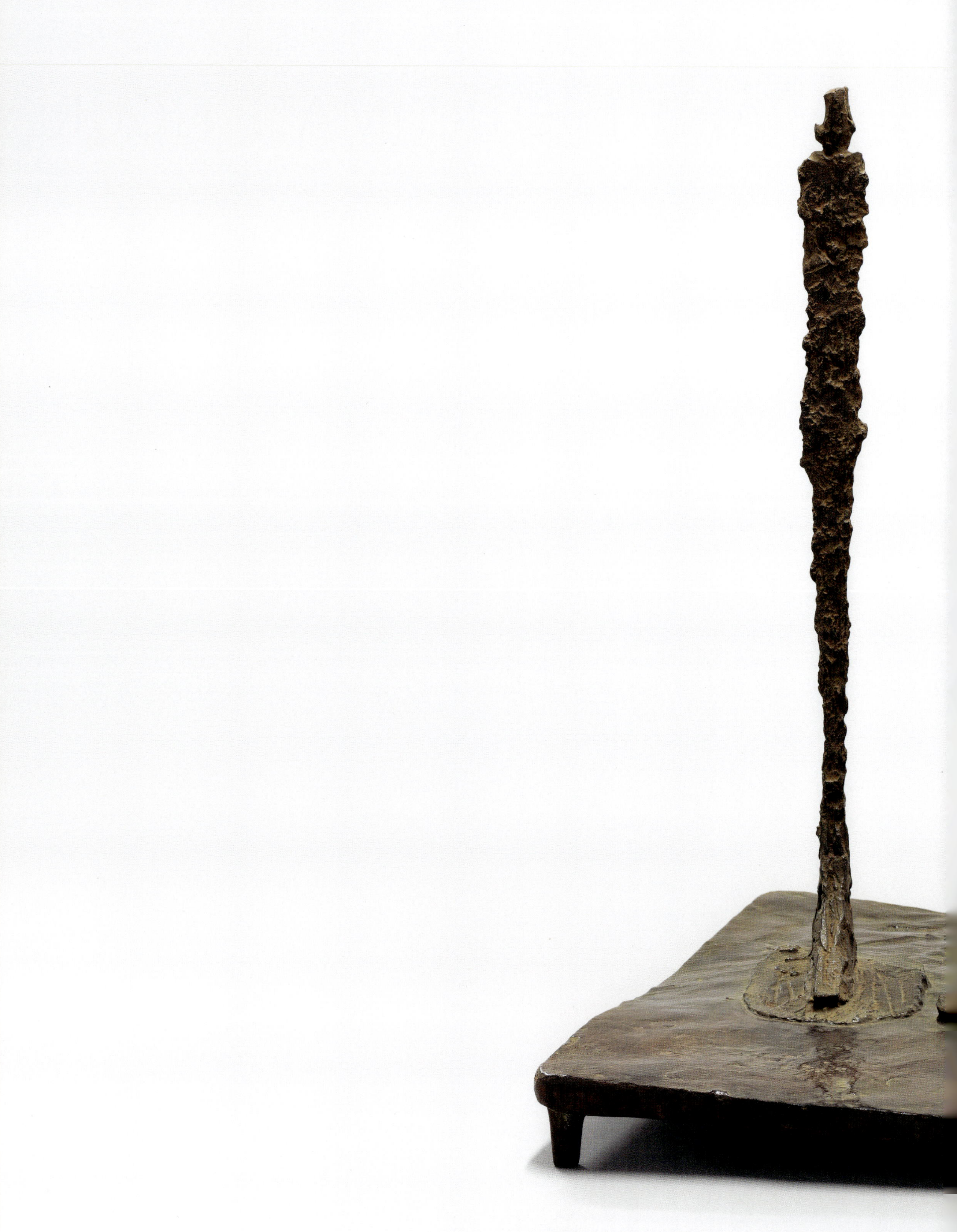

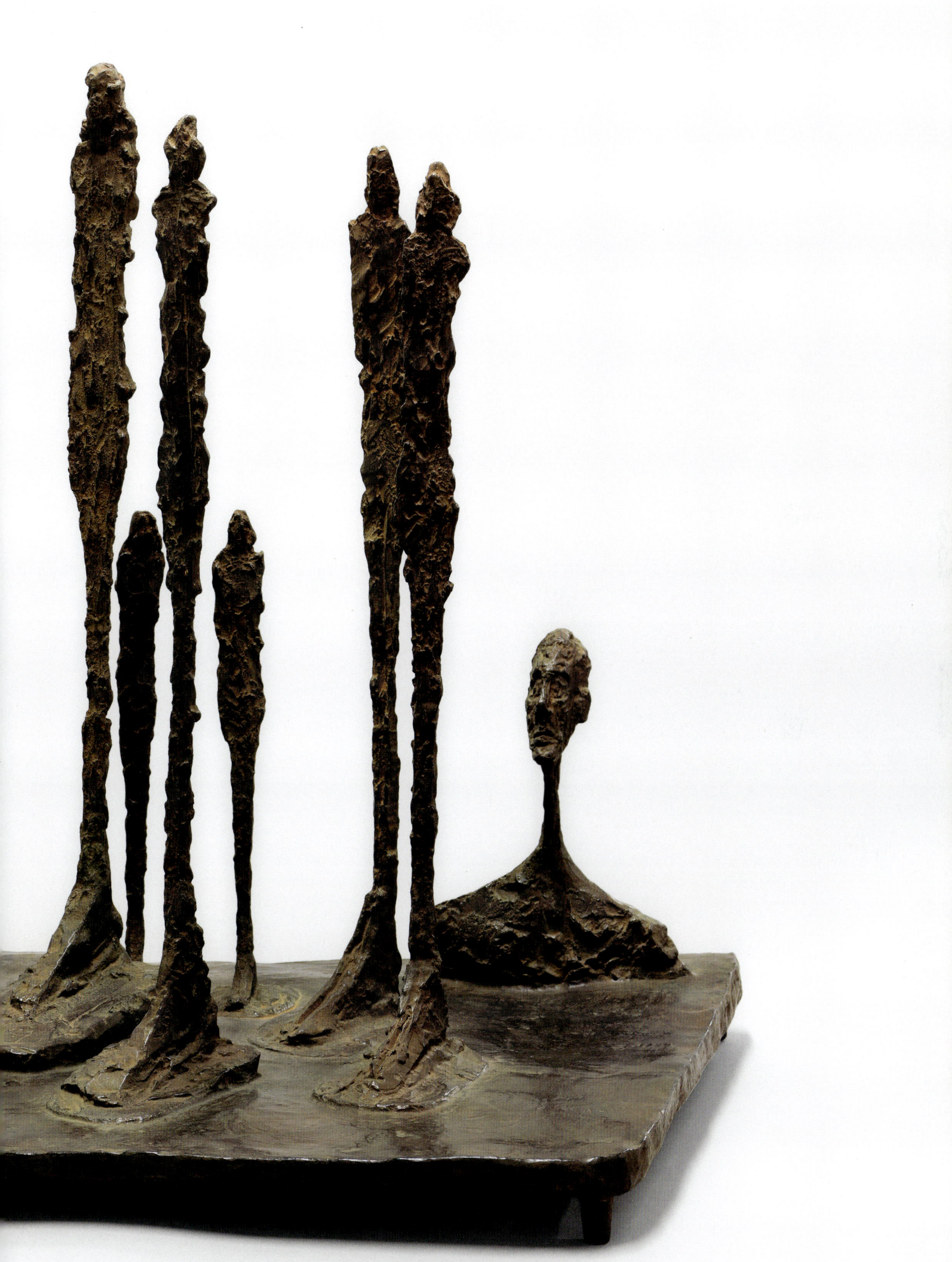

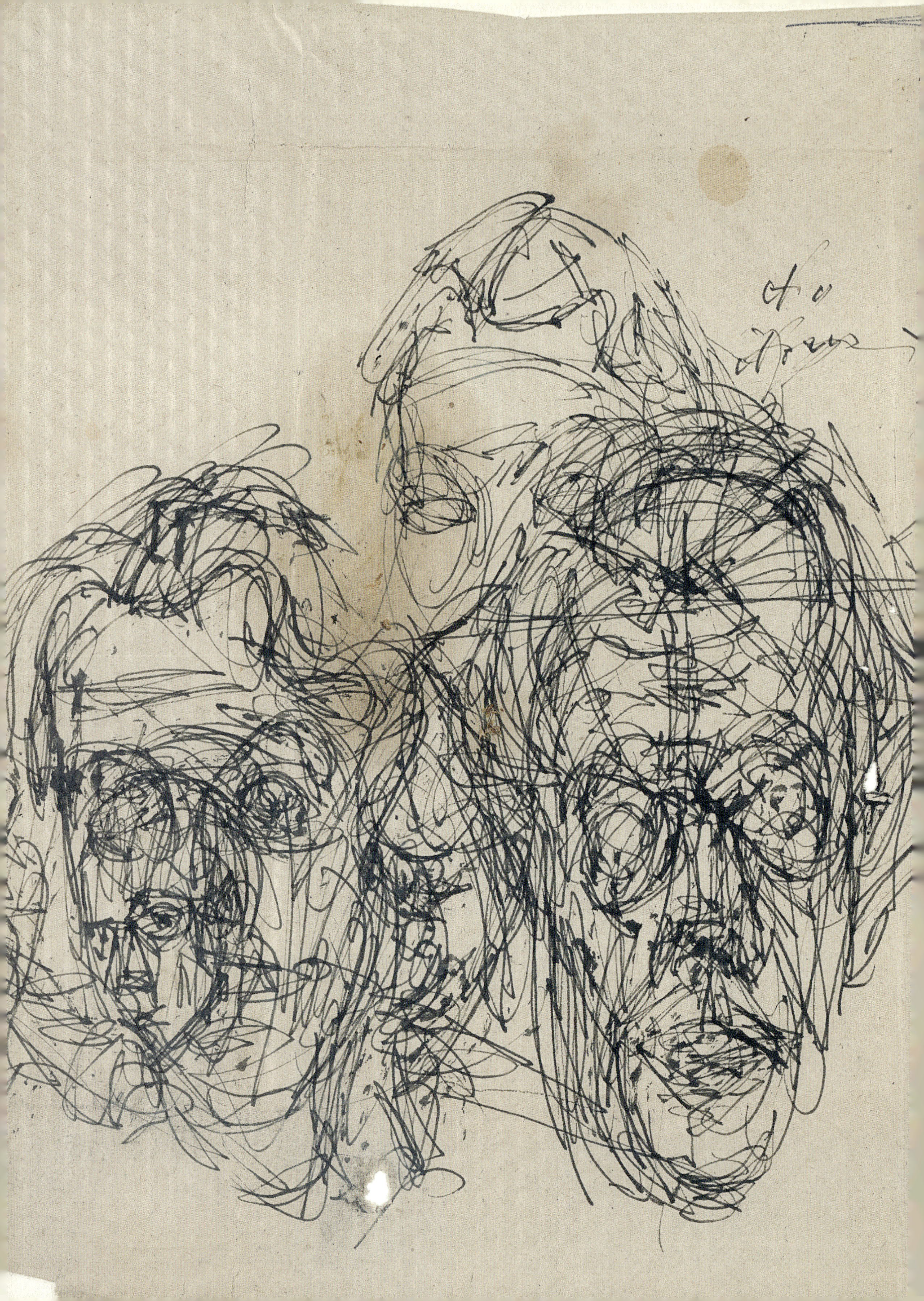

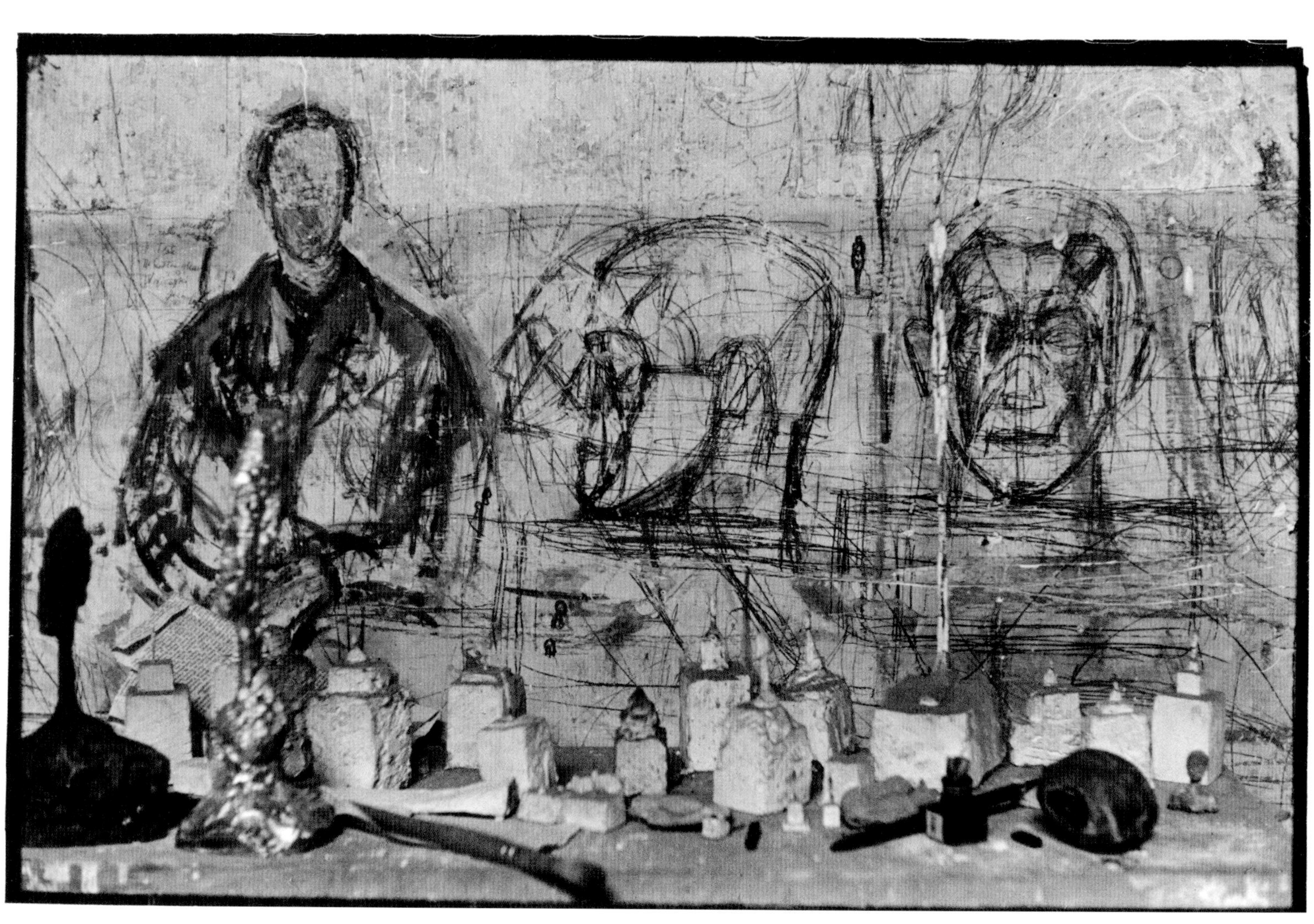

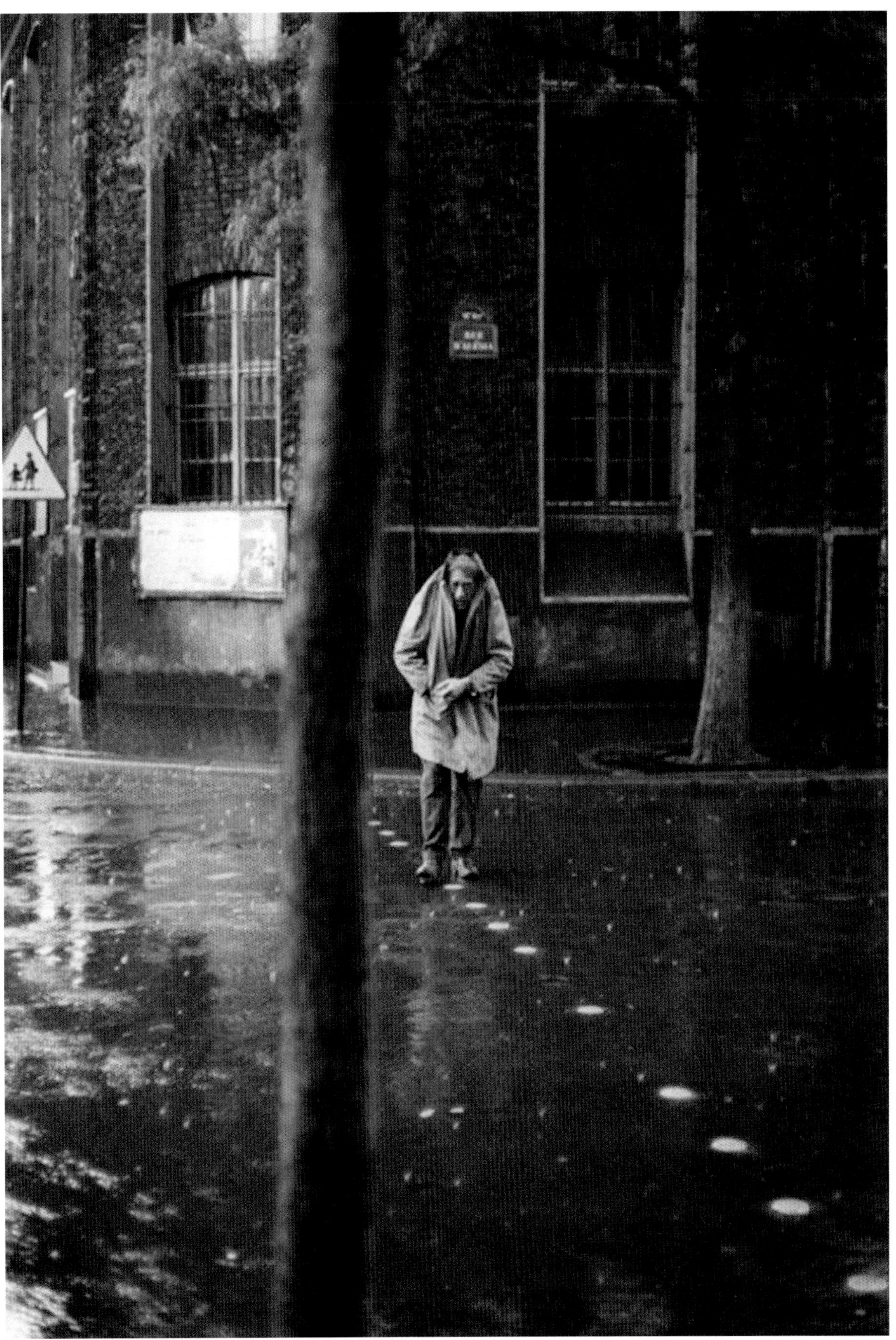

Published on the occasion of the exhibition *Alberto Giacometti: Toward the Ultimate Figure*, on view at the Cleveland Museum of Art from March 12 to June 12, 2022; the Seattle Art Museum from July 14 to October 9, 2022; the Museum of Fine Arts, Houston, from November 13, 2022, to February 12, 2023; and the Nelson-Atkins Museum of Art, Kansas City, from March 19 to June 18, 2023.

Alberto Giacometti: Toward the Ultimate Figure is co-organized by the Cleveland Museum of Art and the Fondation Giacometti.

FONDATION-
GIACOMETTI

Generous support is provided in memory of Helen M. DeGulis, by Malcolm Kenney, and by Mr. and Mrs. Frank H. Porter Jr.

All exhibitions at the Cleveland Museum of Art are underwritten by the CMA Fund for Exhibitions. Generous annual support is provided by an anonymous supporter, Dick Blum and Harriet Warm, Dr. Ben H. and Julia Brouhard, Mr. and Mrs. Walter R. Chapman Jr., the Jeffery Wallace Ellis Trust in memory of Lloyd H. Ellis Jr., Leigh and Andy Fabens, Michael Frank in memory of Patricia Snyder, the Sam J. Frankino Foundation, Janice Hammond and Edward Hemmelgarn, Eva and Rudolf Linnebach, William S. and Margaret F. Lipscomb, Tim O'Brien and Breck Platner, Anne H. Weil, and the Womens Council of the Cleveland Museum of Art.

ISBN: 978-0-300-26391-6

Library of Congress Control Number: 2021921701

All measurements are in centimeters; height precedes width precedes depth.

Texts by Émilie Bouvard, Catherine Grenier, Hugo Daniel, and Romain Perrin translated by Catherine Petit and Paul Buck.

Produced by the Cleveland Museum of Art
Heidi Strean, Chief Exhibition, Design, and Publications Officer
Thomas Barnard, Director of Publications
Exhibition managed by Emily Mears
Publication managed by Rachel Beamer
Copyedited by Sheri Walter
Proofread by Kathleen Mills
Color management by Maurizio Brivio, Milan
Printed and bound by SYL L'Art Gràfic Premium, S.L. in Barcelona, Spain

The Cleveland Museum of Art
11150 East Boulevard
Cleveland, OH 44106-1797
www.clevelandart.org

Distributed by
Yale University Press
302 Temple Street
P.O. Box 209040
New Haven, CT 06520-9040
www.yalebooks.com/art

Cover: Digital proof sheet

Page 1: *Seated Woman* (detail), 1956. Bronze; 51.3 x 15.6 x 23.7 cm. Fondation Giacometti (page 91)

Page 2: *Four Figurines on a Stand (London Figurines)* (detail), 1950–65. Bronze; 157.5 x 42 x 32 cm. Fondation Giacometti (page 192)

Pages 4–5: *The Forest*, 1950. Bronze; 57 x 61 x 49.5 cm. Fondation Giacometti (page 173)

Pages 6–7: *Heads of Annette and Diego, Eyes, and House* (detail), c. 1955. Blue ink on paper napkin; 29 x 51 cm. Fondation Giacometti (page 128)

Page 8: Studio of Alberto Giacometti, 1951. Ernst Scheidegger (Swiss, 1923–2016). Archives, Fondation Giacometti. © 2022 Artists Rights Society (ARS), New York / ProLitteris, Zurich

Page 9: Alberto Giacometti crossing the rue d'Alésia, 1961. Henri Cartier-Bresson (French, 1908–2004). Archives, Fondation Giacometti. © Fondation Henri Cartier-Bresson / Magnum Photos

12 Fondation Giacometti Foreword
13 Directors' Foreword
14 Acknowledgments

INTRODUCTION

16 **Alberto Giacometti, to the US and Back**
Émilie Bouvard

ESSAYS

29 **Force Fields**
Serena Bucalo-Mussely and Catharina Manchanda

39 ***Walking Man***
Catherine Grenier

46 ***The Nose*: The Surrealist Background, between Breton and Sartre**
William H. Robinson

58 ***The Chariot*: Varying Meanings**
William Keyse Rudolph

65 **The All-Consuming Drawing Practice of Alberto Giacometti**
Hugo Daniel

PLATES

74 **Stampa: A Family of Artists**
Ann Dumas

86 **Paris: Life in a Studio in Montparnasse**
Romain Perrin

106 **Obsessed with Heads**
Romain Perrin

136 **Into Thin Air**
Romain Perrin

148 **On Solid Ground**
Romain Perrin

160 **The Artist, the Wife, and the Brother**
Romain Perrin

170 **Other Spaces: Landscapes**
Romain Perrin

182 **Poets, Writers, and Books**
Romain Perrin

196 **Grappling with the Real**
Romain Perrin

202 **Walking Man, Standing Woman**
Romain Perrin

220 Chronology
230 Checklist of the Exhibition
233 Selected Bibliography
236 Contributors and Fondation Giacometti
237 Boards of Trustees

Fondation Giacometti Foreword

Alberto Giacometti first traveled to the United States in 1965, three months before his death in 1966. Nevertheless, early in his career he had received recognition in the country, having been exhibited in the 1930s at the Museum of Modern Art thanks to Alfred Barr and defended with passion by his gallerist Pierre Matisse during the postwar period. In the 1950s, the artist enjoyed retrospectives in some of the era's leading American museums—namely, the Arts Club of Chicago, the Santa Barbara Museum of Art, and the Solomon R. Guggenheim Museum and MoMA in New York—and his work became part of notable private collections. In that respect, Giacometti can be considered an important figure in the history of modern art in the United States.

Since the 1970s, there have been few retrospectives dedicated to the artist in the United States, especially outside New York. Thus, the Fondation Giacometti has collaborated with the Cleveland Museum of Art, the Seattle Art Museum, the Museum of Fine Arts, Houston, and the Nelson-Atkins Museum of Art in Kansas City to organize a vast and ambitious traveling exhibition. *Alberto Giacometti: Toward the Ultimate Figure* gathers more than sixty iconic works and around fifty photographs from the Fondation Giacometti's collection, mainly pieces that had been retained by the artist. Focused on the last twenty years of his life and practice, the exhibition gives the public the chance to discover, through a fresh perspective, an ever-evolving creative practice: Giacometti's relentless quest for the essential form.

Catherine Grenier
Director
Fondation Giacometti, Paris

Directors' Foreword

A towering figure in the history of twentieth-century art, Alberto Giacometti spent a lifetime struggling to resolve the tension between thought and matter, and in the end produced a powerfully distinctive body of work that simultaneously engages universal issues concerning the human condition and speaks to the anxieties of the modern era. *Alberto Giacometti: Toward the Ultimate Figure* is published on the occasion of the United States tour of a selection of the artist's most significant works fifty-six years after his death. The project, which brings together research by French and American curators, focuses on his major achievements of the postwar years (1945–66). Encompassing all media—sculptures, paintings, and drawings—the show surveys a central, animating aspect of Giacometti's oeuvre: his extraordinary, singular concern with the human figure.

Co-organized by the Fondation Giacometti and the Cleveland Museum of Art, the exhibition draws upon the deep resources of the artist's personal collection, and we are delighted to share it with the communities of Cleveland, Seattle, Houston, and Kansas City.

This accompanying volume brings forward in-depth consideration of Giacometti's exploration of the human form in the evolution of his sculptures, ranging in scale from intimate to life-size, and in his lesser-known paintings of the Swiss landscape, drawings imitating the work of other artists, and frenetic ballpoint-pen drawings of overlapping figures and faces.

The Fondation Giacometti is entrusted with the legacy of the artist, which had been overseen by his wife, Annette, who ensured the survival of the works presented in the exhibition. We are fortunate to include contributions by director Catherine Grenier, Émilie Bouvard, Serena Bucalo-Mussely, Hugo Daniel, and Romain Perrin. Their profound knowledge of the artist and their advocacy for his work shaped the exhibition and accompanying publication. The Fondation's generosity in sharing its collection with an American audience will no doubt inspire artists and art historians, as well as members of the general public, all of whom will have the benefit of seeing this extraordinary body of work, held by the artist in his own studio in Paris through the end of his life.

Amada Cruz
Illsley Ball Nordstrom Director and Chief Executive Officer
The Seattle Art Museum

William M. Griswold
Director and President, Sarah S. and Alexander M. Cutler Chair
The Cleveland Museum of Art

Gary Tinterow
Director and The Margaret Alkek Williams Chair
The Museum of Fine Arts, Houston

Julián Zugazagoitia
The Menefee D. and Mary Louise Blackwell Director and Chief Executive Officer
The Nelson-Atkins Museum of Art, Kansas City

Acknowledgments

The organizing museums are grateful to the Fondation Giacometti for making this project possible, and for bringing to it the passion, knowledge, and advocacy for further study of the work of Alberto Giacometti. Under her directorship, Catherine Grenier has led a world-class staff in the development of a United States exhibition tour and an ambitious scholarly publication, all against the backdrop of a worldwide pandemic. Her reserve, encouragement, and generosity guided the tone of this complex collaboration.

Émilie Bouvard, lead curator and editor of this volume, introduces the artist through the lens of his brief (and only) visit to the United States in 1965, providing context for the reader to take in the perspectives of the contributing curators from the American museums. She has fostered a better understanding of the artist's work; we are grateful to her, to Serena Bucalo-Mussely, to Romain Perrin for the humanizing imagery around the artist's many obsessions, and to Sabine Longin and Soizic Wattinne, who contributed to the realization of this project. Hugo Daniel's essay on Giacometti's all-consuming drawing practice is illuminating.

The Cleveland Museum of Art, led by William M. Griswold, director, president, and the Sarah S. and Alexander M. Cutler Chair, is proud to serve as the lead organizer for the tour of *Alberto Giacometti: Toward the Ultimate Figure*. Heather Lemonedes Brown, the Virginia N. and Randall J. Barbato Deputy Director and Chief Curator, supported the exhibition's development, while Emily Mears, director of exhibitions, brought together the teams of the American museums and attended to the intricate administrative duties. Registrars Elizabeth Saluk and Laura Ziewitz ensured the safe travel of the works, managing the logistics between each venue. William Robinson, senior curator of modern art, contributes an essay on *The Nose*; he organized Cleveland's presentation in collaboration with Émilie Bouvard.

Following Cleveland, the exhibition is to be presented at the Seattle Art Museum, led by Amada Cruz, the Illsley Ball Nordstrom Director and Chief Executive Officer, and Catharina Manchanda, the Jon and Mary Shirley Curator of Modern and Contemporary Art, who tailored the exhibition for their audience; Manchanda co-authors an essay with Serena Bucalo-Mussely, co-curator of the exhibition, on Giacometti's vision of the figure in space. All aspects of the installation and planning were managed by Tina Lee, senior manager for exhibitions and publications, with Lauren Mellon, director of museum services and chief registrar.

As the third venue for the exhibition, the Museum of Fine Arts, Houston, led by Gary Tinterow, director and the Margaret Alkek Williams Chair, promises an elegant installation conceived by Ann Dumas, curator of European art, in collaboration with Hugo Daniel; Dumas shares here a biographical vignette on the artist. With aplomb, Deborah L. Roldán, associate director, exhibitions, and John Obsta, exhibitions registrar, managed the presentation and logistics of the exhibition on-site and the transfer to the final venue.

Through the initial conversations of Julián Zugazagoitia, the Menefee D. and Mary Louise Blackwell Director and Chief Executive Officer at the Nelson-Atkins Museum of Art, the exhibition came into being; his infectious enthusiasm for the potential of this project led to the formation of this tour. The Nelson-Atkins collection features *The Chariot*, which William Keyse Rudolph, deputy director, curatorial affairs, takes on in his essay. Their presentation is organized by Zugazagoitia and Rudolph, in collaboration with Romain Perrin and supported by Jill Thompson, head, registration, and Tiara L. Paris, manager, exhibition planning.

This publication was developed by the Cleveland Museum of Art's Publications Department, and designed by Thomas Barnard, director of publications. Image rights and administrative details were handled by publication project manager Rachel Beamer in close collaboration with Philippe de Saint Martin Beyrie of the Fondation Giacometti.

The Fondation Giacometti is deeply grateful to Franck Giraud, Ronald S. Lauder, Daniella Luxembourg, Eyal and Marilyn Ofer, the Don Quixote II Foundation, and the other patrons who wish to remain anonymous.

Alberto Giacometti installing his exhibition, Galerie Maeght, Paris, 1961
Henri Cartier-Bresson (French, 1908–2004). Archives, Fondation Giacometti.

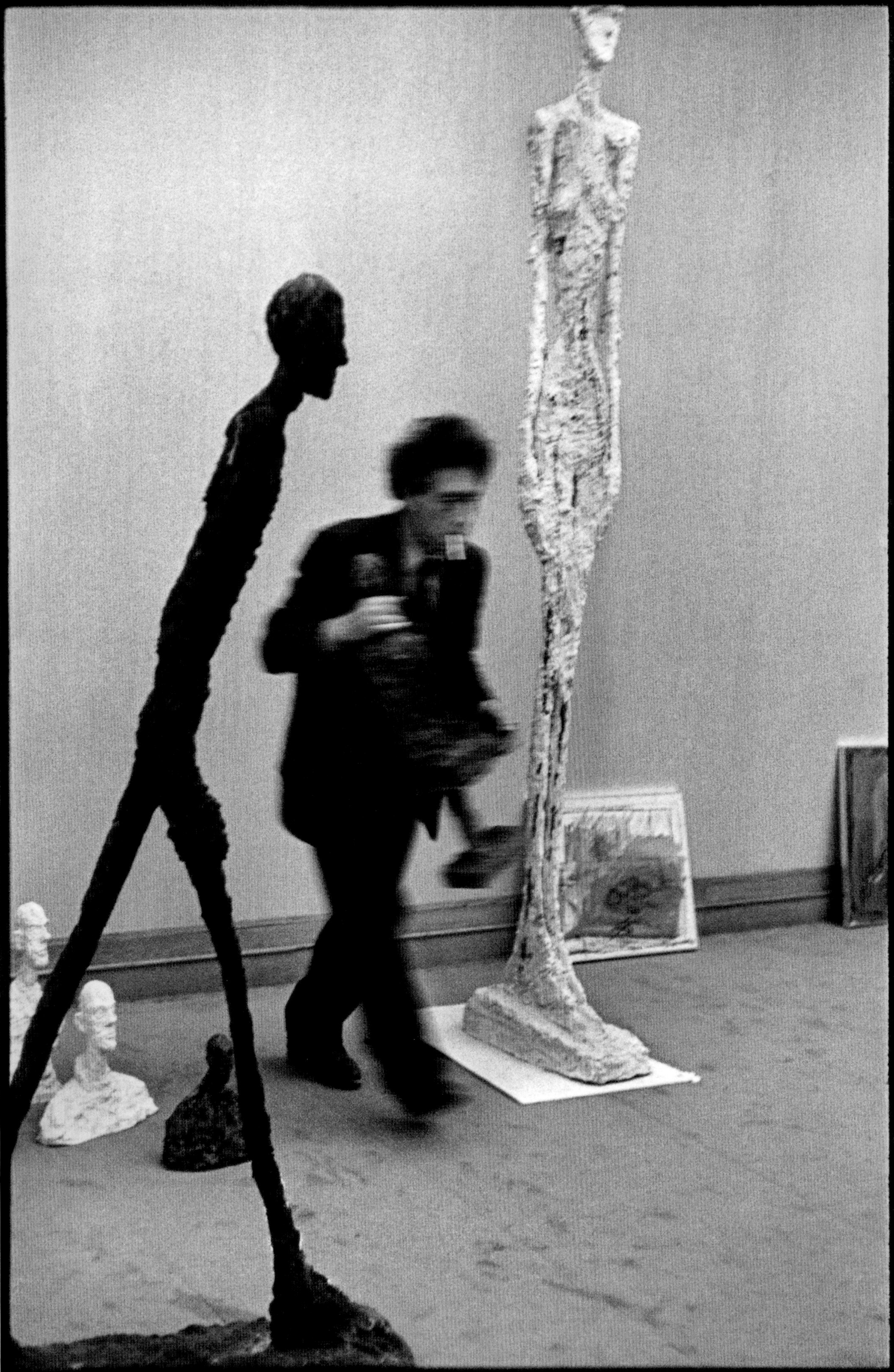

Alberto Giacometti, to the US and Back

ÉMILIE BOUVARD

And look where Giacometti in a room
Dim as a cave of the sea, has built the man
We are, and made him walk:
Towering like a thin
Coral, out of a reef of plaster chalk,
This is the single form we can assume.

[. . .] no nakedness so bare
As flesh gone in inquiring of the bone.

He is pruned of every gesture, saving only
The habit of coming and going. Every pace
Shuffles a million feet.
The faces in this face
Are all forgotten faces of the street
Gathered to one anonymous and lonely.

No prince and no Leviathan, he is made
Of infinite farewells. [. . .]

(From "Giacometti," Richard Wilbur, 1950)

Alberto Giacometti appealed to many photographers during his Surrealist period at the beginning of the 1930s and even more after the war. His growing recognition by the artistic and intellectual milieus, as well as by the public, generated an increase in photo reportages. Brassaï, then Henri Cartier-Bresson, Sabine Weiss, and Ernst Scheidegger, documented the artist's work, as did amateur photographers in the entourage of the sculptor. The majority of photographs of Giacometti and his oeuvre focus on his studio, on the mythical 24 square meters at 46 rue Hippolyte-Maindron that the sculptor occupied from December 1926 until his death in 1966. Mostly in black and white, they aspired to show the artist at work, and the oeuvre in situ, in the atmosphere and surroundings that bore witness to its birth.

In that collection of photographs, one series makes an exception. In color for the most part, the images show a sixty-year-old Giacometti with his elbows resting on the rail of a cruise ship, his hair blowing in the wind. In some he is accompanied by his wife, Annette; by his New York gallerist, Pierre Matisse; or by Patricia Matisse. In others, he is inspecting the ship or holding the navigation instruments. The pictures, taken by Patricia, who already had photographed the studio several times since 1947, were shot, for the first series, on board the Cunard's RMS *Queen Elizabeth*, which left Cherbourg for New York on September 28, 1965, and for the second series, on the SS *France* that brought the Giacomettis back to France in mid-October 1965 (figs. 1, 2). Between those two voyages, ten days or so, was the time of the artist's only stay in the United States. He was on his way to visit, before its closure on October 10, his biggest solo exhibition and retrospective curated by Peter Selz at the Museum of Modern Art (MoMA) in New York, which opened in June (fig. 3a, b).[1]

Giacometti was not a traveler. In his youth, he went on a grand tour of Italy, where he returned a few times, often from his native Val Bregaglia, in Switzerland, on the border of Italy. He stayed regularly in the South of France, but in reality, over forty years, his main trips, once a year on average, took him from Paris to Switzerland. Nevertheless, in July 1965, he went to London to set up his retrospective curated by David Sylvester at the Tate Gallery, then to the United States three months later; as soon as he returned, he departed for Humlebaek, in Denmark, to see his third

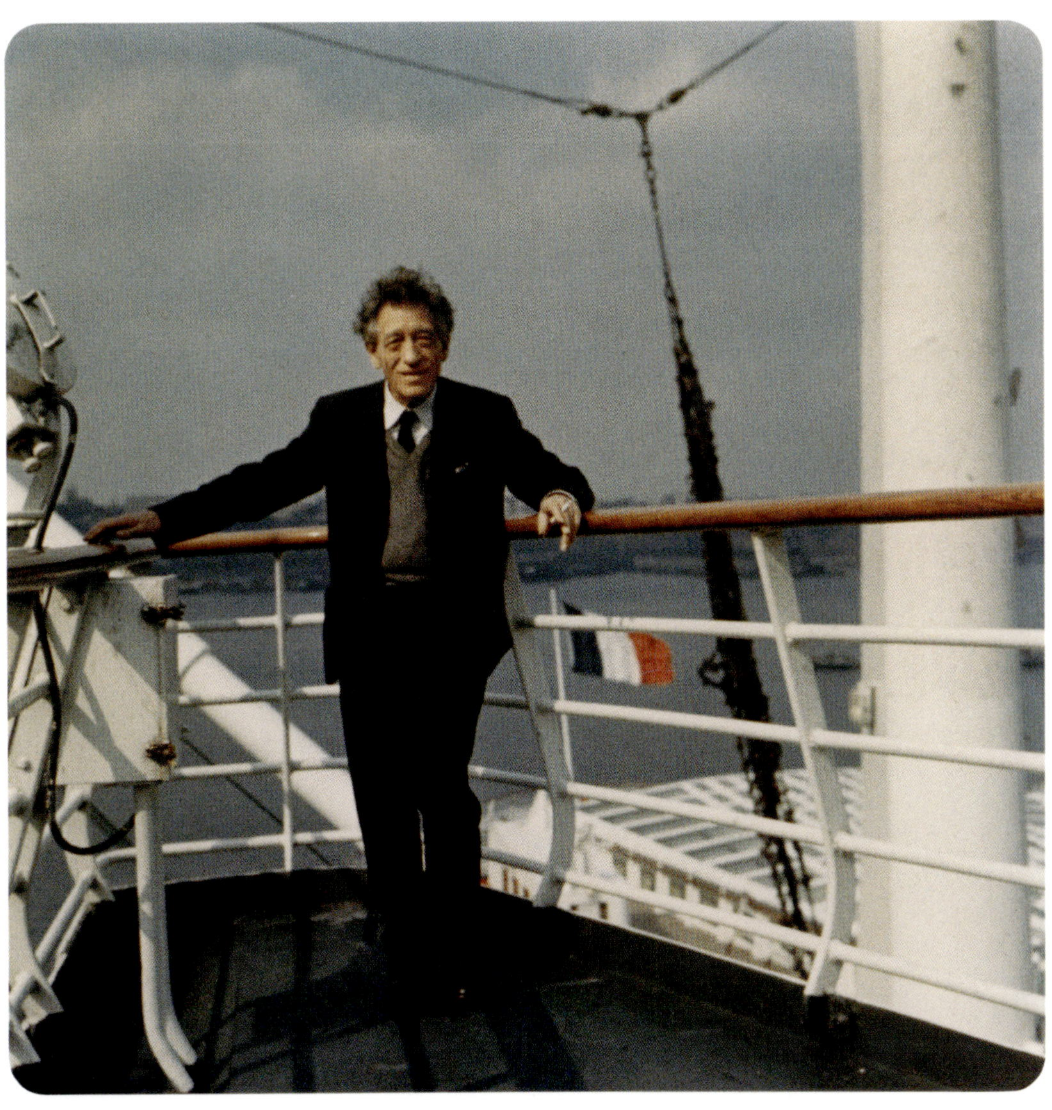

1 Alberto Giacometti on the *France*, 1965
Patricia Matisse
(American, 1923–1972).
Archives, Fondation Giacometti

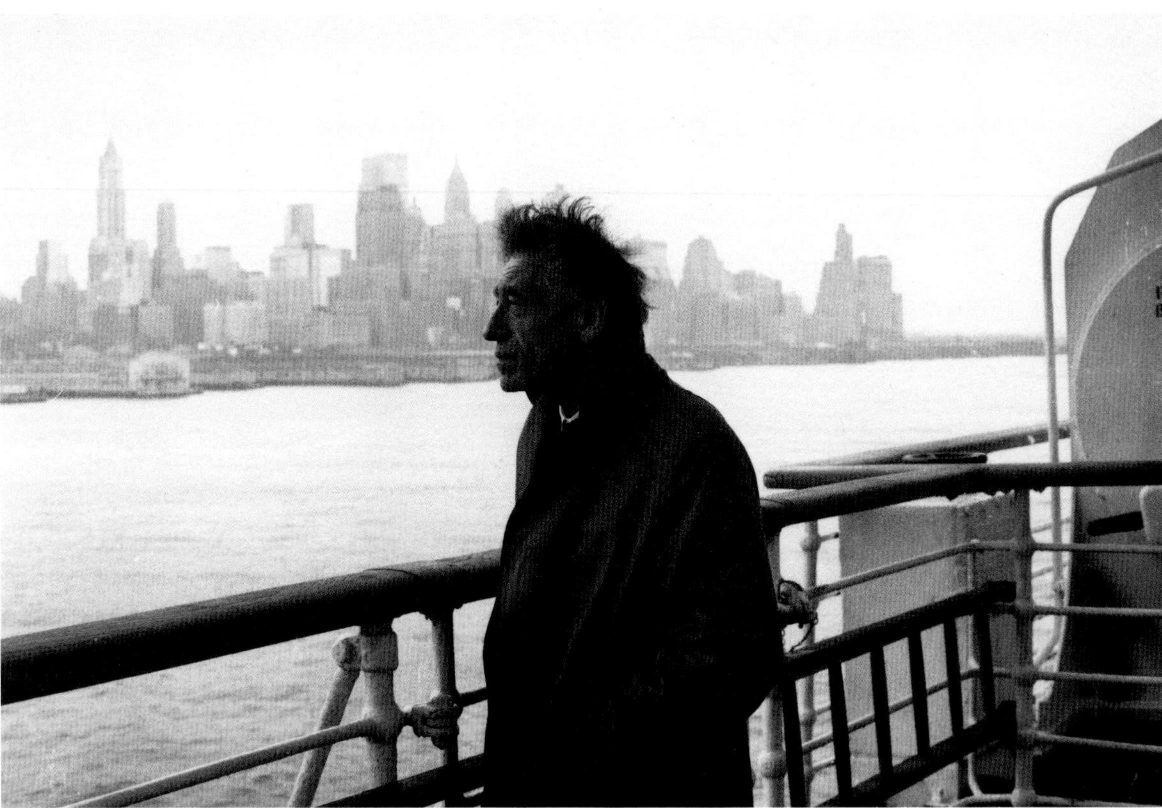

2 Alberto Giacometti on the *Queen Elizabeth*, 1965
Patricia Matisse.
Archives, Fondation Giacometti

solo exhibition of the year, at the Louisiana Museum of Modern Art, before heading home via Hamburg and Cologne. Those trips, motivated perhaps by the desire to see his major retrospectives and even to take part in the installations, as in London, were to be the last. Giacometti died a few weeks later, perhaps following bronchitis, at the Chur hospital in Switzerland.

The 1965 retrospective at MoMA is at the heart of a rich history, that of the relationship—at a distance—between Giacometti and the United States. The artist had many opportunities to set foot on American soil before 1965. Throughout his life, he took part in around 400 exhibitions; nearly 120 occurred in the United States—that is more than a quarter, of which 14 were solo exhibitions (mainly in New York), against 22 in the rest of the world. Giacometti's oeuvre was known to the various art milieus, and even to the American public early on, thanks to the work of several personalities and institutions like gallery owner Julien Levy; MoMA, with Alfred Barr and Peter Selz; Peggy Guggenheim; the Solomon R. Guggenheim Museum, with James Sweeney and Thomas M. Messer;[2] and, finally, Pierre Matisse.[3] Because of them, Giacometti fully integrated into his work the great modernist narrative that was written in the United States and even, due to Selz, some alternative versions. In what measure was the artist aware of, if not actively working at, his own inclusion in the history of American modern art?

Giacometti mainly trained in the studio of sculptor Antoine Bourdelle at the Académie de la Grande Chaumière in Paris during the mid-1920s. Those are the years of a transformation of a young Post-Impressionist painter into an avant-garde sculptor. At the end of the 1920s, Giacometti experimented with the avant-gardes who founded modern art. He made post-Cubist sculptures and brushed with abstraction. His pieces were enthusiastically praised by Hans Arp, André Masson, and the group surrounding Georges Bataille's magazine *Documents*. He befriended writer Michel Leiris and art critic Carl Einstein. The following year, he exhibited *Suspended Ball* at the Galerie Pierre, a piece that made a lasting impression on André Breton and Salvador Dalí, who, as a result, made it the archetype of the "objects with a symbolic function." The young Swiss sculptor, having discovered the avant-gardes who preceded him, was assimilated for the first time into the currents representing the art of his time, and he suddenly was accepted by his peers. Giacometti was considered an important member of the Surrealist group and took part in their activities. The letters addressed to his family show he was very much aware of that turning point in his practice and career.[4]

He made his way into the American art world in the wake of Surrealism. Giacometti wrote to Levy after the latter had organized the first exhibition of the movement in the United States (*Surrealism*, in 1932).[5] The first solo exhibition of the young sculptor took place from December 1, 1934, to January 1, 1935.[6] At the same time, Levy presented a bigger exhibition devoted to Dalí,[7] which was well publicized in the press and eclipsed Giacometti's exhibition, whose commercial

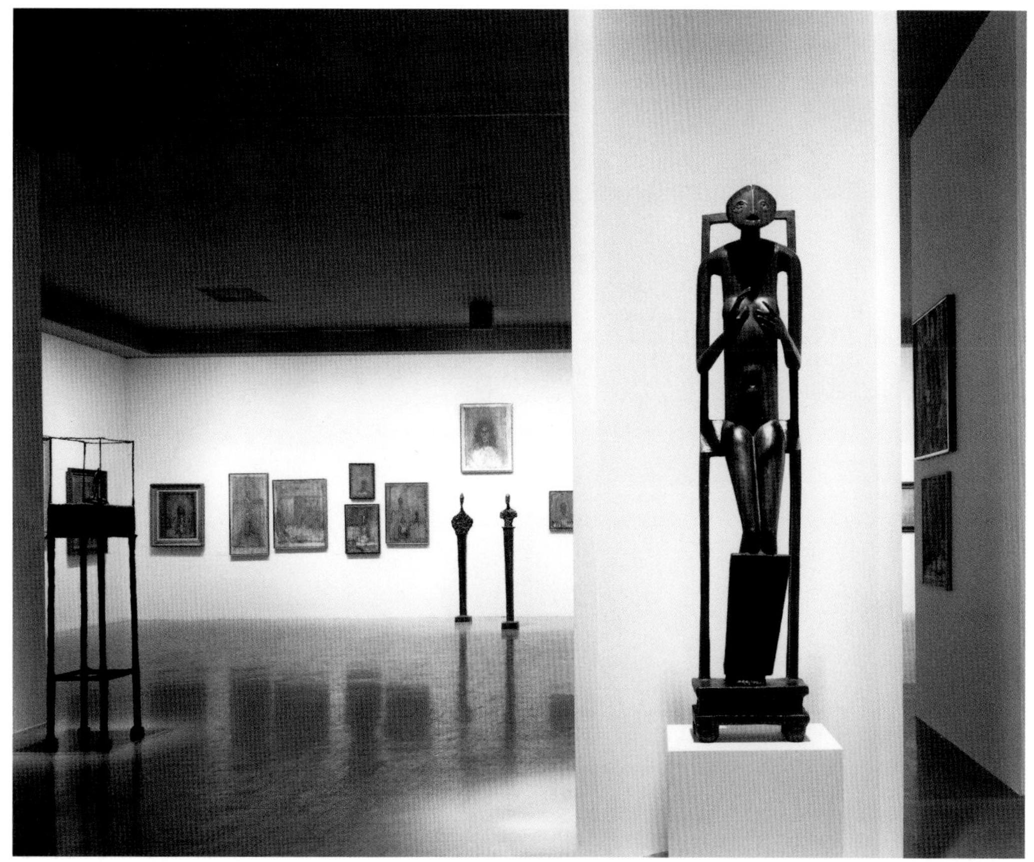

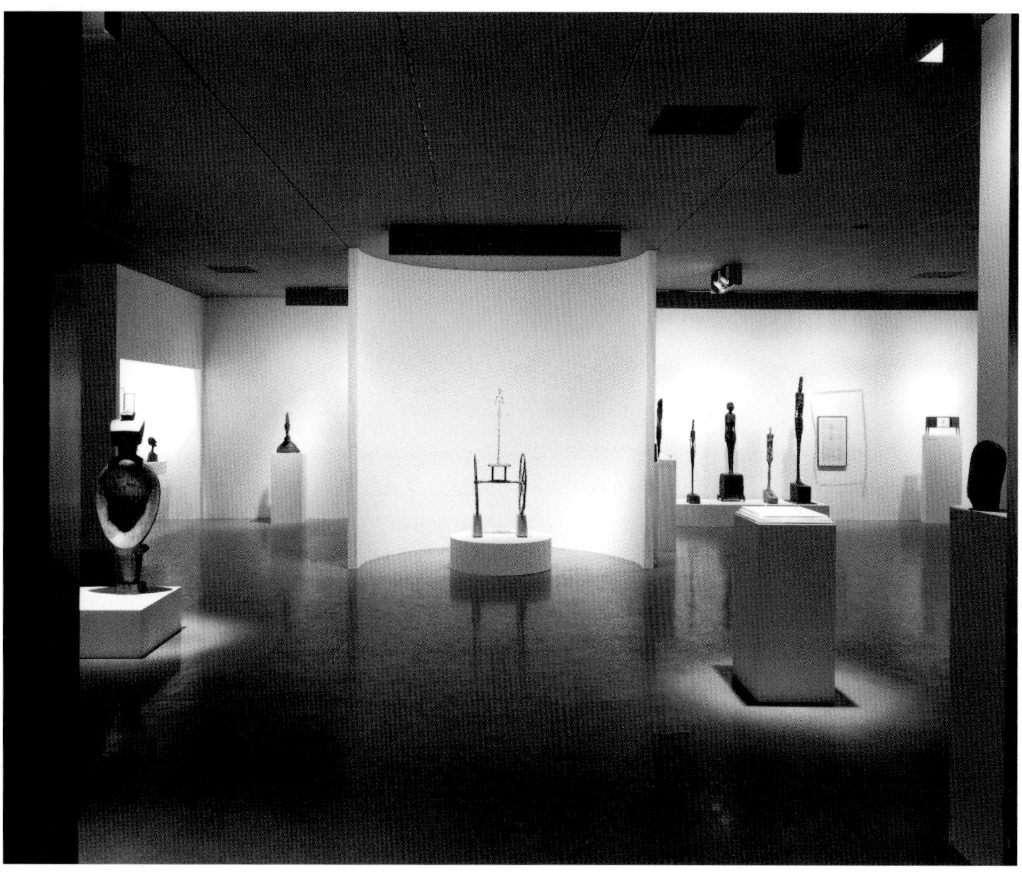

3a, b Installation views
Alberto Giacometti, The Museum of Modern Art, June 9–October 10, 1965. Alexandre Georges. Archives, Fondation Giacometti

4 Installation view
Fantastic Art, Dada, Surrealism, The Museum of Modern Art, December 7, 1936–January 17, 1937, with *The Palace at 4 a.m.* Photographic Archive, The Museum of Modern Art Archives, New York, IN55.1B. Soichi Sunami (American, 1885–1971). Digital Image © The Museum of Modern Art / Licensed by SCALA / Art Resource, NY

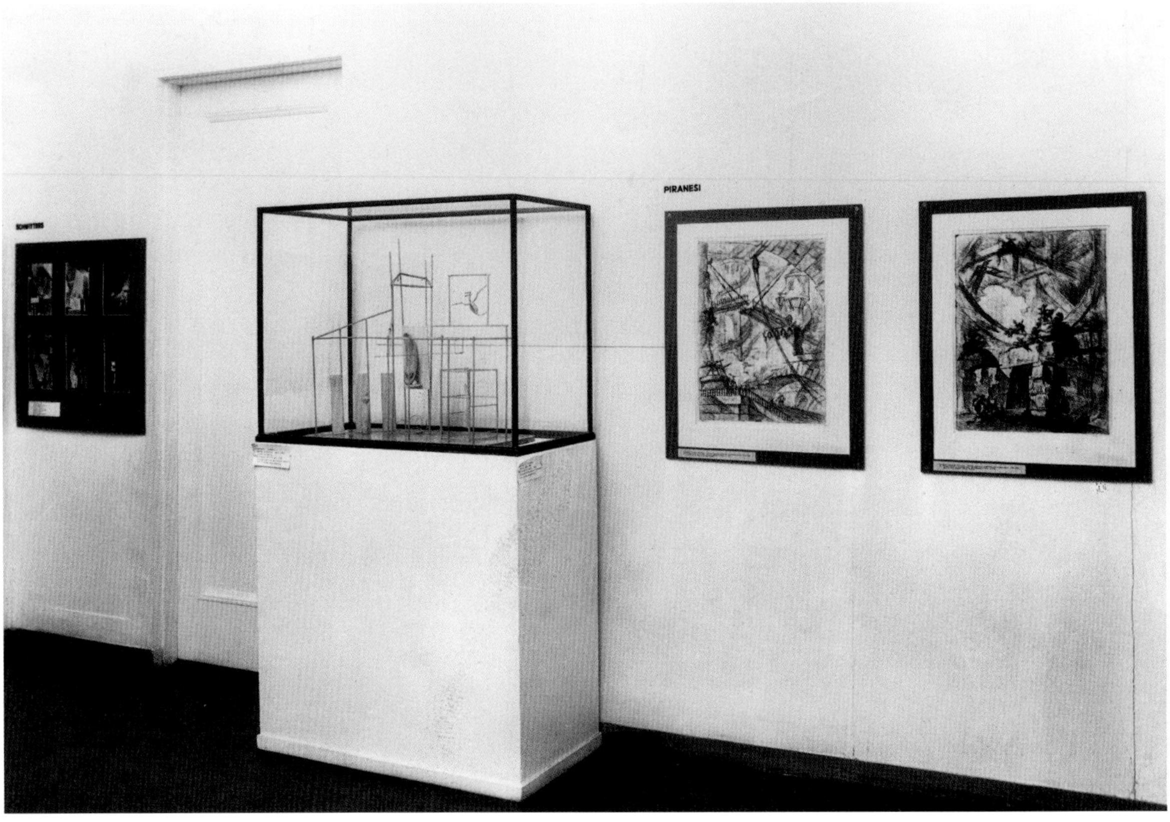

success did not materialize; the critics were mostly negative.[8] However, its title, *Abstract Sculpture by Alberto Giacometti,* gave him a position that was to remain for years to come in the United States. While even the Swiss and French institutions manifested a certain indifference toward him, MoMA, under Barr, placed him at the heart of the history of modern art that he was creating, immediately comprehending what motivated his work. Giacometti took part in the exhibition *Cubism and Abstract Art* in 1936. He exhibited five pieces from the end of the 1920s to the middle of the 1930s, more than Henri Laurens, and as many as Fernand Léger.

He was fairly assessed by Barr in view of his production at the time, in the "younger generation" of "abstract tendencies in Surrealist art." In that saga of modern art drawn up by Barr, Giacometti's place was appropriate, as he had just assimilated Cubism, abstraction, and Surrealism.[9] The catalogue presented him as "the official Surrealist sculptor," while underlining his ability, with *Head-Landscape* and the model for *Project for a City Square,* which were exhibited to question biomorphic abstraction and to solve a point—"namely the composition of isolated form" taken on, among others, by Arp. Giacometti appeared capable of synthesizing several visual art issues and artistic attitudes (Surrealist and even Dalían taste for illusion and for double images, and abstract biomorphism). That same year, three of his works were included in the exhibition *Fantastic Art, Dada, Surrealism* at MoMA.[10] They were placed in the section "Dada and Surrealism" (fig. 4). While Giacometti, involved now in figuration, distanced himself from the movement to finally be excluded from it in 1935, he was presented in the United States as a Surrealist sculptor then and for a few more years.

That association was confirmed by his presence in the collection belonging to Peggy Guggenheim,[11] who acquired *Woman with Her Throat Cut* (1932–33) in 1940 in Paris, cast especially by the artist for her—and for Pierre Matisse. The sculpture figured prominently in the group exhibition at the Art of This Century Gallery in New York that the Guggenheim opened in October 1942, next to the plaster of *Walking Woman* (1932), sold by Pierre Matisse to the collector in 1941 and named "Beheaded Woman"—a title reminiscent of a famous series of etchings by Max Ernst and thus still associated with Surrealism.[12] After that, the Guggenheim acquired the wooden model for *Project for a City Square* (1932) (named "Model for a Garden"). While Giacometti, in Paris and then in Geneva from 1938 to 1945, created tiny human figures, the Guggenheim organized a solo exhibition, gathering nine works from his Surrealist period, from February 10 to March 10, 1945, at the Art of This Century Gallery.[13] These works mainly came from, besides Peggy Guggenheim's private collection, the collections of Roberto Matta, Levy (he loaned *On ne joue plus*), and architect Philip Johnson.[14] When the war ended, and though Giacometti met up once more with Jean-Paul Sartre and Simone de Beauvoir in Paris, and immersed himself in the existentialist atmosphere of the Liberation, he was, for everyone in the United States, a sculptor associated with Surrealism.[15] His output of that time was not known about.[16]

One understands, in that context, the event the exhibition represented when it opened on January 19, 1948, at the Pierre Matisse Gallery, which was to champion Giacometti on American soil until his death (fig. 5). In close collaboration with the artist, Matisse expertly built in the confined space of his gallery a real retrospective. Giacometti's Surrealist works were there, some on loan,[17] but also his most recent pieces, figurative works, and those made specifically for the exhibition, which had stimulated his creativity: some "small figures" as well as *The Nose*, *Walking Man*, and *Man Pointing*, from 1947; tall hieratic female figures; and two paintings, showing another facet of his work unknown until that date in the United States. This exhibition generated a big change of paradigm. Sartre, the founder of existentialism, which permeated French culture in the postwar years, wrote the remarkable preface "The Search for the Absolute," which swept away, at least for several years, any Surrealist reading, insisting on the relationship of figures to space, shifting Giacometti's sculpture toward issues around perception and a deep humanist commitment. Despite that text by an author who had not yet made his mark on the other side of the Atlantic, the immediate reaction of the press showed how hard it was to change an interpretative paradigm. The density of the works in the gallery—the cohabitation of milky plasters whose matter seemed so crumbly, dark bronzes, and Surrealist and figurative works—the whole conferring an impression of strangeness to the exhibition, also explained, in part, that reluctance.

Though it was a commercial success, and Giacometti was feted in *Harper's Bazaar* and *Vogue*, the critics were divided. Henry McBride, in the *New York Sun*, wrote that "these very odd statues" and "these sculptures are the queerest that have ever come from abroad. . . . They are thin to the point of stringiness and do not invite you to touch for they have been built in sticky white plaster which results in picky surfaces. Happily you are not asked to touch."[18] Sam Hunter, in the *New York Times*, wrote that this "new show at the Matisse Gallery takes dehumanization a step further and risks clarity, even sanity in doing so," and "the naturalistic debris of Dada is rejected for a nearly pathological, dream-reality of grisly, elongated club-footed prophetic figures, always threatening to dematerialize into meaningless plaster drippings and just saved by the faintest poetic suggestion."[19] Clement Greenberg, in *The Nation*, after having underlined the significance of Giacometti's Surrealist sculpture, lamented its new direction. It was a "sad falling-off from his previous standard. . . . Gone is the bold, rough geometry that gave Giacometti's former flights of imagination their motive power; gone the audacious inventiveness that shocked the spectator's vision only to stabilize it on a higher and secure level."[20] Only the critic for *ARTnews* showed enthusiasm: the sculptures "are fixed in space and hold the spectator, too, to the one spot where they are immediately grasped, realized, and wholly astonishing."[21] In his letters to the artist, Matisse comforted Giacometti, declaring his trust in the future.[22]

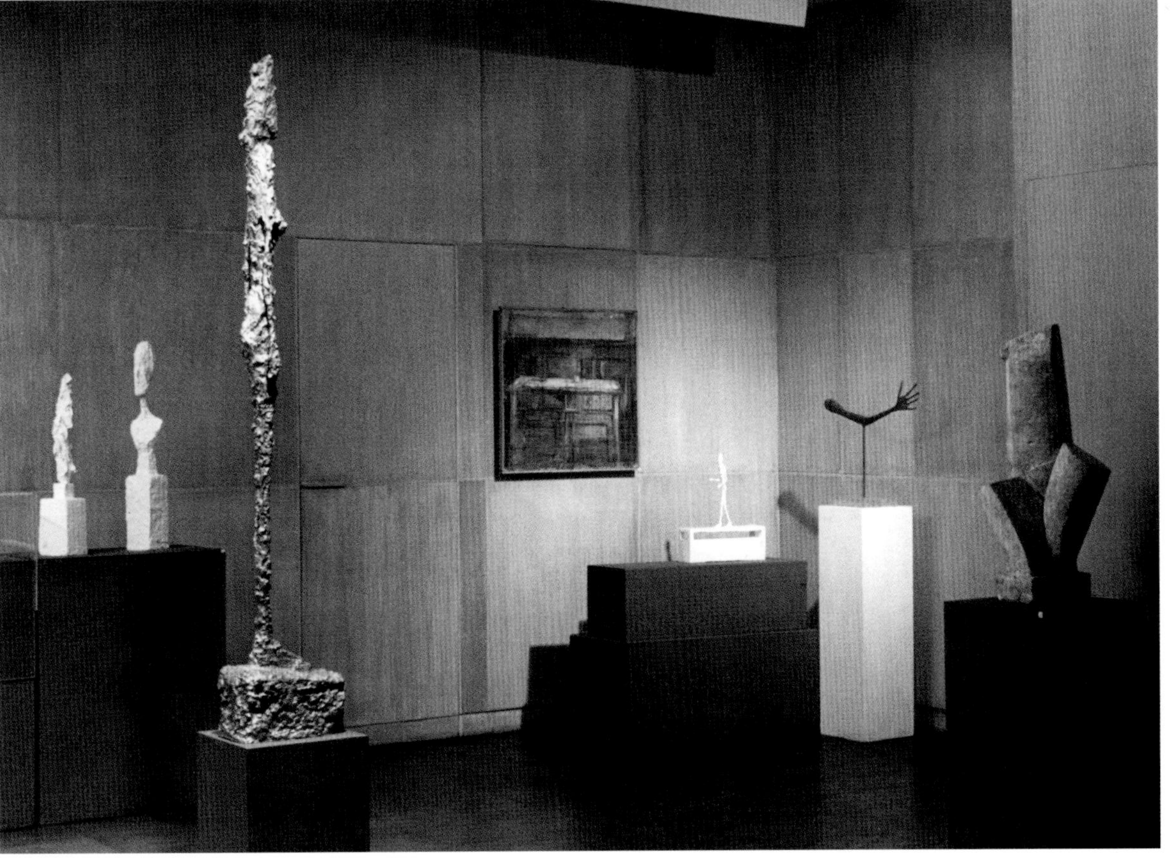

5 Installation view
Alberto Giacometti, Pierre Matisse Gallery, January 1948. Patricia Matisse. Archives, Fondation Giacometti

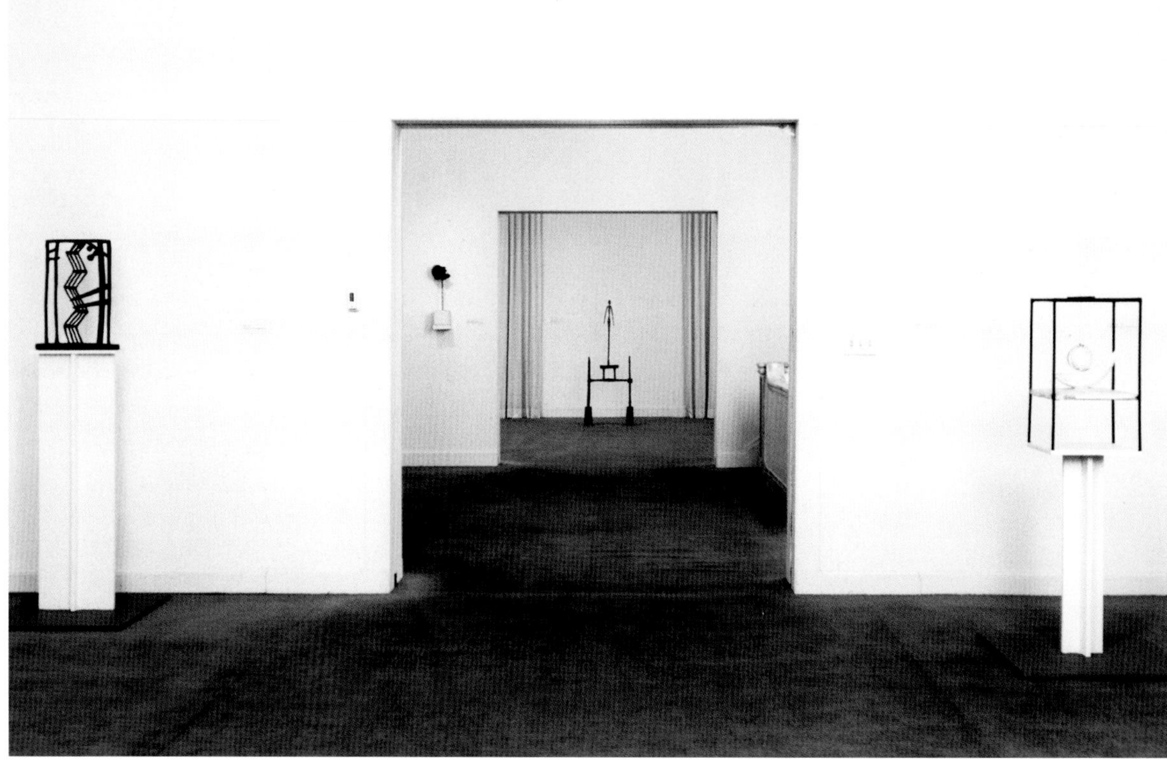

6 Installation view
Alberto Giacometti, Solomon R. Guggenheim Museum, June 1955. Archives, Fondation Giacometti

The exhibitions, both solo and group shows, that followed in the coming years established Giacometti as one of the great modern artists of the postwar era.[23] Matisse showed him sometimes with artists associated with Surrealism, but as many times, and in the same exhibitions, next to Jean Dubuffet, Pablo Picasso, Georges Braque, Balthus, André Derain, and Henri Matisse. Other gallery owners, particularly Sidney Janis, also showed Giacometti's work, whose postwar style gradually gained recognition with the American public. He was included in group exhibitions in museums and in public and private collections. His first retrospective in a museum in the United States took place in 1955 at the Guggenheim (fig. 6).[24] The exhibition presented 24 paintings, 19 drawings, and 47 sculptures, from the 1920s to the 1960s, mainly loaned by gallerists Pierre Matisse and Maeght; by a few museums, including MoMA and the Baltimore Museum of Art; and by private collectors, mainly Mr. and Mrs. J. W. Alsdorf for a great many paintings and drawings, as well as G. David Thompson for several sculptures (fig. 7).[25] In 1958, he was commissioned to produce a piece for the Chase Manhattan Plaza in New York, a project he gave up after creating several models of *Walking Man*, *Tall Woman*, and *Large Head* (fig. 8).[26]

The way MoMA incorporated him into the narrative around the history of art of the postwar years truly shows that evolution. While Giacometti was represented in its collections and displays mainly through his works from the 1930s, and MoMA still acquired in 1949 a bronze of *Woman with Her Throat Cut*, it gradually chose to acquire the postwar masterpieces, sometimes via Pierre Matisse. The museum bought a *City Square* (1948) in 1949, a *Chariot* (1950) in 1951, a *Man Pointing* (1947) in 1954 thanks to a donation by Blanchette Hooker Rockefeller, a *Dog* (1951) in 1958 through the A. Conger Goodyear Fund, and the painting *The Artist's Mother* (1950). Then, until 1966, the acquisition of works by Giacometti, all from the postwar years, took place due to donations by prominent collectors, among them Tristan Tzara, Thomas Hess, Sidney and Harriet Janie, and Pierre Matisse. At the same time, other acquisitions, purchases, and donations started to flood American museums, a testimony to the entrance of Giacometti into American private collections in the previous years, thanks to his gallerist.

MoMA's acquisition of these sculptures was the sign of a new reading of the artist's work, which became apparent in 1959. Selz curated the exhibition *New Images of Man*, whose catalogue cover showed the plaster of *Tall Figure II* (1948–49, Fondation Giacometti) (fig. 9). After ten years or so of abstract art dominating in the United States, perceived as the ultimate degree of "modernism," Selz opted in this exhibition for the "Great Figurative artists" of the postwar period, underlining, in direct opposition to majority opinion, the persistence of the representation of the human figure, through the works of artists of Giacometti's generation (Willem de Kooning, Jean Dubuffet, Francis Bacon, and Germaine Richier—the only female artist exhibited) or younger (Karel Appel, César, and Leon Golub).

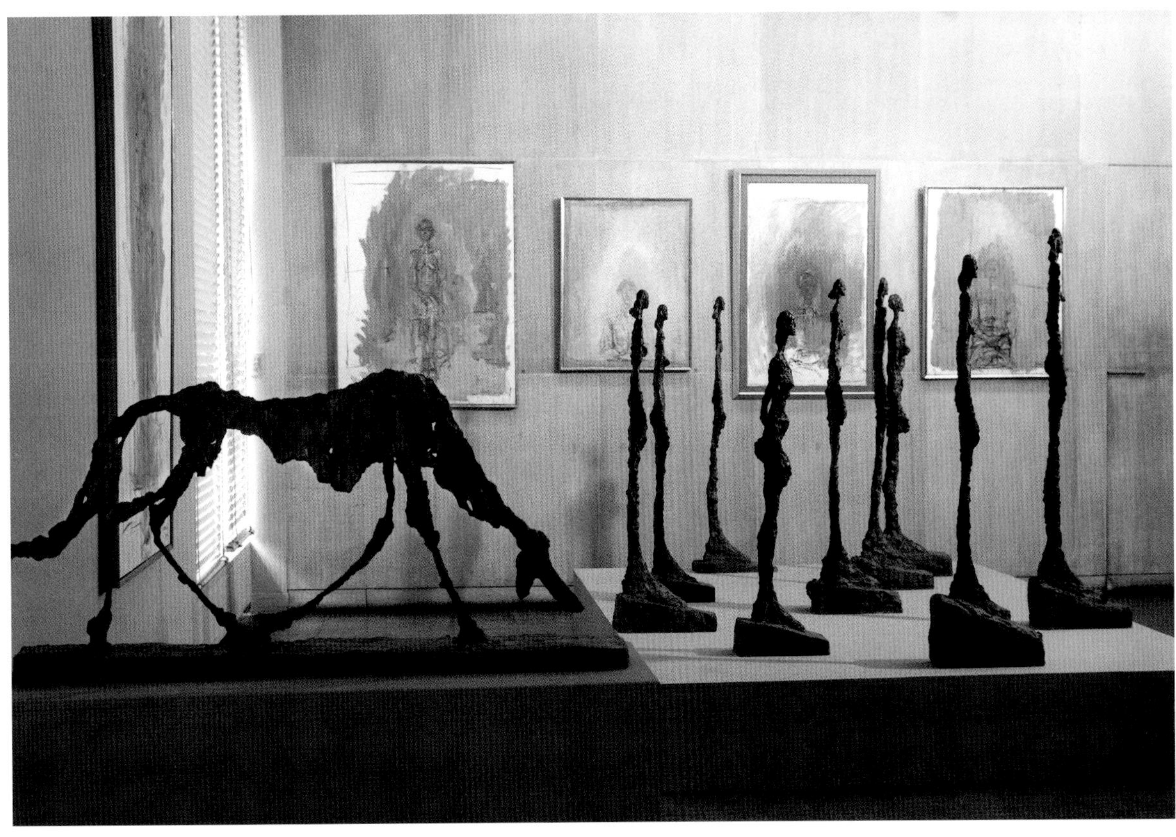

7 Installation view
Giacometti: Sculptures, Paintings, Drawings from 1956 to 1958, Pierre Matisse Gallery, May 1958. Herbert Matter (Swiss American, 1907–1984). Archives, Fondation Giacometti

On the theme of Marsyas, Apollo's unfortunate rival, according to Selz's preface, the exhibition gathered artists who were seeking the language of the "wounds of existence." Associating Apollonian "abstraction" with the representation of "essence," Selz declared he exhibited those who saw themselves on the side of an "existence" dominated by angst: "the face of Marsyas has the dread of existence, the premonition of being flayed alive. . . . Some of these artists have what Paul Tillich calls the 'courage to be,' to face the situation and to state the absurdity."[27] Selz established a strong link between those expressions and the philosophies of existence (Kierkegaard, Heidegger, and Camus), but he also connected them to Romanticism—evoking the importance in them of the "passion, the emotion, the break with both idealistic form and realistic matter, the trend towards the demoniac and the cruel, the fantastic and the imaginary"—to Cubism and its reinvention of anatomy, to Expressionism and its "mystical faith in the power of the effigy,"[28] to the Dada break, and to the Surrealist taste for dreams and automatism.[29]

Finally, it was their work on the material (clay and pigments), their formal work on the surface, that

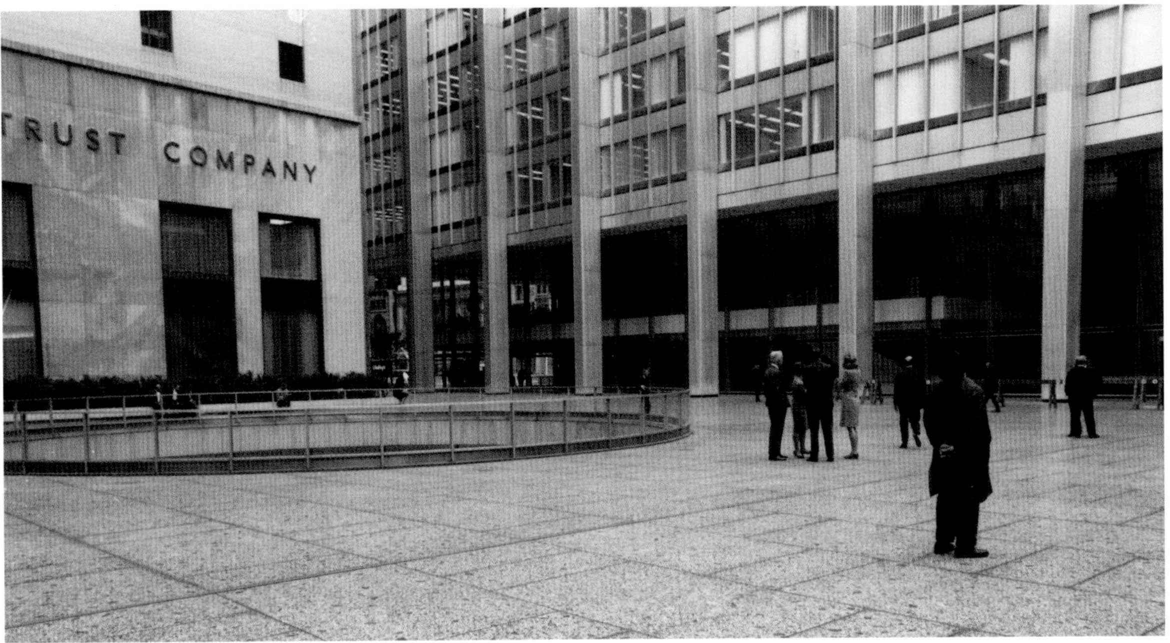

8 Alberto Giacometti at the Chase Manhattan Building, New York, 1965
Patricia Matisse. Archives, Fondation Giacometti

connected them and associated them with the abstract artists of their time.[30] Those elements are in many respects consistent with Giacometti's artistic journey and his own sources and influences; they show a reception of his work assimilating the existential reading, dominant in Europe at the time. Even though he was the "youngest member" of the Surrealist group, he appeared to be, in that exhibition, the leading figure of an ensemble of practices that formed neither a group, nor a current, but rather a choice and a shared attitude, those of a path that was not that of abstraction and a figuration in tension with the modern world. Six sculptures and two paintings were presented,[31] all coming from MoMA or American private collections. For the catalogue, Giacometti published a statement in which he confirmed his simple, "traditional" quest to represent what he saw. The questioning developed in that short text took on an existential dimension at the end:

> It may be that all this is nothing but an obsession, the causes of which I do not know, or a compensation for a deficiency somewhere. In any case, I recognize now that your question is much too vast or too general for me to answer in a precise manner. By asking this simple question you have, in fact, put everything into question, so how to answer it?[32]

In his note, Selz added his reflection on Sartre's essay "The Search for the Absolute," emphasizing the issues around perception, distance, and the right scale of the sculptures, but also insisted, with poetic sense, on the fact that the sculptures were "simply human beings—alone, inaccessible, and therefore inviolate"—who—"erect, distant and immutable—can stand or pace but never rest." Selz concluded his text by quoting the poem by Richard Wilbur in tribute to Giacometti, and René Char offered a poem describing and animating Giacometti's sculptures in a natural setting.

The interpretative shift accompanying the discovery and recognition of Giacometti's oeuvre on the other side of the Atlantic was completed with the 1965 retrospective organized by Selz at MoMA.[33] It presented 81 sculptures, 35 paintings, and 35 drawings.[34] The majority of loans came from American public and private collections (among them, Joseph Hirshhorn's), confirming that Giacometti's works had entered the United States, as well as from the Pierre Matisse Gallery and the artist himself. The works were displayed in a kind of visual simultaneity with no attempt at

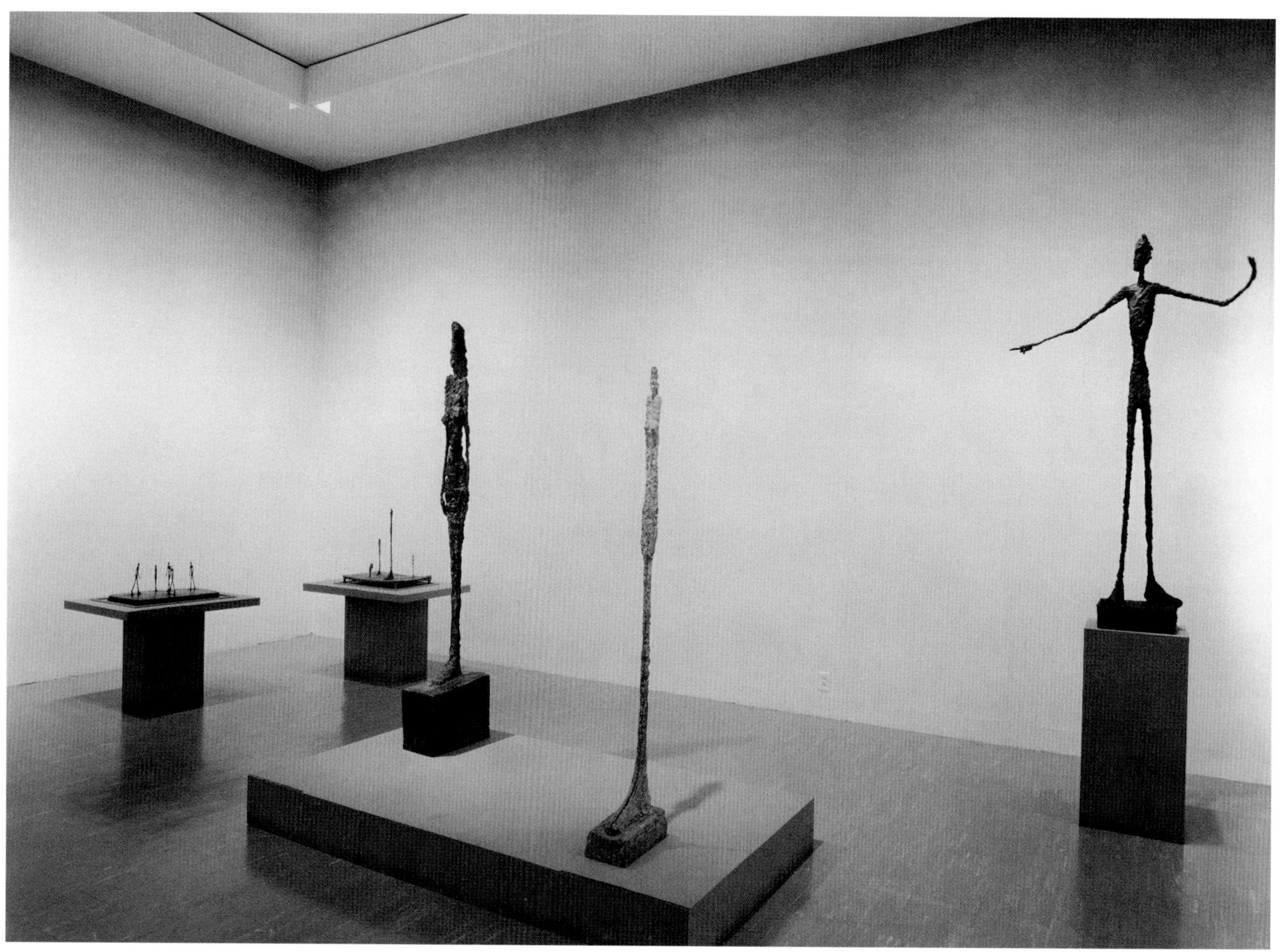

9 Installation view
New Images of Man, The Museum of Modern Art, September 30–November 29, 1959. Photographic Archive, The Museum of Modern Art Archives, New York, IN651.12. Soichi Sunami. Digital Image © The Museum of Modern Art / Licensed by SCALA / Art Resource, NY

respecting a strict chronology. The preface of the exhibition catalogue gathers key elements still pertinent to the understanding of his oeuvre:[35] a sculpture dominated by the question of the point of view, the gaze, if not the "eye"; the issues of perspective and distance, giving an "absolute" presence to the figures; the relentless character of the working process; the destruction and the reworking of pieces, looking more toward "the adventure" than the "result"; the importance of copying old masterpieces; the intimate relationship between the artist and his models, who, however, after hours of sitting, looked like "strangers"; and the importance of Stampa. It depicted Giacometti's journey from his absorption of the avant-gardes to 1965, mentioning the decorative arts, and clearly relying on the conversations published by the artist and evoking the familiar myths of the sculptor's accounts that were circulated that way.

The portrait was completed with the publication of Giacometti's letter to Matisse in 1947, in which the artist related and outlined his development, just before what was his first real retrospective in the United States in 1948. He was then writing a first-person story that would be published when he was still alive to accompany the major exhibition at MoMA. Not only the works but also the image of the artist—the mythical figure he himself created throughout the years in his texts, conversations, and photographic portraits, especially by famous American photographers—were finally established on the other side of the Atlantic.

Since 1966, in a rather counterintuitive way, and despite the presence of Giacometti's works in countless public and private collections in the United States, few retrospectives devoted to the artist have been arranged.[36] The exhibitions, co-organized with the Fondation Giacometti, taking place in 2022 and 2023 at the Cleveland Museum of Art; the Seattle Art Museum; the Museum of Fine Arts, Houston; and the Nelson-Atkins Museum of Art finally address an absence—that of important recent comprehensive exhibitions devoted to the artist in the United States. Focusing mostly on the last period of Giacometti's oeuvre, on his path "toward the ultimate figure," the exhibitions also aim to stress the importance of those final twenty years, which still need to be further examined and rediscovered.

Installation view
Alberto Giacometti: A Retrospective Exhibition, The Cleveland Museum of Art, 1974. Organized by the Solomon R. Guggenheim Museum, New York. Courtesy CMA Archives

Translated by Catherine Petit and Paul Buck

1. The exhibition then traveled to the Art Institute of Chicago, the Los Angeles County Museum of Art, and the San Francisco Museum of Art.

2. Thomas M. Messer was responsible for the major posthumous retrospective of 1974, organized by the Solomon R. Guggenheim Museum.

3. From 1951, Giacometti was represented in France by the Galerie Maeght. In New York, gallery owner Sidney Janis also presented his work several times, in group exhibitions gathering other major modern artists. The gallery owner, who had welcomed the exhibition *First Papers on Surrealism* in 1942, included him in the book *Abstract and Surrealist Art in New York* (New York: Reynal and Hitchcock, 1944); in 1968, thanks to his donation to the Museum of Modern Art, an exhibition was organized, and following that, three works by Giacometti entered the collection (*Three Men Walking I*, 1948–49; *The Artist's Wife*, 1954; and *Annette*, 1962).

4. See Giacometti to his parents, June 21, 1931, in *Lettres à sa famille* (Paris: Éditions Bernard Chauveau and Fondation Giacometti, 2021), 20.

5. See https://auction.tajan.com/pdf/2004/4481.pdf, 19.

6. Eleven sculptures were exhibited, among them *On ne joue plus* (1933), whose image was reproduced on the invitation card and which later entered the dealer's private collection, and *Object without Base* (1931), which is perhaps *Disagreeable Object to Be Thrown Away*. See Patricia Phegan, "Alberto Giacometti's First Exhibition in the United States, 1934–35," in *Alberto Giacometti and America*, ed. Tamara S. Evans, Pro Helvetia Swiss Lectureship 2 (New York: The Graduate School and University Center, City University of New York, 1984), 35–41.

7. Julien Levy also exhibited Pavel Tchelitchew.

8. One critic judged his abstraction excessive, another "silly." Only one (Henry McBride, *The New York Times*) emphasized the unsettling strangeness of those both simple and complex pieces. Phegan, "Giacometti's First Exhibition in the US," 38.

9. The biography that presents him in the catalogue notes: "GIACOMETTI, Alberto. Sculptor. Born in Stampa, Switzerland, 1901. Painted, 1913–1921. First sculpture, 1915. Studied Geneva School of Art and Sciences, 1920. Italy, 1921–22; Paris, 1922. Joined Surrealists about 1930. Lives in Paris." The works exhibited were "*Standing Figure*, c. 1927, artist's collection"; "*Sculpture*, 1927, collection A. E. Gallatin, New York" (today, in the collection of the Philadelphia Museum of Art); "*Disagreeable Object*, private collection, New York" (today, promised gift to the Museum of Modern Art); "*Head-Landscape*, 1932, artist collection, New York" (reproduced in the catalogue; today, in the collection of Musée National d'Art Moderne–Pompidou Centre); and "*Project for a City Square*, 1932, artist's collection" (acquired by Peggy Guggenheim at a later date). Albert Eugene Gallatin—a major American collector, member of the Anonymous Society, and founder of the Gallery, then the Museum of Living Art—had most certainly bought the "sculpture" from 1927 in Paris during a trip in summer 1934.

10. Those sculptures were *Disagreeable Object* and *Head-Landscape*, previously exhibited (see note 9), and *The Palace at 4 a.m.* (1933), which, in the catalogue, is noted as being in the collection of the Museum of Modern Art, which had just bought it. All three are reproduced in the catalogue.

11. At her death, Peggy Guggenheim's Venice collection contained six sculptures by Giacometti.

12. This piece, however, was presented as a mannequin bearing a head in the shape of a cello and neck and hands in the shape of feathers and a flower at the Galerie Pierre Colle in 1933. The removal of its "head" and its "arms" marked in 1936 Giacometti's departure from Surrealism and his interest in other figurative forms (here, clearly referencing ancient Egyptian statuaries and archaic Greek figures of the Cyclades).

13. The works presented were "1. *The Palace at 4 a.m.*, 1932–33 (wood), loaned by the Museum of Modern Art; 2. *On ne joue plus*, 1934 (marble), loaned by Mr Julien Levy; 3. *Female Figure* [*Invisible Object*], 1935 (plaster), loaned by Matta; 4. *Construction* [*Three Characters outside*, exhibited in 1929 at the Galerie Bernheim, Paris], 1935 (bronze), loaned by Mr Philip Johnson; 5. *Two Figures* [*Mother and Daughter*], 1935 (bronze), loaned by Miss Ann Resor; 6. *Woman with Her Throat Cut*, 1931 (bronze), Art of this Century; 7. *Model for a garden* [*Model for a Square*], 1932 (wood), Art of this Century [ill.]; 8. *Statue of a headless woman* [*Walking Woman*, 1932–36], 1934 (plaster), Art of this Century; 9. *Disagreeable Object*, 1931 (wood), anonymous loan."

14. Johnson continued acquiring works by the artist in the postwar years. *The Night* (1947) had a prominent place in his "Glass House."

15. It is more than likely that in the art circles, informed by Breton and the Surrealists in exile, they would have heard about Giacometti's break with Surrealism as early as 1935.

16. It was shown for the first time in France in the double issue of the publication *Cahiers d'art* for 1945–46.

17. The lenders were the owners cited in note 13. Giacometti also exhibited *Suspended Ball* (1930) and *Fleur en danger* (1932).

18. Henry McBride, "Distance Brought Nearer," *New York Sun*, January 28, 1948.

19. Sam Hunter, "Arts," *New York Times*, January 25, 1948.

20. Clement Greenberg, "Arts," *The Nation*, February 7, 1948.

21. T. B. H., "Giacometti," *ARTnews* 46, no. 12 (February 1948).

22. Pierre Matisse to Giacometti, end of January 1948, Fondation Giacometti. "The exhibition is very popular, and generates many discussions, from what I've heard. The artists in general like it a lot, the public, which is not so sure, doesn't know yet what to think. The critics have been moronic, a little unsettled by Sartre's preface, or to be more precise, by the presence of Sartre right next to you. It was the risk we took. But to be honest, there's little harm done."

23. See the chronology in this catalogue.

24. See Karole P. B. Vail, "Giacometti and the Guggenheim," in *Giacometti*, ed. Megan Fontanella and Vail, exh. cat. (New York: Solomon R. Guggenheim Museum, 2018), 18–25. The exhibition catalogue only listed the works exhibited.

25. This exhibition showed the public the importance of the Pittsburgh collection, which, acquired by the Kunsthaus Zurich in 1965, forms the core of the Alberto Giacometti-Stiftung.

26. See Catherine Grenier's essay in this catalogue.

27. Peter Selz, *New Images of Man* (New York: Museum of Modern Art, 1959), 12.

28. Ibid., 13.

29. The image of *The Palace at 4 a.m.* was reproduced in the preface and compared in the text with *The Square*, an existential transcending of Surrealism. It is mentioned again in the overview of the artist in the catalogue.

30. In reality, in the period just after the war, Giacometti was already seen and appreciated by the Abstract Expressionists he would eventually meet in New York in the 1960s.

31. *Man Pointing* (bronze, 1947), The Museum of Modern Art (gift of Mrs. John D. Rockefeller); *Tall Figure* (bronze, 1947), private collection; *Tall Figure* (painted bronze, 1949), collection of Mr. and Mrs. James Thrall Soby; *City Square* (bronze, 1949), collection of Mr. and Mrs. Pierre Matisse; *Composition with Three Figures and a Head (The Sand)* (painted bronze, 1950), collection of Philip Johnson; *The Artist's Mother* (oil on canvas, 1950), The Museum of Modern Art; *Man Seated* (oil on canvas, 1950), collection of Mr. and Mrs. Richard Deutsch; *Head of Diego* (bronze, 1954), collection of Mr. and Mrs. Sidney F. Brody.

32. Selz, *New Images of Man*, 68.

33. In 1961, Giacometti won the Carnegie International Prize for sculpture.

34. See https://assets.moma.org/documents/moma_master-checklist_387316.pdf?_ga=2.146345588.1341766655.1614355821-1998086743.1612693561.

35. Peter Selz, "Introductory Note," in *Alberto Giacometti*, exh. cat. (New York: Museum of Modern Art, 1965), 8–11.

36. After 1966, only five solo exhibitions in the United States devoted to Giacometti have been organized: at the Solomon R. Guggenheim Museum in New York in 1974 and 2018, the Portland Museum of Art in 2000, the Museum of Modern Art in New York in 2002, and the Bechtler Museum of Art in Charlotte in 2012, some of which toured to other venues, including the Cleveland Museum of Art in 1974.

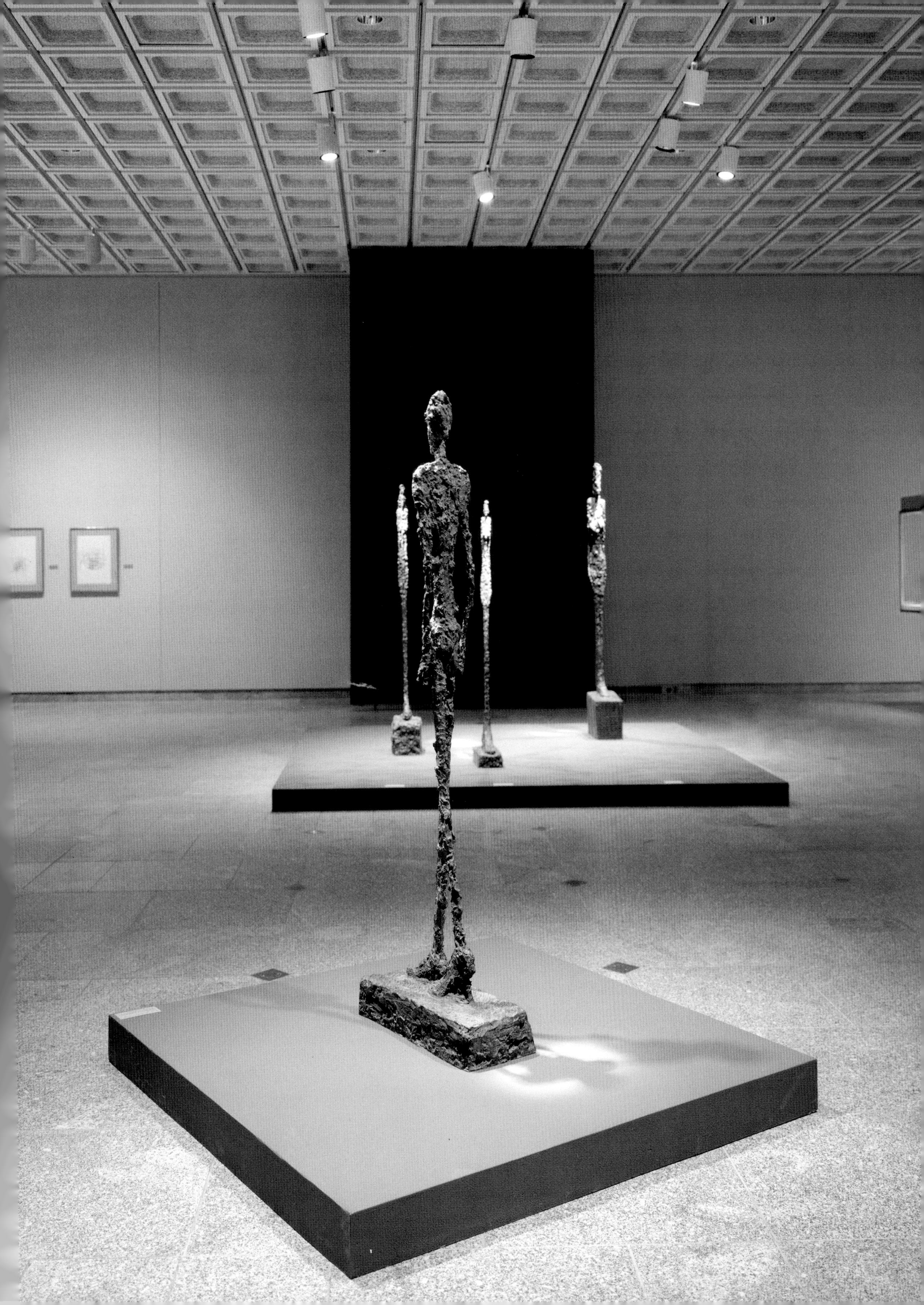

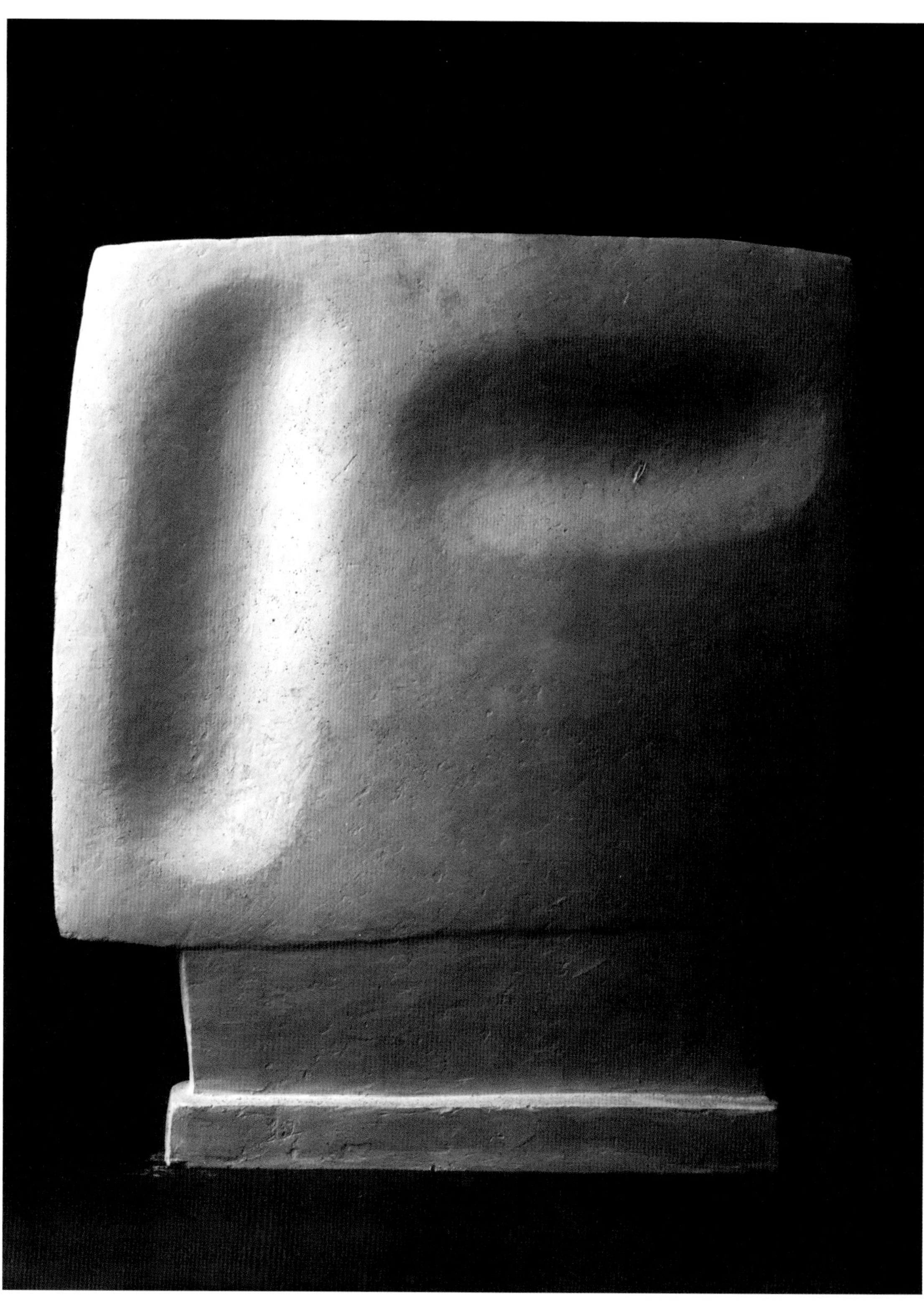

10 ***Gazing Head* in plaster, 1929**
Marc Vaux (French, 1895–1971).
Archives, Fondation Giacometti

Force Fields

SERENA BUCALO-MUSSELY AND CATHARINA MANCHANDA

> [T]he polelike figures are the core of the space surrounding them; the empty space appears to push inward on the figures, compressing them into an obdurate shaft. The dual definition is one of nothingness and meaning. Protuberances in a figure are not projections so much as they are residual points left by lines cutting inward.[1]
>
> —Donald Judd

Alberto Giacometti's interest in spatial concepts became increasingly prominent in the late 1920s and early 1930s, a time when he moved among the vanguard artists and writers in Paris. Over the next two decades, he began to articulate artistic concerns that would grow beyond sculpture to include the surrounding space. By the late 1940s and 1950s, he had developed a highly complex visual program centered on his unique vision of the figure in space.

Giacometti's journey began when he moved to Paris in 1922. His fascination with spatial relationships arose in part from the challenges posed by leading developments in painting and sculpture in the 1910s and 1920s, which collapsed traditional understandings of Western perspectival rendering. At the time, Paris was a hub of artistic experimentation and attracted artists from around the world. The portrait and the human figure were at the center of Giacometti's practice, and during the 1920s, he took an increasingly abstract approach. The first indicators of this new direction appeared in 1928, where facial markers such as an eye or a nose became so abstracted that they could be interpreted as topographic landscapes (fig. 10). Similar architectonic qualities continued to surface in the following years. In sculptures such as *Reclining Woman Who Dreams* (1929), he daringly moved away from the figure as a solid, unified form (fig. 11). Instead, he created open structures, to be looked at and looked through. This and related works seem to carry within the memory of Cubist painting, pioneered by Pablo Picasso and Georges Braque, nearly twenty years earlier, as they had championed the fragmentation of a figure and its dispersal in the surrounding pictorial space.[2] Picasso's *Ma Jolie* (1911–12) is one prominent example where the viewer intuits, rather than sees, a figure as a ripple in space (fig. 12). A push toward

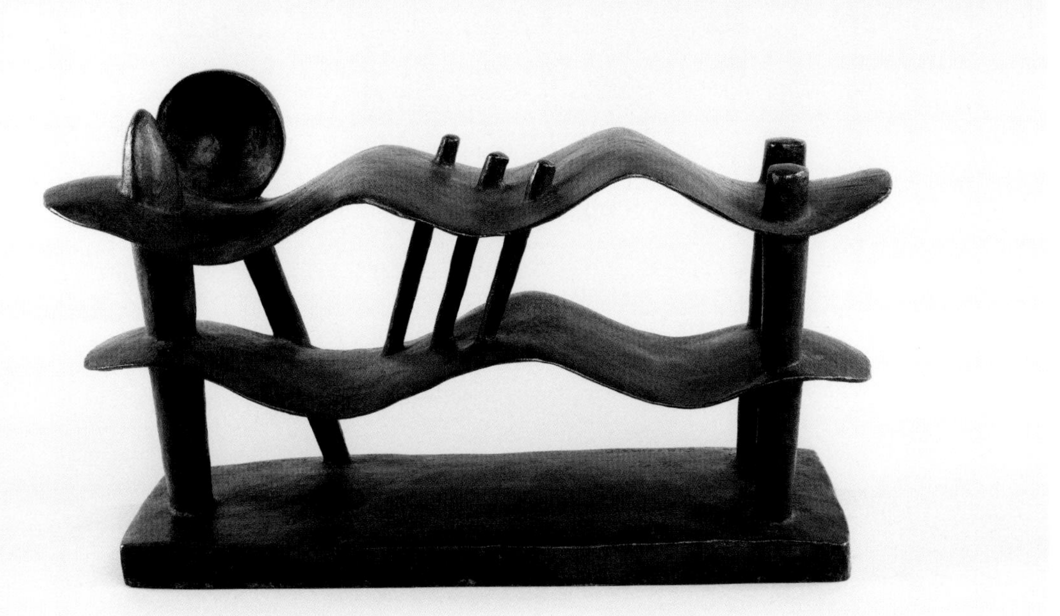

11 *Reclining Woman Who Dreams*, 1929
Bronze; 23.7 x 42.6 x 13.6 cm.
Fondation Giacometti

radical innovation in sculpture had also been gathering momentum throughout the 1910s and 1920s, with the Italian Futurists, Russian Constructivists, and other practitioners of Cubism (Juan Gris, Jacques Villon, and Jean Metzinger, among others) contributing important ideas that relate to the perception of space and time.[3] Additionally, certain shared concerns with Giacometti's open structures from the late 1920s can be found in Picasso's welded sculptures from the same decade, which look like three-dimensional drawings in space.

In 1930, Salvador Dalí and André Breton discovered Giacometti's abstract sculptures and drew him into the Surrealist group of artists and writers, whose interest in dreams and the unconscious opened new possibilities for spatial imagination. Giacometti swiftly expanded on the architectonic possibilities of his abstracted heads in a fascinating move toward tabletop sculptures, such as his *Model for a Square* (1931–32) (fig. 13).[4] Here, abstract forms are arranged in a parkour-like constellation similar to monuments or architectural features on an empty plaza. Giacometti also realized this work on a much larger scale in plaster, offering the viewer a physical experience, rather than just a visual one. In the tabletop model, the objects have a fixed position, but in the large-scale version, they do not (see page 88). This allowed the artist to create an oneiric space where he could arrange the pieces in different configurations.[5] *Model for a Square* conjures an associative field of possibilities not unlike the metaphysical paintings concerned with time and space created in the 1910s by Italian artist Giorgio de Chirico, another figure greatly appreciated by the Surrealists. De Chirico's paintings of empty plazas ringed by somnolent buildings with an occasional monument impart a vastly different aesthetic and melancholy mood, but both artists employ a stagelike conception of space, as if awaiting the arrival of protagonists (fig. 14). It is this latent, provisional aspect of Giacometti's *Model for a Square*, repeated in other works from this period, that foreshadows future developments.

One of the most intriguing sculptures that continues this idea is *The Palace at 4 a.m.* (1932), an open, quasi-architectural space built with thin wooden sticks inhabited by four objects arranged to look like stage props (fig. 15). In 1933, the artist described his mode of production in alignment with Surrealist methods: rather than create from nature, he could see works of art fully formed in his mind. Written like the recollection of a dream, his description dovetailed with the Surrealists' interest in the unconscious as a site of ready-made imagery and ideas.[6] Giacometti identified the objects in his palace as a cage with a fragile vertebra, a skeletal bird, a statue of a standing woman before curtains, and an oblong object attached to a vertical board, not further defined but an object to which he related. The text touched on the interconnectedness between sexuality, death, and violence—key themes explored by the Surrealist circle of artists and writers.[7] Each object inside Giacometti's *The Palace at 4 a.m.* is evocative, and the early hour suggests a nocturnal and associative scene, a dreamscape conceived in the form of a stage set.

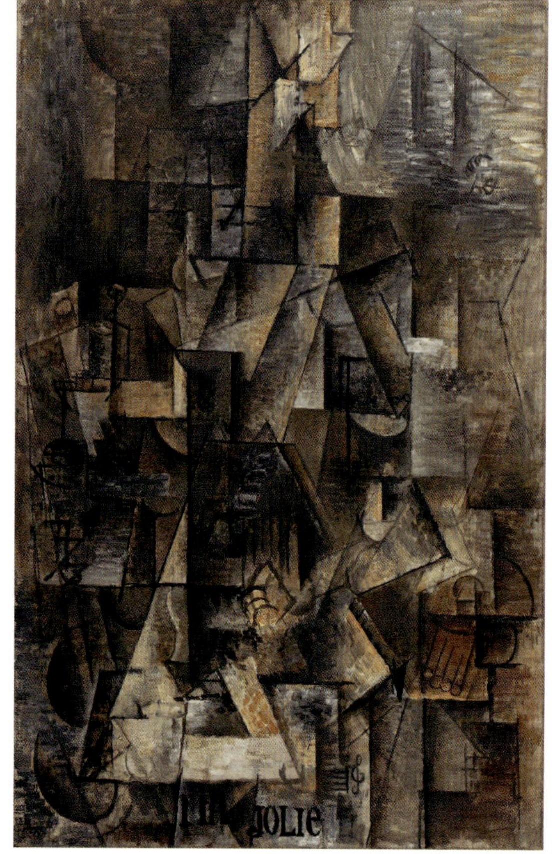

12 *Ma Jolie*, winter 1911–12
Pablo Picasso (Spanish, 1881–1973). Oil on canvas; 100 x 64.5 cm. The Museum of Modern Art, New York, Acquired through the Lillie P. Bliss Bequest. Digital Image © The Museum of Modern Art / Licensed by SCALA / Art Resource, NY. © 2022 Estate of Pablo Picasso / Artists Rights Society (ARS), New York

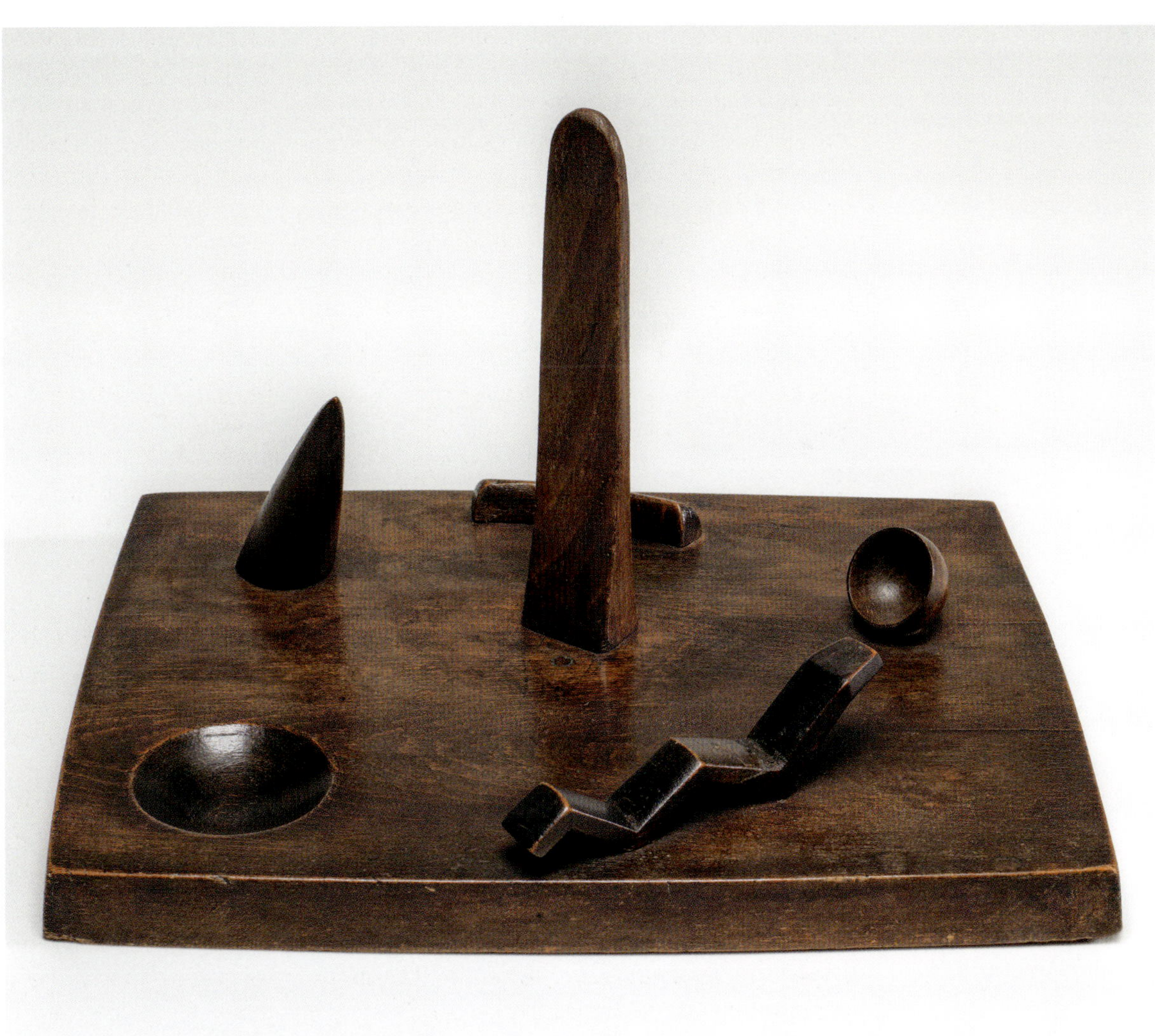

13 ***Model for a Square*, 1931–32**
Wood; with base: 19.4 x 31.4 x 22.5 cm. Peggy Guggenheim Collection, Venice (Solomon R. Guggenheim Foundation, New York), 76.2553 PG 130

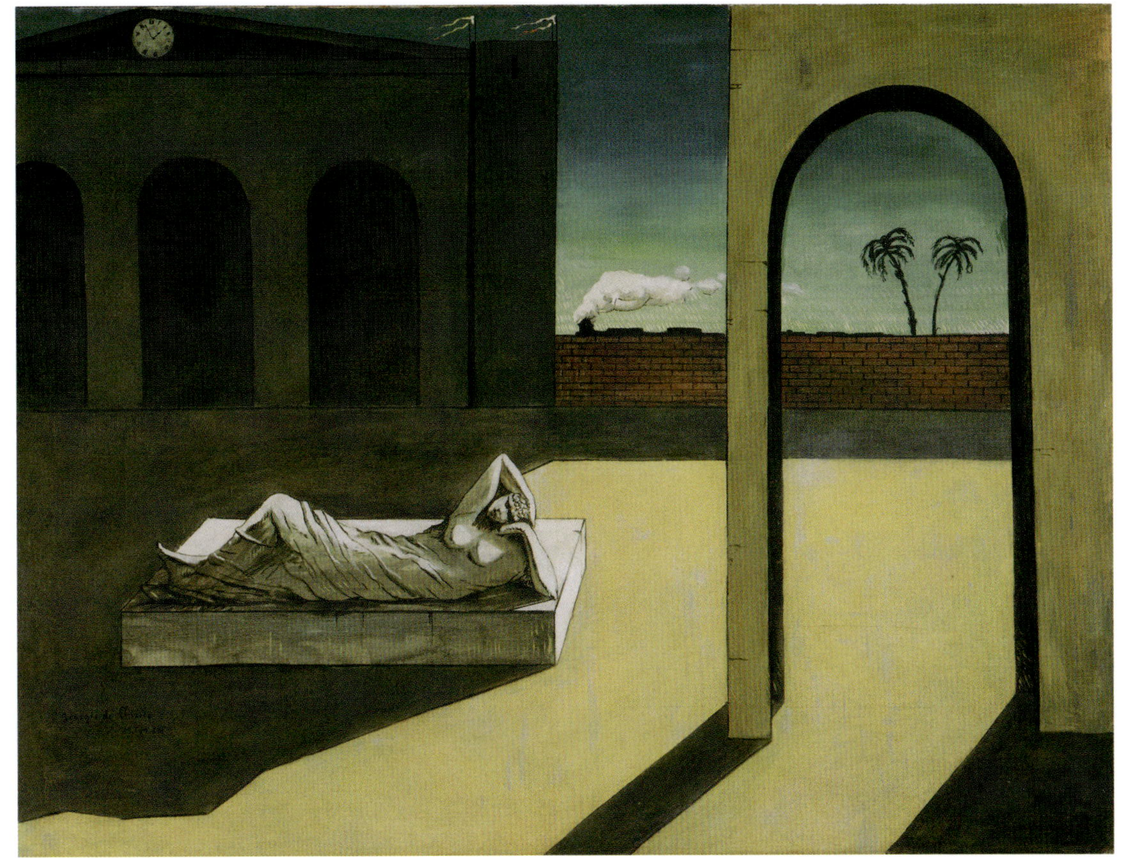

14 ***The Soothsayer's Recompense*, 1913**
Giorgio de Chirico (Italian, 1888–1978). Oil on canvas; 135.6 x 180 cm. The Philadelphia Museum of Art, The Louise and Walter Arensberg Collection, 1950. Photo: The Philadelphia Museum of Art / Art Resource, NY. © 2022 Artists Rights Society (ARS), New York / SIAE, Rome

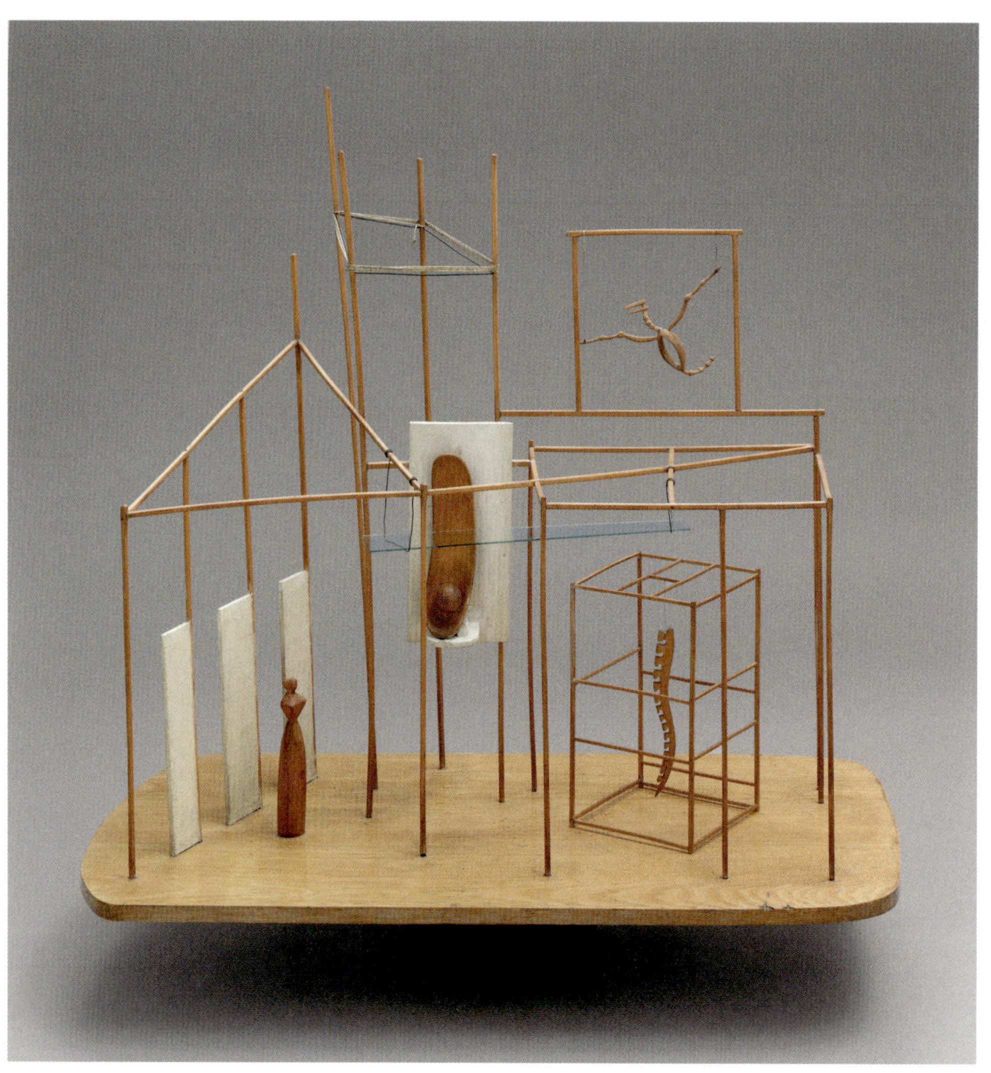

15 ***The Palace at 4 a.m.*, 1932**
Wood, glass, wire, string; 63.5 x 71.8 x 40 cm. The Museum of Modern Art, New York. Photo: Digital Image © The Museum of Modern Art / Licensed by SCALA / Art Resource, NY

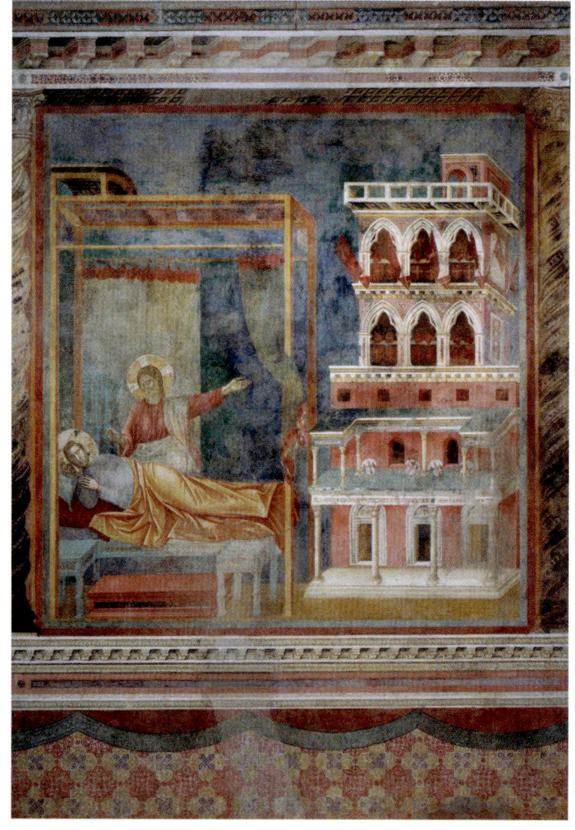

16 ***Dream of the Palace, Legend of Saint Francis*, 1297–99**
Giotto di Bondone (Italian, c. 1266–1337). Fresco; 270 x 230 cm. Basilica of Saint Francis, Assisi. Photo: Scala / Art Resource, NY

Giacometti's treatment of space in this work might have had other sources of inspiration. When the artist was young, he spent time in Italy, where he admired ancient art he had only known through books in his father's library. He also discovered the frescoes of Italian Renaissance artists and their interest in perspectival space—in particular, Giotto di Bondone, whose work he encountered in Padua and Assisi. As an early practitioner of perspectival renderings, Giotto frequently set his religious figures within delicately painted architectural spaces with strong symbolic connotations. One example of interest here is Giotto's *Dream of the Palace*, where a four-post bed frames his religious protagonist (fig. 16). Giacometti may have been mindful of the Renaissance artist when he created *The Palace at 4 a.m.*, and he continued to make similar use of open architectural structures at this time and in later works. One example is *The Cage* (1930–31), in which a wooden, open box imprisons a tight ensemble of objects. Tangled and piercing as if in a violent struggle, the elements are suggestive of forms connected to vegetables and animals. Similarly, *Suspended Ball* (1930), a work laced with erotic suggestion, uses thin metallic bars for a framework architecture that contains a ball suspended by a rope swinging over a crescent (fig. 17).

Here, the implication of movement is destabilizing and upends the viewer's expectations of sculpture as static.

His brief, productive association with Breton and his Surrealist group came to an end in 1935 when Giacometti started to work again with live models.[8] In a later conversation with Pierre Schneider, the artist recalled his search for a new beginning centered on the human figure. He thought he would work from a model for eight days and then be armed with studies to create a new body of work. Instead, he found himself absorbed and confounded by the empirical investigation of a head and by the details of a body, which he rendered in ever smaller sculptures.[9] A few years later, the artist began to make miniature busts and figures, such as *Small Bust on a Double Base* (1940–41) and *Small Bust of Silvio on a Double Base* (1943–44), that sit atop heavy bases that take on a quasi-architectural quality (pages 138 left, 139). In a letter to gallerist Pierre Matisse in 1947, Giacometti summarized his recent artistic developments and his decision to move away from live models and to work again from memory:

> Wanting to produce from memory what I had seen, to my horror, the sculptures were becoming smaller and smaller, they only bore any resemblance [to the model] when they were small and yet these dimensions made me rebel and, untiringly, I started afresh, only to arrive after some months at the same point.[10]

The bases became an important element in this endeavor. When he made the miniature heads, the comparatively monumental bases of these miniscule sculptures created a delimited space and an anchor. They became an integral part of his work going forward; as the artist experimented with variations of their shape and proportion, each time the surrounding space was defined in a new way.

Since the early 1930s, Europe's authoritarian governments had been cultivating monumental aesthetics: public buildings that dwarf the human figure, together with a preference for idealized realism in painting, sculpture, photography, and film. By contrast, Giacometti's solitary, tiny busts and figurines ambiguously rise from or disappear into their heavy pedestals. Compared with the architectural monumentalism of the period, they spell out a form of aesthetic resistance. These small-scale sculptures opened the door to the artist's mature style, which developed more fully when he returned to Paris in 1945.

17 *Suspended Ball*, 1930 (1965 version)
Plaster, painted metal, string; 61 x 35.6 x 36 cm. Fondation Giacometti

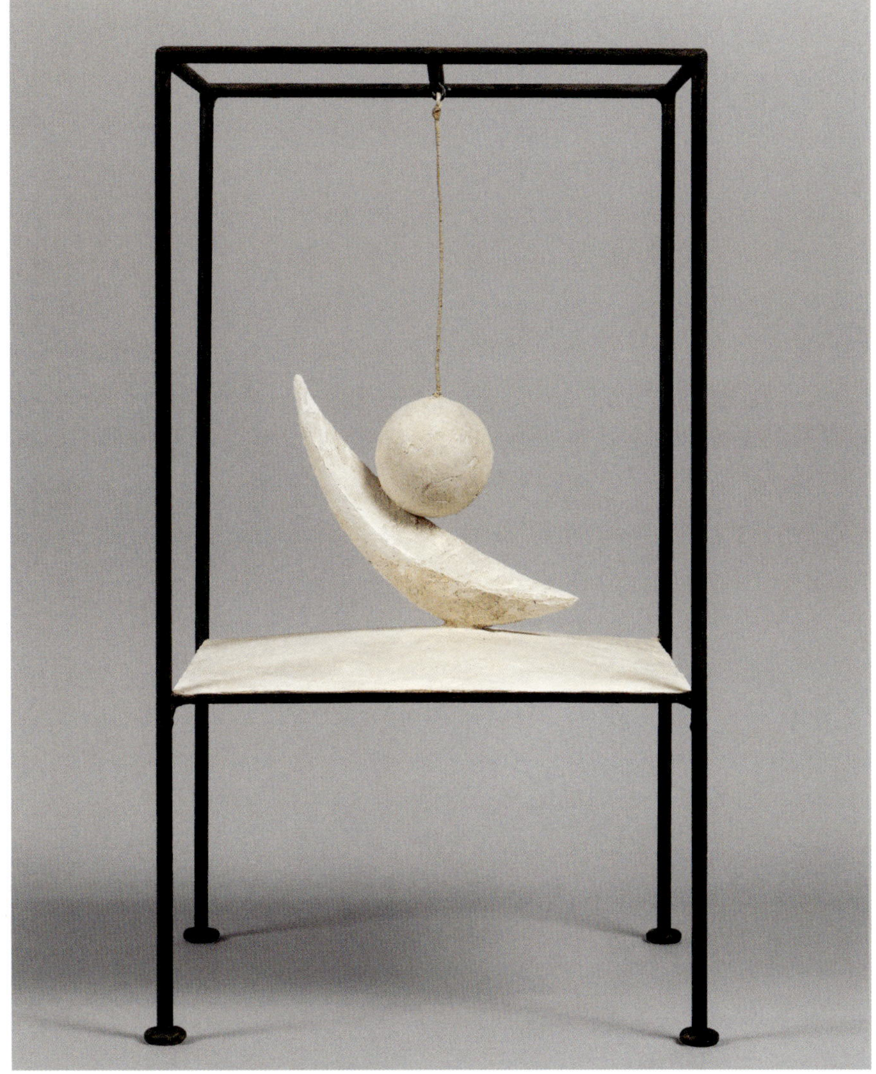

18 *Falling Man*, 1950
In the exhibition *Alberto Giacometti. Plastiken. Gemälde. Zeichnungen*, Wilhelm Lehmbruck Museum, Duisburg, 1977. Anonymous photographer. Archives, Fondation Giacometti

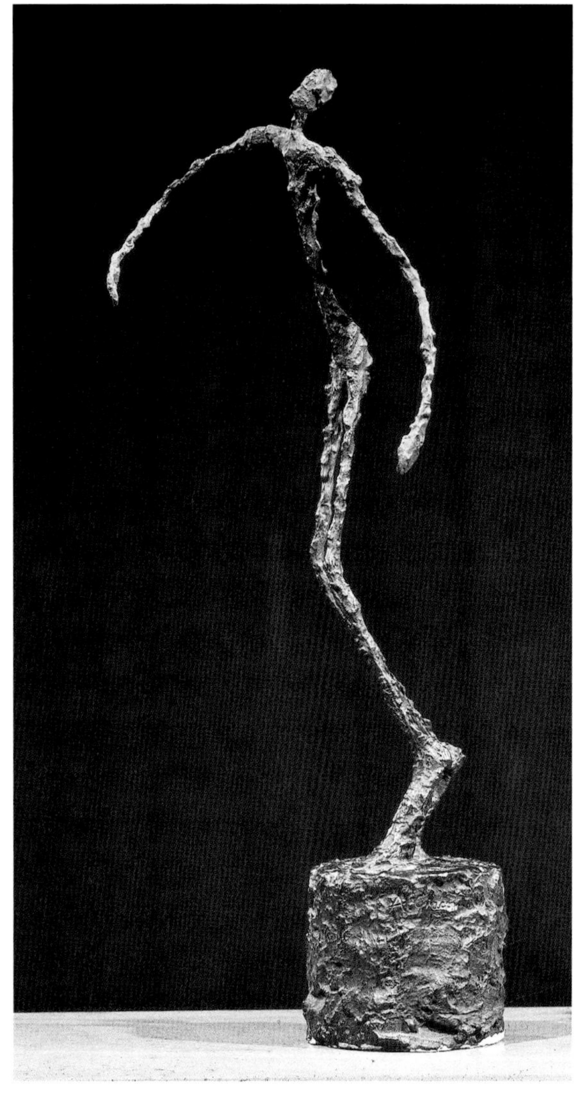

The rough, lumpy surface quality of Giacometti's postwar sculptures was a central element of his new vision and another form of resistance. In the 1920s and early 1930s, he had used a variety of materials, including marble, wood, plaster, and bronze, at times creating highly finished surfaces that invite sensuous and erotic associations. When Giacometti used materials such as clay, he decided to build his works incrementally. This method remains legible in his finished sculptures; the rough surfaces and extremely elongated limbs of his standing women give them a spectral appearance.

A visual memory from a time before World War II, and recounted later, became central to Giacometti's subsequent work and conception of space. The recollection centered on seeing a friend walk away at night, the gestalt gradually disappearing into space; this vision preoccupied the artist for the rest of his career.[11] Going forward, he fundamentally questioned and reconsidered perception; it is a recurring theme in his writings and interviews. His interest in spatial relationships manifests in several key themes: the issue of scale relative to the viewer, a figure's relationship to the pedestal or plinth, and the connection between a sculpture and the surrounding space. In all these developments, the highly textured surfaces of his sculptures have an effect similar to an Impressionist painting. From a distance, we see the posture or movement of a figure in space (fig. 18), but up close the gestalt disintegrates into particulate matter. Writer Jean-Paul Sartre, whose insightful essay accompanied Giacometti's 1948 exhibition at the Pierre Matisse Gallery in New York, described the experience of seeing Giacometti's sculptures:

> You can't approach one of Giacometti's sculptures. Don't expect a belly to expand as you draw near it; it will not change, and you on moving away will have the strange impression of marking time. We have a vague feeling, we conjecture, we are on the point of seeing nipples on the breasts; one or two steps closer and we are still expectant; one more step and everything vanishes.[12]

As Sartre understood, the perception of forms in space is not only revealed by the distance between the spectator and the sculpture, but also dependent on the view. Giacometti's heads, when seen in profile, appear three-dimensional, but when seen frontally, they become slender like the blade of a knife, and the arc of a head's cranium disappears. This effect is especially evident in works such as *Tall Thin Head* (1954), *Head on a Base* (known as *Head without Skull*), (c. 1958), and *Thin Bust on a Base* (known as *Amenophis*) (1954) (pages 144–45, 156).

Between 1946 and 1950, Giacometti made another artistic leap and embarked on a highly productive series of sculptures, vastly different from anything he had made up to this point. He created figures moving in space in varying heights. Among these works are a few tabletop sculptures, such as *The Square* (1948), where a group of slender figures walk in different directions across a plaza, with a single standing figure among them. *Three Men Walking* (1948) is a sculpture of medium height and shows figures drawing close to and walking away from one another (page 194). The flat base on which the figures are positioned captures the scene of an urban plaza with solitary characters. They appear as if seen from a distance, which is a confounding visual experience as the viewer approaches. Related works situated within a natural landscape are *The Glade* (1950) and *The Forest* (1950), where spindly silhouettes rise like trees, straight and still, reminiscent of the forests of his native Switzerland (pages 172, 173). "The composition [of *The Forest*] with seven figures," Giacometti recalled, "reminded me of a forest corner seen for many years (that was during my childhood) where trees with their naked and slender trunks, limbless almost to the top and behind which could be seen granite boulders, had always appeared to me like personages immobilized in the course of their wanderings and talking among themselves."[13]

Cage and *Suspended Ball* had introduced the idea of the enclosure as a framing device nearly twenty years earlier, but by the late 1940s, Giacometti began to think of this more deeply in relation to the self-referential interior of the sculpture compared to its surroundings. A key example is *The Nose* (1947) (page 47). Here, a grotesque head with a Pinocchio-type nose is suspended from a metal structure. The prominent nose protrudes from the boxlike enclosure and connects the "interior" with the surrounding space of the gallery. They are directly linked but also set the "interior" apart from the viewer. These filiform structures became the jumping off point for several related works, among them *The Cage, First Version* (1949–50). Similar to a display case, the upper portion presents a figure and a bust as if laid out in a vitrine (fig. 19 and page 191). The standing figure is not proportional to the considerably larger head, thus disrupting a reading of these figures within a conventional perspectival space. Placed at the outer edge, the standing figure holds onto the armature that marks the perimeter, looking out beyond. Giacometti gave the cage the same nubby texture as the figure, making no material distinction between them. In close proximity, the head rises from the platform of the display, gazing in a different direction, into the void of the surrounding space. The head models the act of looking and establishes a relationship with the standing figure. More importantly, it implicates the artist in the act of looking, as well as the viewer. The empty, open space below the cage provides an abstract measure of volume that relates to the proportions of the surrounding room.

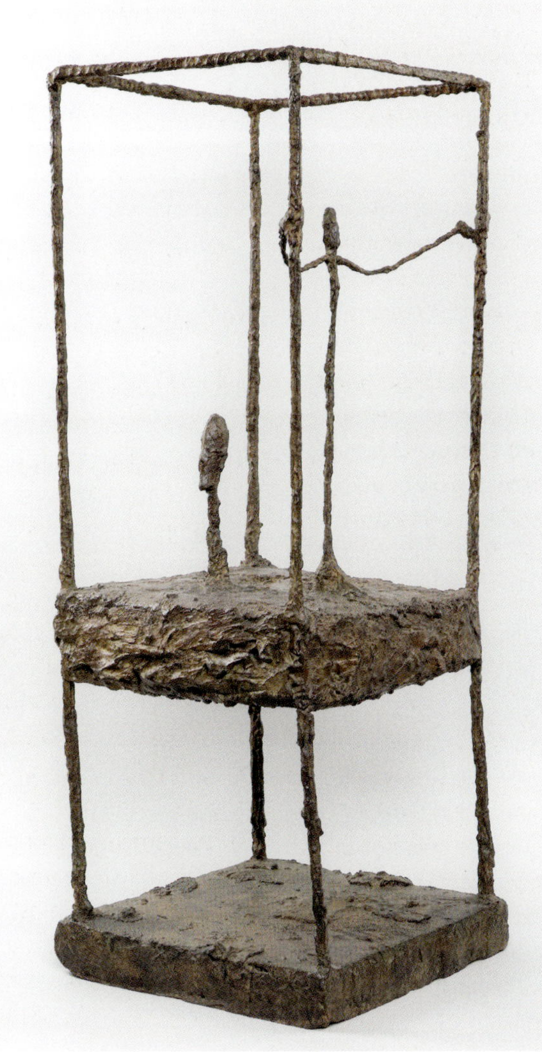

19 ***The Cage, First Version*****, 1949–50**
Bronze; 90.5 x 36.5 x 34 cm.
Fondation Giacometti

In painting as in sculpture, Giacometti used this architectural device to demarcate the scene represented. A painted frame is a way to surround (and outline) the space of his vision. Starting in 1948, he focused on live models. His brother Diego began to sit for him again, as did his spouse, Annette (fig. 20). When painting, Giacometti used one or several frames of neutral color and drew his subjects either with thin black lines or sketched them in broad strokes. The two-dimensional frames played with the viewer's perception, putting more or less distance between them and the painted or sculpted space on the canvas. Windows open onto the scene represented, inviting us to enter the intimate exchange between the artist and the model, while also creating a barrier. Behind his painted figures, the space of the studio is often loosely sketched with a network of lines on a background formed with quick strokes.

Even when working in two dimensions, he was confronted with the challenge of his physical distance in relation to the model, and his perception of the latter in space. When Giacometti painted, he sometimes moved closer to the model, then stepped back, so as to measure the space separating him from the sitter and to establish the proper distance and relational perspective. The same need to reduce or to increase the distance is subconsciously demanded of the viewer when looking at his paintings. Writer Jean Genet, who was Giacometti's friend and model, described this in his emblematic text *L'Atelier d'Alberto Giacometti* (*The Studio of Alberto Giacometti*): "As I move away, the face, with all its contours, appears to me, imposes itself, comes to meet me, swoops down on me, and hurries back into the canvas from which it came, becomes a terrible presence, reality, and form. . . . Seen twenty meters away, each portrait is a small mass of life which could effortlessly feed a hundred other portraits."[14] When drawing, Giacometti likewise focused on the subject represented, which takes up only a small fraction of the white sheet of paper. The rest remains blank. Sartre aptly described Giacometti as the artist of the void, and he understood that Giacometti's figures occupy an imaginary space. The artist's deep interest in the act of seeing can be understood in the significance accorded to the gaze of the model. To him, the expression of a person's eyes is of utmost importance, a portal to the physical and spiritual "resemblance" of the person before him.

20 ***Annette*, 1954**
Oil on canvas; 65 x 54.4 cm. Staatsgalerie Stuttgart. Photo courtesy of Staatsgalerie Stuttgart

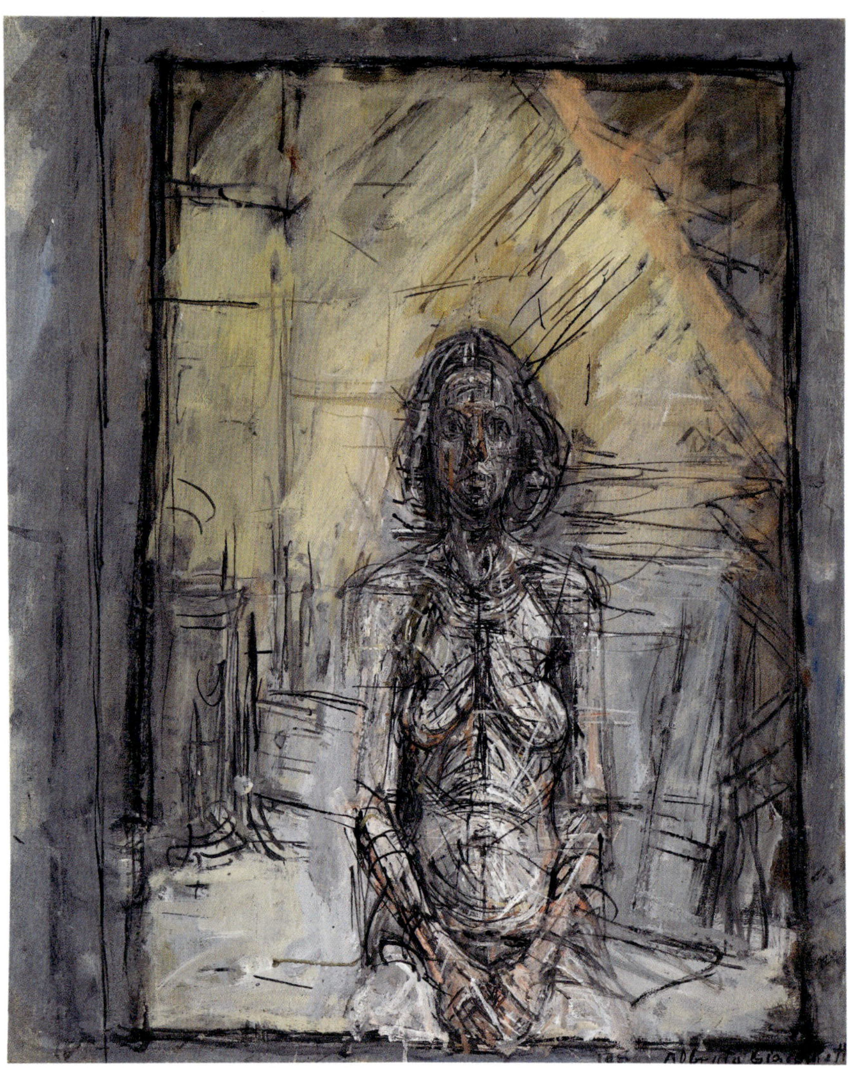

With works such as *Four Figurines on a Stand (London Figurines)* (1950–65), the artist merged the elevated armature of *Cage* with a wide pedestal on which four small, solitary female figures stand like guardians of a temple (page 192). The frontal, hieratic posture of these figures becomes a hallmark of his mature style, and combines austerity with extreme fragility. A profound tension is established by the stark contrast between the monumental scale of the figures in relation to their supporting architecture, the gravitas of their formal posture, and their linear arrangement on the crest of the pedestal compared with their apparent fragility and diminutive scale relative to the viewer's own.

Like many of his artistic contemporaries in Paris, Giacometti had been studying African art since the 1920s, as well as the sculpture and artifacts of ancient cultures of the Middle East, accessible in Paris museums. Ancient Egyptian sculpture and architectural renderings, notably the monumental scale of funerary monuments, would have been highly significant to Giacometti's own artistic explorations. The scale and the placement of objects within a given architecture, especially if elevated, create hierarchies that register both physically and psychologically. It is in this context that Giacometti's figures, standing motionless on their imposing bases or mid-stride on platforms, need to be understood. Genet noted that he was moved and bewildered by these statues, frozen in their walk. They captivate the viewer in an optical illusion.

In the aftermath of World War II, Giacometti searched for an artistic solution that could reclaim the figure in a different dimension. His artistic reply was his solitary and elongated forms, more silhouette than body, fragile but archaic, as if an artifact from a different era.[15] Sculpture had always existed in relation to architecture, often helping to complete elaborate visual programs of an encompassing vision, starting with ancient architecture. Traditionally, sculpture was inscribed into the architecture and had to correspond to the established proportions, set into alcoves and flanking entrances, thus reinforcing and embellishing an architectural vision. Giacometti's astounding insight is that he could produce figures that allowed him to frame surrounding space, independent of a building's scale. More importantly, he draws viewers' attention to the sculptures in relation to the overwhelming weight of the surrounding space. Regardless where they appear, his figures stand up against the void.[16]

Giacometti's shift from sculpture as a self-contained unit to space itself is possible because his figures are spectral rather than representational, and this effect is heightened when they appear in white interiors. A viewer might expect that Giacometti's sculptures would be swallowed by the surrounding space, but the visual and spatial effect, increased by the patina of the bronzes, creates a surprising optical resistance. It is this dynamic exchange between his figures (at times barely there) that invariably asserts their presence: Giacometti creates an electrified stage on which the viewer enters. This is qualitatively different from 1960s Minimalism in the United States. Artists like Carl Andre, Donald Judd, and Sol LeWitt mapped the space of a gallery with serial repetition of a preconceived module, such as a grid of metal tiles on the floor, a stack of wall-mounted shelves, or a cluster of white open cubes that make the surrounding space observably measurable. These installations provide a mathematical, factual quantification of space and volume. Giacometti, by contrast, allows the viewer to understand space intuitively—the weight and power it exerts on a single figure and by implication the viewer. His solemn, hieratic standing women magically reinscribe the architectural surroundings as a sacred space, as if translating Giotto's painted "space within a space"—the sanctum surrounding his holy protagonist—into three dimensions.

1. Donald Judd, "Alberto Giacometti," *Arts Magazine* (February 1962): 42.

2. For additional works that do away with a sculpture's solid core, see Giacometti's *Man (Apollo)* (1929), *Three Figures Outdoors* (1929), and *Cage* (1930). *Three Figures* and *Cage* are especially interesting for their frame and box, respectively, where forms are dynamically piercing and interacting within the confines of a delineated space.

3. For an intriguing and alternative view of the concepts of space and time in relation to the development of modern art, viewed through new scientific discoveries and their connection to Theosophy and other spiritual and spiritualist theories, see *Okkultismus und Avangarde: Von Munch bis Mondrian 1905–1915* (Ostfildern: Schirn Kunsthalle Frankfurt, 1995).

4. These works have been reviewed at length in relation to principles of chance and play. For a discussion of these themes' connection with different Surrealist tenets, see Rosalind E. Krauss, "A Game Plan: The Terms of Surrealism," in *Passages in Modern Sculpture* (Cambridge, MA: MIT Press, 1994), 105–46.

5. This work no longer exists, but photographs taken in Giacometti's studio by Hungarian French photographer Brassaï offer a glimpse. They show the individual objects on a large scale: a stele, cone, circle, semisphere, and snake motif.

6. Ángel González, *Alberto Giacometti: Works, Writings, Interviews* (Barcelona: Polígrafa, 2006), 131.

7. For an overview of key ideas, see Krauss, *The Originality of the Avant-Garde and Other Modernist Myths* (Cambridge, MA: MIT Press, 1985).

8. "The Surrealists consider this change to representation a betrayal. In late 1934 or early 1935, Giacometti is called to account by Breton at a group meeting and charged with disloyalty to Surrealism owing to his design work for Jean-Michel Frank." See "Chronology," in *Alberto Giacometti* (New York: Museum of Modern Art; Zurich: Kunsthaus Zurich, 2001), 284.

9. Pierre Schneider, "*Ma longue marche* par Alberto Giacometti," *L'Express*, no. 521 (June 1961): 48–50; reprinted in Alberto Giacometti, *Écrits: Articles, notes et entretiens* (Paris: Hermann and Fondation Giacometti, 2007), 236.

10. Letter from Giacometti to Pierre Matisse, in González, *Alberto Giacometti*, 133.

11. Pierre Dumayet, "Le drame d'un réducteur de tête," *Le Nouveau Candide*, no. 110 (June 6–13, 1963): 9; reprinted in Giacometti, *Why I am a sculptor* (Paris: Hermann and Fondation Giacometti, 2017), 44.

12. Jean-Paul Sartre, "The Search for the Absolute," in *Alberto Giacometti: The Origin of Space*, exh. cat. (Ostfildern: Hatje Cantz, 2011), 235.

13. Giacometti, in *Alberto Giacometti*, exh. cat. (New York: Museum of Modern Art, 1965), 55.

14. Jean Genet, *L'Atelier d'Alberto Giacometti* (Décines: Barbezat, 1958), 57. A translation can be found in Charlotte Mandell and Jeffrey Zuckerman, *The Criminal Child: Selected Essays by Jean Genet* (New York: NYRB Classics, 2020), 81. Genet sat for two portraits painted in 1954 and 1955. In 1957, Giacometti made a third painted portrait of the author.

15. There is a melancholy element in the elongation of his limbs, a proportional ratio that has a precedent in the sculptures of Wilhelm Lehmbruck.

16. This is a fundamental and existential relationship that leads to fruitful conversations with playwright Samuel Beckett and their collaboration for the 1960 stage set for *Waiting for Godot*, for which Giacometti created the tree, the central prop.

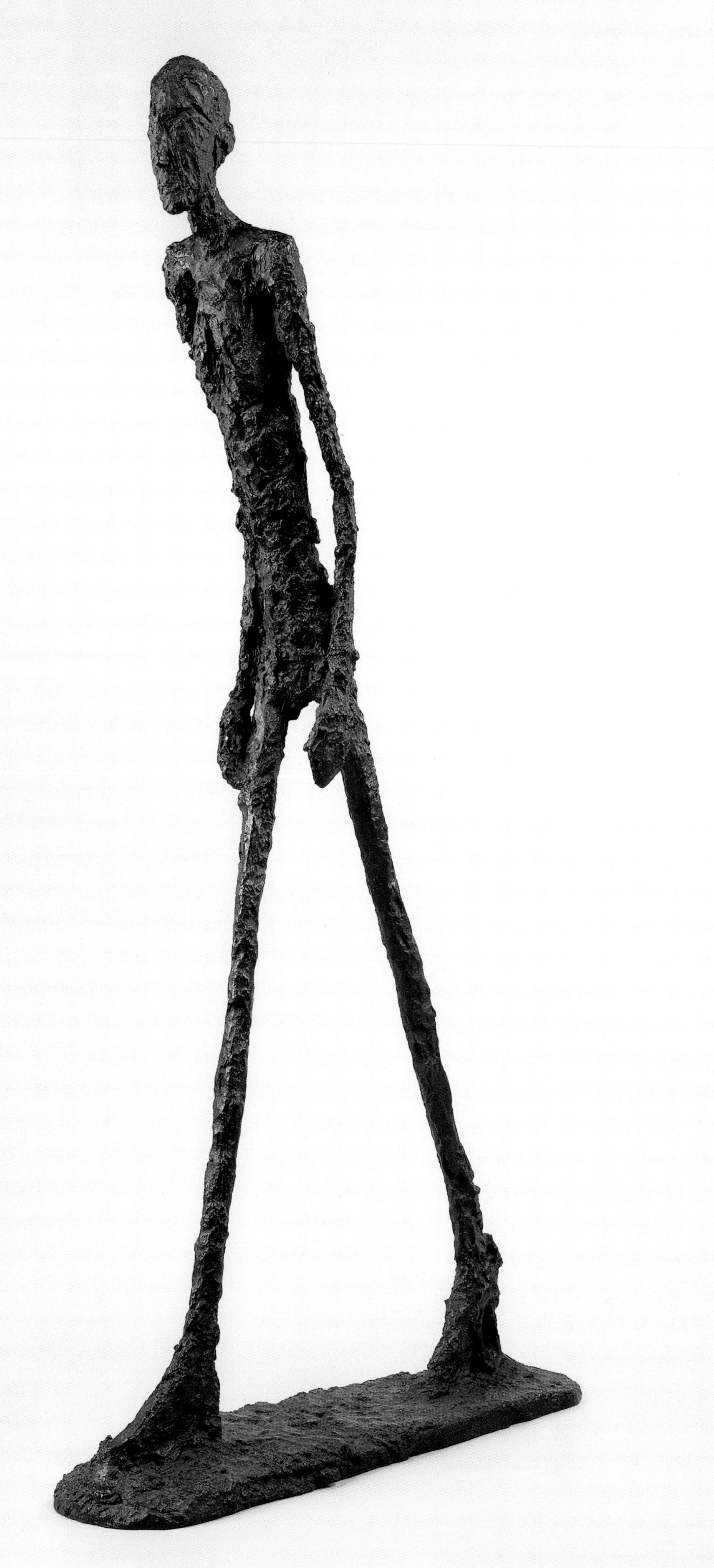

Walking Man

CATHERINE GRENIER

***Walking Man I*, 1960**
Bronze; 180.5 x 27 x 97 cm.
Fondation Giacometti

Walking Man (page 216) is the most well known of Alberto Giacometti's works. More than a famous sculpture, more even than a masterpiece, it is a contemporary icon. With that theme, treated by many others before him, but which he approached in his own distinct style, Giacometti succeeded in concentrating the expressive energy of his oeuvre and in representing the most powerful aspiration of his time: to humanize the world, history, and art. In this symbolic sculpture, the artist conveyed everything about the human being with the greatest economy of means and effects: a matter compressed to its limit; an attitude devoid of pathos, essentially human in its simplicity; a symbol without emphasis; a title without lyricism. This representation of humanity, particularly precious in the present time, places this work among the most celebrated in the world and, in correlation, among the dearest.

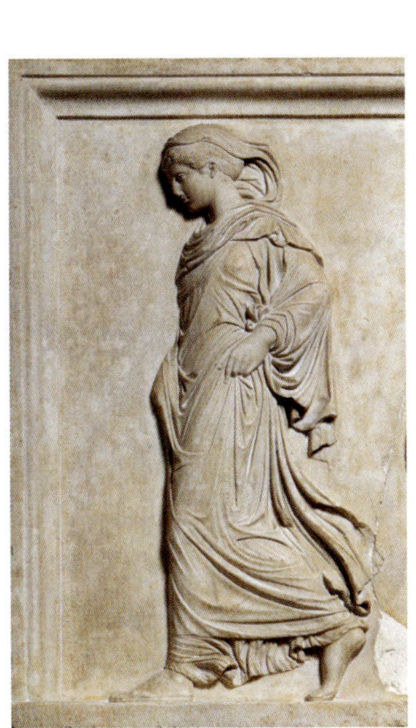

21 Bas-relief known as "Gradiva," detail of a Roman copy after a Greek original from the 4th century BC
Marble. Museo Chiaramonti, Vatican Museums, Vatican State. Photo: Scala / Art Resource, NY

In its first stage, *Walking Man* was *Walking Woman*, the title of the first work that took on this theme. Created in 1932 during the artist's Surrealist period, that sculpture reasserted the importance of the human figure within his production of works, which had lost direct connection with figuration. After the naturalism of his early works, followed by a short neo-Cubist phase that took him to the doors of abstraction, in 1929 the young artist acquired a reputation with works steeped in symbolic connotations that persuaded the Surrealists to invite him to join their ranks. After three years of creating "objects with a symbolic function"—an expression coined by Salvador Dalí, who enthused about his work—*Walking Woman* (1932) reconnected with a more traditional representation. However, the desire to depict again the human body did not bring the artist back to the living model, but led to a composition based on imagination that goes back to the principles and postures of Egyptian motifs. Headless and armless, the slender body is similar to an archaeological find; the aesthetics of that androgynous character are also reminiscent of the Symbolist sculpture the artist was familiar with in his youth. The theme is given a Surrealist undertone and should be connected to the fascination Dalí had for *Gradiva*, the "woman who moves forward" from Wilhelm Jensen's novel, famous for the use Sigmund Freud made of it in his study on the workings of dreams and the analytical cure (fig. 21).

Giacometti used this motif a second time to represent a hieratic and static character, a strange female figure sitting on a throne (*Invisible Object*), which was the last of its type. After having struggled to give form to his idea, the artist showed his dissatisfaction for a work of imagination that still produced two masterpieces. He decided to go back to working from the live model, which accelerated his breakup with André Breton's movement in 1935. The following year he nevertheless agreed to present *Walking Woman* at the Pierre Matisse Gallery in New York. To adapt this sculpture to his new principles, he decided to rework the original model by accentuating the silhouette's natural style. He devoted several months to this transformation, removing the mysterious cavity made in the thorax of the original version and remodeling the back and the chest in a more naturalistic way. "It is probably the best thing I've ever made," he wrote to his mother. "I started it in 1932 and gradually I worked on it a lot."[1] This plaster sculpture was sold to Peggy Guggenheim. Roland Penrose, who had exhibited its first version at the Surrealist exhibition presented in London, commissioned a copy. Giacometti was now involved in a new practice, and he was not tempted by the growing public success of his oeuvre from the Surrealist period to make works in the same vein, and that despite unanimously positive reactions.

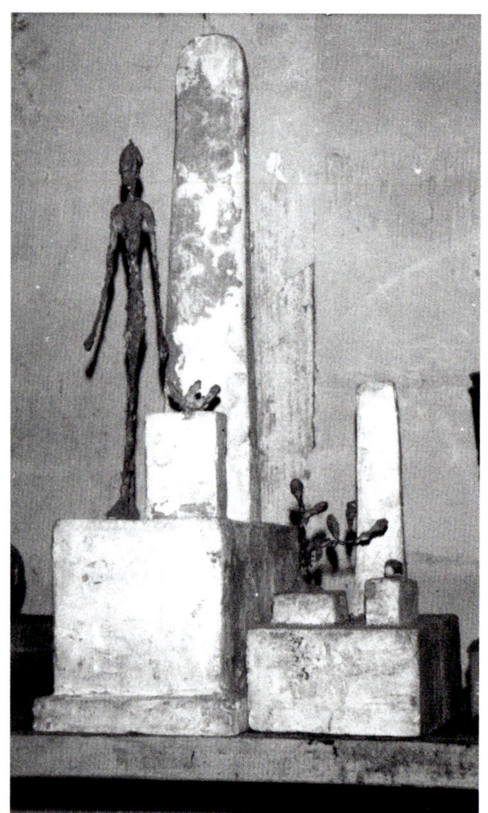

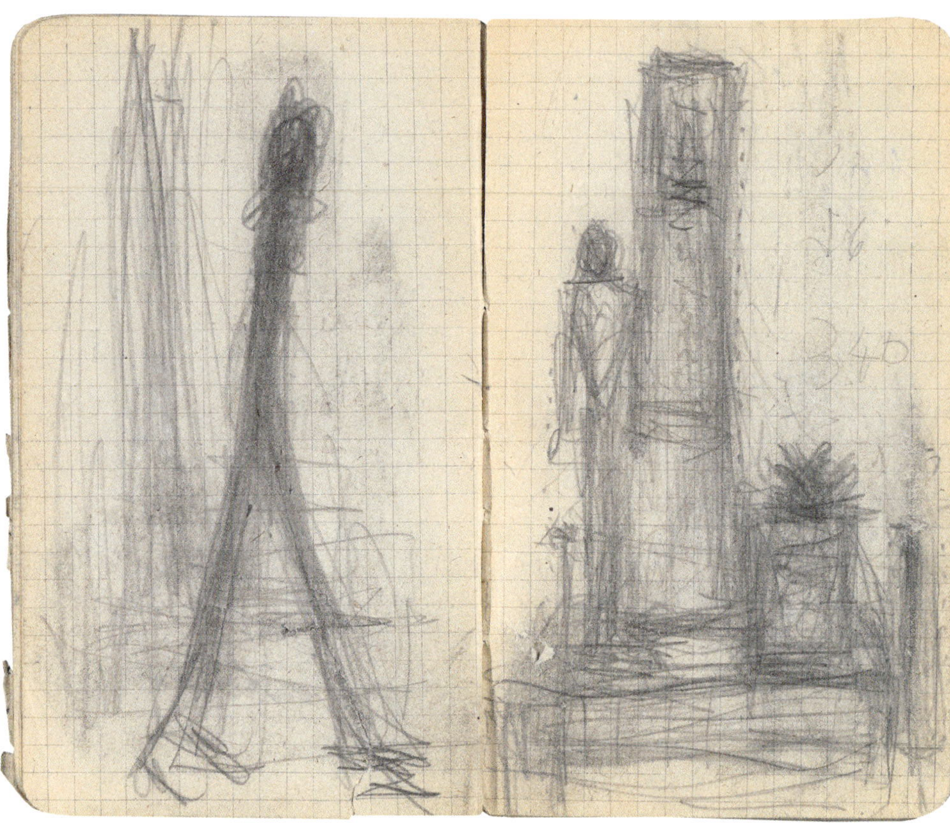

22 Two projects for monuments in memory of Gabriel Péri (plaster casts of 1946), in the studio of Diego Giacometti
Archives, Fondation Giacometti

23 *Sketches for a Project for a Monument in Memory of Gabriel Péri*
Pencil on notebook;
14.4 x 17.8 cm.
Fondation Giacometti

The theme of the walking figure only reappeared after the war. As soon as he was back from Geneva, where he stayed for more than three and a half years, commissions came in steadily. In December 1945, he was approached by the City of Paris to create a monument commemorating Jean Macé,[2] who promoted secular schools. According to communist writer André Thirion's memoirs, he imagined "a wonderful spindly character," who was refused and whose model is not known today.[3] Perhaps it is the sculpture *The Night*, the fragile silhouette of a naked woman walking on a long, high board. This plaster work, made at the same time, was indeed publicized in 1946 under the title *Study for a Monument*.[4] Giacometti described it to Pierre Matisse as "a skinny young woman fumbling in the dark."[5] The slender figure, which he subsequently enlarged and placed on a higher base, lost its hands and female attributes in the second version. A few months later, the Communist Party invited him to take part in a competition for a monument honoring the memory of Resistance fighter Gabriel Péri (figs. 22, 23). This project didn't materialize either, but the research accomplished for the occasion led him to represent a universal human figure. The experiments he undertook for those commissions were a crucible of ideas for new pieces: "Whether the statue is made or not, I still have the sculpture," he wrote about the monument to Péri.[6]

The quest for a commemorative image to be set up in a public space induced him to imagine sculptures with simple forms, like graphic signs unfurling in space. For the monument to Péri, he made a walking man. A massive plaster base, surmounted by a stele in the same material, served as the foundation for that slender bronze figure. A second model for the stand was made by an architect friend, Paul Nelson, who placed the figure on a more dynamic base. Too imposing, and not in harmony with the form and lightness of the walking man, neither of those bases successfully exhibited the qualities required for a monument. The motif, on the other hand, appeared in many sculptures made during the following years.

In 1947, Giacometti created two walking figures purposefully without a stand; a thin platform integrated into the sculpture made it possible to place it directly on the ground. Represented life-size, the first of these walking men is so thin that he is almost invisible full face. The narrow width of the step and the static aspect of the body seem to be once again a reference to Egyptian art. The original plaster used to cast the piece having been damaged, this sculpture was only made in an edition of one. Despite the artist's wish for the model to be restored so that the casting could be continued,[7] this project was left aside to make room for others. Although it is called *Walking Man*, the character represented in this sculpture doesn't have strong gender-related features.

At the time, the issue on the artist's mind was not so much that of androgyny, a theme connected to Surrealist circles, as that of the stripping of all that was not essential to the representation, which distinguishes his work after the war. This figure, like those that followed, shows no distinctive characteristics or anecdotal elements. Nothing connects it to a person in particular, or to a special period, whether in the hairstyle, the clothes, or any other detail. The second version, made in smaller dimensions (67 cm high), is a bronze of which certain parts have been enhanced with color by the artist. But those highlights, which were mainly applied to the hair and the details of the face, tend to epitomize the sculpture rather than resemble a specific model. A link to ancient art appears here too, mainly to sculptures painted in archaic antiquity.

Several years had passed before the artist went back to the motif of the life-size walking man. The theme had not been abandoned, though, as it was used in sculptures of smaller dimensions that introduced a more direct connection with reality: the walking figure no longer refers to a stereotype of the representation but to the perception of an occurrence in daily life. In the street, on a square, Giacometti staged the common man and the fleeting vision of life that is embodied in the movement of people walking in the distance. The titles of pieces echo this character of daily life: *The Square* (1948), *Me Walking Quickly under the Rain* (1948), *Man Walking in the Rain* (1949), *Man Crossing a Square* (1949), and *Man Crossing a Square on a Sunny Morning* (1950) are indicative of the desire to restore the immediacy of the movement. The bases, integrated into the sculptures, follow the idea of sampling reality at a given time. The slender walking figure is supported by the fragment of space on which it is moving.

In *The Square*, of which the artist made two versions, several figures move on a large quadrangular terrace. The four other pieces show isolated characters on an oblong terrace. A ring of three figures on a tiny portion of ground, *Three Men Walking* (1948) revisits the old model of a group sculpture. The poetic *Figurine between Two Houses* (1950) goes back to the female figure. The piece gives greater importance to the fragment of reality associated with the sculpture, a kind of pierced box on feet that the title describes as "two houses." All these sculptures, developed horizontally, are distinguished by the idea of movement introduced by the characters, a movement all the more accentuated; in *The Square*, one of the figures—a female—stands still in the middle of the moving figures.

As in *Gradiva*, "a Pompeian fantasy" in which the figure from an antique bas-relief is incarnated in a living woman, the Egyptian model of Giacometti's first *Walking Man* has been given movement, and has changed into a contemporary silhouette. The effect is even more striking since during that same period, he produced countless female sculptures of hieratic appearance, still and with arms alongside their bodies, as in *The Square*, whose representation is at the opposite of reality: a reflection on ancient art on the one hand, and a vision from a café terrace on the other. The contrast between the two forms of representation reinforces the specificities of both. Giacometti was trying to reconcile the art of imagination with the art of perception, past and present. Like many artists, he responded to the stimulation that the animated image and the realism of cinema provided, and he chose to do it by exploring the limits of representation. As a sculptor, he exploited at the same time the virtues of permanence that fix movement at its peak and the movement of the spectator that animates the motif in a subjective way.

In 1951, he presented at Galerie Maeght a new model of *Walking Man* in large format, *Walking Man IV*, whose figure evolved this time on a tall base on feet in the shape of a box. The disappearance of this plaster work has been explained by the artist's dissatisfaction, but it could also be that the model's deterioration prevented it from being cast. Whatever the reason, it marked his abandonment of the sculpted motif of the walking man for several years. A special occasion was needed for the sculptor to return to it. In November 1958, Giacometti received a proposition that filled him with enthusiasm: to compete for the installation of an outdoor artwork in front of the Chase Manhattan Bank in New York.

For the whole of 1959 and part of 1960, Giacometti worked on various ideas for that project. The main aspect was quickly decided on: as in *The Square*, he planned to have sculptures of various natures in dialogue—a very tall standing woman, a walking man, and a large head—all directly placed on the ground. He worked relentlessly and was preoccupied with the issue of proportions. Giacometti had never been to New York; he had never experienced physically the monumentality of American buildings. He decided on the proportions of each sculpture based on pedestrians, rather than trying to adapt to the scale of the city. "He's making three big plaster sculptures," wrote Annette Giacometti to their friend Isaku Yanaihara in June 1959, "a large stationary woman standing 2 m 75 high, a walking man (2 m 20, I think) and a huge head (as big as he can make it), the three sculptures will be placed in relation to one another."[8]

Three months later, the artist wrote to Gordon Bunshaft, the architect commissioning the work: "I was very happy about what you thought of my sculptures during your visit here, but since then, things haven't been happening as planned. I thought I could finish the sculptures in fifteen days, but in reality, I had to pull them apart and remake them several times. I had to start on a new head, a new woman and a new walking man."[9] Although he had begun to work directly on the plaster aggregated around the frame, he decided to change his technique: "He has abandoned plaster and started again on the head and the large woman with clay. I think he's happy with the walking man now," Annette wrote.[10] The studio had never been so cluttered with works and material piled up. "I removed all the plaster from the studio," Annette explained. "I filled five bags, the studio is full of things, on top of the plaster sculptures, there are new ones in clay."[11] But Giacometti was not fully satisfied with any of these sculptures, as his wife noted: "He started all over again with clay, and the sculptures, for the moment, are becoming smaller and smaller, the head particularly, you know, the big head, it has now become much smaller."[12]

The artist then went back to work with plaster. That project forced him to confront new challenges. His tiny studio was little suited to the making of large sculptures, and he was not used to working in large dimensions. To make *Tall Woman*, of which he created several successive models, he had to climb on a ladder to form the material directly. While working on the sculpture, he sprayed the surface with a plaster milk that soiled all the pieces surrounding it. To see the sculptures better and evaluate their scale, he carried them into the courtyard or the street. Giacometti was more worried than usual about the difficulties he encountered, and he became increasingly perplexed.

At the beginning of the following year, after another visit by Bunshaft to Paris, Giacometti seemed more positive. He made two models for *Walking Man*, a *Tall Woman*, and a *Large Head*. "Yesterday evening I spoke on the phone for almost an hour with Alberto who is very happy," Annette said. "He says that this time it's working, and that he's going to finish it all this week, and that he'll be able to finally come to Stampa for a little while to rest. I hope that this time it's going to work, and that all those large sculptures will leave for the foundry and then for New York."[13] The sculptures were finally sent to the foundry, and the artist went to Stampa, then to Rome with Annette. On his return, though, he was dissatisfied with the result. "You're going to be disappointed, and probably angry too, and Bunshaft also," he wrote to Matisse. Giacometti continued:

> The sculptures have been cast. I looked at them at the foundry, I had them burnished, looked at them again on the pavement, in the street in front of the foundry, had them transported to Garches into the Susse garden, the bronzes and the plasters, everything, cast and not cast. All of them are good in some respect, perhaps, but all very far from what I wanted (or thought I wanted), so wide of the mark, so bad that it's out of the question for me to send them, I'd rather never again make any sculpture, I'd rather die than send those bronzes to New York now. I worked on them for a whole year, and on top of that, had done nothing else, I dropped everything for that and the spring exhibition, I have never worked so hard, until the night before my departure for Stampa. I had them cast, four instead of three, I couldn't have done more. I can see they are a failure, or rather, they are not fully achieved, they are all wide of the mark in a big way. . . . I'm not going to leave them, I'm going to start the tall woman and the head all over again as quickly as possible, and I want to have good results as quickly as possible. Walking man is more complicated, I don't know yet if I can make it again. I'm going to try one more time anyway.[14]

But nothing will do. In the summer, he made a *Tall Woman* and a *Walking Man* in plaster that were never cast in bronze. He then gave up on the commission. In total, he had four models of giant female figures, two models of *Walking Man*, and two of *Large Head* cast in bronze. They were individually shown in exhibitions that followed.

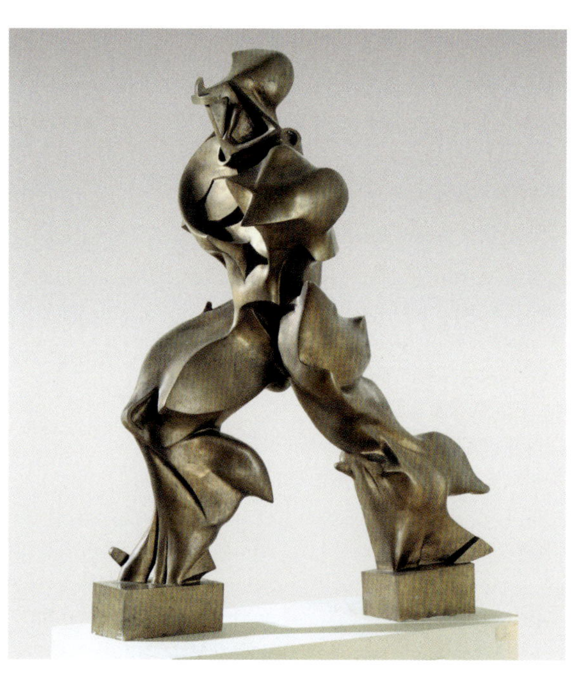

24 ***Unique Forms of Continuity in Space*, 1913**
Umberto Boccioni (Italian, 1882–1916). Bronze; 111.2 x 88.5 x 40 cm. Museo del Novecento, Milan. Scala / Art Resource, NY

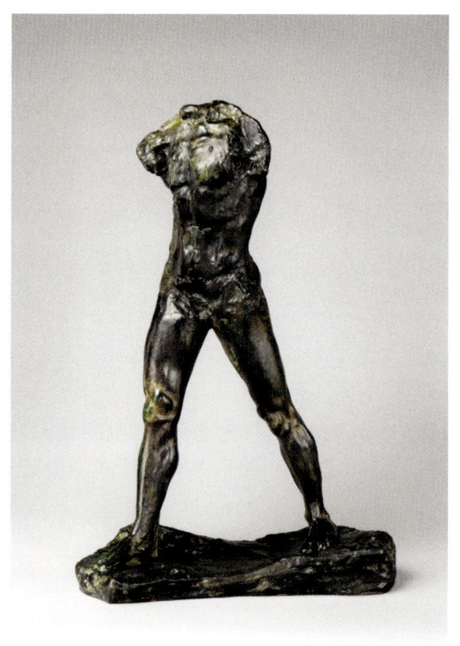

25 ***The Walking Man*, modeled before 1900, cast before 1914**
Auguste Rodin (French, 1840–1917). Bronze, green patina; h. 85.1 cm. The Metropolitan Museum of Art, Gift of Miss G. Louise Robinson, 1940, 40.12.4

26 *Walking Man*, c. 1957
Lithographic pencil on paper; 28.7 x 19.2 cm.
Fondation Giacometti

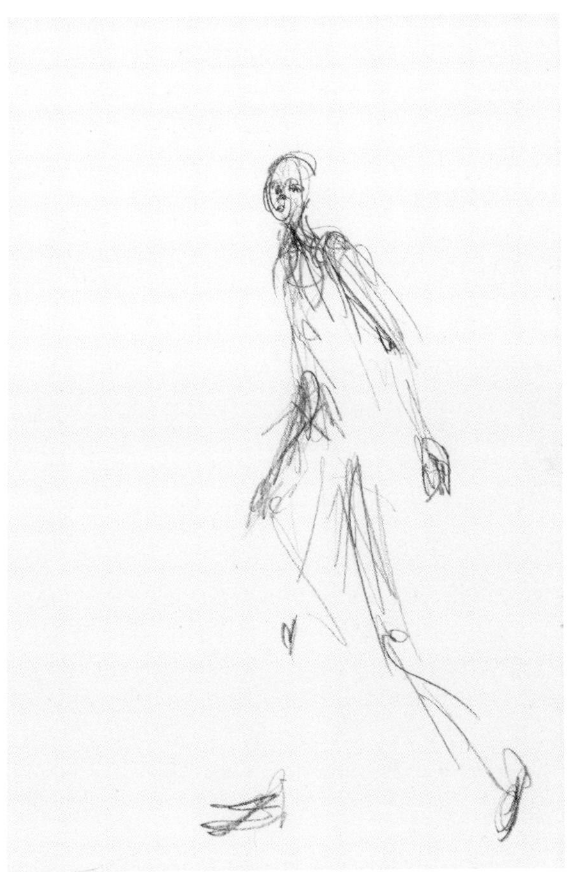

Paradoxically, those sculptures that, in his disappointment he thought were "a failure," were very quickly considered his most symbolic works. Once again, the commission for a sculpture to be placed in a public space provided the right conditions for the creation of exceptional pieces. The extreme concentration he showed during those several months of work was reflected in the sculptures. The two models of *Walking Man*, slightly bigger than the life-size one and whose step is wide and confident, offer the vision of a human at the same time fearless and fragile. Public recognition was immediate. The Carnegie Prize was awarded to him in 1961 for *Walking Man I*, and the sculpture figures among the Carnegie Museum of Art's masterpieces.

To be confronted with the motif of *Walking Man* was a challenge for an artist who had the greatest respect for the works of antiquity and the history of sculpture. Egyptian figures and Greek kouroi but also Umberto Boccioni's modern *Unique Forms of Continuity in Space*, Auguste Rodin's famous *The Walking Man*, or Germaine Richier's *The Walking Man* are illustrious models that he endeavored to follow by imposing on them his own distinctive mark (figs. 24, 25). Unlike all these antecedents, the figure he created doesn't have the anatomy of a hero. Not realistic, epic, or futuristic, it belongs to a different order of representation: that of a figurative sculpture halfway between representation and sign, figuration and abstraction. Giacometti's *Walking Man* reaches the essence of movement, obtained through the synthesis of the various positions of a walking body. As Edgar Degas had done before in his paintings of galloping horses, Giacometti chose the truth of perception experienced by the spectator rather than the faithfulness to nature objectified by photography. In a period when abstract art was at its peak, Giacometti invented the conditions for a figuration that is not a return to tradition. Though he refuted the "devaluation of reality"[15] that he thought *informel* art was, he was nonetheless contemporary with that style, which values sensation over description. He too explored the possibilities of expression through matter and the universe of symbols.[16] "Sculpture where I want / not abstract / or conventional / something else / but what?" he wrote in a notebook around 1949.[17] He considered that the main role of art is to reflect reality, particularly through the image of the human body, but he did not hesitate pushing representation to its limits. The numerous drawings he made of the same motif show the simplification he carried out in his sculptures. More or less minimal, those sketches made with a pencil or a ballpoint pen are closer to the real observation of someone walking than the sculptures. In many of them, the natural movement, the inclination of the body, the folding of the leg show that they are drawings made while looking at scenes in the street (fig. 26). In sculpture, on the contrary, coherence and harmony of the motif are privileged.

All the *Walking Men* made as part of the project for the Chase Manhattan Plaza display the same posture: a foot placed on the ground and the other raised, the legs stiff, the body in the continuity of the back

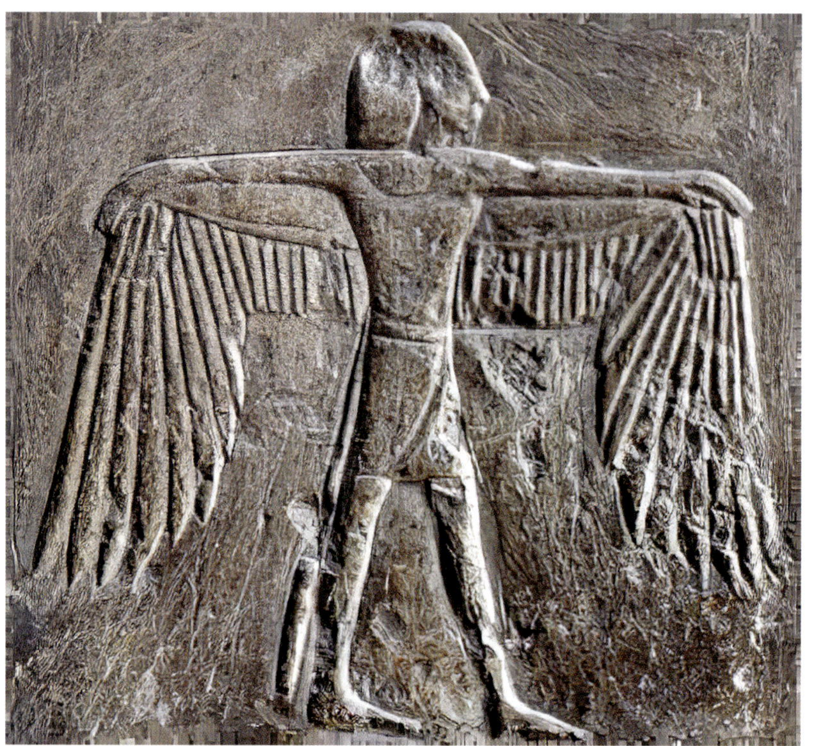

27 Carved hieroglyph on a wall of the funerary temple of Sety I, Abydos, Egypt

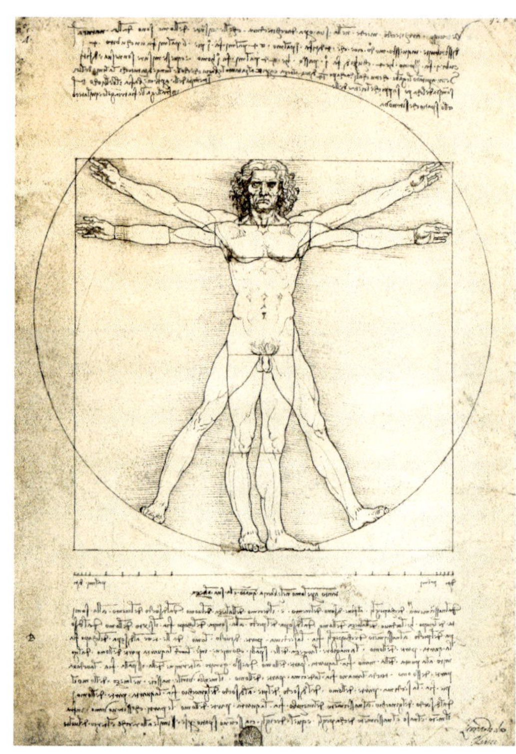

28 *The Vitruvian Man*, c. 1489–90
Leonardo da Vinci (Italian, 1452–1519). Metal nib, pen and brown ink on paper; 34.5 x 24.6 cm. Gallerie dell'Accademia, Venice

leg. In his Surrealist period, Giacometti witnessed the development of anthropology and ethnography, and he was sensitive to the symbolic and ritual dimension of body representation. An admirer of cave paintings and the stylization of Egyptian art, he placed the human reference at the heart of his system of representation and was inspired by the visual power of the pictogram (fig. 27). *Walking Man* is the expression of a desire to reaffirm an anthropology of the image, like the famous illustration *The Vitruvian Man*, which Leonardo da Vinci elevated to the symbol of humanism (fig. 28). Le Corbusier pursued a similar goal when he created *Le Modulor* (fig. 29), based on the principle decreed by the Athens Charter (1941): to regulate the dimensioning of all things according to the human scale. With *Walking Man*, Giacometti revisited the archetypes that he freed from the myth in order to create a symbolic image of modern man: a sensitive, liberated being moving toward the future but who stays connected with the profundity of history (fig. 30). For the artist had held for a long time the conviction that the archetype does not betray objective reality but reveals it:

> Any of us resembles much more an Egyptian sculpture than any other sculpture ever made. And it's the same thing for exotic arts, for African or Oceanic sculpture. People like them because they think them entirely invented, and because they refute the outside world, the common view on reality. On the opposite, people look down on a classic head, a Greco-Roman, because it has a likeness, which is not very interesting at all. I like sculpture from New-Guinea because I find it resembles much more anyone, you or me, than a Greco-Roman head or a conventional head. Style gives us the most accurate vision.[18]

The making of *Walking Man* shows us that with this symbolic representation, Giacometti had succeeded in both style and truth.

29 ***Le Modulor*, 1945**
Le Corbusier (Swiss, 1887–1965). Fondation Le Corbusier, Paris. Photo: Banque d'Images, ADAGP / Art Resource, NY.

30 ***Sketch of a Walking Man and Copy after an Egyptian Sculpture in* Die Antike Kunst: Ägypten und Vorderasien**
Pencil on book; 28.5 x 22 cm.
Alberto Giacometti-Stiftung, Zurich

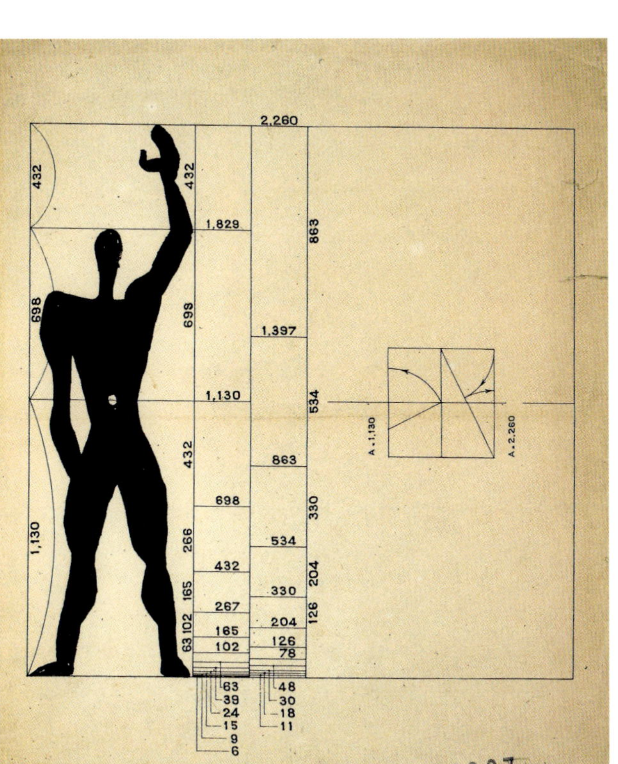

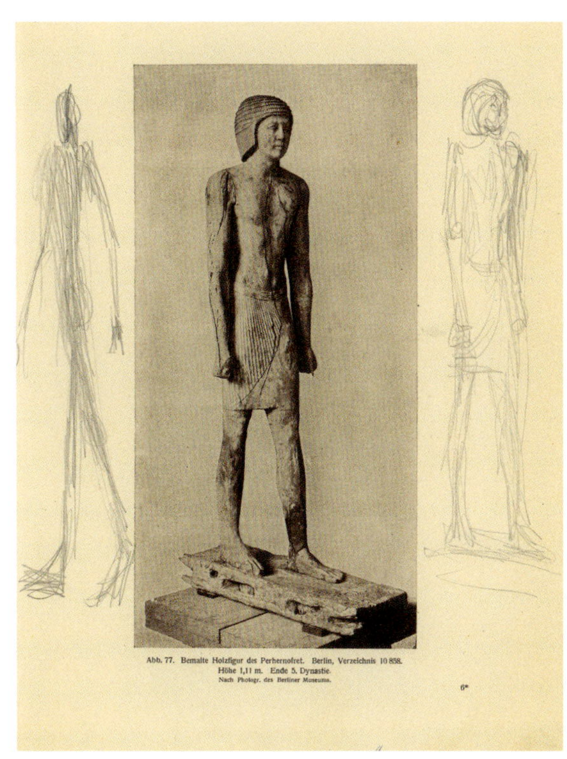

A variation of this essay appears in Grenier, Catherine, ed. *L'Homme qui marche*. Lyon: Editions Fage; Paris: Fondation Giacometti, 2020.

Translated by Catherine Petit and Paul Buck

1. Alberto Giacometti to his mother, October 21, 1936, Archives Alberto Giacometti-Stiftung, Zurich.

2. Alberto Giacometti to his family, December 31, 1945, Swiss Art Archives, SIK-ISEA, Zurich, inv. HNA 274.A.2.1.221.

3. André Thirion, *Révolutionnaires sans révolution* (Paris: Robert Laffont, 1972), 546.

4. Caption of the illustration in *Cahiers d'Art* (1945–46): 258.

5. Alberto Giacometti to Pierre Matisse, October 27, 1947, Pierre Matisse Gallery Archives, The Morgan Library & Museum, New York, box 11, folder 7, item 11.

6. Alberto Giacometti to his family, January 8, 1946, Swiss Art Archives, SIK-ISEA, Zurich, inv. HNA 274.A.2.1.222.

7. Alberto Giacometti to Pierre Matisse, June 9, 1954, Pierre Matisse Gallery Archives, The Morgan Library & Museum, New York, box 11, folder 20, item 113.

8. Annette Giacometti to Isaku Yanaihara, June 5, 1959, Yanaihara Archives, Private collection.

9. Alberto Giacometti to Gordon Bunshaft, September 13, 1959, photocopy, Fondation Giacometti Archives, Paris.

10. Annette Giacometti to Isaku Yanaihara, October 27, 1959, Yanaihara Archives, Private collection.

11. Ibid.

12. Annette Giacometti to Isaku Yanaihara, November 30, 1959, Yanaihara Archives, Private collection.

13. Annette Giacometti to Isaku Yanaihara, February 9, 1960, Yanaihara Archives, Private collection.

14. Alberto Giacometti to Pierre Matisse, April 29, 1960, Pierre Matisse Gallery Archives, The Morgan Library & Museum, New York, box 11, folder 37, item 169.

15. Antonio del Guercio, "L'art dans la société d'aujourd'hui: Entretien avec Alberto Giacometti," *Rinascita*, no. 8 (June 23, 1962): 32; reprinted in Alberto Giacometti, *Écrits: Articles, notes et entretiens* (Paris: Hermann and Fondation Giacometti, 2007), 261–62.

16. Giacometti knew Michel Tapié, who promoted *informel* art. A photograph shows them in Giacometti's studio on rue Hippolyte-Maindron in 1954 (Archives, Fondation Giacometti). He was also connected to several *informel* artists represented, like him, by Galerie Maeght.

17. Alberto Giacometti, Notebook, 1949–50, Fondation Giacometti. See Giacometti, *Écrits*, 541.

18. Alberto Giacometti, quoted in Pierre Schneider, "Au Louvre avec Alberto Giacometti," *Preuves*, no. 139 (September 1962): 23–30; reprinted in Giacometti, *Notes on the copies* (Paris: Hermann and Fondation Giacometti, 2021), 19.

The Nose: The Surrealist Background, between Breton and Sartre

WILLIAM H. ROBINSON

***The Nose*, 1947–49**
Bronze, painted metal, cotton rope; 80.9 x 70.5 x 40.6 cm.
Fondation Giacometti

The Nose holds a special position in Alberto Giacometti's art as the great pivot between his engagement with Surrealism in the 1930s and the highly personal style he developed in the late 1940s. This iconic sculpture features a slender head hanging by a rope from the top of a metal cage. The large, gaping mouth seems either to scream in agony or to laugh with a comic shriek. The figure's tenuously long nose extends outside the cage, making it the only part of his body to escape the metal prison. His grotesquely attenuated neck ends abruptly, leaving the figure suspended in midair. Hanging precariously by a rope, the head can sway with air currents, but not far enough to escape the cage. Trapped between potential movement and stagnation, the figure exists in a perpetual state of ambiguity and tension, its delicate nose subject to potential damage or destruction by outside forces.

Giacometti began working on *The Nose* while writing a short essay for the review *Labyrinthe* titled "Le Rêve, le Sphinx et la mort de T." (The Dream, the Sphinx and the Death of T.). The essay and the sculpture are closely connected. The essay describes a series of traumatic dreams, memories, hallucinations, and real events. It begins with Giacometti recalling a terrifying dream of seeing an enormous furry spider hanging by a single thread over his bed and imagining it suspended over his head. The nightmare is juxtaposed in the essay with thoughts about the recent death of "T.," an elderly man who lived in a room adjacent to Giacometti's in the small house they shared on rue Hippolyte-Maindron in the Montparnasse district of Paris. The corpse remained in the house for days. Giacometti recalled the shock of seeing the emaciated body stretched out on the man's bed at 3:00 a.m., his belly swollen, the head flung back, the mouth open. "Never had any corpse seemed to me so non-existent, pathetic remains to be tossed into the gutter like a dead cat," the artist observed.[1] The next day, Giacometti was seized by the terrifying thought that the dead man was no longer in his body but everywhere in the room, and at any moment he might feel the touch of an icy hand on his arm. Giacometti soon began seeing people in the cafés and on the streets as if alive and dead at the same time. "I screamed in terror, as if I had just crossed a threshold," he remembered, "as if I were entering a totally unknown world."[2]

This haunting experience brought back traumatic memories of an earlier death. In 1921, Giacometti was traveling through Italy with an older man, Peter Van Meurs, who suddenly became ill and died in a hotel room. While watching Van Meurs stretched out on his bed in the process of dying, the twenty-year-old artist was struck by how "his nose became more and more attenuated, his cheeks grew hollow, his almost motionless mouth barely breathing."[3] The experience filled Giacometti with a horrifying obsession that changed his life. Later, while writing his spider dream essay, he developed the feeling that "all of these events existed simultaneously around me," prompting him to draw sketches of a circular concept of time.[4]

While the spider dream essay provides essential context for understanding *The Nose*, Giacometti also borrowed key elements from his Surrealist sculptures of the 1930s. Around 1928, he began moving away from his blocky, Cubist-inspired sculptures toward strange, erotic, sexually violent images incorporating aspects of African and Oceanic art. The introduction of symbolic, metamorphic forms and references to dreams began to align with the Surrealist ideology of the movement's leader, André Breton. This new direction in Giacometti's art became publicly known when he presented *Suspended Ball* at a joint exhibition with Joan Miró and Hans Arp at the Galerie Pierre in Paris in the spring of 1930 (see fig. 17). Giacometti's provocative sculpture features a plaster ball hanging by a rope inside in a metal cage, effectively establishing the basic conceptual format for *The Nose* of 1947. The suspended plaster ball in the earlier sculpture hangs over a curved, crescent shape resting on a thin horizontal platform and has a long notch gouged in the surface. Suspending the ball over the crescent form places the two abstract shapes in a tense, erotic relationship. Wildly enthusiastic about the sculpture, Salvador Dalí proclaimed it the prototype for a new form of art known as the "symbolically functioning object." Writing in the journal *Le Surréalisme Au Service De La Révolution*, Dalí interpreted the gouged

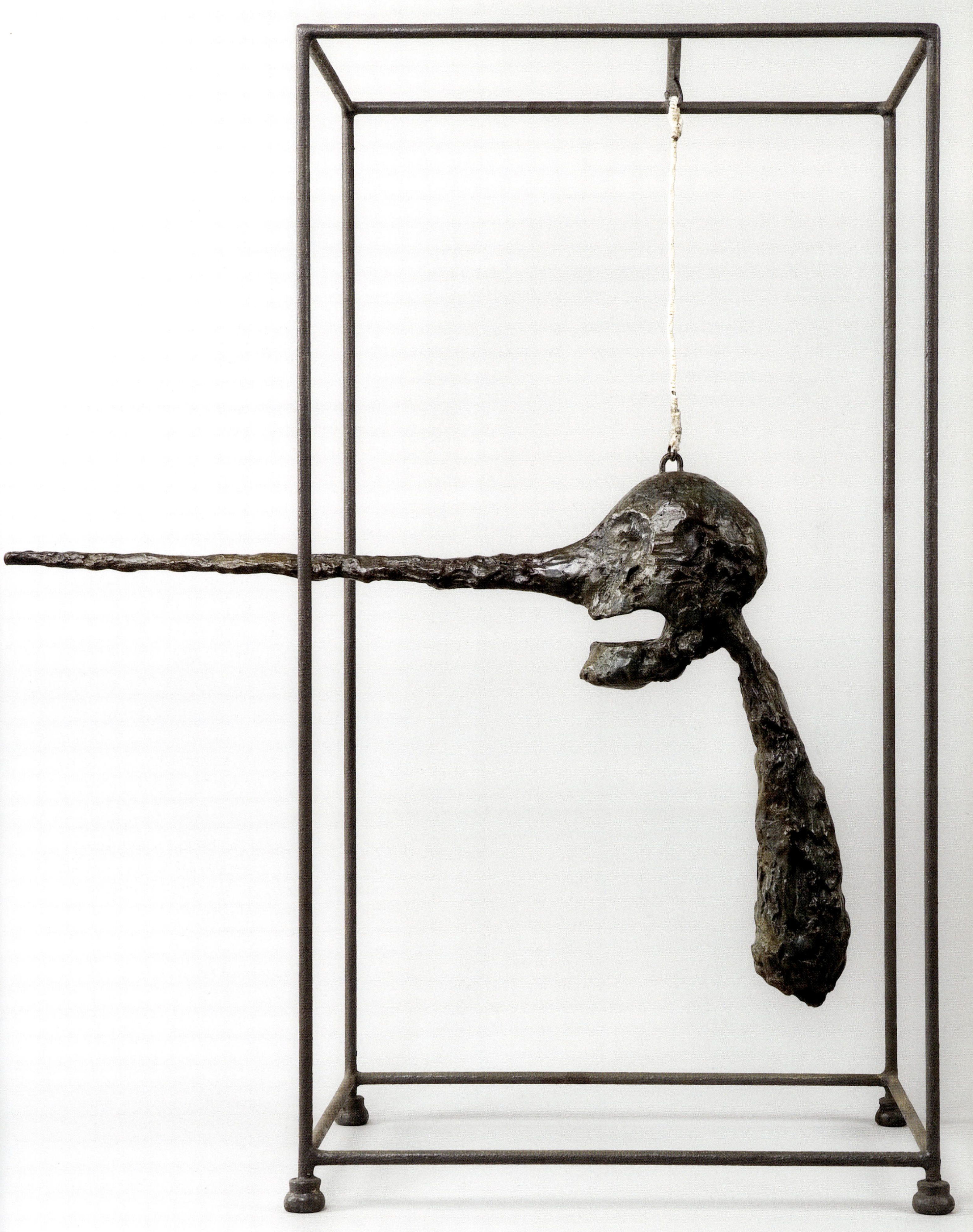

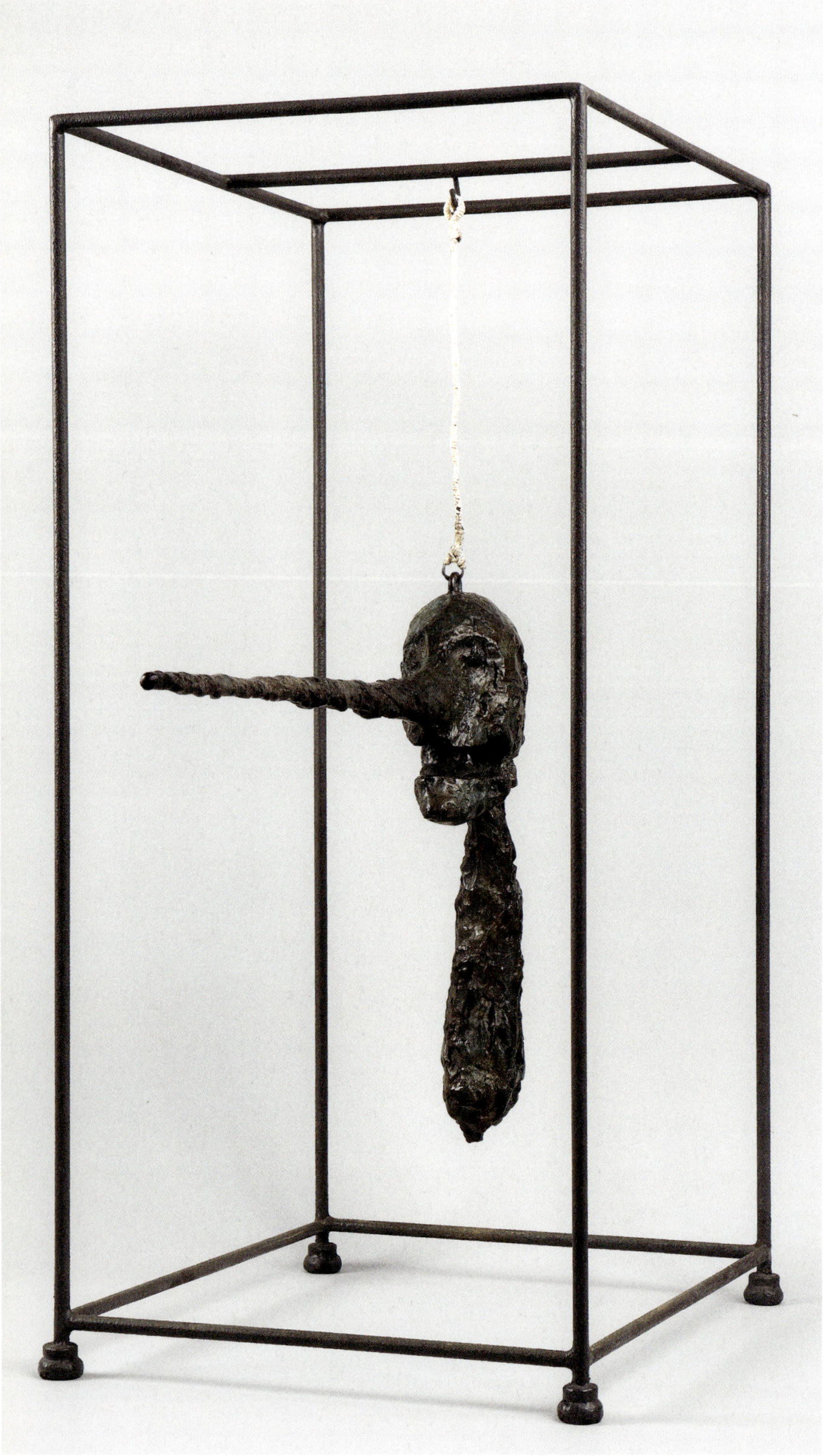

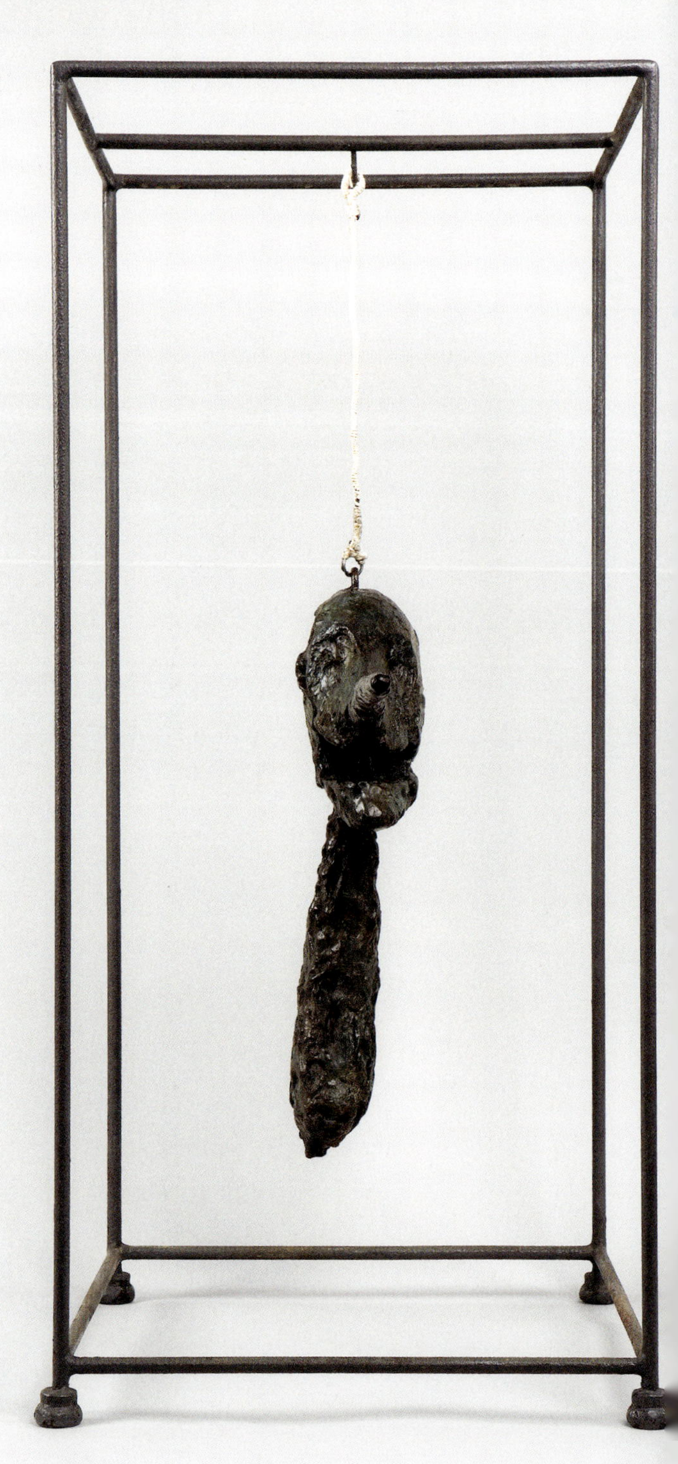

***The Nose*, 1947–49**
Bronze, painted metal, cotton rope; 80.9 x 70.5 x 40.6 cm.
Fondation Giacometti

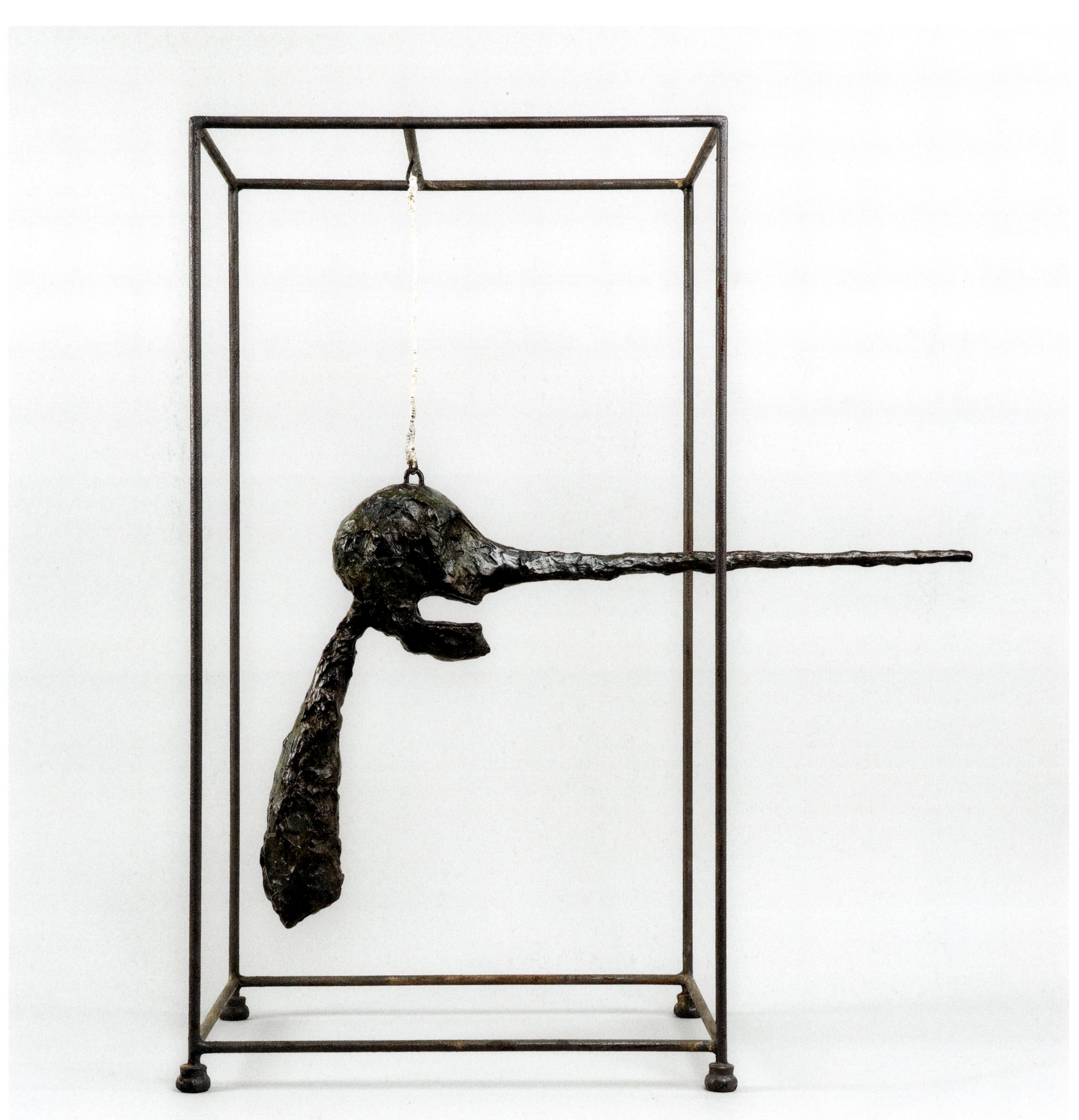

31 ***Disagreeable Object to Be Thrown Away*, 1931**
Bronze; 22.8 x 34.3 x 25.9 cm.
Fondation Giacometti

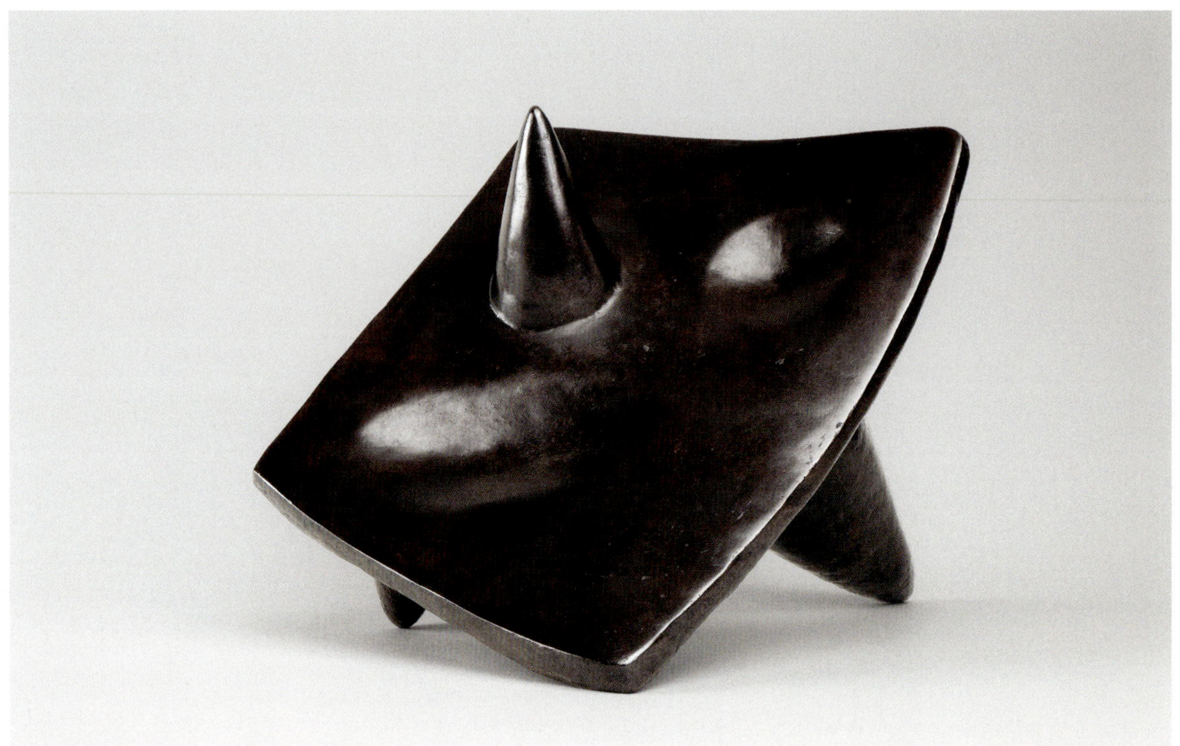

notch that brushes against the crescent shape as a "female slit," observing that the work elicits feelings of both sexual excitement and frustration, as "the beholder instinctively feels the urge to slide the ball over this edge, something the length of the string makes it possible to do only to an extent."[5]

After seeing Giacometti's sculptures at the Galerie Pierre exhibition, Breton visited the artist in his studio, initiating one of the most consequential relationships in the artist's life. Giacometti soon began attending Surrealist meetings and participating in their exhibitions. By 1933, Giacometti and Breton were exchanging visits almost daily, prompting the artist to comment in a letter to his father: "He is by far the most intelligent and sensitive person I know and the only one from whom I learned so much."[6] The relationship provided Giacometti with deeper insights into Freudian psychoanalysis and techniques of exploring the unconscious through free association. Breton's influence is strongly felt in the automatic text Giacometti wrote to accompany his sketches in "Objets Mobiles et Muets" (Mobile and Mute Objects), a two-page spread published in *Le Surréalisme Au Service De La Révolution* in 1931. Three years later, Giacometti wrote another free-flowing, semiautomatic essay, "Hier, Sables mouvants" (Yesterday, Quicksand), published in the same journal, which combines childhood memories with violent sexual fantasies.

32 ***Point to the Eye*, 1931**
Plaster and metal; 13.5 x 59.5 x 31 cm. Fondation Giacometti. Partial reconstitution realized in collaboration with the Alberto Giacometti-Stiftung, Zurich

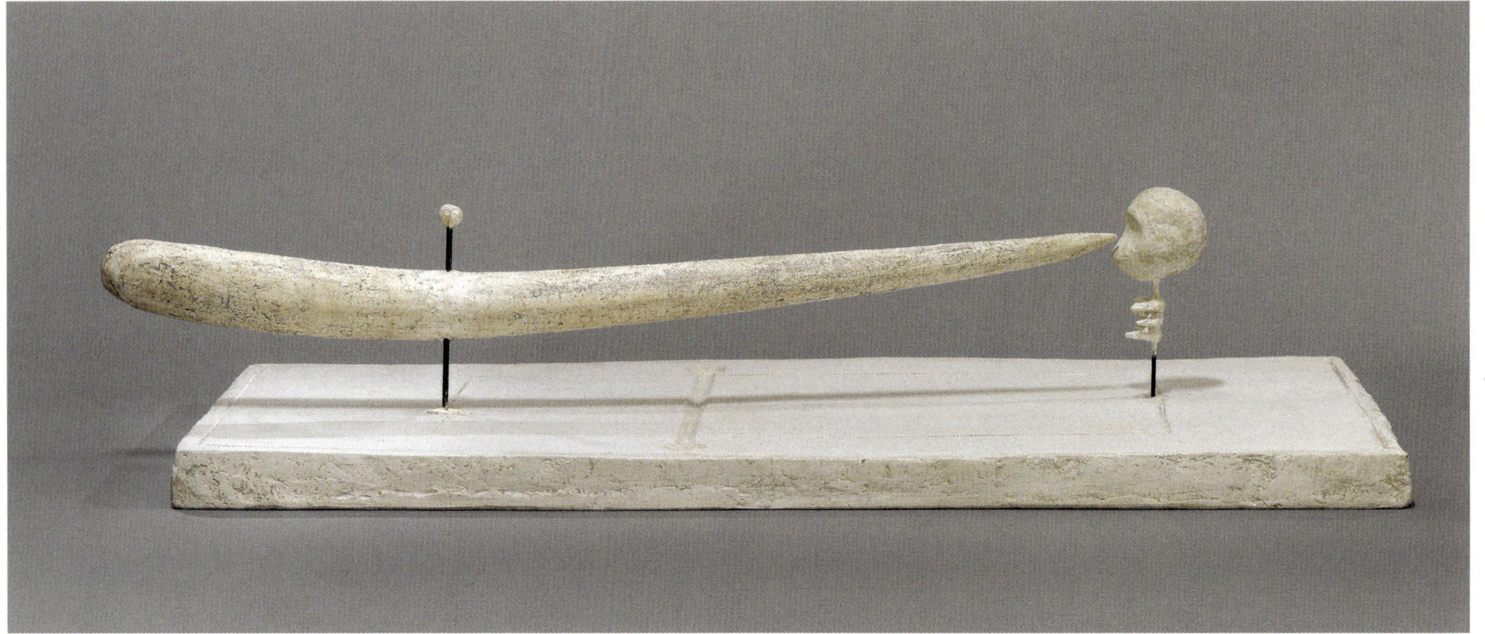

During his Surrealist period, Giacometti stopped working from live models in favor of exploring dreams, memories, and hallucinations through sculptures that combine abstract forms with vague figural references. Objects trapped in cages and sharply pointed forms allude to sublimated desires, fears, anxieties, and sadistic sexual fantasies. The threatening pointed forms in *Disagreeable Object to Be Thrown Away* and *Point to the Eye* (figs. 31, 32) anticipate the attenuated proboscis in *The Nose*. Man Ray's photograph *Woman Holding Giacometti's Disagreeable Object* makes the phallic connotations of the crescent shape in *Disagreeable Object* and *Suspended Ball* more explicit (fig. 33).

In 1934–35, Giacometti returned to working from a live model, precipitating a bitter clash with Breton and his Surrealist allies. Unable to resolve their disagreement, Giacometti was effectively expelled from the Surrealist movement. He stopped attending their meetings but continued to lend his works to their exhibitions so long as he was identified as a "former Surrealist."[7] From around 1938 to 1945, Giacometti spent long hours working on small figural sculptures, often focusing obsessively on small heads and figures seen from a distance. Neither fully naturalistic nor abstract, his works from this transitional period reflect his search for a new path that was more closely tied to ordinary, daily experience.

Giacometti was in Switzerland when the Germans invaded Poland in September 1939. Later that fall, he returned to his studio on rue Hippolyte-Maindron and remained in Paris for over a year. In December 1941, he slipped out of France and spent the rest of the war in Switzerland producing mostly small figural sculptures, with one notable exception, along with paintings and drawings. In September 1945, four months after the war in Europe ended, he returned to Paris, once again establishing himself in the studio on rue Hippolyte-Maindron.

The intellectual and cultural climate in Paris changed dramatically during the postwar years. Living in the

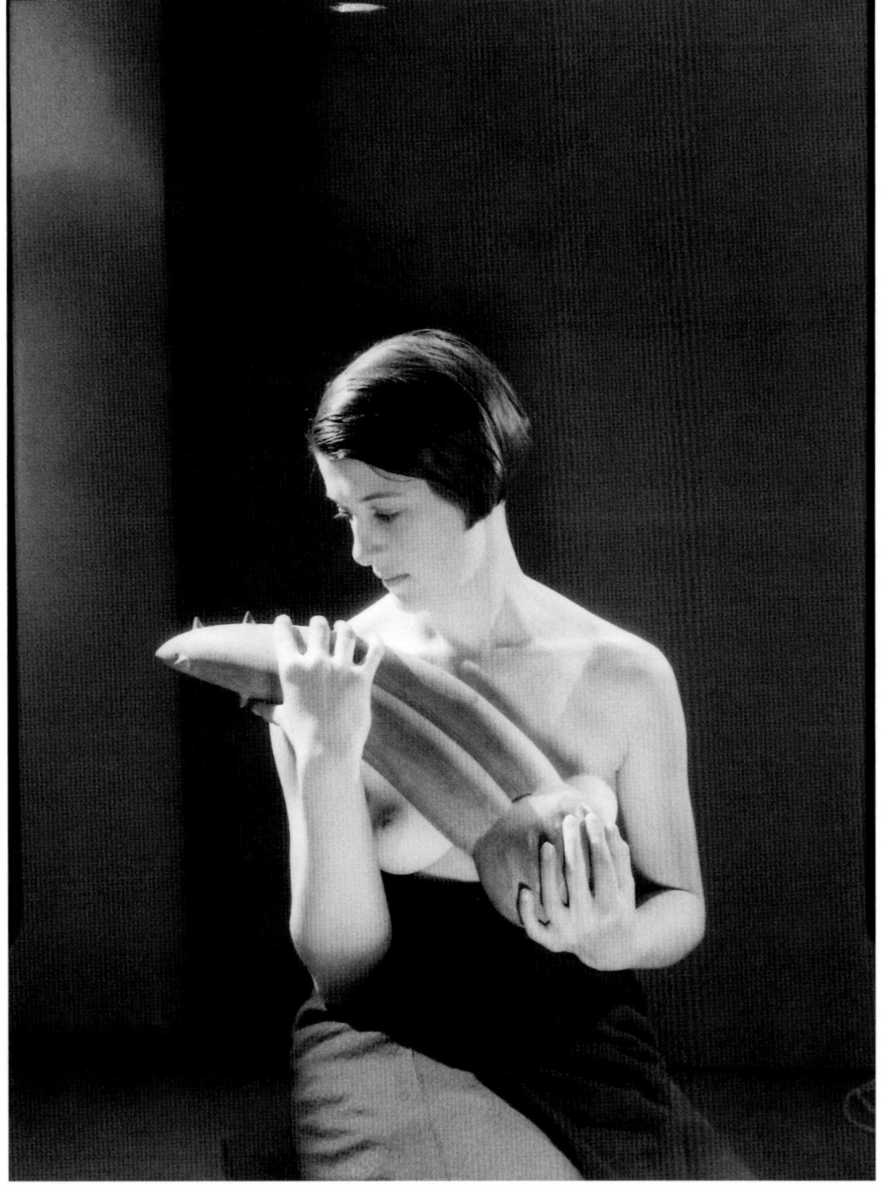

33 *Woman Holding Giacometti's Disagreeable Object*, 1931
Man Ray (American, 1890–1976). Gelatin silver print. Archives, Fondation Giacometti. © Man Ray 2015 Trust / Artists Rights Society (ARS), NY / ADAGP, Paris 2022

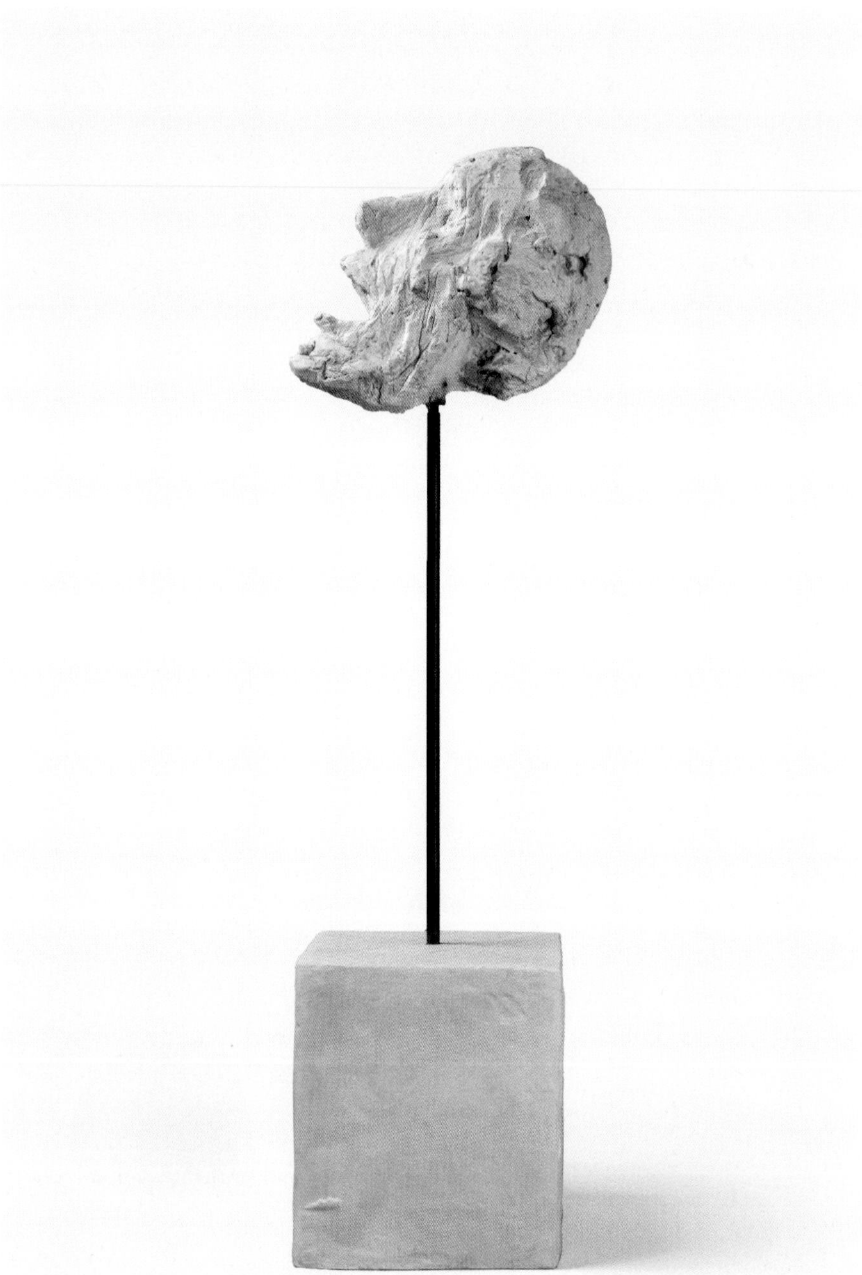

34 ***Head of a Man on a Rod,*** **c. 1946–47**
Plaster reworked with pocketknife and painted; 54 x 19 x 15 cm. Fondation Giacometti

shadow of the war and the Holocaust, and under rising Cold War tensions, artists began to question everything, even the nature and meaning of existence. It was in this climate of uncertainty and anxiety that Giacometti developed his attenuated figures, often portrayed alone or in groups, yet separated enough to convey feelings of psychological isolation and alienation. One of the earliest works from this period, *Head of a Man on a Rod* (fig. 34), is closely related to *The Nose*. Like the latter, *Head of a Man on a Rod* was partly inspired by Giacometti's experience of encountering the corpse of his dead neighbor stretched on his bed at 3:00 a.m., "his head thrown back, his mouth open," already a pathetic "non-existent" cadaver ready to be thrown into the gutter. Compared with Giacometti's earlier portraits, there is a new pathos to *Head of a Man on a Rod*. The roughly worked surfaces gouged with knife marks seem burnt and scarred, evoking associations with the victims of the gas chambers and the living dead of Hiroshima and Nagasaki, casualties of unearthly fire and radiation sickness. The figure's agonized expression also recalls the distressed women in Pablo Picasso's *Weeping Woman* series (1937) and the screaming women fleeing burning buildings in *Guernica* (May–June 1937). The similarities may not be accidental considering Giacometti's close relationship with Picasso. Yet, unlike Picasso's terrified figures, Giacometti's *Head of a Man on a Rod* exists in an indeterminate state between life and death, the mouth eliciting a scream, while the eye sockets seem hollow and lifeless.

In 1947, while preparing for his exhibition at the Pierre Matisse Gallery in New York, Giacometti made a new plaster version of his Surrealist sculpture *Suspended Ball*, a project that provided a direct stimulus for *The Nose*. Although *The Nose* borrows the idea of suspending a form from a rope inside a metal cage, it humanizes the earlier sculpture by replacing the abstract ball

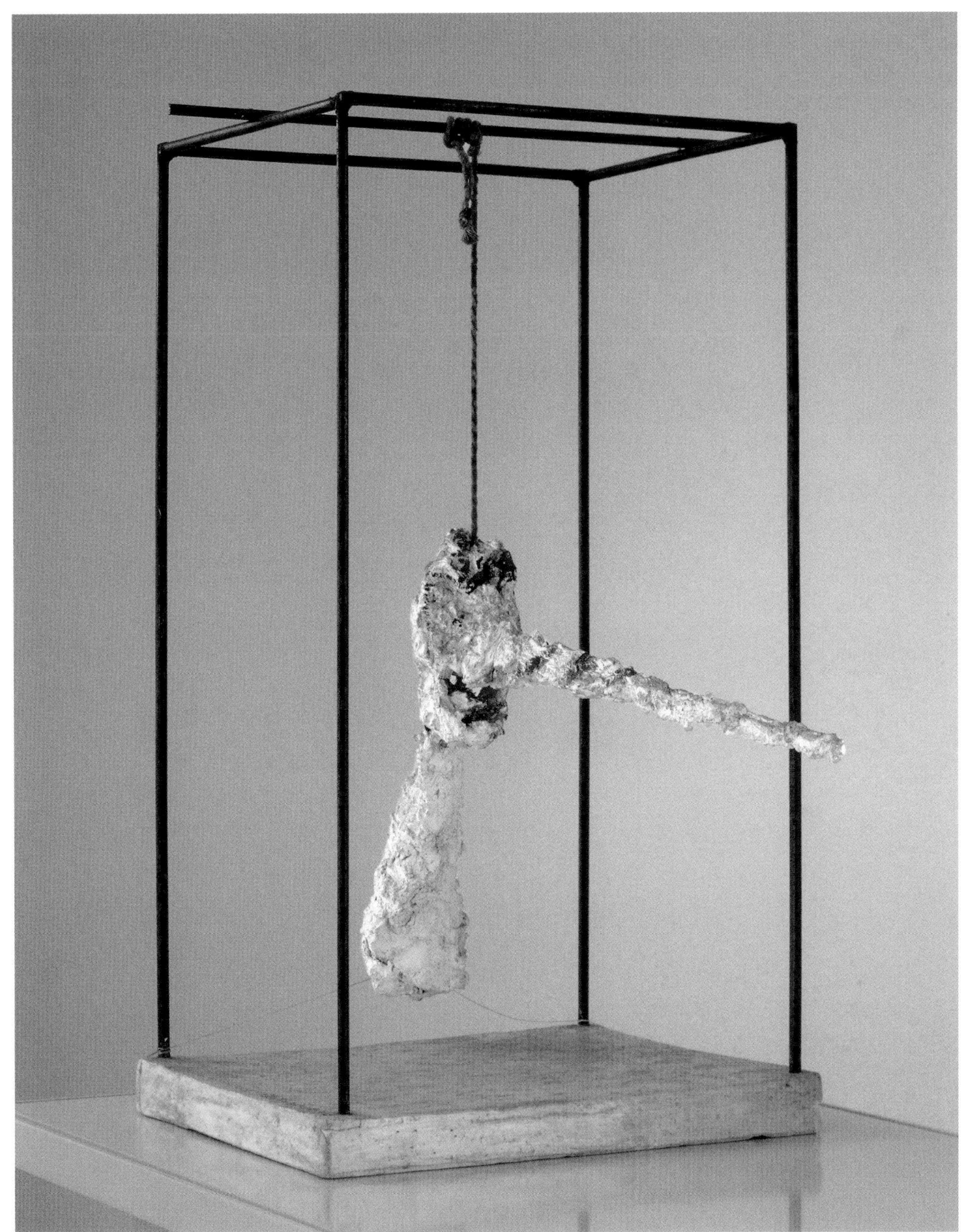

35 *The Nose*, 1947 (first version)
Painted plaster, rope, metal, wooden plate; 82 x 40.5 x 45 cm. Kunstmuseum Basel, on permanent loan from the Alberto Giacometti-Stiftung. Photo: Kunstmuseum Basel / Martin P. Bühler

and crescent shape with the head of a man whose attenuated nose protrudes outside the cage, thereby introducing an element of danger and uncertainty.

Always seeking to refine his works, Giacometti made several versions of *The Nose* in which he varied the figure's facial expression and made subtle adjustments to the cage. The first version features a plaster head with a tongue sticking out of the mouth and a painted stripe spiraling along the entire length of the nose (fig. 35). Associating the spiral with New Year's Day and Carnival masks, art historian and former museum director Jean Clair observes that the stripe has long been a mark of exclusion or transgression, linked during the Middle Ages with the devil, death, and madness.[8] Clair also notes that long, decorated noses in Oceanic masks are symbolic of rites of passage and rituals of life and death. He speculates that the attenuated nose in Giacometti's sculpture may have been inspired by masquerade masks, characters in the Commedia dell'arte, *Pinocchio* (published 1882), and Venetian Carnival masks, in which grotesquely obscene noses are thought to ward off death and evil. Clair provocatively describes the elongated noses on such masks as an "obstinate erection in the middle of a cadaver" and "a sign of virility that mocks death."[9]

A photograph of 1948 shows another version of *The Nose* resting on the floor of Giacometti's studio (fig. 36). This version also has a stripe spiraling around the nose and seems related to a drawing of a suspended head with open eyes, a lively tongue, and protruding ears (fig. 37). The suspended head in the sketch has an almost comical expression and seems fully alive, unlike the indeterminate state of the agonized figure in *Head of a Man on a Rod*. Giacometti made another version of *The Nose* in 1949 that served as the prototype for a series of bronze casts (fig. 38). The new head is more

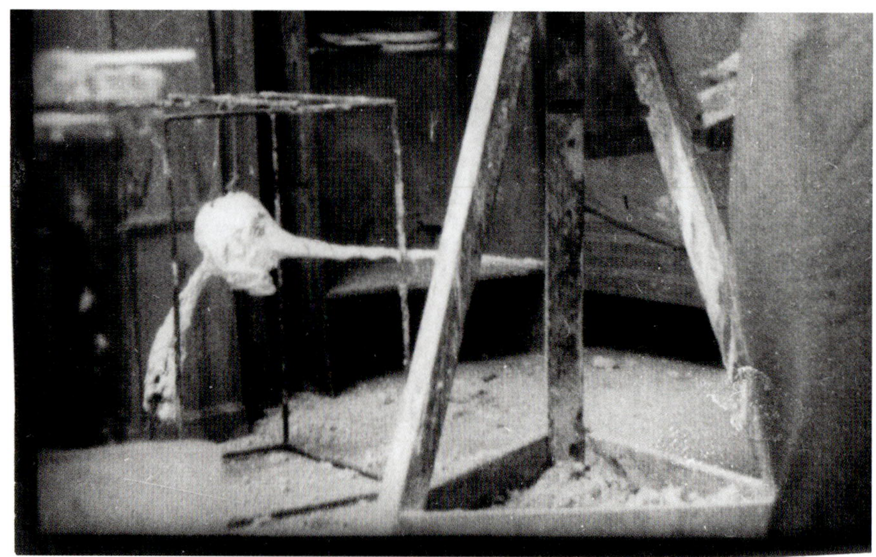

36 *The Nose* in Giacometti's studio (detail), May 20, 1948
Richard Winther (Danish, 1926–2007). Archives, Fondation Giacometti

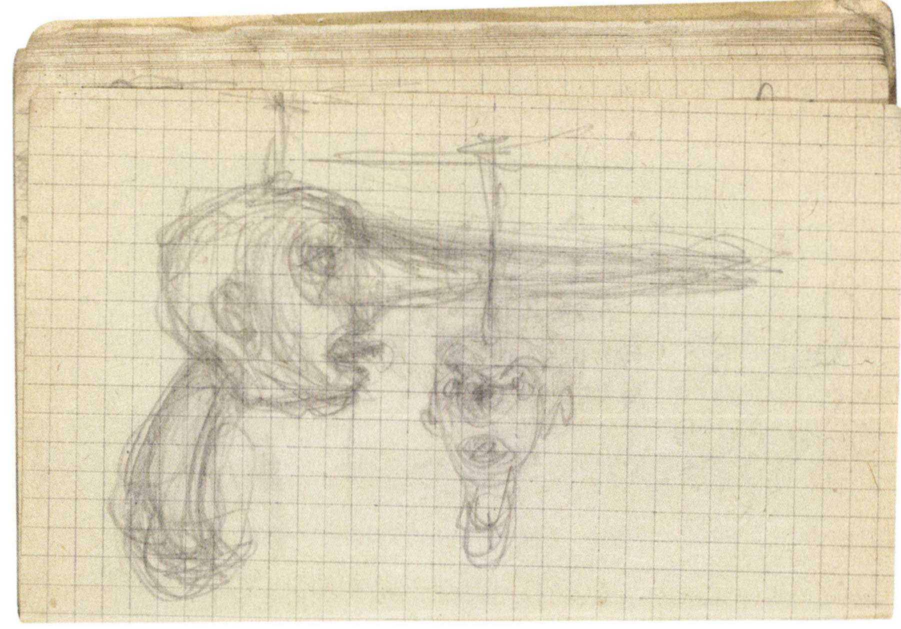

37 *The Nose, Face and Profile*, 1946–47
Pencil on notebook page; 10.7 x 16.2 cm.
Fondation Giacometti

tragic: the painted nose stripe has been deleted, the tongue and ears eliminated, the eyes replaced by the sunken sockets of a death's head, and the gaping mouth made larger and more animated, as if screaming in horror or pain.

As Giacometti developed different versions of *The Nose*, he also made subtle adjustments to the metal cage. In the first or 1947 version of the sculpture, the cage rests on a plaster slab or sculptural platform that gives the work a sense of permanence and stability (see fig. 35). Giacometti eliminated the plaster platform in the 1949 version and replaced it with a horizontal metal band stretched around the four legs near the base of the cage, so the head now hangs precariously over an empty rectangle like the open trapdoor of a gallows. Giacometti also hung the head slightly higher in some versions and added small feet to the four legs of the cage (page 47).

The Nose set the precedent for a series of sculptures Giacometti produced in the late 1940s containing figures trapped inside a cage (pages 190, 191). It was during the same period that he developed his attenuated walking figures, often portrayed alone, and at other times in groups of multiple figures standing or walking through empty spaces. Although freed from the cage, the figures remain firmly attached to a square or rectangular platform, like insects caught on sticky paper. Although their striding posture may suggest movement, the figures are fixed in time and place, frozen in an ambiguous state between movement and stasis, metaphorically caught between exercising free will and contravening forces. In this sense, the base or plinth performs a parallel symbolic function to the cage.

38 ***The Nose*, 1947 (1949 version)**
Painted plaster, string, metal; 82.6 x 77.5 x 36.7 cm. Musée national d'art moderne, Centre Georges Pompidou, Paris, AM1992-358. Photo: CNAC / MNAM, Dist. RMN-Grand Palais / Art Resource, NY / Adam Rzepka

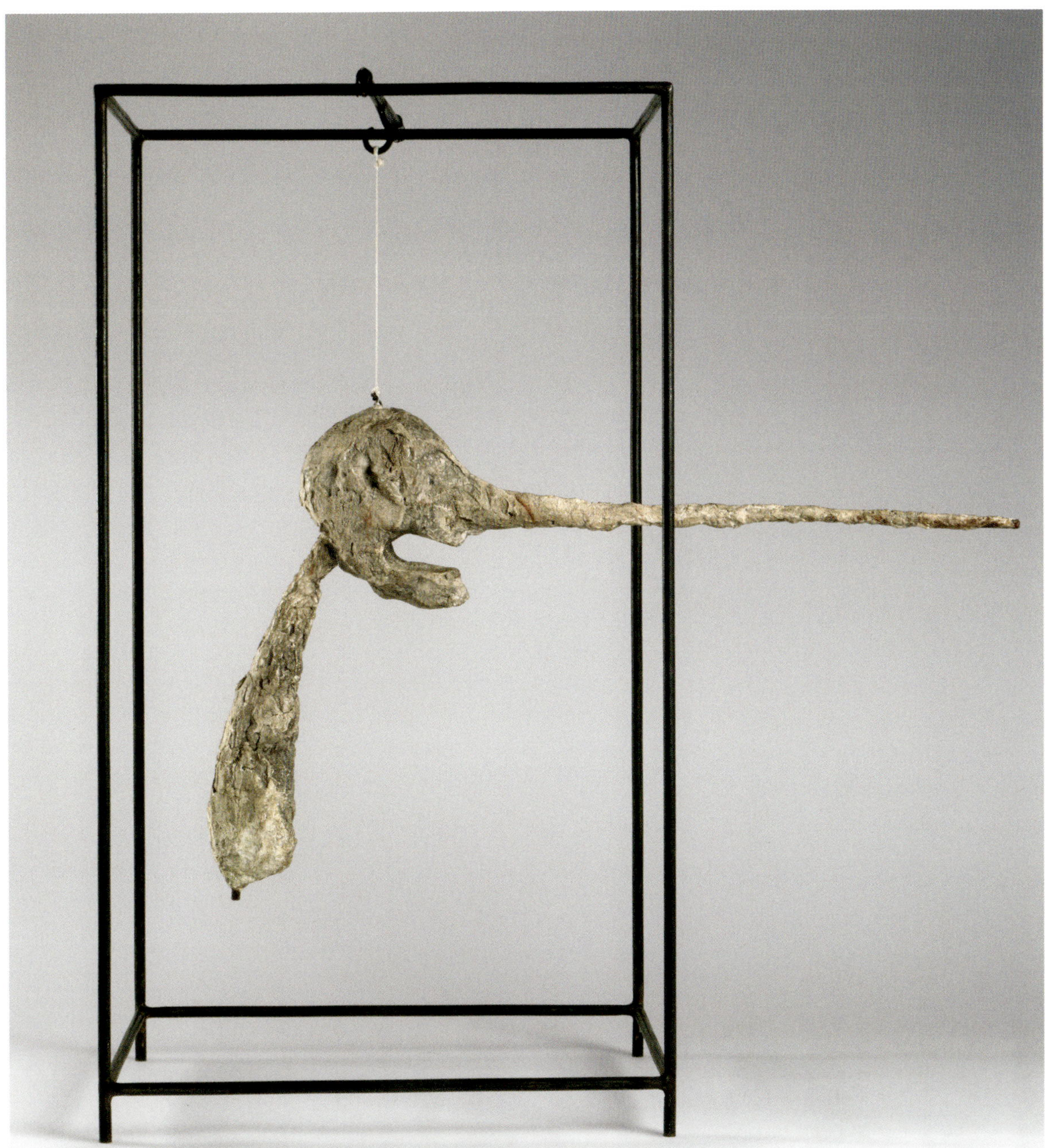

Giacometti's contemporaries interpreted his postwar sculptures in the context of existentialism, a philosophy that can be understood as an ethical inquiry into the human condition.[10] The association between his sculptures and existentialism is not fortuitous. In 1941, Giacometti developed a close relationship with two of the movement's leading theorists, Jean-Paul Sartre and Simone de Beauvoir.[11] Sartre's seminal text, *Being and Nothingness* of 1943, examines the nature of consciousness and asks how we can survive in an irrational, amoral universe that constantly forces us to make ethical decisions unique to our individual circumstances. Sartre posits that our "essence" or "real nature" is not fixed, but instead determined by our choices.[12] Confronted with an absurd universe, we live in a state of perpetual anxiety and seek possibilities for affirming our existence through an awareness of our being and by exercising free will. Sartre observes that we remain aware of our existence even when confronted with the most difficult circumstances. "The existence of consciousness," he asserts, "comes from consciousness itself."[13]

In 1947, Giacometti asked Sartre to write the catalogue introduction for his upcoming exhibition at the Pierre Matisse Gallery in New York scheduled to open in January 1948. Sartre's introductory essay, "The Search for the Absolute," considers Giacometti's sculptures both through the lens of existential philosophy and within the context of contemporary life. While noting that Giacometti's attenuated figures may allude to the world around us, Sartre marvels at their capacity to transcend ordinary experience:

> At first glance we seem to be up against the fleshly martyrs of Buchenwald. But a moment later we have quite a different conception; these fine and slender

natures rise up to heaven, we seem to have come across a group of Ascensions, of Assumptions; . . . [w]hen we have come to contemplate this mystic thrust these emaciated bodies expand, what we see before us belongs to earth.[14]

Knowing that Giacometti was troubled by the issue of representation, Sartre praises the artist for confronting the question of whether it is possible to make sculptures under current circumstances. Sartre pointedly asks whether it is conceivable to "mold a man in stone without petrifying him?"[15] In the philosopher's view, Giacometti addressed the crisis by placing himself "at the beginning of the world" and by creating sculptures that remind us of the primordial moment of inception.[16] Sartre describes the artist's elongated figures as "moving outlines, half-way between nothingness and being, always modified, bettered, destroyed, and begun once more, setting out at last on their own."[17] In this context, Sartre interprets Giacometti's elongated figures as signs of the "original movement of creation, that movement without duration, without parts," and notes that "man is the indissoluble unity and the absolute source of his movements."[18] For Sartre, the artist's slender figures that almost disappear when viewed from a distance or from certain angles exist in a precarious state between being and nonbeing. "In accepting relativity from the very start," Sartre writes of Giacometti, "he has found the absolute."[19]

Inspired partly by personal experiences, but at the same time engaging broader concerns echoed in Sartre's discourse, *The Nose* stands at a crucial juncture when Giacometti was moving beyond the hermetic symbolism of Surrealism toward a more accessible, humanistic vision informed by postwar attitudes and anxieties. Although Giacometti held strongly leftist political views, his postwar sculptures convey a more general response to a world in crisis. The unprecedented destruction of the war and the immense barbarity of the Holocaust had exposed the full measure of mankind's capacity for cruelty and evil. Equally frightening was the specter of nuclear annihilation and the question of whether the human race would extinguish itself. This precarious situation undercut the Enlightenment principles at the heart of Western civilization and signaled a widespread loss of confidence in political and religious systems of thought, leaving many people feeling adrift in a world devoid of values, beliefs, and meaning.

Confronted by this unprecedented crisis, Giacometti responded by exploring a humanistic vision of elemental figures in states of psychological distress and uncertainty. The elongated proboscis in *The Nose* that extends precariously into a zone of risk and danger has its parallel in the artist's elongated figures walking or standing in space, their emaciated bodies eaten away as if evaporating into air, their surfaces often gouged or painted with slashing, gestural marks. They seem highly vulnerable, on the precipice of annihilation, caught between the capacity to exercise free will and forces that deny their freedom. As if constantly resisting preordained destruction, their animated forms infuse them with a life-sustaining élan comparable to the gestural brushstrokes of Abstract Expressionist action painting, in which the creative process itself becomes an act of self-affirmation.

Giacometti's attenuated figures seem to exist outside any specific time or narrative. Yet, as so powerfully conveyed by *The Nose*, they embody the attitudes and psychological complexities of an era of existential crisis, when events challenged conventional assumptions about the human condition. *The Nose* played a crucial role in this moment of transition toward a more humanistic vision informed by the postwar need to validate the authenticity and autonomy of the individual. It cries out and affirms its presence through a concrete act of defiance by resisting if not mocking the absurdities of our short, precarious, earthly existence.

1. Alberto Giacometti, translated by Barbara Wright, "The Dream, the Sphinx, and the Death of T.," *Grand Street*, no. 54 (1995): 146–54, https://doi.org/10.2307/25007933. The Sphinx refers to a brothel Giacometti frequented in Paris.

2. Ibid., 150.

3. Ibid., 152.

4. Ibid.

5. Salvador Dalí, "Objets à fonctionnement symbolique," *Le Surréalisme Au Service De La Révolution*, no. 3 (1931): 2.

6. Catherine Grenier, *Alberto Giacometti: A Biography* (Paris: Flammarion, 2018), 123.

7. Grenier, *Alberto Giacometti,* 144.

8. Jean Clair, *Le Nez de Giacometti: Faces de Carême, Figures of Carnaval* (Paris: Gallimard, 1992), 24.

9. Ibid., 65, 67, 75–79.

10. The *Encyclopedia Britannica* cites the following key tenets of existentialism: (1) Existence is always particular and individual—always *my* existence, *your* existence, *his* existence, *her* existence. (2) Existence is primarily the problem of existence (i.e., of its mode of being); it is, therefore, also the investigation of the meaning of Being. (3) That investigation is continually faced with diverse possibilities, among which the existent (i.e., the human individual) must make a selection, to which he must then commit himself. (4) Because those possibilities are constituted by the individual's relationships with things and with other humans, existence is always a being-in-the-world—i.e., in a concrete and historically determinate situation that limits or conditions choice. See Nicola Abbagnano, "Existentialism," *Encyclopedia Britannica*, October 20, 2020, https://www.britannica.com/topic/existentialism.

11. Giacometti first met Sartre and Beauvoir in the 1930s. See Grenier, *Alberto Giacometti*, 152–53.

12. Paul S. MacDonald, *The Existentialist Reader: An Anthology of Texts* (New York: Routledge, 2001), 6.

13. Jean-Paul Sartre, *Being and Nothingness: A Phenomenological Essay on Ontology*, trans. Hazel E. Barnes (New York: Washington Square Press, 1992), 16.

14. Jean-Paul Sartre, "The Search for the Absolute," in *Alberto Giacometti: Sculptures, Paintings, Drawings*, exh. cat. (New York: Pierre Matisse Gallery, 1948), 16, 20.

15. Ibid.

16. Ibid., 4.

17. Ibid., 4–5.

18. Ibid., 3, 14.

19. Ibid., 11.

The Chariot: Varying Meanings

WILLIAM KEYSE RUDOLPH

The Chariot commands a position of importance within Alberto Giacometti's oeuvre. Its scale—over four feet tall—broke with the past. Its evocative subject, an attenuated female figure astride a wheeled vehicle, is one of only two works with wheeled bases.[1] Known through six casts,[2] the work has accumulated intense critical and market interest. As James Lord, the artist's biographer, wrote: "There are many extraordinary sculptures of 1940 and 1950. Among them all, however, there is one, perhaps, more extraordinary than the others by reason of having required him [Giacometti] to be extraordinary. It asks the beholder to be extraordinary, too."[3]

At the most recent sale, a version of *The Chariot* (cast 2/6) fetched $101 million with premium, making it one of a handful of sculptures to crack the $100 million mark.[4] That price tag reawakened interest in *The Chariot*, and commentators speculated about the identity and business practices of its purchaser and what the sale said about the "current overheated art market."[5]

This essay explores how *The Chariot* has assumed importance for generations of writers, viewers, and collectors, with particular reference to the Nelson-Atkins Museum of Art's cast.

INTERPRETATIONS

Giacometti unveiled *The Chariot* in 1950 in New York at the Pierre Matisse Gallery. The show was originally scheduled for February but delayed until December because the artist was still completing the works.[6] The exhibition catalogue maintained that inspiration struck the artist while recuperating in the hospital from a traffic accident suffered on October 18, 1938, at the Place des Pyramides in Paris. While crossing the street, Giacometti had been hit by a car, breaking his foot. The catalogue reproduced a letter from Giacometti to Pierre Matisse that located the work's genesis in that stay: "1938 at the Bichat Clinic, I was all amazed at the clinquant pharmacy wagon being wheeled around the room. In 1947 I saw the sculpture as if it had been made in front of me, and in 1950 it was already situated in the past, but this is not the sole reason which prompted me to do this sculpture."[7] Giacometti elaborated to Matisse in an additional letter, also in the catalogue, that "I could also name the *Chariot*, *Pharmacy Wagon*, because this sculpture comes from the clinquant wagon of the Bichat hospital which was wheeled in the rooms and which astounded me in 1938."[8]

In foundational texts on Giacometti throughout the 1950s and 1960s, as *The Chariot* was further exhibited and published, commentators on the sculpture stressed the biographical linkage that transformed a pharmacy cart into an artistic vehicle.[9] Subsequent scholars amplified associations with the 1938 accident. Thus, the sculpture's gold patination and composition recall the gilded statue of Joan of Arc at the Place des Pyramides that the wounded Giacometti would have seen while lying in the road (fig. 39).[10] Or it is part of a trilogy that works through the experience of personal injury and trauma, with the *Walking Man* expressive of the artist immediately before the accident, the *Falling Man* representative of the accident itself, and *The Chariot* functioning as the movement toward life afterward.[11]

But biographical interpretation has not been universal. Scholars have cautioned that Giacometti also stated: " . . . [T]his [the pharmacy wagon] is not the sole reason which prompted me to do this sculpture."[12] As Véronique Wiesinger has pointed out, not only did pharmacy carts not possess large wheels, but Giacometti only spent one night at the Bichat Hospital, October 19 to 20, 1938. Thus, the famous description of the cart "is another one of those many red herrings that Giacometti, like Duchamp, enjoyed dishing up to his viewers since the 1930s, as if to test their vigilance."[13] Perhaps the form of *The Chariot* comes from Giacometti's known interest in prehistoric art. Competing candidates from Egyptian, Etruscan, Celtic, and Nordic cultures—which Giacometti is known to have seen either in public collections or in books he owned—all make the potential short list of visual influences (fig. 40).[14]

Symbolic magic might play into the design. The female figure's outstretched arms could express the

***The Chariot*, 1950**
Painted bronze; 142.9 x 61.6 x 68.6 cm. The Nelson-Atkins Museum of Art, Kansas City, MO, Gift of the Hall Family Foundation, Acquired from the Patsy and Raymond Nasher Collection, F99-33/7. Photo: Nelson-Atkins Media Services / Jamison Miller

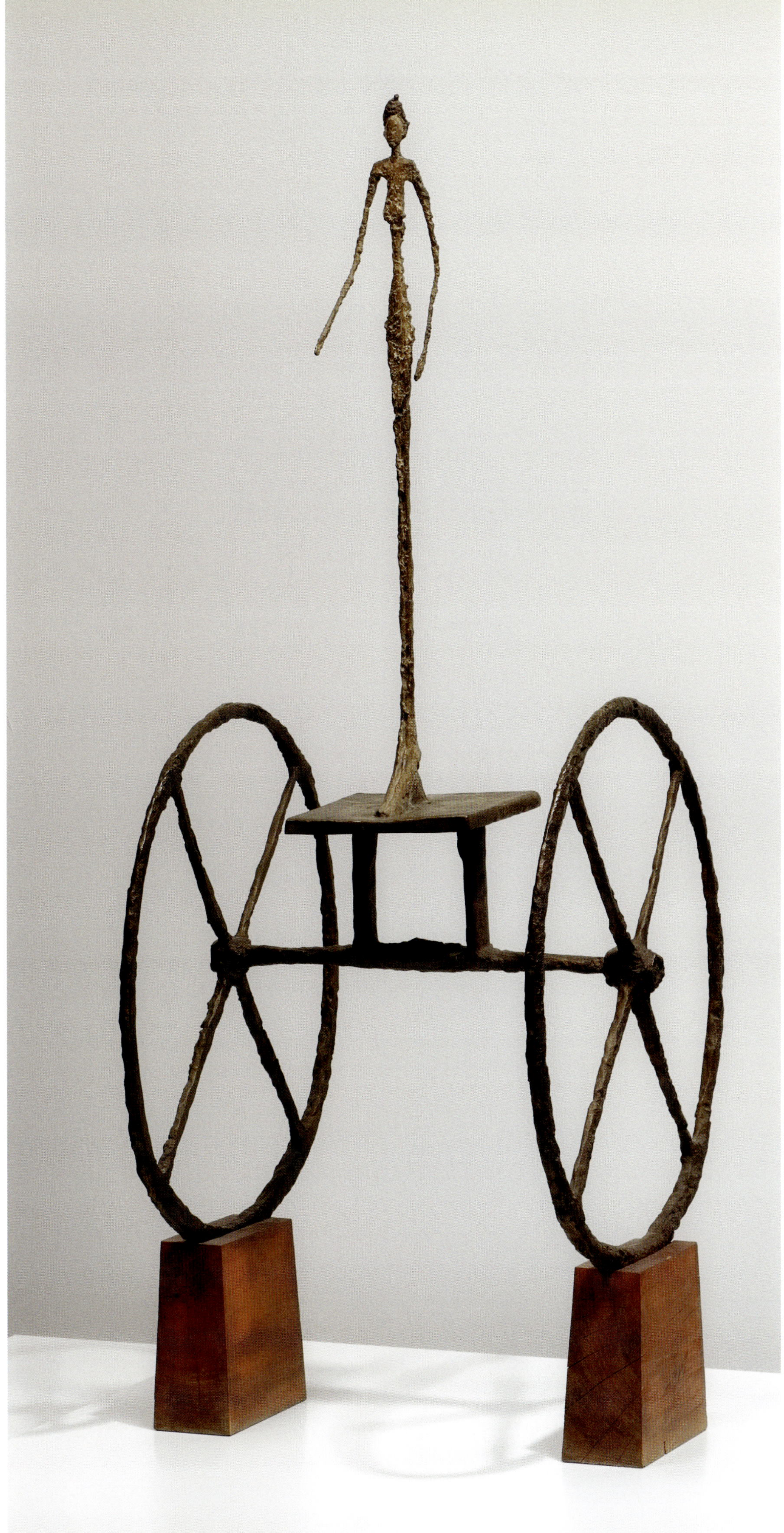

39 Statue of Joan of Arc in the Place des Pyramides, Paris, 1874
Emmanuel Frémiet (French, 1824–1910). Gilded bronze. Photo: © Vanni Archive/ Art Resource, NY

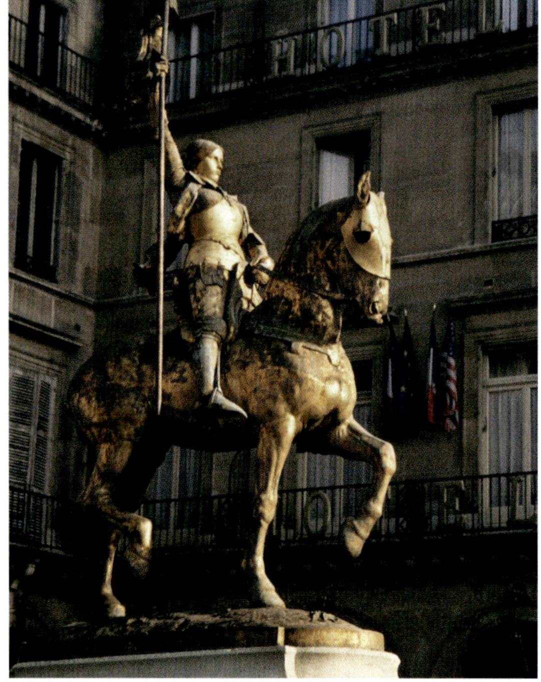

movement of the sun across the heavens, evoking figures as disparate as the Goddess Sekhmet outside the tomb of Tutankhamun or Venus Anadyomene.[15] In this vein, Valerie Fletcher commented: "[H]is rigid female nudes stand like symbols of the irreducible essence of humanity, unapproachable and indestructible."[16]

Scholars who are reluctant to dabble in psycho-biographical or symbolic waters[17] have shifted focus to *The Chariot*'s function, specifically how its base affects reception. Here they seem to have been guided by Giacometti's statement to Matisse that "*The Chariot* was realized by the necessity again to have the figure in empty space in order to see it better and to situate it at a precise distance from the floor."[18] By being on wheels on blocks, the sculpture is both set apart in space from and grounded in relation to the viewer. It can move, yet doesn't move, creating tension between object and viewer, one perhaps also inflected by the rough surface's oscillation between clarity and indeterminacy.[19]

As David Sylvester noted: "Throughout most of his working life Giacometti was concerned with the problem of creating sculpture that would involve the beholder in its spatial continuum, sculpture that, rather than seeming to pursue a self-sufficient life in a notional space apart, would seem to imply a beholder's presence, as if this were necessary to its being."[20]

The interest in bases, per Alex Potts, may not be exclusively Giacometti's preoccupation, but part of a larger modernist project of the 1940s, in which David Smith and Henry Moore also grappled with "how to articulate the juncture between a work and the ground on which it was placed."[21] It has also been suggested that *The Chariot* is the legacy of a rejected commission from Giacometti by the City of Paris to replace a memorial to educator Jean Macé (1815–1894) destroyed during the Nazi Occupation. Archival research, however, cannot confirm this hypothesis.[22]

Most recently, *The Chariot* has been linked with the earlier *Woman with Chariot* (1943–45) (fig. 41). This association comes from compositional qualities: as mentioned earlier, the two are the only Giacometti sculptures with wheeled bases. Moreover, as the organizers of a 2010 exhibition argued, the model for both works is not Annette Arm, Giacometti's muse, companion, and eventual wife,[23] but British artist Isabel Lambert Rawsthorne (1912–1992). Indeed, Giacometti was on his way home from visiting her at the Hotel Saint-Roman on rue St. Roch when he suffered the accident—further support for Isabel as the model.[24]

THE NELSON-ATKINS *CHARIOT*

The first owners of the Nelson-Atkins Museum of Art's cast were Fernand and Beatrice Reiter Leval. Fernand was a Swiss-born, naturalized US citizen who was board chairman of the Louis Dreyfus Corporation of international grain merchants.[25] Beatrice had spent time in Paris in the 1920s, where she developed an

40 Egyptian war chariot
Museo Archeologico Nazionale di Firenze, Florence. Photo: Scala / Art Resource, NY

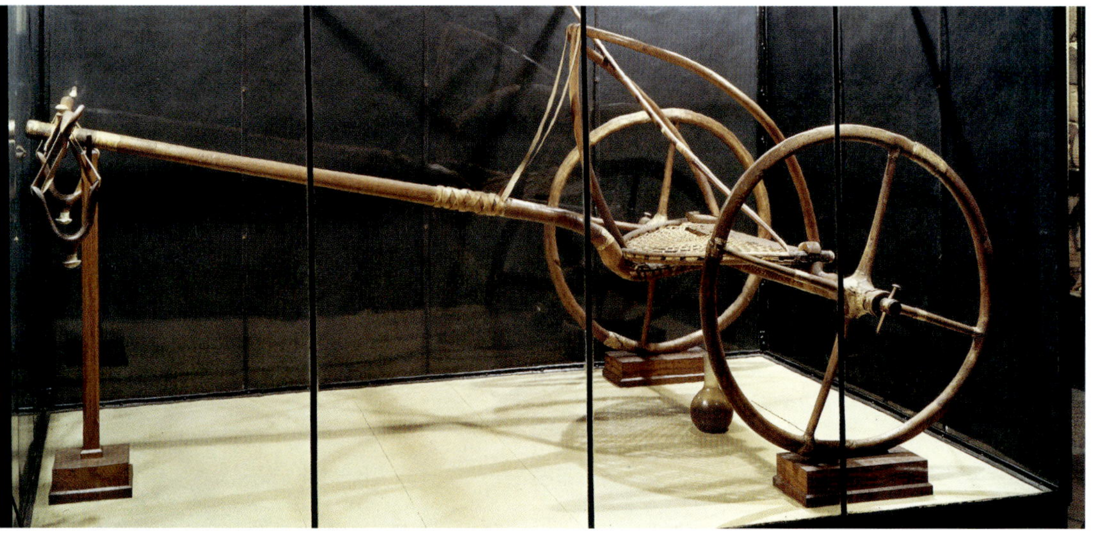

41 *Woman with Chariot*, 1943–45
Plaster, wood; 163.5 x 38 x 36 cm.
Fondation Giacometti

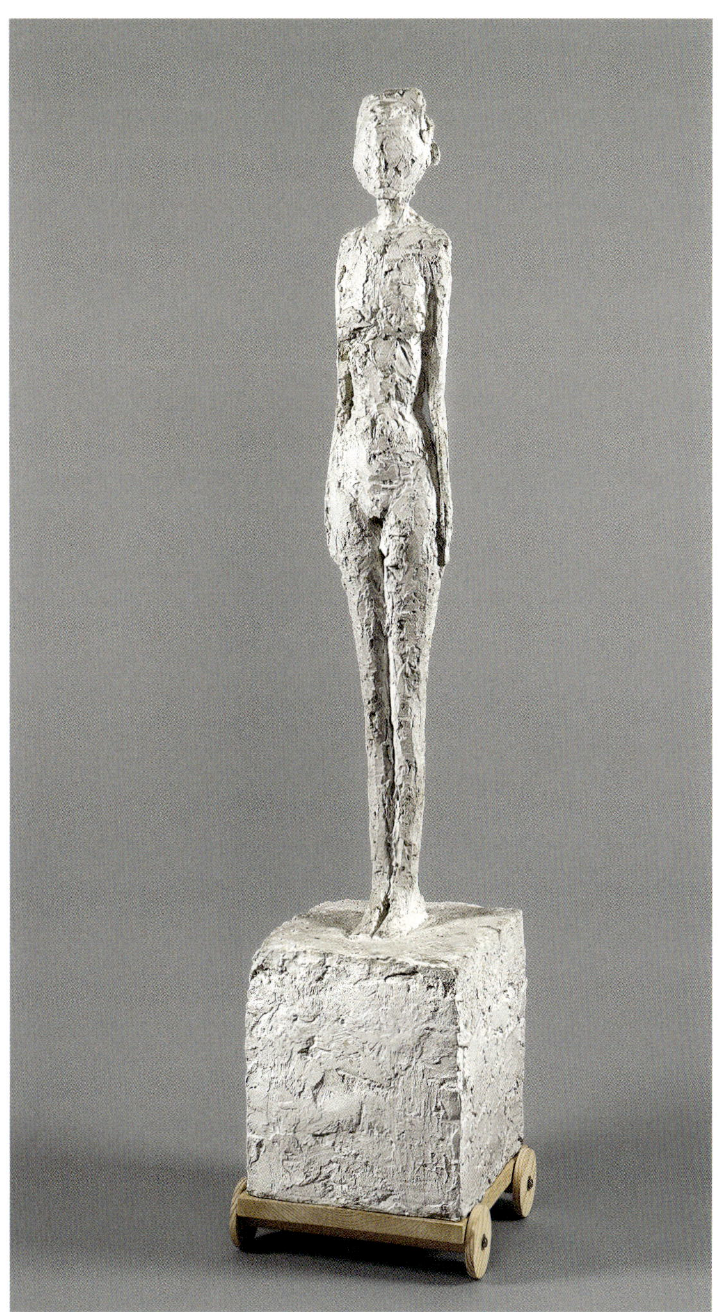

appreciation for contemporary art. The Levals steadily collected Impressionist, Post-Impressionist, and modernist art, often acquired through annual summer trips to France, except during the war years.[26]

In 1952, in Paris, the Levals went to the Galerie Maeght, which their son Pierre recalled was an anomaly for the couple. During that visit, proprietor Aimé Maeght kept ordering around a "big burly guy" named Sandy to help retrieve works for consideration. They later learned this gallery assistant was American sculptor Alexander Calder (1898–1976), who had been visiting the gallery that morning. The Levals did not acquire one of "Sandy's" works; they left instead with two works by Giacometti: *The Chariot* and *La Clairière* (1950).

With the exception of a loan to the Solomon R. Guggenheim Museum in 1955 for the artist's retrospective, *The Chariot* assumed pride of place in the Levals' home, first at 120 East End Avenue until 1959 and then at 660 Park Avenue, where it occupied a white marble foyer.[27] Near *The Chariot*, Beatrice staged stark, dramatic furniture by British designer Terence Harold (T. H.) Robsjohn-Gibbings (1905–1976), then the leading interior designer in New York, whose simplified aesthetic based on classical Greek prototypes attracted clients such as Alfred A. Knopf, Doris Duke, and Aristotle Onassis.[28] The overall effect was "bold," as Pierre remembers; Susana Torruella Leval, the couple's daughter-in-law and later director of the Museo del Barrio, recalls the figure's monumental presence: "It was an incredible thrill to see her, a very quiet thrill—and it made the viewers quiet."[29]

In 1983, twenty years after her husband's death, Beatrice sold *The Chariot* at auction, from which it was acquired by Dallas couple Patsy and Raymond

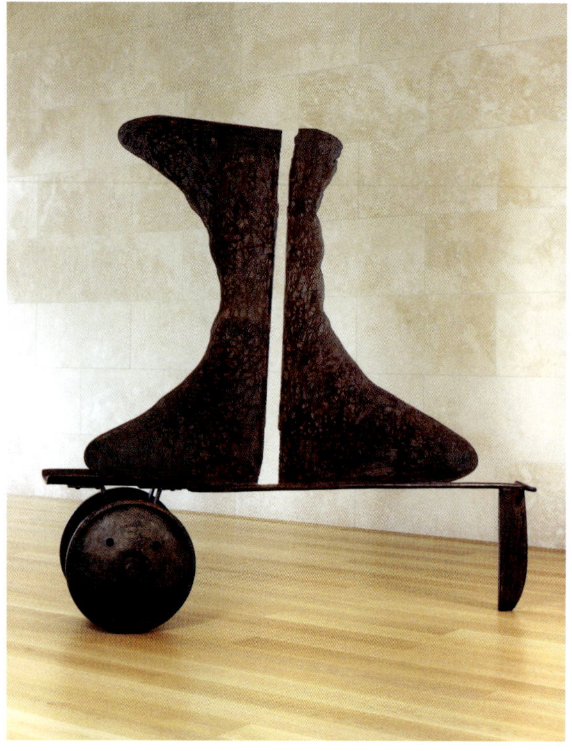

42 *Voltri VI*, 1962
David Smith (American, 1906–1965). Steel; 251.1 x 259.7 x 61 cm. Raymond and Patsy Nasher Collection, Nasher Sculpture Center, Dallas, NC.1978.A.04. Photo: Tom Jenkins. © 2022 The Estate of David Smith / Licensed by VAGA at Artists Rights Society (ARS), NY

Nasher, who were building what would become one of the most significant private collections of modern sculpture in the United States.[30] The Nashers, who were instrumental in spearheading postwar Dallas's residential and retail growth north of its traditional boundaries, initially began collecting pre-Columbian art in the 1950s. They pivoted to modern sculpture in the 1960s, concurrent with their development of NorthPark Mall, which incorporated sculpture into its spaces.[31] As E. Luanne McKinnon, art historian and former consultant to the couple, recalled the Nashers' taste, "Everything was geared to the monumental." In addition, Patsy also believed in collecting in depth.[32] According to Steven A. Nash, founding director of the Nasher Sculpture Center, she responded avidly to Giacometti, whose work she acquired broadly, both Surrealist and figurative. Nash speculated that the opportunity to own *The Chariot* would have been tempting. She simply "couldn't resist the masterpiece. It had all the fingerprints on it."[33] McKinnon confirmed that "Patsy set her sights" on *The Chariot*, which she triumphantly bought in the salesroom in New York, announcing "We got it!" in a call back to Dallas and gently correcting the misconception that it had gone for seven figures ("You got the zeros wrong.").[34]

Inside the Nashers' light-filled home, *The Chariot* dominated the main living room, near a grand piano adorned with a bust by Raymond Duchamp-Villon. McKinnon remembered that Patsy linked *The Chariot* with David Smith's *Voltri VI* (1962), believing that both pieces, being wheeled, evoked antiquity. She installed the Smith sculpture on the patio just outside the Giacometti, maintaining a visual adjacency (fig. 42). *The Chariot* would not stay long in the Nasher Collection. During one of the periodic recessions endemic to Dallas's boom-or-bust cycles at the beginning of the 1990s, the now-widowed Raymond, as the owner of NorthPark National Bank in Dallas, needed to maintain capital reserves and made the difficult decision to sell art.[35]

Thus, in May 1991, *The Chariot* was acquired by the Hall Family Foundation, the philanthropic organization created by the founding family of Hallmark, Inc., which was amassing a collection of modernist sculpture as part of their support of the Nelson-Atkins Museum of Art. The foundation purchased four additional works from the Nasher Collection by Carl Andre, Constantin Brancusi, Max Ernst, and Henry Moore.[36] As then-president Bill Hall recalled, "We saw the Brancusi [*Portrait of Nancy Cunard*] and the Giacometti as the two great items."[37] The Hall Family Foundation immediately placed the ex-Nasher works on loan to the museum in 1991, donating them nine years later.

In its histories, the Nelson-Atkins *Chariot* has been an unexpected purchase that played a dramatic role in a domestic environment; in another collection, it amplified understanding of Giacometti's oeuvre, additionally suggesting shared affinities. Finally, its time-honed status as a masterpiece, as well as its provenance, made it attractive for public-focused artistic philanthropy.

Is it also the memory of a mistress, a goddess, a symbol of postwar Europe, a spatial perception exercise, possibly a rejected monument, or even an index of the state of the market in a new century? *The Chariot* may indeed be all or none of these things. Nearly three quarters of a century after its creation, this sculpture continues to testify to the artist's accomplishment.

1. Véronique Wiesinger and Gottlieb Leinz, foreword to *Alberto Giacometti: Die Frau auf dem Wagon, Triumph und Tod*, trans. Véronique Wiesinger, exh. cat. (Munich: Hirmer, 2010), 7. Note: All page numbers refer to the English translation published on CD-ROM included with the catalogue.

2. The Nelson-Atkins Museum of Art's curatorial files originally listed seven casts at the time *The Chariot* entered the collection, from 0/6 to 6/6, but the majority of the literature only documents six. Nelson-Atkins Museum of Art, Curatorial Files, subsequently referred to as NAMA Curatorial Files. This replicates information contained in Steven A. Nash, ed., *A Century of Modern Sculpture: The Patsy and Raymond Nasher Collection*, exh. cat. (New York: Rizzoli, 1987), 157. The documented casts are at the Nelson-Atkins Museum of Art (5/6); the Museum of Modern Art (1/6); the National Gallery of Art, Washington, DC (6/6); the Kunsthaus Zurich (3/6); and in two private collections.

3. James Lord, *Giacometti: A Biography* (New York: Farrar, Straus, Giroux, 1985), 304.

4. Incidentally, the other record-breakers were also by Giacometti: *Walking Man* and *Pointing Man*. Susan Moore, "The Art Market," *Apollo: The International Magazine for Collectors* 181, no. 627 (January 2015): 72; "Alberto Giacometti's 1950 bronze sculpture 'Chariot' sells for $101M at Sotheby's New York," Artdaily.com, November 5, 2014, https://artdaily.cc/news/74084/Alberto-Giacometti-s-1950-bronze-sculpture--Chariot--sells-for--101m-at-Sotheby-s-New-York#.X7Fkky2caYU. On *Walking Man*, see Carol Vogel, "At London Sale, a Giacometti Sets a Record," *New York Times*, February 3, 2010, C-1. On *Pointing Man*, see Daniel McDermon, "Steven A. Cohen Was Buyer of Giacometti's 'Pointing Man' for $141 Million," *New York Times*, June 9, 2015, C-3.

5. See Robert Frank, "Steve Cohen just bought this $101 million sculpture," CNBC News, November 11, 2014, https://www.cnbc.com/2014/11/11/steve-cohen-just-bought-this-101-million-giacometti-sculpture.html; Felix Salmon, "The Not So Special Hundred-Million-Dollar Giacometti," *New Yorker*, November 5, 2014, https://www.newyorker.com/business/currency/the-hundred-million-dollar-giacometti; and Carol Vogel, "Steven A. Cohen Was Buyer of Giacometti's 'Chariot,' for $101 Million," *New York Times*, November 10, 2014, https://artsbeat.blogs.nytimes.com/2014/11/10/steven-a-cohen-was-buyer-of-giacomettis-chariot-for-101-million/?searchResultPosition=1.

6. Véronique Wiesinger, "Giacometti's *Woman with Chariot*: Between Epic and Myth," trans. Anthony Allen, in Wiesinger and Leinz, *Alberto Giacometti*, 9.

7. *Alberto Giacometti: November 1950*, exh. cat. (New York: Pierre Matisse Gallery, 1950), 13; letter illustrated, 12.

8. Ibid., 3.

9. The letter is also reproduced in Ernst Scheidegger, *Alberto Giacometti: Schriften, fotos, zeichnungen* (Zurich: Der Arche, 1958); the quotation is also reprinted in *Alberto Giacometti*, exh. cat. (Basel: Galerie Beyeler, 1964), n.p., and Giacometti, *Alberto Giacometti*, exh. cat. (New York: Museum of Modern Art, 1965), 60.

10. The 2014 sales catalogue repeats this frequently expressed claim. See "Alberto Giacometti. Chariot," Sotheby's New York, November 4, 2014, 33.

11. Yves Bonnefoy, *Alberto Giacometti: A Biography of His Work*, trans. Jean Stewart (Paris: Flammarion, 1991), 361–62.

12. *Alberto Giacometti: November 1950*, 13.

13. Wiesinger, "Giacometti's *Woman with Chariot*: Between Epic and Myth," in Wiesinger and Leinz, *Alberto Giacometti*, 17.

14. For the broadest ranging discussion of these chariot prototypes, see Gottlieb Leinz, "*Woman with Chariot:* From the 'Haycart' to the 'Great Fortune,'" trans. Jeremy and Petra Gains, in Wiesinger and Leinz, *Alberto Giacometti*, 29–53; see also Reinhold Hohl, ed., *Alberto Giacometti: A Retrospective Exhibition*, exh. cat. (New York: Solomon R. Guggenheim Museum, 1974), 26–27; Nash, *A Century of Modern Sculpture*, 157; and Suzanne Pagé, ed., *Alberto Giacometti: sculptures, peintures, dessins*, exh. cat. (Paris: Musée d'art moderne de la Ville de Paris, 1991), 220.

15. Laurie Wilson, referenced in "Alberto Giacometti. Chariot," Sotheby's, 33, 36; *Giacometti: Giovanni, 1868–1933, Augusto, 1877–1947, Alberto, 1901–1966, Diego, 1902–1985*, exh. cat. (Mexico City: Centro Cultural / Arte Contemporaneo, A. C., 1987), 83. For Venus, see Franz Mayer, *Alberto Giacometti, Eine Kunst existentieller Wirklichkeit* (Fraunefeld and Stuttgart: Huber, 1968), 174.

16. Valerie J. Fletcher, "Giacometti family," *Grove Art Online*, 2003, https://doi.org/10.1093/gao/9781884446054.article.T032017.

17. See Christian Klemm et al., preface to *Alberto Giacometti*, ed. Christian Klemm, exh. cat. (New York: Museum of Modern Art, 2001), 7.

18. Giacometti to Pierre Matisse, in *Alberto Giacometti: November 1950*, 3.

19. Alex Potts, "Giacometti and the Basis of Sculpture," in *Giacometti: Critical Essays*, ed. Peter Reed and Julia Kelly (Burlington, VT: Ashgate, 2009), 139. See also Ann Umlaud, referenced in "Alberto Giacometti. Chariot," Sotheby's, 40, 43.

20. David Sylvester, *Looking at Giacometti* (New York: Henry Holt, 1994), 61. Sylvester also echoes Reinhold Hohl, *Alberto Giacometti: Sculpture, Painting, Drawing* (London: Thames and Hudson, 1972), 134.

21. Potts, "Giacometti and the Basis of Sculpture," in Reed and Kelly, *Giacometti*, 131.

22. Hohl, *Alberto Giacometti*, 135; Nash, *A Century of Modern Sculpture*, 157; Wiesinger disagrees, in "Giacometti's *Woman with Chariot*: Between Epic and Myth," in Wiesinger and Leinz, *Alberto Giacometti*, 21–22.

23. Bonnefoy, *Alberto Giacometti*, 364.

24. Wiesinger, "Giacometti's *Woman with Chariot*: Between Epic and Myth," in Wiesinger and Leinz, *Alberto Giacometti*, 18–19, 20–21. On Rawsthorne, see Carol Jacobi, "Muse and Painter: Isabel Lambert, 1912–1992," in Wiesinger and Leinz, *Alberto Giacometti*, 55–68.

25. "Fernand Leval, Grain Executive. Ex-Head of Louis Dreyfus Corporation Dead at 70," *New York Times*, July 7, 1963, 52. See also Francine du Plessix Gray, *Them: A Memoir of Parents* (New York: Penguin, 2006), 270.

26. Pierre Leval and Susana Torruella Leval, interview with the author, December 28, 2020.

27. Ibid.

28. Ibid. On Robsjohn-Gibbings, see Danielle Ohad Smith, "T. H. Robsjohn-Gibbings: Crafting a Modern Home for Postwar America," *Journal of Interior Design* 34, no. 1 (September 2008): 39–55.

29. Ibid.

30. "Impressionist and Modern Paintings and Sculpture," Christie's New York, November 15, 1983, lot 79, 88. NAMA Curatorial Files.

31. See "History," https://www.nashersculpturecenter.org/visit/about-the-nasher.

32. E. Luanne McKinnon, interview with the author, December 28, 2020.

33. Steven A. Nash, interview with the author, October 22, 2020.

34. McKinnon, interview with the author, December 28, 2020.

35. Nash, interview with the author, October 22, 2020.

36. Scott Cantrell, "Five New Pieces, in Many Styles. Nelson Gallery's Acquisitions represent artists of the 20th Century whose unique visions are vastly different," *Kansas City Star*, June 23, 1991, I-1, I-8.

37. Alice Thorson, "Sale Lifts the Value of Nelson's 'Chariot,'" *Kansas City Star*, November 23, 2014, A-1, A-9; quote from A-9.

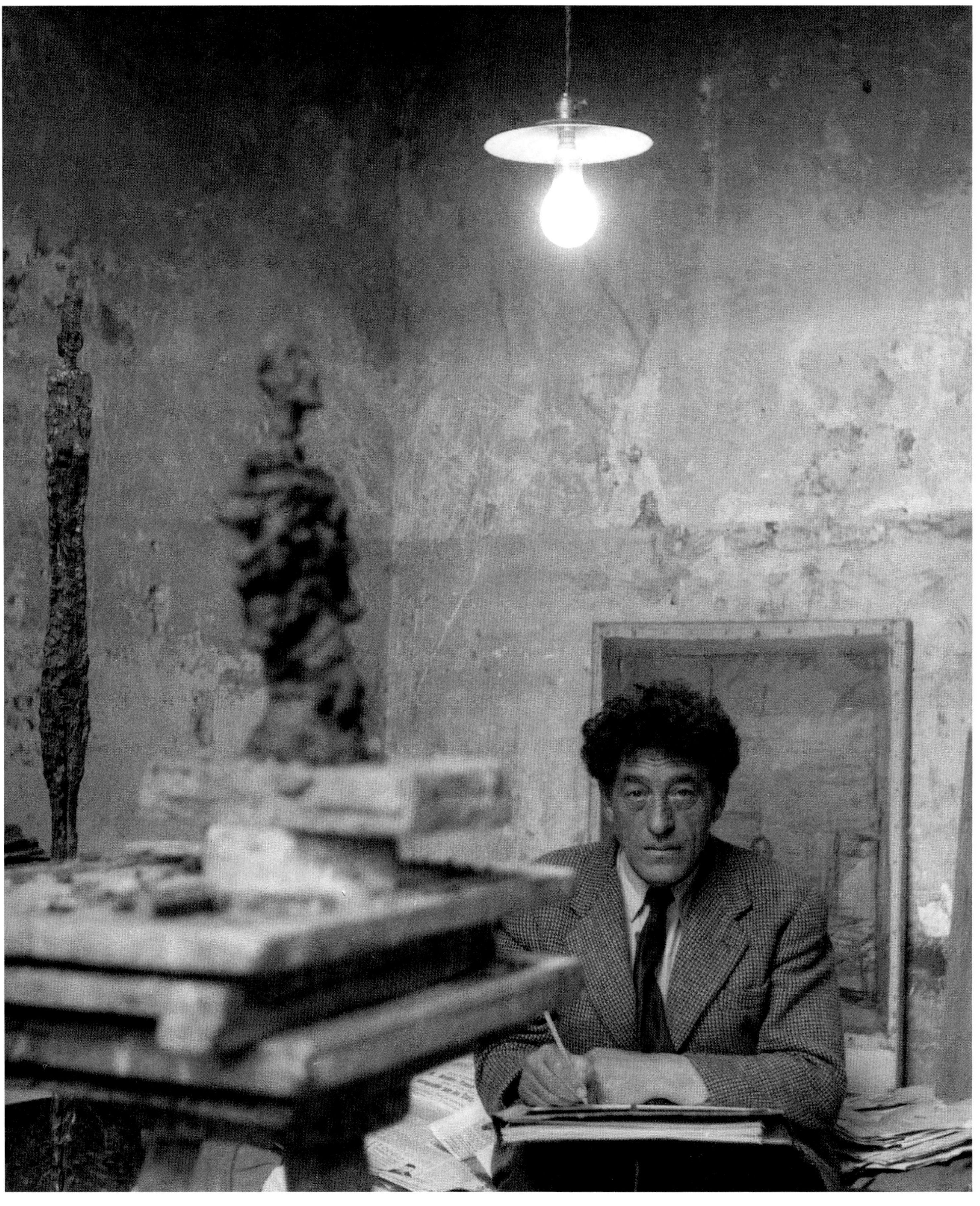

The All-Consuming Drawing Practice of Alberto Giacometti

HUGO DANIEL

Alberto Giacometti drawing in the studio, July 1954
Sabine Weiss (French, b. Switzerland, 1924–2021).

"Drawing is the basis for everything."[1] Alberto Giacometti never ceased reiterating, particularly in the second part of his life, the prominence he gave to the practice of drawing. One should however question what he was referring to, in that all-encompassing gaze, as "the basis for everything"—as well as question what is the "basis" as much as what is the "everything." The huge volume of the corpus of pictorial works alone shows the importance of the practice of drawing for the artist.[2] But in Giacometti's works, with a few rare exceptions, drawing was not a preliminary step to paintings and sculptures, as can be deduced when reading his statement. If it is a basis, it is not a preparatory work (sketch, underlying drawing, etc.), but in a sense at the same time broader, looser, and more fundamental. The artist's declaration calls to mind another in which he attested that "attempts are everything."[3] Drawing existed for him not as a work prior to another, but as an essential register in the formulation of the art experience apprehended as an attempt—on par with sculptures, for example—rather than what would be its execution.

In Western psyche since the Renaissance in particular, drawing has been associated with the intellect, in an assimilation with the "idea" about which art historian Erwin Panofsky underlined the link with a theology of creation that implied the execution in the *disegno* of a divine plan. A notion fashioned in the Renaissance, the *disegno*, considered both a plan and a representation of that plan taking the form of the outline (drawing), became the foundation of a theory of art that placed the intellect in the foreground of the creative process. Giorgio Vasari made the practice of drawing the "father of all arts" (because it is its first step), and following that notion defined the place that drawing occupies in the Academy.[4] From Cennino Cennini[5] and Vasari to Henri Matisse and writer Paul Valéry, the drawing practice remains assimilated not only to a *project*, but also to the edge of the work, an isolated *place*, associated with the thought in the process of development, in which would be formulated the burgeoning idea, the intention, as extrapolated by the theory of the *disegno*. Drawing as practice would take precedence over the other practices in the system that the Academy chose to classify under the category of "arts of drawing"—architecture, painting, and sculpture—because the drawing practice was an essential preliminary stage.

To that ideal conception of drawing, Giacometti opposed a more material reality, more immediate and perhaps necessary. He practiced an economy of drawing different from the tradition, which does not valorize the sketch and the fragment such as Romanticism had developed (against that same tradition). That economy is detectible in his notes where drawing is mentioned, with a remarkable regularity—on equal footing with painting and sculpture—in the trilogy "painting, sculpture, drawing," to which he sometimes added writing. For Giacometti, the drawing "is the basis" because it is first and foremost a fundamental activity where the experience of looking, which was for him the artistic experience per se, was played out again and again.

Giacometti's relationship to drawing began with an *imitation* practice, in two respects. First, he started to draw when still very young, in the manner of his father, in his studio; second, his initial drawings were copies of illustrations (among the first were images from *Snow White*).[6] It is significant that one of the first copies that remains is that of Albrecht Dürer's famous etching *The Knight, Death, and the Devil* (1915) (fig. 43), made when he was 14. Giacometti reproduced a seminal work in the history of illustrative arts, an ambitious demonstration in the detail and precision of the outline, and a model in the imitation of nature. Through its

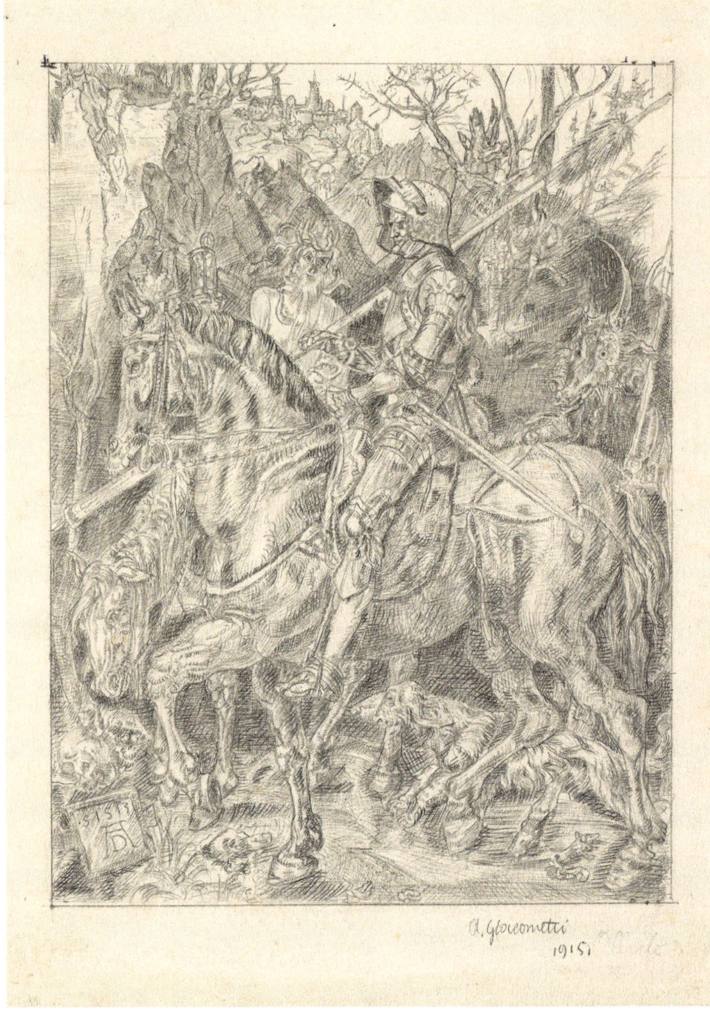

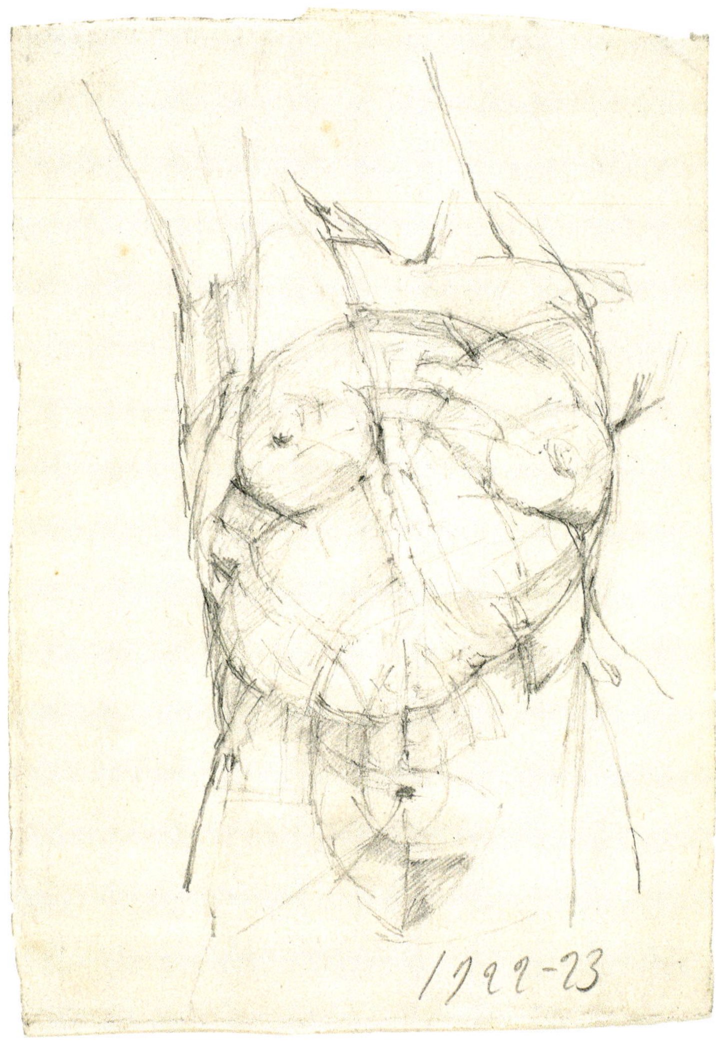

43 ***After Dürer's* The Knight, Death, and the Devil, 1915**
Pencil on paper; 31.2 x 23.6 cm.
Fondation Giacometti

44 ***Torso of Naked Woman*, 1923–25**
Pencil on paper; 17 x 12 cm.
Fondation Giacometti

details, the attention to proportions, the density, and the aspect of the visual material, *The Knight, Death, and the Devil* expresses his visual mastery and ability to convey, in drawing, realist elements. By duplicating it meticulously,[7] by searching for the smallest details, Giacometti reappropriated a line that tries to convey everything. He carried on learning through other copies and completed his training with skillful drawings of scenes from daily life and the mountainous landscapes of the Grisons.

This practice was to continue throughout his life. When he began, a certain easiness prevailed: "I drew landscapes. I drew to communicate, to dominate. My pencil was my weapon. I had the impression I was reproducing and appropriating what I wanted. I became big-headed. Nothing could resist me."[8] He finished training between 1922 and 1927 while studying classic drawing at the Académie de la Grande Chaumière (fig. 44). There, he broadened his knowledge by experimenting in depth with a direct relationship with the model, a confrontation that remained essential to his practice. It was in that tension of a line in direct contact with real life that he found the power and singularity of his own line. After he completed his first year at the Académie, he sought a volumetric construction, the learning of drawing for a sculptor, which is conveyed with a subtle faceting of bodies, whose sharp and appealing character was eventually replaced by a more nervous line, a more direct line. The tension between the desire to represent the volume and the urge to apprehend more directly the motif would always be there.

Undoubtedly more than at any other time, his Surrealist period (1930–35) was that of inventive drawing, an exploratory field for the imaginary, which left him dreading he would end up losing himself. In his notebooks, on loose sheets, the outline, in a combinatory of shapes, seems to be the immediate expression of the imaginary. The figures, multiplied and associated on the same sheet or in the same notebook, are linked by free associations, making explicit, in that prolific period, the similarities between sculptures, decorative art objects,[9] and the imagined forms that accompany them, without being necessarily destined to become anything else but an execution on paper (fig. 45). Besides a certain visual freedom that favored the association of those more linear drawings, during that Surrealist period Giacometti increasingly made use of "cages," frames or polyhedrons that convey the exploration of a mental space (fig. 46).

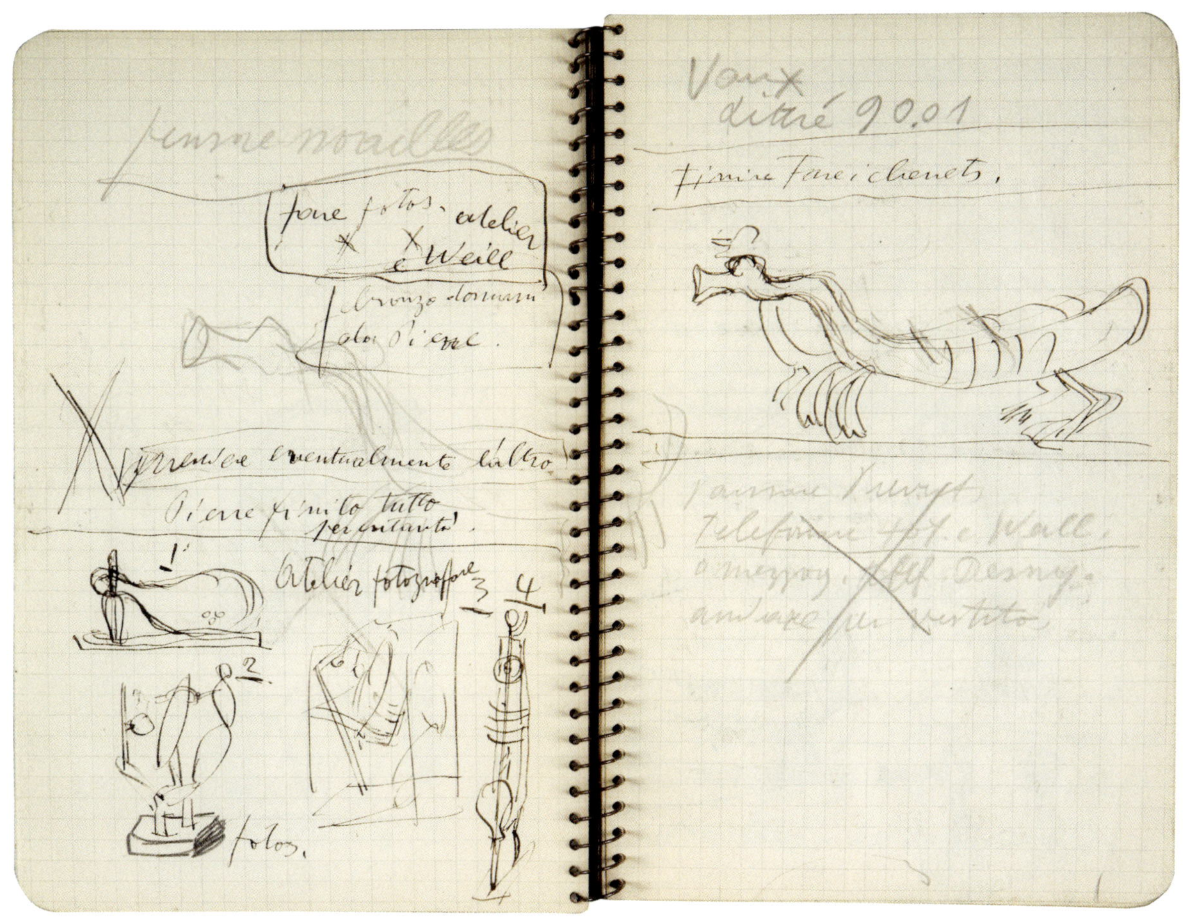

45 ***Projects for Andirons, Sculptures, and Notes*, 1929–30**
Pencil and ink on page of notebook; 17.1 x 22.4 cm.
Fondation Giacometti

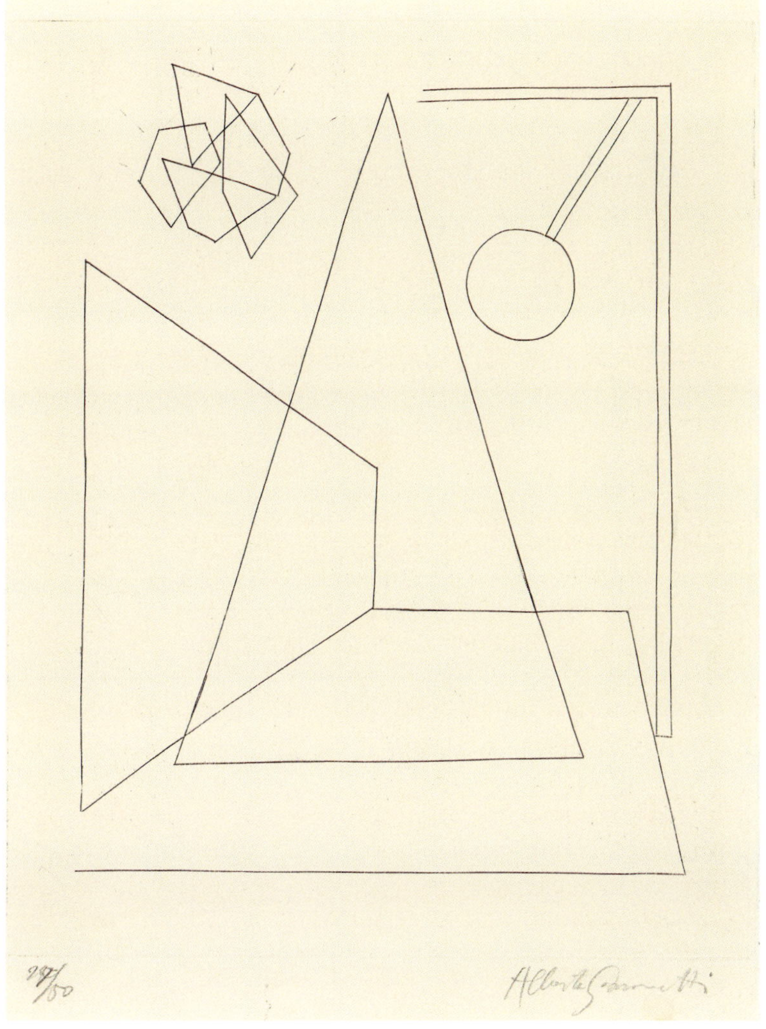

46 ***Composition II* (for Anatole Jakovski's portfolio, 23 engravings, Paris: H. Orobitz, 1935), 1935**
Chisel, pencil on paper; 65.5 x 49.9 cm.
Fondation Giacometti

Consequently, his line became redefined. As in the sculptures from the end of the 1920s, Giacometti tried to pare down his drawing, in a style that was only temporary, marking the middle of the 1930s. His search for a sharp line is made explicit in one of his notebooks: "one line only, not to go over it, sharply defined."[10] But that search, evident in the etchings he made with the engraver Samuel Hayter, did not last beyond the projects to illustrate the collection of poems *L'air de l'eau* (1934) by André Breton, and the portfolio set by critic Anatole Jakovski.[11] In this research is expressed the sudden awareness of an economy of means and an immediacy proper to drawing, close to the automatisms that the Surrealists experienced in their various drawing games, including exquisite corpses and telephone whispers. Giacometti did not play those games, but he recognized their immediacy, an interest proved by the rare copy of children's drawings—one copy, still. "Children's chalk drawings on the pavement of the Boulevard Villemain, they cover the whole width of the pavement," he wrote on the sheet on which he recorded, in 1932, that childish drawing whose schematic and flowing character had caught his eyes (fig. 47).

Giacometti stopped participating in the Surrealist group to respond to the urge to work from the live model again in the studio to explore, in his drawing and sculpture practice, that tension with real life. From then on, and until the end of his life, without abandoning completely drawing from imagination (he always practiced that), his drawing became more refined and dense in the confrontation with reality, gradually evolving toward a more pronounced style, in which surfaced a more incisive and repeated line, and a concentration on certain elements. Repetitive and sharp, his drawing is the opposite of a drawing by Matisse or Pablo Picasso, who often sought the stripped-down or pure line; here, the repetitions, the multiplication of lines instead convey a practice of the line directly connected to the creation of the form (fig. 48).

For Giacometti, drawing was as much a physical experience of confrontation with the object as a mental one. It was a necessity not only intellectual, not only psychological, but also *organic*. In the 1940s, his drawing acquired characteristics that were more accentuated, that of the style with which he was immediately identifiable in the postwar years. He concentrated on

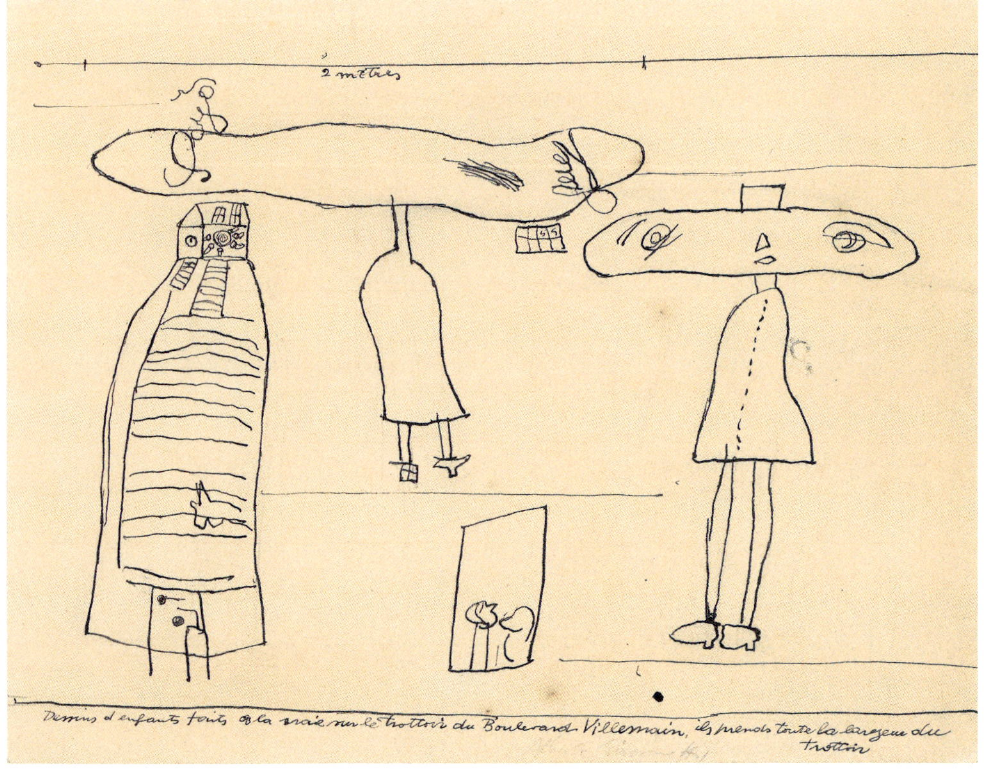

47 *Copy after Children's Chalk Drawings on the Sidewalk of the Boulevard Villemain*, 1932
Black ink, pencil on loose sketchbook page; 17.2 x 22.6 cm. Fondation Giacometti

a few models: his brother Diego, then after 1945 his wife, Annette. And the multiplication of portraits, human figures, and interiors marked a delimited but inexhaustible field for experimentation that he maintained until the end of his life. Giacometti spoke very little about his drawing practice—there was no theorization as with Matisse regarding it. In 1945, he commented on the etchings of Jacques Callot, which he compared to those of Francisco de Goya. We can see, in the attention he brought to the pictorial matter, what he looked for in his own drawing practice:

> Callot's etchings represent very often big spaces, vast empty landscapes seen from a certain height, diagonally, from a perspective close to the one we have in front of an anthill. In those spaces a multitude of tiny characters swarm and move about, characters outlined with a sharp avarice of incisive and precise lines and which often stand out as torn shadow puppets on the empty and impassive white. (There would be much to say on the dimensions of those etchings.)[12]

It is a yearning that is expressed here, already perceptible in the choice of Dürer's engravings, for meticulous drawings, and for that visual "anthill" he commented on, and which he also practiced. These few sentences are very important to understanding Giacometti's drawings. The artist reveals how he considered the practice of drawing. He made a connection between the formal aspects of the work (the materiality of the outline and the vacuum left) and not only the subject but its meaning. How to not perceive the same association in his own sharp drawings? That link between the "incisive and precise lines" that stand out on a white background and the violence of Callot's drawings is not fortuitous. Giacometti confirmed it further on in his text, recalling still that "Goya has also represented the horrors of the war, and the bullfights too, whose big vacuums and sharp lines are reminiscent of Callot."[13] The association between visual expression and the subject's violence is made explicit by the artist at the end of his article, when he emphasized: "The greatest or smallest visual quality is only ever the sign of the more or less significant obsession of the artist for his subject; the form is always proportional to that obsession."[14]

Several characteristics mark the development of Giacometti's drawings in the postwar era, in an

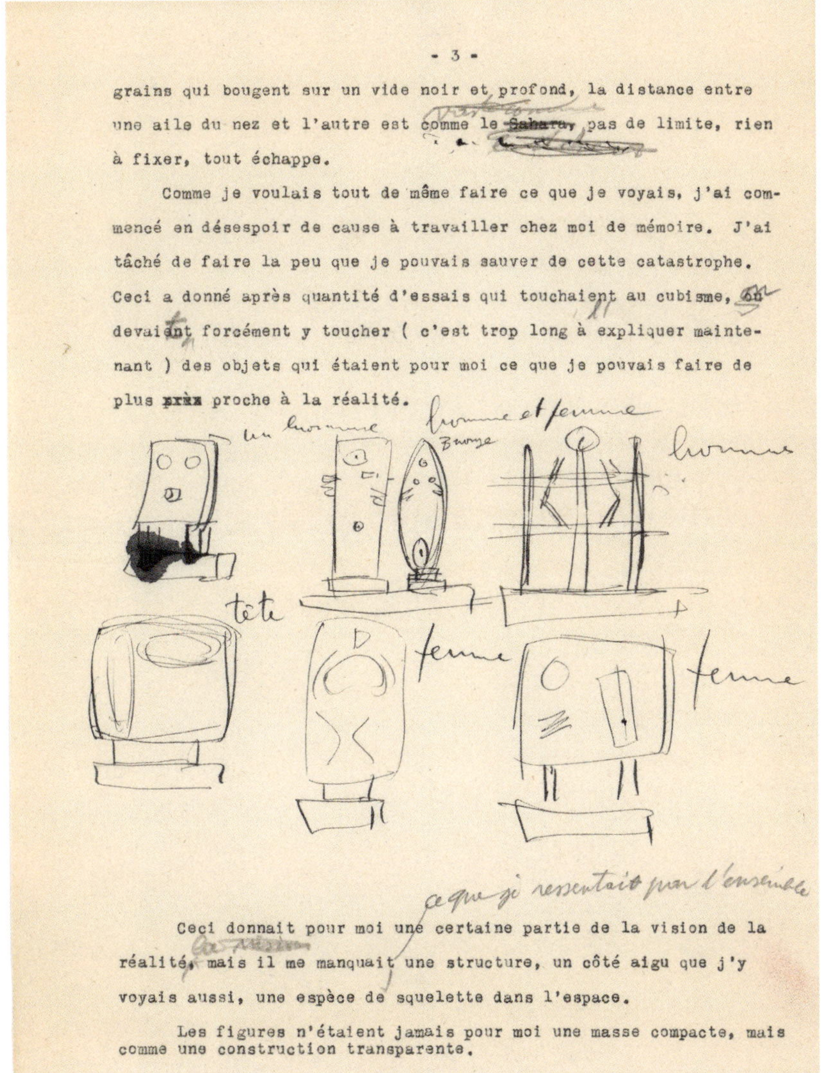

- 3 -

grains qui bougent sur un vide noir et profond, la distance entre une aile du nez et l'autre est comme le ~~Sahara,~~ pas de limite, rien à fixer, tout échappe.

Comme je voulais tout de même faire ce que je voyais, j'ai commencé en désespoir de cause à travailler chez moi de mémoire. J'ai tâché de faire la peu que je pouvais sauver de cette catastrophe. Ceci a donné après quantité d'essais qui touchaient au cubisme, on devaient forcément y toucher (c'est trop long à expliquer maintenant) des objets qui étaient pour moi ce que je pouvais faire de plus ~~près~~ proche à la réalité.

Ceci donnait pour moi une certaine partie de la vision de la réalité, mais il me manquait une structure, un côté aigu que j'y voyais aussi, une espèce de squelette dans l'espace.

Les figures n'étaient jamais pour moi une masse compacte, mais comme une construction transparente.

48 Letter to Pierre Matisse, tapescript with drawings, 1947
Ink, pencil on letter paper;
27 x 21 cm.
Fondation Giacometti

49 ***Heads of Men and Figures*, c. September 1959**
Blue ballpoint pen;
18.3 x 13.6 cm.
Fondation Giacometti

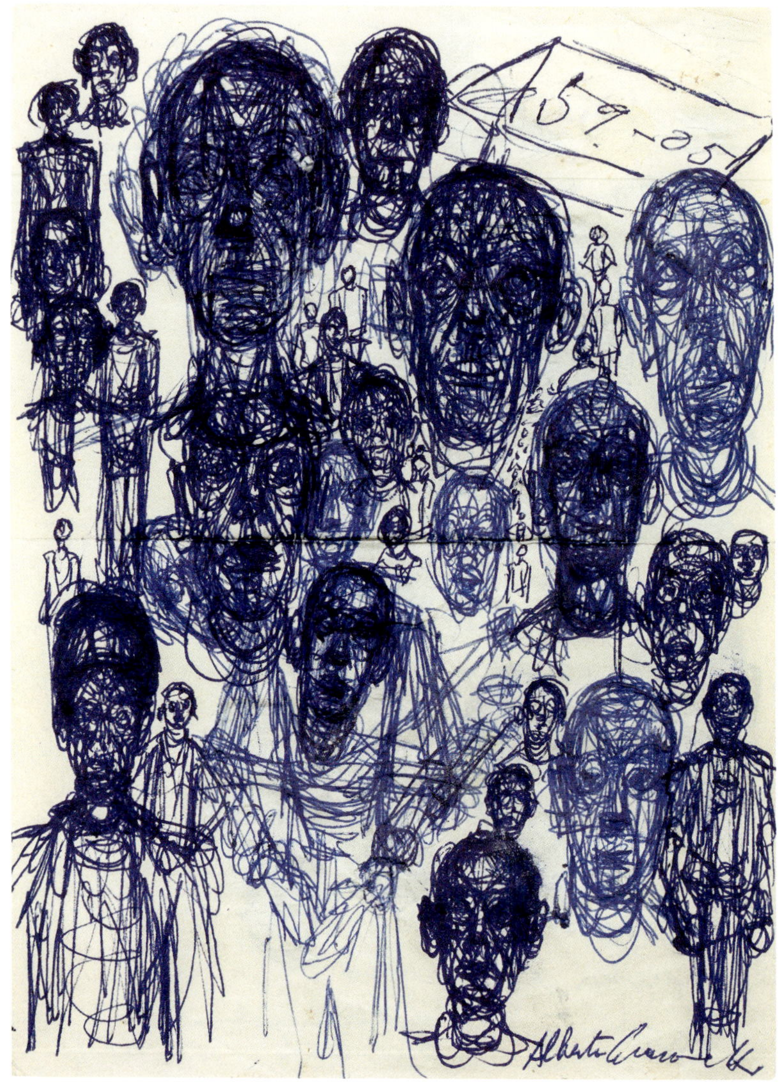

evolution that only went forward: the progressive concentration on some aspects of the subject (the gaze and the eyes, for example, in the portraits); the important expanse of white, called "reserve"; the use of frames; and the emergence of an outline made from repeated lines. Most of those characteristics lead to a concentration. Those qualities, which the artist commented on in Callot's and Goya's art, influenced his contemporaries—the use of the reserve, for example—especially in the postwar years. André du Bouchet mentioned it, using the metaphor of the landscape: "Drawings by Alberto Giacometti—in cold blocks detached from a glacier whose facets cut;"[15] Jean Genet noticed that the lines "are only there to give form and solidity to the white spaces."[16] In their confrontation with real life, Giacometti's drawings bear the mark of carving, and express even in their iteration and sharp character—Michel Leiris saw in them "accumulated scratches"[17]—the obsession around the intrusion of reality. Genet conferred on them the hardness and precision of diamonds:

> It seems to me that for him, a line is a man: he treats it as an equal. The broken lines are sharp and give to his drawing—due to the granitic and paradoxically softened substance of the pencil—a gleaming appearance. Diamonds. Diamonds even more because of the way he uses the white spaces. . . . Extraordinarily chiseled gems. And it is white—the white piece of paper—that Giacometti has chiseled.[18]

Giacometti explicitly formulated in his text on Callot the connection he later made between the outline and the expression of an obsession. Where is it to be found? Undeniably, for he who admitted his fascination with the human head, one has to look for that obsession, even more than in the way it is expressed in his paintings and sculptures, in the human figure. "To bite into reality":[19] that's what had characterized the easy and carefree pleasure of his first drawings. Though Giacometti's drawing delves into real life, his drawings made in biro, a tool he used as soon as it was commercialized at the beginning of the 1950s, express better than any other his obsession.

In the multiplication of sheets, involving all supports—envelope, letter, newspaper, book, magazine—the drawings in biro express the irrepressible, quasi-organic urge to bite with the tip, the artist having found in the human head the focal point of this obsession (fig. 49). As with Antonin Artaud, that visual urgency sometimes happened to the detriment of the paper, pierced by the insistence of the tip. Some drawings that have made the paper soft with overuse acquire sculptural qualities. In the various testimonies about sitting for the drawings, such as those of his brother Diego, Isaku Yanaihara, Genet, and Igor Stravinsky, the strong tension he maintained with his models became apparent, so that the creative act addresses a double register, mixing what is fixed on paper and the exchange, in the intensity of the gaze and the words that sometimes accompany it, between artist and model.

Prolific, he developed his drawings in series, in the taking of breath between capturing a moment, as in the series of portraits he made of Matisse in 1954 (fig. 50), and the longer continuity connects the major themes throughout the decades: the human figures, the heads, the interiors linked to daily life, a few landscapes. Gradually, from the 1940s to the 1950s, in an evolution that was confirmed in the 1960s too, perhaps with a greater awareness of his obsessional functioning, Giacometti's drawing takes on his aspiration to consume reality and proceeds by concentration and by ellipse, densifying the detail in support of an increasingly larger white reserve of paper, to the point that finally the sketch of the eye is enough to convey not only a whole face, but a whole person. In that evolution is also expressed the consummation that the artist's drawing represents: it imposes its own temporality, the expression of its organic evolution.

In one of his most remarkable texts, Giacometti recalls the "basis" that the necessary practice of drawing represents for him. In the middle of the Atlantic Ocean, on the ship bringing him back from New York where the Museum of Modern Art had presented his major retrospective, he wrote a few "notes on the copies," those countless drawings from great masters of the

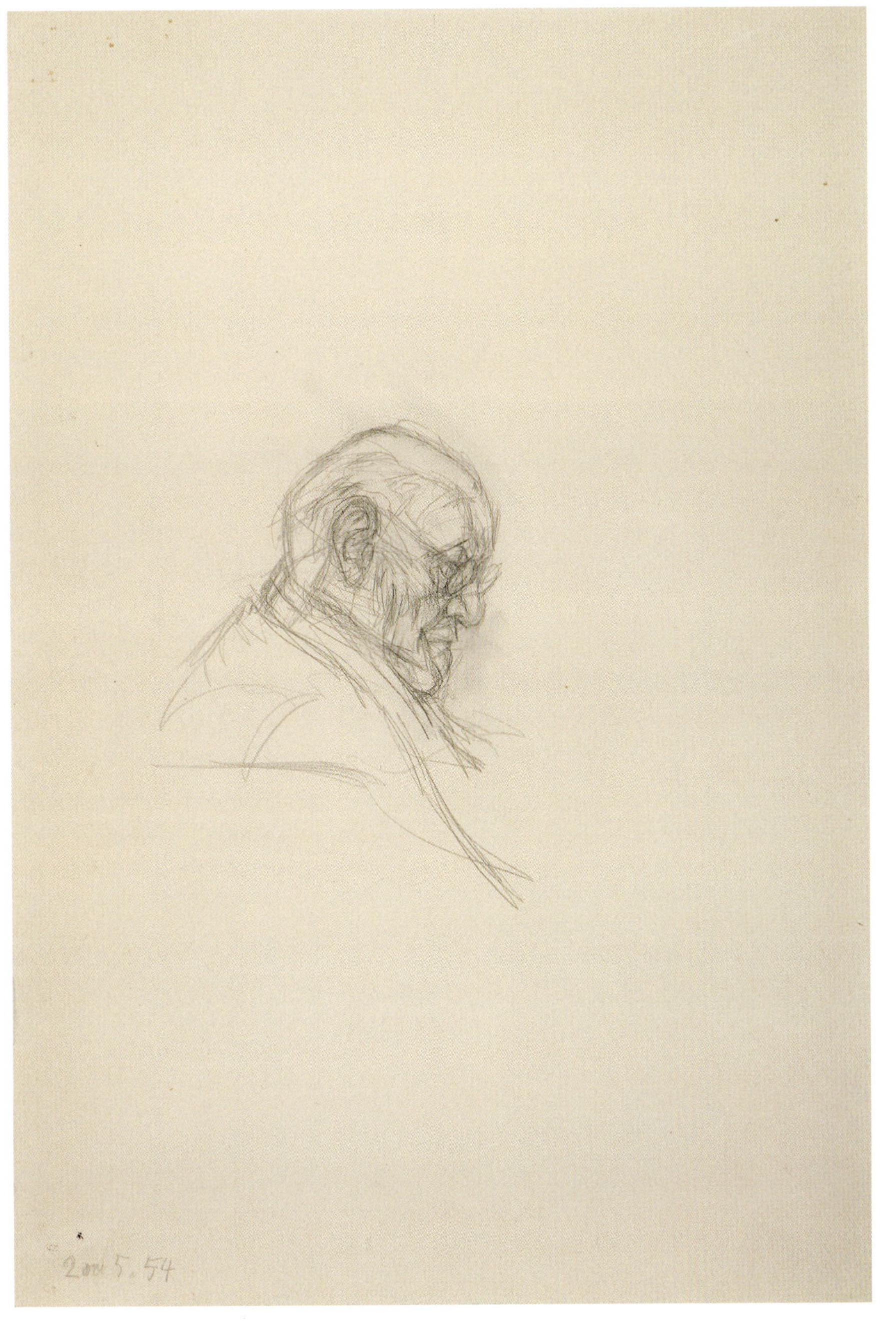

50 ***Henri Matisse*, July 2–5, 1954**
Pencil and rubber on paper;
44.6 x 32 cm.
Fondation Giacometti

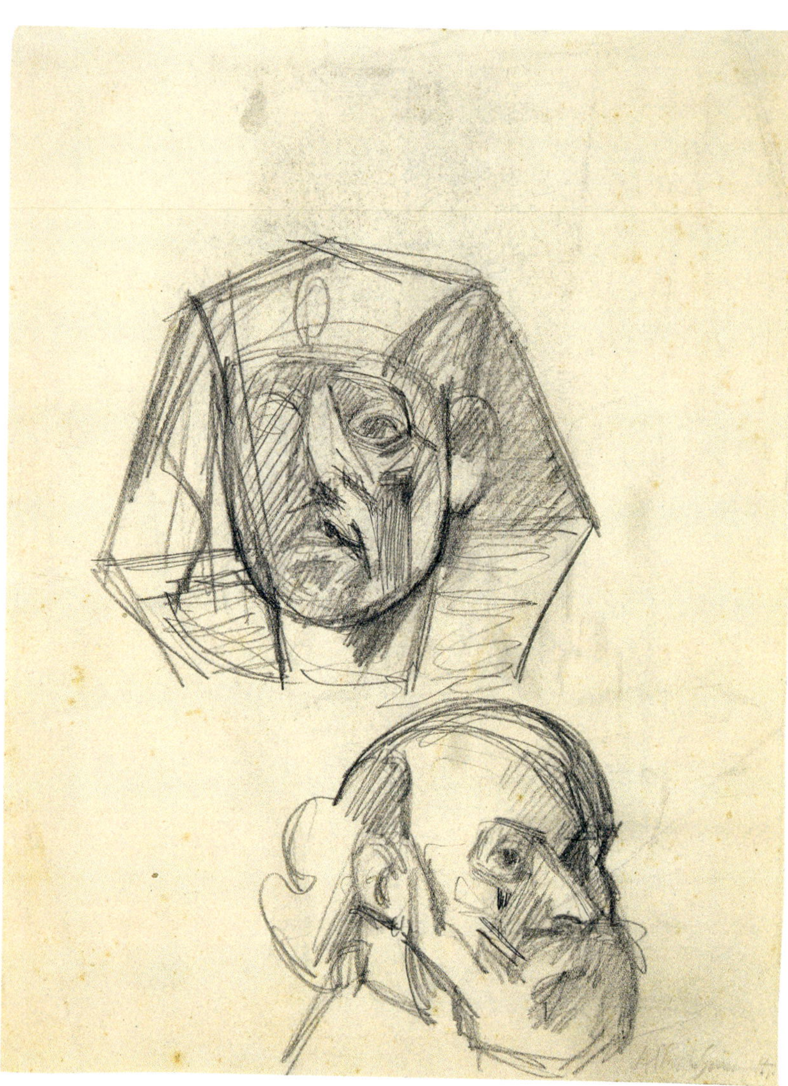

51 ***Copies after the Head of Senwosret III and after Cézanne's Self-Portrait*, 1937**
Pencil on paper; 32.8 x 25.3 cm.
Fondation Giacometti

past, as well as from his fellow artists, whom he had never stopped sketching since his childhood (fig. 51). In these notes, he gave a portrait of the artist as a copyist:

> Suddenly I see myself in Rome in the Borghese Gallery copying a Rubens, one of the great discoveries of the day, but at the same moment, I see myself simultaneously in my whole past: in Stampa next to the window around 1914, focused on the copy of a Japanese print, I could describe it in every detail, and in 1915, Rembrandt's *The Supper at Emmaus*, then a Pinturicchio that suddenly comes to mind and all the Quattrocento's paintings in the Sistine Chapel, but I also see myself [forty] years later, coming back in the evening to my studio in Paris, leafing through books and copying this or that Egyptian sculpture or a Carolingian miniature, but also some Matisses. How to say it all? . . . The memories of the artworks are mixed with personal memories, memories from my own work, from my whole life. . . . All those copies are today on the same level, as if space has taken the place of time. They are so part of my life, of my practice since my most distant childhood. . . . I began copying before I even wondered why I was doing it, probably to give a reality to my predilections.[20]

Copying condenses and absorbs the indisputable pictorial necessity, the expression of a desire endless because it has no other object than life itself. It leads to the point when drawing is copying, for the artist ends up contemplating "copying a nose from life."[21]

The drawing is everything, for it consolidates and develops the art practice, by bringing, like copies, realities and experiences on the same plane, compressing space and time in a fine and sharp-edged form.

Translated by Catherine Petit and Paul Buck

1. Alberto Giacometti to David Sylvester, in *L'Éphémère*, no. 18 (Paris, November 1971); reprinted in Giacometti, *Écrits* (Paris: Hermann, 1992), 287.

2. The collection belonging to the Fondation Giacometti, which keeps the drawings that were in the artist's possession at his death, numbers nearly two thousand drawings on loose sheets (to which must be added more than a hundred notebooks, as well as drawings on books, newspapers, and magazines). An estimate of drawings attributed to the artist, not counting his etchings and notebooks, would be five thousand.

3. "All that is not much, all paintings, sculptures, drawings, writing, or rather / literature. / All that has its place, and nothing more. / Attempts are everything." Giacometti, handwritten note, 1965, in Giacometti, *Écrits: Articles, notes et entretiens* (Paris: Hermann and Fondation Giacometti, 2007), 599.

4. Erwin Panofsky, *Idea: A Concept in Art Theory* (New York: Harper & Row, 1968), 106 and following. The notion, in the treatises of the 14th century, such as Cennino Cennini's *Libro dell'Arte*, which already distinguished the idea from its execution by opposing the "mental drawing" with the "natural drawing," was reclaimed by his most famous advocate, Giorgio Vasari, in the perspective of an elaboration of art history as a discipline in its own right. The definition of the *disegno* by Zuccari in 1607 associated the "internal drawing" (*disegno interno*)—that is, the idea in the sense of the plan—with the "external drawing" (*disegno esterno*)—that is, the outlined form. Zuccari's ideas on the *disegno* are included in his major work *L'Idea de'pittori, scultori ed architetti*, published in 1607.

5. Cennino Cennini, *Libro dell'Arte* (Padua, late 1300s). First published as *Libro dell'Arte*, ed. Roma (1821).

6. "The oldest drawing I remember was not at all from nature, it was the illustration for a story. Snow White in her little coffin, surrounded by the dwarfs. As a child, I wanted to illustrate stories. Then, quite quickly, I began drawing from nature." Pierre Schneider, "*Ma longue marche* par Alberto Giacometti," *L'Express*, no. 521 (June 1961): 48–50; reprinted in Giacometti, *Écrits* 2007, 230.

7. We are familiar with two reproductions of that masterpiece by Giacometti. The first, not so successful and undoubtedly not finished, only copies the contours of the drawing, while the second searches for details in the engraving. As an adolescent, Giacometti identified with Dürer, whose monogram he had copied.

8. Giacometti, "Conversation with Jean Clay" (1963), in Giacometti, *Écrits* 2007, 310.

9. From 1930, Giacometti collaborated with interior designer Jean-Michel Frank to create decorative art objects such as lamps and vases. That activity, providing him with a means to make a living, echoes the sculptures, often called "objects," that he created at the same time. In his drawings, the distinction between the two different outcomes (sculptures or decorative objects) faded significantly.

10. Giacometti, notebook, quoted in *Alberto Giacometti, Catalogue raisonné des estampes*, ed. Mathilde Lecuyer and Eberhard Kornfeld (Paris: Fondation Giacometti; Berne: Eberhard W. Kornfeld, 2017), 1:36.

11. Made of twenty-three etchings from different artists, the portfolio by Jakovski conveys his desire to find a common ground between abstraction and Surrealism. The "Composition" with abstract accents made by Giacometti for the project is undoubtedly one of the artist's most linear and geometric drawings.

12. Giacometti, "A propos de Jacques Callot" (1945), in Giacometti, *Écrits* 2007, 63.

13. Ibid., 64.

14. Ibid., 65.

15. André du Bouchet, "Sur le foyer des dessins d'Alberto Giacometti," in *Alberto Giacometti, dessins, 1914–1965* (Paris: Maeght, 1969), 30.

16. Jean Genet, *L'Atelier d'Alberto Giacometti* (Paris: L'Arbalète, 1957), 63.

17. Michel Leiris, [Ce qui m'émeut par-dessus tout . . .], in *Alberto Giacometti: Dessins*, exh. cat. (Paris: Galerie Claude Bernard, 1975), n.p.

18. Genet, *L'Atelier d'Alberto Giacometti*, 63.

19. Giacometti, "Je fais certainement de la peinture . . ." (1957); reprinted in Giacometti, *I certainly practise painting* (Paris: Hermann and Fondation Giacometti, 2021), 20.

20. Giacometti, "Notes sur les copies" (1965); reprinted in Giacometti, *Notes on the copies* (Paris: Hermann and Fondation Giacometti, 2021), 4.

21. Ibid., 8.

Stampa: A Family of Artists

ANN DUMAS

Alberto Giacometti (1901–1966) was born into a close-knit Swiss family of exceptional artistic talent. His father, Giovanni Giacometti (1868–1933), the son of a rural innkeeper, became a noteworthy Post-Impressionist painter and printmaker (fig. 52). His mother, Annetta Giacometti-Stampa (1871–1964), was from a prominent family of the region. They settled in Stampa, in the beautiful alpine area Val Bregaglia, near the Italian border.

Giovanni first studied art in Munich, and from 1888 to 1891 he continued his training in Paris, mostly at the Académie Julian, in the company of fellow Swiss painter Cuno Amiet (1868–1961). Back in Stampa, in the 1890s, Italian Symbolist painter Giovanni Segantini (1858–1899) taught him his distinctive Divisionist technique of applying paint in systematic strokes and dots. In 1907, he was profoundly influenced by the work of Cézanne that he saw at the Paris Salon d'Automne. This, combined with his earlier absorption of the Pont-Aven group's bold, flat colors, resulted in a personal and energetic variant of Fauvism. His admiration for the German Die Brücke artists was particularly evident in the woodcuts that he began making around 1907. After 1916, there was a marked shift in Giovanni's style. Although he remained a colorist, his compositions became more descriptive and lyrical. His late work would influence his son Alberto.

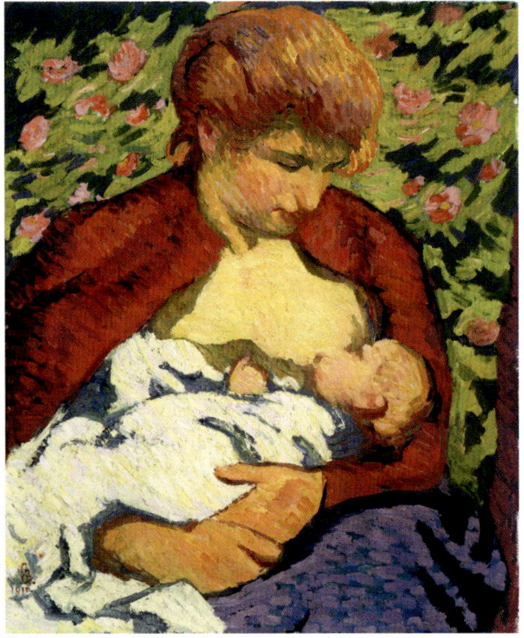

52 *Young Mother*, 1910
Giovanni Giacometti (Swiss, 1868–1933). Oil on canvas; 65.4 x 55.9 cm. The Museum of Fine Arts, Houston, John A. and Audrey Jones Beck Collection, Gift of Audrey Jones Beck, 98.283

Giovanni's cousin Augusto Giacometti (1877–1947) was a painter and decorative artist who studied in Zurich and Paris, where, under the influence of Eugène Grasset, he began working in a stylized, Art Nouveau manner. From 1902 to 1915, he studied Renaissance painting in Florence and developed his signature style of colorful abstractions with spiritual and Symbolist undertones. In 1915, he settled in Zurich, where he was much sought after for large-scale decorative commissions, particularly in mosaic and stained glass. In the 1950s, his paintings earned him a reputation as a pioneer of abstraction. He was compared to Wassily Kandinsky, the European Tachistes, and the American Abstract Expressionists.

Alberto's closest artistic relationship was with his brother Diego (1902–1985). Diego joined Alberto in Paris in 1925, and from 1929 he helped his older sibling with technical aspects of his work, carving stone and making bronze and plaster casts. In the 1930s, he assisted with Alberto's commissions for lighting fixtures and vases for interior decorator Jean-Michel Frank. His greatest achievement, however, was the production of highly original decorative objects in bronze beginning in the 1950s. He created designs for lamps and furniture in a geometric style, often adorned with animal motifs. Among his major commissions were those from the Fondation Maeght, in Saint-Paul-de-Vence, and, in the mid-1980s, from the Musée Picasso, in Paris, for furniture and light fixtures in bronze and resin.

Another younger brother, Bruno (1907–2012), was an important modernist architect who built the Swiss pavilion for the 1952 Venice Biennale and the natural history museum in Chur. The least-known member of the family, the brothers' sister, Ottilia (1904–1937), who died in childbirth, had practiced weaving in her youth.

Alberto Giacometti's early life, spent in a supportive family environment, whose inner circle included the greatest Swiss artists of the day—Cuno Amiet and Ferdinand Hodler (1853–1918)—had a lasting impact on him (fig. 53). He retained close ties with his family home in Stampa, and during regular summer visits from Paris, he would work in the wooden barn that his father had turned into a studio. Today, this structure forms part of the Museo Ciäsa Granda, in Stampa.

53 The Giacometti family on the occasion of Annetta's 38th birthday: (left to right) Alberto, Diego (front), Bruno, Giovanni, Ottilia, Annetta, 1909
Andrea Garbald (Swiss, 1877–1958). Bündner Kunstmuseum Chur, Deposit of the Fondazione Garbald. © Fondazione Garbald, Castasegna

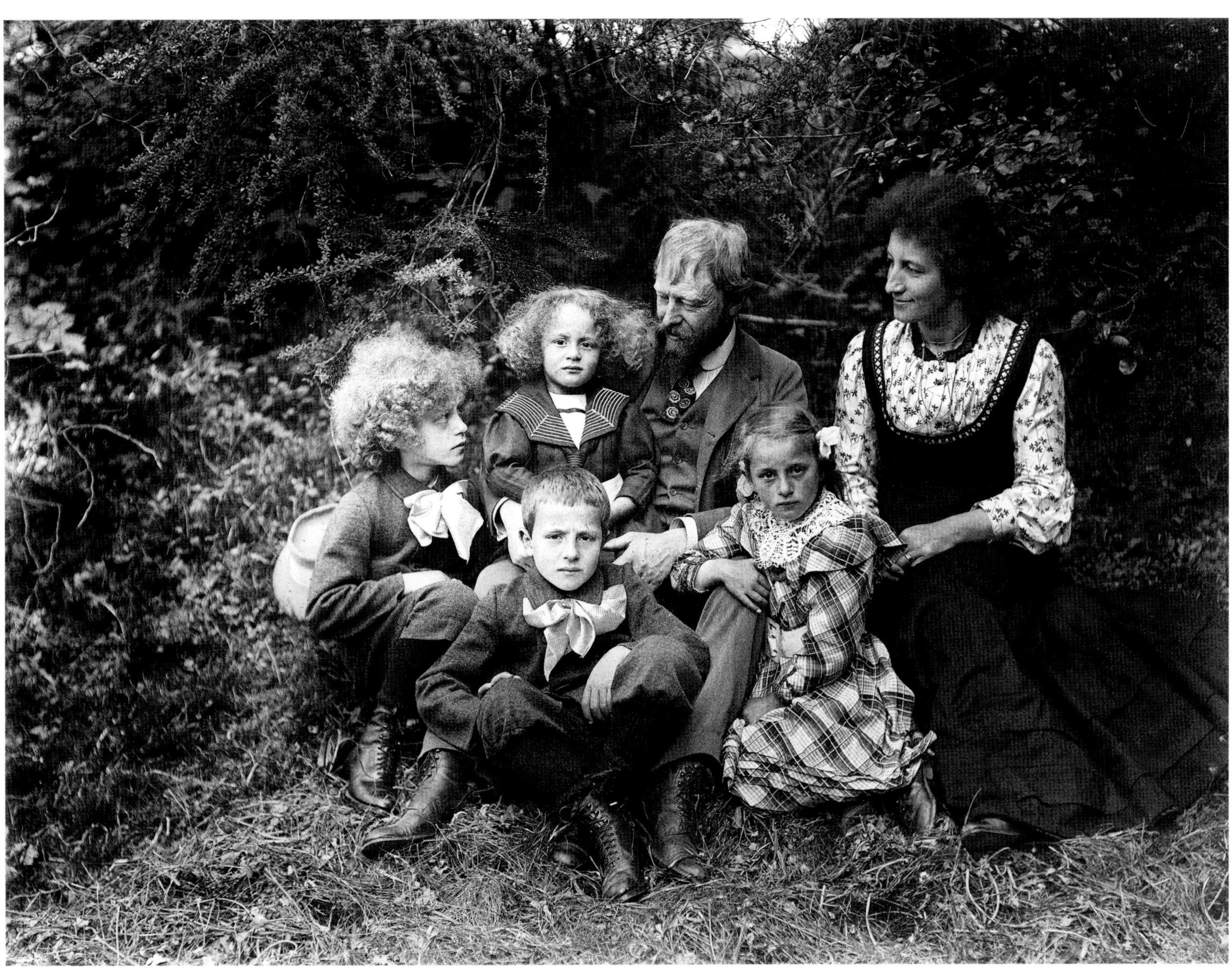

***View of Stampa*, c. 1919**
Black ink on paper; 16 x 24 cm.
Fondation Giacometti

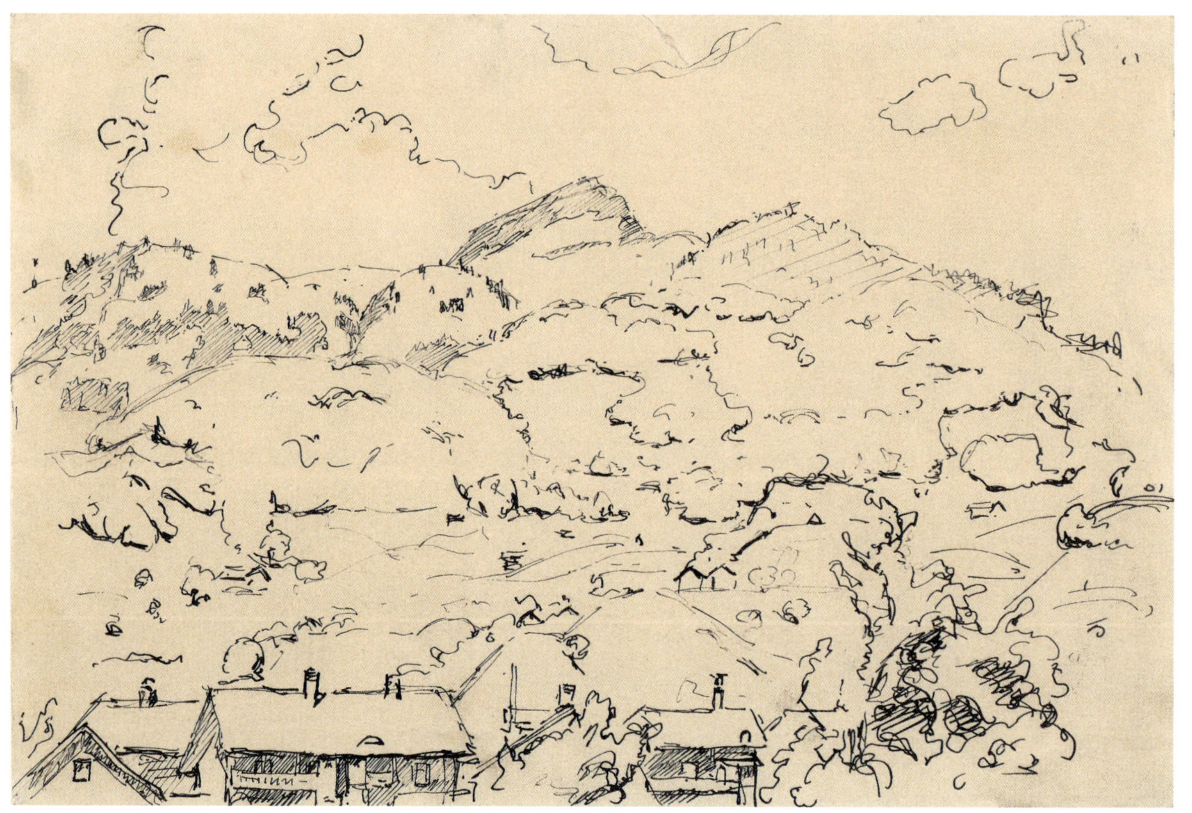

***Street of Stampa in the Winter*, c. 1917**
Blue ink on paper; 34 x 21.7 cm.
Fondation Giacometti

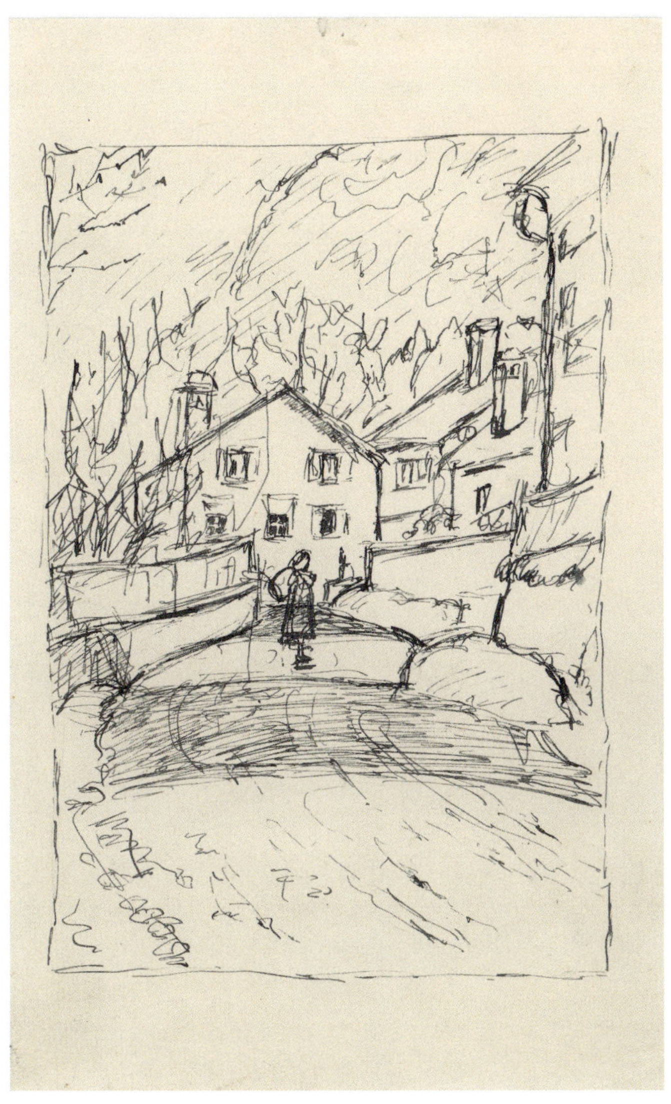

Stampa, 1961
Anonymous photographer.
Archives, Fondation Giacometti

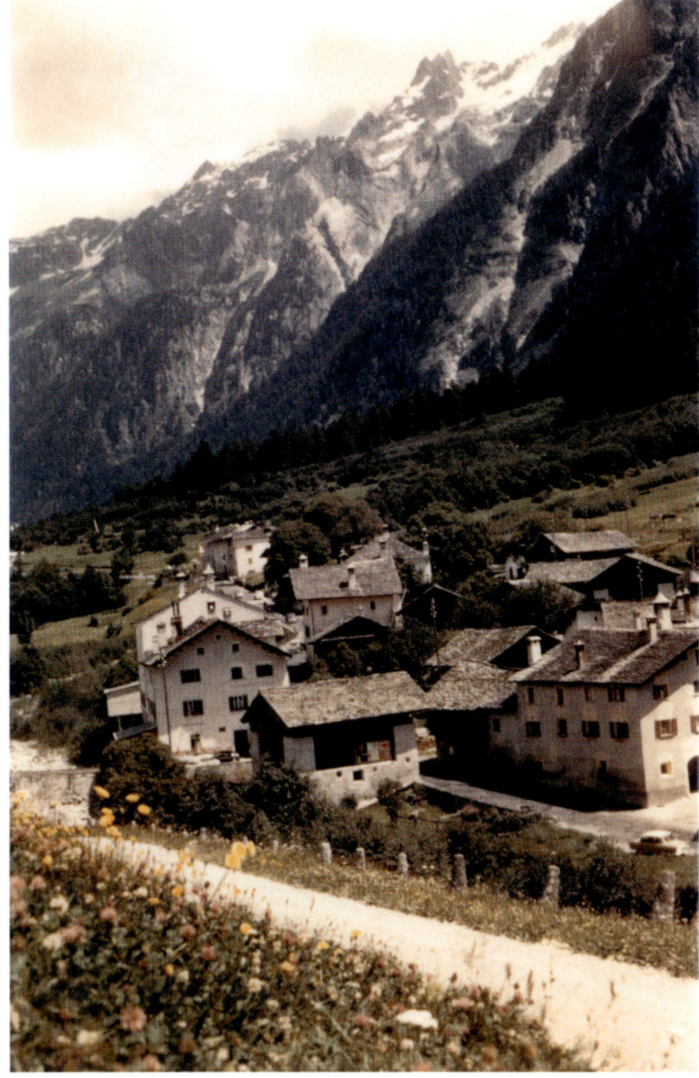

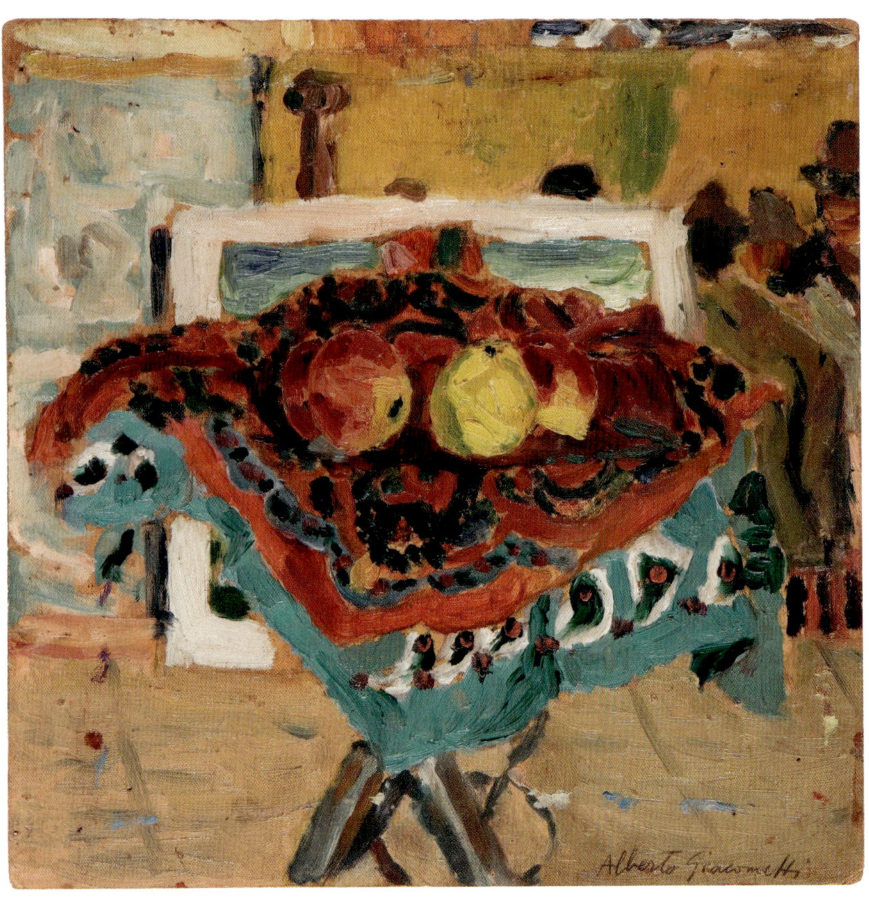

***Still Life with Apples*, c. 1915**
Oil on cardboard; 36.2 x 36.6 cm.
Fondation Giacometti

***Mountain at Stampa*, 1917–20**
Oil on cardboard; 36.6 x 36.2 cm.
Fondation Giacometti

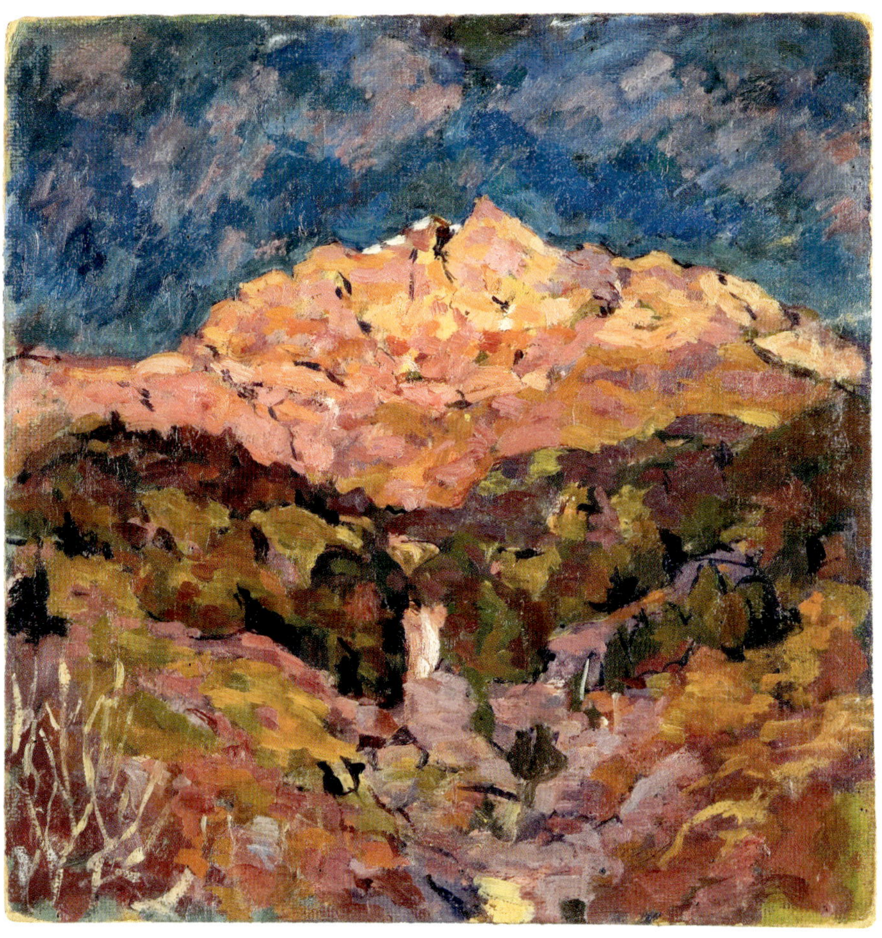

***The Mountain Road*, c. 1919**
Watercolor and pencil on
paper; 22 x 29 cm.
Fondation Giacometti

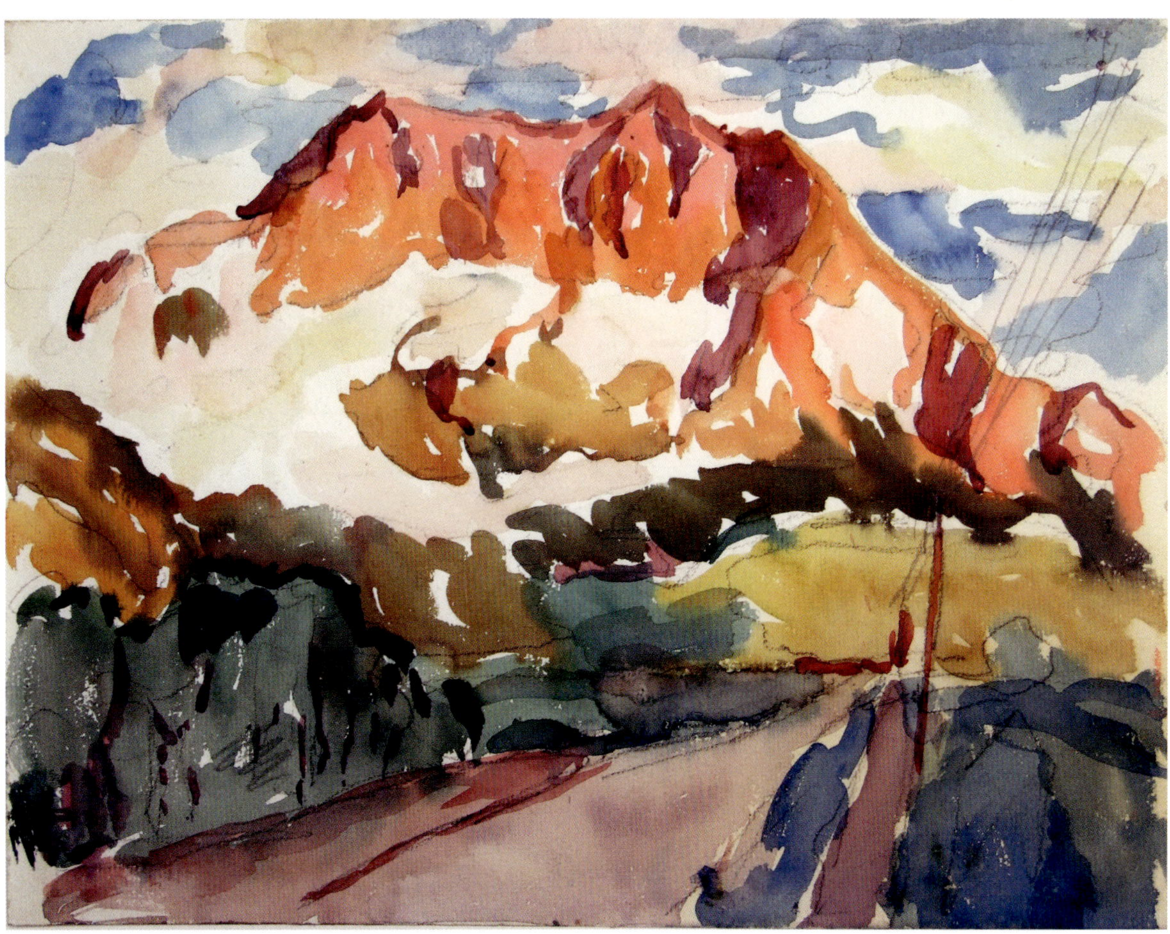

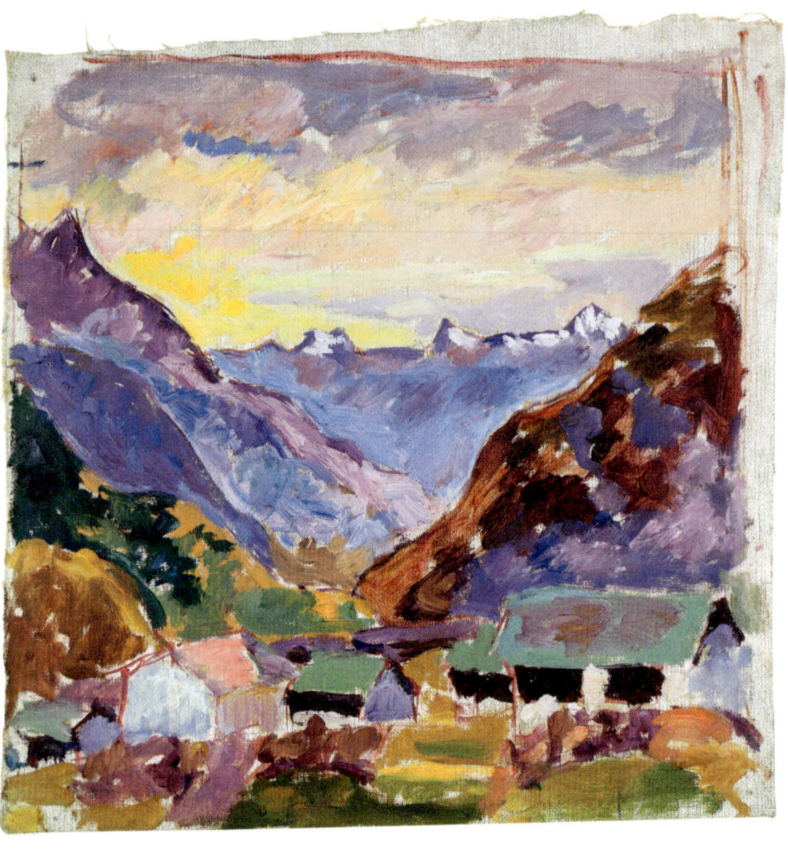

***Mountain Landscape at Coltura*, c. 1920**
Oil on cut canvas; 30.4 x 30.2 cm.
Fondation Giacometti

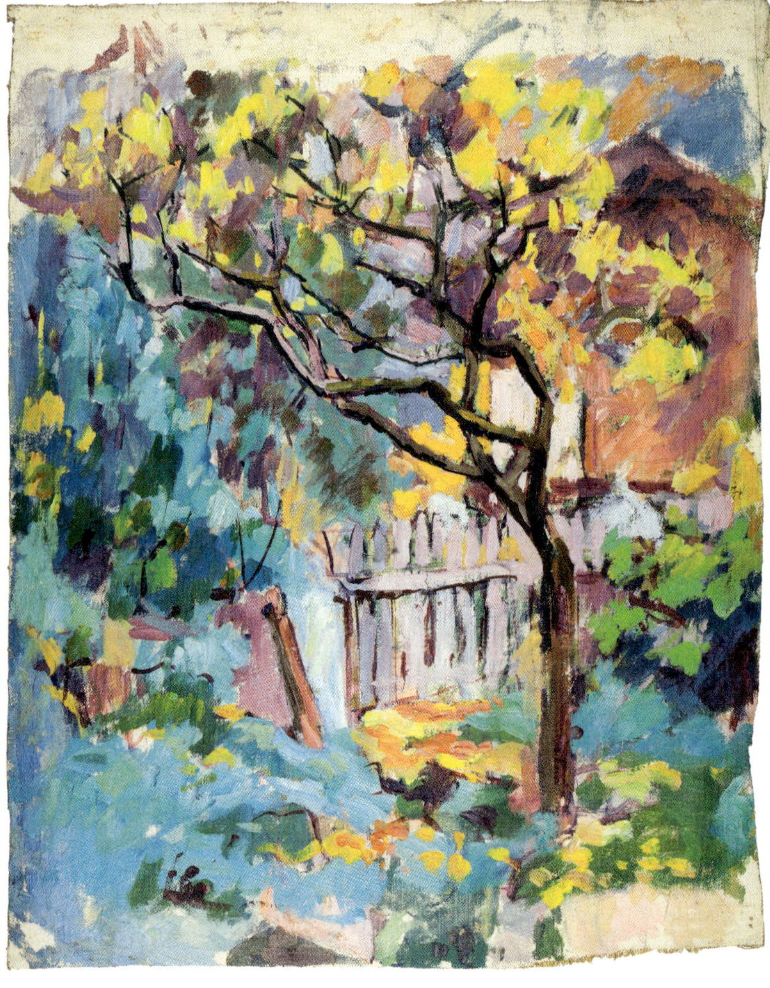

***Landscape*, c. 1920**
Oil on cut canvas; 47.2 x 38.6 cm.
Fondation Giacometti

***Mountain Landscape*, c. 1921**
Oil on canvas; 60.3 x 50.1 cm.
Fondation Giacometti

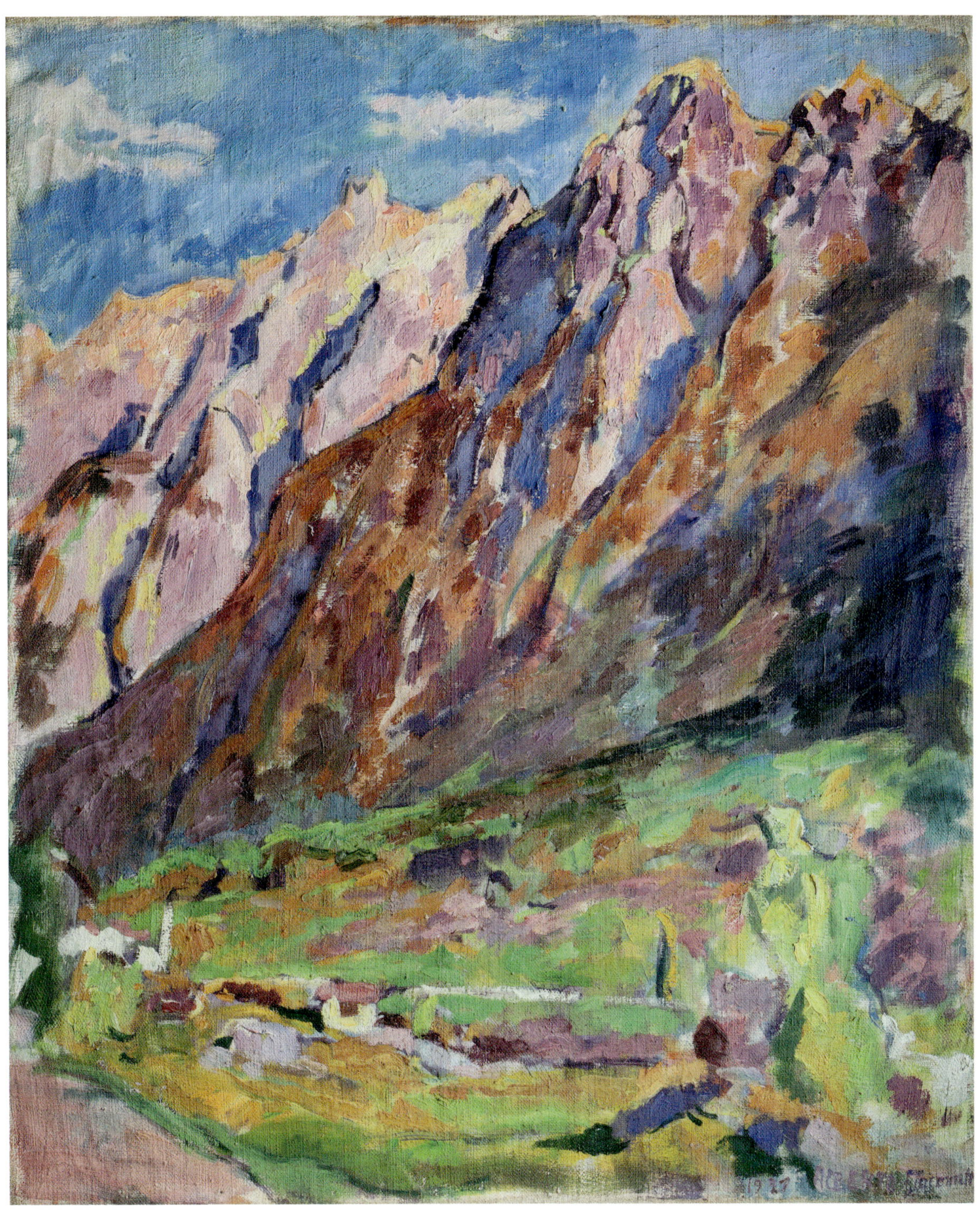

***Diego in Profile and Copy after Cézanne's Self-Portrait*, c. 1918**
India ink and graphite pencil on paper; 34 x 25.7 cm.
Fondation Giacometti

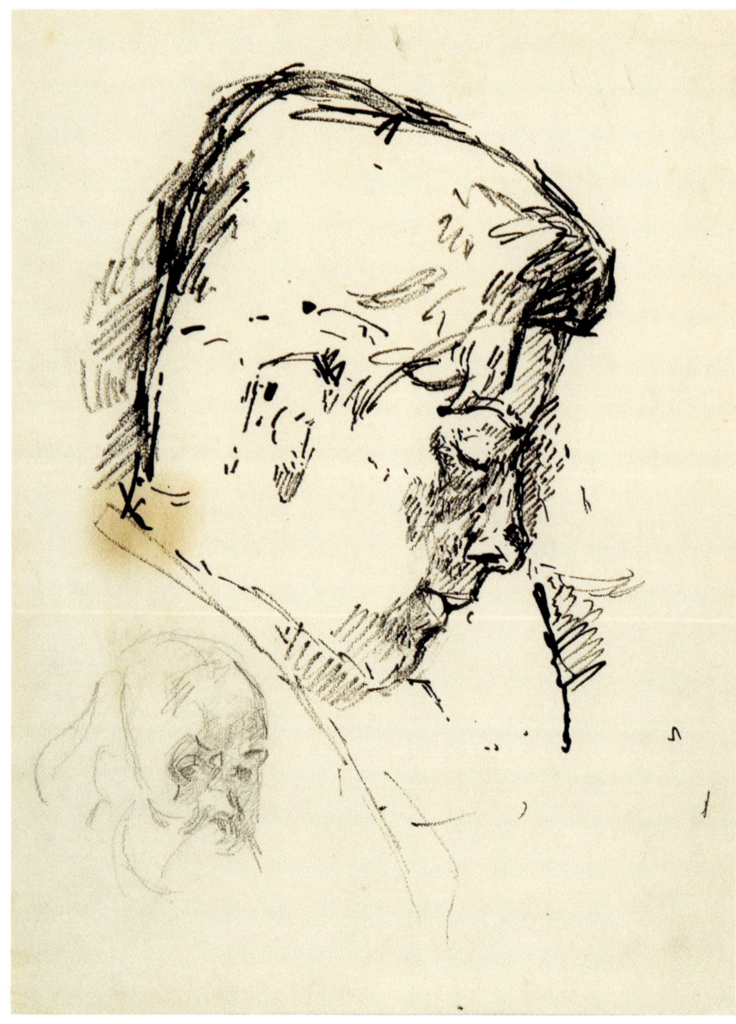

***Bruno*, c. 1918**
Blue ink and graphite pencil on paper; 29 x 22.5 cm.
Fondation Giacometti

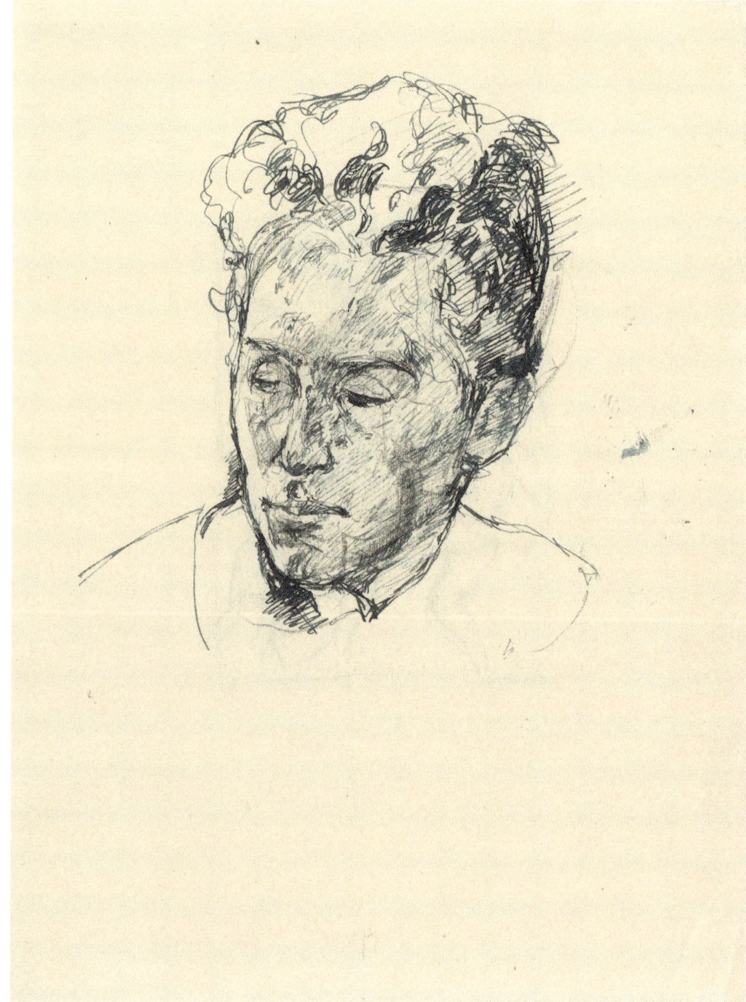

***Portrait of a Woman Seated on a Chair, Three-Quarter View*, c. 1918**
Black ink on paper; 48.1 x 35.1 cm.
Fondation Giacometti

***Woman Sewing (Maria)*, c. 1925**
Black ink on paper; 48.8 x 33.2 cm.
Fondation Giacometti

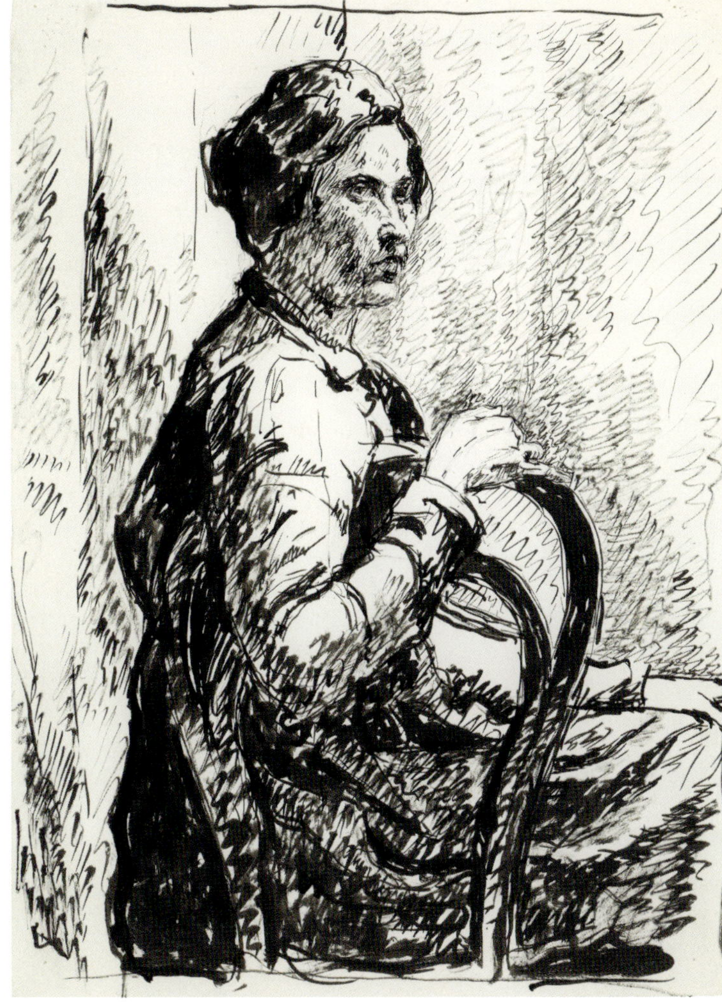

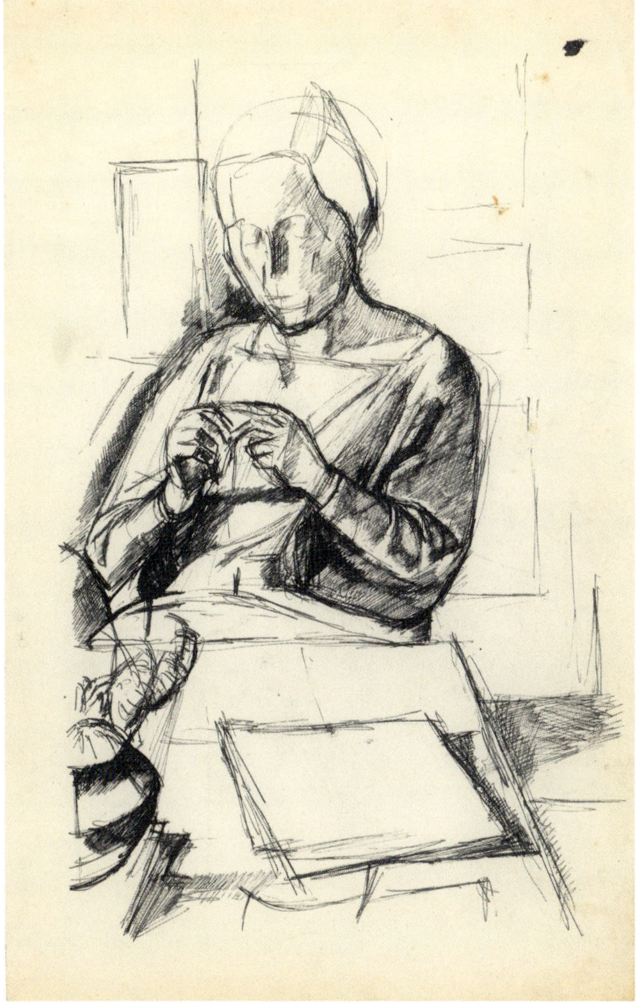

***Apples in a Fruit Dish on the Table*, 1947**
Graphite pencil on notepaper;
29.7 x 21 cm.
Fondation Giacometti

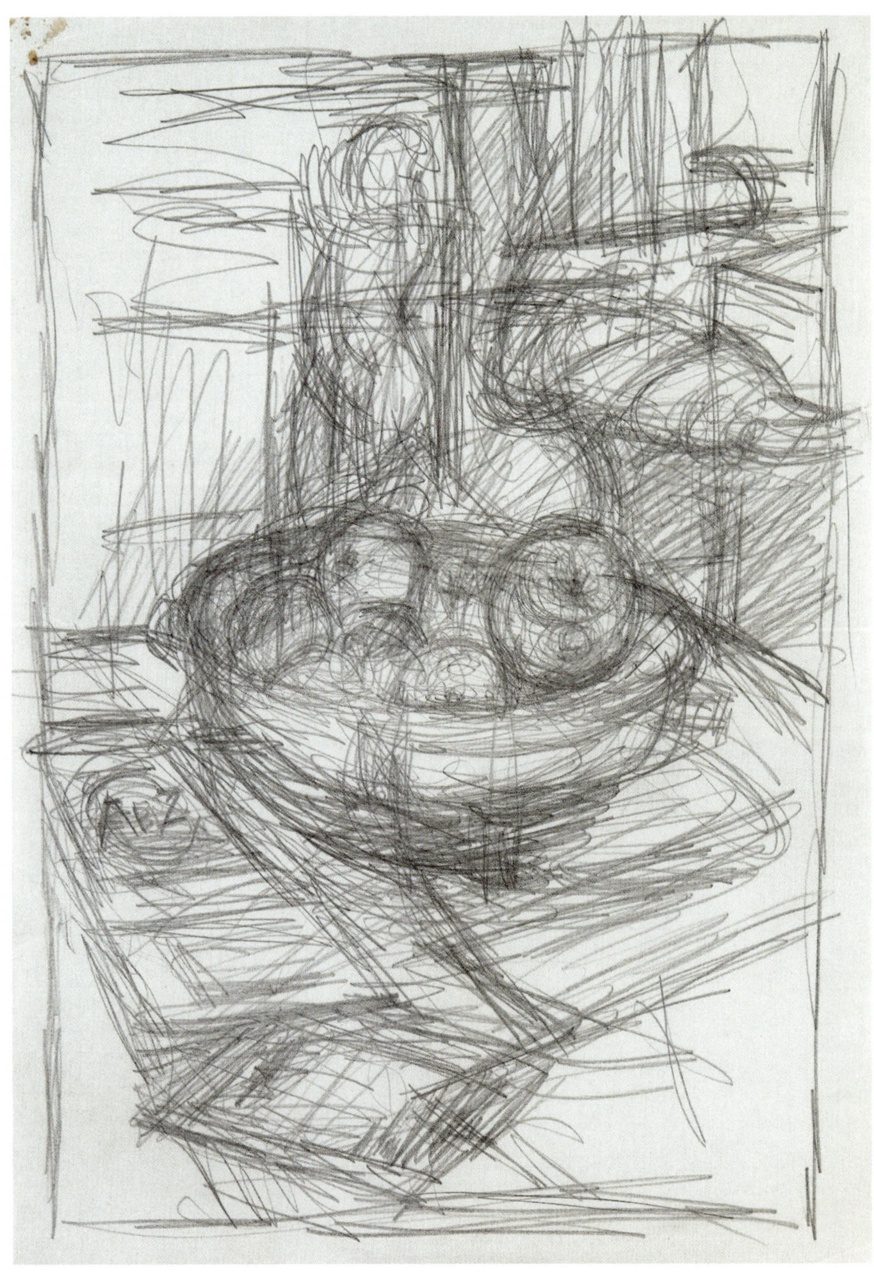

***The Mother of the Artist in Stampa*, c. 1959**
Graphite pencil and rubber on paper; 50 x 32.8 cm.
Fondation Giacometti

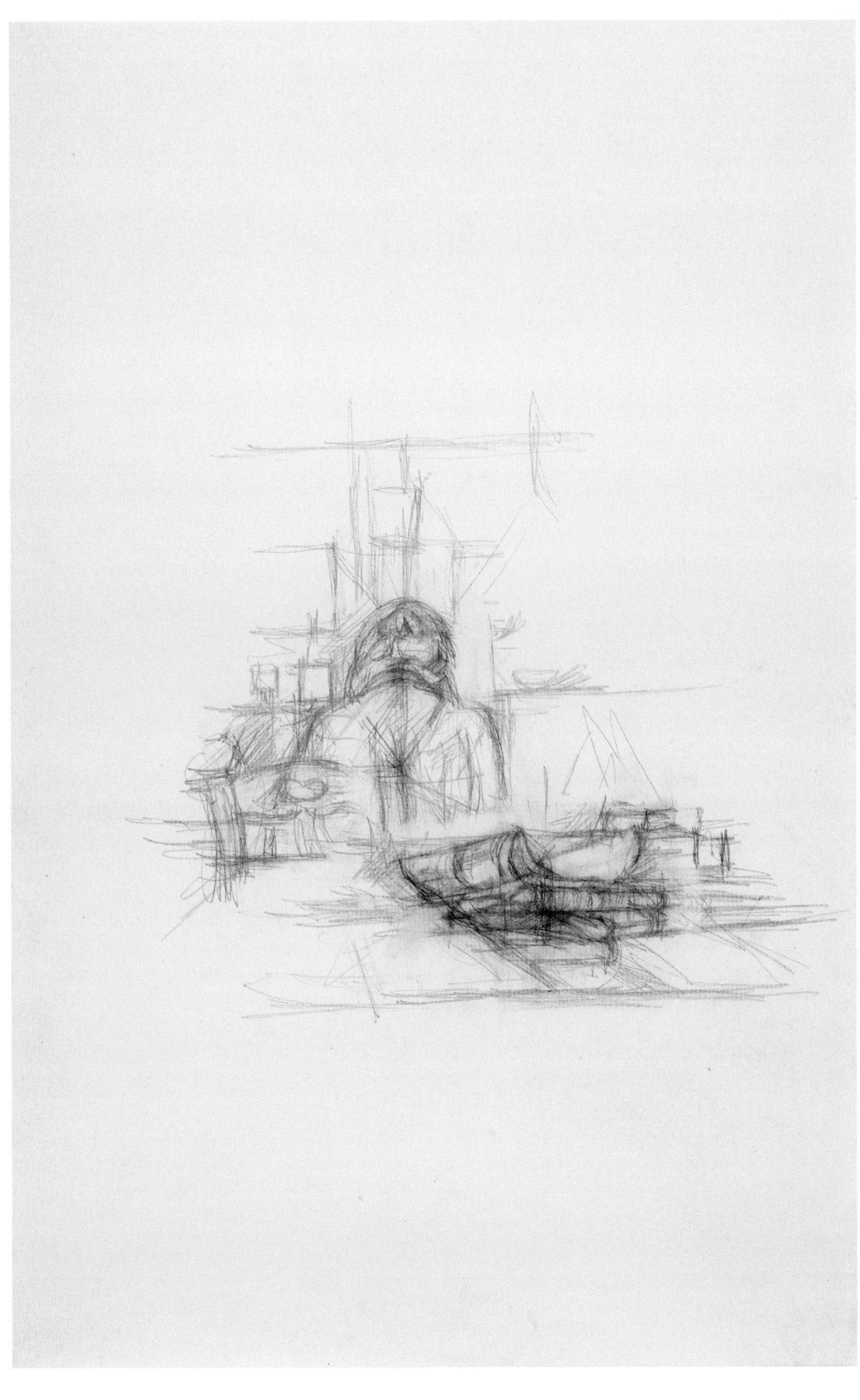

Paris: Life in a Studio in Montparnasse

ROMAIN PERRIN

Alberto Giacometti at the street entrance of the studio courtyard, 1948
Emmy Andriesse (Dutch, 1914–1953). Leiden University Libraries. © Leiden University / Joost Elffers

When Alberto Giacometti arrived in Paris in 1922, he joined the sculpture class taught by Antoine Bourdelle at the free Académie de la Grande Chaumière. He lived in a hotel, and rented at least two studios, one of which was the studio of sculptor Alexander Archipenko. In December 1926, wanting his own studio, Giacometti settled at 46 rue Hippolyte-Maindron, in the heart of Montparnasse, then the epicenter of bohemian cultural life. This settling in the French capital corresponded to a time when the young man began asserting himself as an artist.

Giacometti's studio belongs to those places intimately mixed with the people who inhabited them, because it relates so much to the myth that built up around him. The artist never left it, despite its narrowness and the lack of comfort that characterized that room of barely 23 square meters, to which was added a mezzanine, and in which the light came through a glass wall opening up to a long courtyard shared with other studios. There was no running water, the house was badly heated, and the roof leaked in many places. Its prewar state is only known through a few drawings and photographs, some taken by well-known individuals in the entourage of the Surrealists, but the studio seems to have changed little throughout the years. Though Giacometti gradually rented the adjacent units to settle his brother Diego in 1929, to bring the comfort of a separate bedroom to his young bride Annette Arm in 1947, and to store his sculptures in 1957, he continued leading an ascetic existence, the consequence of a life exclusively focused on work.

In the postwar years, the photographers who entered the studio—like Henri Cartier-Bresson, Sabine Weiss, and Ernst Scheidegger, whose pictures were printed in the press—captured a particular atmosphere that the black and white images, as well as the presence of the artist at work or striking a pose, tended to aestheticize. The humble space, cluttered with sculptures in progress or completed, brushes, bottles of turpentine, clay, and plaster, attesting to the artist's relentless work, fascinated all the visitors to the studio, and reinforced a certain romantic vision of art practice.

In a letter addressed to Nelson Algren, writer Simone de Beauvoir speaks of a "studio submerged in plaster"[1] and a "scary" house. The studio became a literary subject, on which poet Georges Limbour was the first to write a piece in 1947, "Le charnier de plâtre d'Alberto Giacometti."[2] The several sittings Jean Genet submitted to between 1954 and 1957 inspired him to write one of the most important texts published on the artist, in which the studio is the place where a dialogue with Giacometti and a reflection on his oeuvre occur.[3] Sketched many times, notably for the collection of lithographs *Paris sans fin* (1959–65), the studio represented for Giacometti a visual motif that one can also discern in the background of his portraits. Beyond that "paper studio," both described and invented, 46 rue Hippolyte-Maindron was a place frequented by intellectuals, in particular those from Paris. Giacometti was always accommodating toward those who wished to visit. The people he mixed with during those long hours of sitting mentioned the silence that reigned in the room, at times broken by the artist's exasperation when he failed in what he was trying to achieve.

Entering the studio, the visitor discovered walls covered in sketches, painted or carved. After the artist's death, the pictorial layers were removed to be preserved, making the place of creation part of his oeuvre, as if Giacometti, like an alchemist, had transmuted, as was suggested by poet Yves Bonnefoy,[4] the crude substance of the studio.

1. Simone de Beauvoir, *Lettres à Nelson Algren* (Paris: Gallimard, 1997), 99–100.

2. Georges Limbour, "Le charnier de plâtre d'Alberto Giacometti," *Action* 24 (September 1947); reprinted in *Dans le secret des ateliers* (Paris: L'Éloquent, 1986), 39.

3. Jean Genet, *L'Atelier d'Alberto Giacometti* (Paris: L'Arbalète, 1957).

4. Yves Bonnefoy, *Remarques sur le regard* (Paris: Calmann-Lévy, 2002), 113.

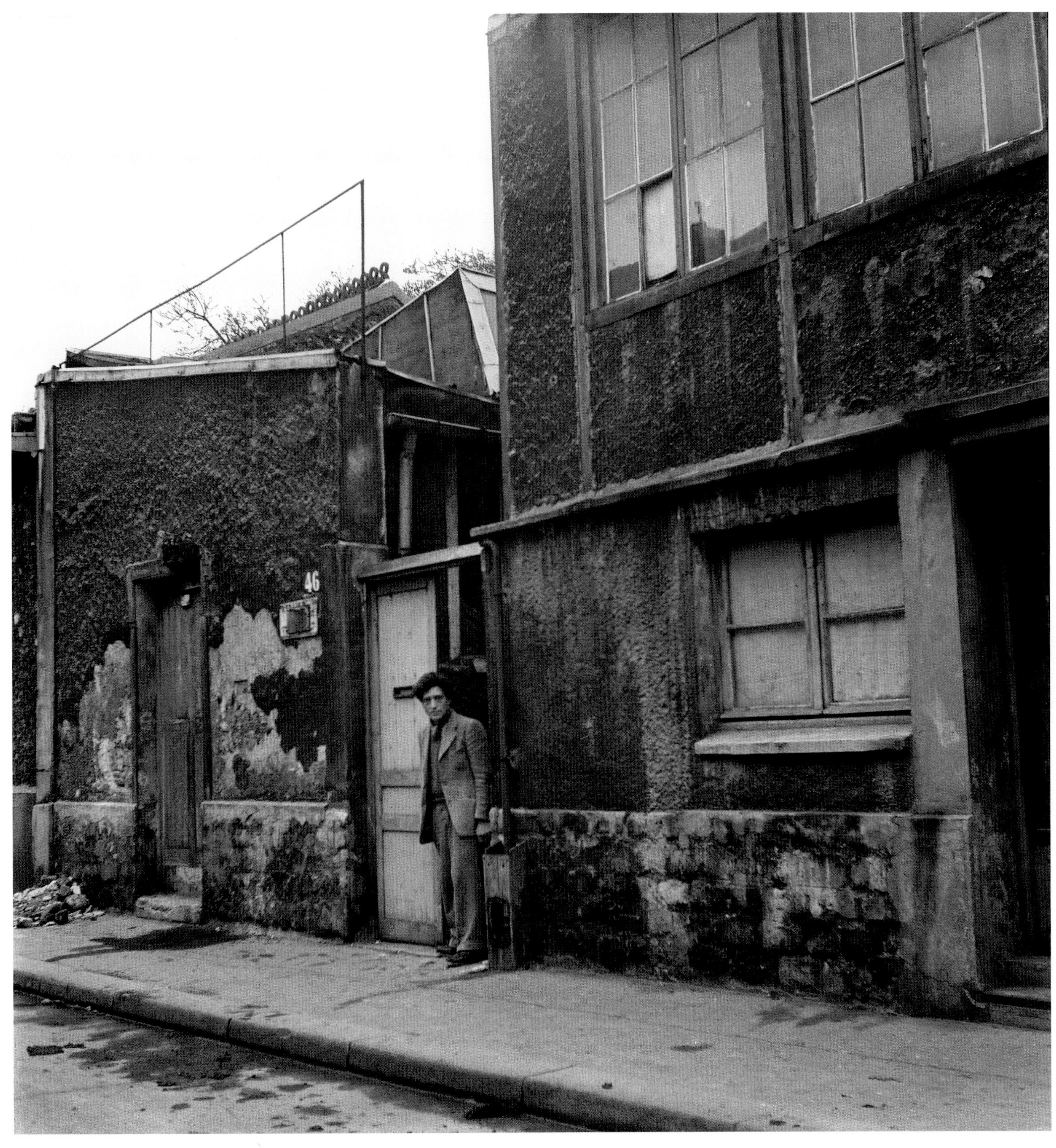
46

Alberto Giacometti in the studio holding one of the elements of the *Project for a City Square*, c. 1932
Anonymous photographer.
Archives, Fondation Giacometti

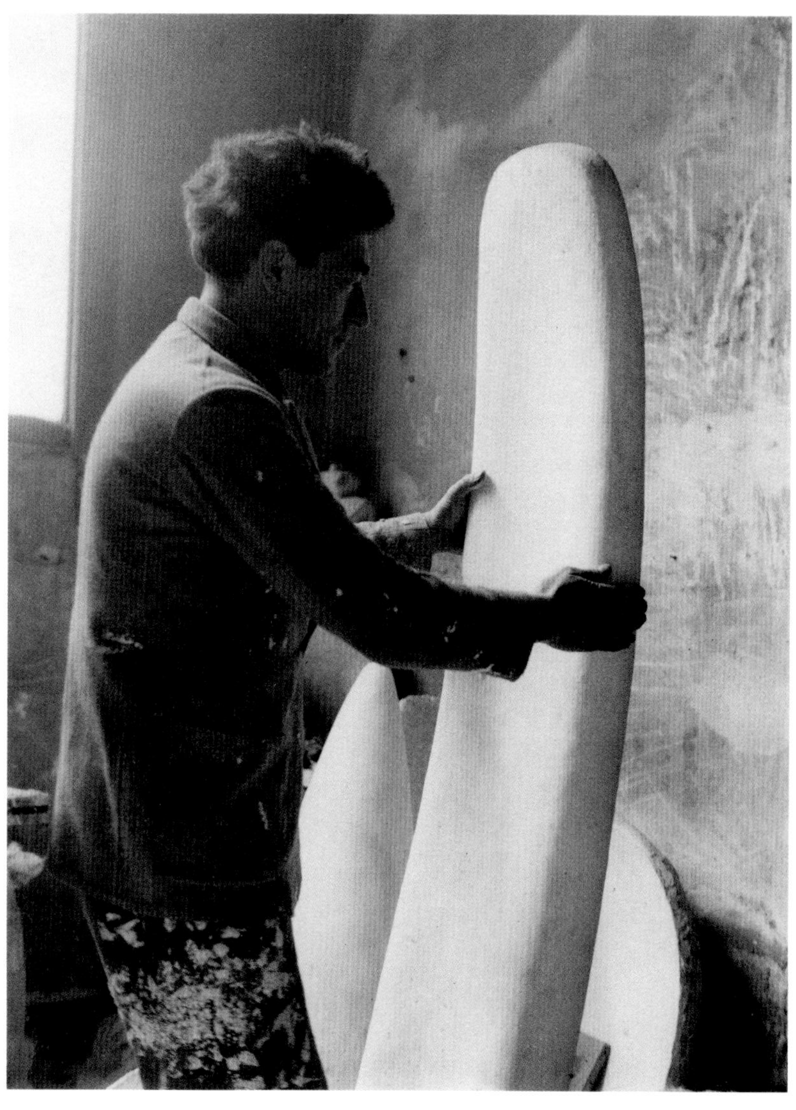

***Woman (Flat V)*, c. 1929**
Bronze; 55.5 x 33.6 x 7.7 cm.
Fondation Giacometti

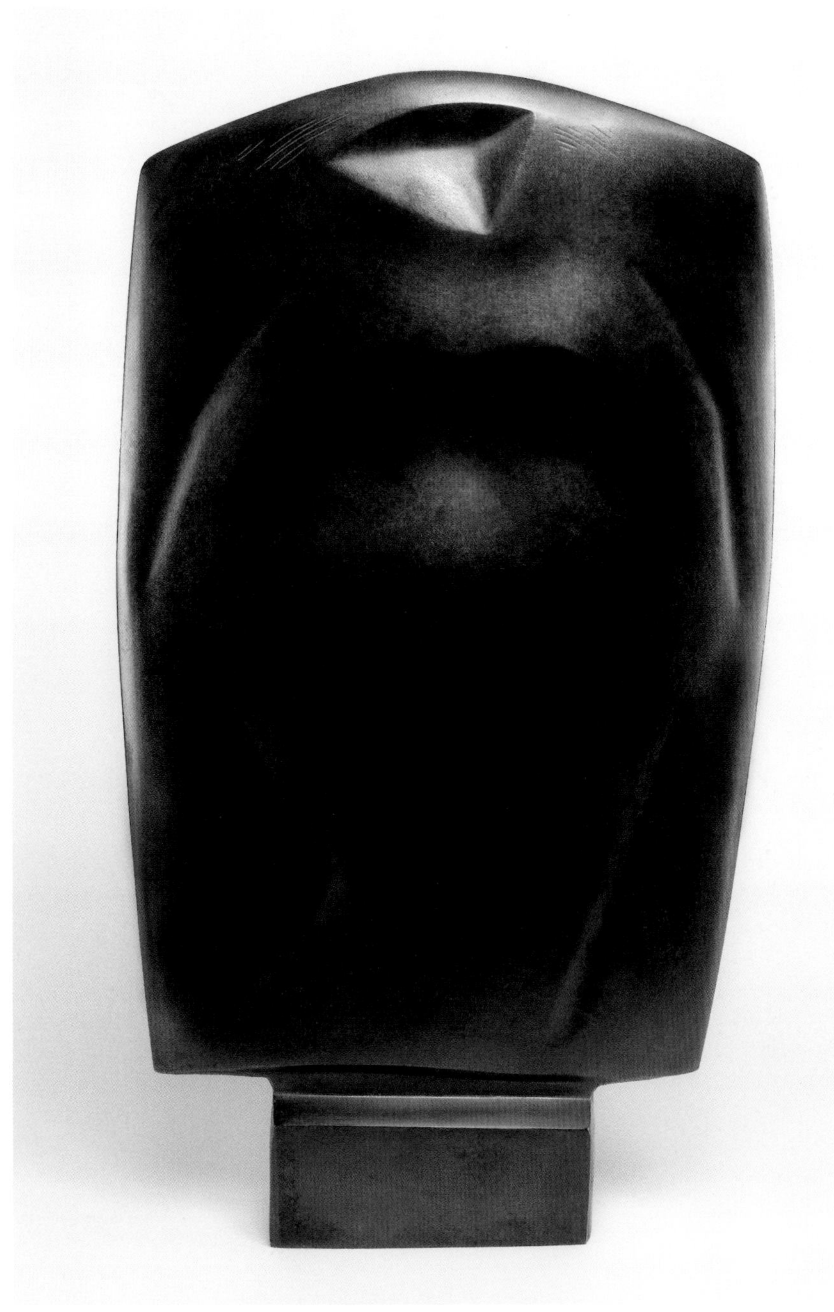

***Sculptures in the Studio VII*, pl. 28, from *Paris sans fin*, 1969**
Printed by Mourlot. Edited by Tériade éditeur, Paris. Lithograph; sheet: 42.5 x 32.5 cm.
Fondation Giacometti

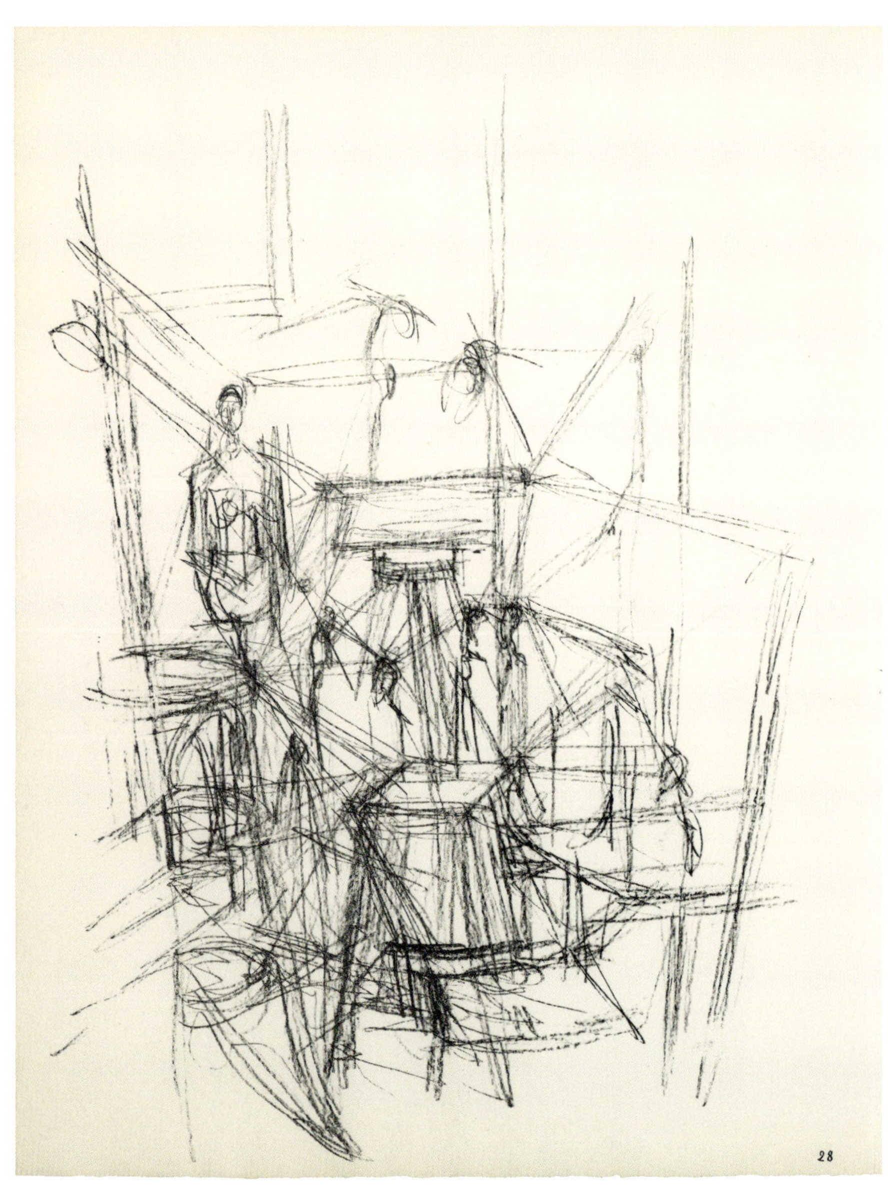

***Seated Woman*, 1956**
Bronze; 51.3 x 15.6 x 23.7 cm.
Fondation Giacometti

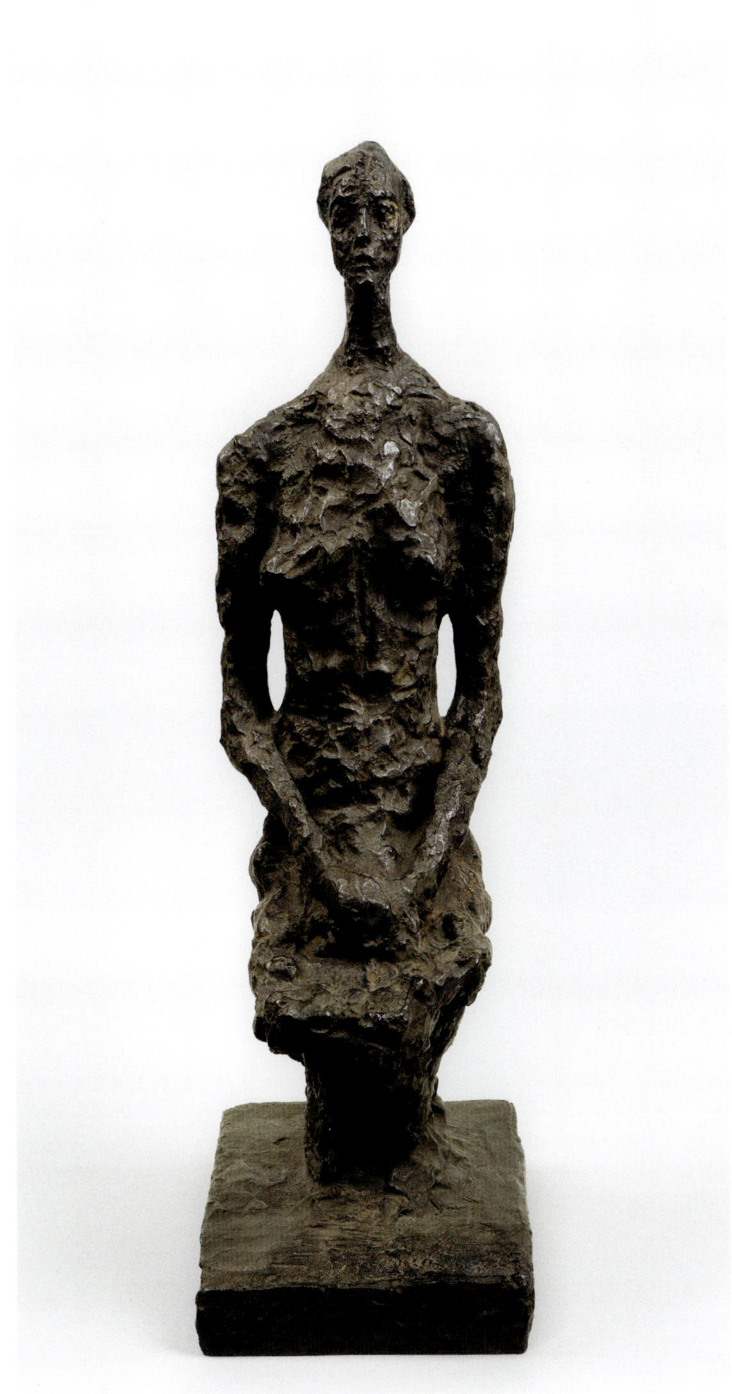

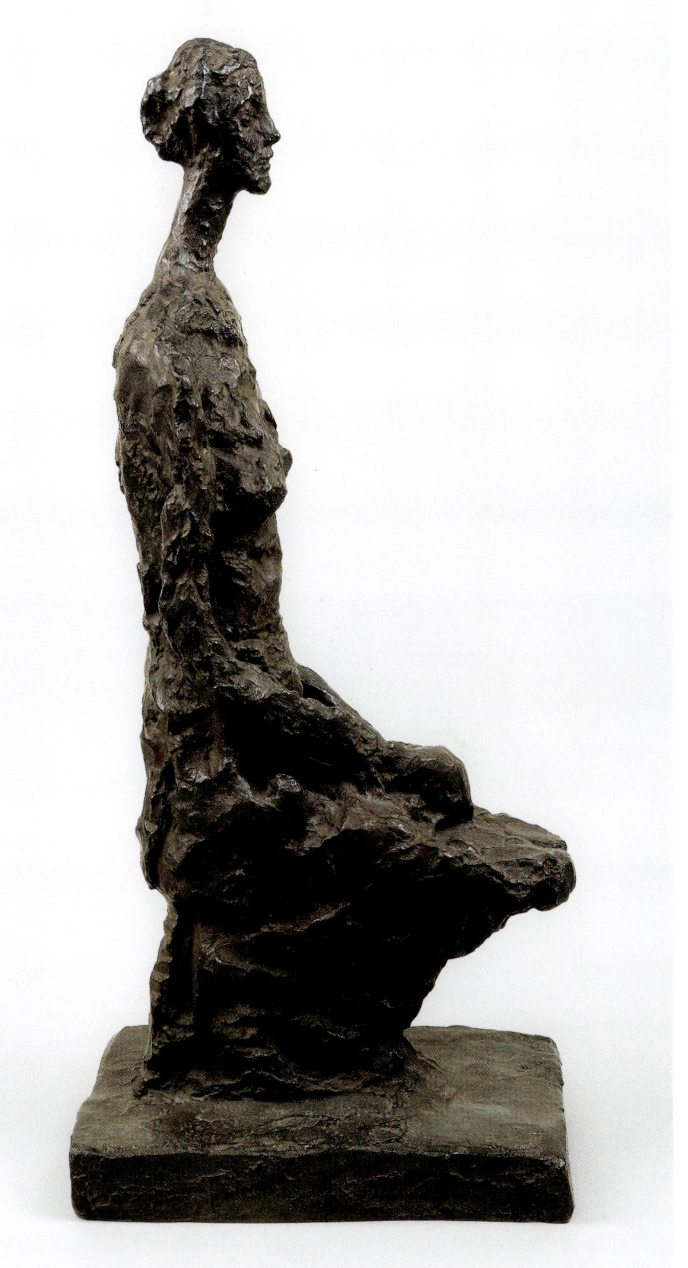

***Sketch for* The Cage, First Version, *Sketch for* Four Figurines on a Stand, *Sketches for* The Chariot *(Two Facing and One Profile)*, c. 1949–50**
Painting on wall on canvas;
124.5 x 107.3 cm.
Fondation Giacometti

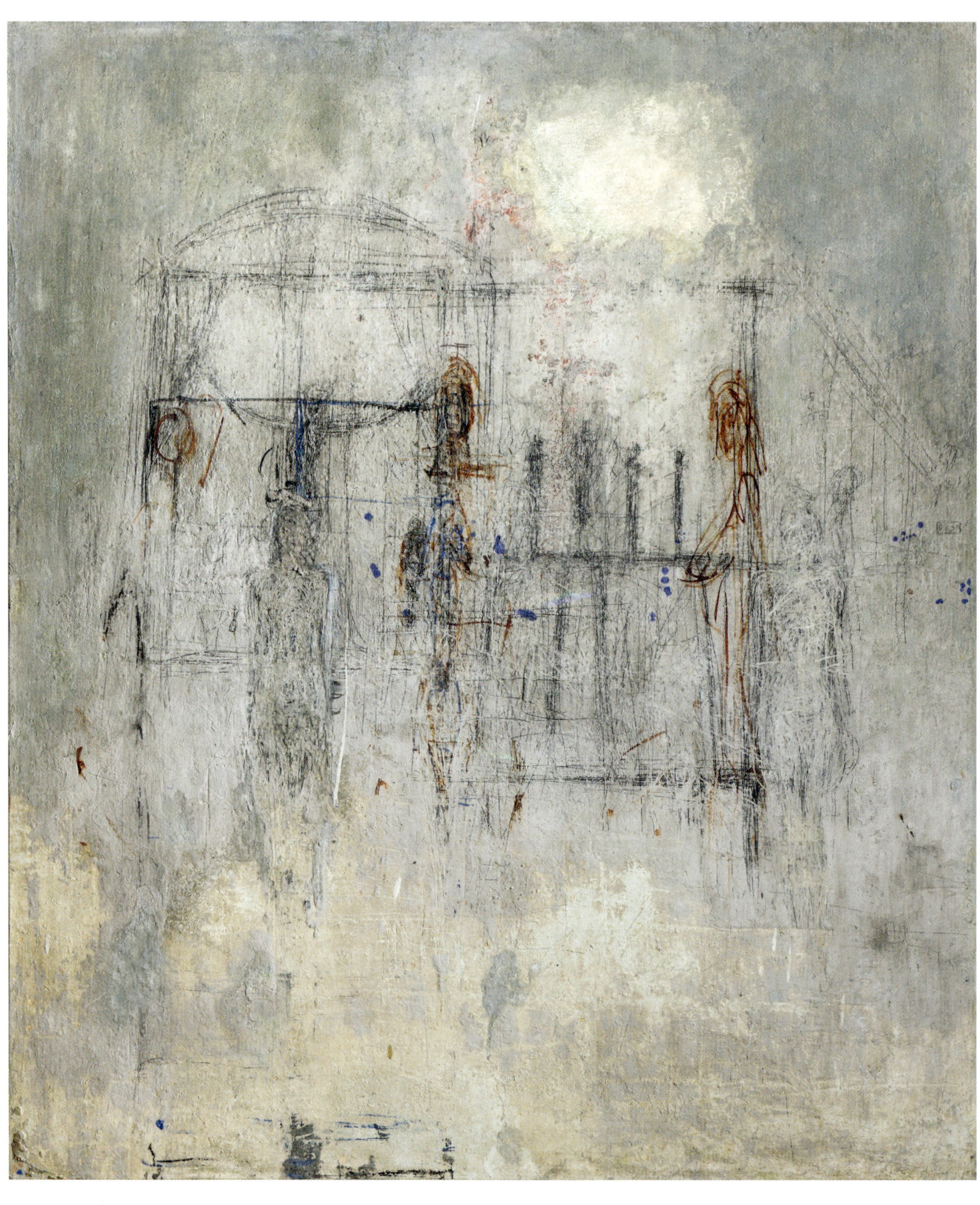

Alberto Giacometti in his studio, Paris, 1954
Sabine Weiss.
Archives, Fondation Giacometti.

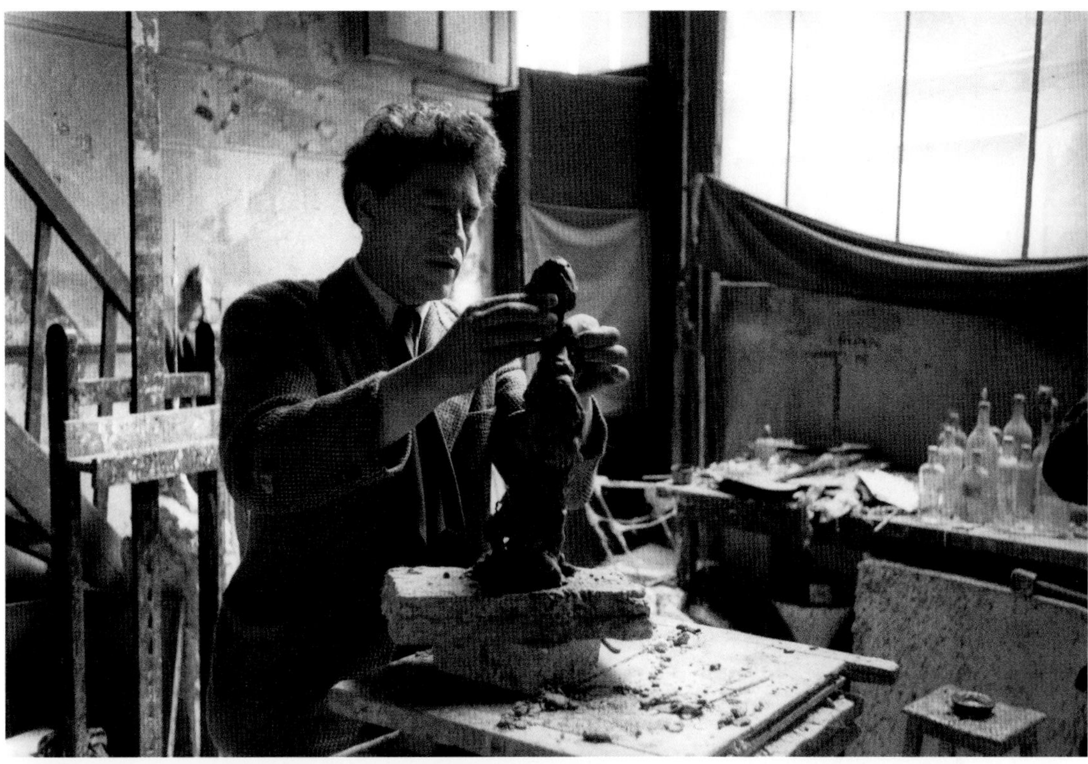

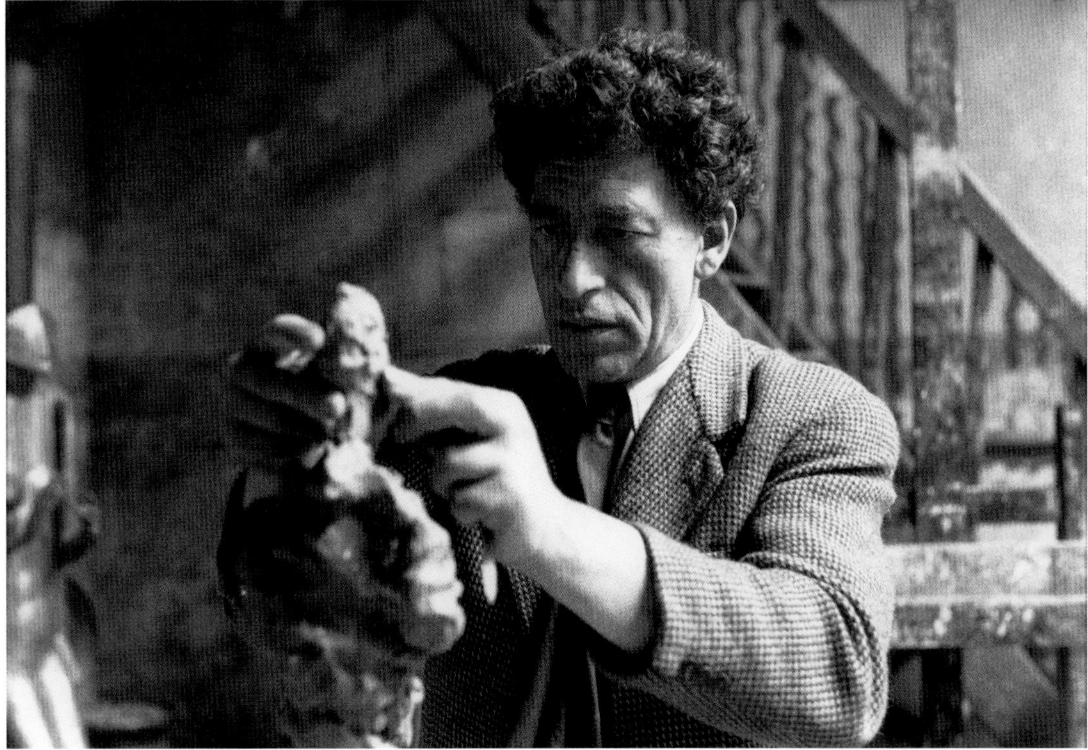

***Sculptures in the Studio IX*, pl. 100, from *Paris sans fin*, 1969**
Printed by Mourlot. Edited by Tériade éditeur, Paris. Lithograph; sheet: 42.5 x 32.5 cm.
Fondation Giacometti

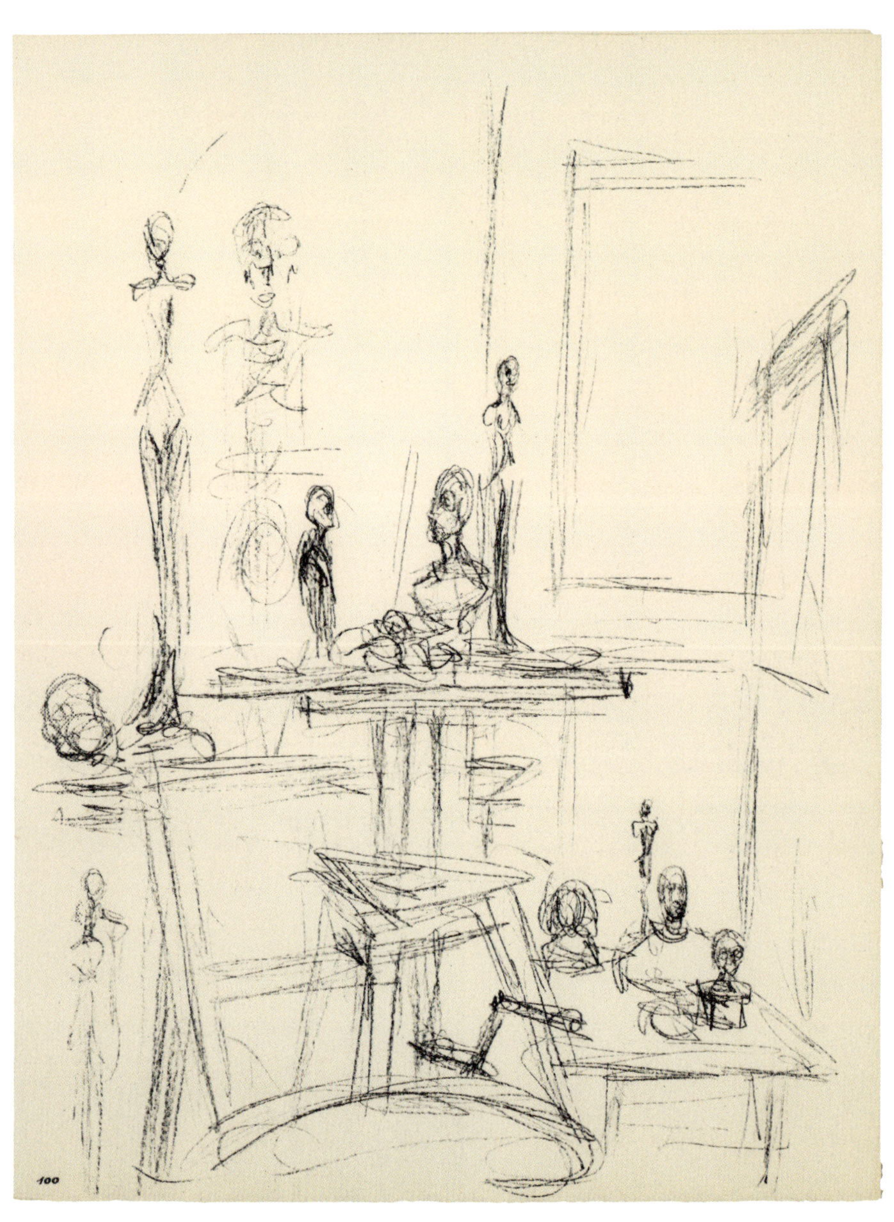

***Bust of Annette*, c. 1950**
Painted plaster; 18 x 16.5 x 9 cm.
Fondation Giacometti

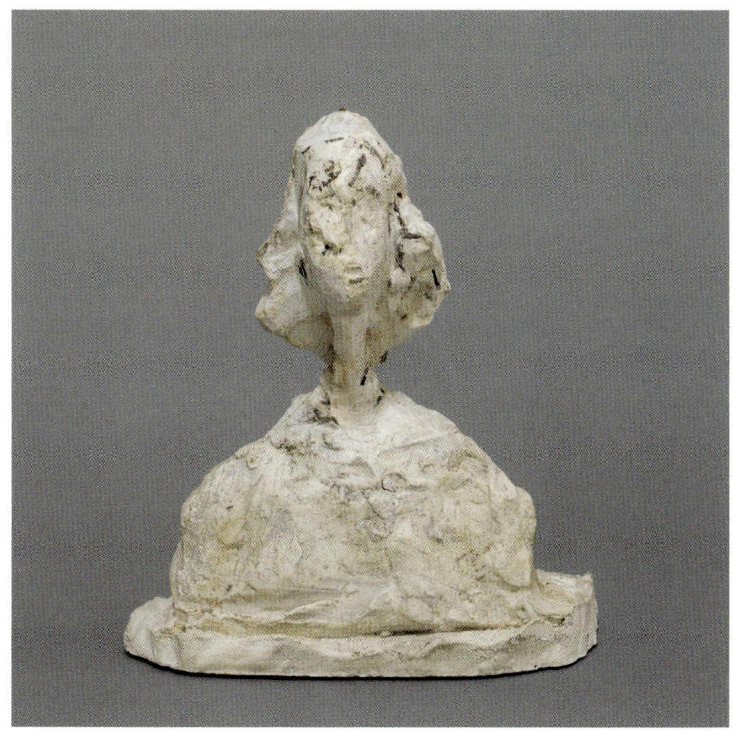

***Small Bust*, c. 1955**
Plaster; 20.8 x 17.5 x 7.8 cm.
Fondation Giacometti

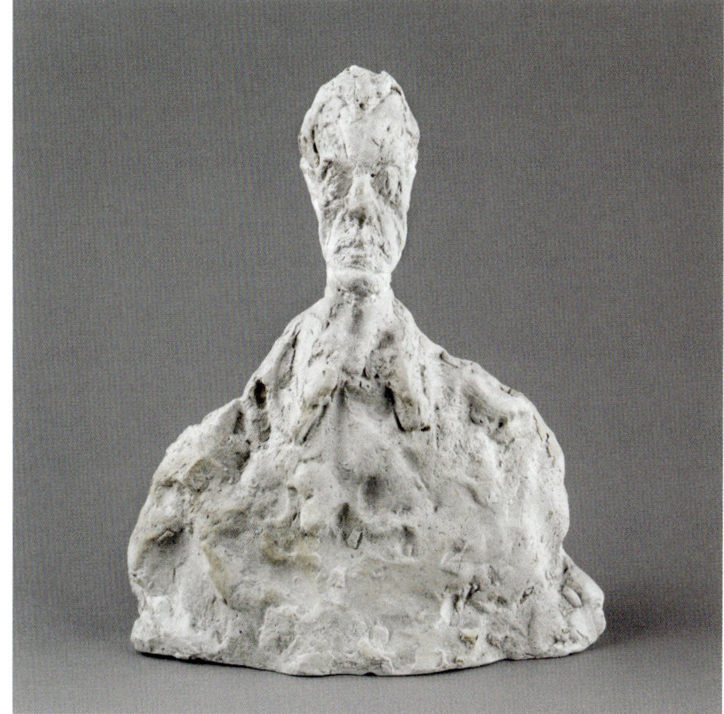

***Sculptures in the Studio X*,**
pl. 101, from *Paris sans fin*, 1969
Printed by Mourlot. Edited by Tériade éditeur, Paris. Lithograph; sheet: 42.5 x 32.5 cm.
Fondation Giacometti

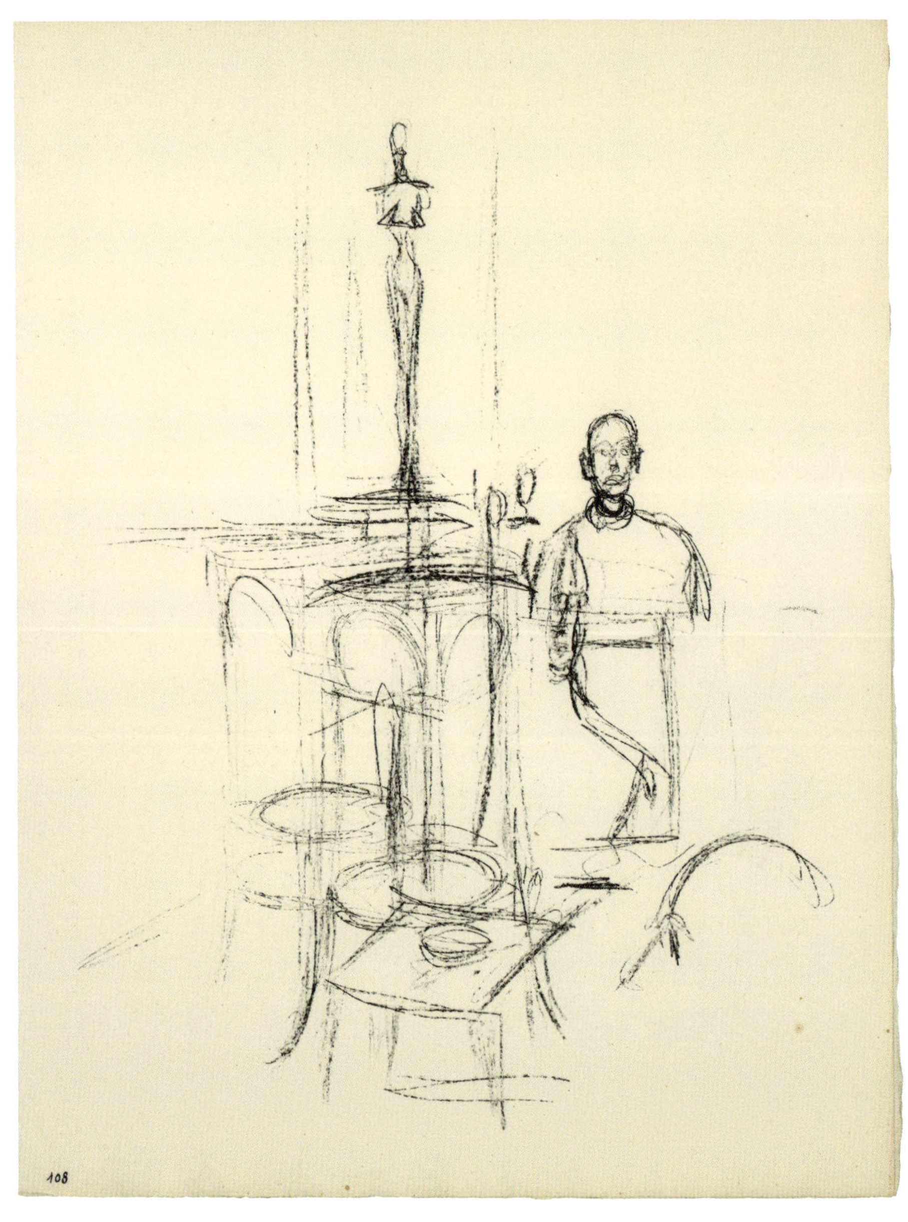

***Bust of Diego from Life*, 1951**
Bronze; 26.8 x 21.5 x 12.1 cm.
Fondation Giacometti

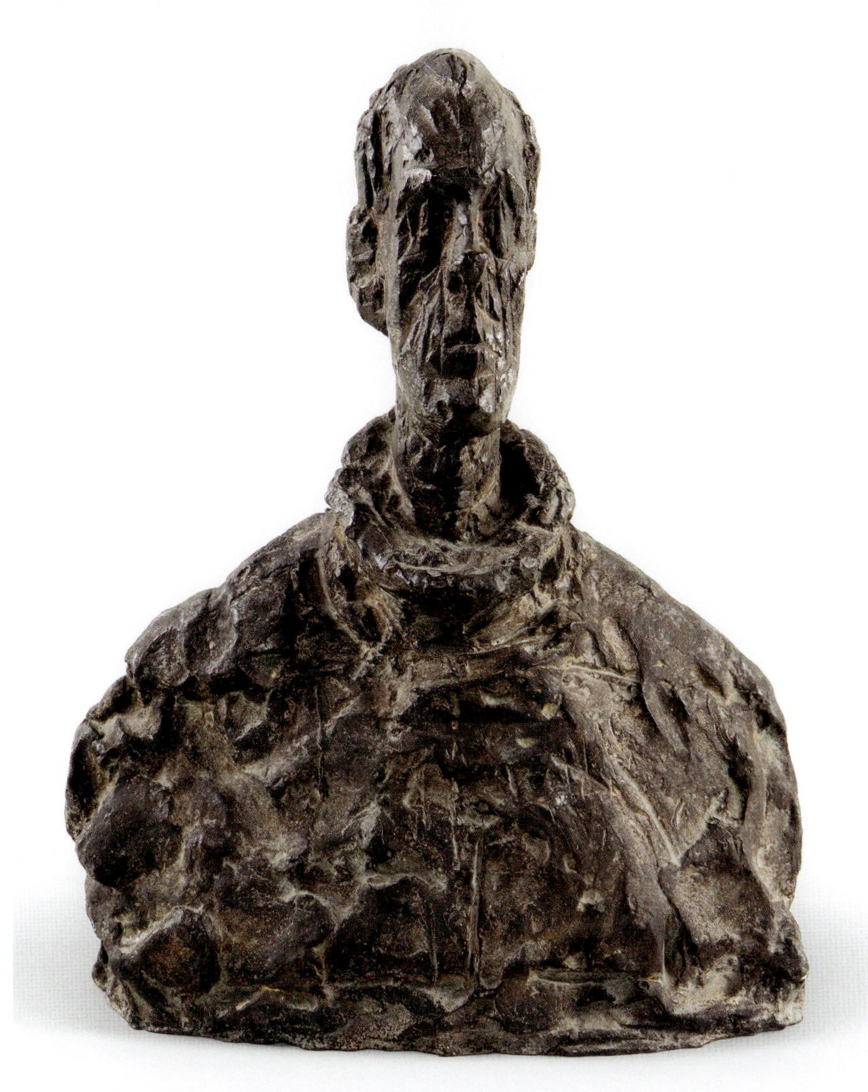

***Standing Woman (Poseuse I)*, 1954**
Bronze; 56.1 x 13 x 18.2 cm.
Fondation Giacometti

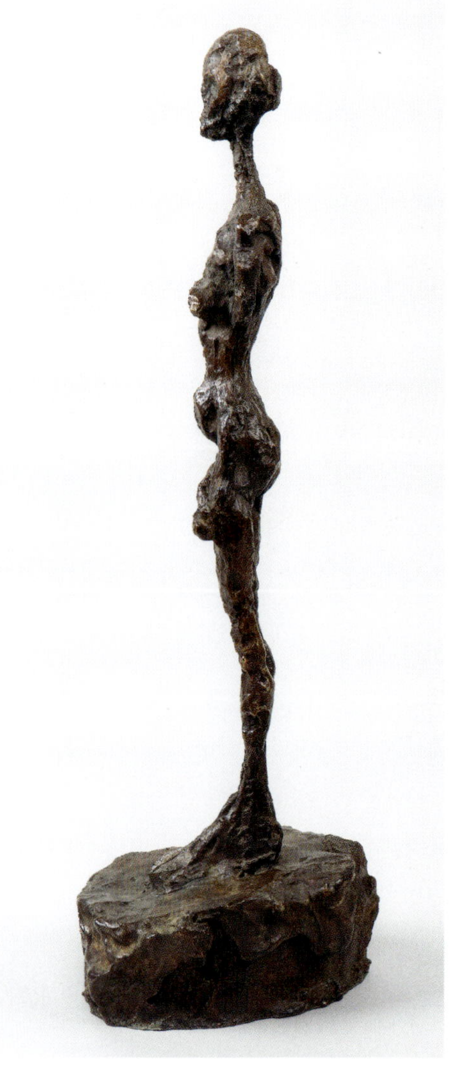

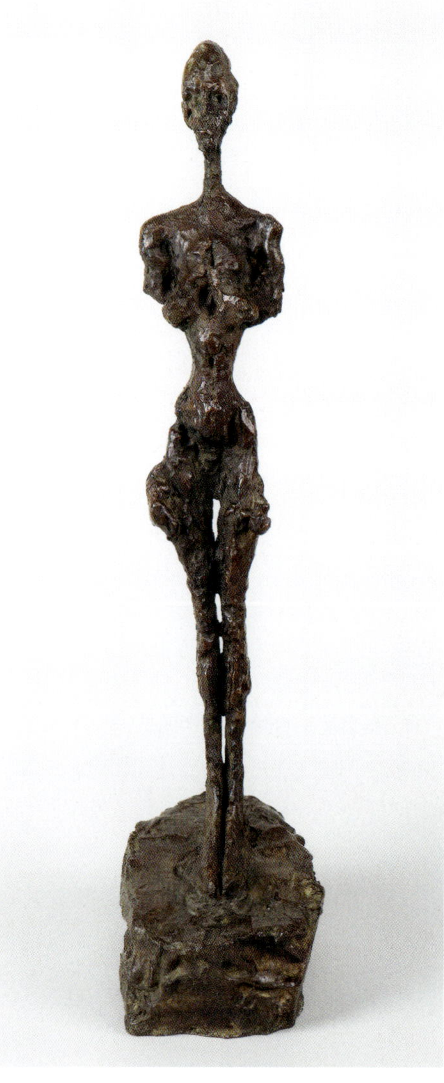

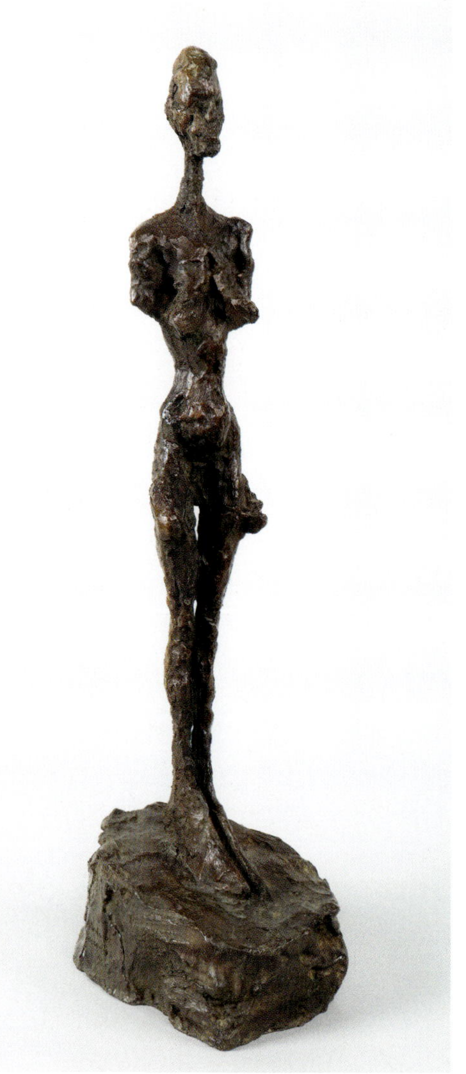

***Sculptures in the Studio VIII*,**
pl. 29, from *Paris sans fin*, 1969
Printed by Mourlot. Edited by
Tériade éditeur, Paris. Lithograph;
sheet: 42.5 x 32.5 cm.
Fondation Giacometti

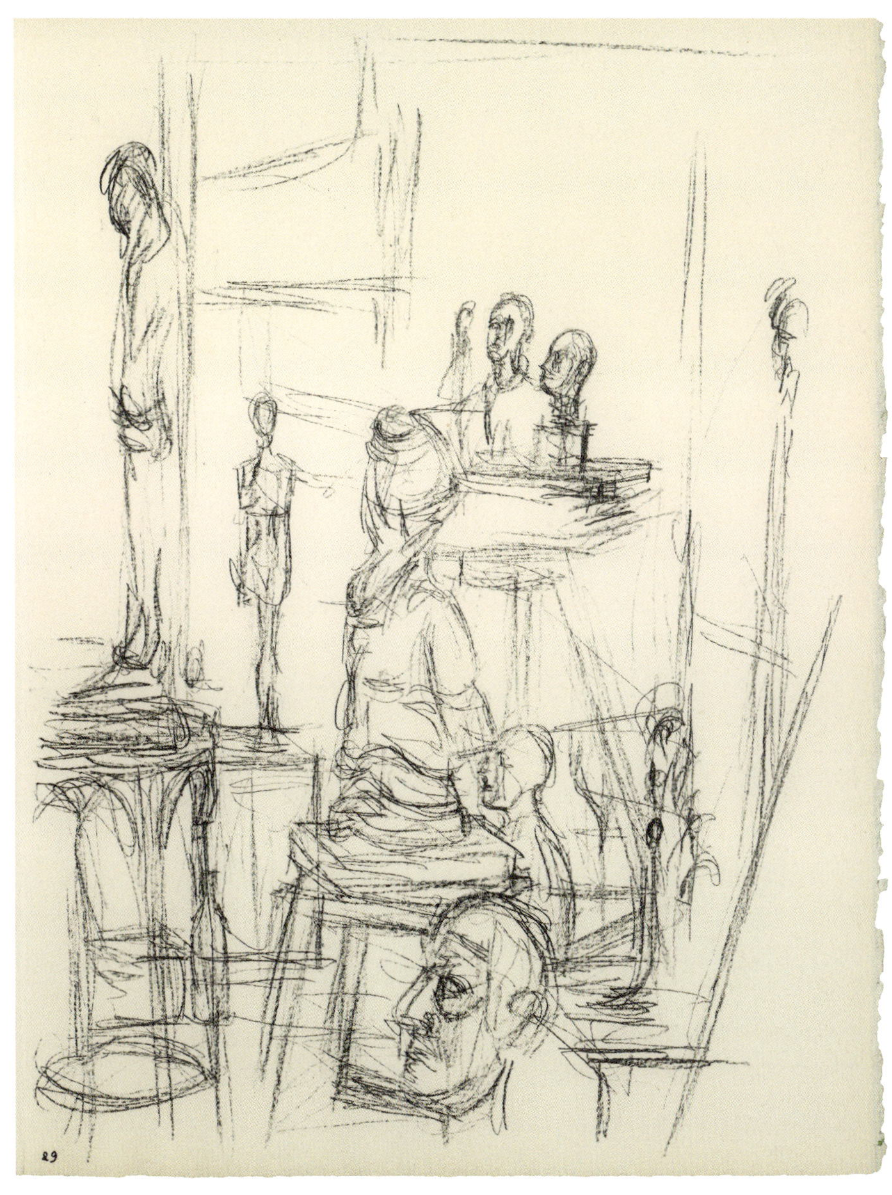

Studio of Alberto Giacometti, 1948
Emmy Andriesse.
Leiden University Libraries.

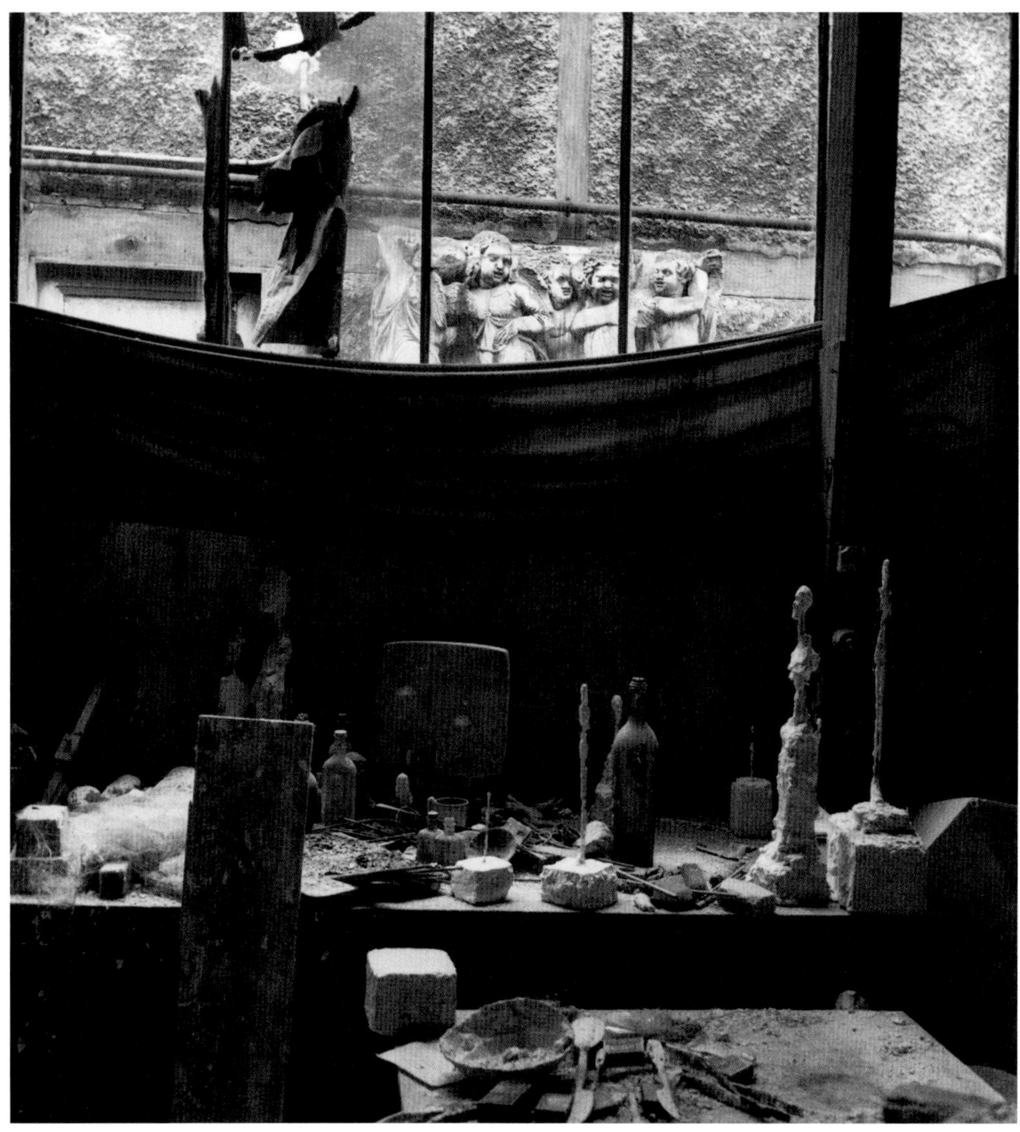

Alberto Giacometti working in his studio, 1951
Ernst Scheidegger (Swiss, 1923–2016).
Archives, Fondation Giacometti.

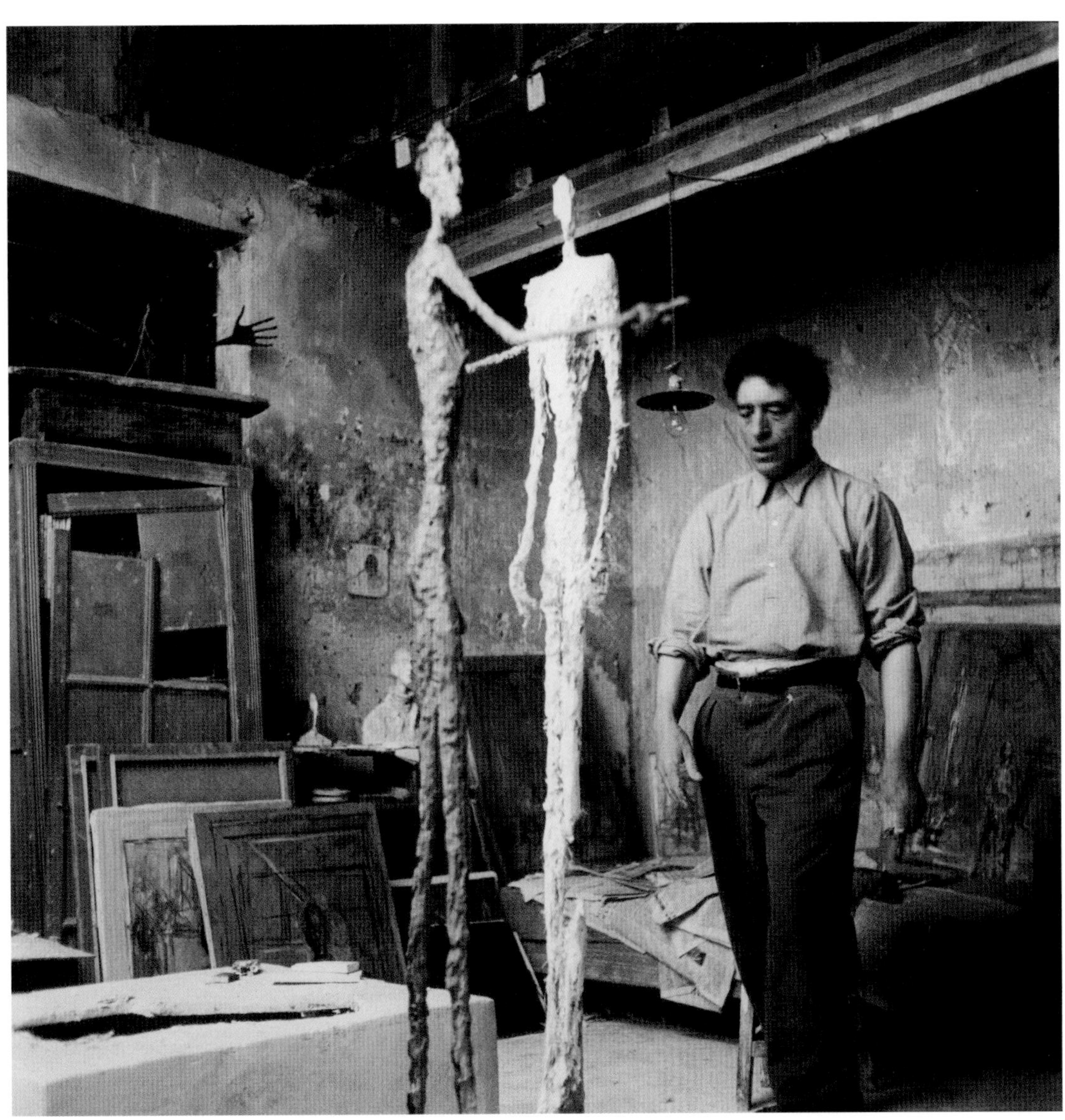

***Sculptures in the Studio XI*,**
pl. 128, from *Paris sans fin*, 1969
Printed by Mourlot. Edited by
Tériade éditeur, Paris. Lithograph;
sheet: 42.5 x 32.5 cm.
Fondation Giacometti

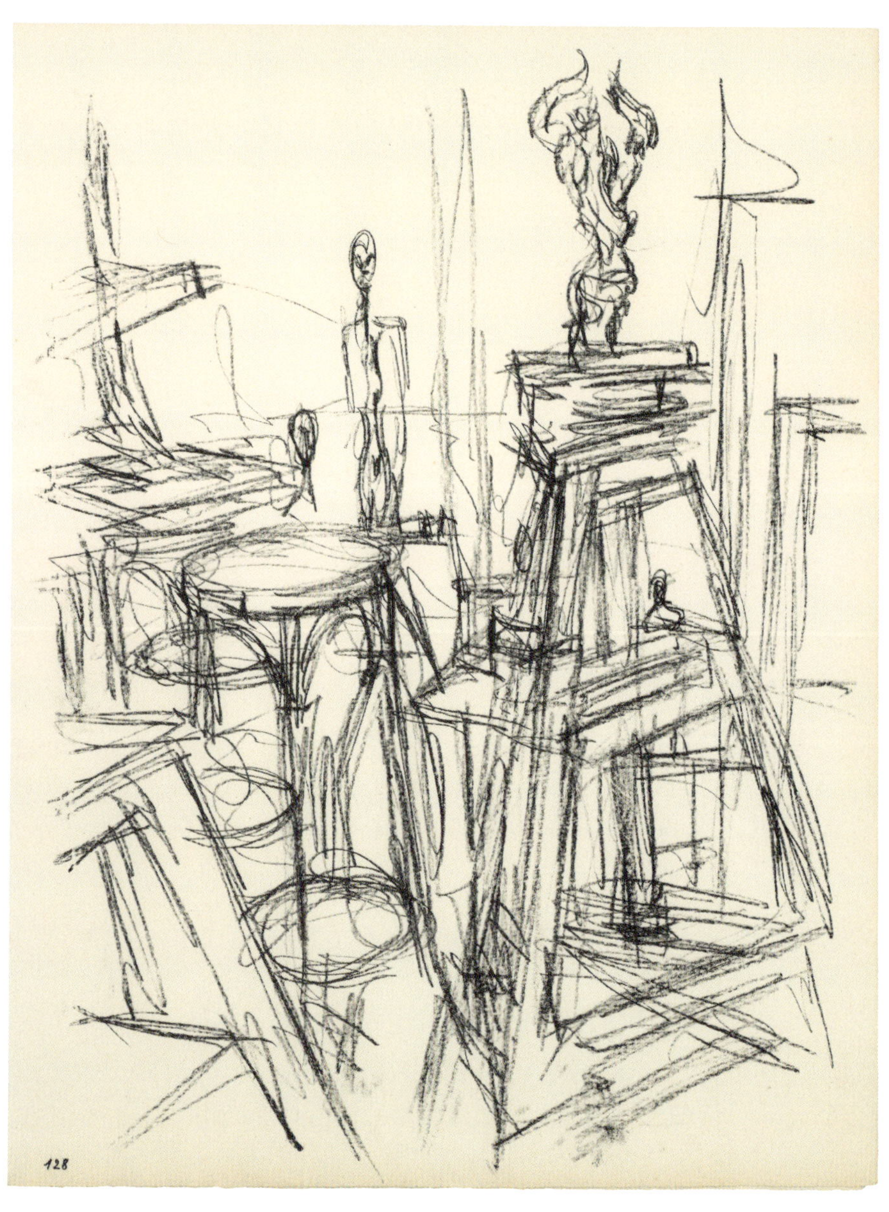

***Figurine*, 1961**
Bronze; 44.4 x 8 x 16.1 cm.
Fondation Giacometti

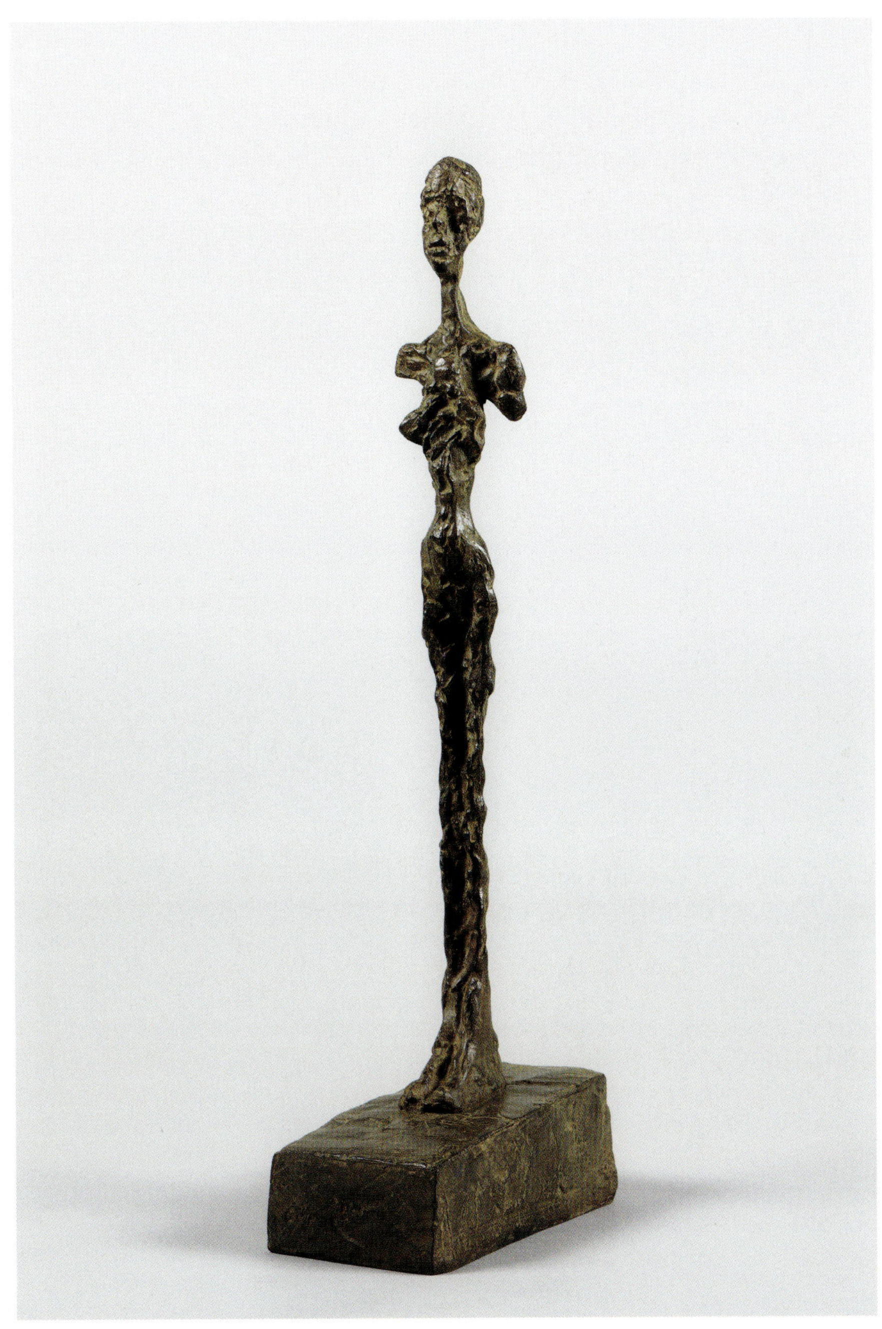

Alberto Giacometti in his studio (detail), 1957
Robert Doisneau (French, 1912–1994). Archives, Fondation Giacometti.

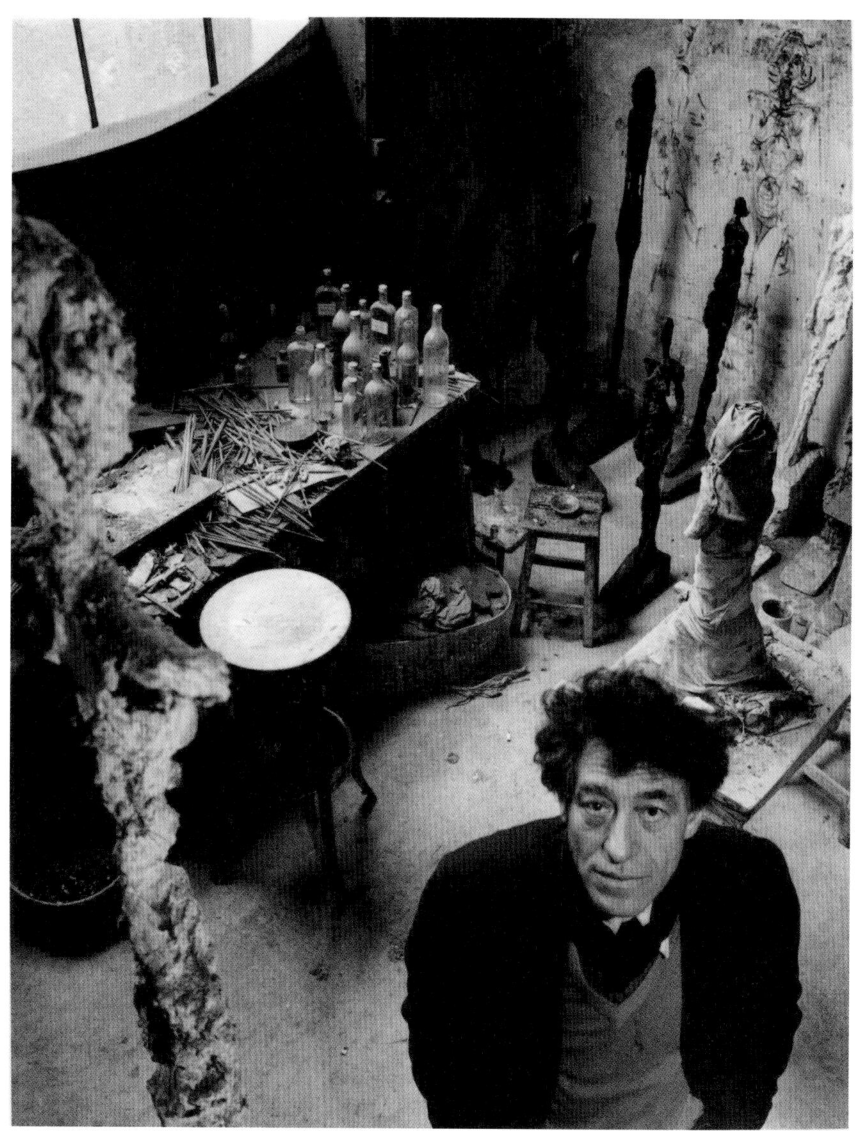

Alberto Giacometti at the entrance of his studio, 1954
Denise Colomb (French, 1902–2004).
Archives, Fondation Giacometti

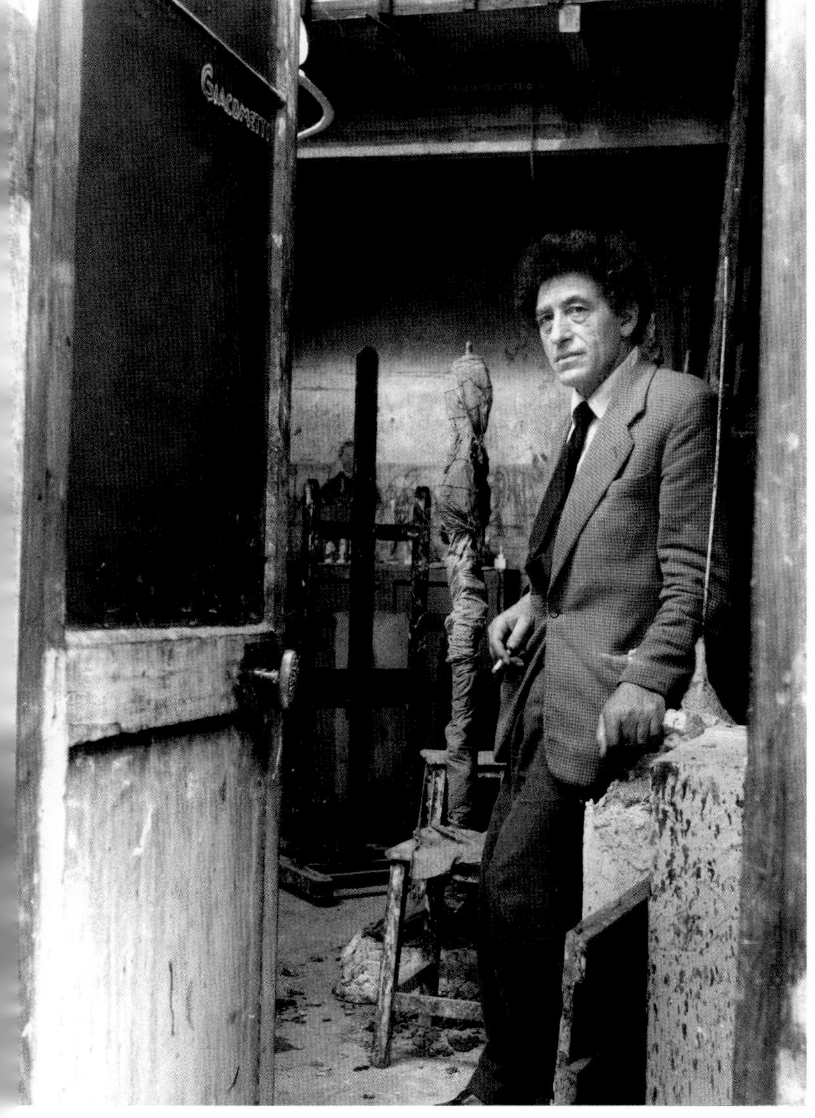

Alberto Giacometti in his studio, c. May 1965
Jack Nisberg (American, 1922–1980).
Archives, Fondation Giacometti.

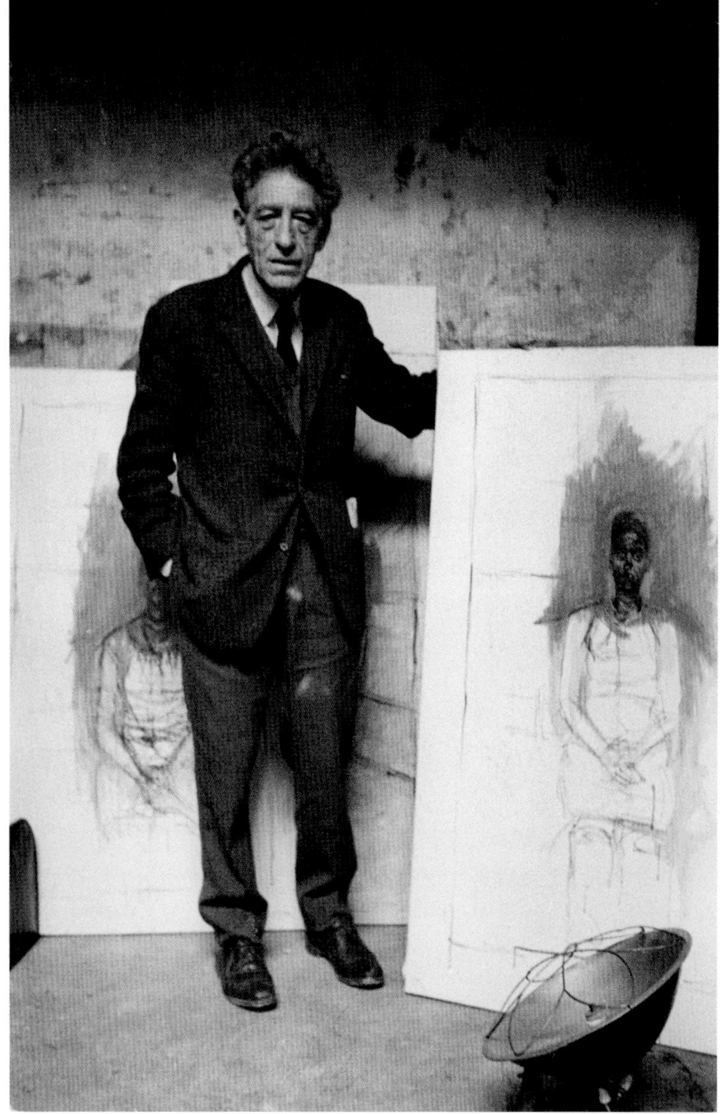

Obsessed with Heads

ROMAIN PERRIN

***Head of Diego* in plaster in the studio in Stampa, summer 1966**
Ernst Scheidegger.
Archives, Fondation Giacometti.

The theme of the portrait, or at least that of the head, is recurrent in Alberto Giacometti's oeuvre. Its importance for the artist is evidenced in the countless sculptures and paintings he made of his wife, Annette, and his brother Diego. If the artist seemed to have been truly obsessed with that subject, it is because on the head is concentrated much more than the question of resemblance: it encompasses the means of representation itself.

Giacometti confronted it early on, when, still young, he modeled with a disconcerting facility—as he would say later—the portrait of Diego, age 12 at the time. After a crisis of confidence about his ability to sculpt a head that looks alive, he adopted, from 1925, the vocabulary of modernity, inspired by the work in planes of Paul Cézanne, as well as by non-Western and archaic statuary. *Head of Woman (Flora Mayo)*, whose details are carved on a flat face, inaugurated those key years that took him to the limits of abstraction (page 108).

After a period in the company of the Surrealists creating "objects," sculptures whose suggestive and ambiguous character echoes inner visions linked to the subconscious and dreams, Giacometti, prey again to doubt, went back to working from a live model. That decision was not to the liking of André Breton, who allegedly declared, in sheer exasperation, during one of those arguments the group was familiar with: "A head, everyone knows what a head is!"[1] Giacometti broke with the Surrealists, but that did not shake his determination to make a head that bore a true likeness to the model's.

From then on, Giacometti began a process of unlearning, relying on what he saw and no longer on what he knew of real life. Diego (page 112) was the first to sit for him again, followed by the young model Rita Gueyfier (pages 110–11), as well as his artist friend Isabel Lambert Rawsthorne (page 113), with whom he had a relationship. Giacometti sculpted portraits of his relatives and friends and, after the war, of the people he knew in the Parisian intellectual milieu. The face of philosopher Simone de Beauvoir is seen in its entirety from a distance the artist imposed on himself in order to capture the essence of his model (page 117). The portrait of collector Marie-Laure de Noailles already bears the marks of the stretching Giacometti would apply to his figures as he searched for another way to sculpt (page 116).

The question of resemblance, in a strict sense, represented an obstacle he needed to overcome; he tirelessly returned to the same subject to try making a head that looked alive. The work was so intense that the artist had the feeling he was no longer looking at the face of his brother Diego, but rather a stranger.[2] The features remain those of the model, but the way the sculptor looked at the moment of creation, in a state of deep concentration, tended to objectify the model. The portraits of Eli Lotar, made in 1964–65, are characterized, beyond the physiognomy, by the force of the gaze that captures the viewer's attention, making the head seem alive (page 135).

The gaze played a fundamental part and gave the head a crucial importance over the rest of the body. The latter even became secondary, as is shown by the many drawings in biro on the most diverse supports. Often without a body, those heads, which seem to appear spontaneously—the lines superimposed as if Giacometti could not stop drawing—reveal an obsession with the head itself, as much as with the gaze that is at its center.

1. Simone de Beauvoir, *La Force de l'âge* (Paris: Gallimard, 1960), 501.

2. Alberto Giacometti, "Le drame d'un réducteur de tête," conversation with Pierre Dumayet, *Le Nouveau Candide*, no. 110 (June 6–13, 1963); reprinted in Giacometti, *Why I am a sculptor* (Paris: Hermann and Fondation Giacometti, 2017), 52.

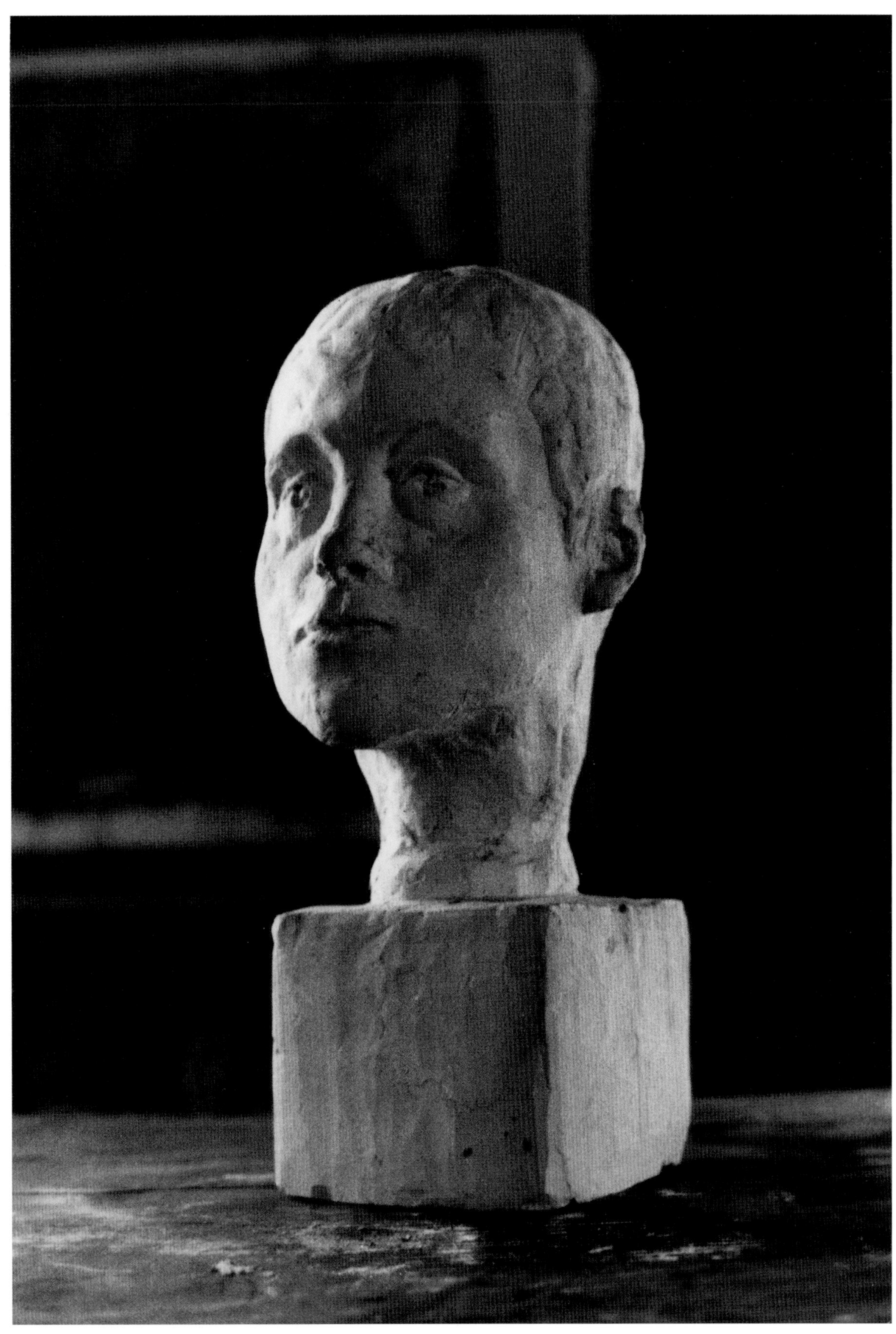

***Head of Woman (Flora Mayo)*, 1926**
Bronze; 30.5 x 22.9 x 8.5 cm.
Fondation Giacometti

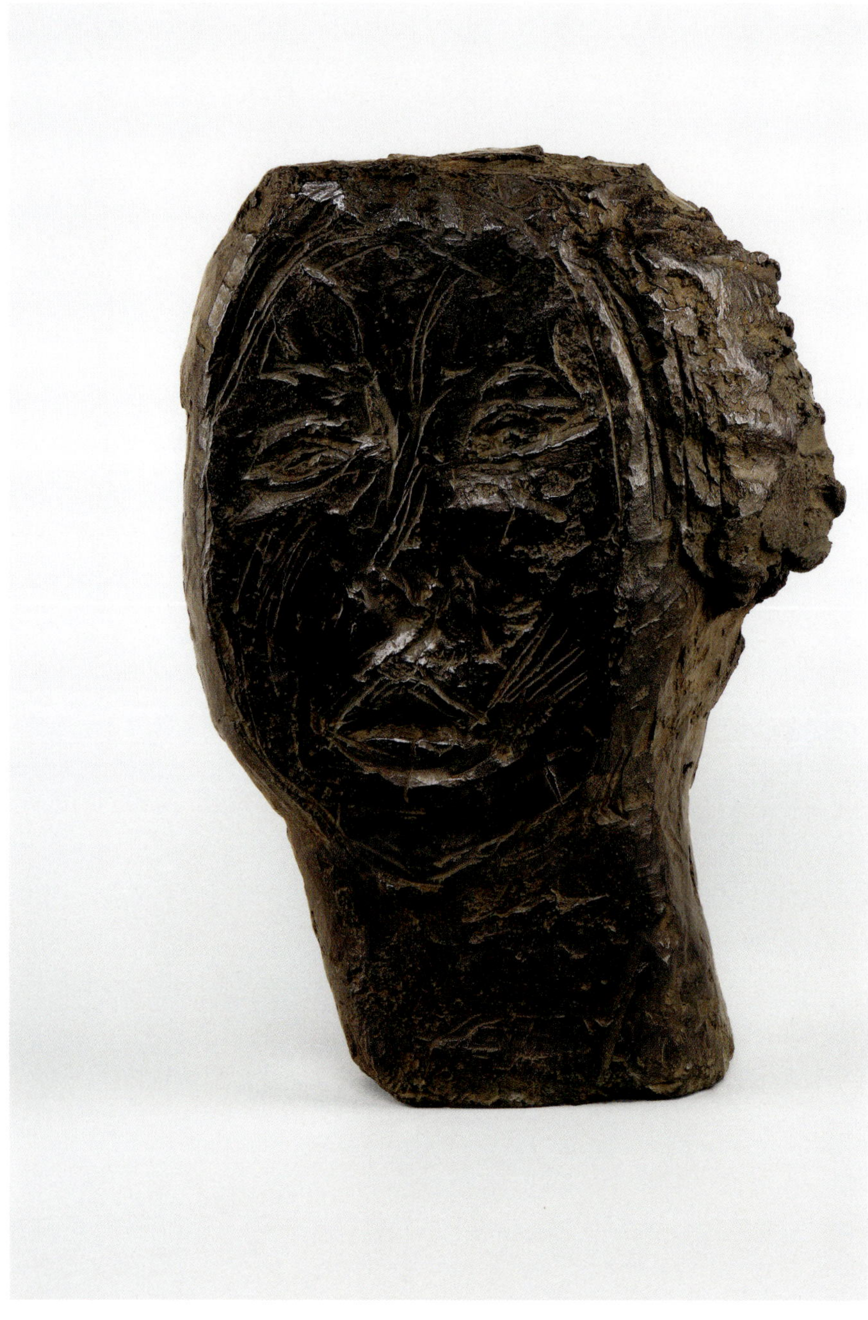

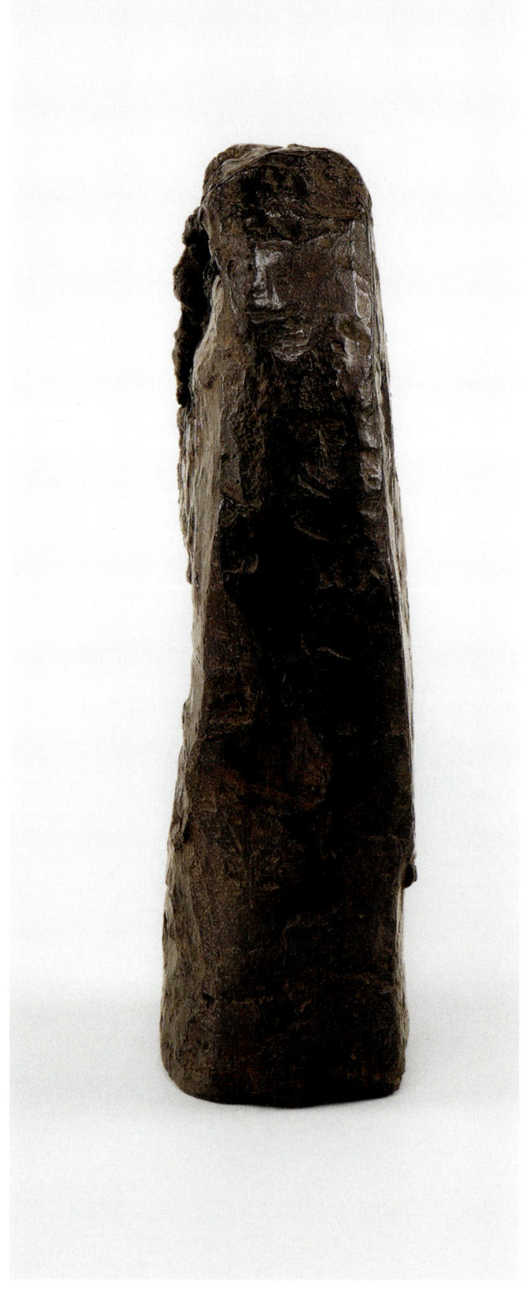

Head of Woman (Denise), c. 1932
Pencil and rubber on paper;
49 x 31.9 cm.
Fondation Giacometti

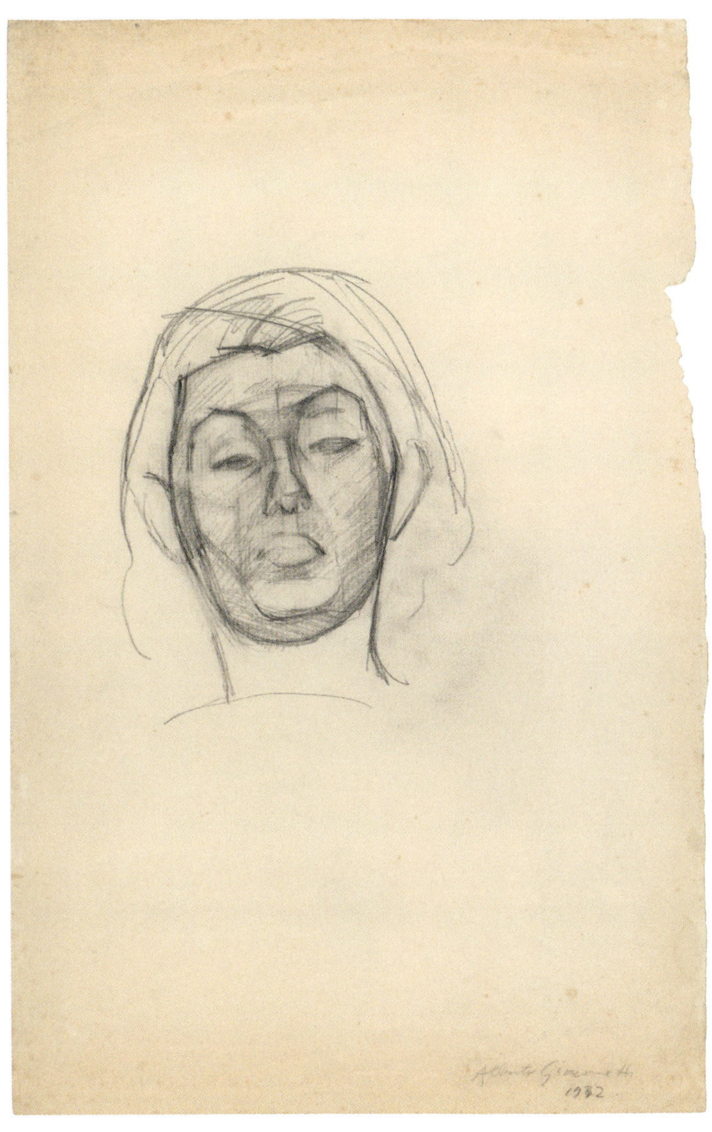

Head of Woman, c. 1935
Pencil on paper; 19.4 x 18.7 cm.
Fondation Giacometti

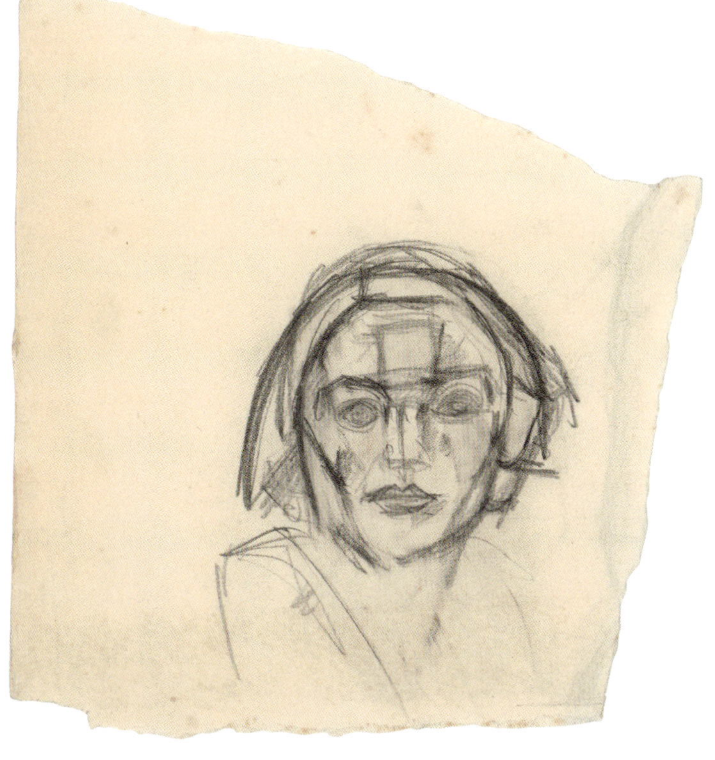

Head of Woman (Rita),
c. 1936
Bronze; 23.9 x 13.8 x 18.3 cm.
Fondation Giacometti

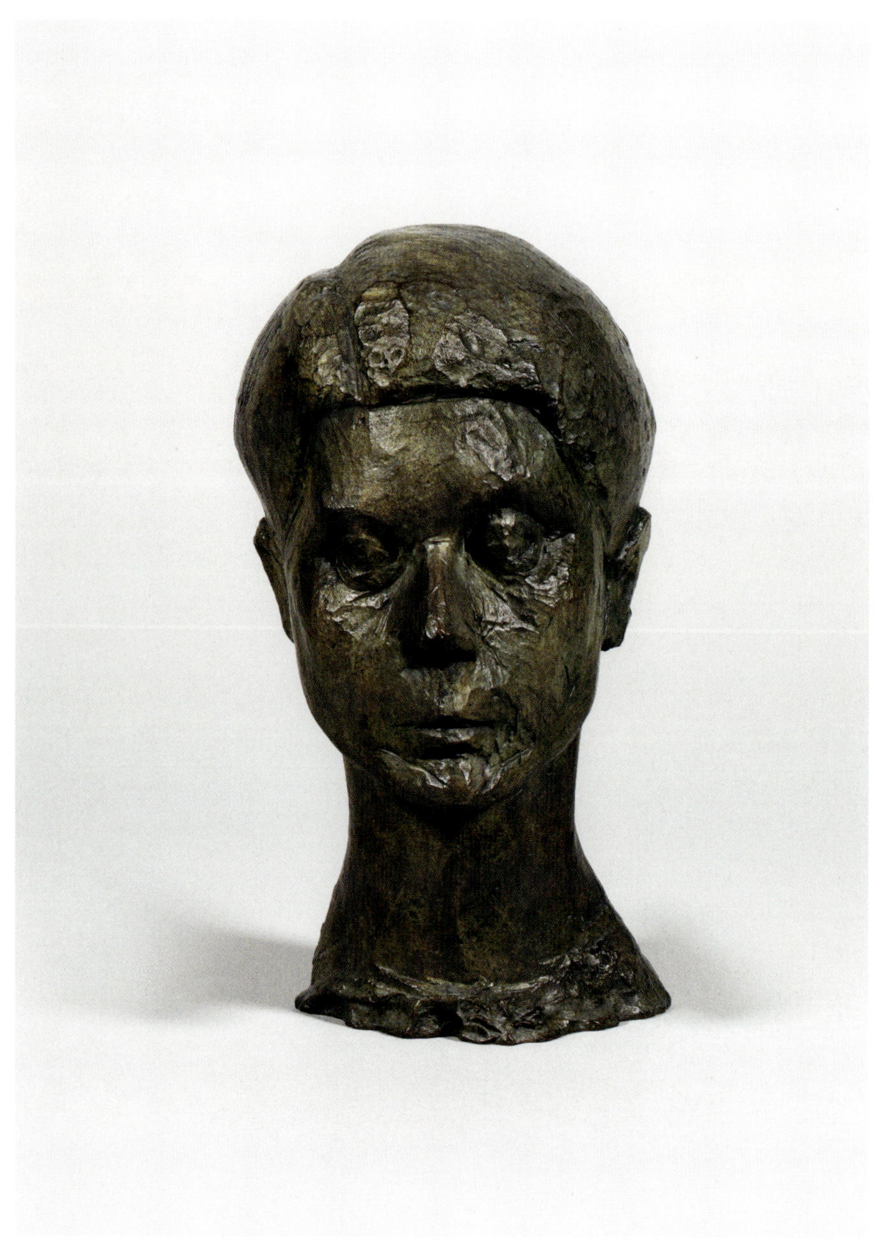

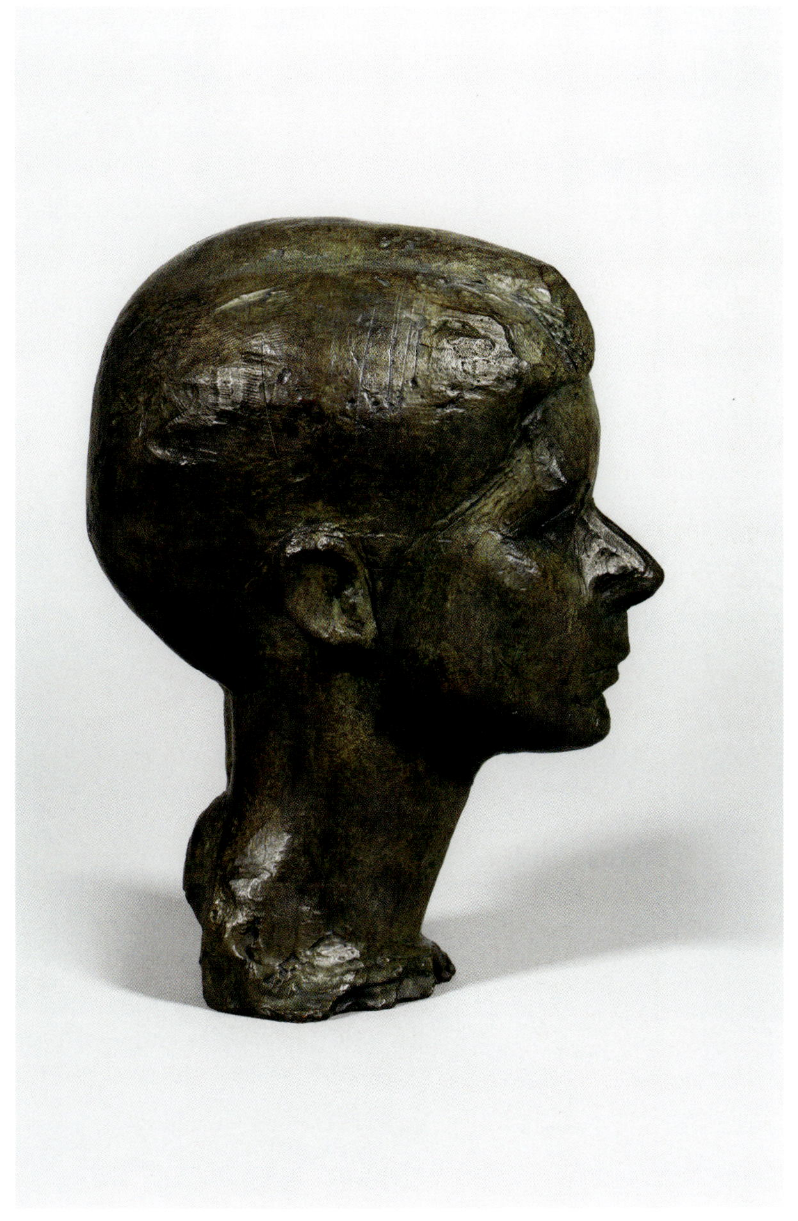

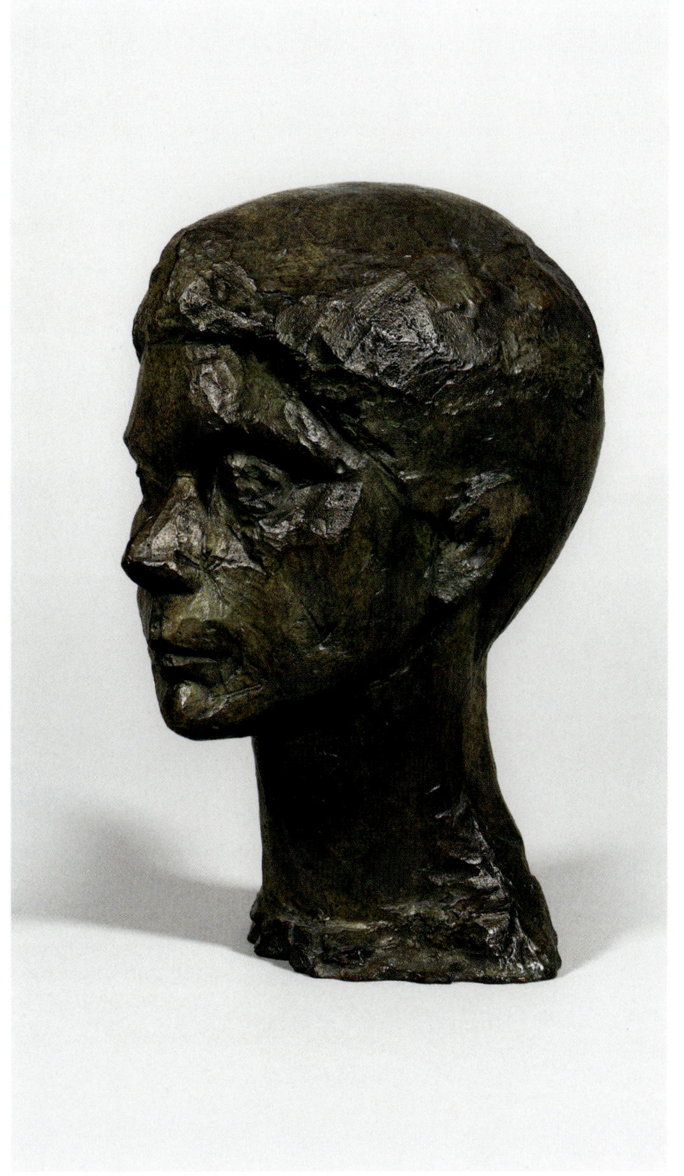

***Head of Diego*, c. 1936**
Plaster; 23.5 x 14.6 x 21.2 cm.
Fondation Giacometti

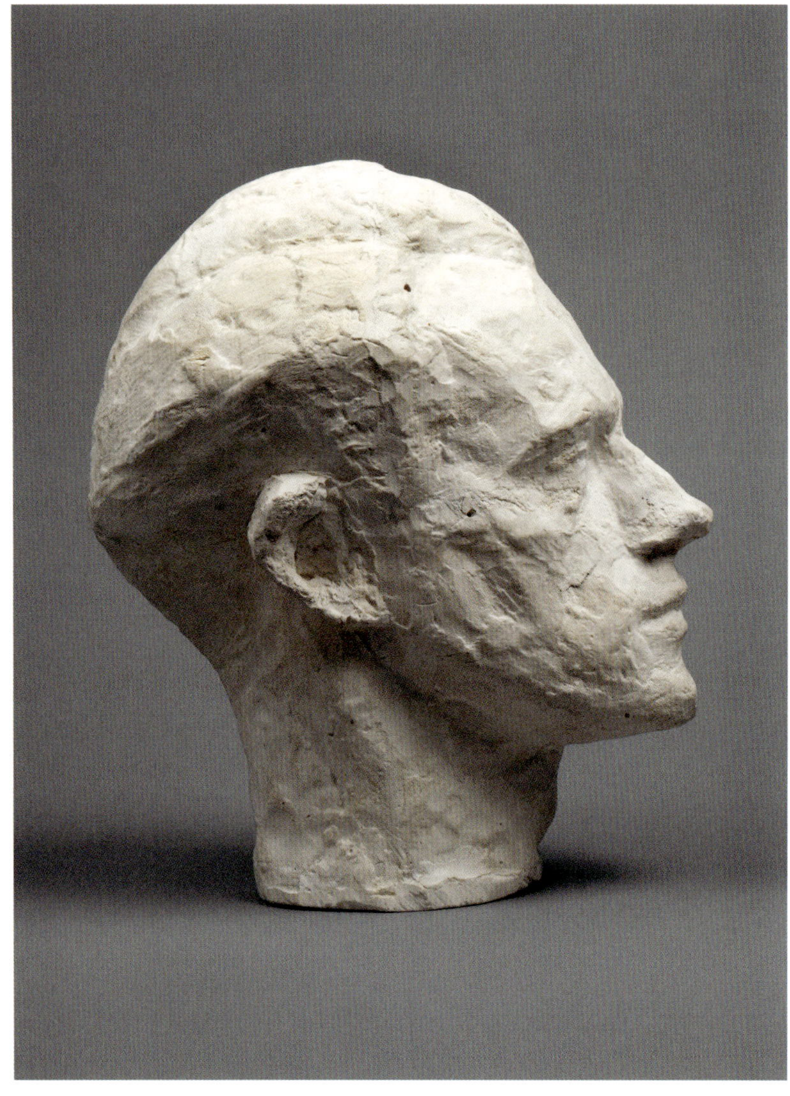

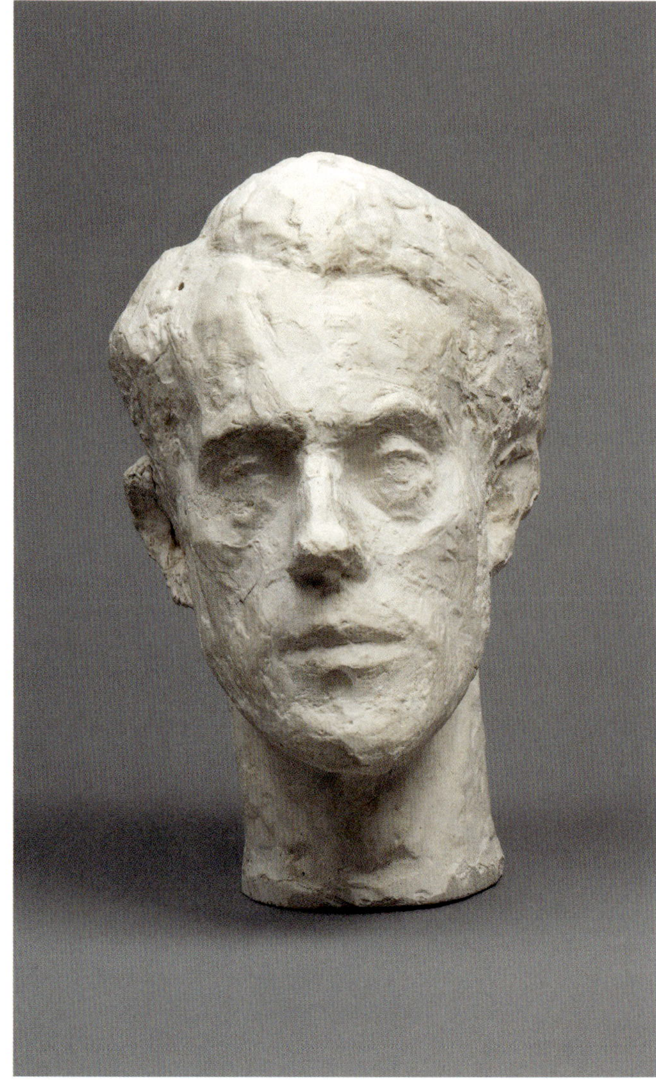

***Head of Isabel*, 1937–38**
Bronze; 21.3 x 16 x 17.2 cm.
Fondation Giacometti

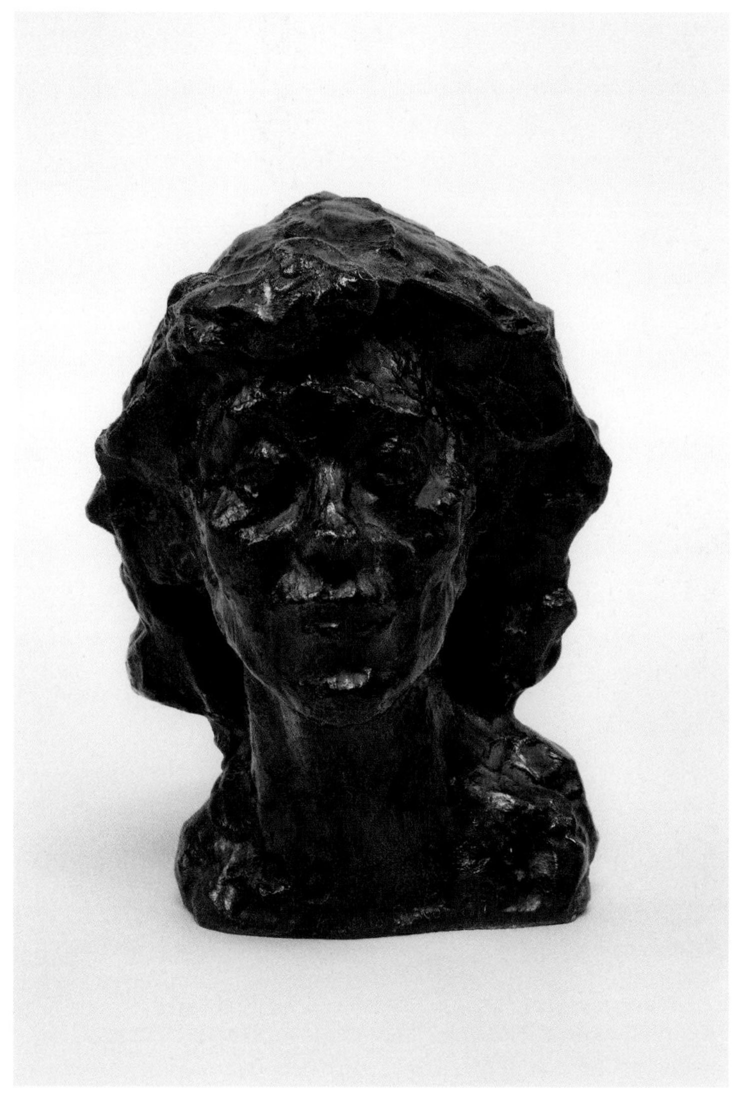

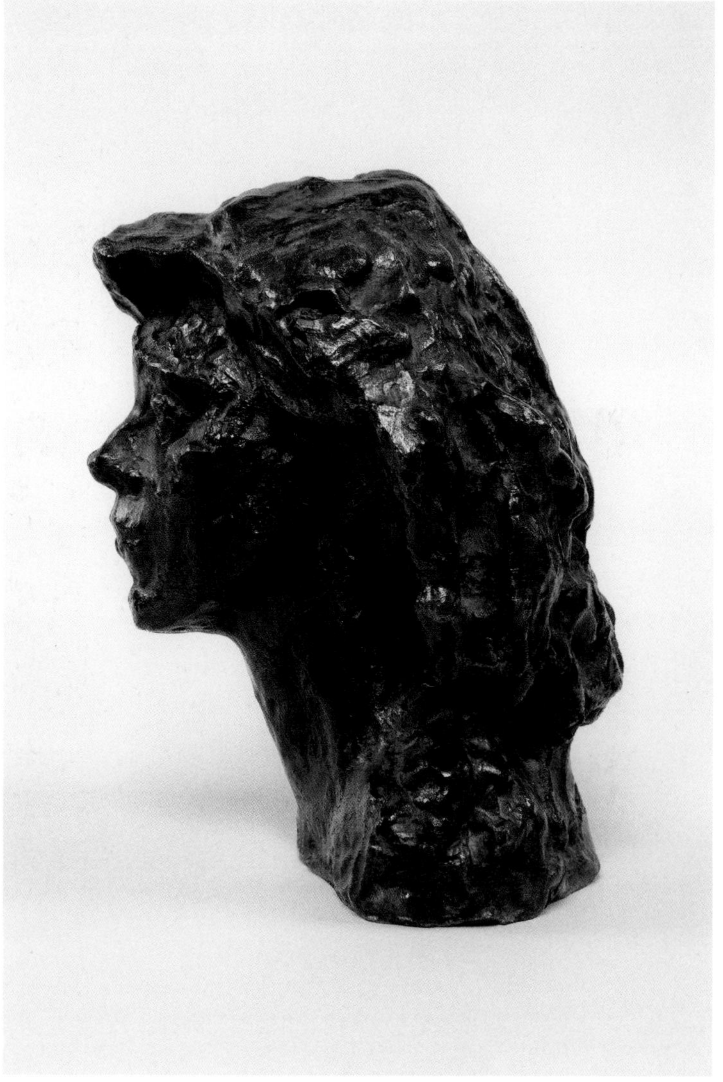

***Head of Diego*, c. 1937**
Bronze; 19 x 11.6 x 16.9 cm.
Fondation Giacometti

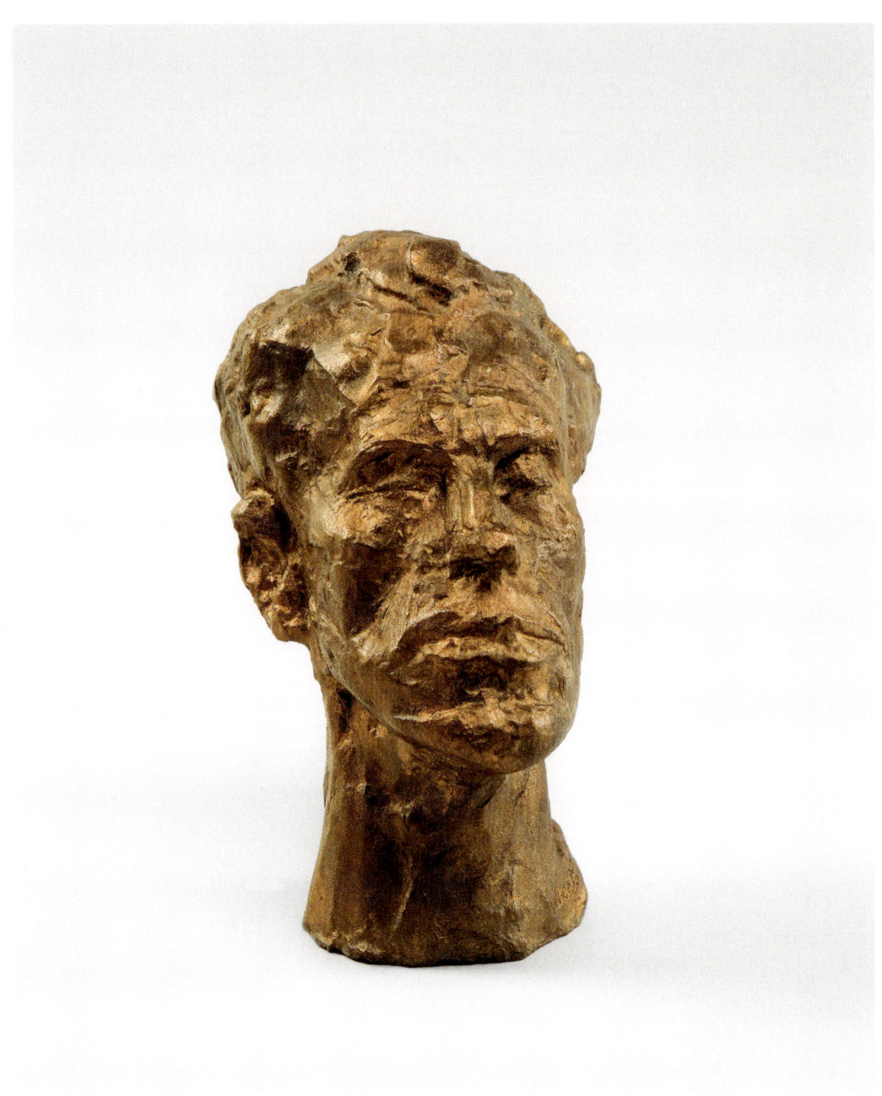

Head of Woman (Rita),
1937–38
Bronze; 22 x 12 x 15.4 cm.
Fondation Giacometti

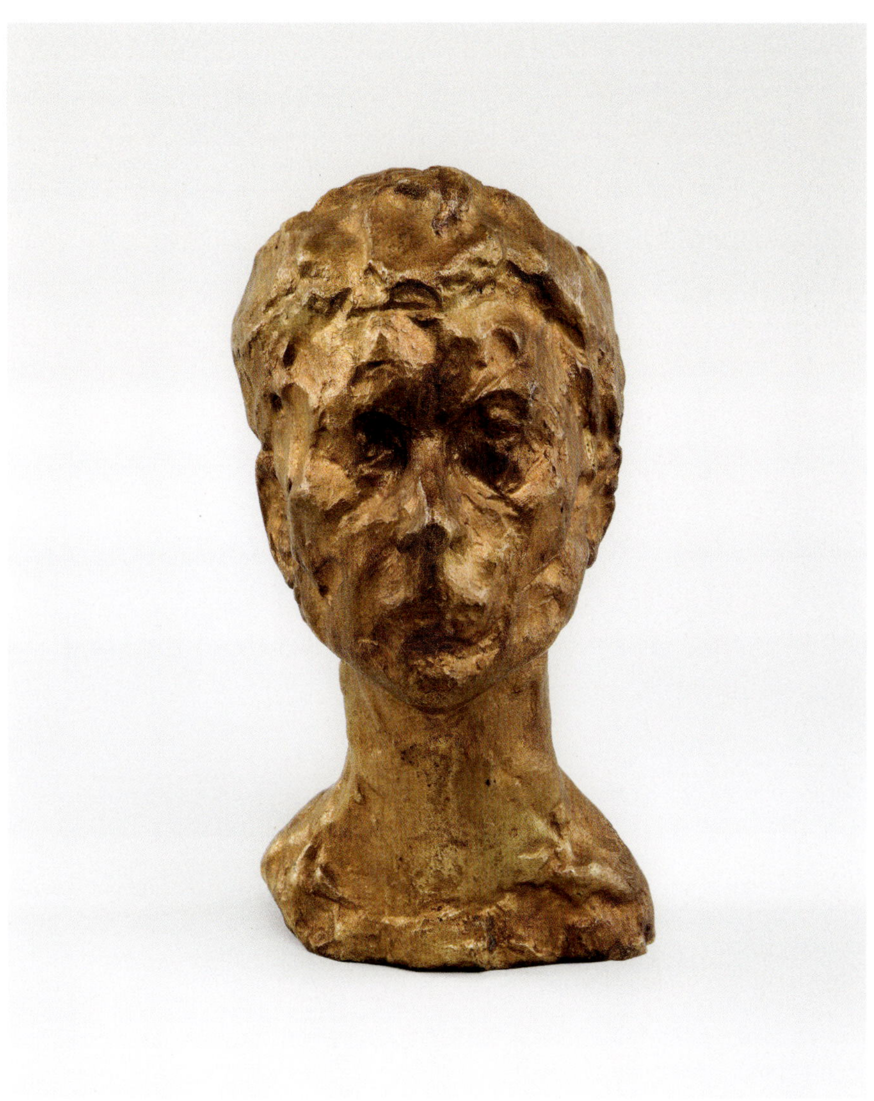

Head of Marie-Laure de Noailles on a Double Base, 1946
Bronze; 30.4 x 8.8 x 10.5 cm.
Fondation Giacometti

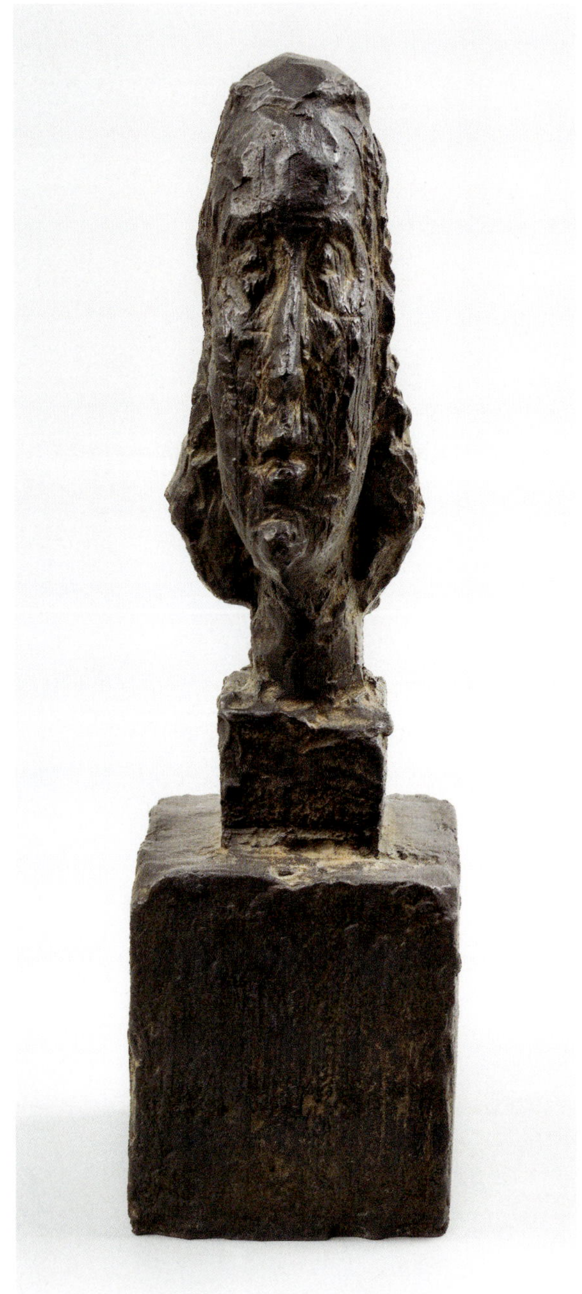

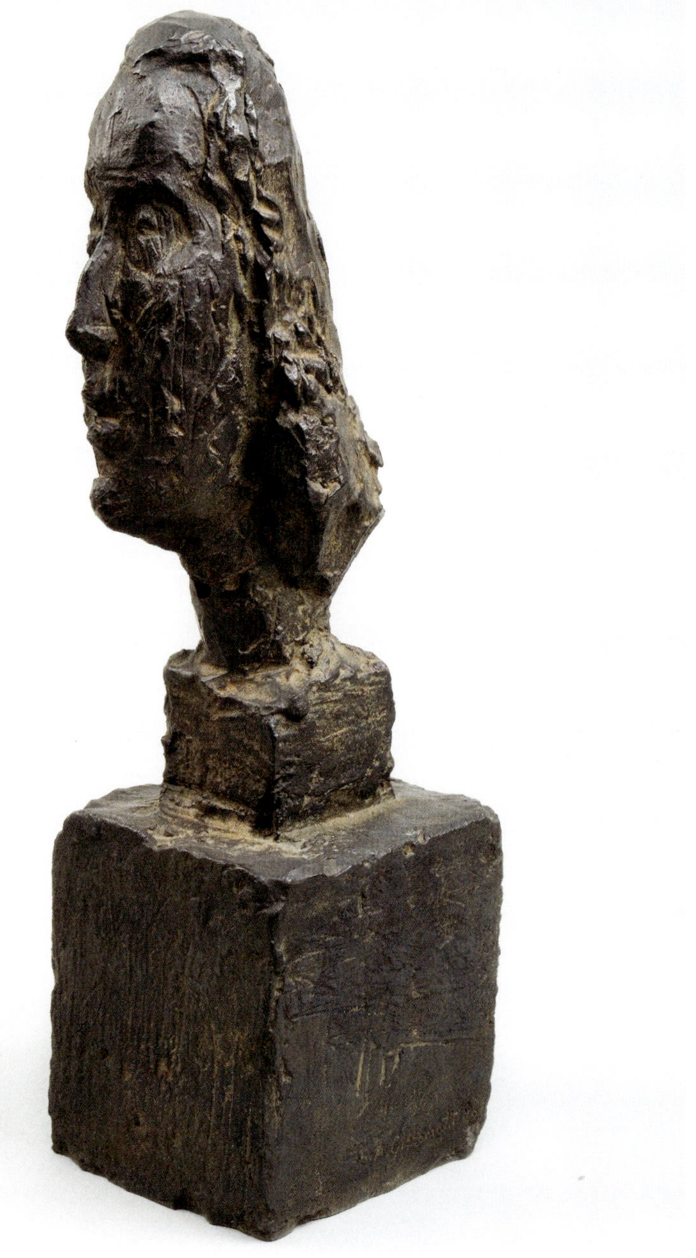

***Simone de Beauvoir*, 1946**
Bronze; 13.4 x 4 x 4.1 cm.
Fondation Giacometti

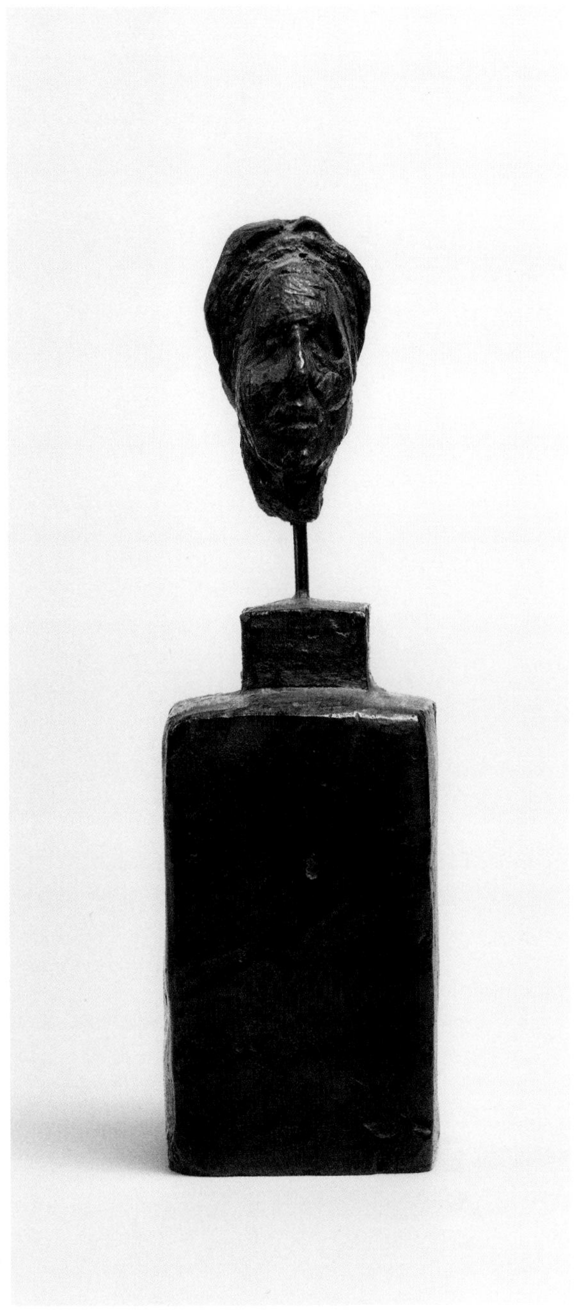

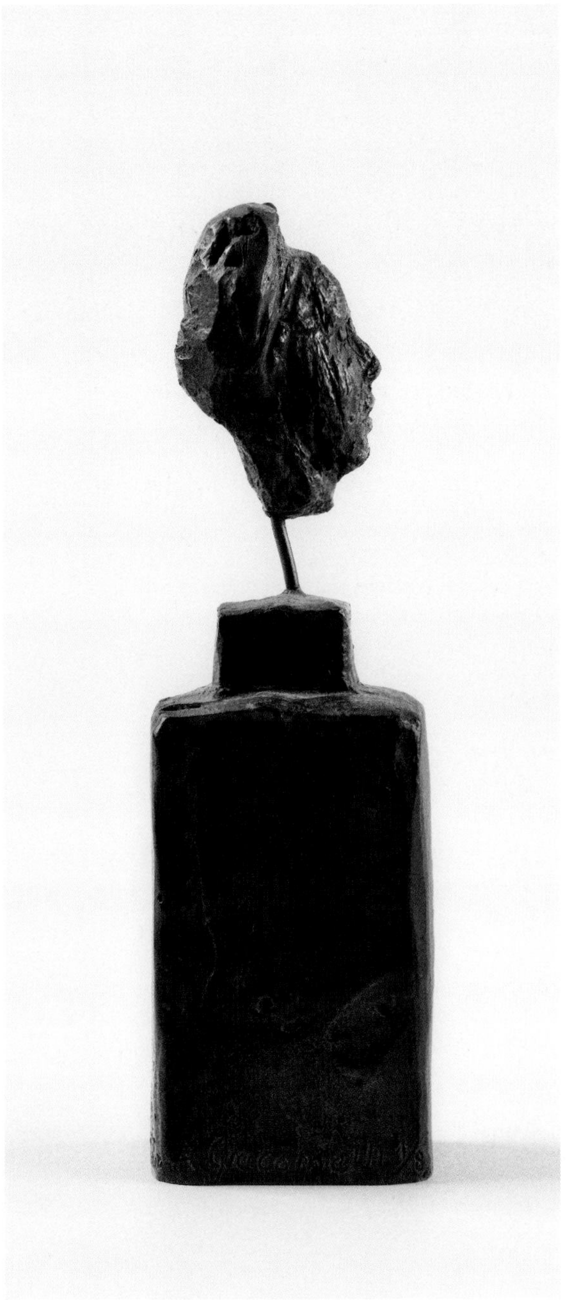

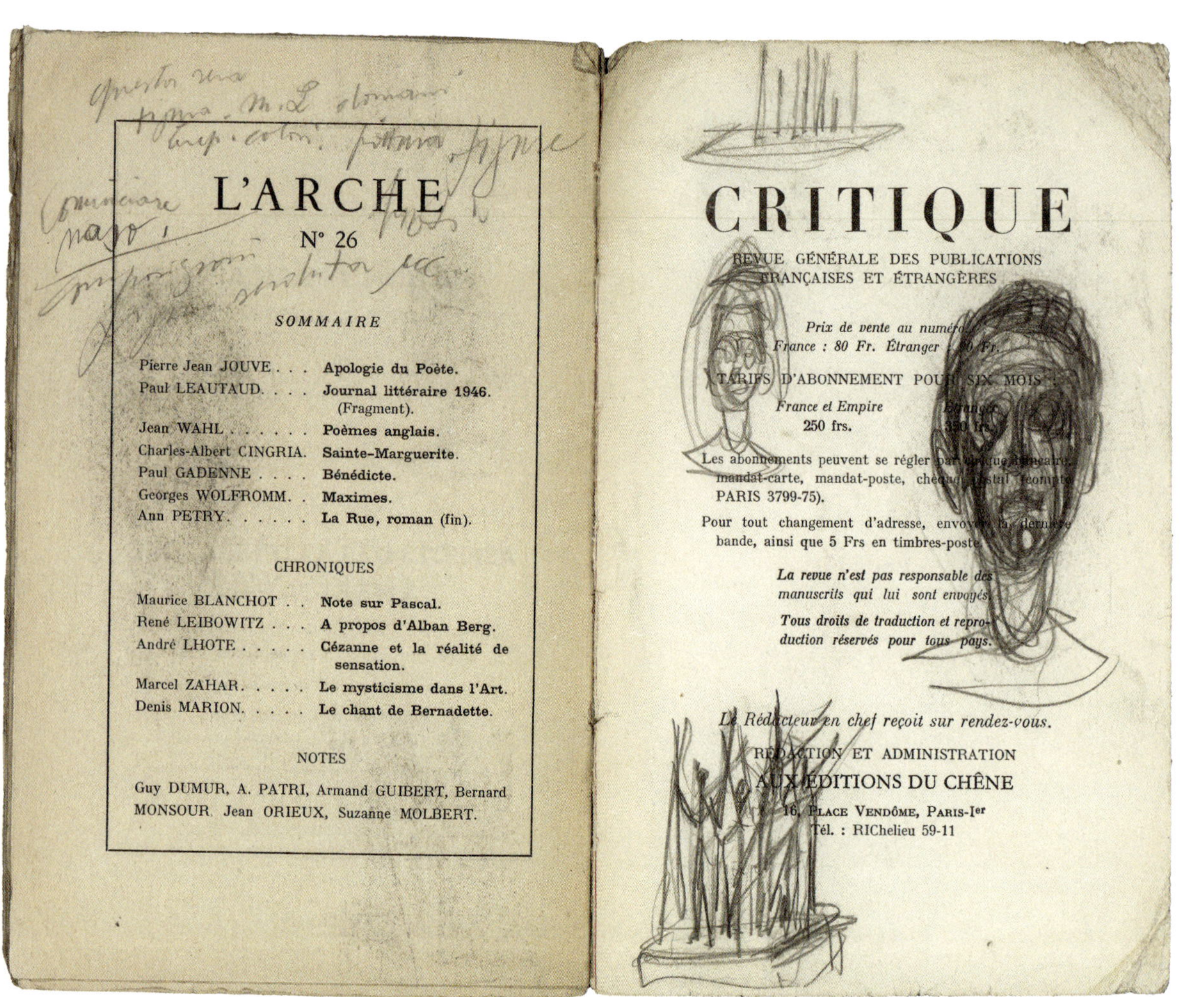

L'ARCHE

N° 26

SOMMAIRE

Pierre Jean JOUVE . . . Apologie du Poète.
Paul LEAUTAUD. . . . Journal littéraire 1946. (Fragment).
Jean WAHL . . . . . . Poèmes anglais.
Charles-Albert CINGRIA. Sainte-Marguerite.
Paul GADENNE . . . . Bénédicte.
Georges WOLFROMM. . Maximes.
Ann PETRY. . . . . . La Rue, roman (fin).

CHRONIQUES

Maurice BLANCHOT . . Note sur Pascal.
René LEIBOWITZ . . . A propos d'Alban Berg.
André LHOTE . . . . . Cézanne et la réalité de sensation.
Marcel ZAHAR. . . . . Le mysticisme dans l'Art.
Denis MARION. . . . . Le chant de Bernadette.

NOTES

Guy DUMUR, A. PATRI, Armand GUIBERT, Bernard MONSOUR, Jean ORIEUX, Suzanne MOLBERT.

CRITIQUE

REVUE GÉNÉRALE DES PUBLICATIONS FRANÇAISES ET ÉTRANGÈRES

Prix de vente au numéro
France : 80 Fr. Étranger

TARIFS D'ABONNEMENT POUR SIX MOIS :
France et Empire 250 frs.

Les abonnements peuvent se régler par chèque bancaire, mandat-carte, mandat-poste, chèque postal (compte PARIS 3799-75).

Pour tout changement d'adresse, envoyer la dernière bande, ainsi que 5 Frs en timbres-poste.

La revue n'est pas responsable des manuscrits qui lui sont envoyés.

Tous droits de traduction et reproduction réservés pour tous pays.

Le Rédacteur en chef reçoit sur rendez-vous.

RÉDACTION ET ADMINISTRATION
AUX ÉDITIONS DU CHÊNE
16, PLACE VENDÔME, PARIS-Ier
Tél. : RIChelieu 59-11

***Head of a Man and Figures on a Base* on Critique, *no. 12, May 1947*, c. May 1947**
Pencil on paper; book open: 22.3 x 28.6 x 1 cm.
Fondation Giacometti

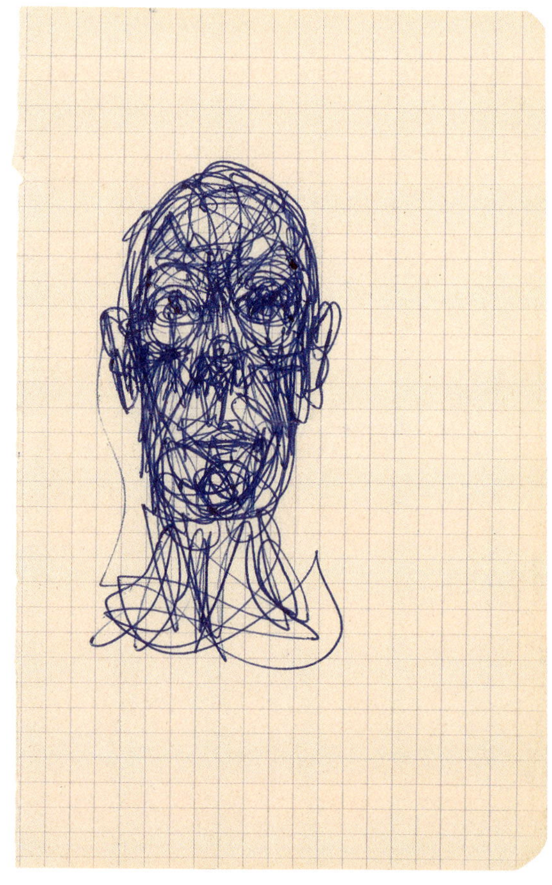

***Head of a Man*, 1959–60**
Blue ballpoint pen on squared paper; 17 x 10.5 cm.
Fondation Giacometti

***Heads of Men*, 1947**
Oil and pencil on cut canvas;
30.5 x 25.6 cm.
Fondation Giacometti

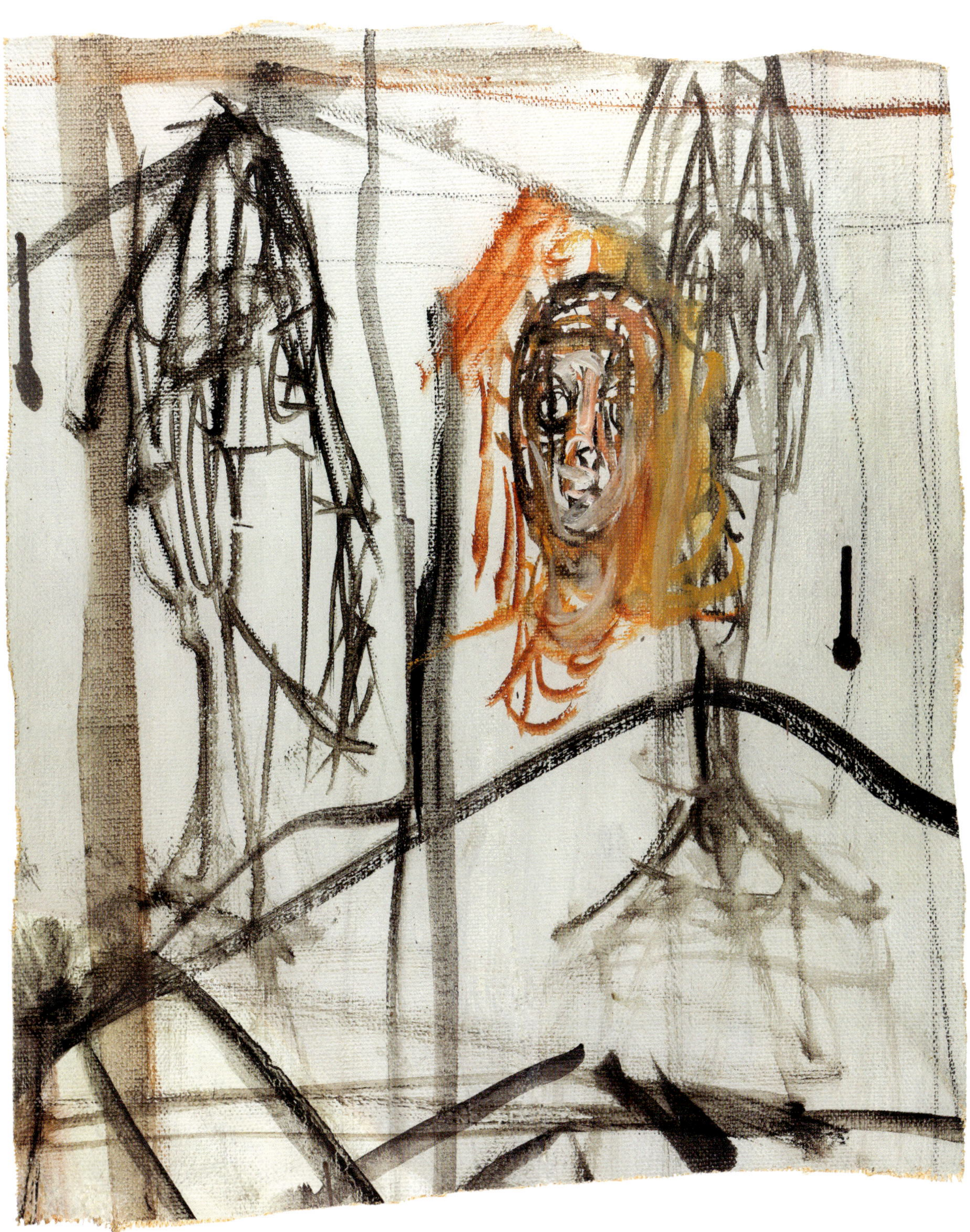

***Standing Man*, c. 1951**
Pencil on paper; 50 x 32.9 cm.
Fondation Giacometti

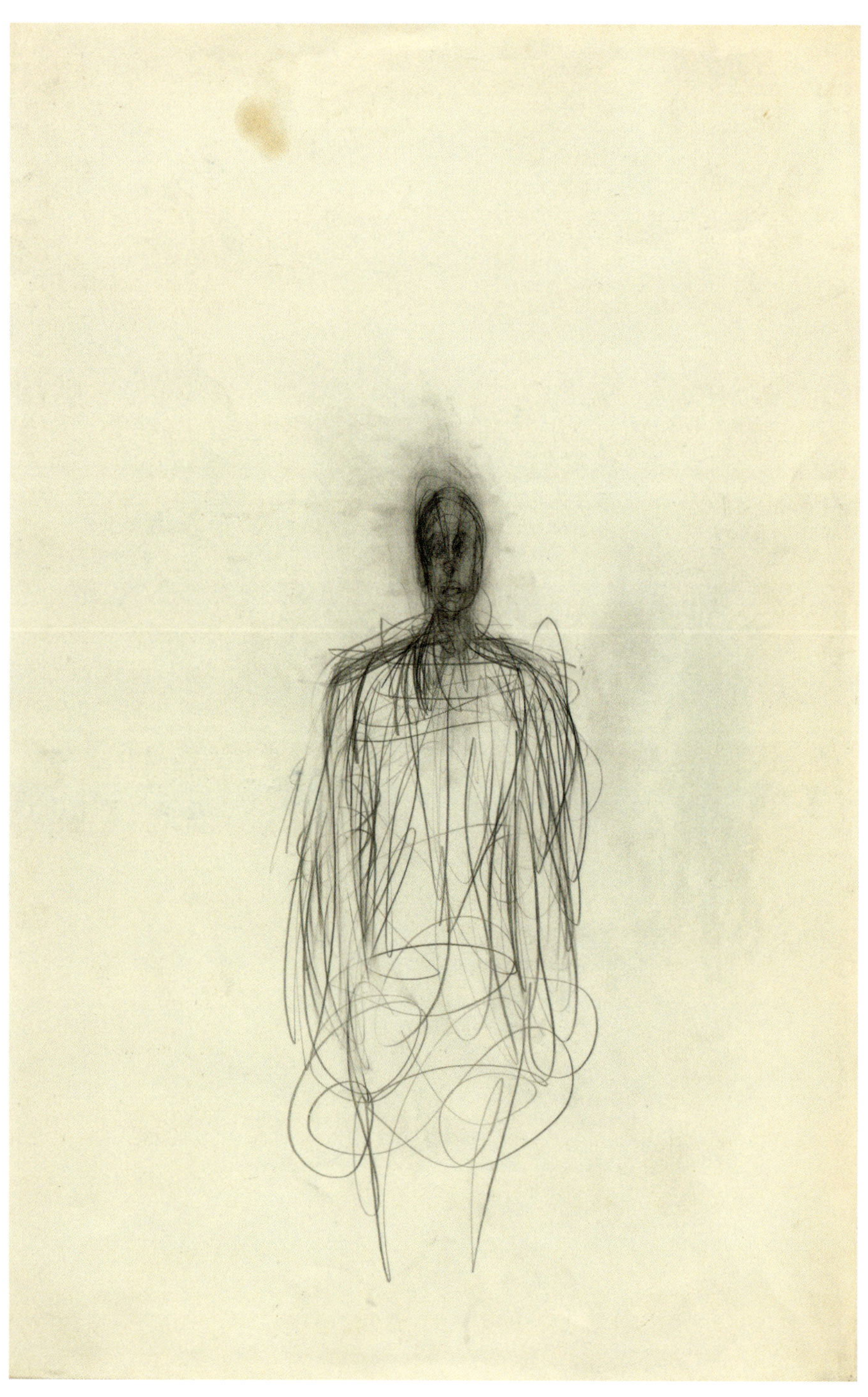

***Head of Diego*, c. 1953**
Aluminum alloy;
13.2 x 5.5 x 8.1 cm.
Fondation Giacometti

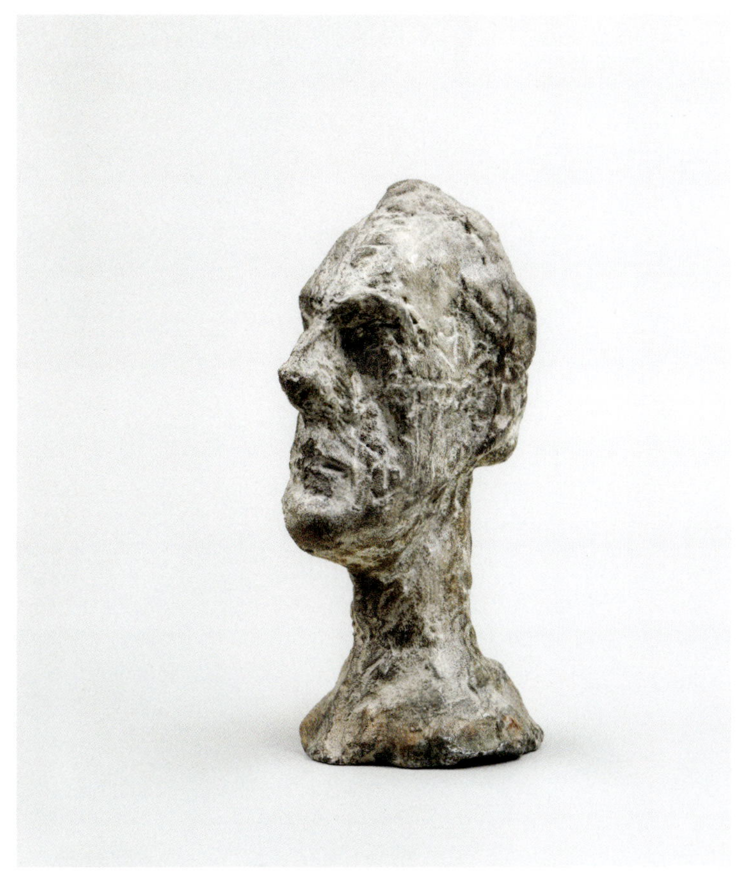

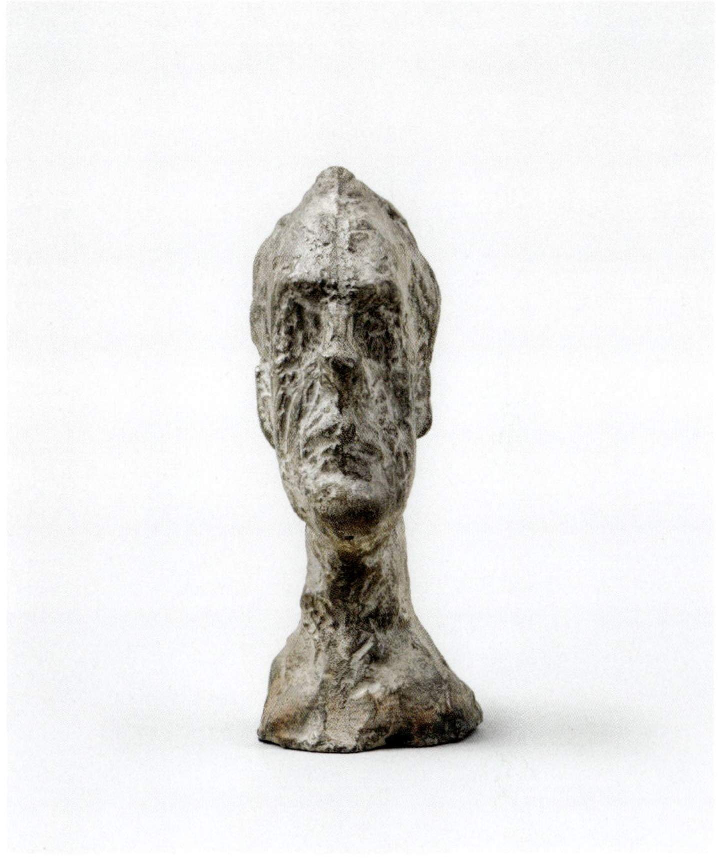

***Heads of Men on the Proof for the Exhibition Catalogue at Pierre Matisse Gallery,* May 1958**
Blue ballpoint pen on cardboard; 26.1 x 42 cm.
Fondation Giacometti

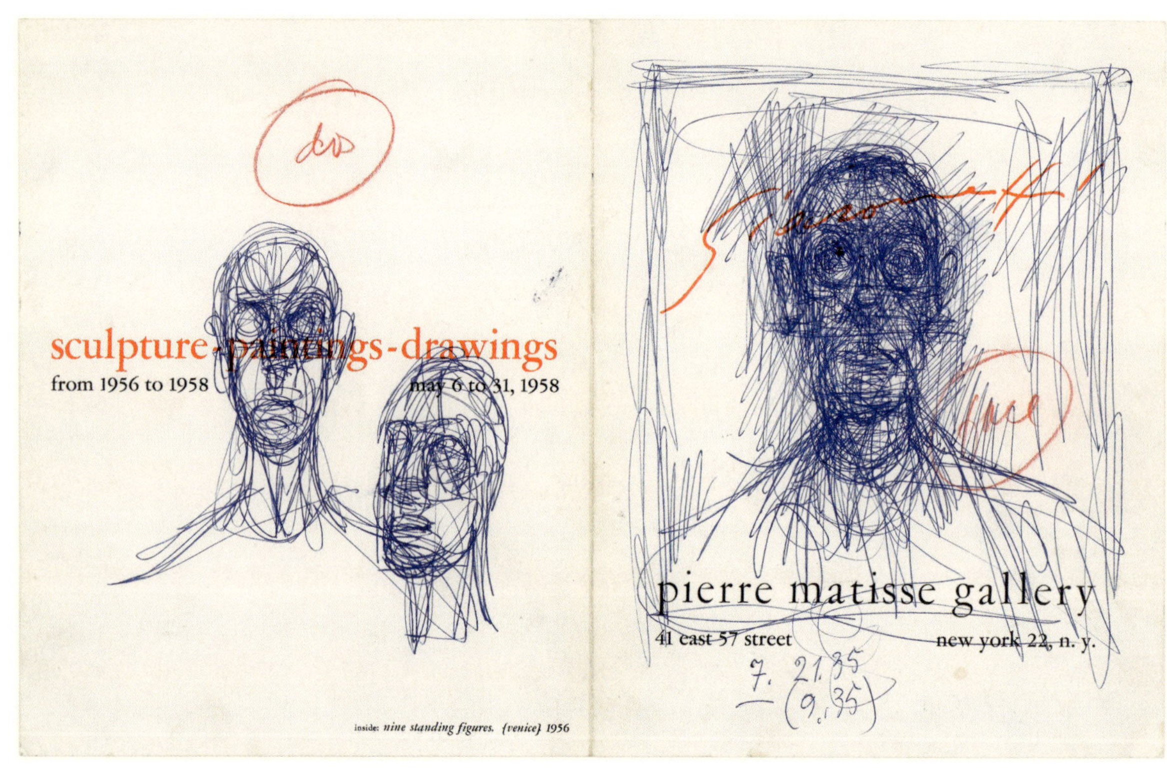

***Heads and Bust of Men,* c. 1963**
Blue ballpoint pen on letter paper; 14.8 x 21 cm.
Fondation Giacometti

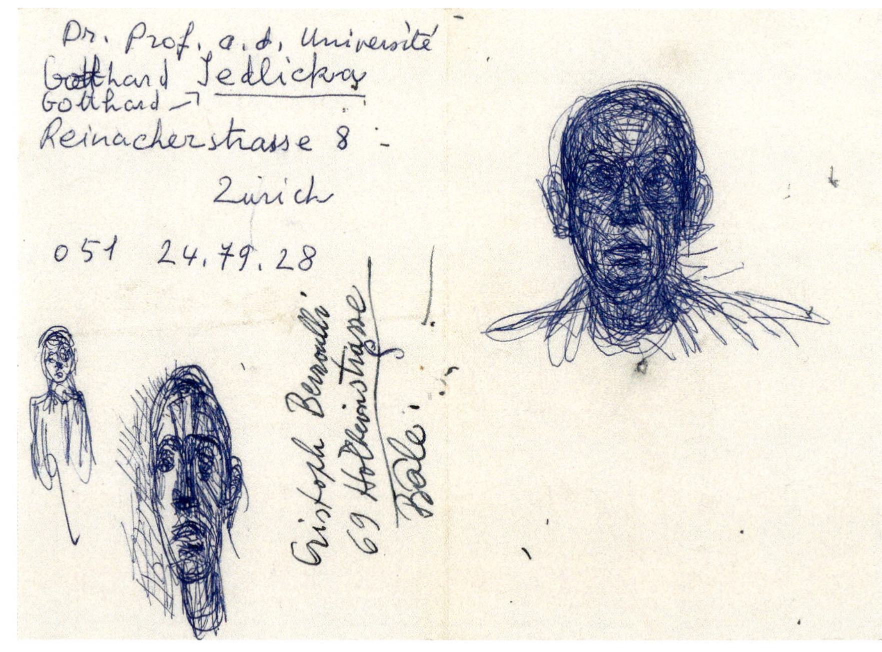

***Copy after Cimabue, Santa Trinita Maestà*, c. 1958**
Blue ballpoint pen on paper;
32.4 x 25.6 cm.
Fondation Giacometti

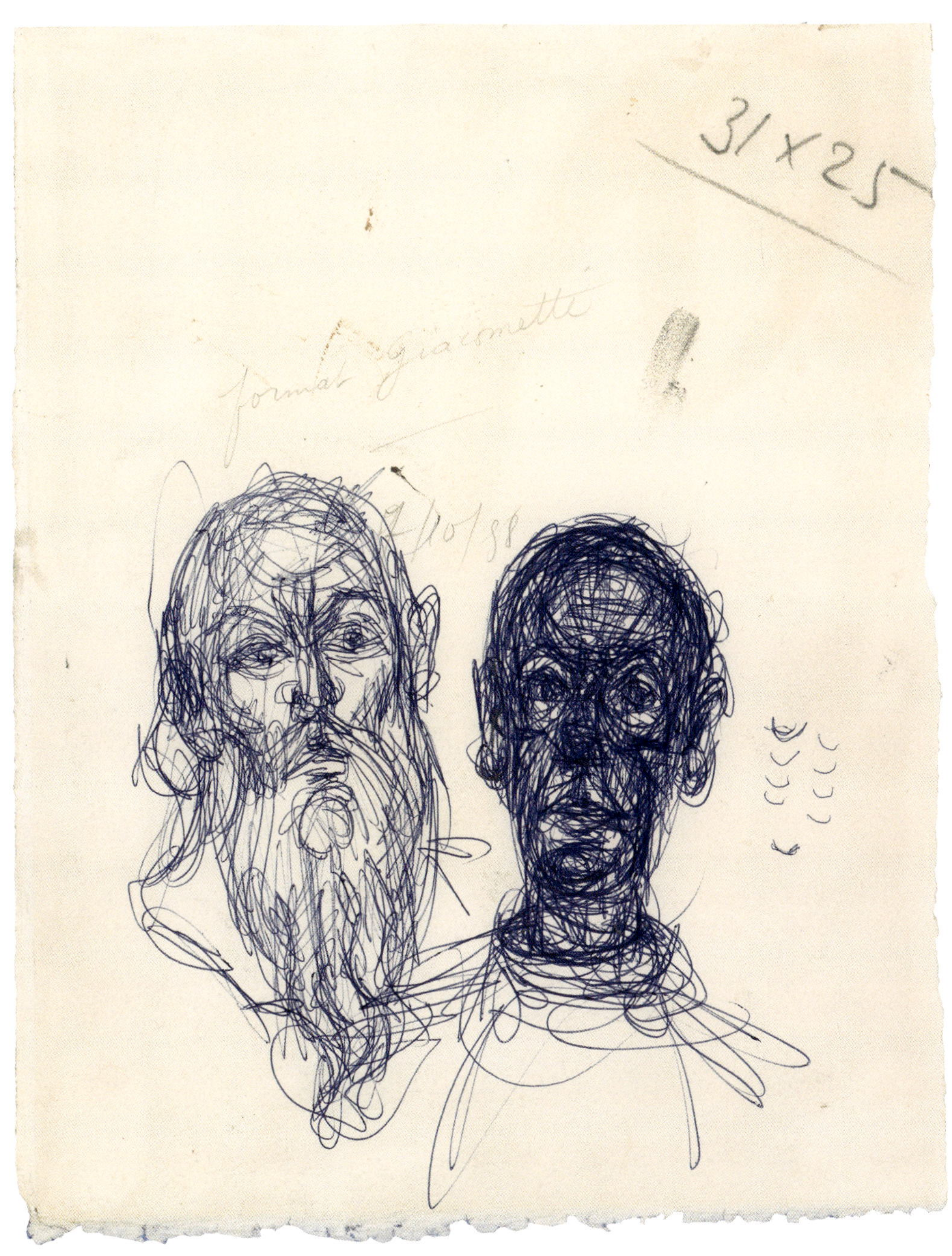

Head of a Man in Profile,
c. 1959
Blue ballpoint pen on paper;
65 x 19.3 cm.
Fondation Giacometti

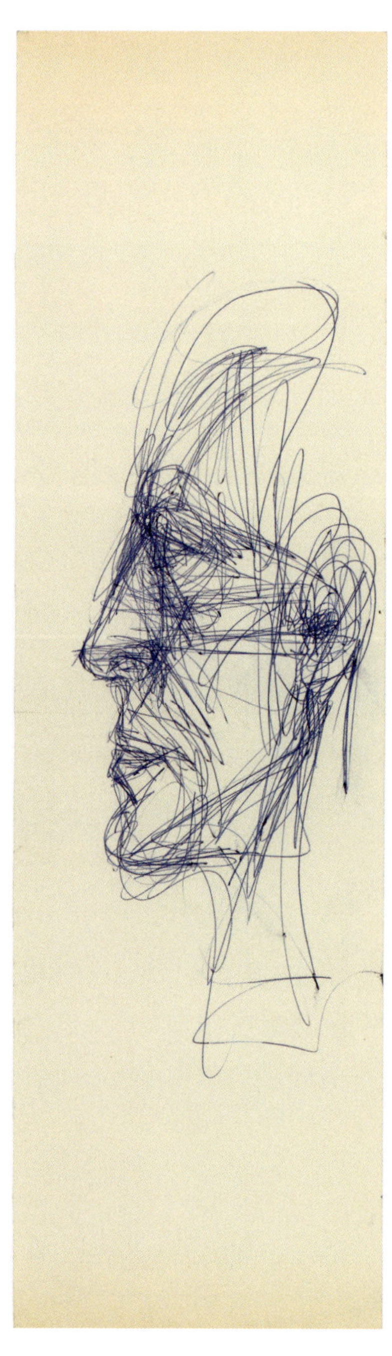

***Head of a Man, Head of a Woman, and Female Figure Standing on a Letter from the Junior Council of the Museum of Modern Art*, c. 1960**

Blue ballpoint pen on paper letter;
27.9 x 21.6 cm.
Fondation Giacometti

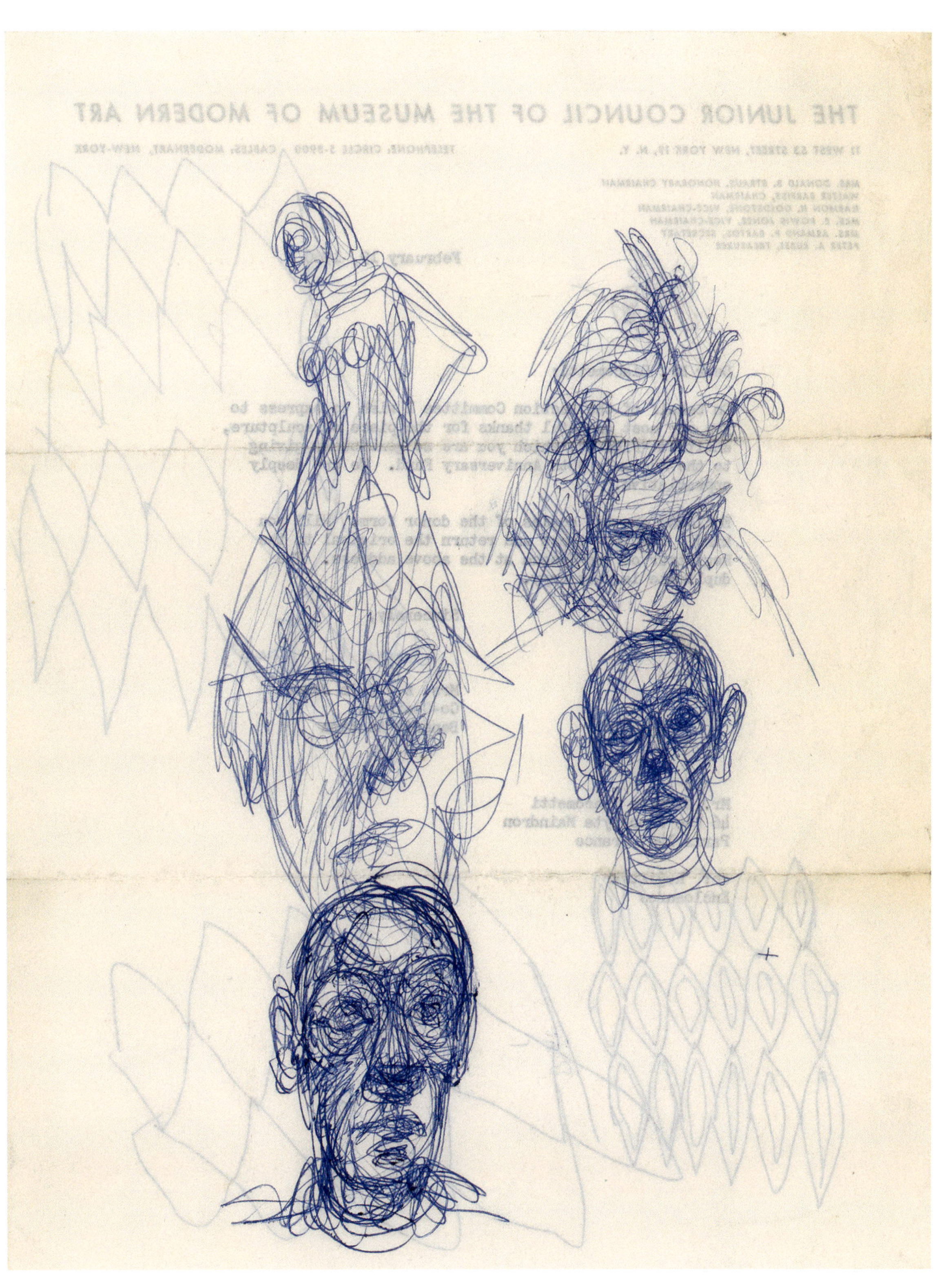

***After Photographic Portraits of Jacques Duclos in* L'Express, *no. 889, November 27, 1958,* c. November 1958**

Blue and black ballpoint pen on newspaper; magazine open: 42.8 x 59.6 cm.

Fondation Giacometti

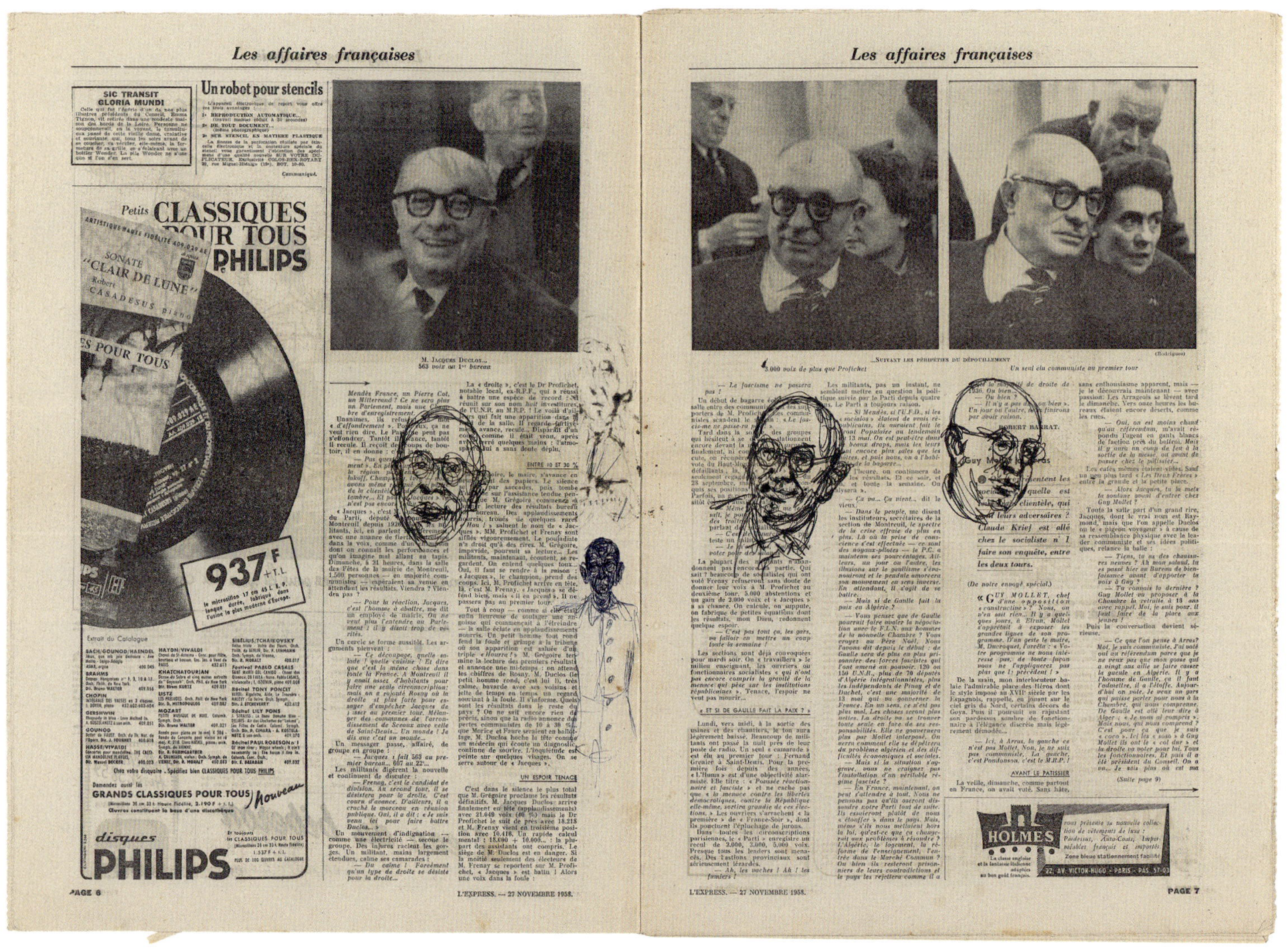
Les affaires françaises

SIC TRANSIT GLORIA MUNDI

Un robot pour stencils

Petits CLASSIQUES POUR TOUS PHILIPS

SONATE "CLAIR DE LUNE"

937 F

GRANDS CLASSIQUES POUR TOUS

disques PHILIPS

M. JACQUES DUCLOS... 563 voix au 1er bureau

ENTRE 10 ET 30 %

UN ESPOIR TENACE

PAGE 6

L'EXPRESS. — 27 NOVEMBRE 1958.

Les affaires françaises

3.000 voix de plus que Profichet

...SUIVANT LES PÉRIPÉTIES DU DÉPOUILLEMENT

Un seul élu communiste au premier tour

« ET SI DE GAULLE FAIT LA PAIX ? »

AVANT LE PÂTISSIER

HOLMES

L'EXPRESS. — 27 NOVEMBRE 1958.

PAGE 7

***Head of Annette*, 1965**
Black ballpoint pen on
notepaper; 27 x 21 cm.
Fondation Giacometti

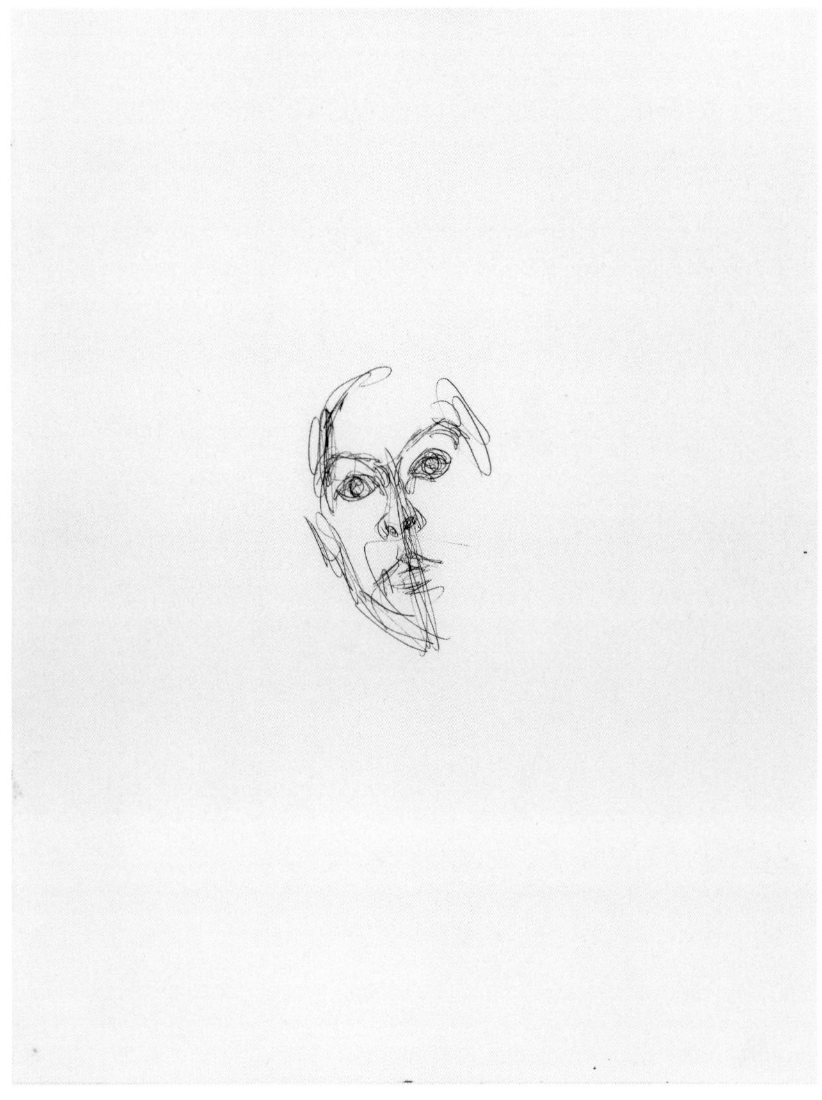

***Heads of Annette and Diego, Eyes, and House*, c. 1955**

Blue ink on paper napkin; 29 x 51 cm.

Fondation Giacometti

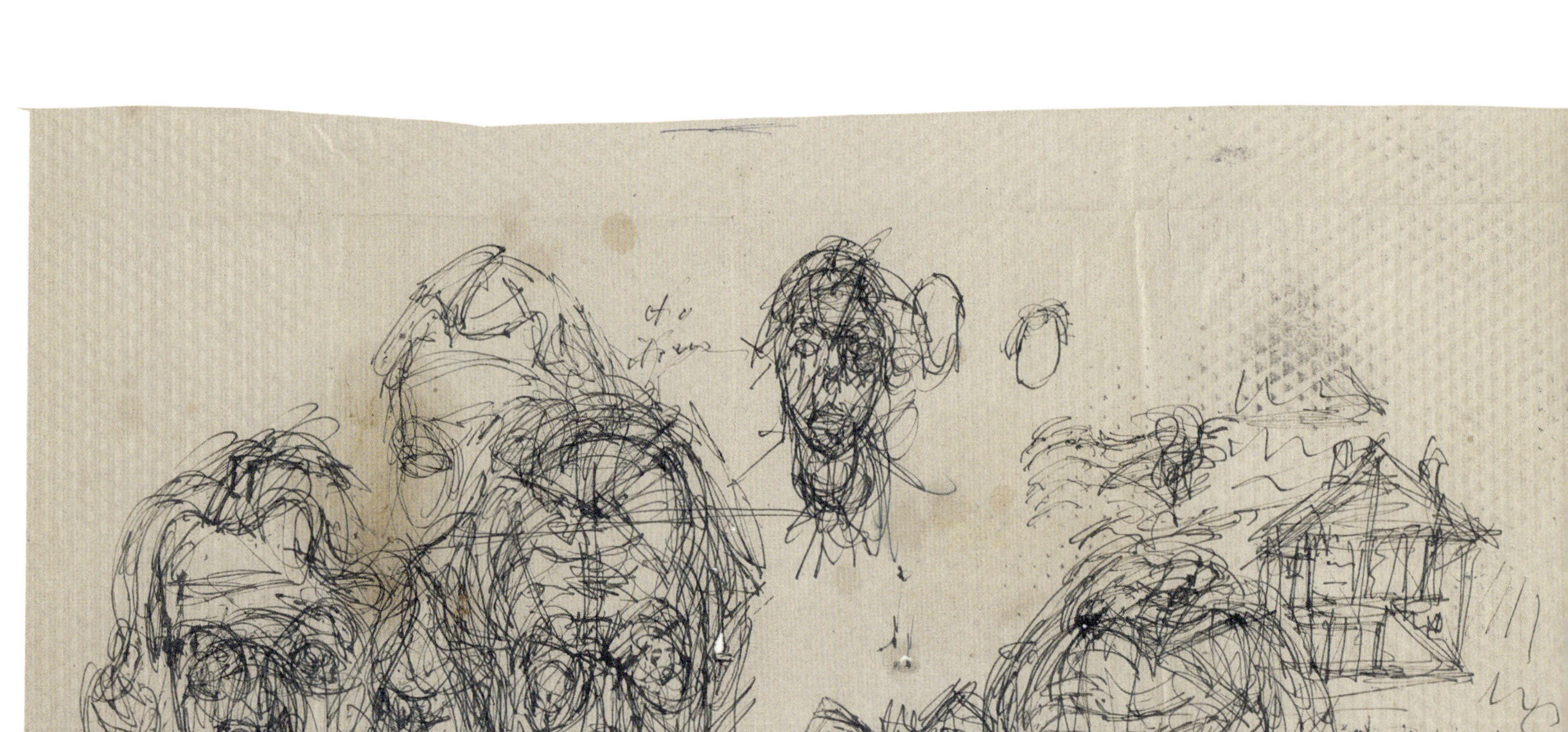

***Heads and Nudes on the Invitation Card for the Exhibition* Georges Braque, dessins, *Galerie Maeght, June 21, 1962*, 1962**
Red ballpoint pen on invitation card; 12.5 x 16.1 cm.
Fondation Giacometti

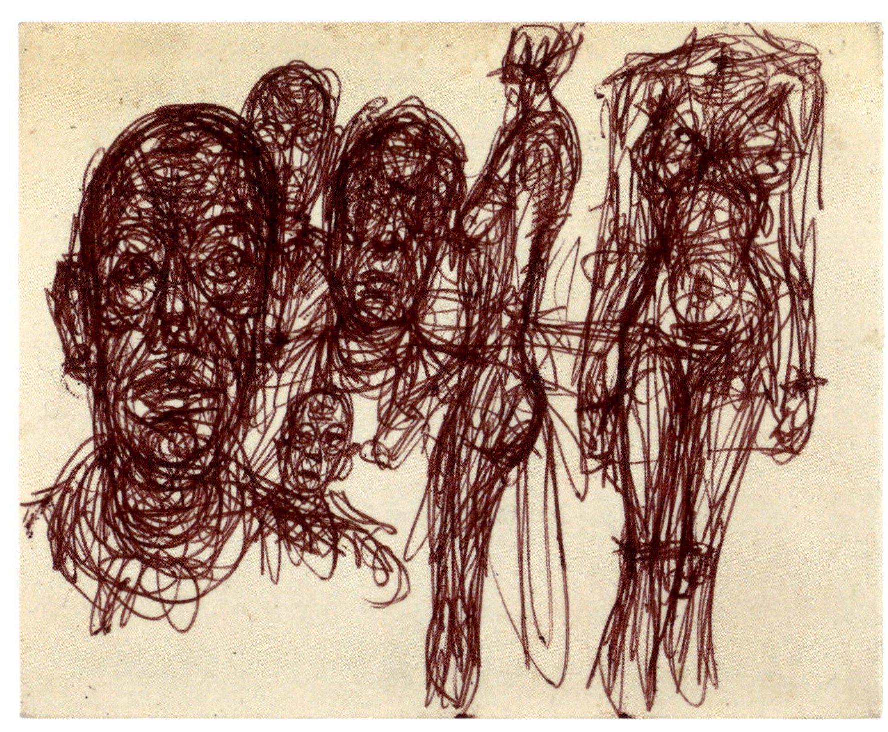

***Head of a Man in* Masterpieces of Mexican Art, *1962*, c. 1962**
Blue ballpoint pen on book;
book open: 21 x 32.6 x 3.8 cm.
Fondation Giacometti

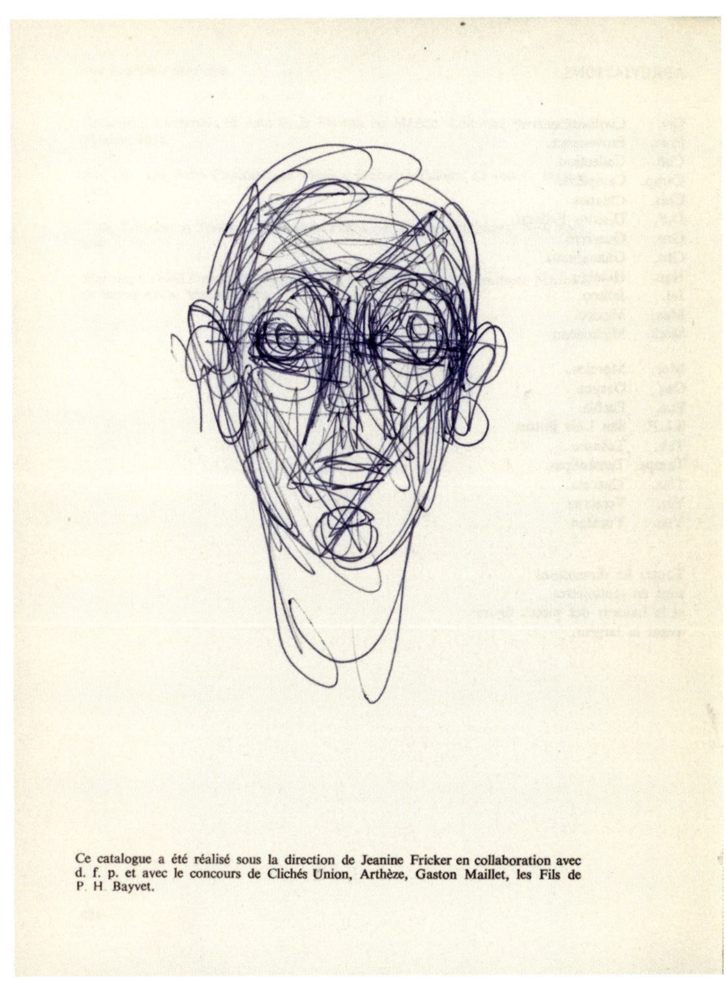
Ce catalogue a été réalisé sous la direction de Jeanine Fricker en collaboration avec d. f. p. et avec le concours de Clichés Union, Arthèze, Gaston Maillet, les Fils de P. H. Bayvet.

***Heads of Men*, c. October 1962**
Red ballpoint pen on paper;
28.5 x 22.6 cm.
Fondation Giacometti

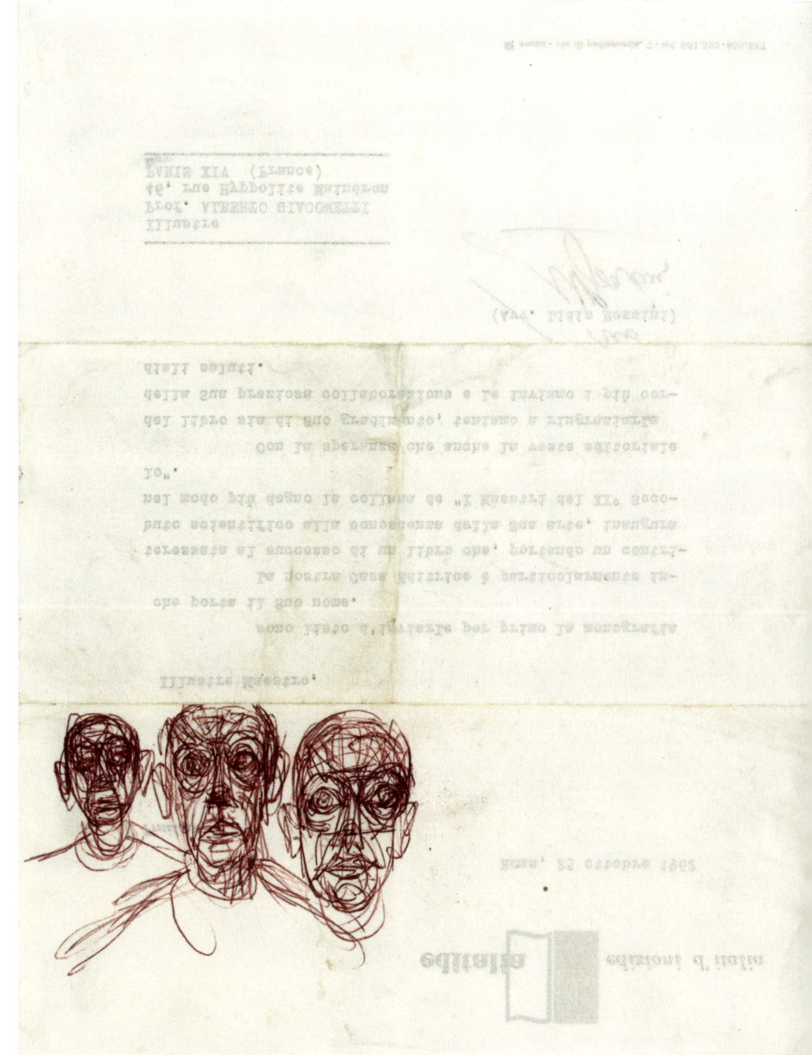

***Heads of Men and a Small Figure*, c. 1962**
Blue ballpoint pen on envelope;
19.1 x 10.2 cm.
Fondation Giacometti

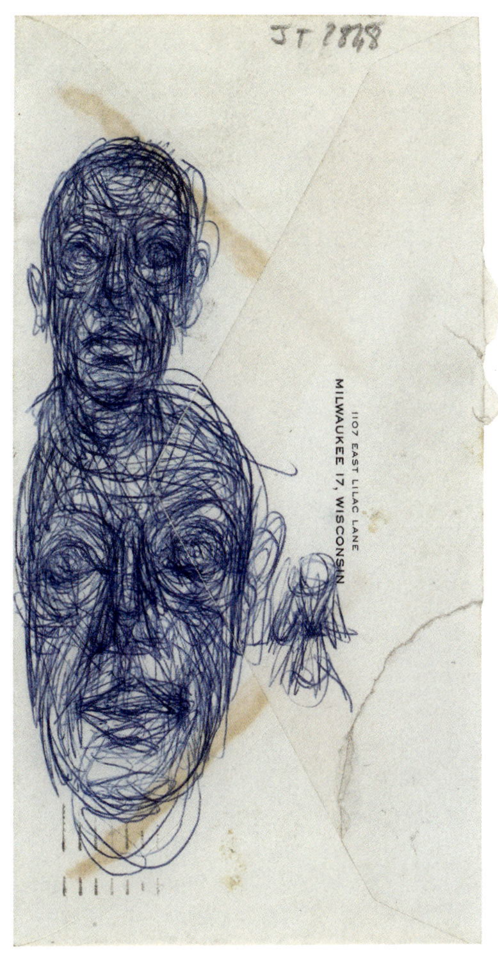

***Heads of Men Front and Profile on the Catalogue of the Exhibition* Sculptures de Duchamp-Villon, *Galerie Louis Carré, June–July 1963*, c. 1963**
Blue and black ballpoint pen on paper; 27.5 x 23.9 cm.
Fondation Giacometti

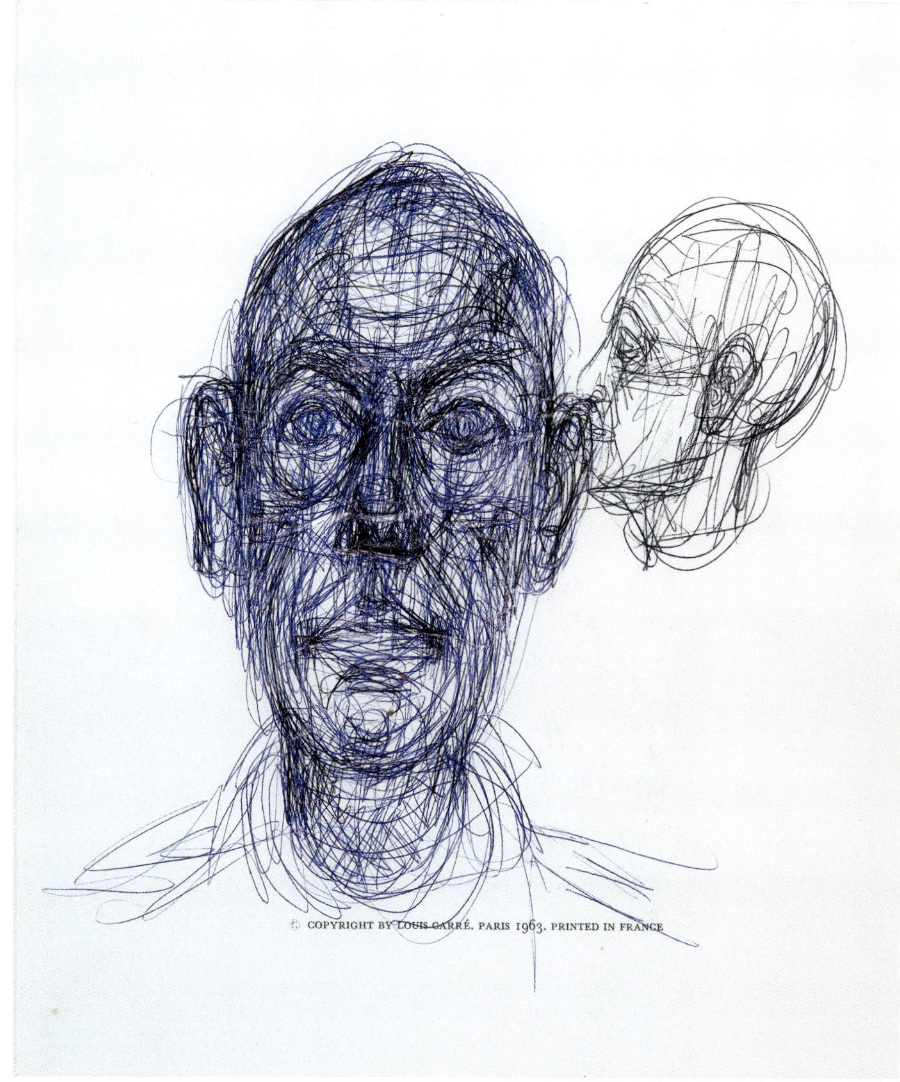

***Portrait of a Man; Portrait of Annette*, 1963**
Blue and black ballpoint pen on notebook; notebook open: 18 x 24.6 cm.
Fondation Giacometti

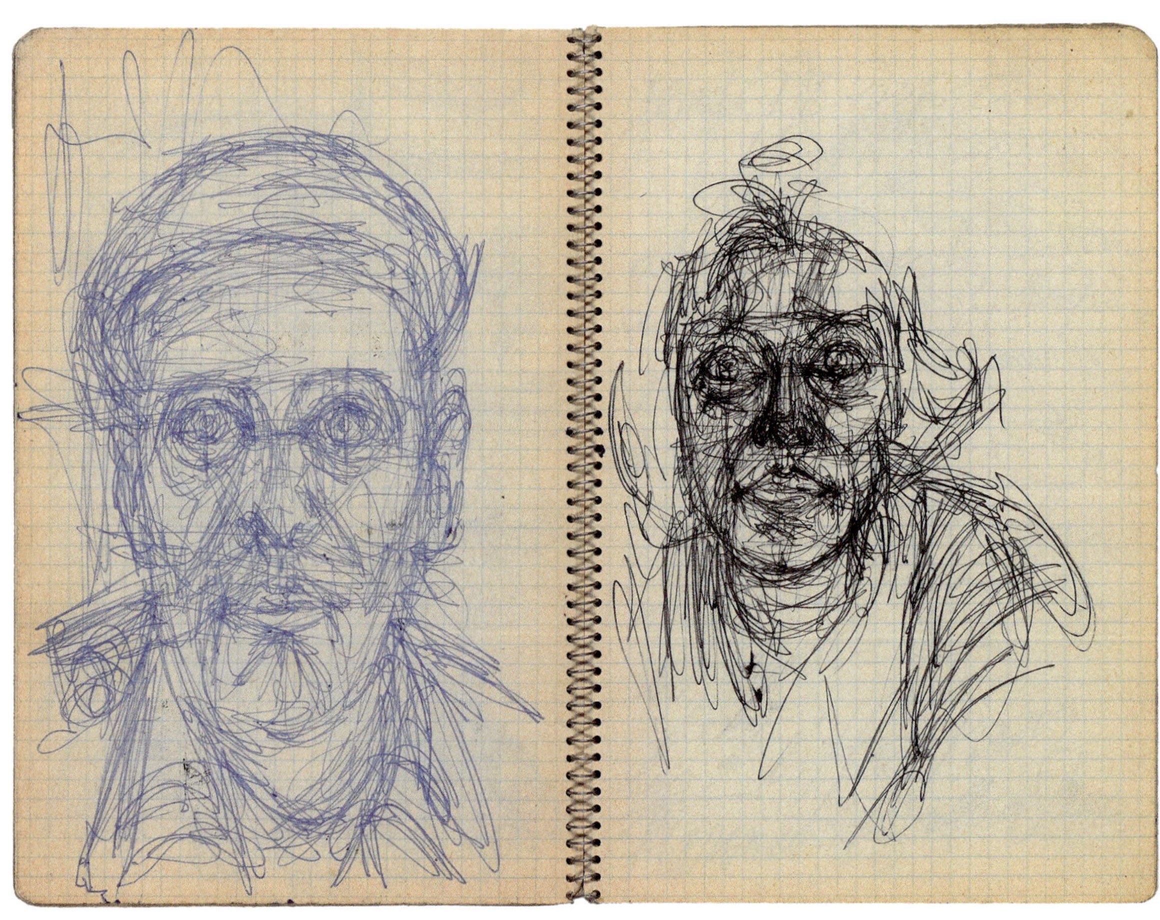

Heads and Busts on the Front Page of the **Lettres Françaises**, *no. 991, August 22–28, 1963*, **c. August 1963**
Blue ballpoint pen on detached newspaper page; 60.5 x 46 cm.
Fondation Giacometti

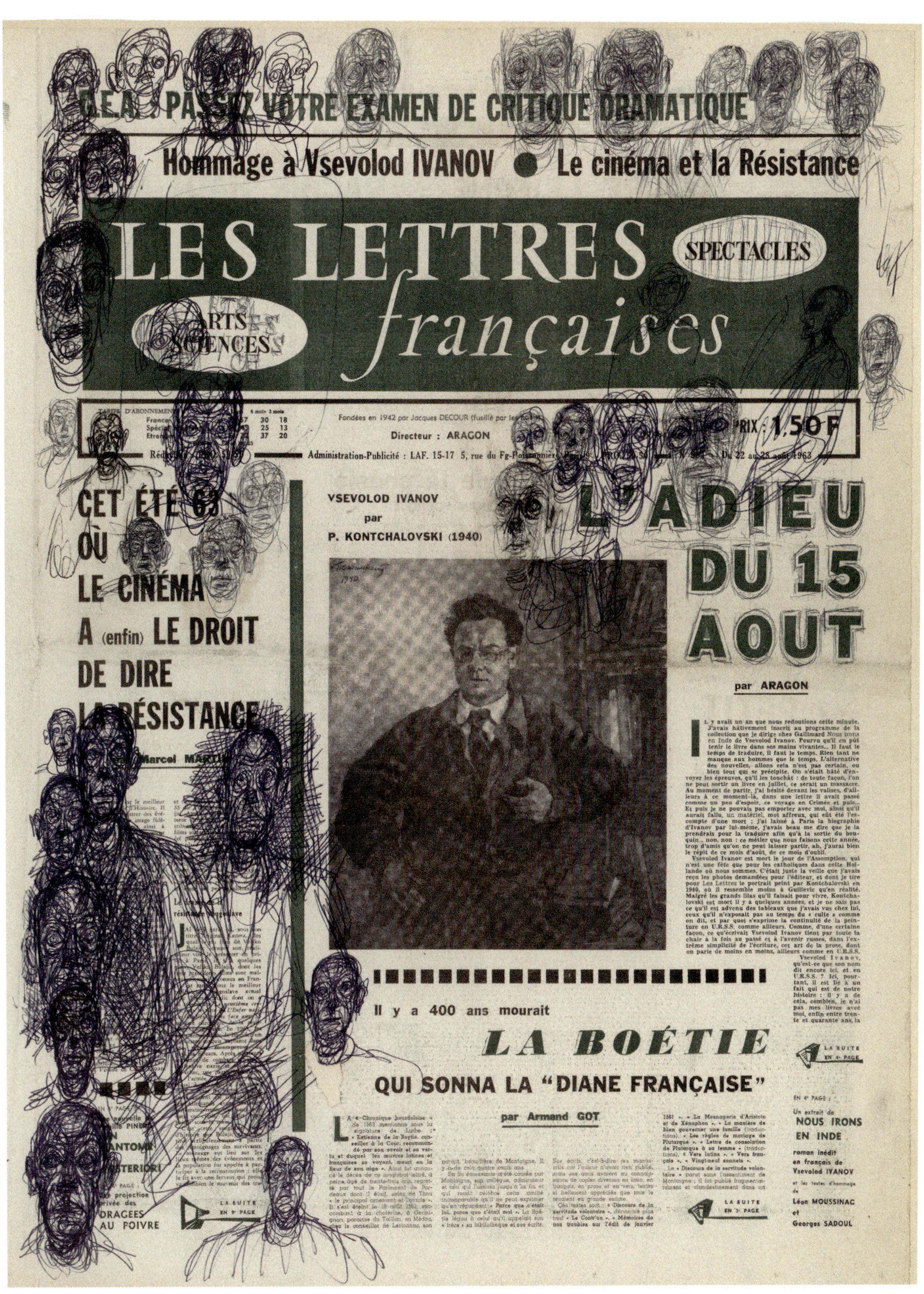

***Heads of Men, Face and Profile*, c. 1960**
Blue ballpoint pen on envelope;
15.3 x 22 cm.
Fondation Giacometti

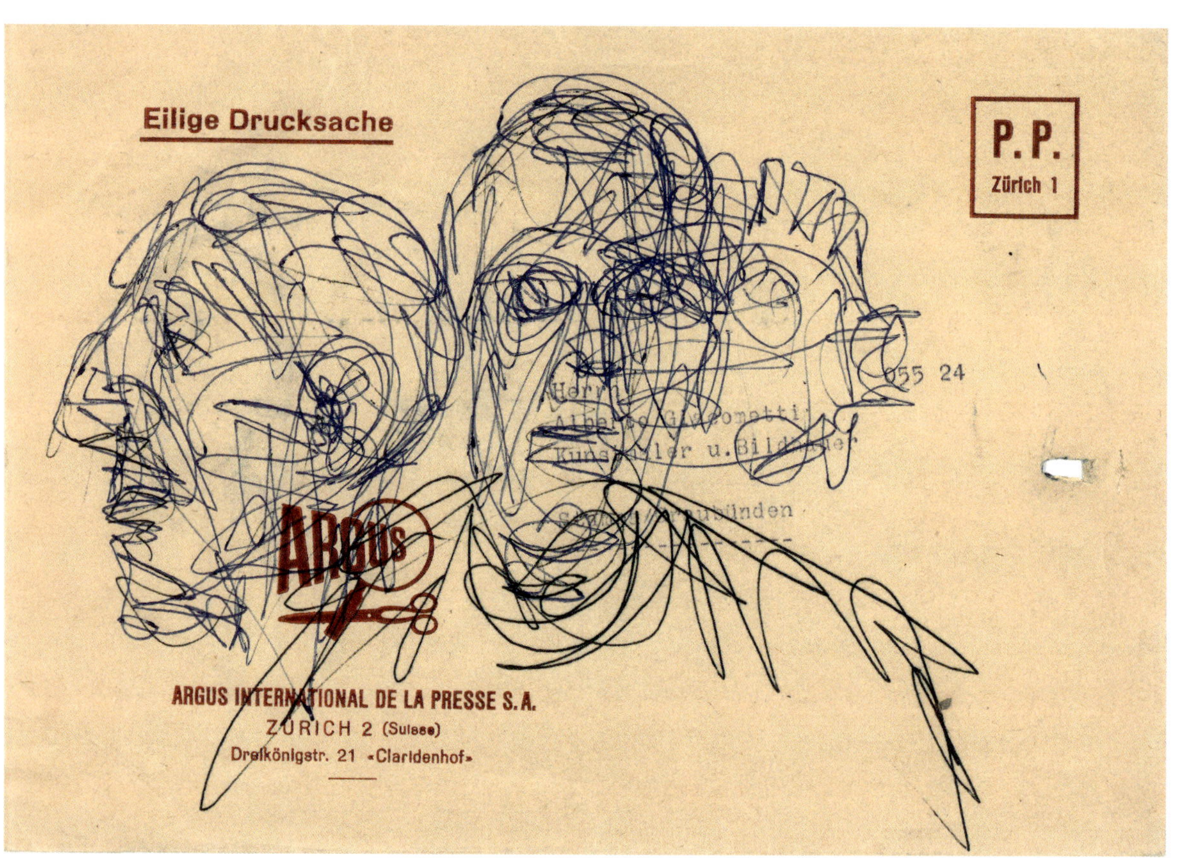

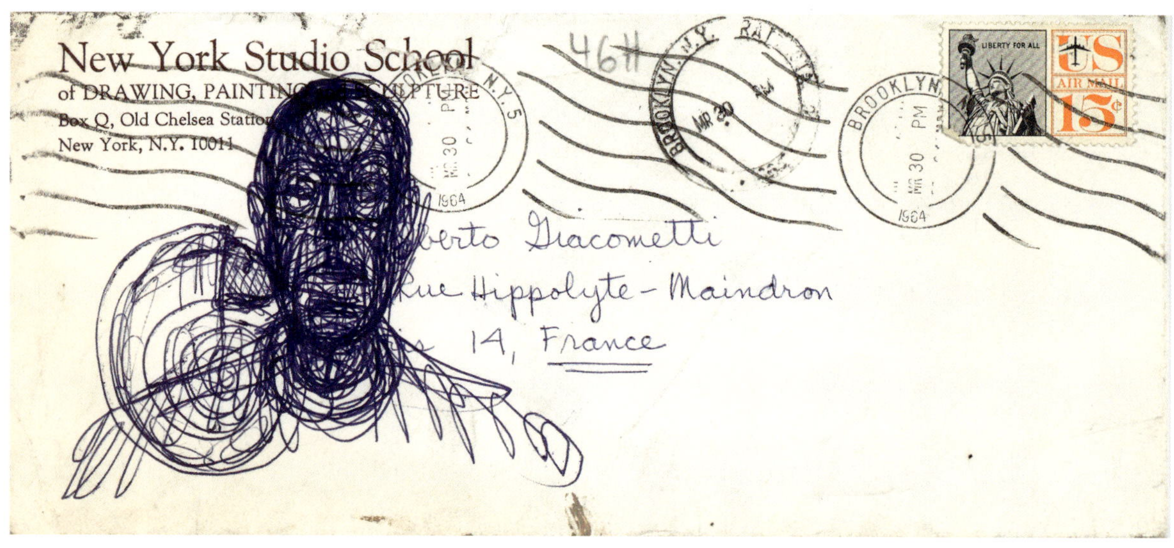

***Bust of a Man and Snail Shell*, 1964**
Blue ballpoint pen on envelope;
10.7 x 24.1 cm.
Fondation Giacometti

***Head of a Man (Lotar I)*, 1964**
Bronze; 25.5 x 28.2 x 13.2 cm.
Fondation Giacometti

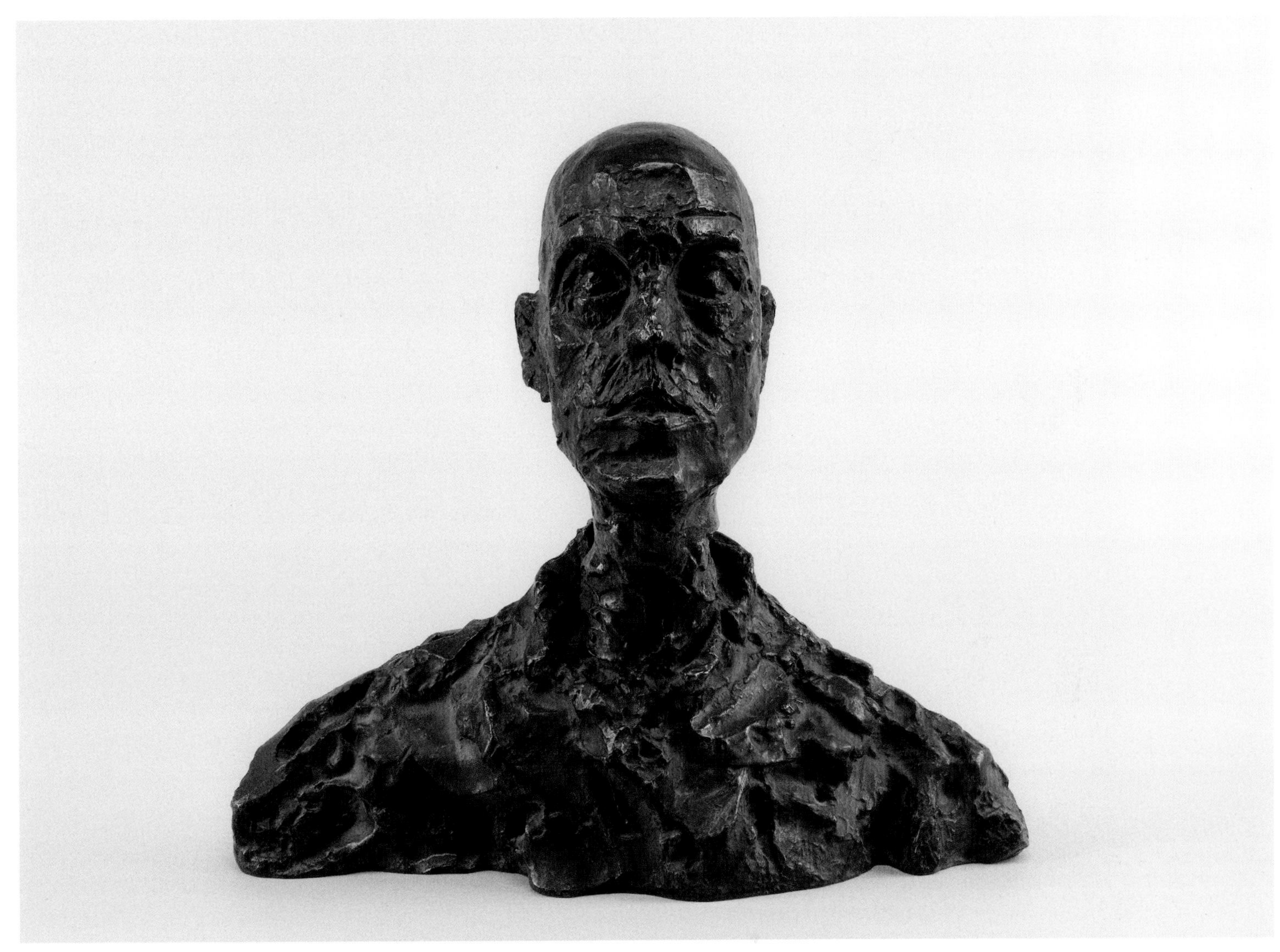

Into Thin Air

ROMAIN PERRIN

Alberto Giacometti in his studio, Paris, 1954
Sabine Weiss. Archives, Fondation Giacometti.

Alberto Giacometti's sculpture was well received in the 1940s and 1950s by the Parisian intellectuals linked to the schools of thought regarding phenomenology and existentialism. His works, in the correspondence between looking and being looked at that they establish with the spectator, share the same questioning of the phenomenon of perception.

In his search for a way to represent his vision of real life, Giacometti, from the end of the 1930s to the 1950s, worked on the relations of distance and perception between the artist and the model, which, almost subconsciously, drove him to gradually reduce the scale of his sculptures. Submerged in too many details, the artist needed to move away from his model in order to capture the form of a head or a body as a whole. In reducing a sculpture, he tried to place "at a real distance" the thing observed, because in the phenomenon of vision, real size no longer exists.[1] In fact, it all seems relative to the space surrounding the model because that "space surrounds us, isolates us."[2] Despite their modest dimensions, the busts of his nephew Silvio (page 139) and of his wife, Annette (page 138 right), made in the 1940s, maintain a strong presence because of their relation to space. Giacometti compared them to prehistoric statuettes, Sumerian or Egyptian, because of "their size which [is] most instinctively close, such as one really sees."[3]

However, that reduction represented only a temporary solution, for the artist dreaded seeing them disappear. To counteract that effect, he decided to stretch them. But by doing so, the statues became excessively thin, like the figurines created at the beginning of the 1950s (pages 140–41), whose matter was lumpy, as if they were coming out of a kiln, in Jean Genet's words.[4] The details that greatly preoccupied Giacometti vanished to be replaced by a universal silhouette, almost a shadow.

In a letter to his New York dealer Pierre Matisse, published in the catalogue of his 1950 exhibition, the artist talked about the sculpture *Four Women on a Base* (page 143) as related to the vision he had one evening of prostitutes in a brothel on rue de l'Échaudé. Giacometti described those four naked women as both "very close and menacing."[5] The "threat" he experienced forced him to keep a distance, and it was that distance that created the scale of the sculpture, a scale that is his own, giving the impression that the statues are at the same time far away and close to the spectator.

Realistic as they may be, Giacometti's sculptures were subjected to distortions, even his busts. Seen full face, Diego's head, the "sharp heads," and the "thin heads," created as early as 1953, give the impression that the artist has flattened the model's head. This representation, which reduces the face in *Tall Thin Head* (pages 144–45) to a vertical line and makes it resemble an anamorphosis, manipulates the space in depth in an aberrant perspective that aims not at depicting real life in an objective way, but at conveying the experience of the artist's original vision.

By trying to produce images in volume such as he saw them, Giacometti seems to create the equivalent, in sculpture, of what Michel Leiris, in his diary, called "pictorial painting"—that is, "fragments of nature—inert or alive—both close and distant."[6]

1. Jean Clay, "Alberto Giacometti: Le long dialogue avec la mort d'un très grand sculpteur de notre temps," *Réalités*, no. 215 (December 1963); reprinted in Alberto Giacometti, *Écrits: Articles, notes et entretiens* (Paris: Hermann and Fondation Giacometti, 2007), 315.
2. Giacometti, *Écrits*, 317.
3. Giacometti, conversation with David Sylvester, *L'Éphémère*, no. 18 (November 1971), 183.
4. Jean Genet, *L'Atelier d'Alberto Giacometti* (Paris: L'Arbalète, 1963), n.p.
5. Giacometti to Pierre Matisse, December 28, 1950, in *Alberto Giacometti*, exh. cat. (New York: Pierre Matisse Gallery, 1950); reprinted in Giacometti, *Écrits*, 102.
6. Michel Leiris, *Journal* [1992], Quarto (Paris: Gallimard, 2021), 798.

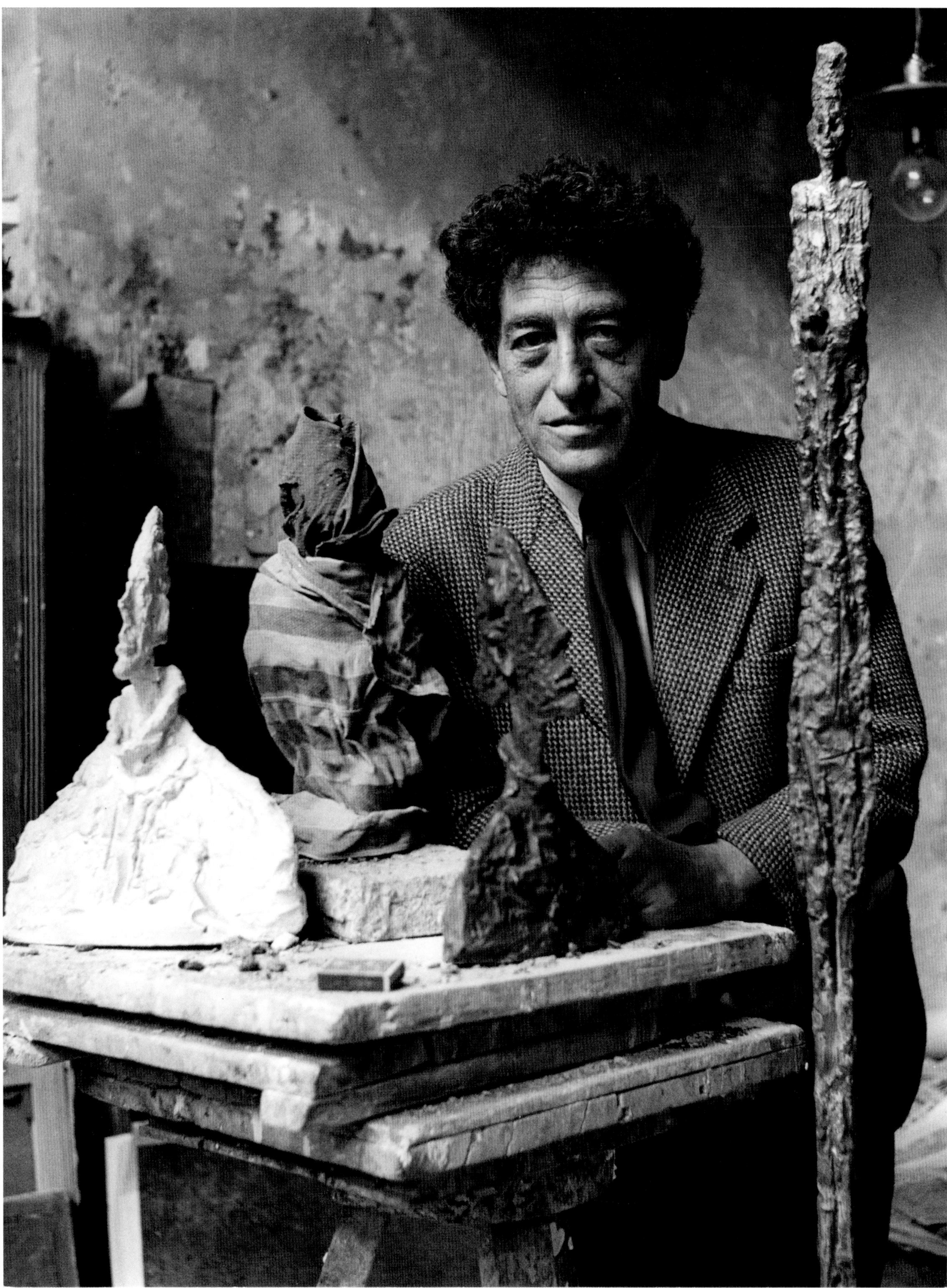

Small Bust on a Double Base,
1940–41
Bronze; 11.6 x 6.2 x 5.4 cm.
Fondation Giacometti

Small Bust of Annette,
c. 1946
Bronze; 16 x 13.6 x 8.5 cm.
Fondation Giacometti

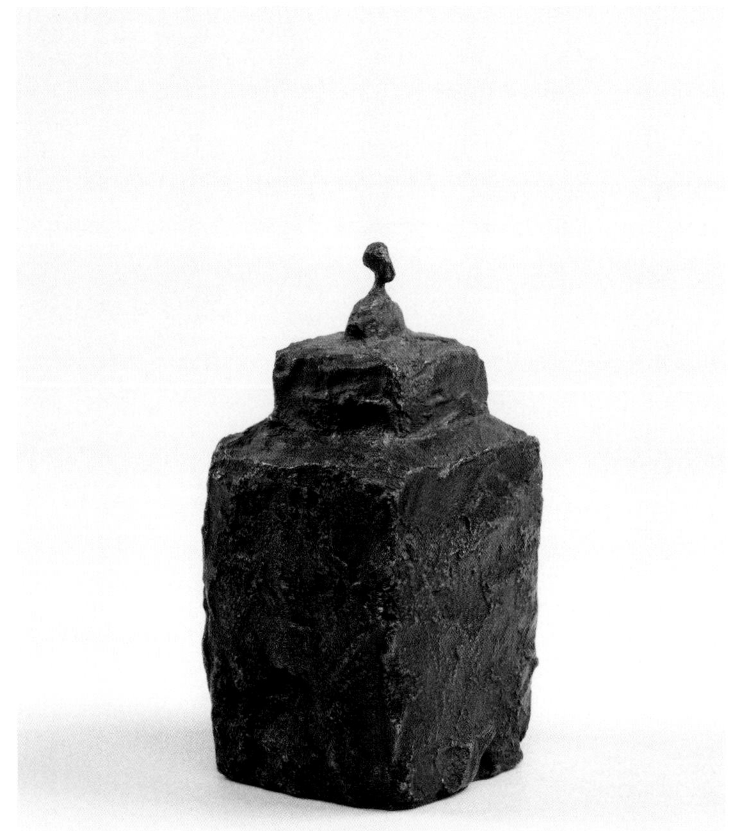

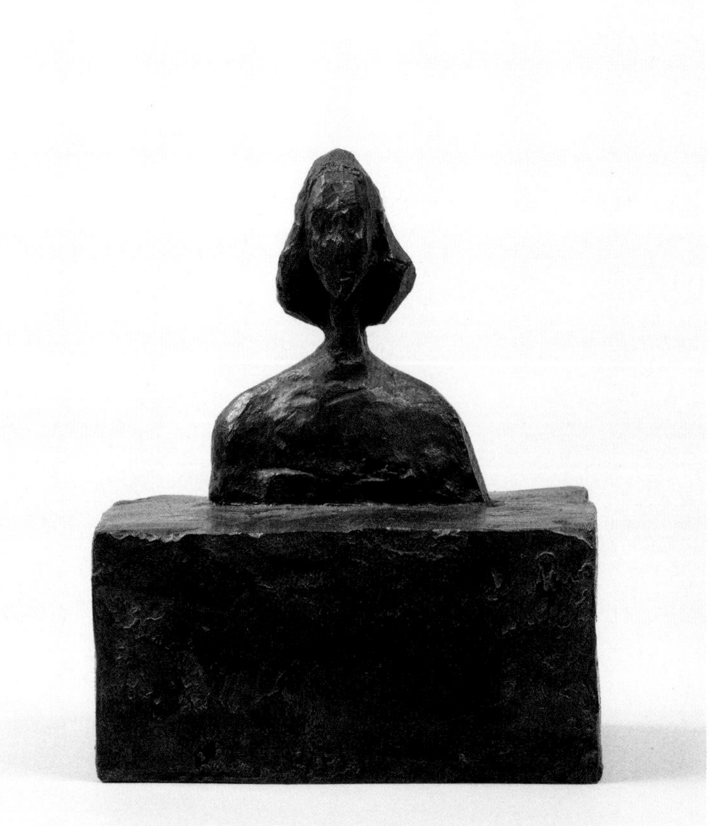

***Small Bust of Silvio on a Double Base*, 1943–44**
Bronze; 18.3 x 12.8 x 11.5 cm.
Fondation Giacometti

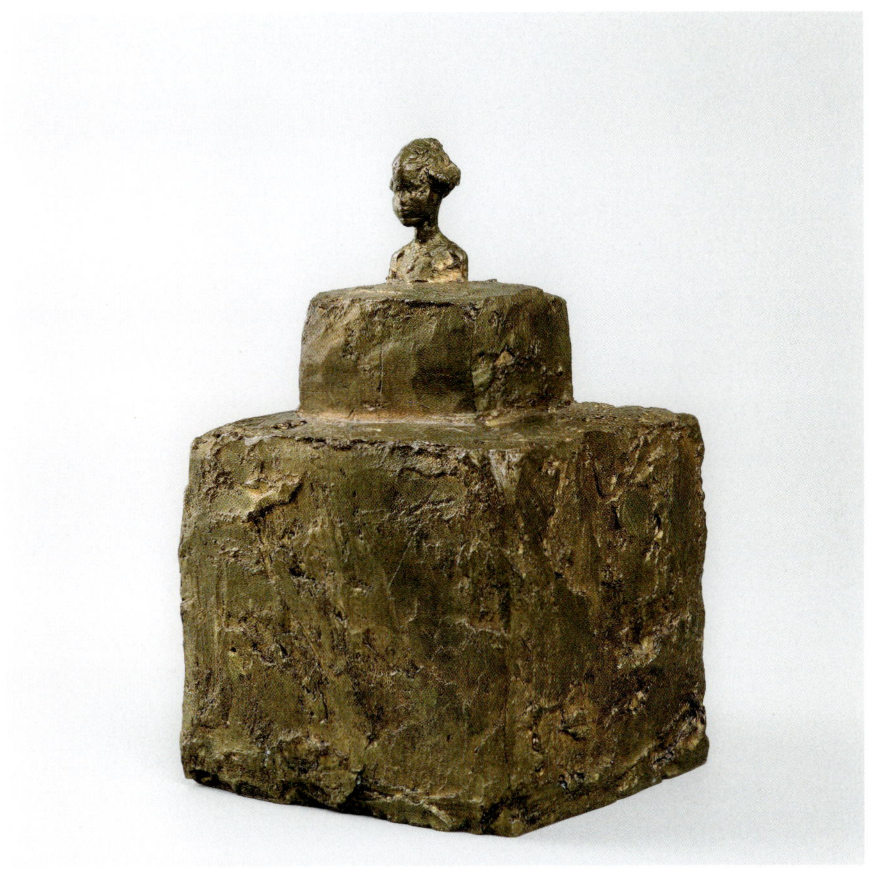

***Figurine*, c. 1947**
Bronze; 28.4 x 9.3 x 10.4 cm.
Fondation Giacometti

***Figurine*, c. 1950**
Bronze; 15.5 x 4.5 x 5.7 cm.
Fondation Giacometti

***Figurine*, 1953–54**
Bronze; 10.7 x 3.4 x 4.1 cm.
Fondation Giacometti

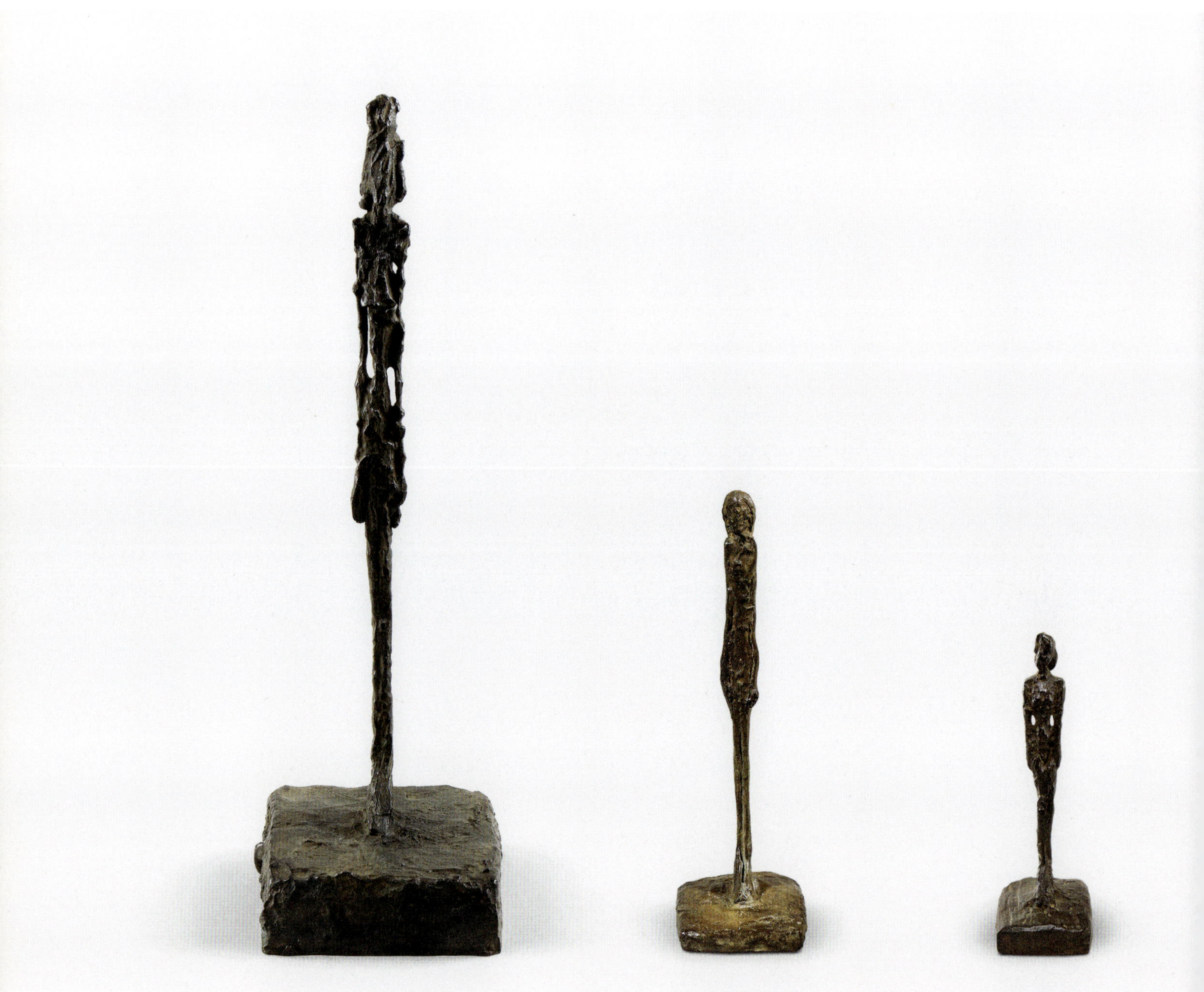

***Figurine*, c. 1954**
Bronze; 14.9 x 4.7 x 6.3 cm.
Fondation Giacometti

***Figurine*, c. 1956**
Bronze; 23.4 x 7 x 10.3 cm.
Fondation Giacometti

***Figurine without Arms*, c. 1956**
Bronze; 12.2 x 4.6 x 6.8 cm.
Fondation Giacometti

***Figurine without Arms*, c. 1956**
Bronze; 14.1 x 6.2 x 7.1 cm.
Fondation Giacometti

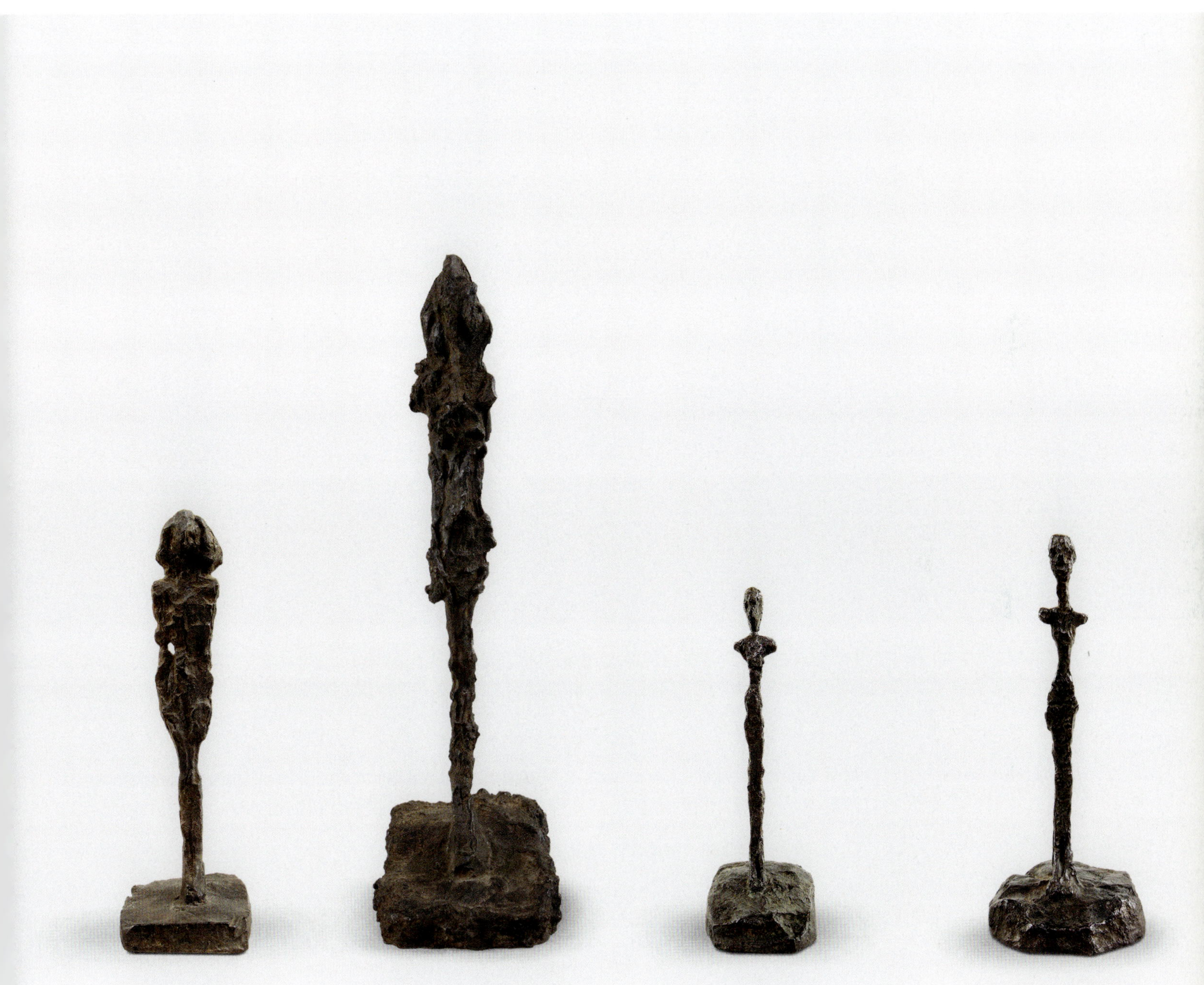

***Woman of Venice III*, 1956**
Bronze; 118.5 x 17.8 x 35.1 cm.
Fondation Giacometti

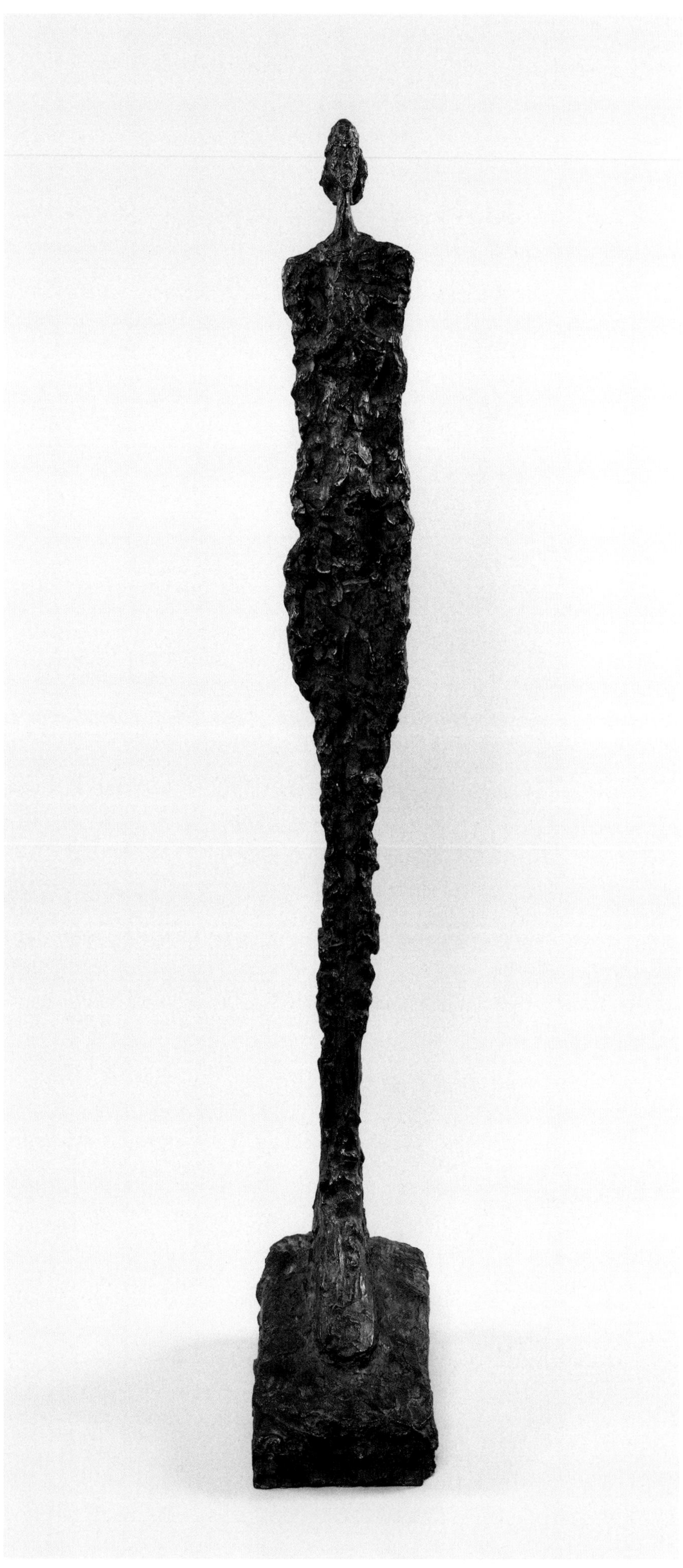

***Four Women on a Base*, 1950**
Bronze; 76 x 41.3 x 16.4 cm.
Fondation Giacometti

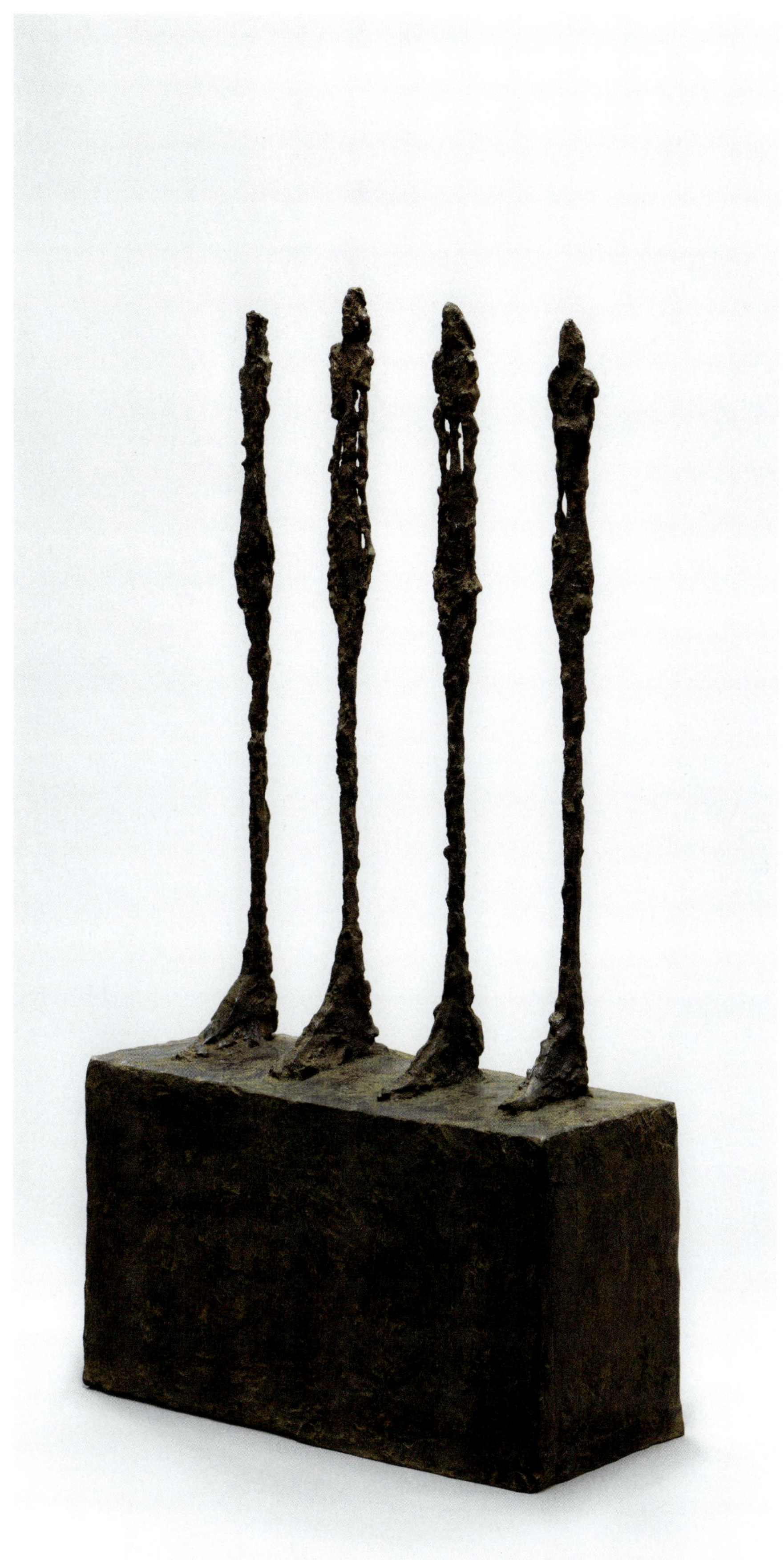

***Tall Thin Head*, 1954**
Bronze; 64.5 x 38.1 x 24.4 cm.
Fondation Giacometti

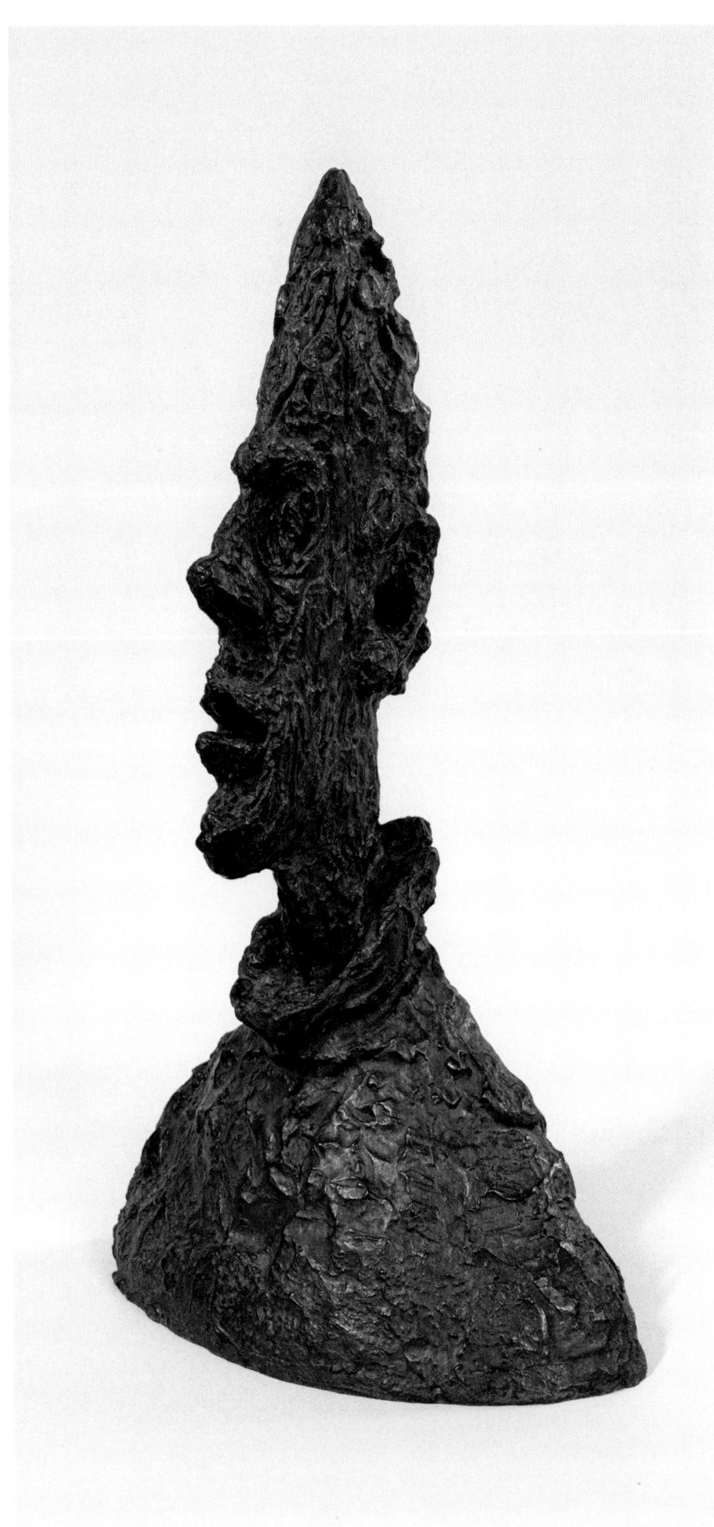

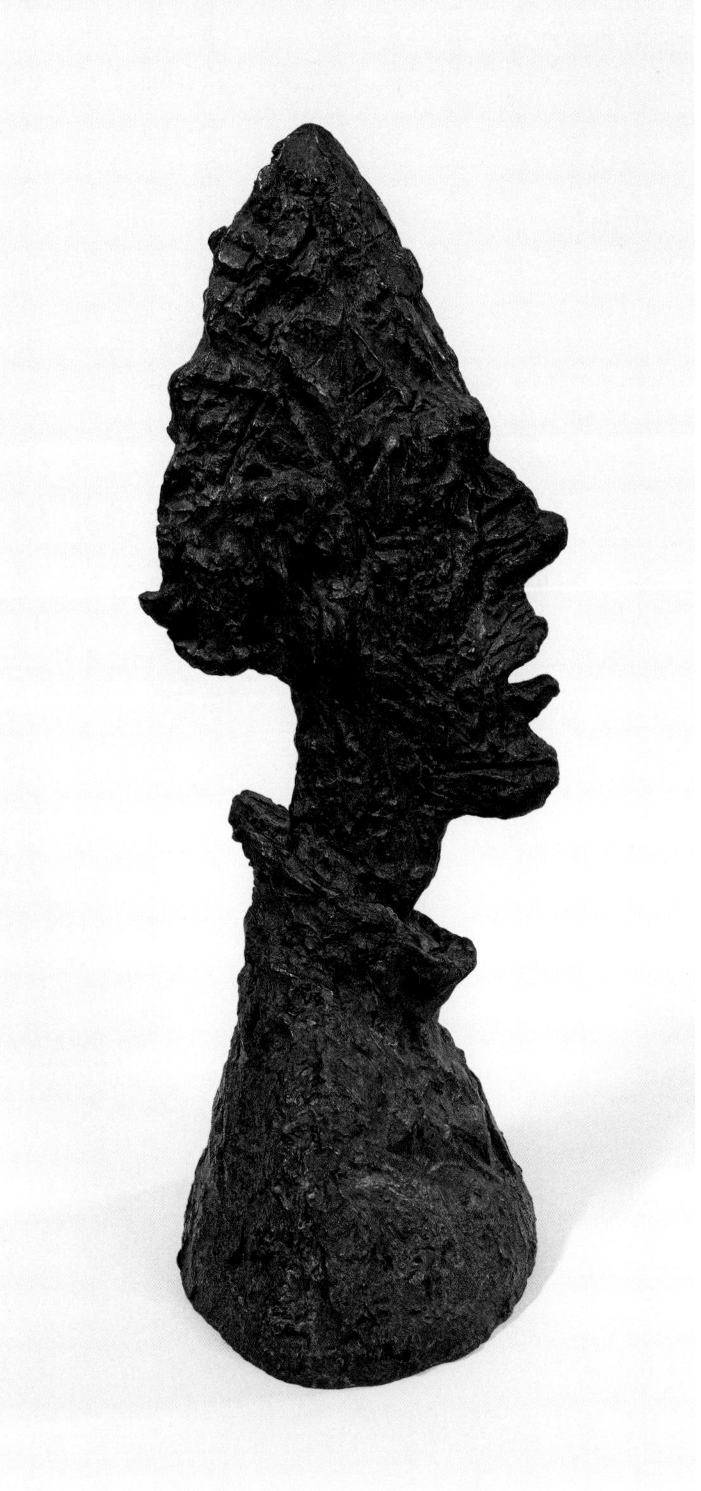

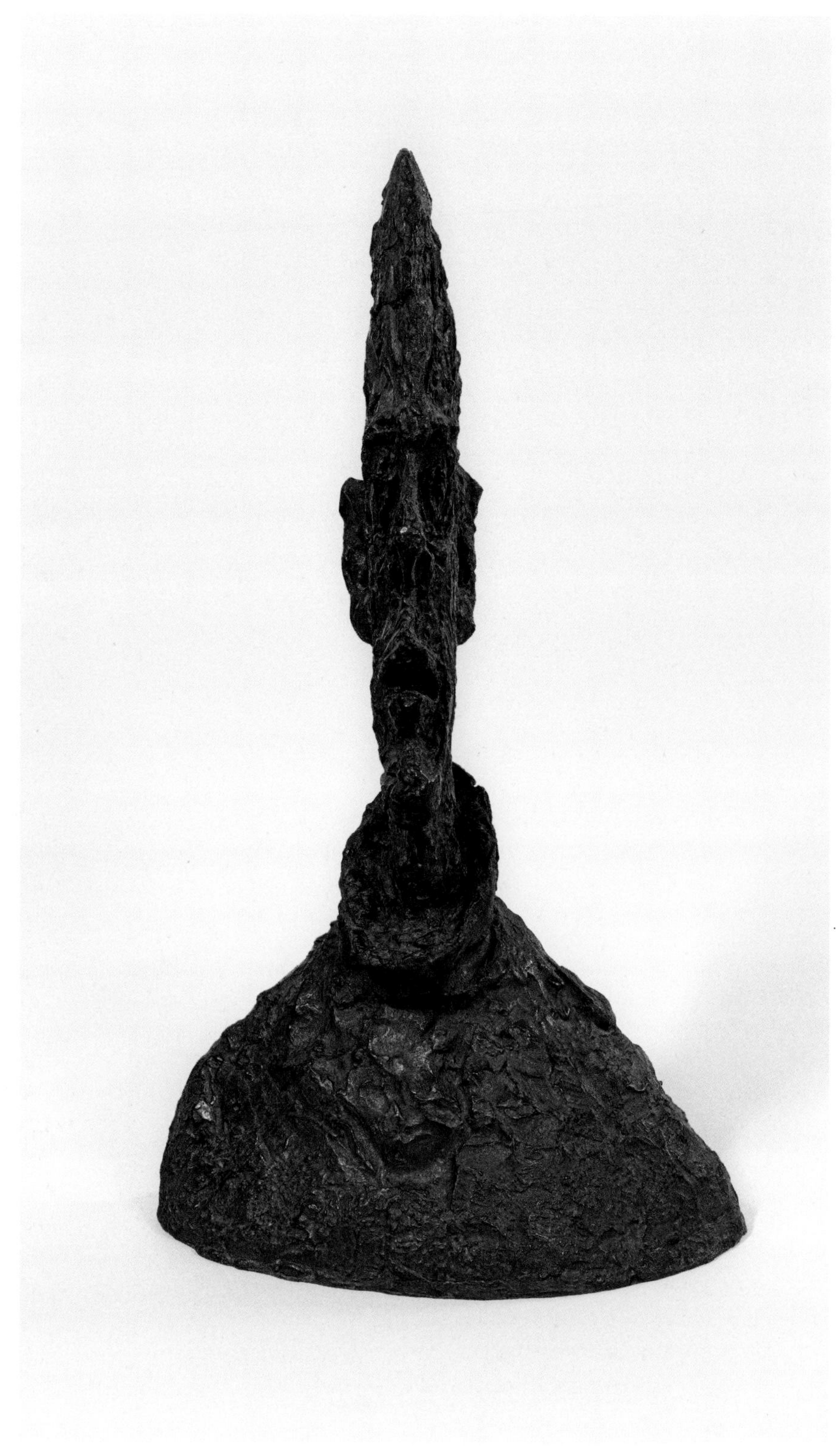

***Bust of a Man*, The Chariot, Head on a Base, *Head of Pierre Loeb for* Regard sur la peinture, 1949–50**
Pencil on paper; 21.7 x 17.5 cm.
Fondation Giacometti

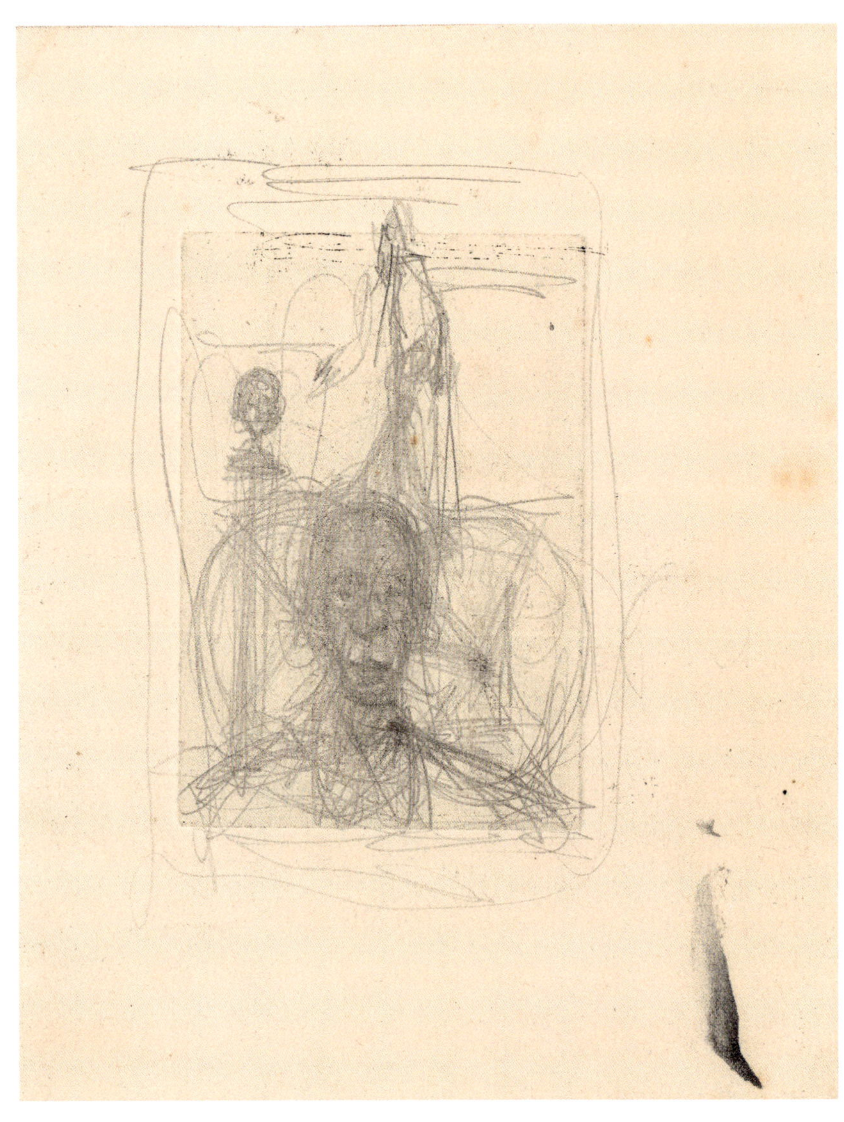

Man Crossing a Square on a Sunny Morning *and* The Chariot, 1957
Blue ink on notepaper;
21 x 26.9 cm.
Fondation Giacometti

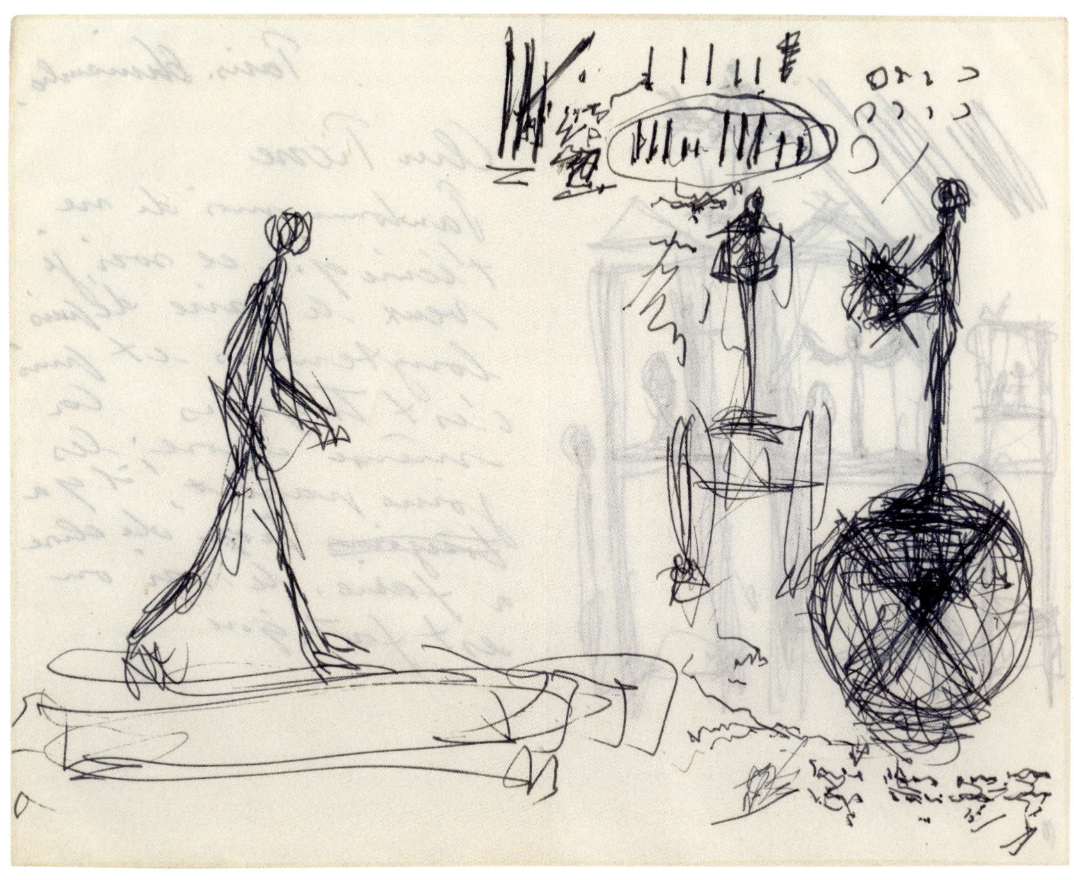

On Solid Ground

ROMAIN PERRIN

***Head of a Woman on a Double Base* in plaster, c. 1946**
Anonymous photographer. Archives, Fondation Giacometti

Alberto Giacometti's sculptures not only impose on the spectator a certain way of looking, because their scale is no longer connected to their environment, but they also show the result of the artist's direct perception. Even though the latter relates to his interest in the way his works were displayed, he tended to leave it to the gallery owners or museum curators. Giacometti seems to have been less concerned about the process of exhibiting his sculptures than about the view they generated. Thus, he began working on the base, the traditional element of the presentation of a statue, whose integration into the piece itself modifies its perception.

If most of the sculptures of the Surrealist period were identified as objects, and consequently did not necessitate bases, the statuettes made in the 1940s, because of their small size, needed to be placed on one, so that they could be seen. Giacometti explained to journalist Pierre Dumayet in 1963 that if he had wanted to make a sculpture of his friend Isabel Nicholas as he saw her on boulevard Saint-Michel one night in 1937—that is, very small—he would have "made a huge pedestal for the whole scene to correspond to his vision."[1] The base is the element that enables the artist to both compensate for the scale of the sculpture and form a device that highlights the work, to the point of making it appear monumental (pages 151, 152). But because of that play with proportions, those statues were not accepted by the commission of the Swiss Pavilion (his brother Bruno, an architect, was a member) for the exhibition of the arts of textile and fashion in Zurich in 1939. Giacometti had made a very small sculpture on a big base that was mistaken for a provocation. In a letter to his family, the artist mentioned this sculpture, saying that it "can make a square meter look vast."[2]

The need to place the figures in a fictional environment drove Giacometti to conceive specific elements of presentation. Thus, the boards, tables, and cages of the 1950s offer a parallel reality, that of the sculptures. Until that time, they burst into the realm of the spectator. From the end of the 1950s, the base of a bust, originally in plaster, was cast with it in bronze, becoming an element of the sculpture, having been taken into consideration by the artist and no longer added as an afterthought (page 156). Giacometti took his work on bases as far as to make them into columns and steles on which the busts were placed at human height (page 157). In that respect he joined Auguste Rodin and the experimentations of Constantin Brancusi. His signature on the base-column evidently shows that the element was planned by the artist from the start.

In his text on Giacometti's studio, Jean Genet describes "the anxiety, the enchantment that comes from that fabulous club-foot."[3] The author refers to the "strange 'pieds' [feet] or pedestals" that form a base of a statue. The theme of the relationship between figure and ground, the connection between a vertical and a horizontal axis, is explored in *Women of Venice* (page 142), as well as in *Standing Woman* and in *Figurines* (pages 158, 159). There is some attempt at eliminating the pedestal: their legs with joined feet melt naturally into the base that supports them, giving the impression that the figures emerge from it like trees, strongly rooted in the ground.

1. Alberto Giacometti, "Le drame d'un réducteur de tête," conversation with Pierre Dumayet, *Le Nouveau Candide*, no. 110 (June 6–13, 1963); reprinted in Giacometti, *Why I am a sculptor* (Paris: Hermann and Fondation Giacometti, 2017), 47.

2. Giacometti to his family, n.d. [August 1939], repr. in Serena Bucalo-Mussely, *Lettres d'Alberto Giacometti à sa famille*, vol. 2, *L'Artiste confirmé, 1930–1945* (Paris: Bernard Chauveau Éditions; Fondation Giacometti, 2021), 66.

3. Jean Genet, *L'Atelier d'Alberto Giacometti* (Paris: L'Arbalète, 1963), n.p.

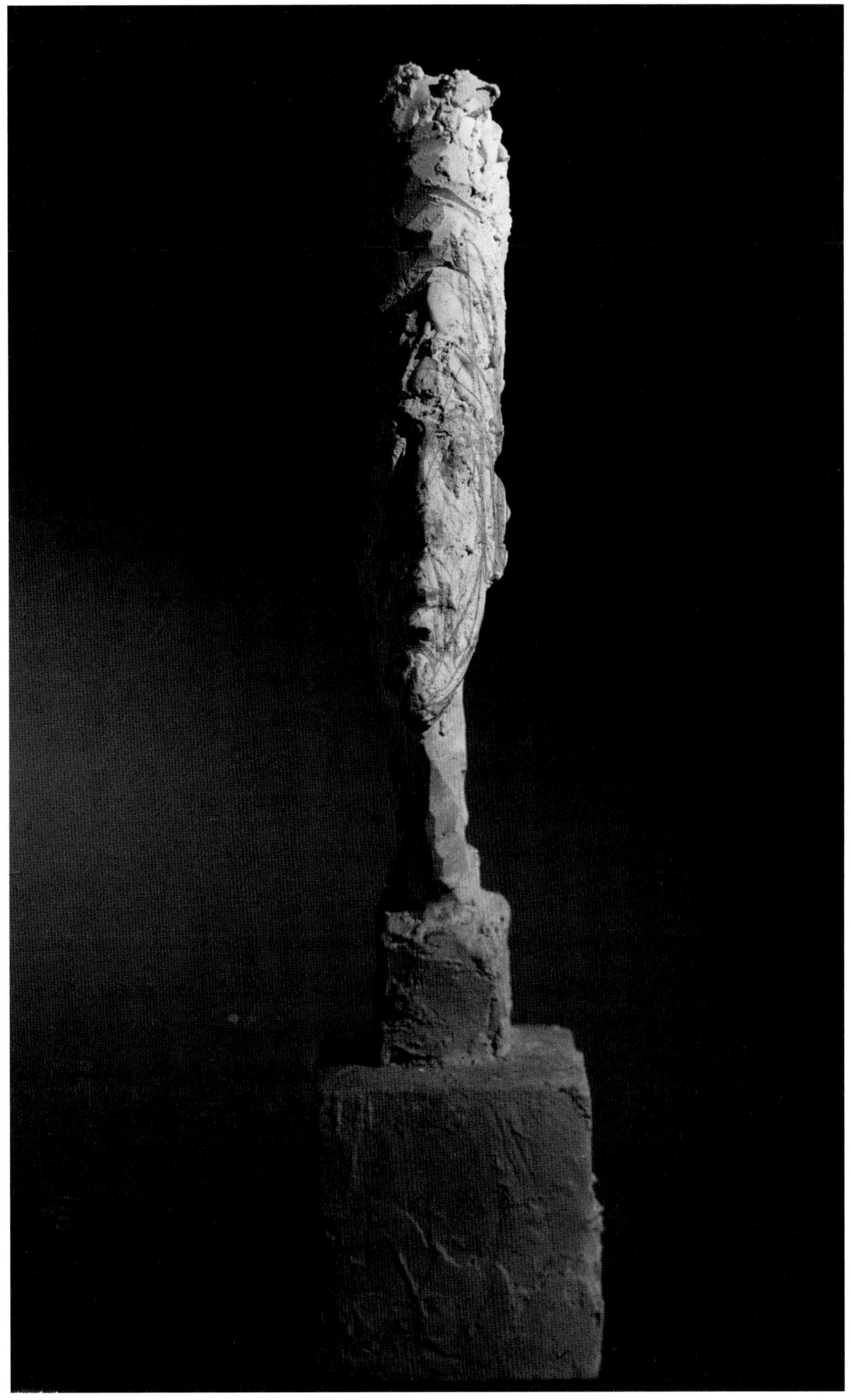

***Diane Bataille*, c. 1947**
Bronze; 47.7 x 13.1 x 13 cm.
Fondation Giacometti

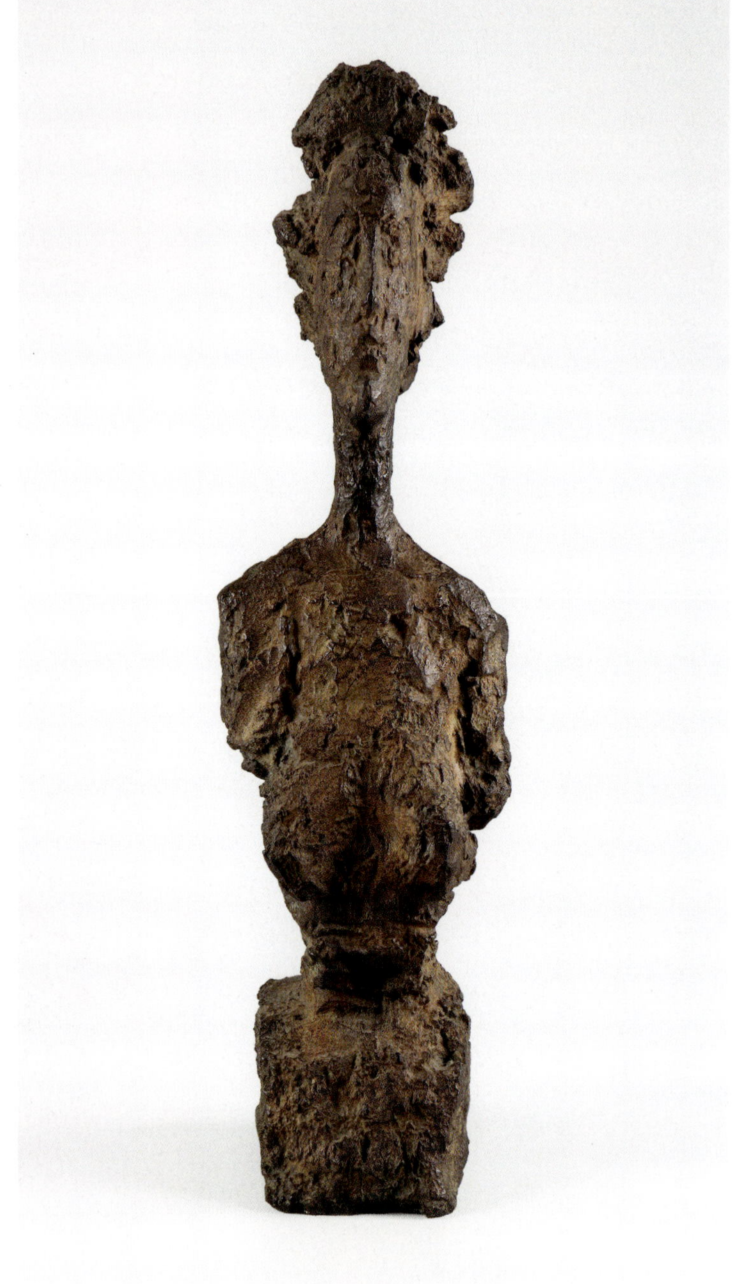

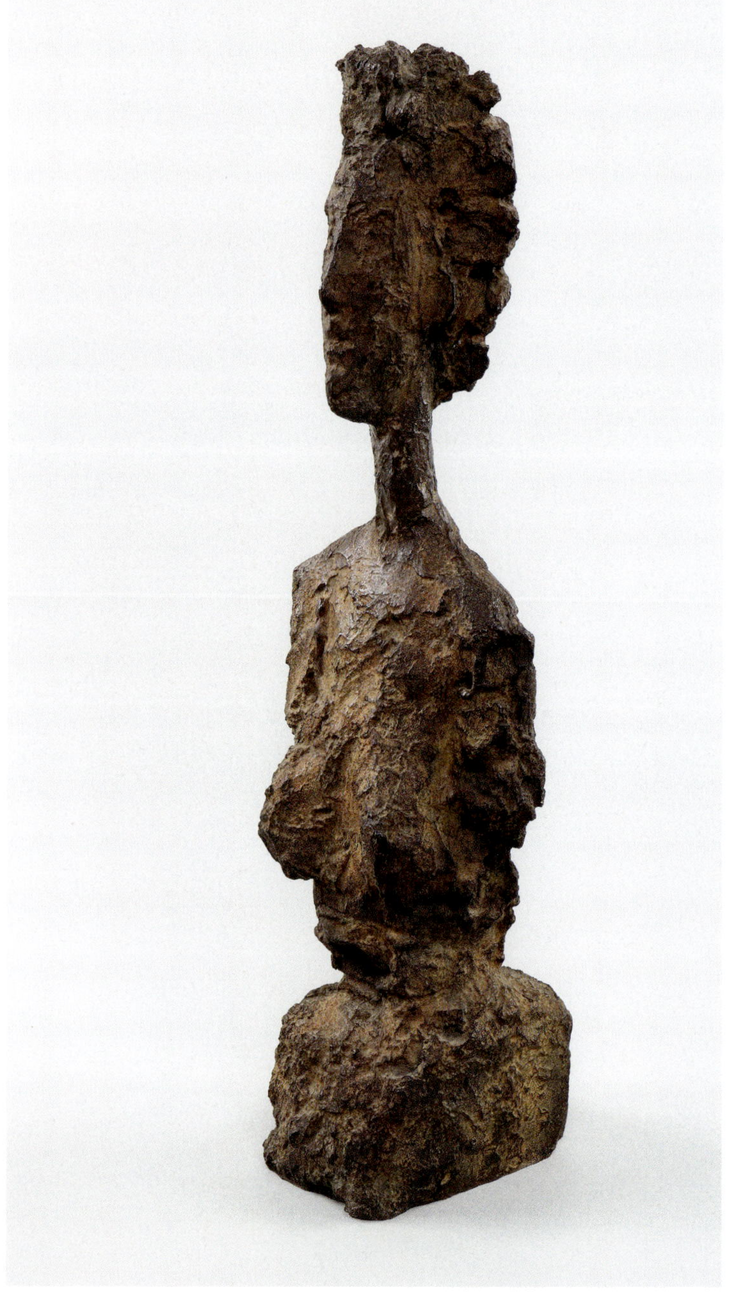

Bust of a Man on a Base,
c. 1947
Bronze; 54.5 x 11.4 x 10.1 cm.
Fondation Giacometti

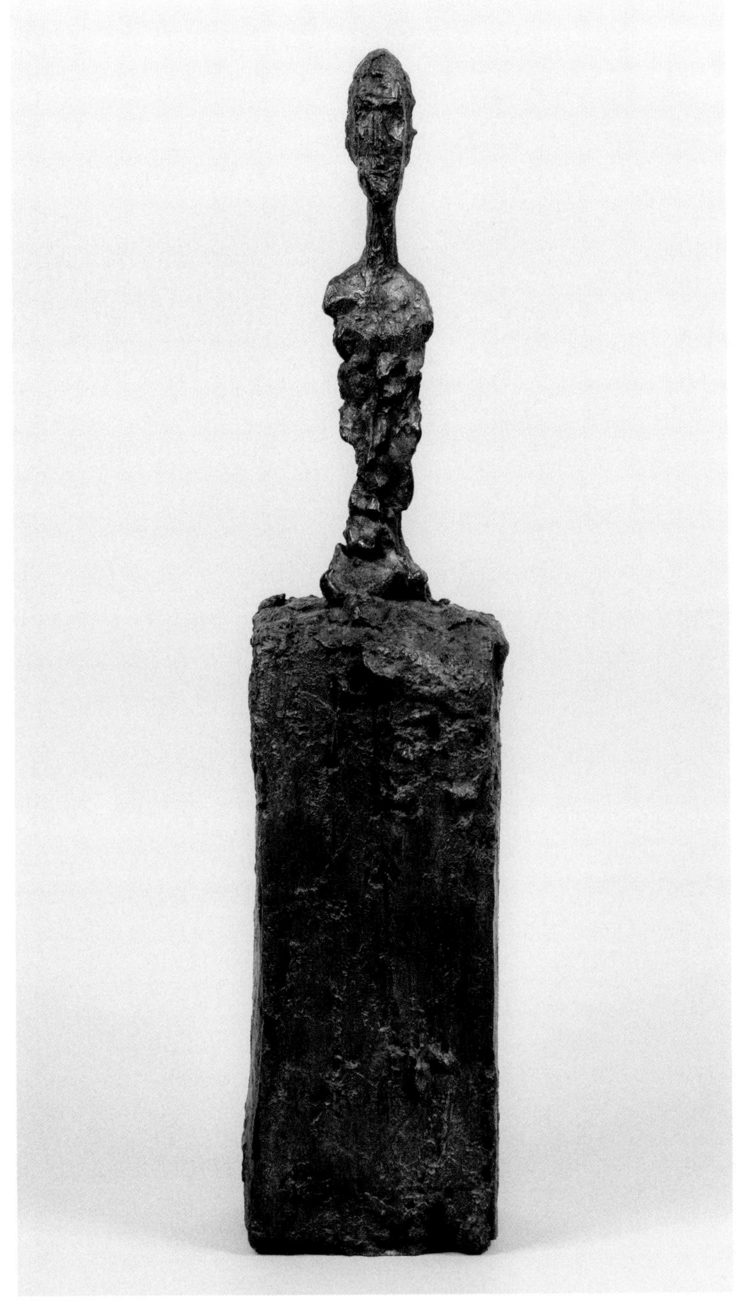

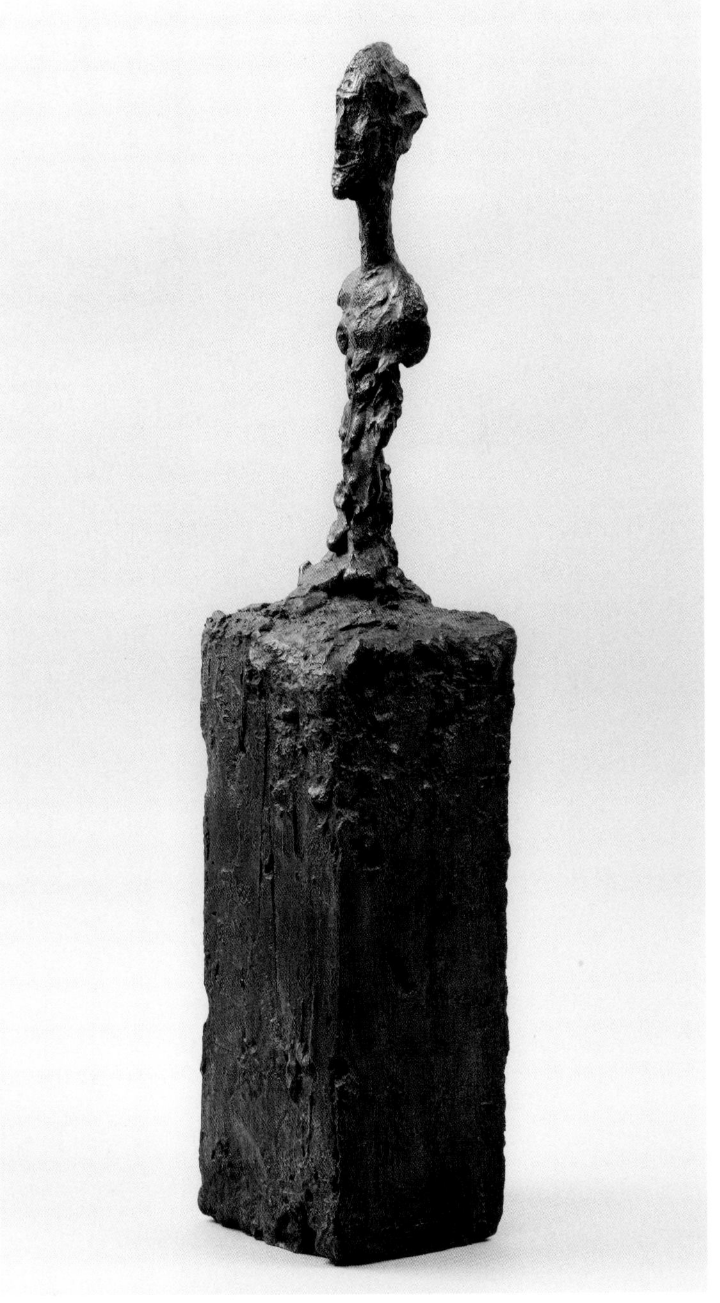

Bust of a Man on a Base,
c. 1948
Bronze; 36.4 x 11.6 x 10.7 cm.
Fondation Giacometti

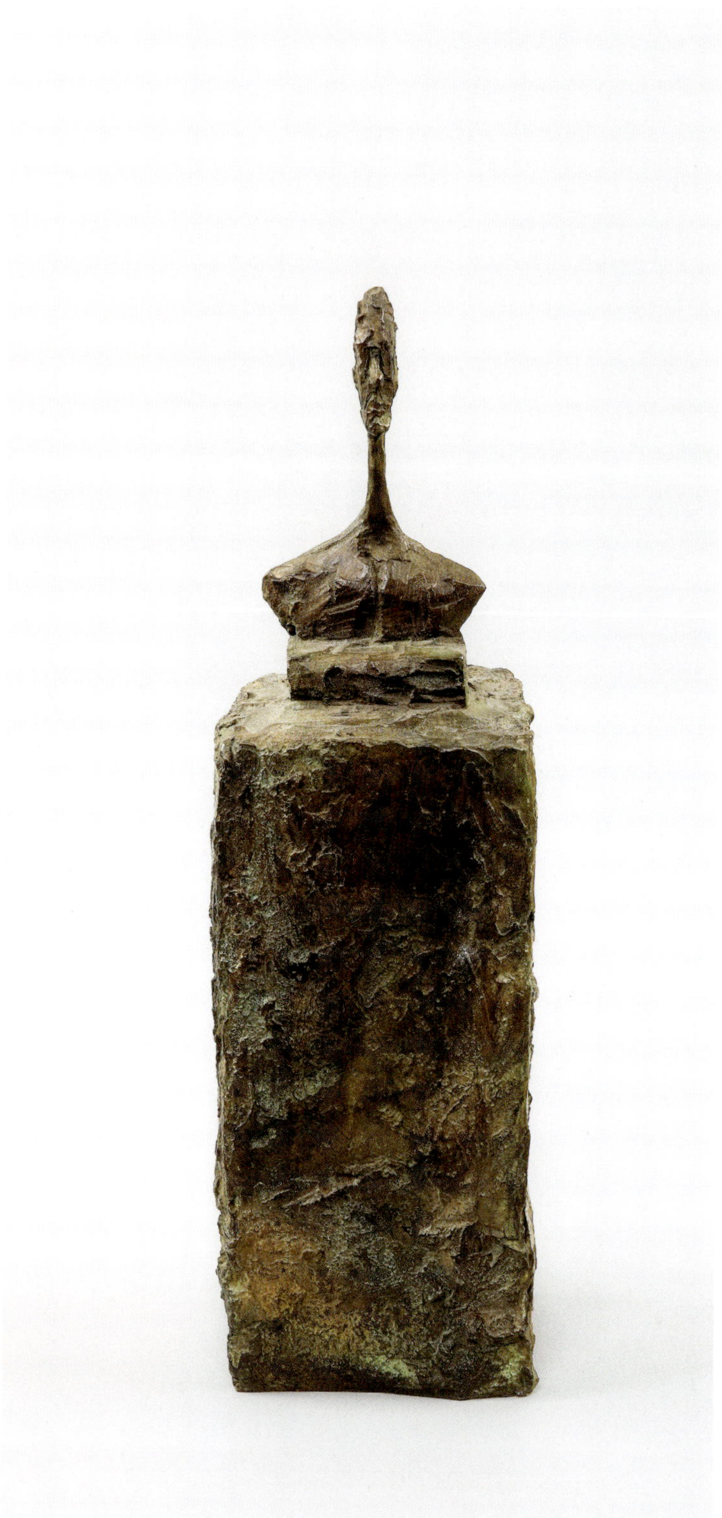

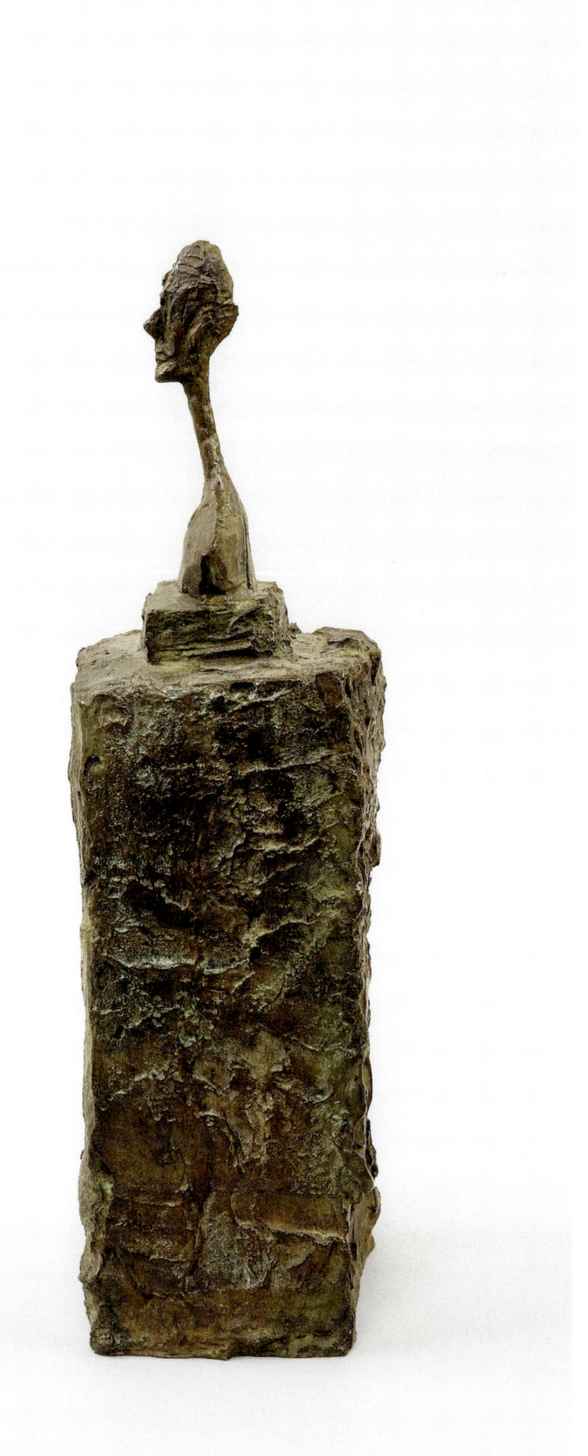

***Bust of a Man*, c. 1950**
Bronze; 56 x 15.5 x 16.7 cm.
Fondation Giacometti

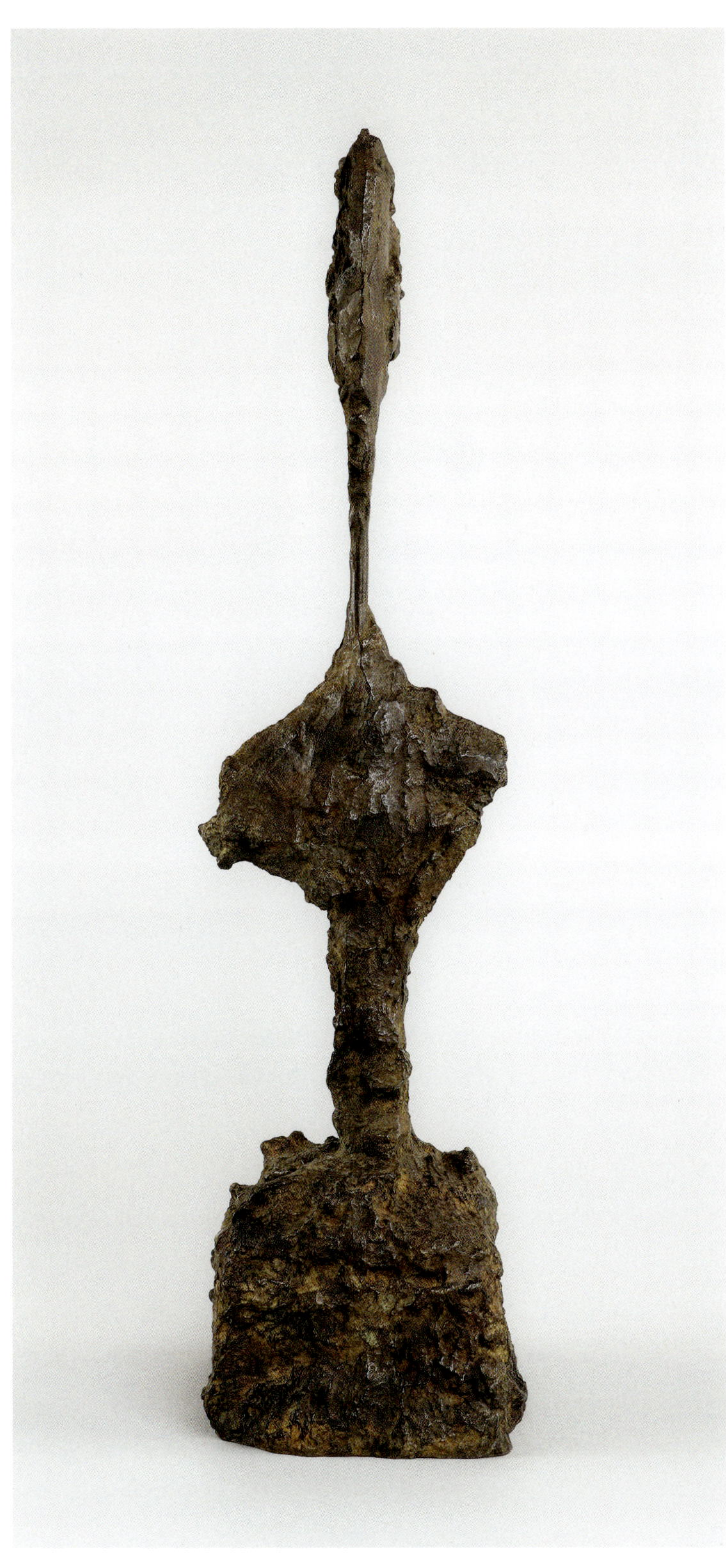

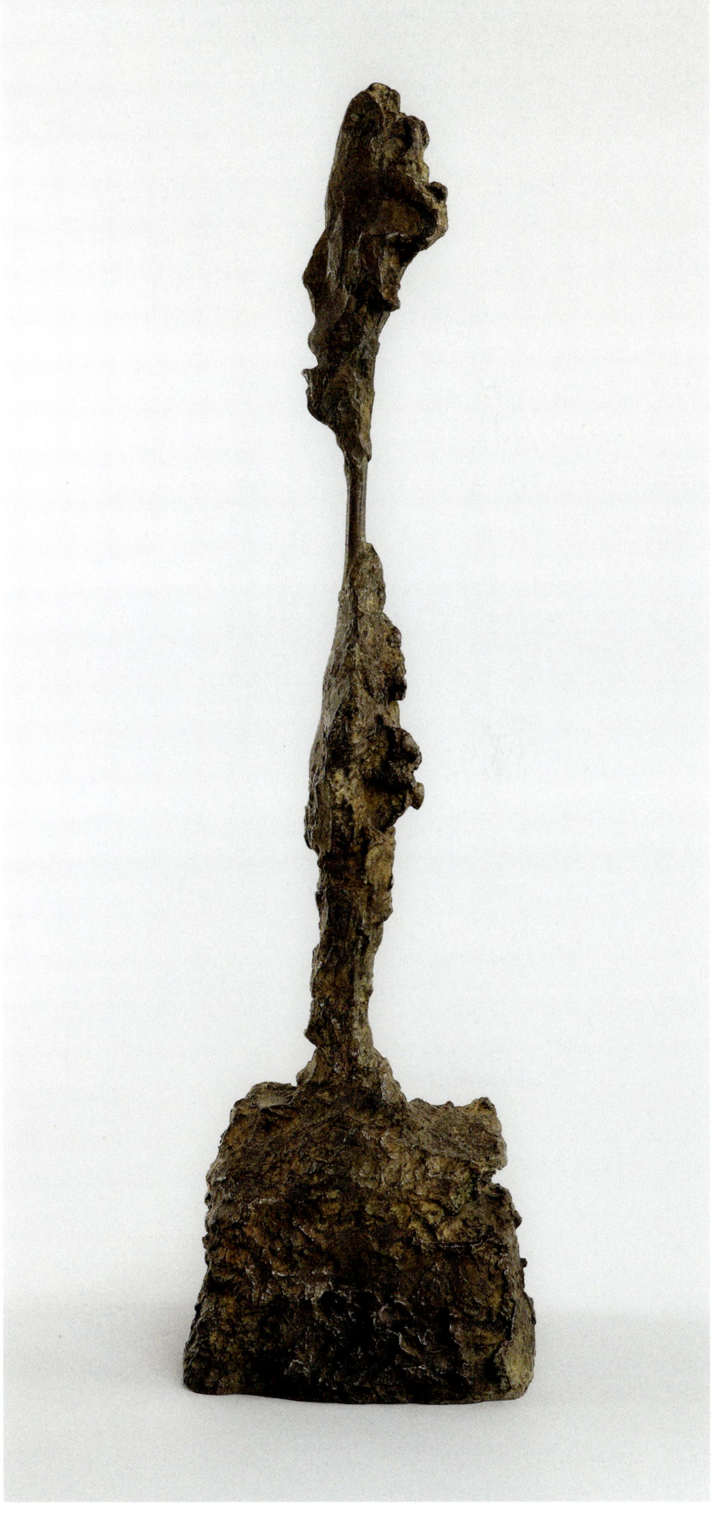

***Standing Nude on a Cubic Base*, 1953**
Bronze; 43.3 x 11.5 x 10.4 cm.
Fondation Giacometti

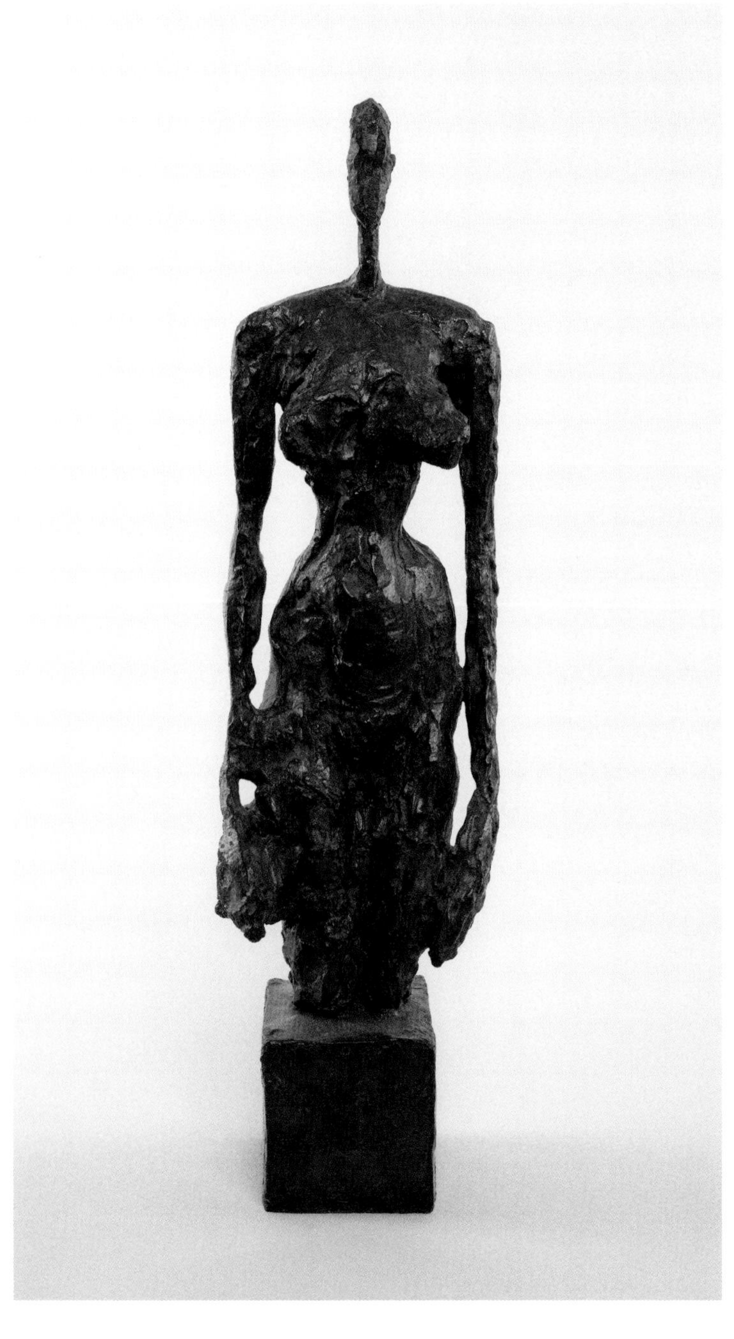

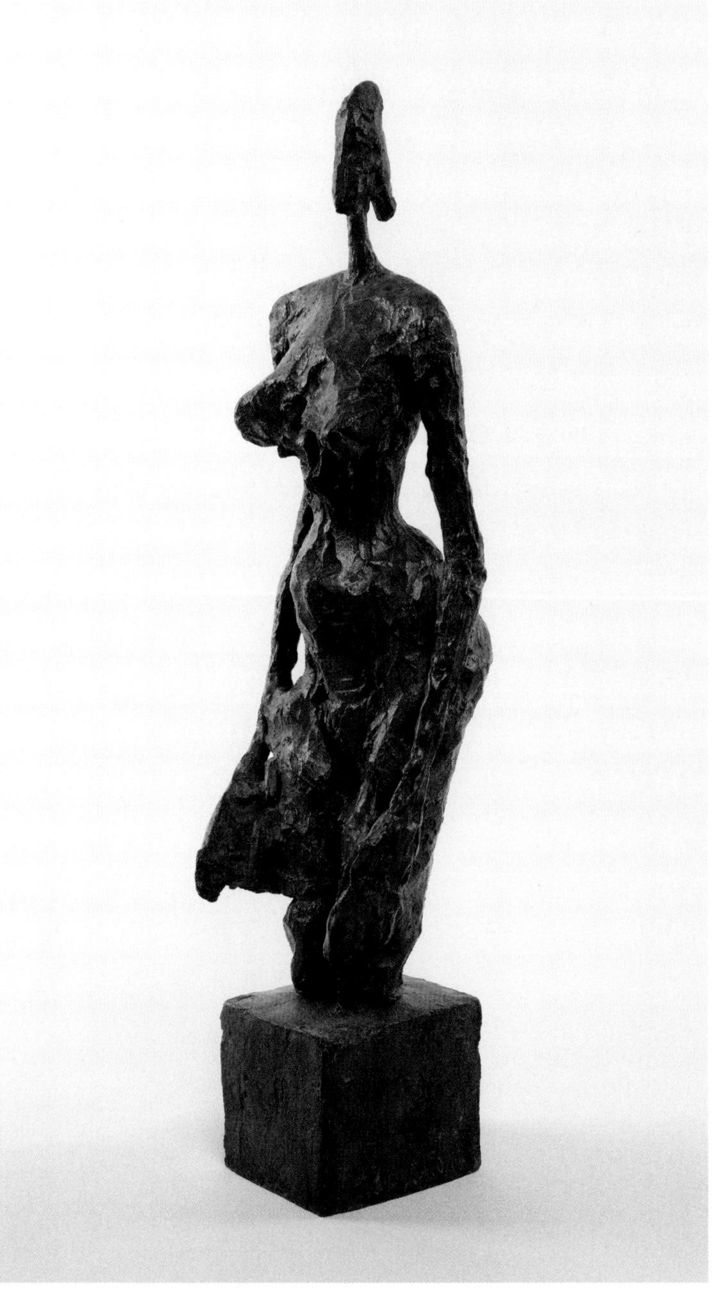

***Annette Standing*, c. 1954**
Bronze; 47.5 x 10.5 x 20.3 cm.
Fondation Giacometti

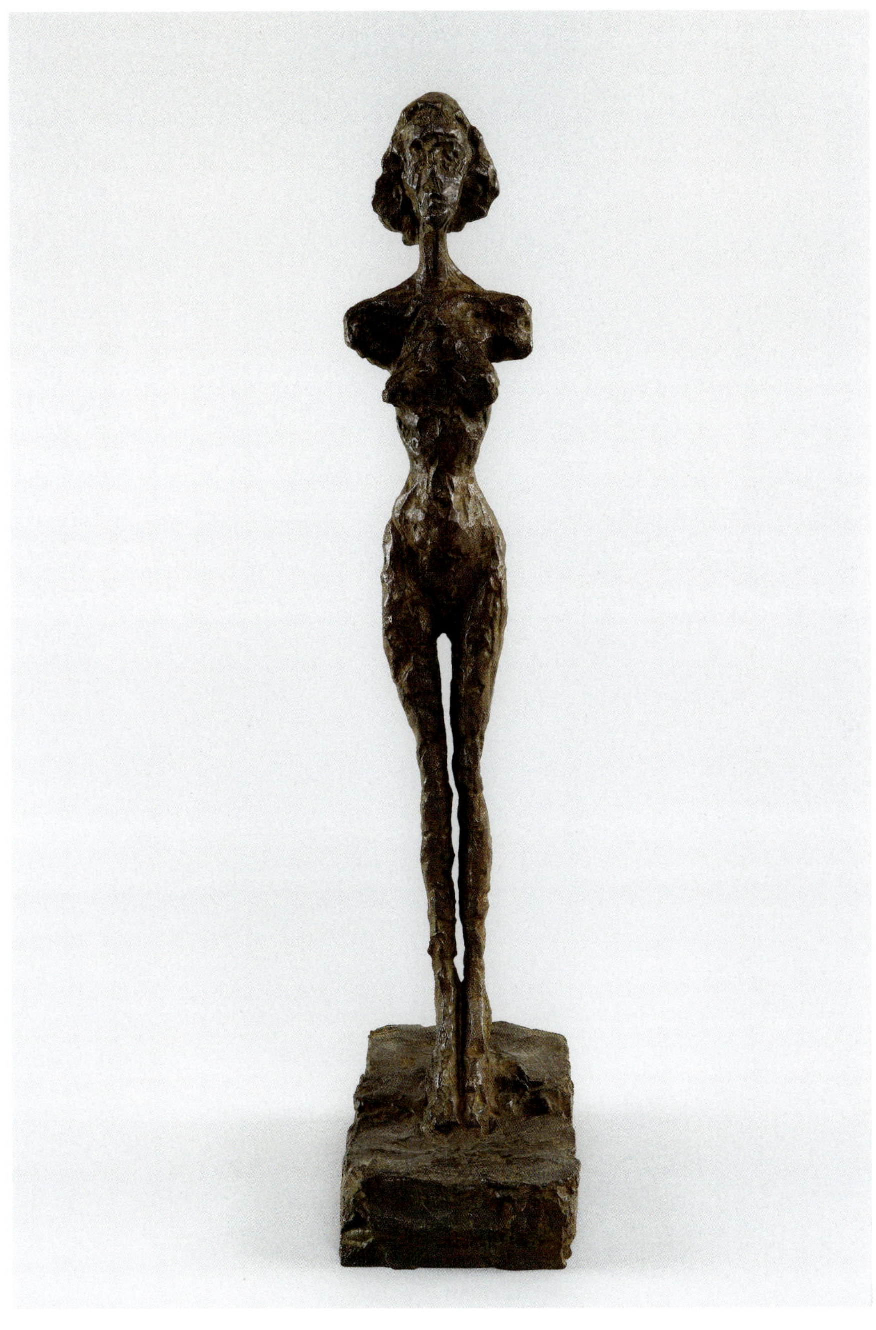

***Head on a Base* (known as *Head without Skull*), c. 1958**
Bronze; 43.3 x 8.1 x 10.6 cm.
Fondation Giacometti

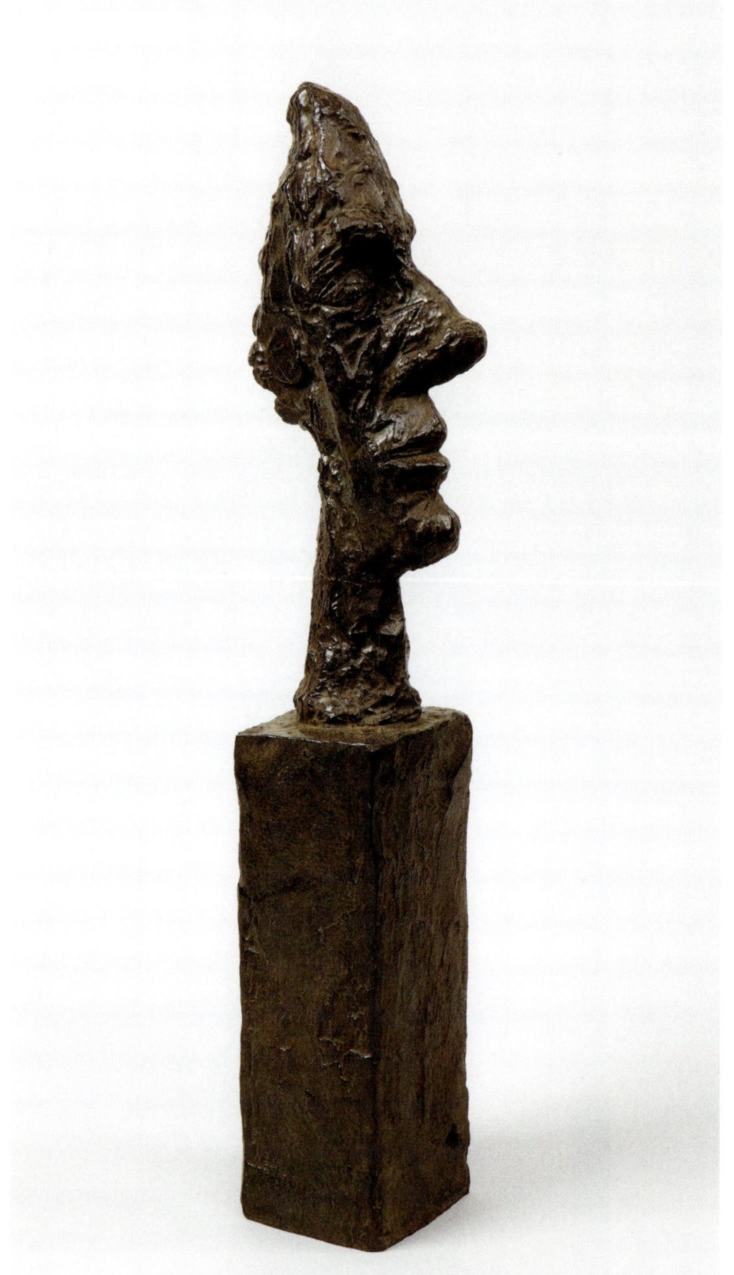

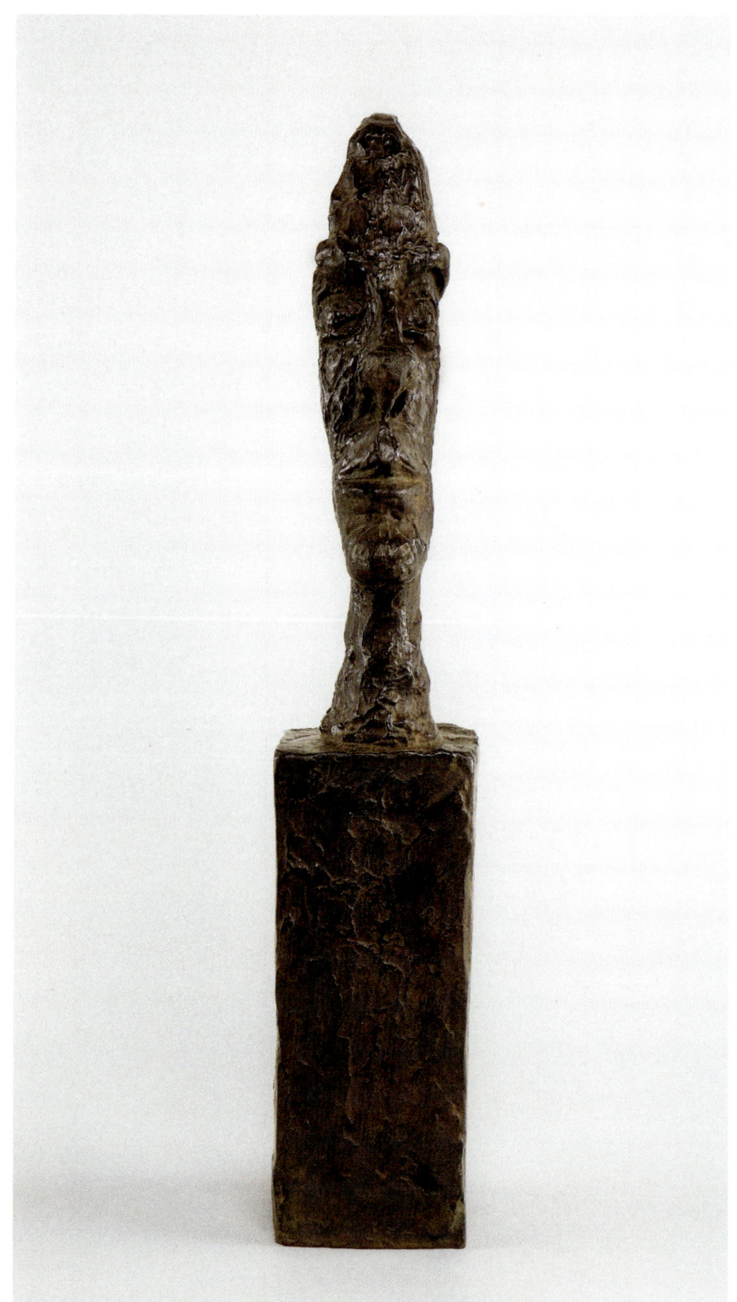

***Small Bust on a Stand,* **
1951–52
Bronze; 152.2 x 21.2 x 22.6 cm.
Fondation Giacometti

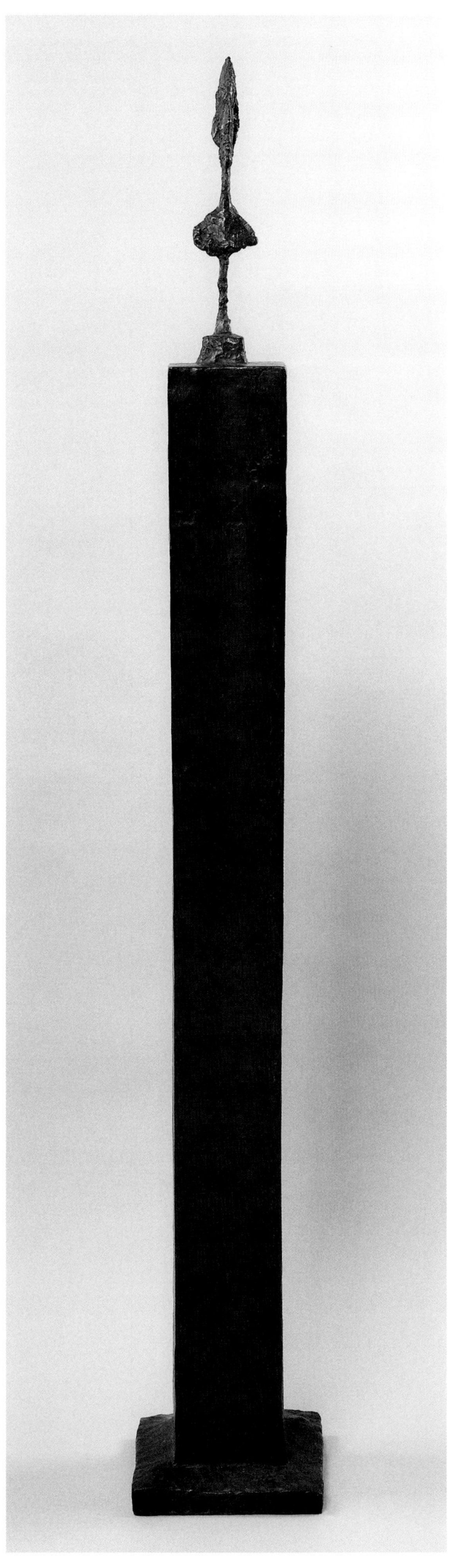

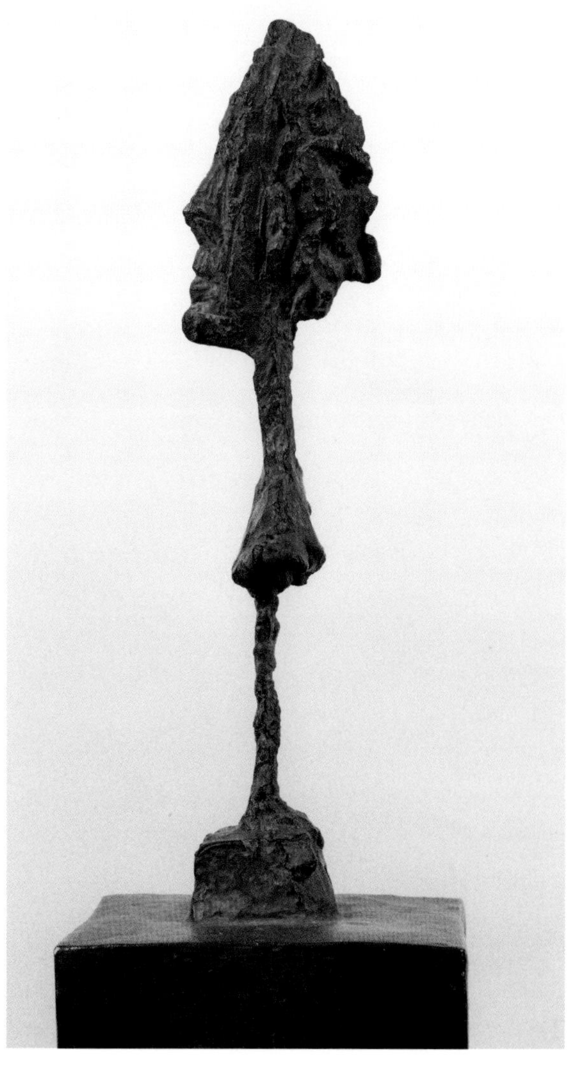

***Standing Woman*, c. 1961**
Bronze; 45.4 x 8.1 x 11.2 cm.
Fondation Giacometti

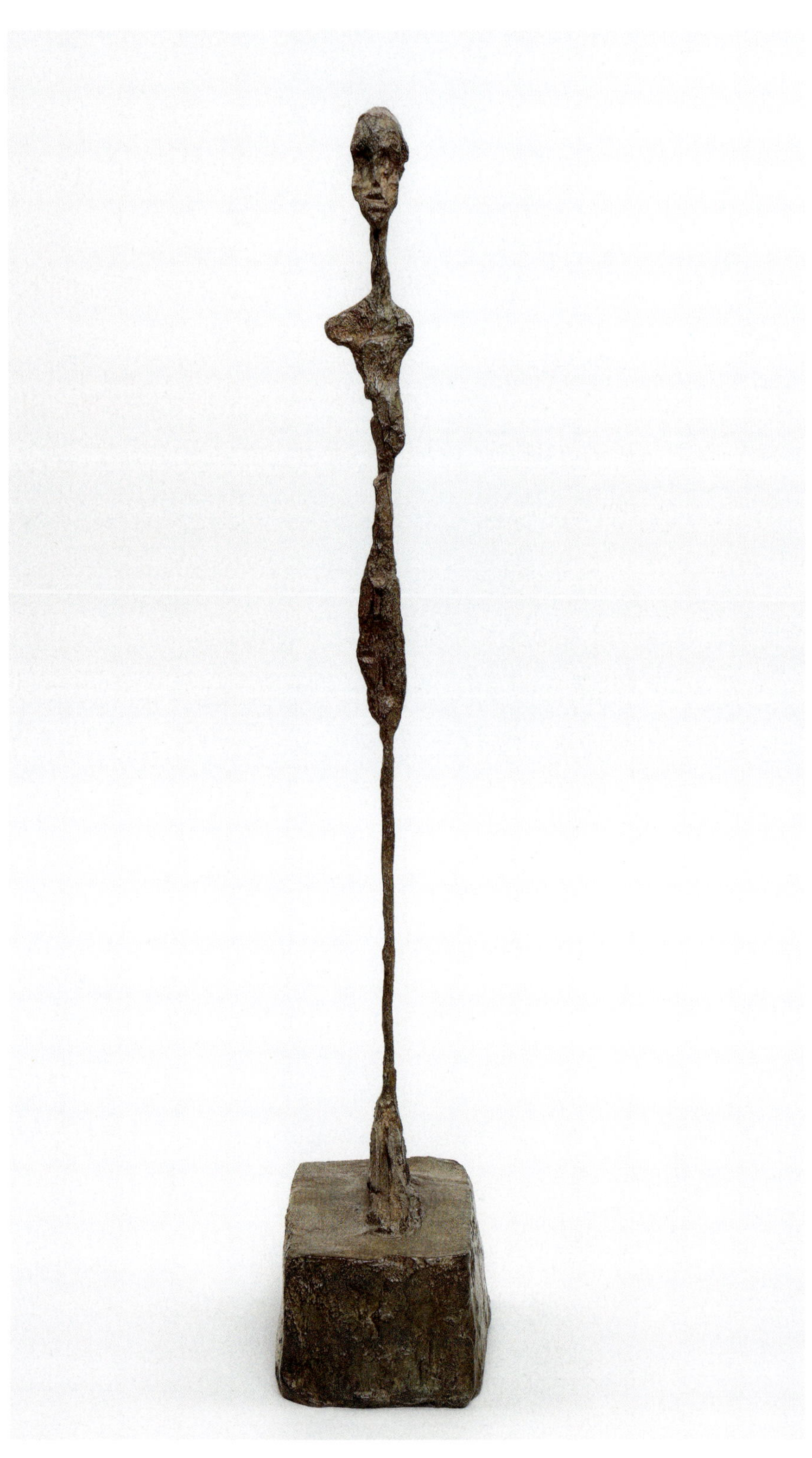

***Figurine of London I*, 1965**
Bronze; 26.5 x 9 x 13.5 cm.
Fondation Giacometti

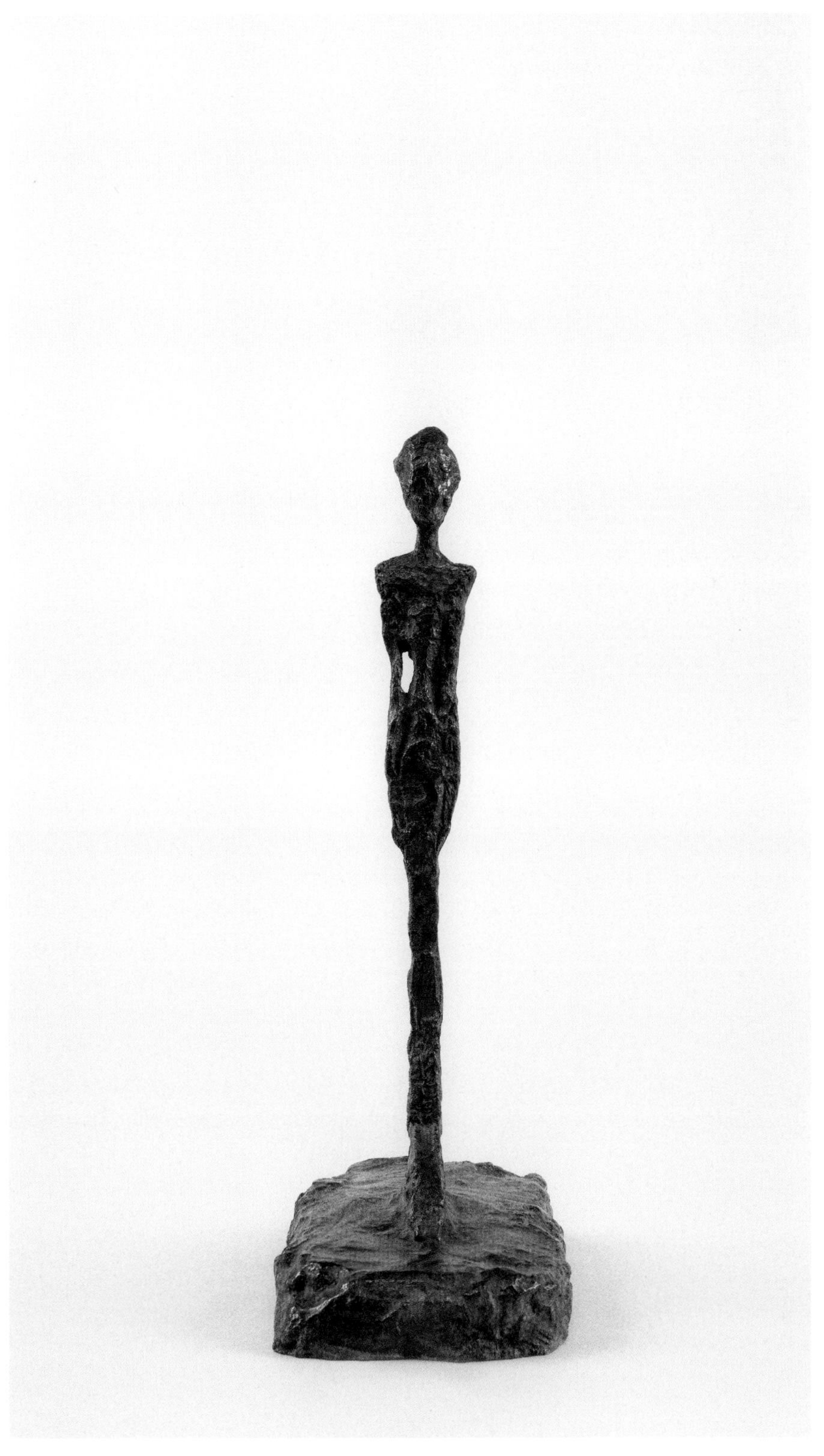

The Artist, the Wife, and the Brother

ROMAIN PERRIN

Alberto Giacometti, his brother Diego, and wife, Annette, in his Paris studio, 1951
Alexander Liberman (Ukrainian American, 1912–1999). Alexander Liberman Photography Archive. Getty Research Institute, Los Angeles, 2000.R.19. © J. Paul Getty Trust

Among modern artists, Alberto Giacometti was without question one who worked with the smallest number of models. His brother Diego and his wife, Annette, appear the most, being the closest to him. In addition, there were his friends, including philosopher Isaku Yanaihara, doctor Theodore Fraenkel, artist Isabel Nicholas, and his mistress, Caroline, as well as some intellectual companions such as Jean Genet and Simone de Beauvoir, and, more rarely still, some collectors. Diego and Annette sat for Giacometti so many times that their features seem to resurface unconsciously beneath his hand whenever he drew or sculpted.

In the monograph that poet Jacques Dupin published in 1962, he offered an explanation to that never-ending return to two members of the artist's inner circle:

> If he were to change models more often, Giacometti would perhaps feel less keenly the necessity to change himself, that is, to progress, to go into depth with each new work. . . . The insistent, obsessive questioning of a human being (or any other subject) ends with stripping what is familiar in them to unveil the stranger within. And the model will let themself be more docilely stripped when the painter holds on less to superficial details, particularities that could distract him in a person he's just met.[1]

The objective Giacometti set for himself was extremely demanding, for it necessitated a regularity in the long term as well as a huge effort on the part of the models who had to stay still, silent, barely breathing. Making oneself available to sit for long hours and tolerating the attitude of the artist—who, exhausted, was at times overwhelmed by sudden despair when he felt his work eluded him—meant that only his brother and his wife could be regular models. Alexander Liberman's photographs, published in *Vogue* in 1955, show that complicit trio whose center was undoubtedly the artist himself.

Diego had been his model since his very first works as a youth in Stampa, and Annette sat for him in the second part of the artist's career, that of his maturity. In addition to the fundamental position of assistant to his brother, Diego was the person who sat the most and the longest, to the point where the physiognomy of his portrait seems etched in Alberto's mind, and resurfaces beneath his hand in numerous busts and heads made without a model: "When I sculpt, paint or draw, I always have him in mind."[2] The artist took Diego as a model when he returned to figuration after his Surrealist period.

Giacometti met Annette Arm in Geneva during the war. Twenty-two years his junior, the young woman came from a Swiss bourgeois family; she joined him in Paris in 1946 to settle at rue Hippolyte-Maindron, easily fitting into the working relationship of the two brothers. Beyond the endless sittings, Annette was important to Giacometti's daily life. Keeping things tidy and looking after the studio, she brought him, more than anyone else, stability when he was totally devoted to his work. At the sculptor's death, she oversaw his art legacy.

The busts of Diego and Annette exhibit the artist's struggle with the material and his perception of the model (pages 162, 163, 165, 166–67, 168). Through them, Giacometti experimented with the possibility of sculpting a portrait.

1. Jacques Dupin, *Alberto Giacometti* (Paris: Maeght, 1962), 76.

2. Alberto Giacometti, "Alberto Giacometti, Fragmente aus Tagebüchern," conversation with Gothard Jedlicka, *Neue Zurcher Zeitung* (April 5, 1964); reprinted in Giacometti, *I certainly practise painting* (Paris: Hermann and Fondation Giacometti, 2021), 12.

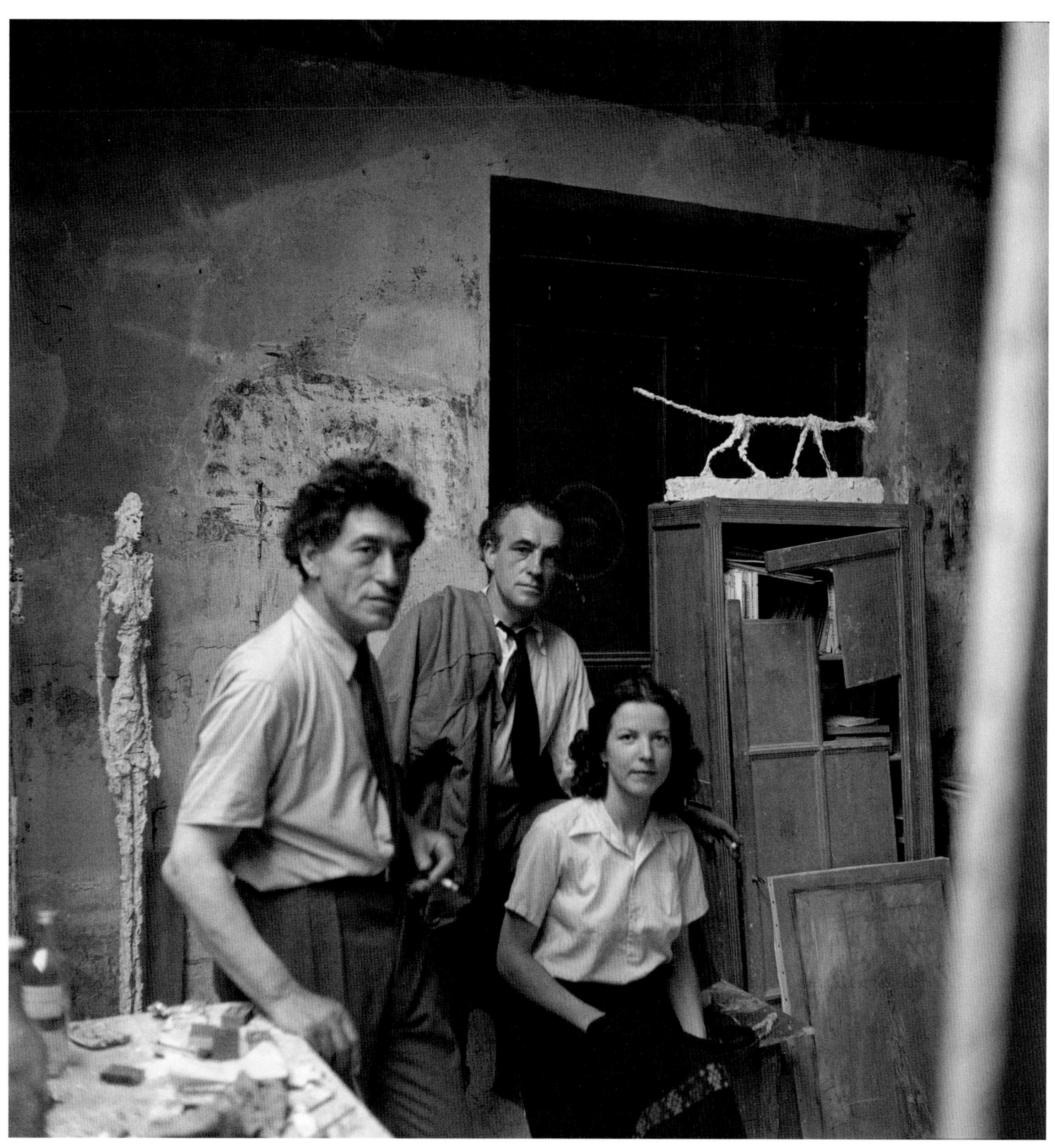

***Bust of Diego*, c. 1954**
Bronze; 25.9 x 20.3 x 11.7 cm.
Fondation Giacometti

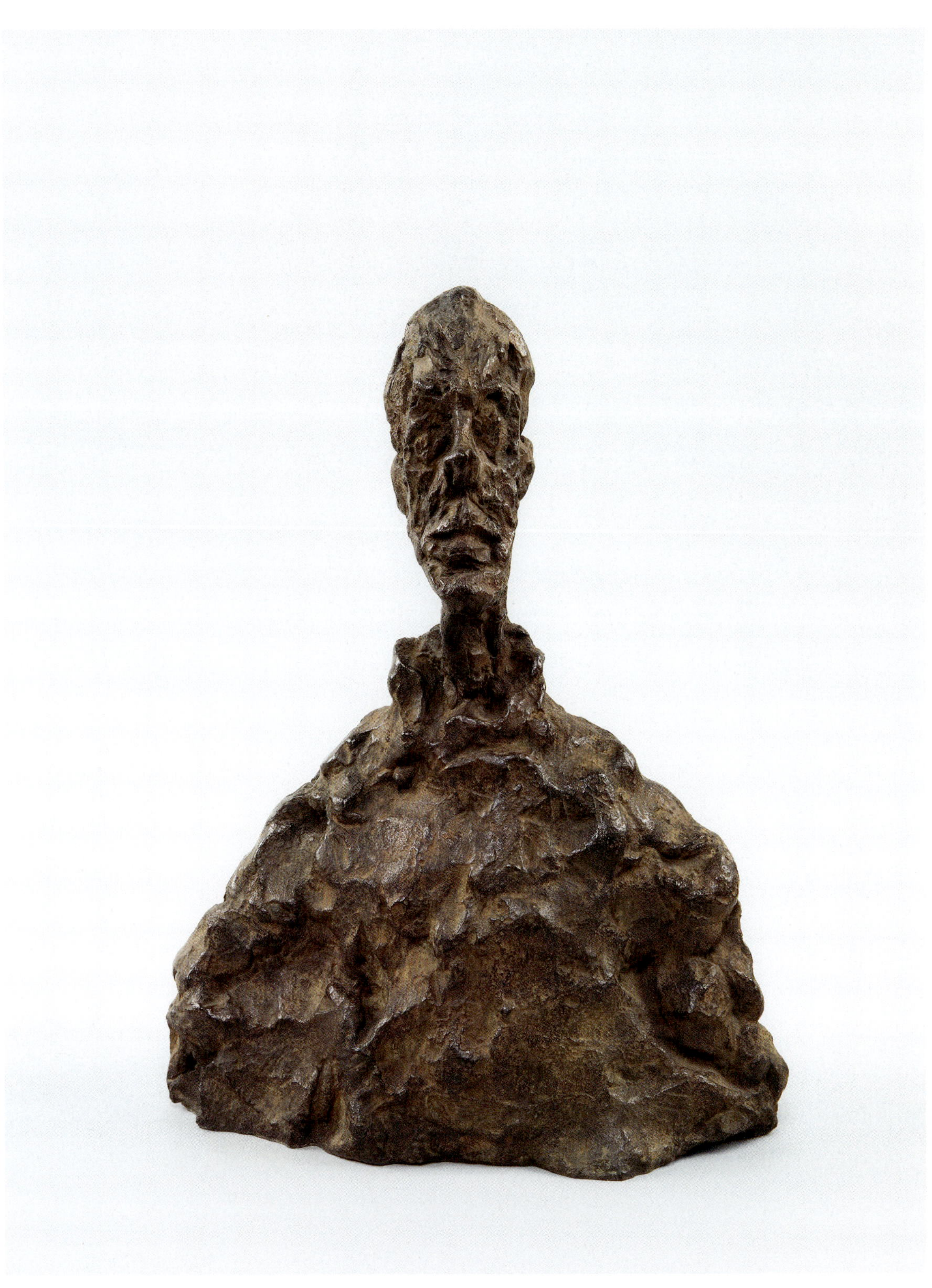

***Diego (Head with a Turtleneck)*, c. 1954**
Bronze; 33.4 x 12.5 x 14 cm.
Fondation Giacometti

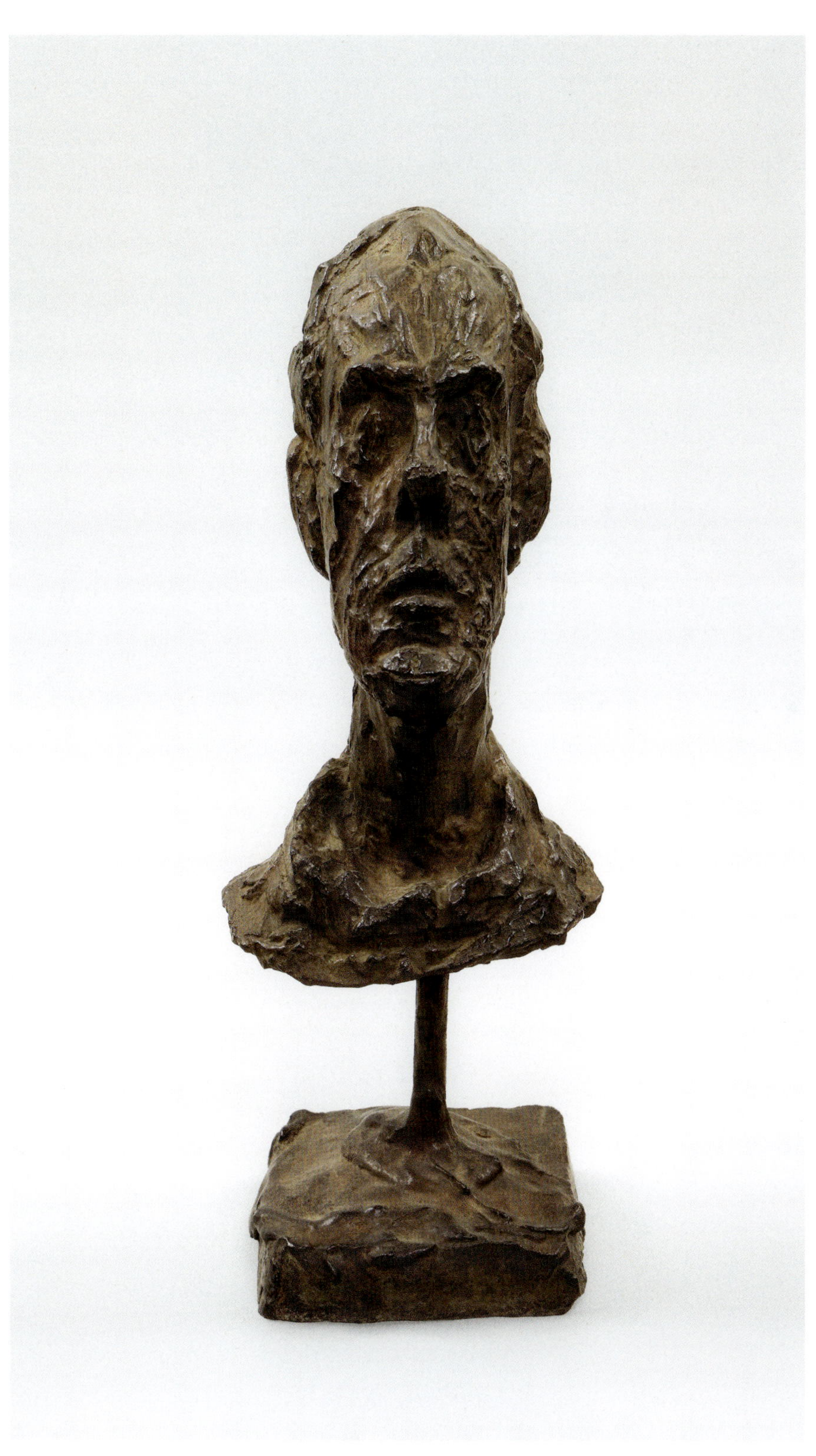

Alberto Giacometti painting Annette's portrait in the studio, 1951
Ernst Scheidegger.
Archives, Fondation Giacometti.

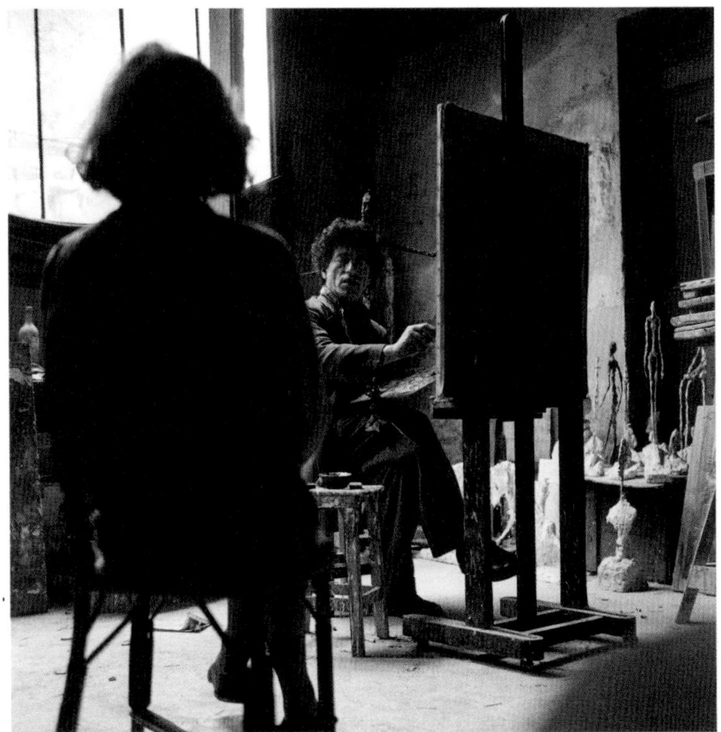

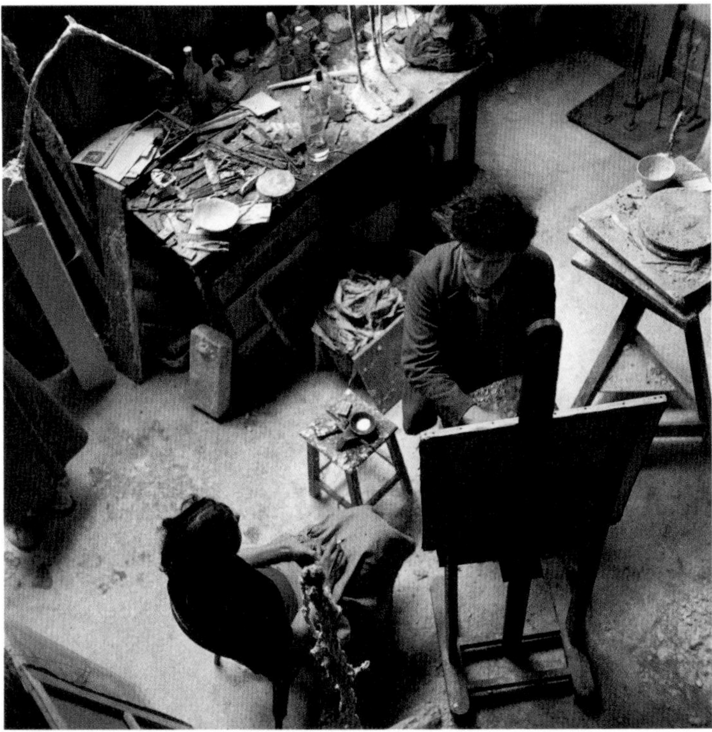

***Bust of Annette VIII*, 1962**
Bronze; 59 x 28.7 x 22.8 cm.
Fondation Giacometti

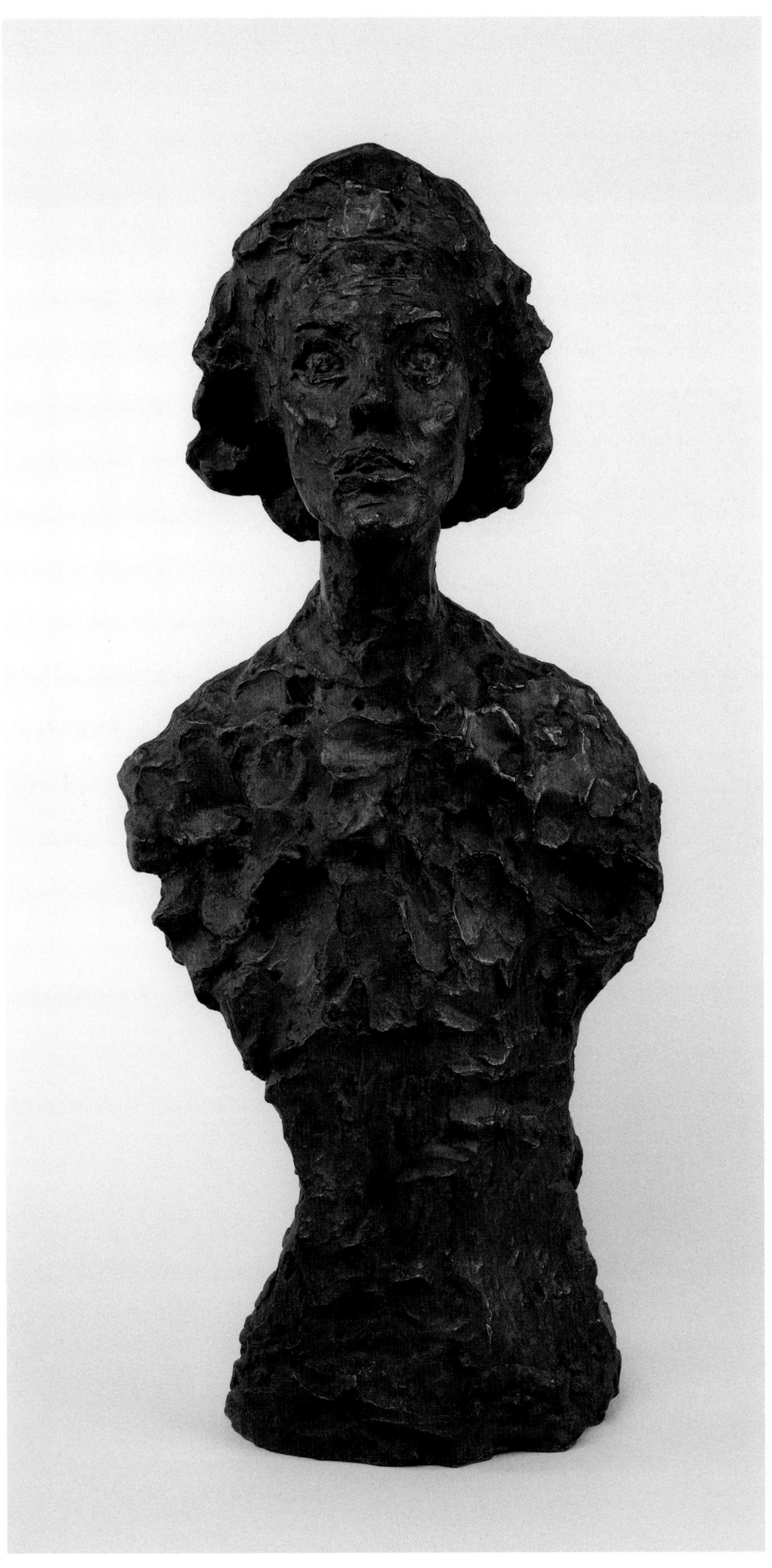

***Bust of Annette* (known as *Venice*), 1962**
Bronze; 46.2 x 26.5 x 16.2 cm.
Fondation Giacometti

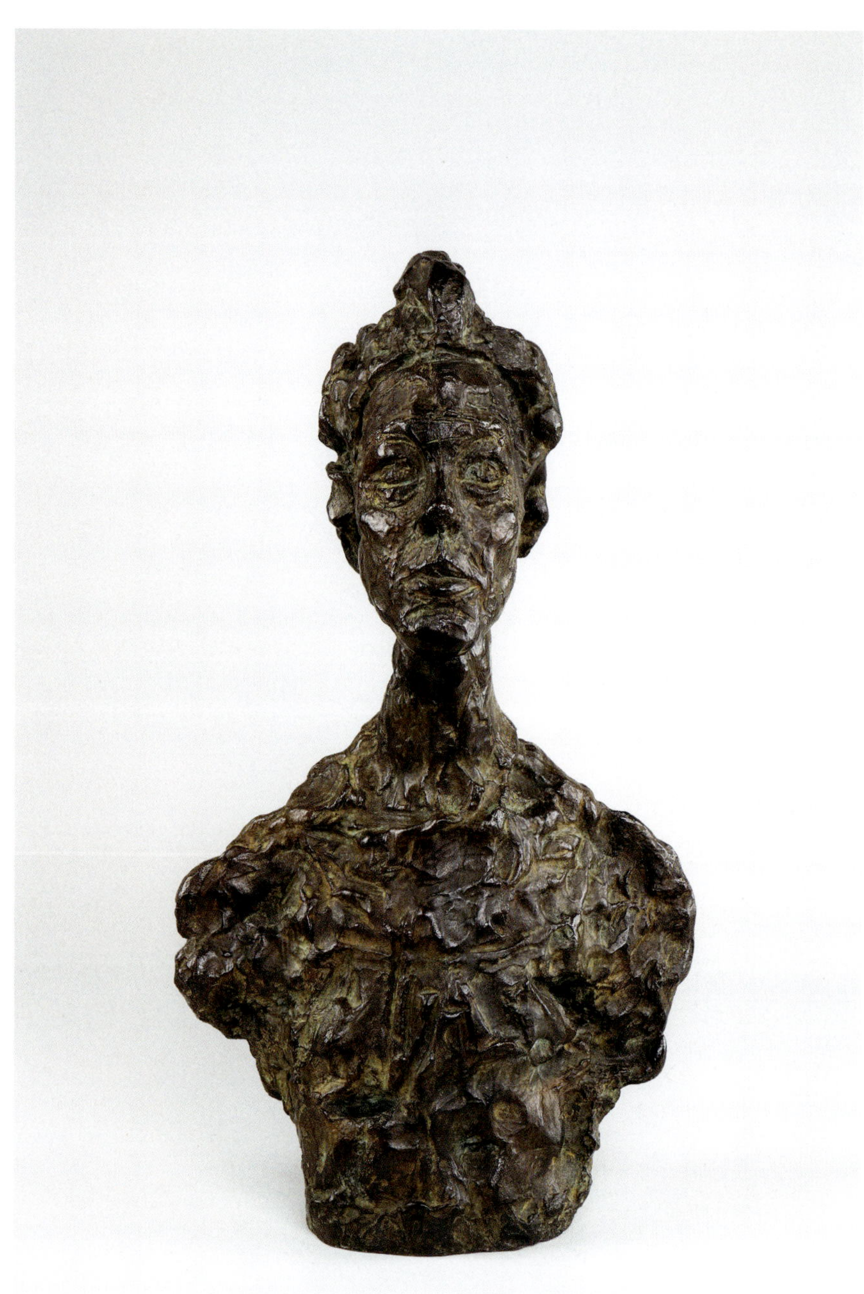

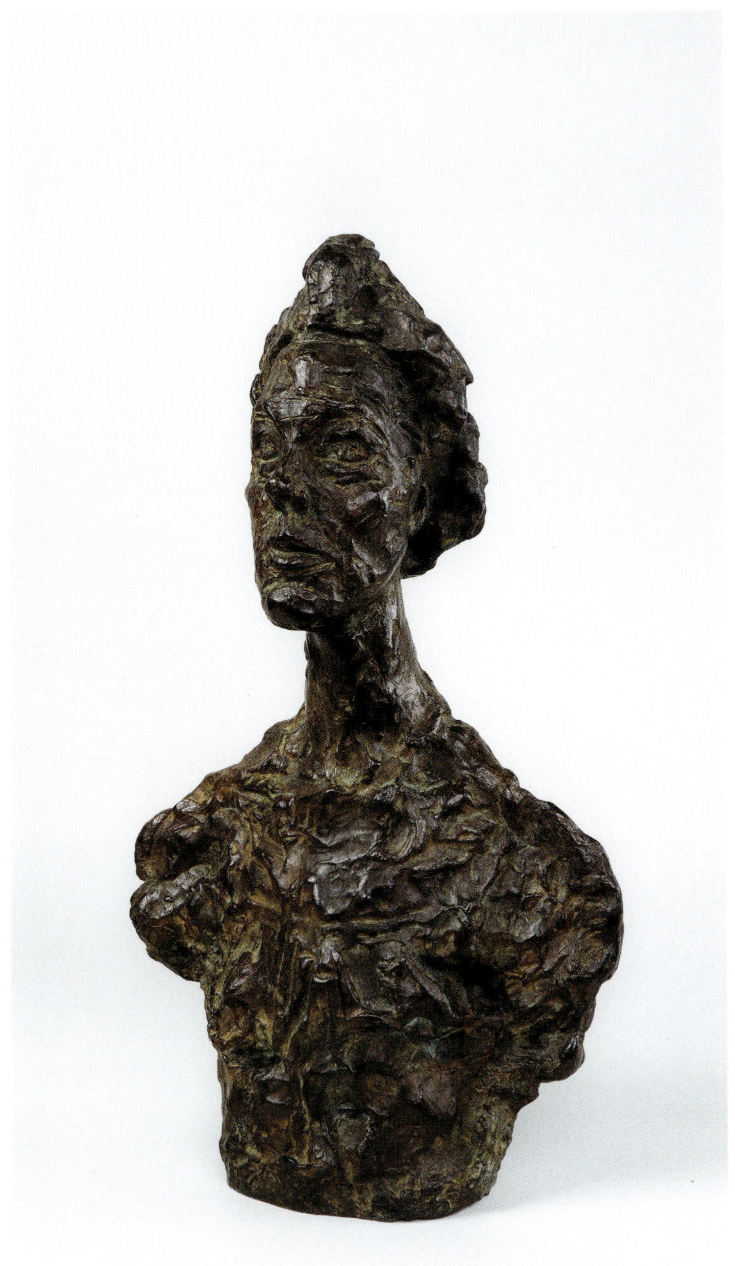

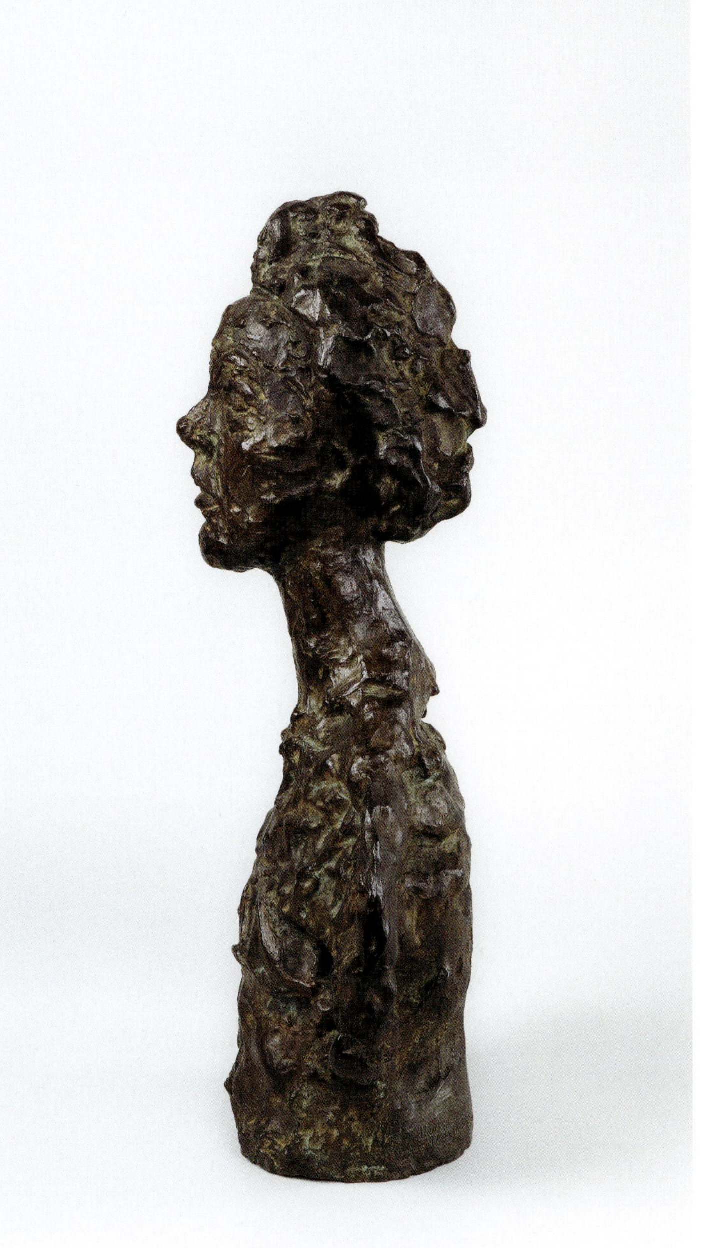

***Bust of Annette X*, 1965**
Bronze; 43.9 x 18.8 x 13.7 cm.
Fondation Giacometti

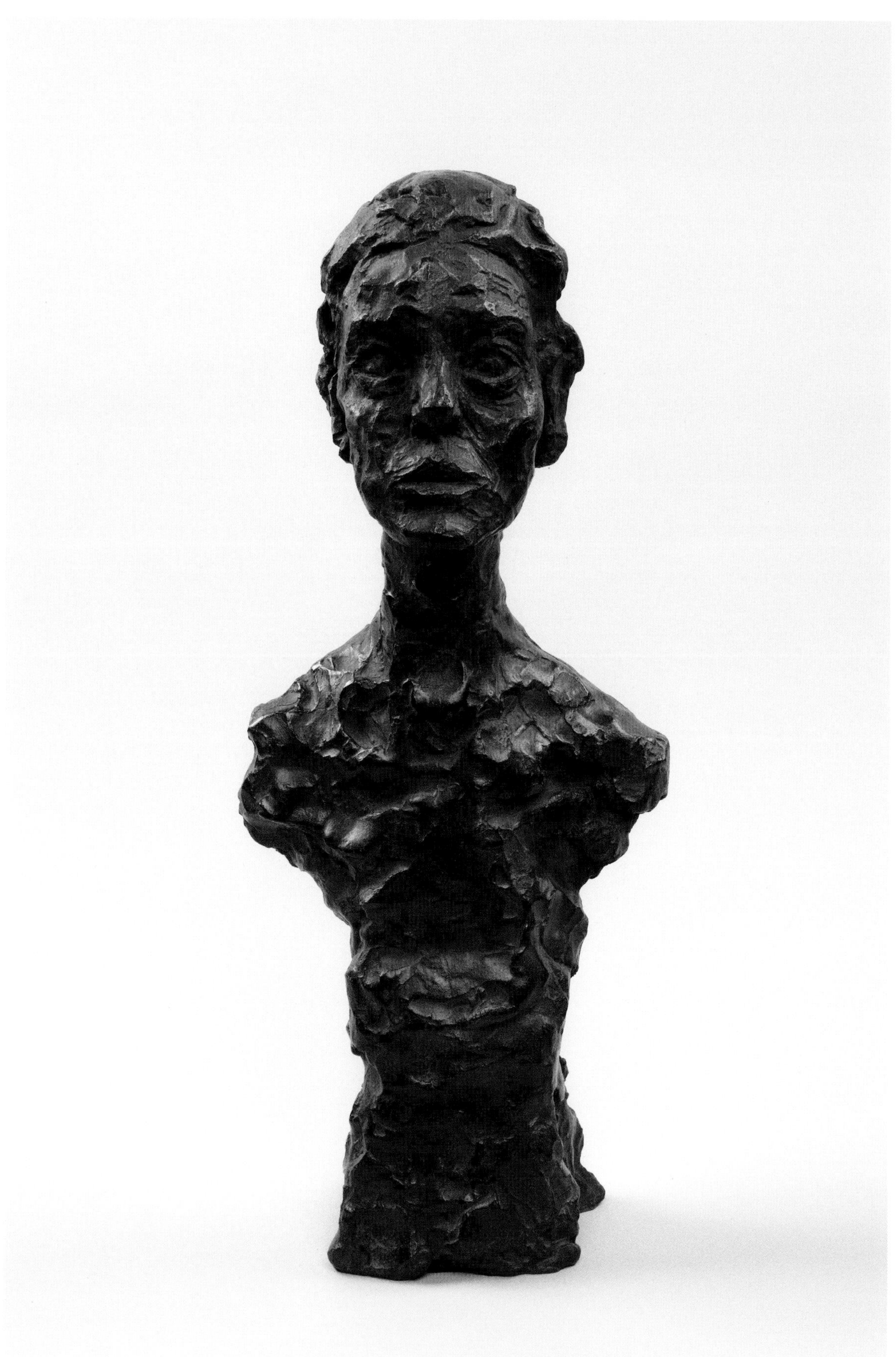

***Self-Portrait with a Woman in a Mirror*, c. 1946**
Pencil and rubber on paper;
49.4 x 32.5 cm.
Fondation Giacometti

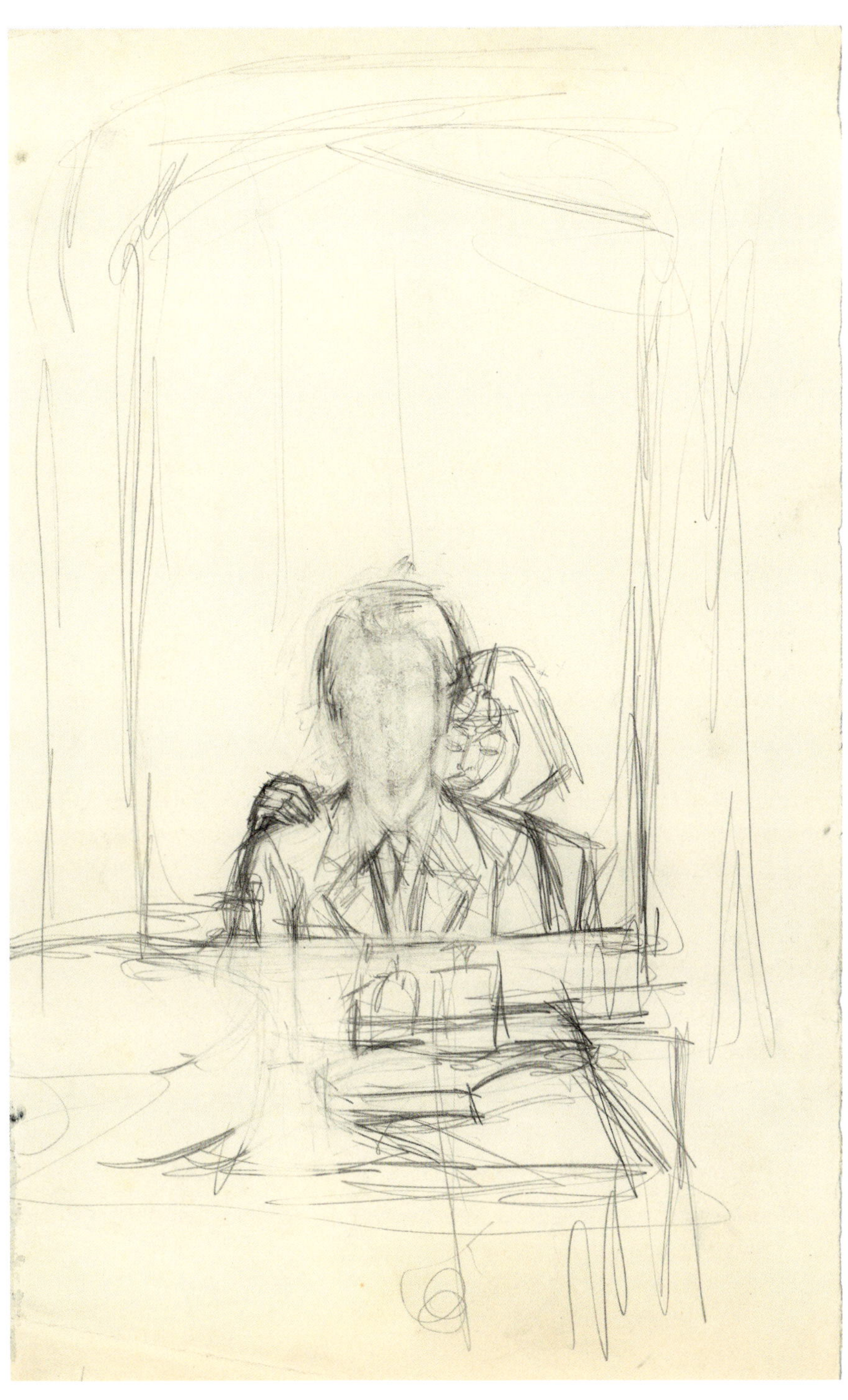

Other Spaces: Landscapes

ROMAIN PERRIN

Alberto Giacometti, September 24, 1965
Yousuf Karsh (Armenian Canadian, 1908–2002). Archives, Fondation Giacometti. © Yousuf Karsh

In his youth, Alberto Giacometti painted many watercolors of landscapes, among them that of the Val Bregaglia, where he grew up. In a Post-Impressionist style reminiscent of his father's, these paintings show a special attachment to his native region, which he never stopped rambling through. Several recurrent elements appear in them—mountains, trees, dwellings, lakes—that together form the essential vocabulary of the landscapes he represented throughout his life, to which were added, from the 1950s, the urban streets of Paris. Though the views of the villages of Stampa and Maloja (pages 78 bottom, 79–81), as well as their surroundings, are predominantly paintings, the representations of the French capital and its suburbs, which were his nearest environment, are predominantly drawings, as in the collection of lithographs *Paris sans fin* (1959–65).

On the other hand, *Man, Tree, and Mountain* does not offer the description of a precise place but appears to be an archetypal landscape in which the human figure is confronted by the immensity of nature (page 179). Giacometti used the painting of romantic landscape to question the human condition, as he did too in the prints for René Char's collection of poetry *Retour amont*, set in Luberon (pages 180, 181). Some have eloquent titles like *Man on the Precipice Looking into the Void*. The human figure, however, is not isolated in that painting, and the perception of a profound unity between the three elements shows how in Giacometti's art the landscape can be seen as a metaphor for the body, as when he wrote, to emphasize the vastness of a detail seen from close up, that "the distance between one side of the nose and the other is like the Sahara."[1]

A central motif in many drawings, the tree almost represents a whole landscape by metonymy. Its surge toward the sky echoes the verticality of the standing body, in particular when the sculptures from the beginning of the 1960s, like *Tall Woman*, give it a monumental dimension. It transpires in *The Glade*, whose nine figures bring forward the impression experienced during a walk along the edge of a forest one autumn day, as he told gallery owner Pierre Matisse (page 172). The slender female silhouettes, still and of various sizes, from *The Forest* resemble the "trees with bare and willowy trunks (branchless right to the top)" of a place he often visited in his childhood, trees that always appeared "to be like characters immobilized in their walk and which talk to one another" (page 173).[2] The head set back from the composition represents the boulder he saw through the trees. Thus, the boulder brings the busts closer to the mineral. Their solid and stony bodies evoke a geological concretion, a stalagmite perhaps, as in *Man with a Windbreaker*, with its tiny head, perched on a mound, of which only the arms stand out (page 177); however, in *Bust of a Man (Lotar II)*, it is the whole body that seems to have turned into a rock (page 174). Through the interpenetration of the mineral with the human in the arrangement of the figures on a board and the modeling of bodies, the question of the landscape, in Giacometti's practice, transcends the strict pictorial field to be transposed into volume in sculpture.

1. Alberto Giacometti to Pierre Matisse, in *Alberto Giacometti*, exh. cat. (New York: Pierre Matisse Gallery, 1948); reprinted in Giacometti, *Écrits: Articles, notes et entretiens* (Paris: Hermann and Fondation Giacometti, 2007), 88.

2. Giacometti to Pierre Matisse, December 28, 1950, in *Alberto Giacometti*, exh. cat. (New York: Pierre Matisse Gallery, 1950); reprinted in Giacometti, *Écrits*, 104.

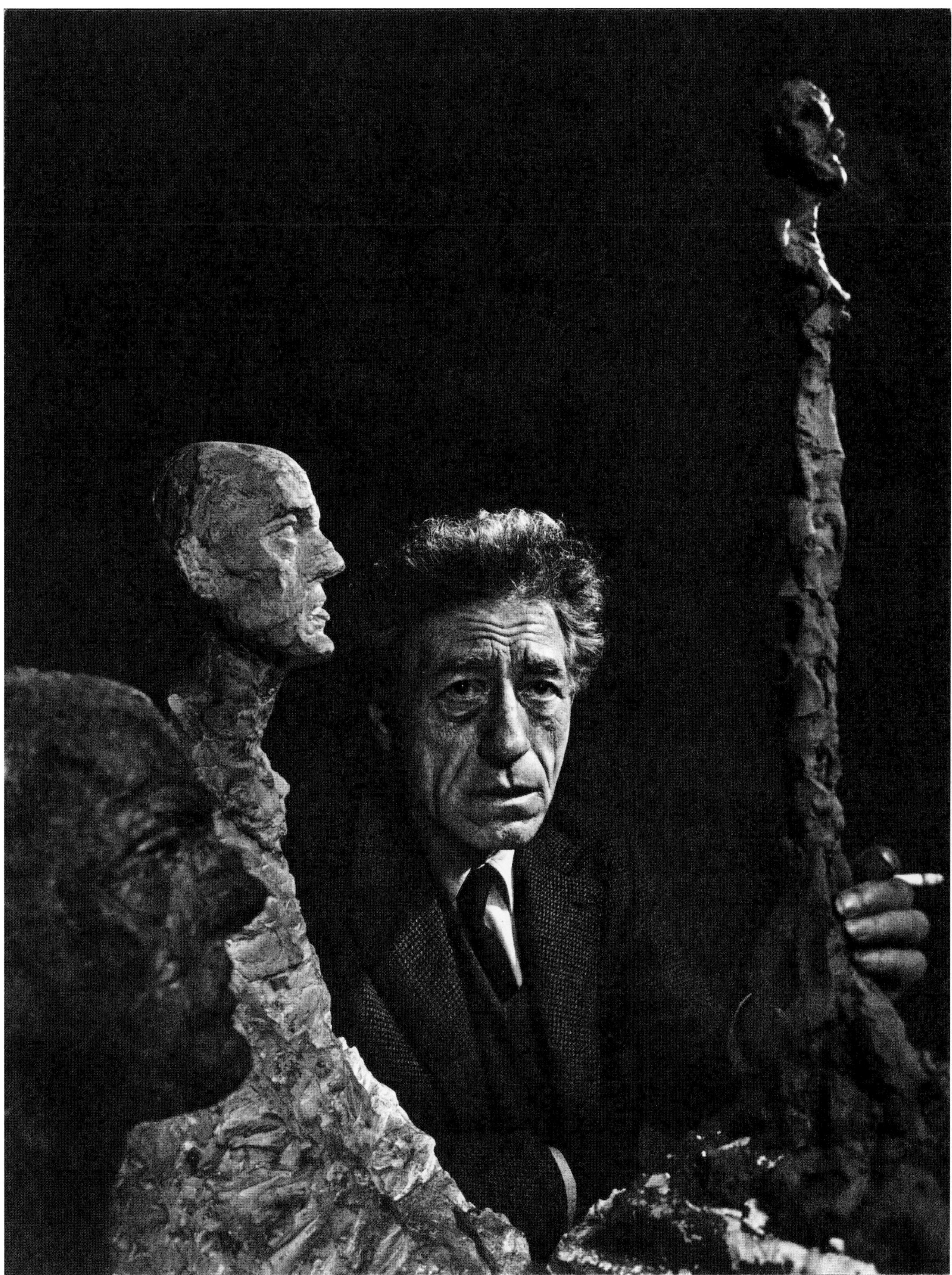

***The Glade*, 1950**
Bronze; 61 x 66 x 53 cm.
Fondation Giacometti

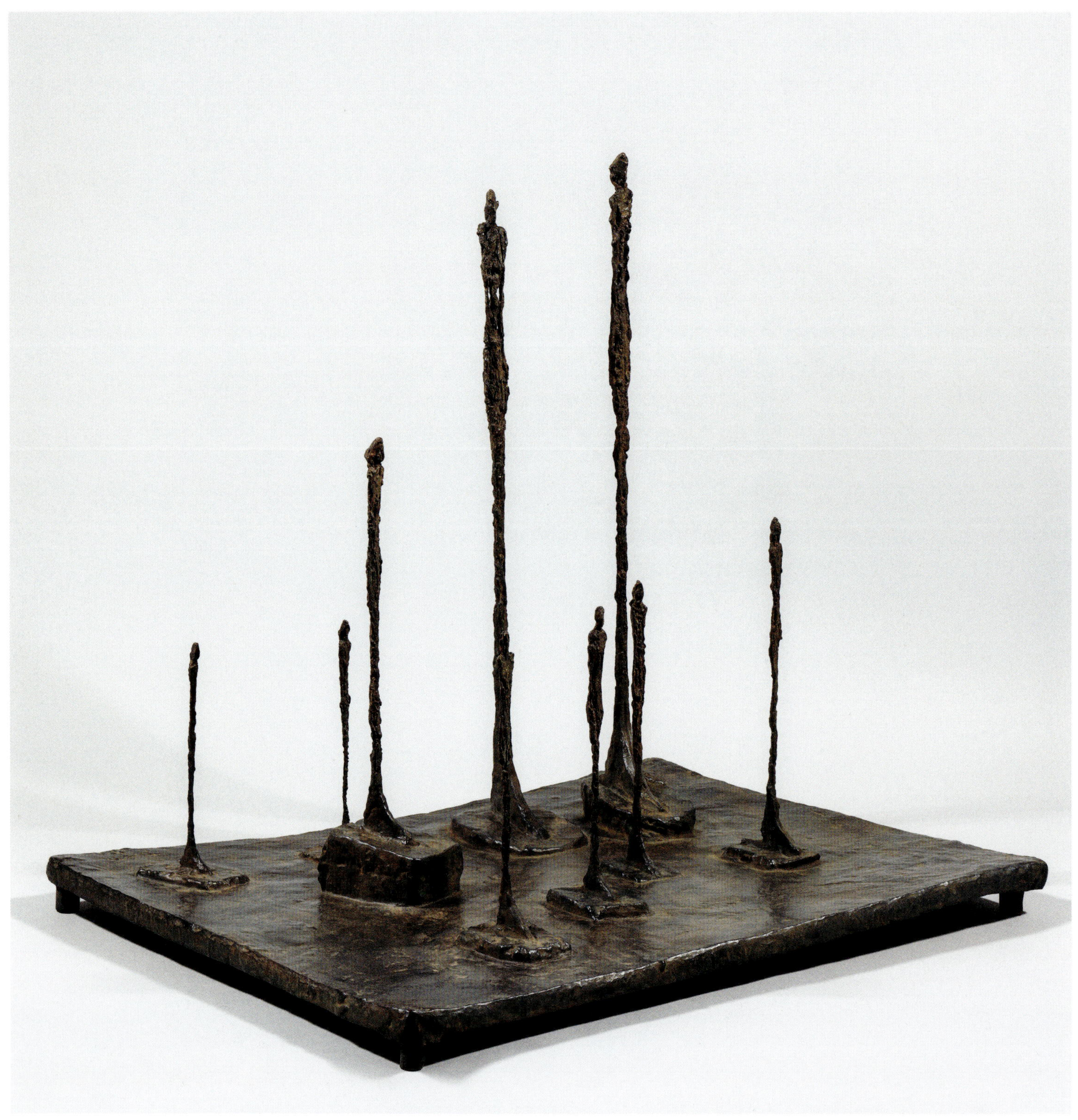

***The Forest*, 1950**
Bronze; 57 x 61 x 49.5 cm.
Fondation Giacometti

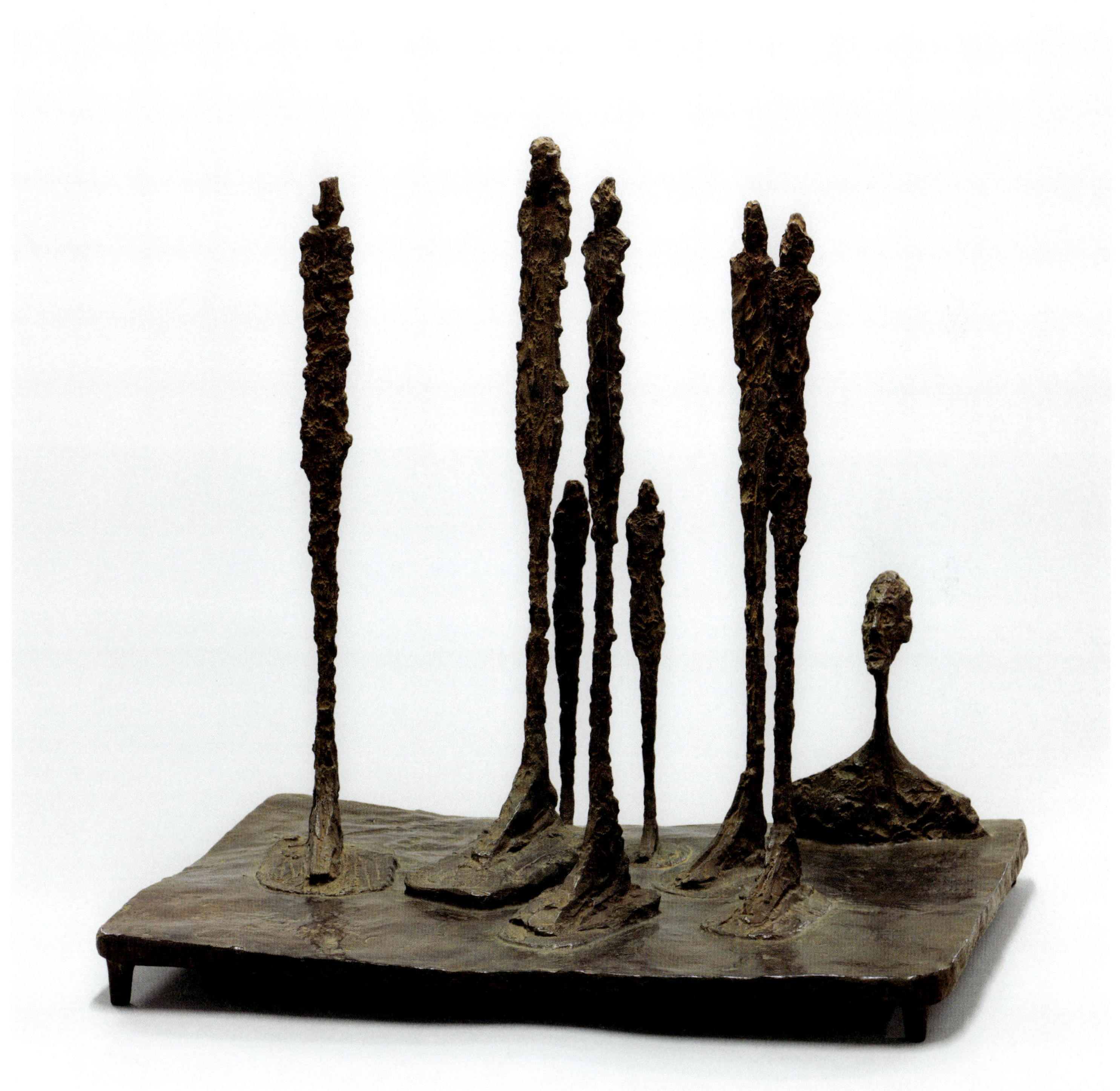

Bust of a Man (Lotar II),
1964–65
Bronze; 57.8 x 38.2 x 25 cm.
Fondation Giacometti

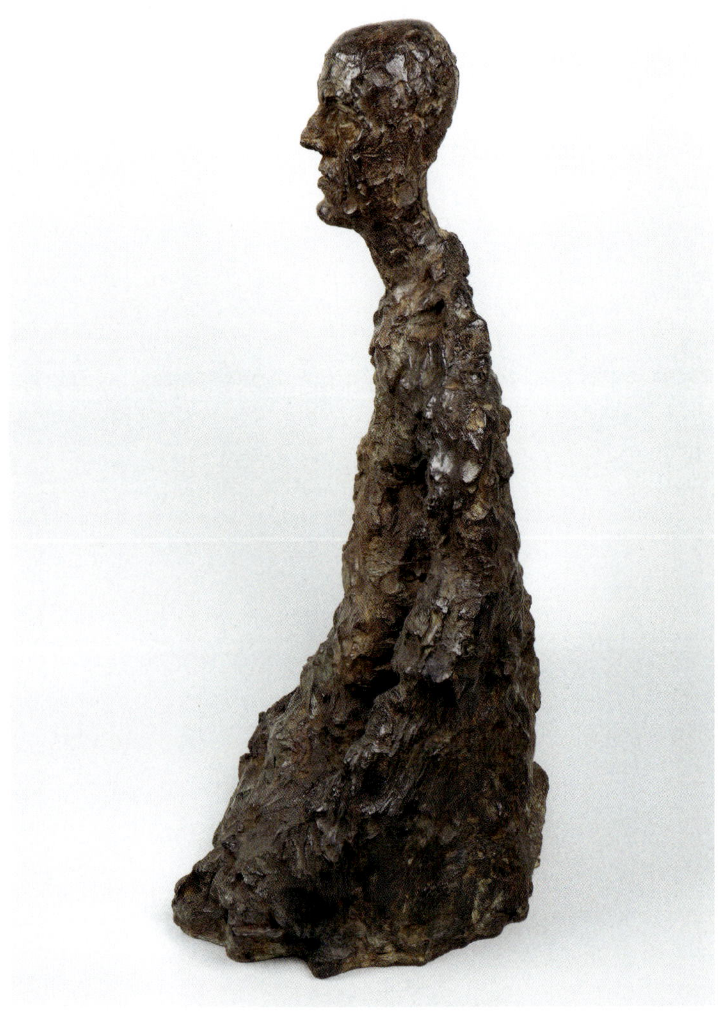

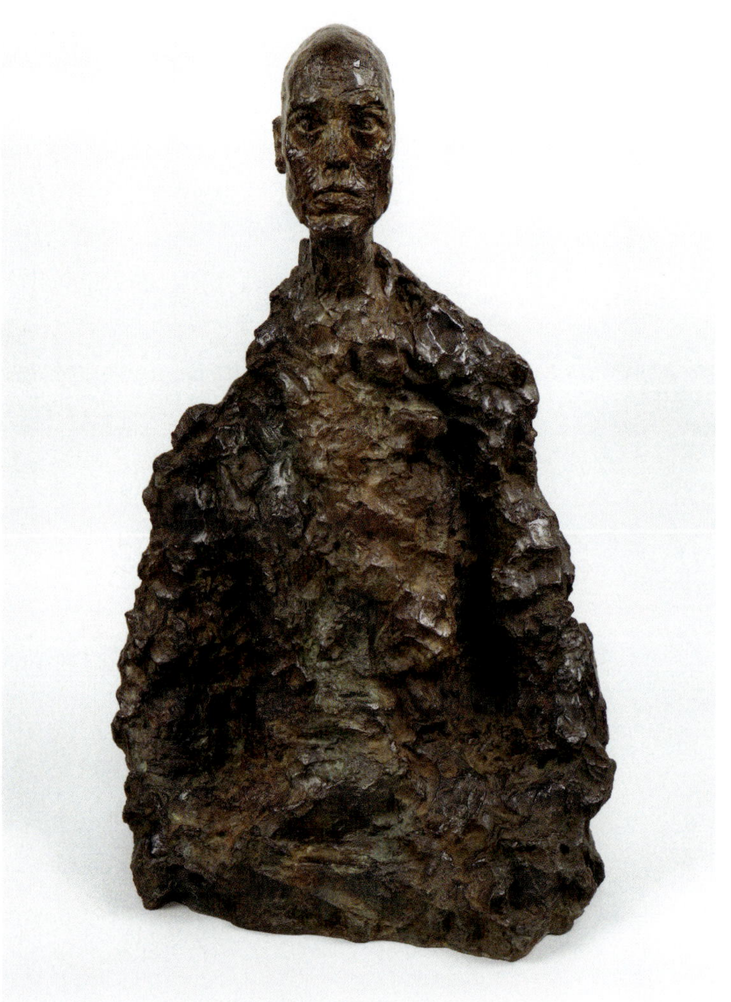

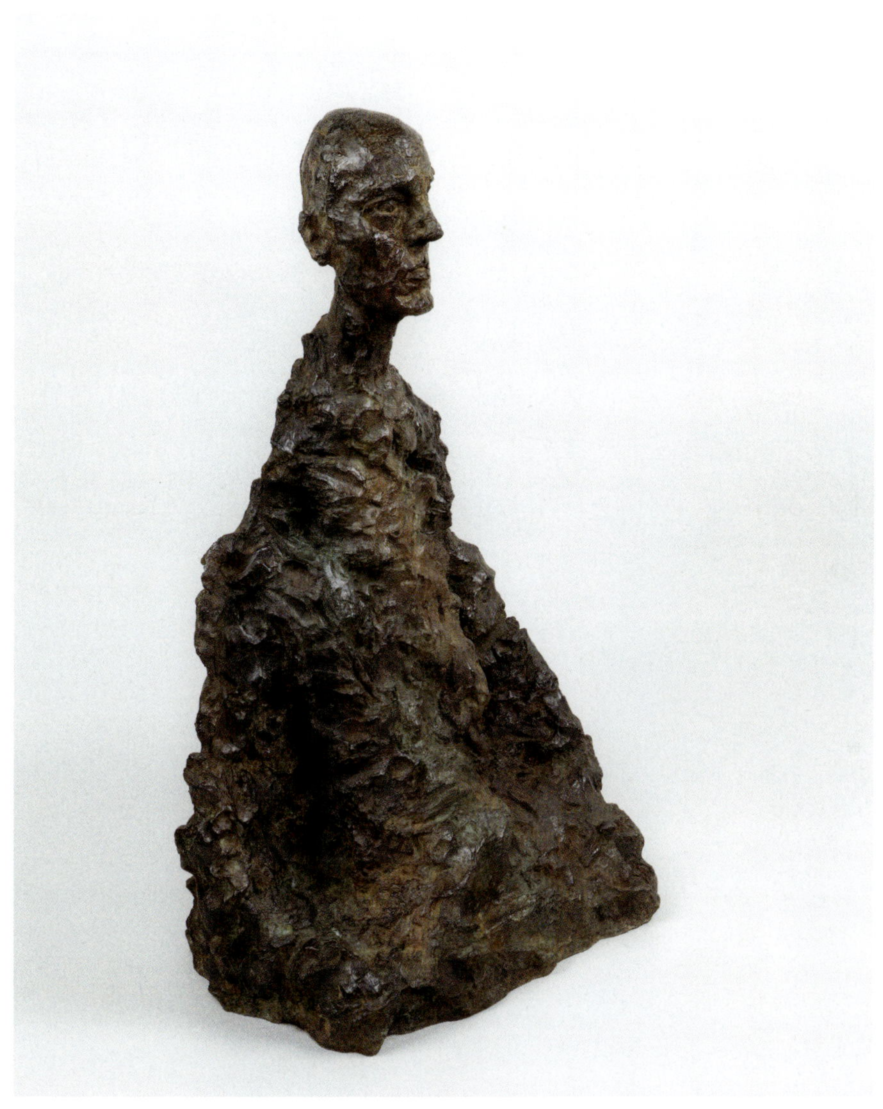

***Landscape in Stampa*, 1964–65**
Printed by Imprimeries de Maeght.
Edited by Maeght éditeur, Paris.
Lithograph; sheet: 65.4 x 48 cm.
Fondation Giacometti

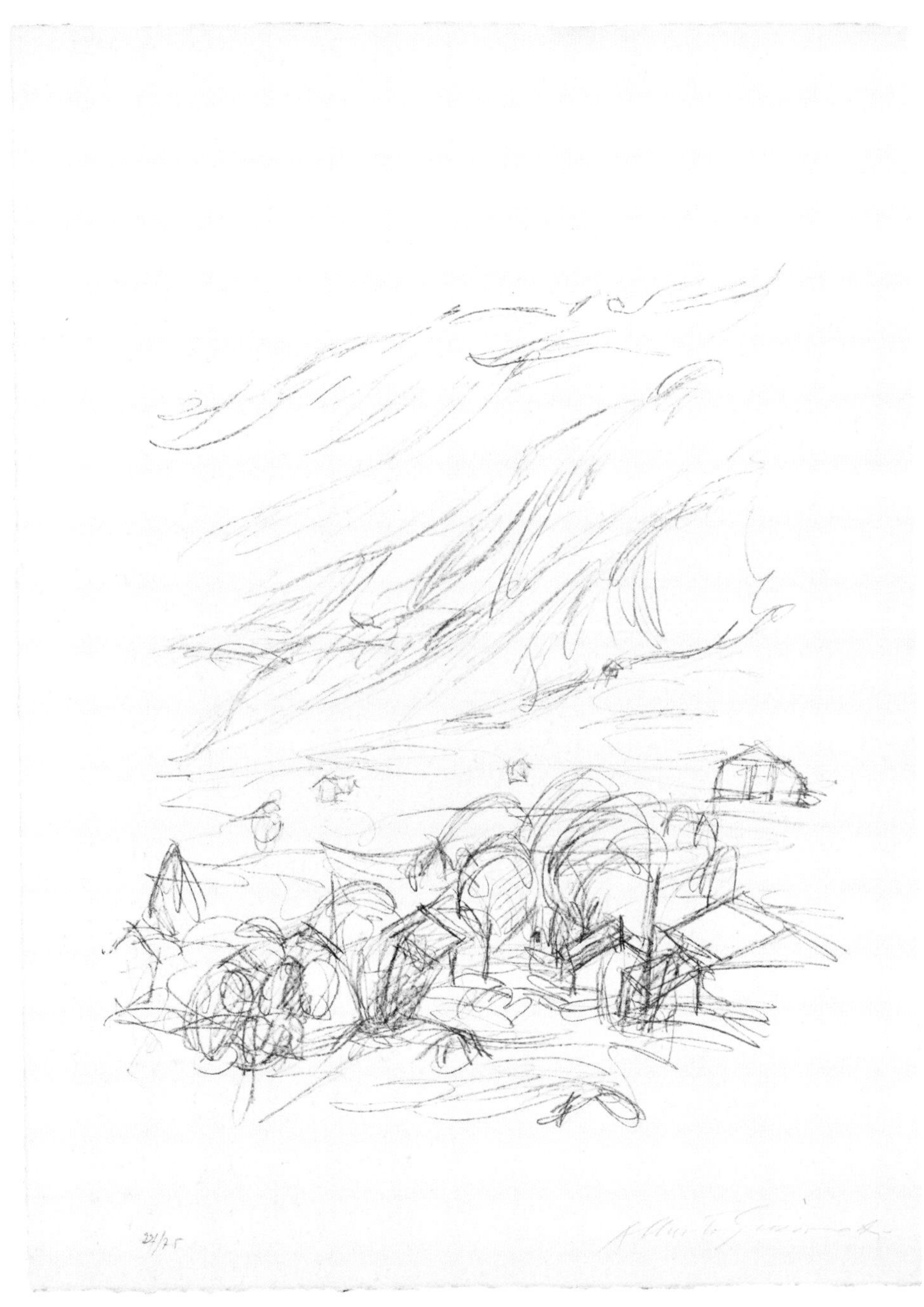

***Man with a Windbreaker*, 1953**
Bronze; 50 x 28.6 x 22.5 cm.
Fondation Giacometti

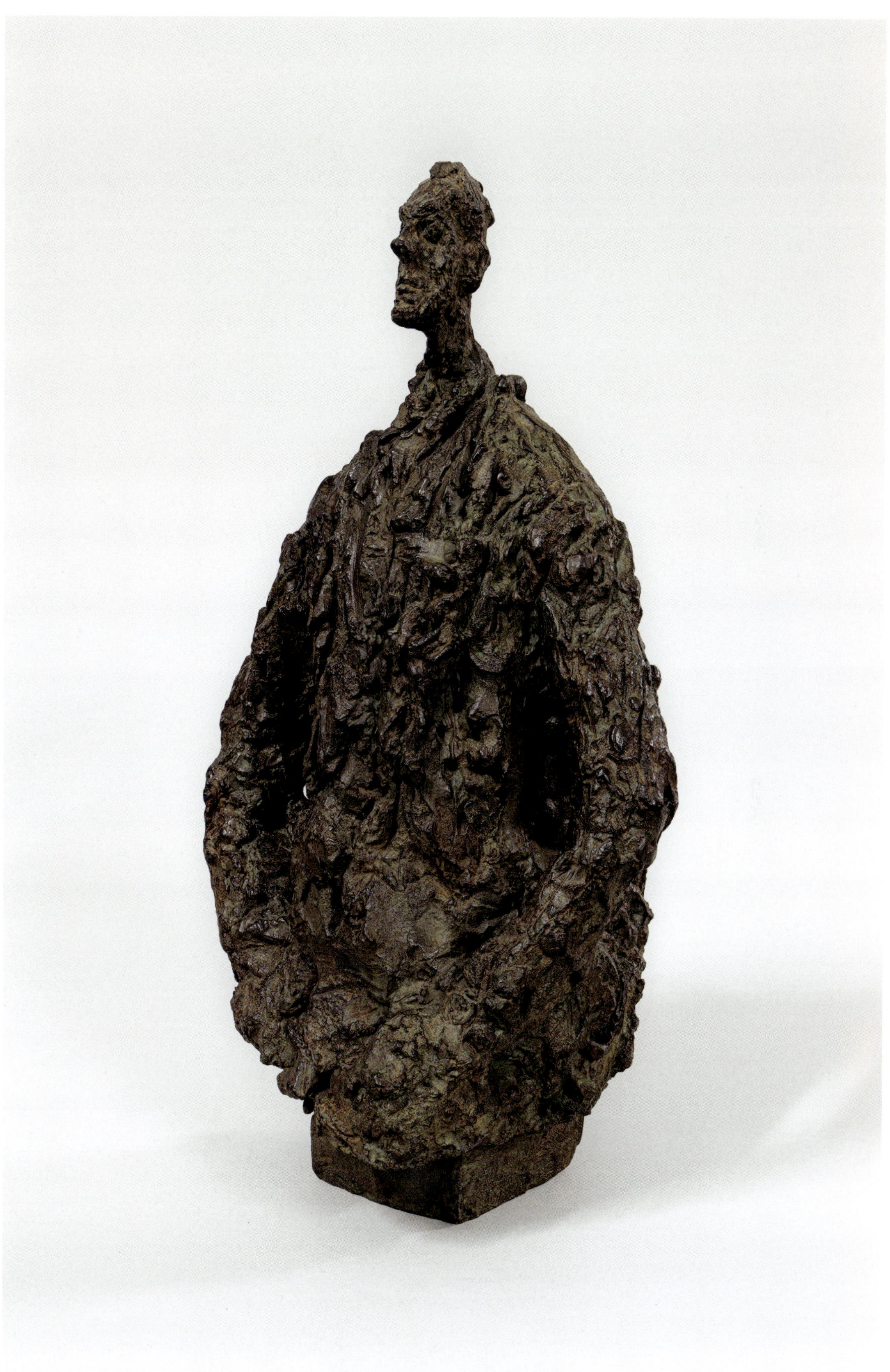

***Conifers, Houses, and Characters*, c. 1951**
Lithographic pencil on transfer paper; 49.8 x 32.6 cm.
Fondation Giacometti

***The Court of the Studio on the Rue Hippolyte-Maindron*, c. 1951**
Pencil on paper; 50 x 32.5 cm.
Fondation Giacometti

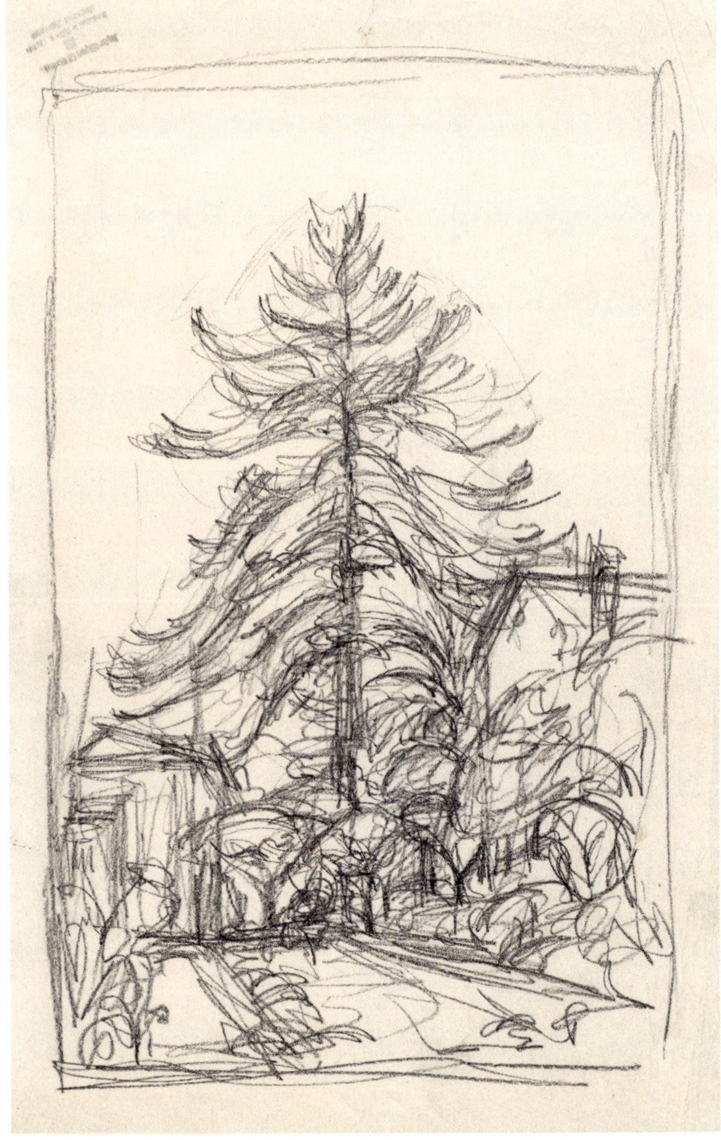

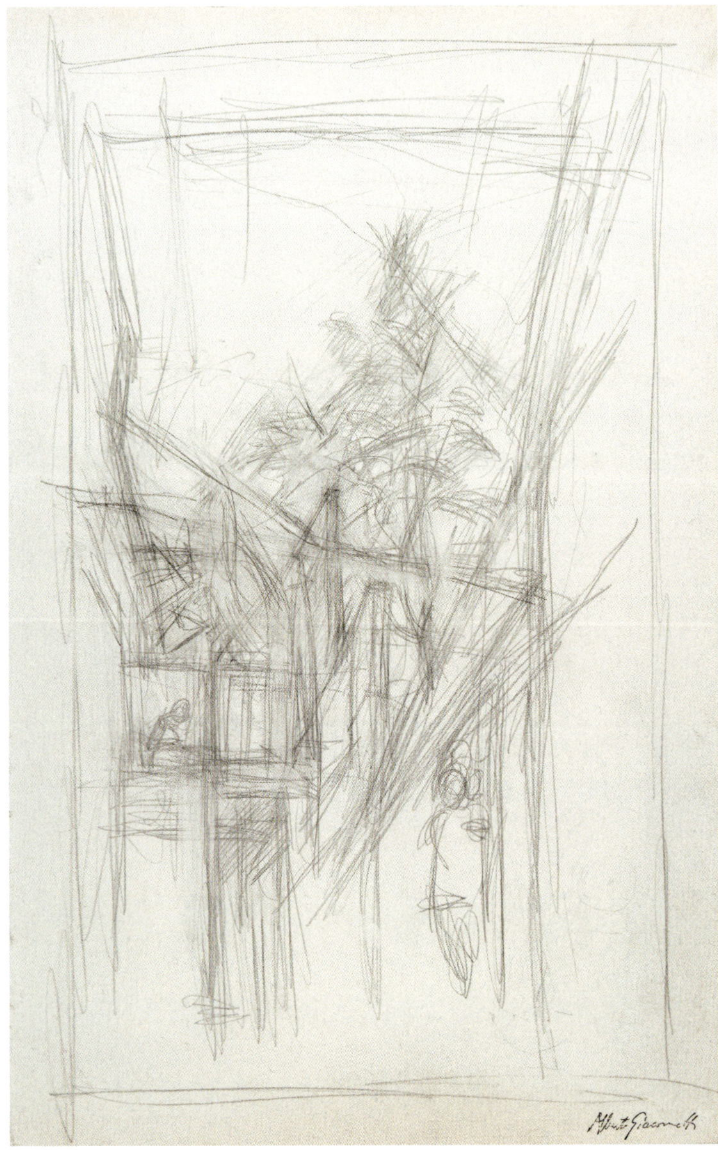

Man, Tree, and Mountain,
1958
Oil on canvas; 60 x 80 cm.
Fondation Giacometti

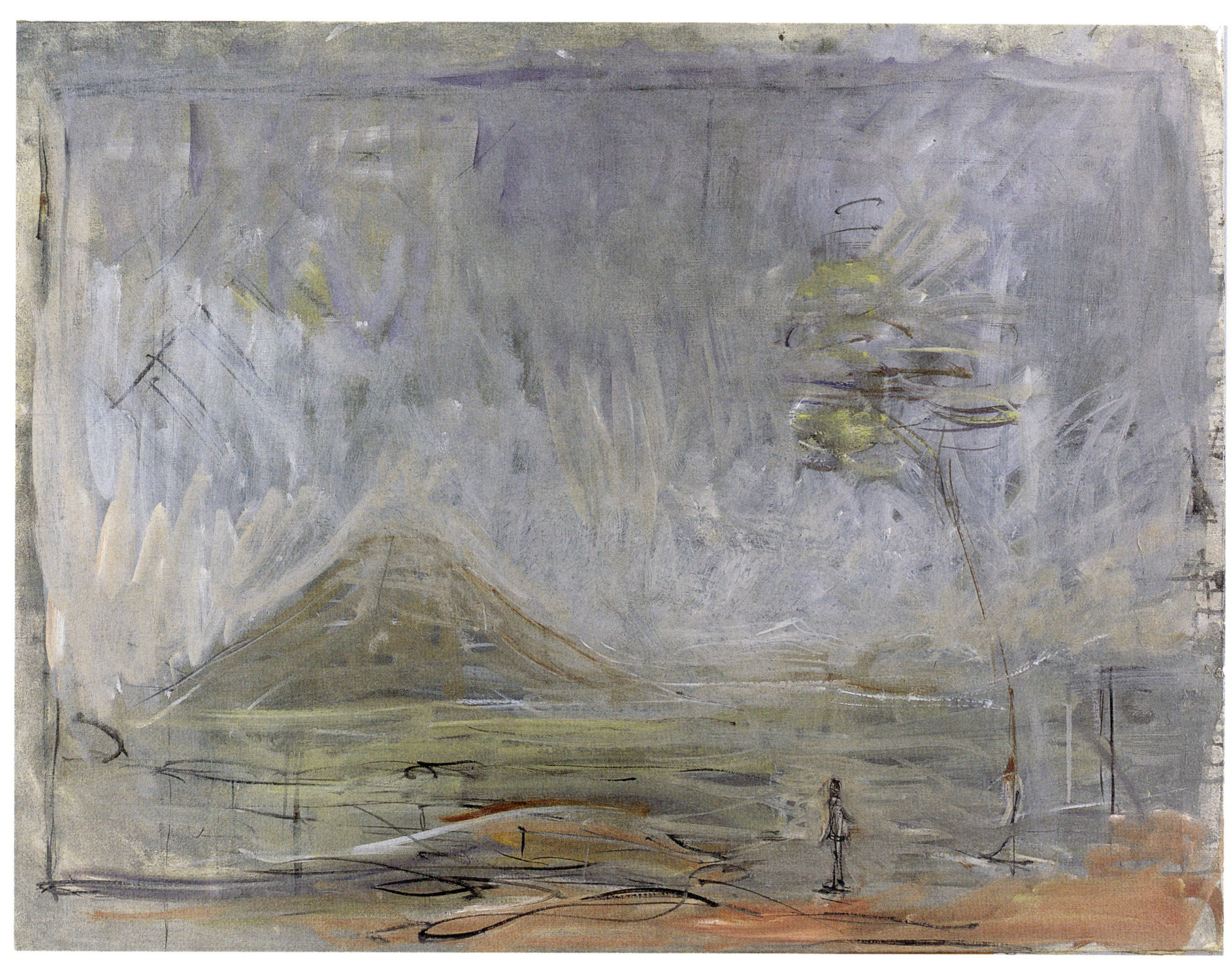

***The Mountain (I)*, pl. 1, from**
***Retour Amont* by René Char, 1965**
Printed by Atelier Crommelynck.
Edited by Guy Levis Mano, Paris.
Aquatint on paper;
sheet: 38.2 x 28.3 cm.
Fondation Giacometti

***Man in the Rocks I*, pl. 3, from *Retour Amont* by René Char, 1965**
Printed by Atelier Crommelynck.
Edited by Guy Levis Mano, Paris.
Aquatint on paper;
sheet: 38.2 x 28.3 cm.
Fondation Giacometti

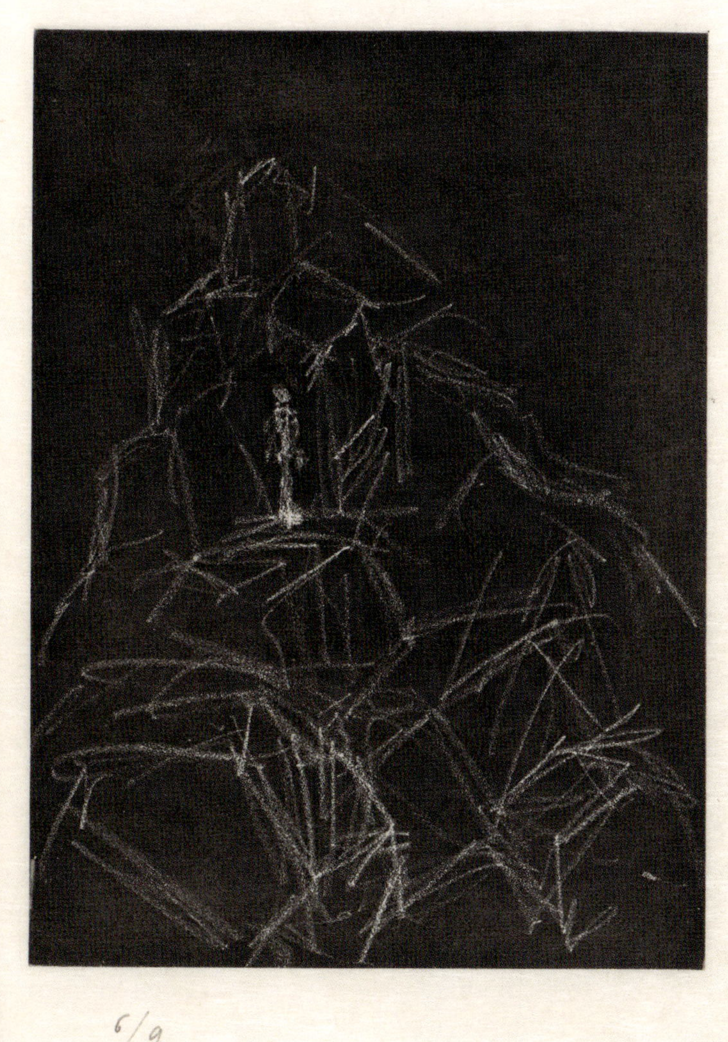

***Man on the Precipice Looking into the Void*, pl. 4, from *Retour Amont* by René Char, 1965**
Printed by Atelier Crommelynck.
Edited by Guy Levis Mano, Paris.
Aquatint on paper;
sheet: 38.2 x 28.3 cm.
Fondation Giacometti

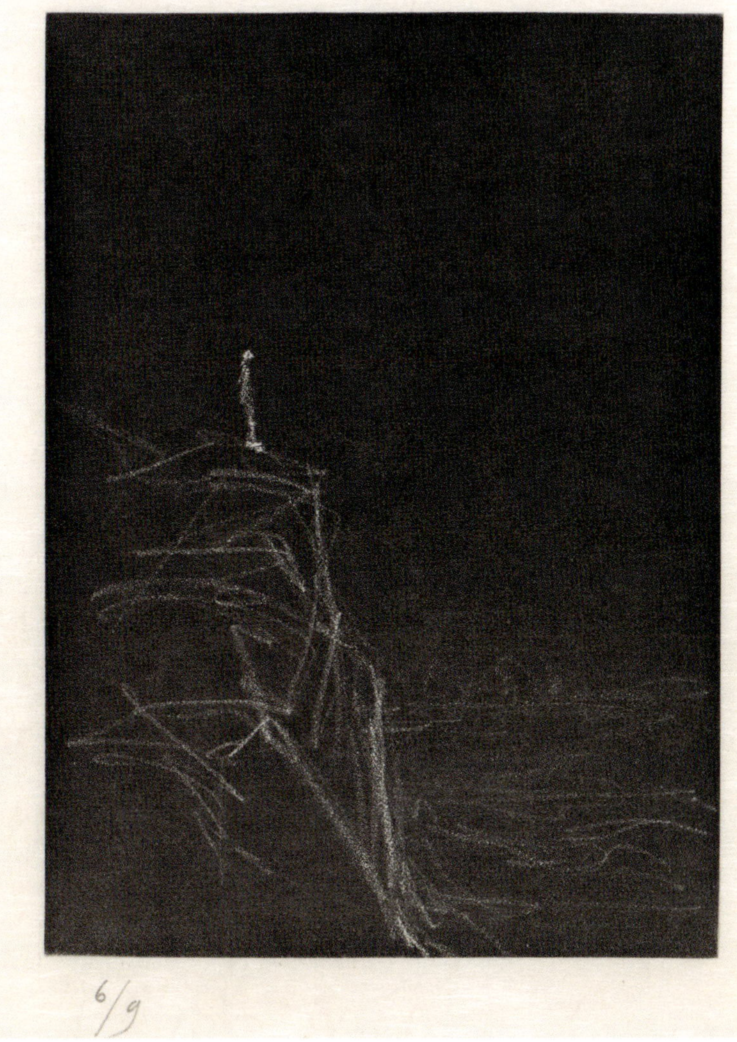

Poets, Writers, and Books

ROMAIN PERRIN

Alberto Giacometti and Samuel Beckett in Giacometti's studio alongside the tree created for *Waiting for Godot*, 1961
Georges Pierre (French, 1921–2003). Archives, Fondation Giacometti

The many books that remain of Alberto Giacometti's library show the artist's deep attachment to literature, especially poetry, as well as to the writers with whom he forged intense friendships throughout his life. Those dialogues developed according to various networks of relationships and together form an intellectual cartography from the interwar period to the 1960s.

The first writers with whom Giacometti had contact, as early as 1929, were in the Surrealist group. Initially, he met the members of the publication *Documents*, including Michel Leiris and Georges Bataille, then those of André Breton's group, among them Louis Aragon and Paul Éluard, to whom he stayed close, even after he broke with the movement.

In 1941, when he felt the need to again confront his sculptures with reality, Giacometti met Simone de Beauvoir and Jean-Paul Sartre. In 1948, the latter wrote "The Search for the Absolute," a famous text that played an important part in how Giacometti's work was perceived and appreciated during the postwar years. The philosopher offered an analysis in which he developed the themes of existential thought.

From 1946, Giacometti received increasingly more commissions for illustrations. The writers of his generation, whom he met before the war, brought him back to Surrealism. Bataille asked him to make a series of prints for *Histoire de rats* (Story of Rats), a narrative text in which the themes of eroticism and transgression call to mind two stories by Giacometti published in magazines, "Hier, Sables mouvants" (Yesterday, Quicksand)[1] and "Le Rêve, le Sphinx et la mort de T." (The Dream, the Sphinx and the Death of T.).[2] Like René Char, with whom he collaborated on several books, the sculptor read the Marquis de Sade. After Leiris's suicide attempt in 1957, the artist watched over the writer and made a series of etchings representing his bedridden friend, which were published in 1961 in *Vivantes cendres, innomées*.

On a request from Jean Genet, whose portrait he had made three times, between 1954 and 1958, Giacometti produced the cover for *The Balcony*, a theater play set in a brothel. That theme was particularly suited to the artist for *Four Figurines on a Stand (London Figurines)*, reminiscent of the back cover, where he wrote, "several naked women seen at the Sphinx,"[3] a place he often visited (page 192).

The themes of the fragility of existence, solitude, the impossibility to communicate, the sense of the absurd, and the grotesque (like that grinning mask of *The Nose* [page 47]) traverse Giacometti's works like those of Samuel Beckett. Though their friendship wavered and did not leave traces other than the collaboration in 1961 for the decor of *Waiting for Godot*—a scraggy bare plaster tree—it was one of the most enduring, from the 1930s until the artist's death. Giacometti's constrained bodies, like the image of the emerging head in the cages (pages 190, 191), seem to anticipate the device used in *Happy Days* (1964), while the choreography of the actors in *Quad* (1981), who move in the space without crossing each other's path, recalls *Three Men Walking* (pages 194–95). The sculptor's attempts at apprehending reality—"I have the feeling, or the illusion, that I'm making progress every day"[4]—echo Beckett's famous saying, "Fail again, fail better."[5]

From the 1950s, Giacometti was the leading light for a new generation of poets. Among them, Olivier Larronde, André du Bouchet, Yves Bonnefoy, and André Dupin were friends and work collaborators. Giacometti's compositions became more narrative, as in the illustrations for the poetry collection of Léna Leclercq, *Pomme endormie* (pages 185–89), which focuses on romantic encounters and separation. These themes inspired Giacometti to create lithographs among the most subdued and mildest he ever produced.

Finally, Giacometti authored several texts and articles, not regularly published, that nourish his oeuvre, shed light on it, and remind us that behind the sculptor, there was undoubtedly a writer.

1. Alberto Giacometti, "Hier, Sables mouvants," *Le Surréalisme Au Service De La Révolution*, no. 5 (May 15, 1933): 44–45; reprinted in Giacometti, *The Dream, the Sphinx and the Death of T.* (Paris: Hermann and Fondation Giacometti, 2021), 28–33.

2. Giacometti, "Le Rêve, le Sphinx et la mort de T.," *Labyrinthe*, no. 22–23 (December 1946): 12–13; reprinted in Giacometti, *The Dream, the Sphinx and the Death of T.*, 4–18.

3. Giacometti to Pierre Matisse, in *Alberto Giacometti*, exh. cat. (New York: Pierre Matisse Gallery, 1948); reprinted in Giacometti, *Écrits*, 101.

4. "Pourquoi je suis sculpteur: Conversation with André Parinaud," *Arts*, no. 873 (June 1962), 1–5; reprinted in Giacometti, *Why I am a sculptor* (Paris: Hermann and Fondation Giacometti, 2017), 38.

5. Samuel Beckett, *Westward Ho* (London: John Calder, 1983), 8.

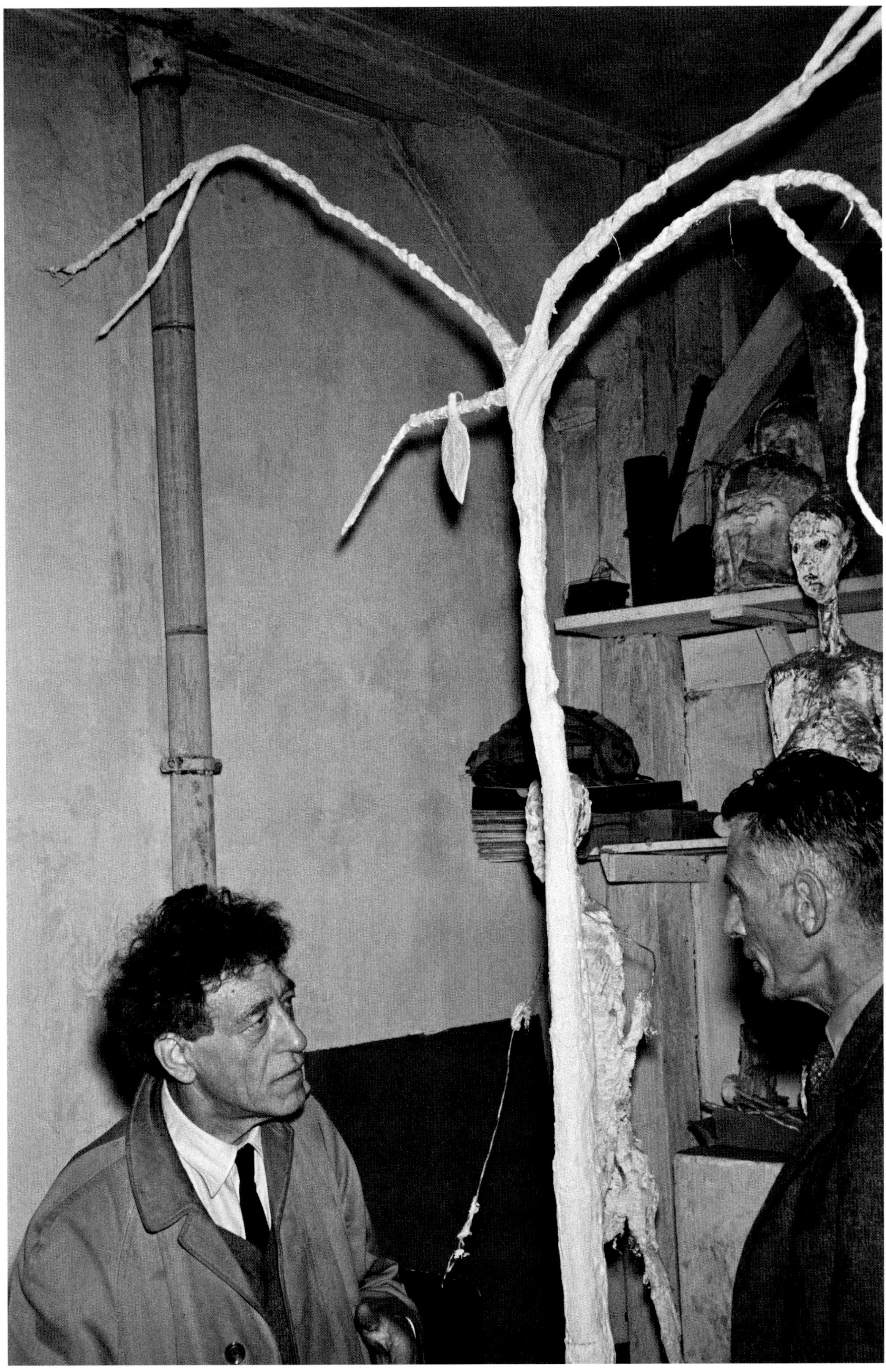

***B Standing in a Cage II*, 1946–47**
Chisel and pen on paper;
28.1 x 22.5 cm.
Fondation Giacometti

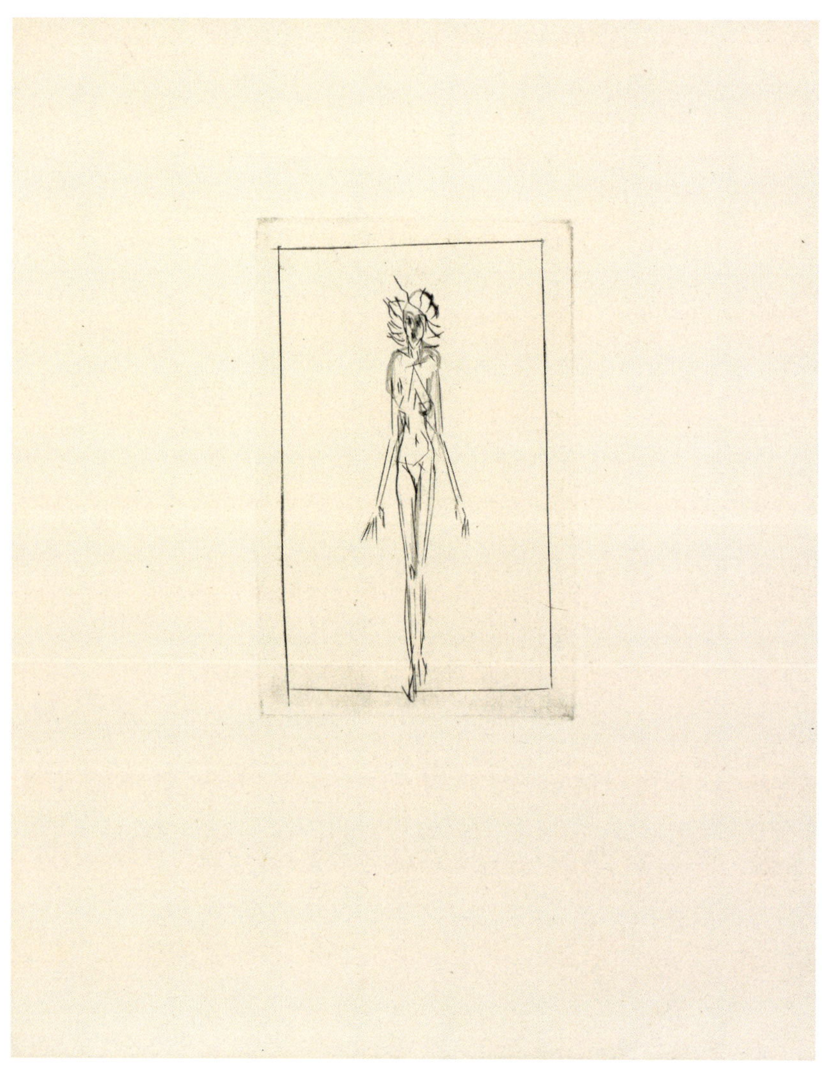

***Illustrations for* Pomme endormie *by Léna Leclercq*, 1961**
Editions L'Arbalète 1958. Illustrated book with 24 lithographs on Japan paper; book open: 32 x 53 cm.
Fondation Giacometti

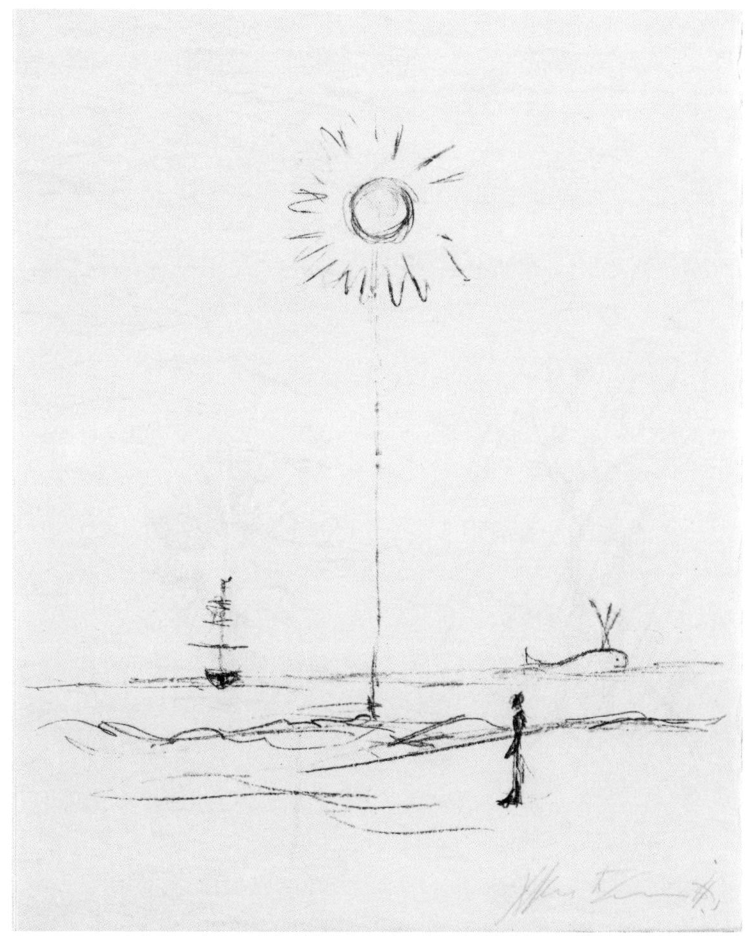

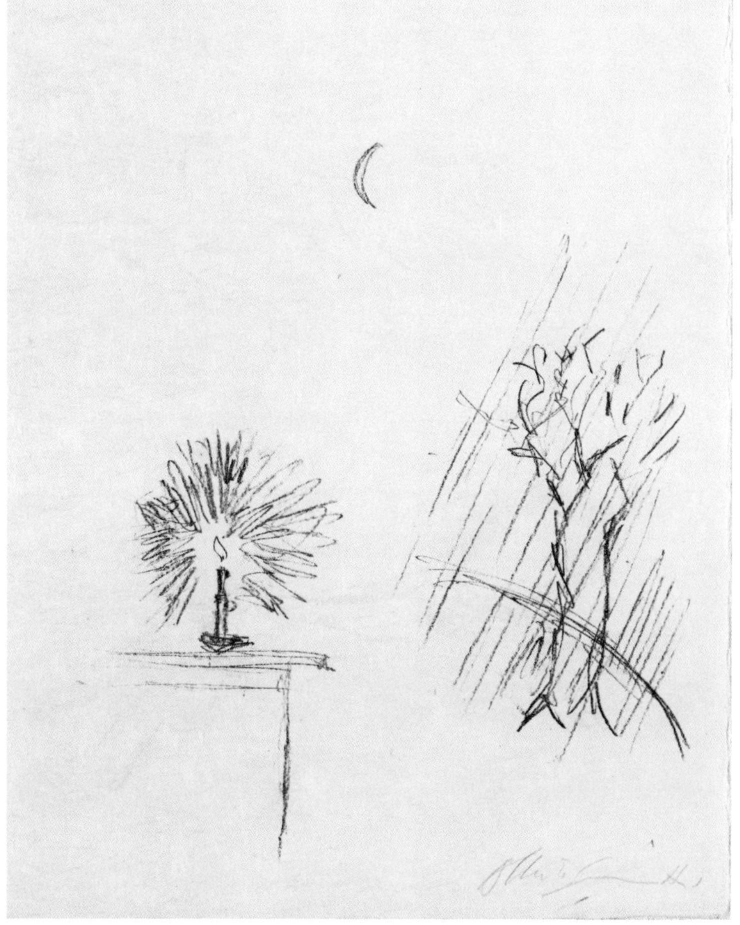

***Illustrations for* Pomme endormie *by Léna Leclercq*, 1961**
Editions L'Arbalète 1958. Illustrated book with 24 lithographs on Japan paper; book open: 32 x 53 cm.
Fondation Giacometti

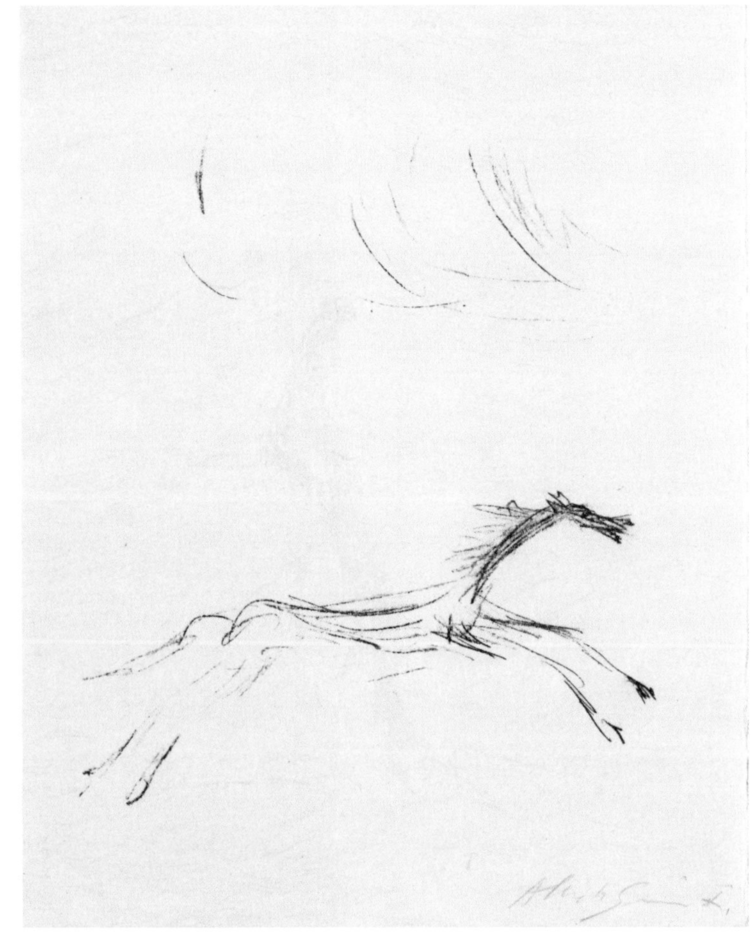

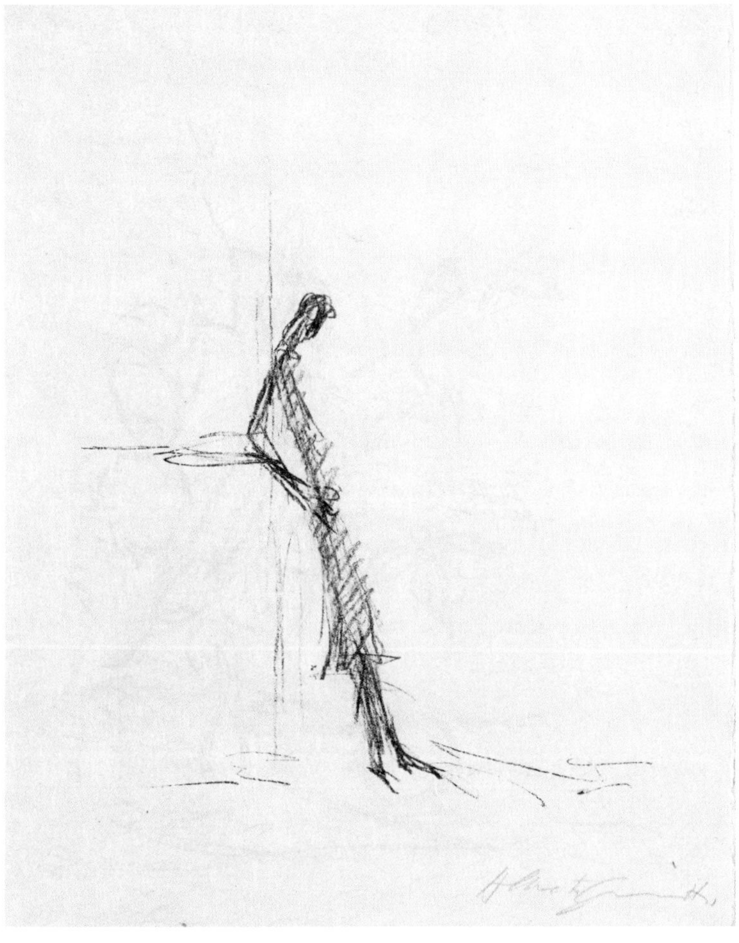

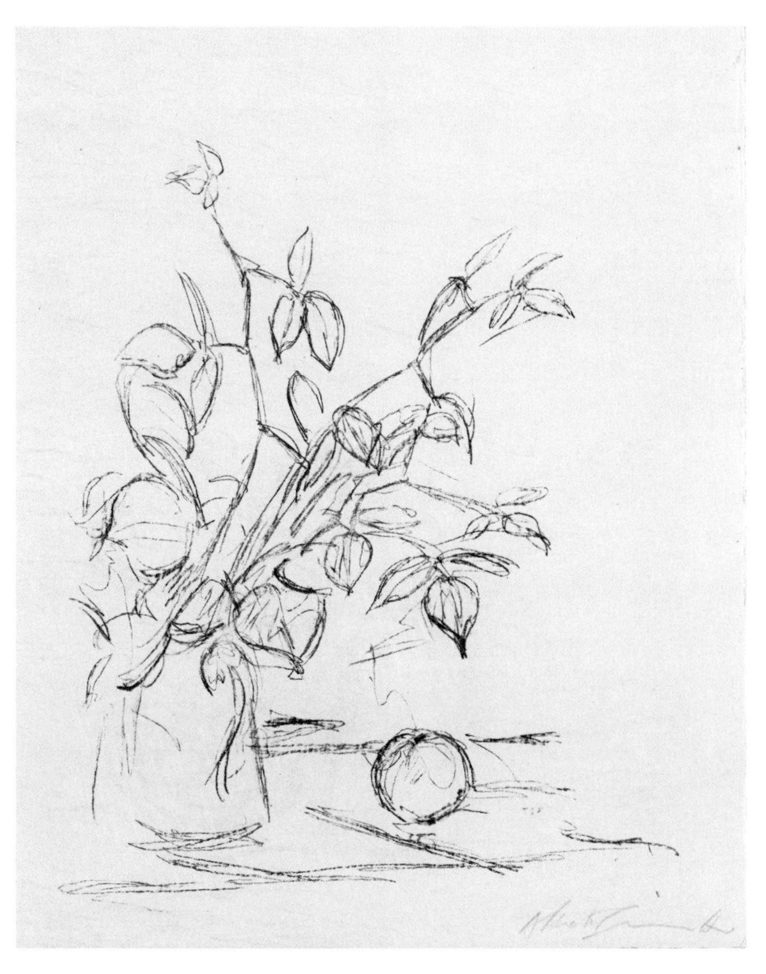

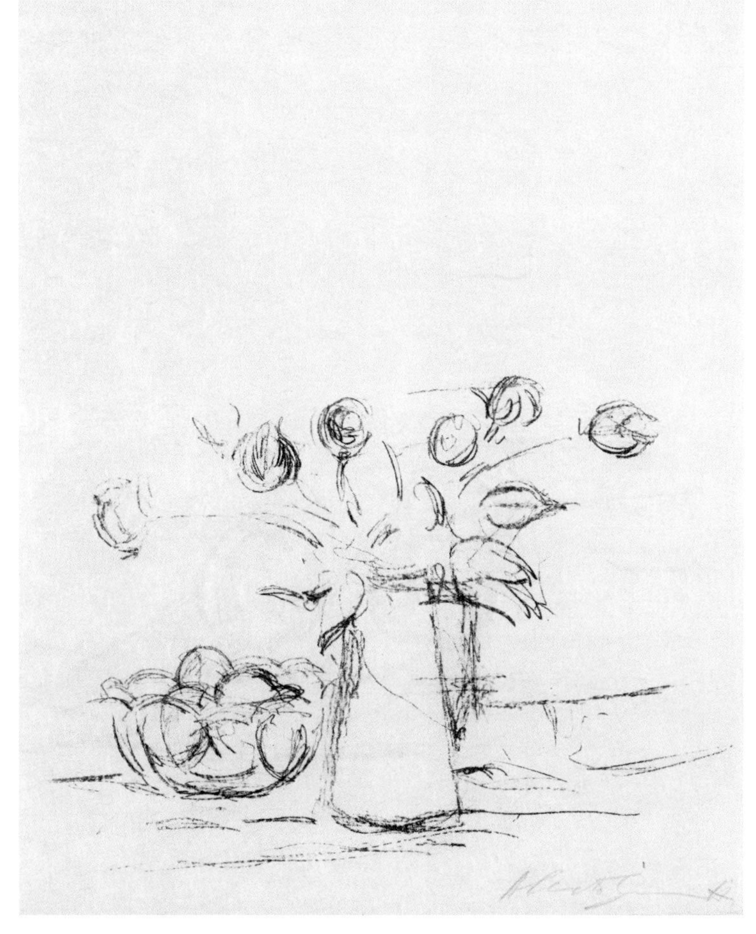

***Illustrations for* Pomme endormie *by Léna Leclercq*, 1961**
Editions L'Arbalète 1958. Illustrated book with 24 lithographs on Japan paper; book open: 32 x 53 cm.
Fondation Giacometti

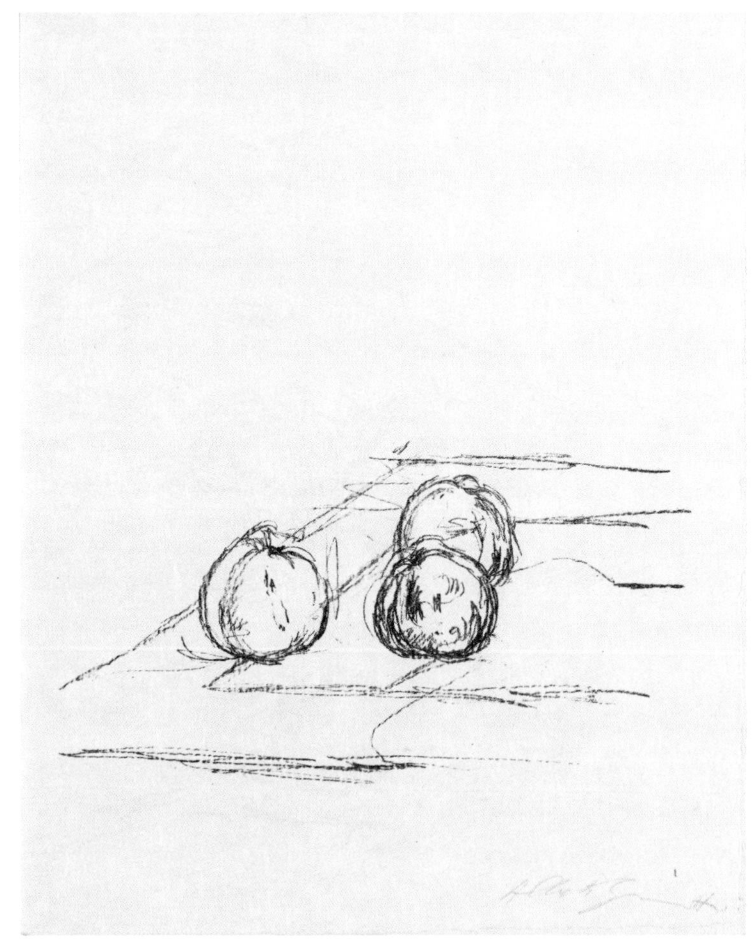

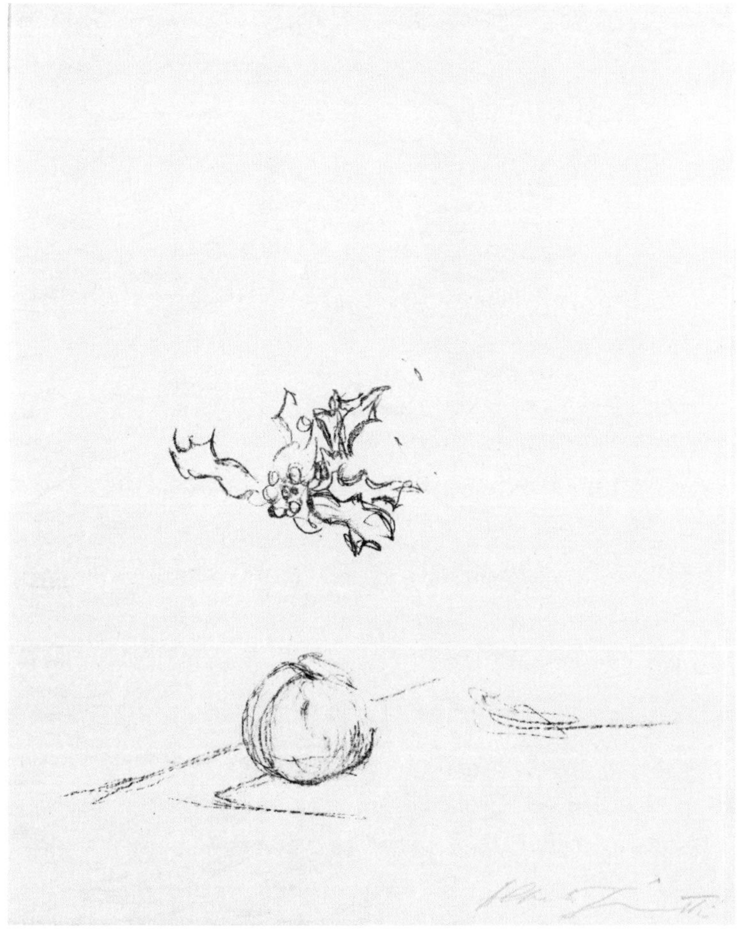

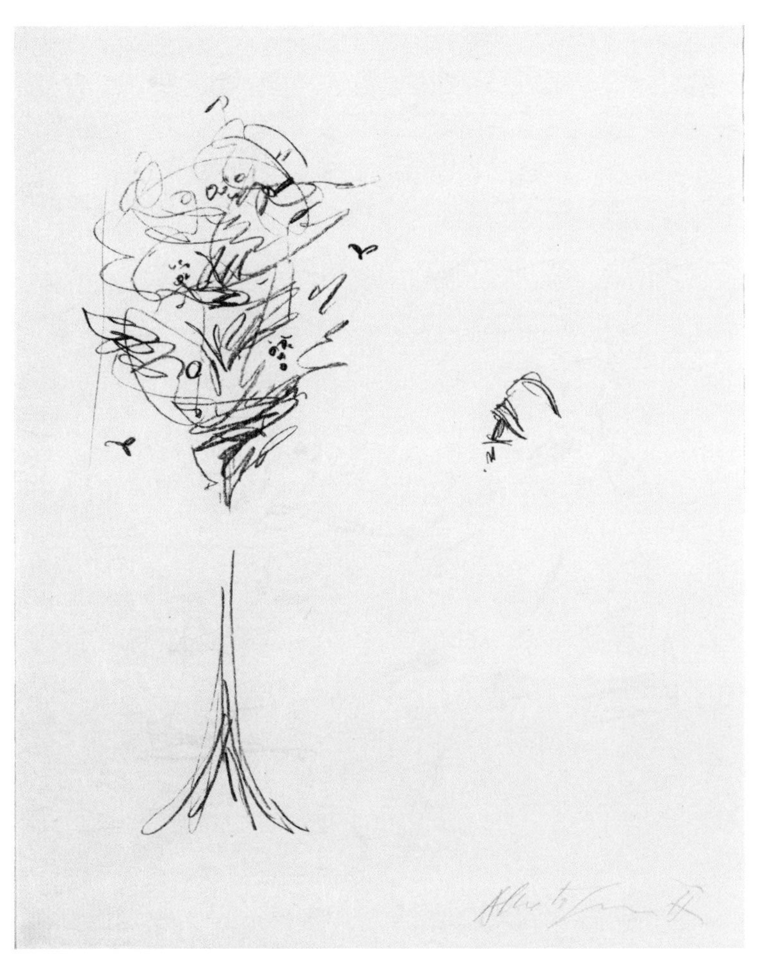

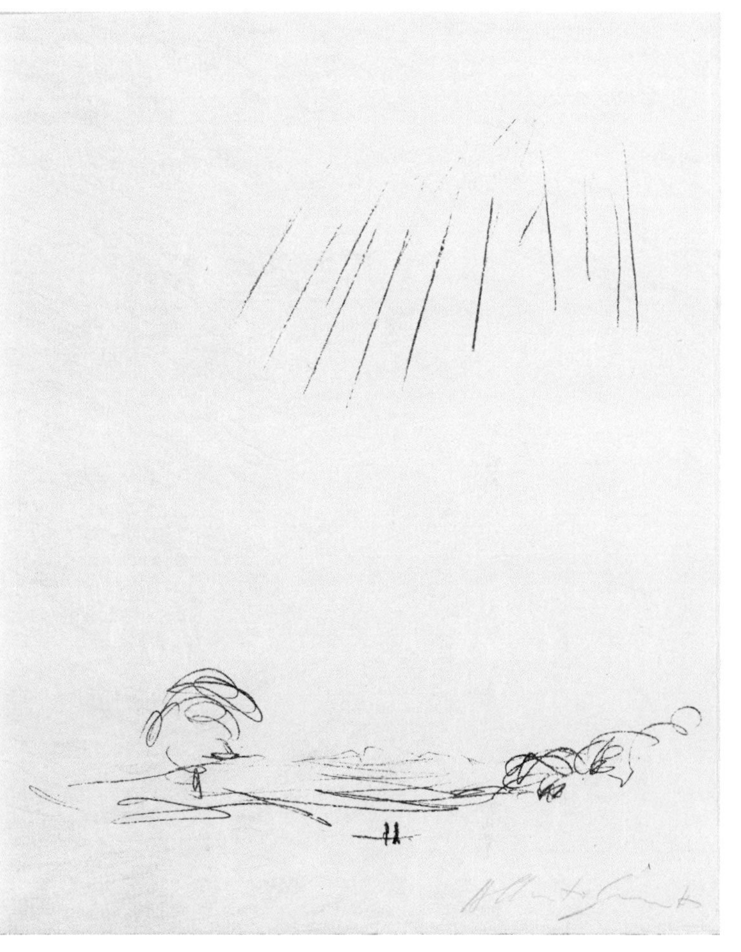

***The Cage*, 1950**
Bronze; 174 x 36 x 40.5 cm.
Fondation Giacometti

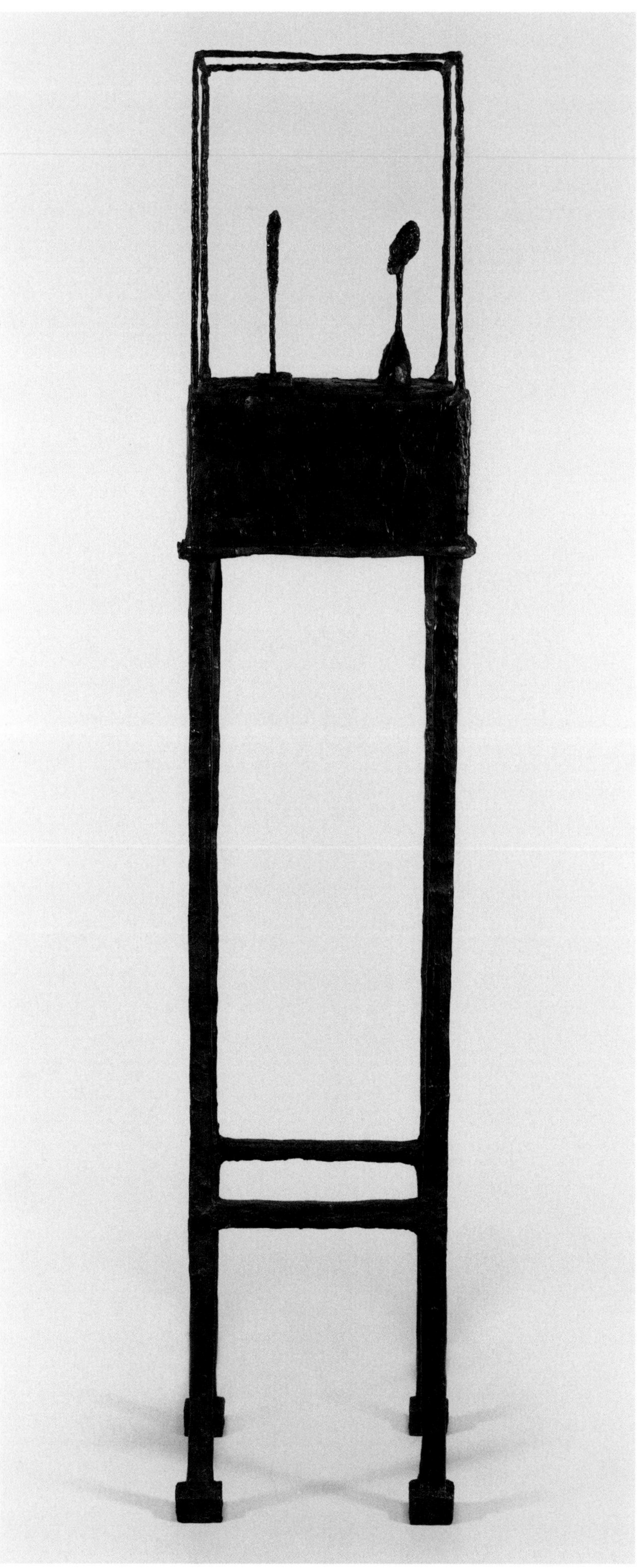

***The Cage, First Version*, 1949–50**
Bronze; 90.5 x 36.5 x 34 cm.
Fondation Giacometti

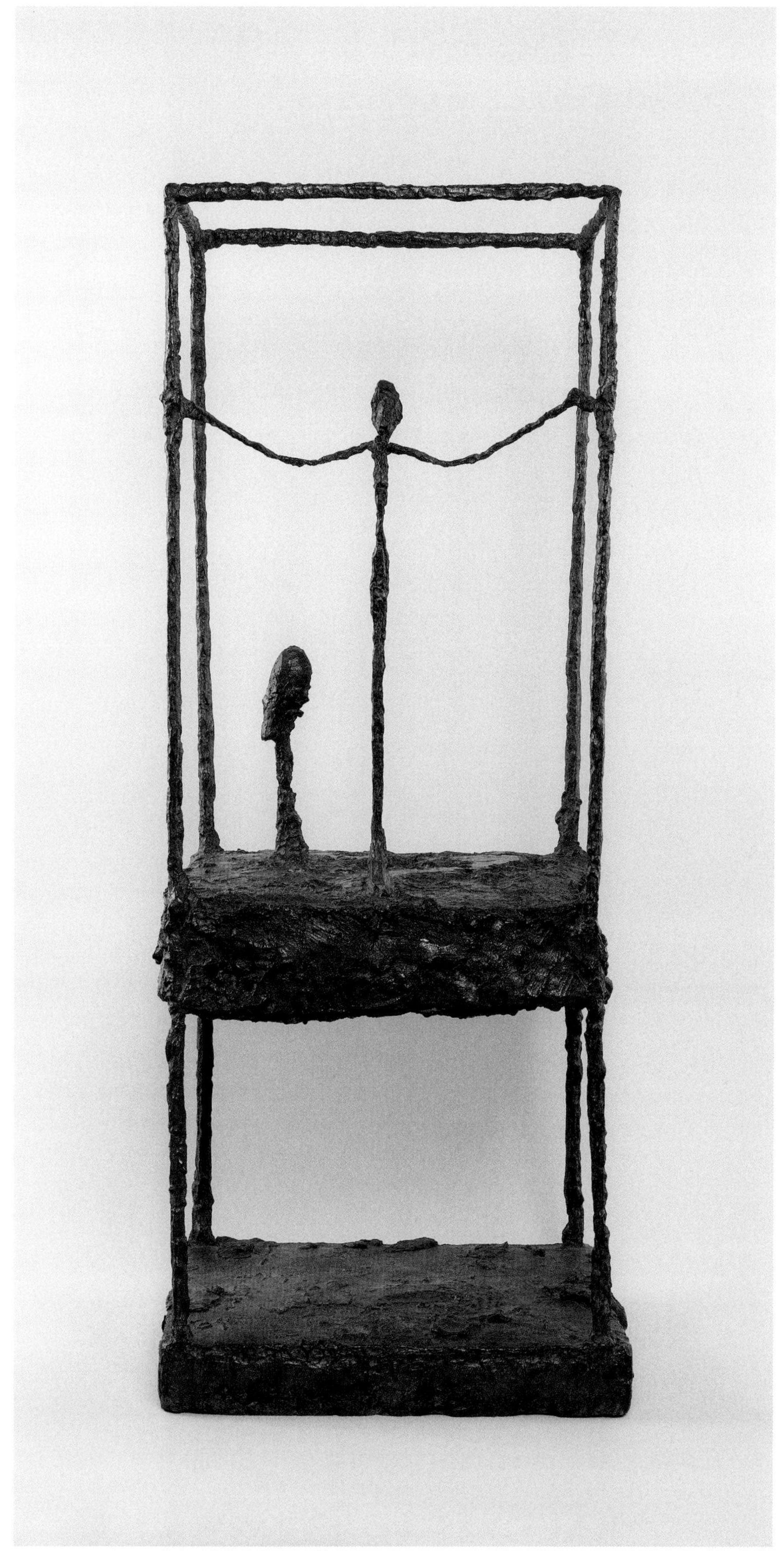

***Four Figurines on a Stand* *(London Figurines)*, 1950–65**
Bronze; 157.5 x 42 x 32 cm.
Fondation Giacometti

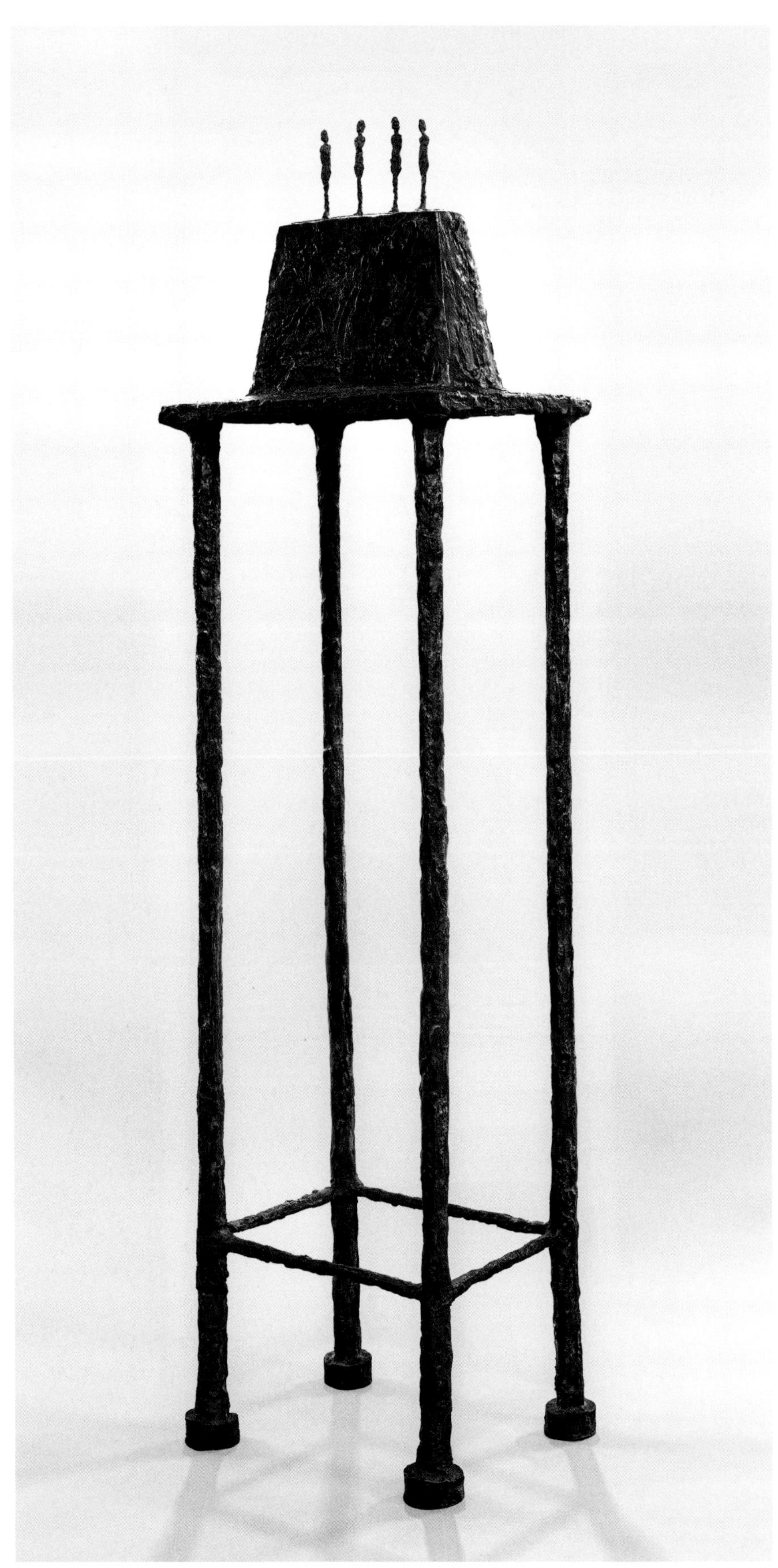

Four Women on a Base, The Chariot, Bust of a Man on a Pedestal, Bust of a Man on a Plinth, Four Figurines on a Stand, Man Crossing a Square on a Sunny Morning, *and* The Cage, 1950
Pencil on a page of notebook;
29 x 22.4 cm.
Fondation Giacometti

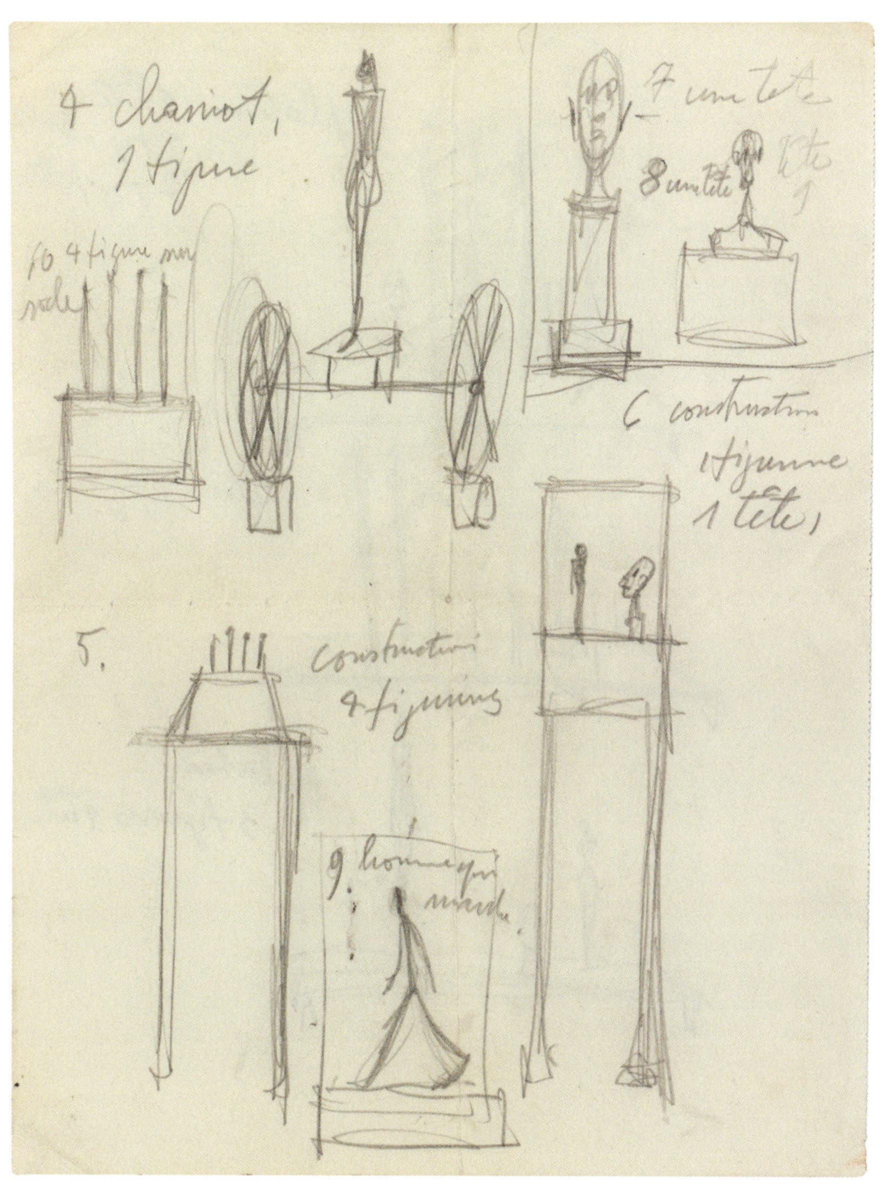

***Three Men Walking*, 1948**
Bronze; 72 x 32.7 x 34.1 cm.
Fondation Giacometti

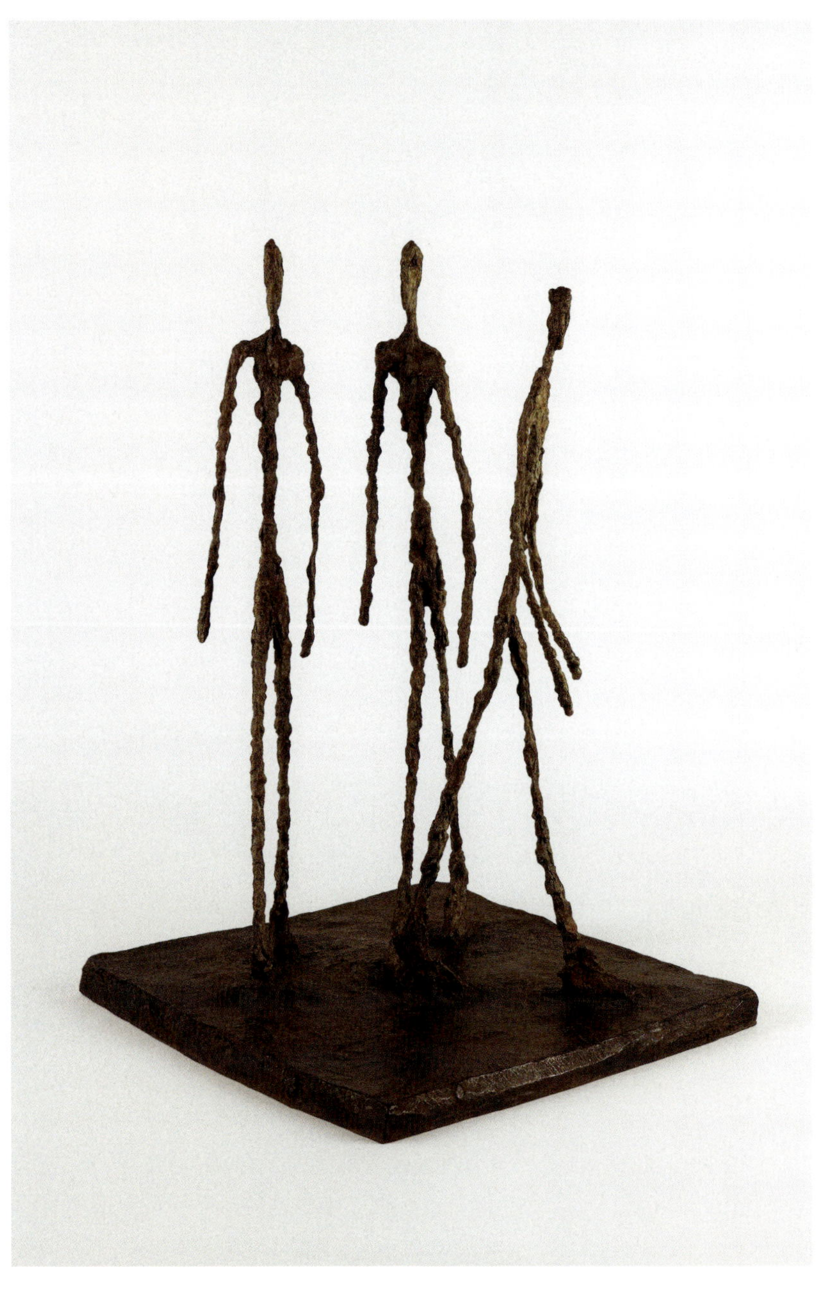

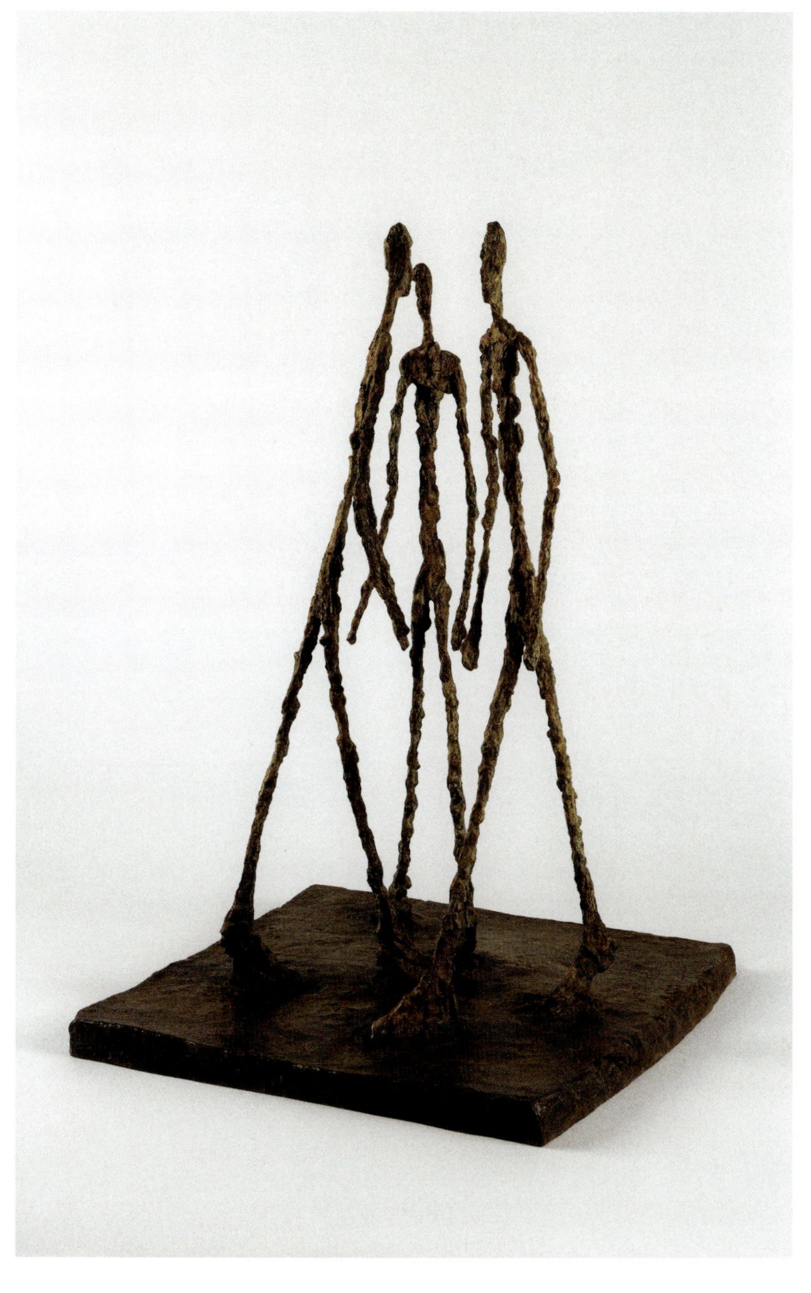

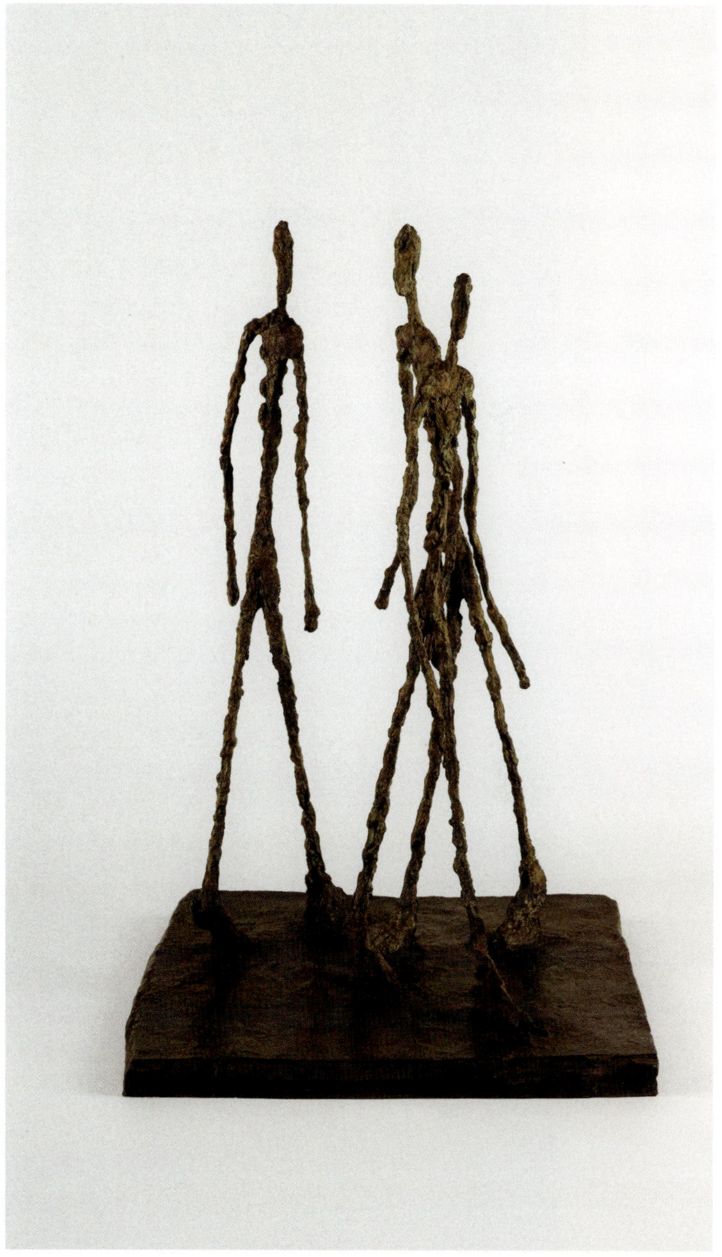

Grappling with the Real

ROMAIN PERRIN

The works Alberto Giacometti made at the end of his life are doubly paradoxical: on the one hand, his desire to depict reality as he perceived it led him to a representation of the model at the limit of caricature, and, on the other, even when the artist reached maturity, he still expressed the necessity to start over again,[1] facing his inability to apprehend the human figure.

That period corresponded to international recognition by institutions, namely the Grand Prix at the Venice Biennale in 1962. Several retrospectives were organized, one after another: at the Kunsthaus Zurich in 1962, then three others in 1965 at the Tate in London, the Museum of Modern Art in New York, and the Louisiana Museum of Modern Art in Humlebaek. The pace at which these exhibitions were organized urged the artist into a dynamic that drove him to work constantly to offer new pieces. The busts of Diego called *New York* were specially produced to be presented in New York, where he headed, crossing the Atlantic Ocean for the first time (pages 198, 199).

Those two sculptures offer a stripping of the human figure that Giacometti had not yet achieved. The resemblance with Diego disappeared under visible stabs made with a pocketknife that recall the incisions made on his female figures. The gesture looks, in certain places, less like modeling than cutting, the artist removing still more matter. The nose, that appendage giving the physiognomy its distinctive character, is emphasized to the point of exaggeration. The result is a scrawny head, a contorted face whose features are so amplified that they verge on the grotesque, as in *Head on a Base* (known as *Head without Skull*) (c. 1958) (page 156). Those pieces seem to relate to a traumatizing image: the memory of a head observed from close up, more than forty years earlier, during a stay in the Tyrol in which his traveling companion suddenly died, as he narrated in "Le Rêve, le Sphinx et la mort de T." (The Dream, the Sphinx and the Death of T.): "I looked at Van M.'s head transforming (the nose more and more accentuated, the cheeks hollowing, the open mouth almost barely breathing and, towards evening, trying to draw that profile, I was suddenly very scared at the thought that he might die)."[2]

A transfer took place between the sculptor and his model, as poet Yves Bonnefoy wrote: "Those terrible gully erosions of the face, in *Bust of a Man (New York I)*, it is self-awareness taking hold of another person's face to experience in it the anxiety of what will be one's death."[3] This anxiety was not new; it already permeated his sculptures from the end of the 1940s and the beginning of the 1950s, but it became more acute with time. The period was, in that respect, grueling: in 1963, Giacometti was operated on for stomach cancer, and Annetta, his mother, one of the pillars of his existence, fell ill and died the following year. From those statues of primitive expressionism comes an intense gaze, which, for Giacometti, is the expression of life, as it gives those busts the quality of strange vanitas.

1. Alberto Giacometti, note dated February 19, 1963, Archive, Fondation Giacometti, published in Giacometti, *Écrits: Articles, notes et entretiens* (Paris: Hermann and Fondation Giacometti, 2007), 571: "To start all over again from scratch as I see beings and things."

2. Giacometti, "Le Rêve, le Sphinx et la mort de T.," *Labyrinthe*, no. 22–23 (December 1946): 12–13; reprinted in Giacometti, *The Dream, the Sphinx and the Death of T.* (Paris: Hermann and Fondation Giacometti, 2021), 28–33.

3. Yves Bonnefoy, *Giacometti: biographie d'une oeuvre* [1991] (Paris: Gallimard, 2018), 374.

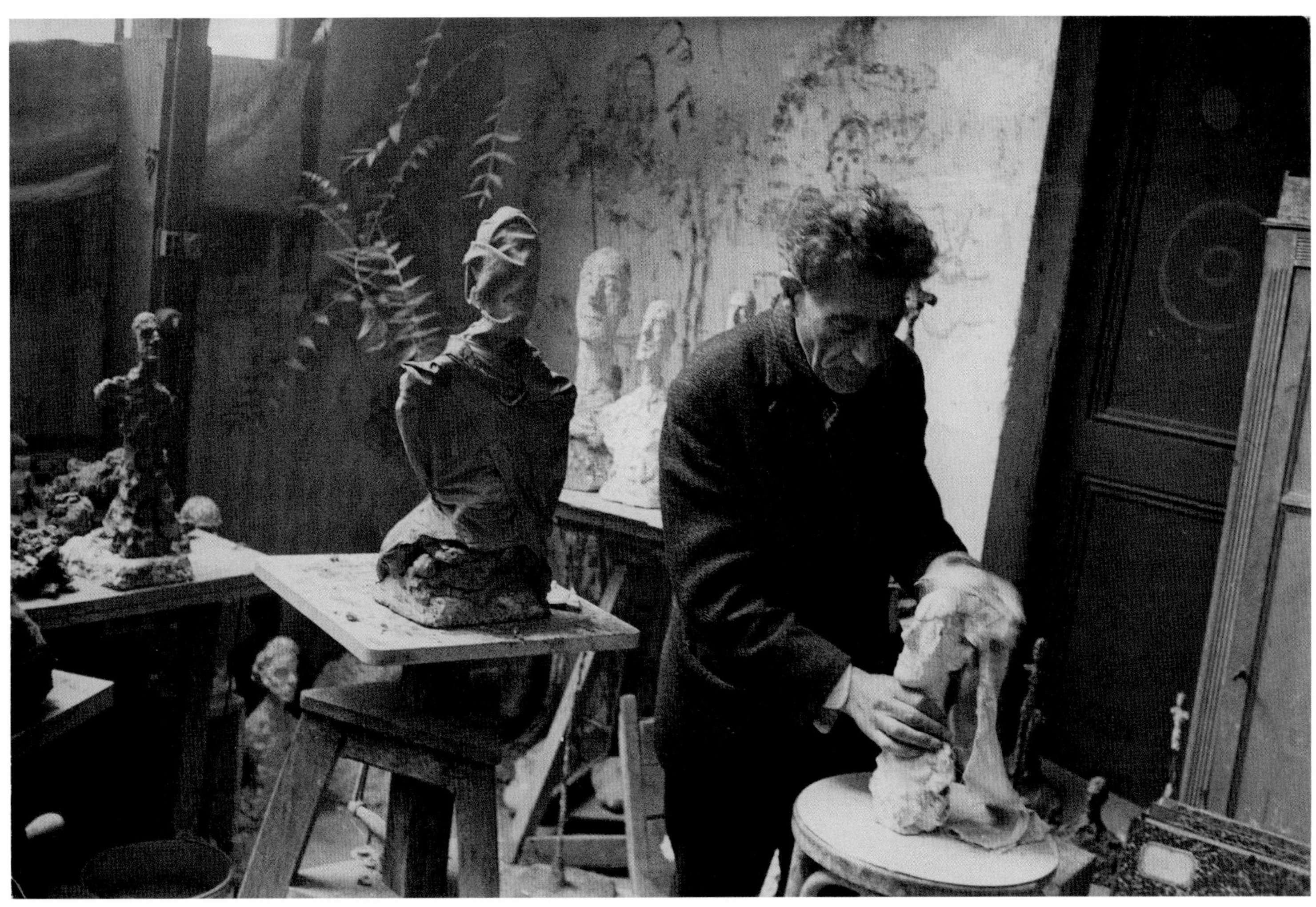

Alberto Giacometti in his studio, c. May 1965
Jack Nisberg.
Archives, Fondation Giacometti.

***Bust of a Man (New York I)*, 1965**
Bronze; 53.9 x 29.4 x 17.8 cm.
Fondation Giacometti

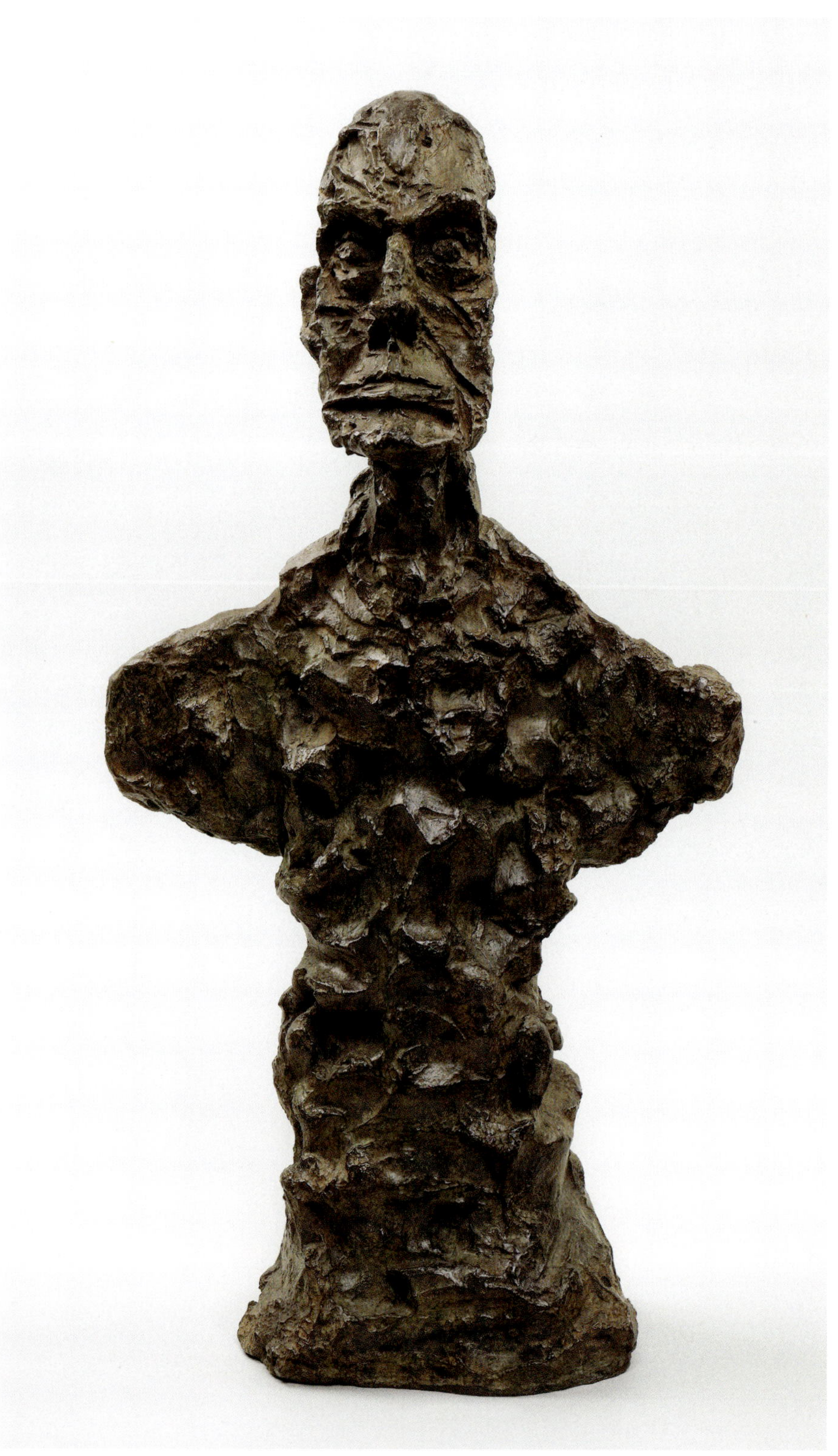

***Bust of a Man (New York II)*, 1965**
Bronze; 46.9 x 24.5 x 15.9 cm.
Fondation Giacometti

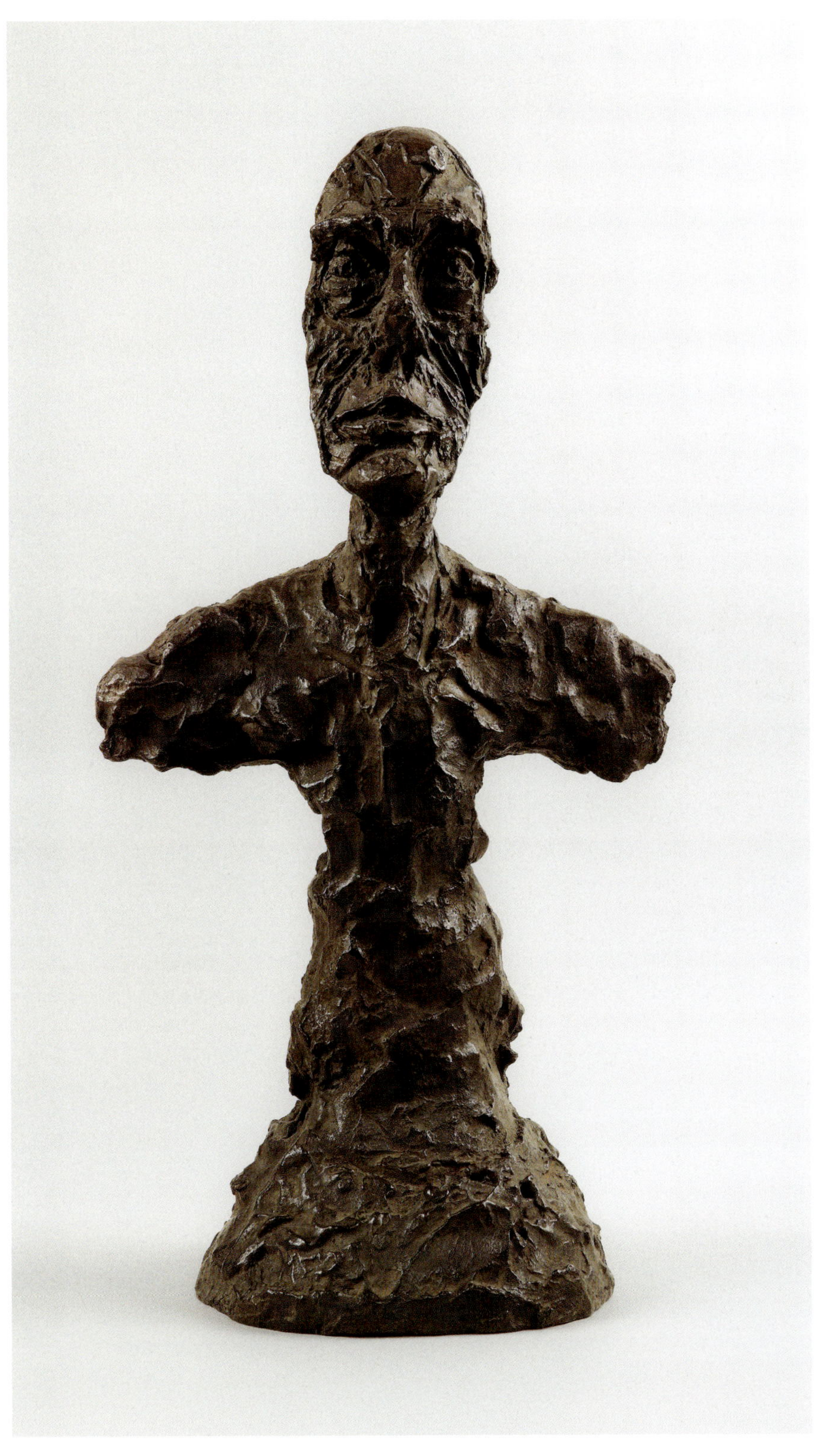

***Half-Length of a Man*, 1965**
Bronze; 59.1 x 19 x 32.1 cm.
Fondation Giacometti

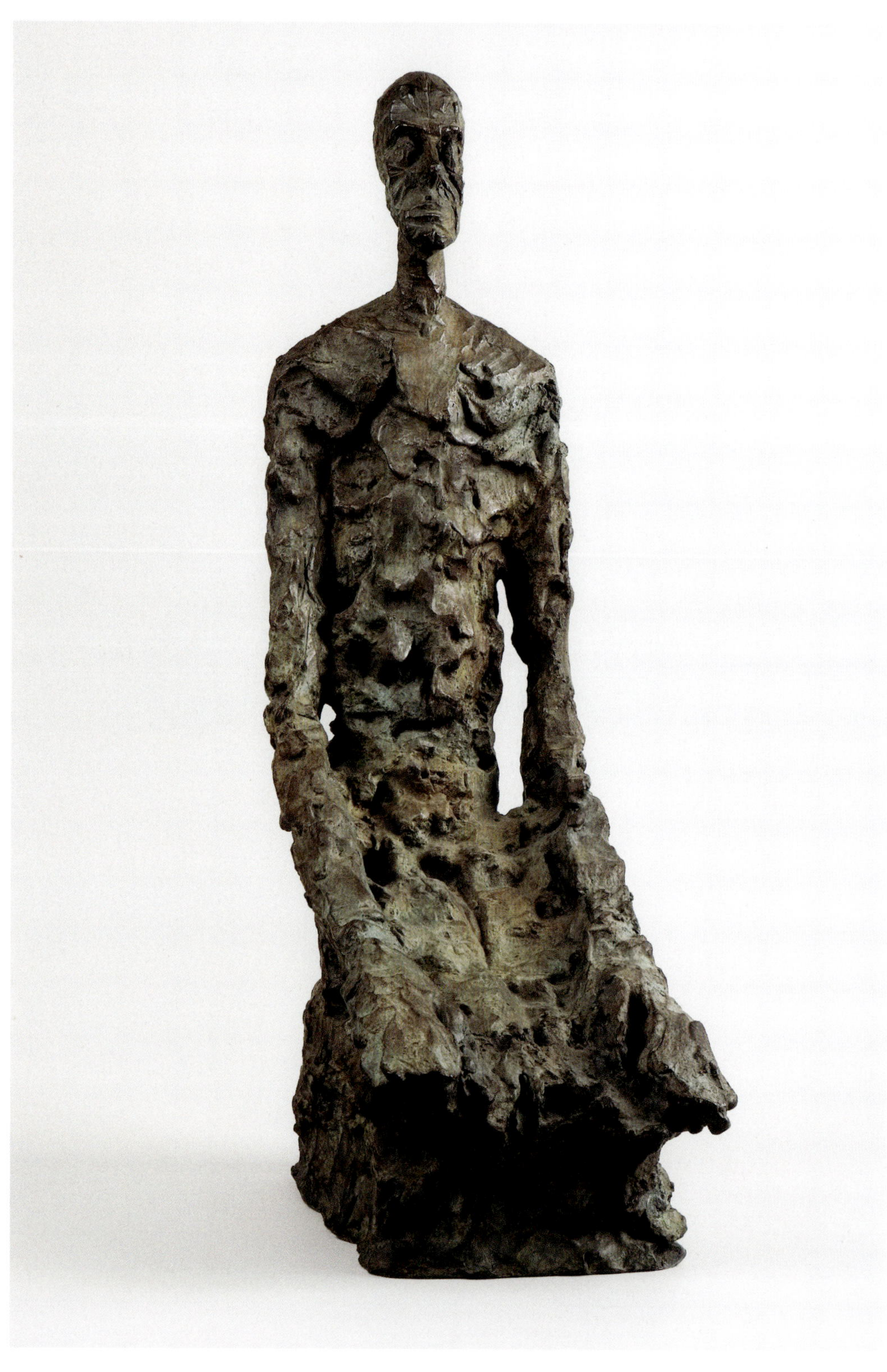

***Standing Nude*, 1961**
Oil on canvas; 69 x 49.5 cm.
Fondation Giacometti

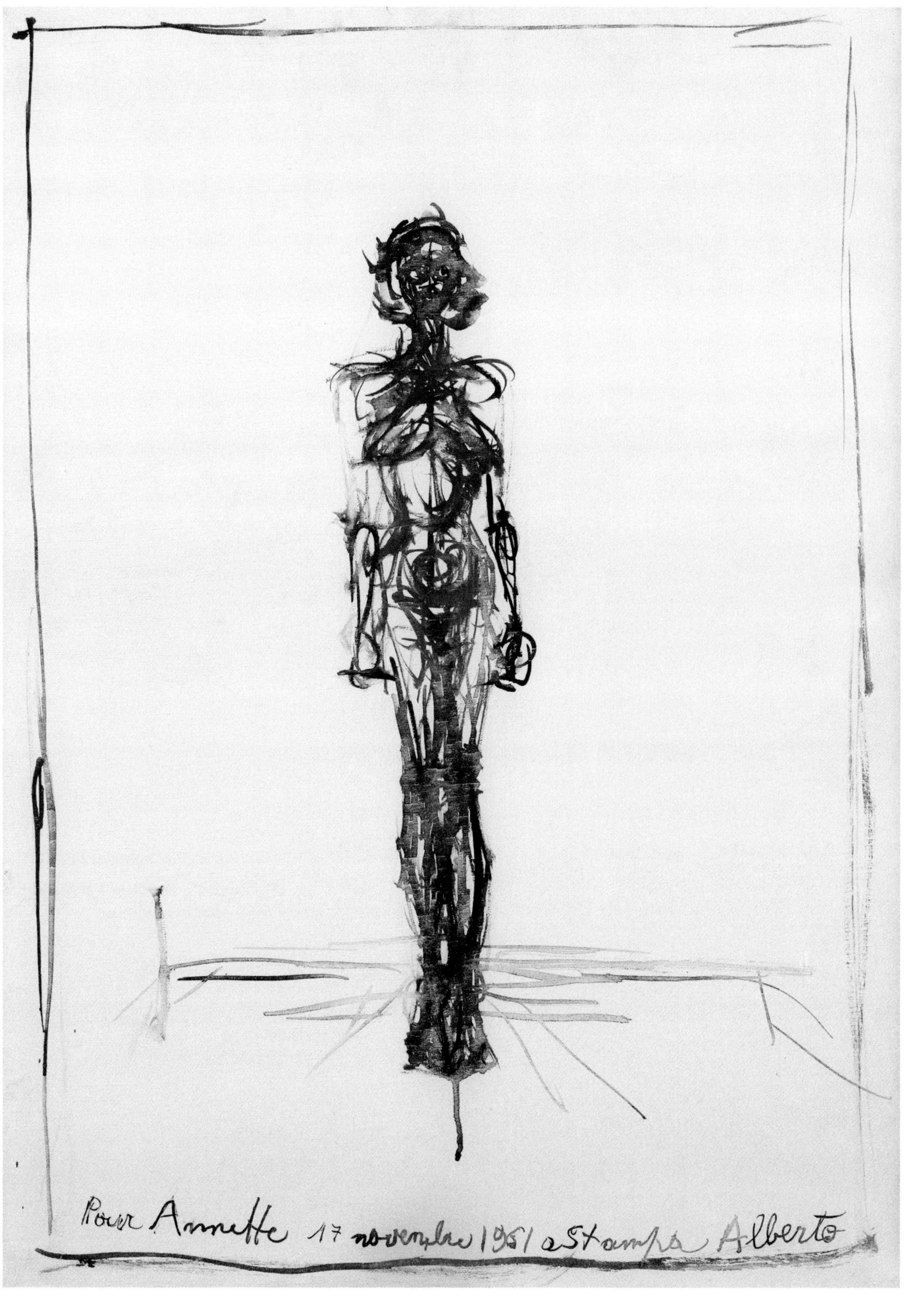

Walking Man, Standing Woman

ROMAIN PERRIN

Alberto Giacometti working on the plaster of the *Walking Man*, 1959
Ernst Scheidegger.
Archives, Fondation Giacometti.

In 1961, in an interview for *L'Express*, Alberto Giacometti declared to critic Pierre Schneider: "I make a woman stand still, but I always make a man walk."[1] It was not a wish to provoke on his part, but a way to record the evolution of his latest works. For if that statement appears like immutable evidence, it was not always the case.

The first walking figure made by Giacometti, then a member of the Surrealist group, was indeed *Walking Woman* (1932), whose gait recalls that of pharaonic Egyptian statues. After the war, the artist described to his New York gallerist Pierre Matisse the sculpture called *The Night* (1946) as "a thin young woman feeling her way in the dark."[2] However, the walking figures that were to follow become androgynous silhouettes before explicitly taking the name *Walking Man* in 1947. During those same years, Giacometti made several female figures whose stillness contrasts with the dynamism of the male subjects and reinforces their respective characteristics. While the standing women, whose hieratic appearance belongs to antiquity, endured, the sculptural motif of the walking man disappeared in 1951 to resurface a few years later for a special occasion.

To look into the motif of walking is to confront art history from antiquity, and particularly the major figure of Auguste Rodin. Like him, Giacometti did not try representing objectively the movement of walking as photography is able to do. On the contrary, he chose to show a synthesis of the various positions of a body to give the impression of movement. During a period marked by a serious concern for abstraction, Giacometti's figures—a walking man or a standing woman, halfway between the sign and the figurative sculpture—show his refusal to abandon representation, which he pushed to its limit.

Tall Woman IV and *Walking Man I* are two sculptures that stemmed from a major project for the square in front of the Chase Manhattan Bank in New York, built by Gordon Bunshaft (pages 214–18). In November 1958, the American architect invited Giacometti to join the competition to create a public sculpture. Full of enthusiasm, the artist worked on it throughout 1959 and for part of the following year. His idea was based on the principle of a dialogue between sculptures of different natures that referred to earlier pieces: a large head, a walking man, and a very tall standing woman (page 204). As Giacometti had never been to New York, and was concerned with questions of scale, he defined the proportions for each sculpture based on the size of passersby, never hesitating to take the pieces from the studio and see how they looked in the street. Giacometti was used to working with dimensions close to the human scale and found himself confronted with new difficulties. In 1961, after several attempts at making his figures again, the artist withdrew from the project, even though some of the models had already been cast. Those were to be shown later in several exhibitions. Despite it all, Giacometti succeeded in creating emblematic sculptures. The year he abandoned his project was the year he was given the Carnegie Prize for *Walking Man I*. By stripping that sculpture of all clues enabling one to assign it within a period or genre, he conferred on it, as in *Tall Woman IV* a universal character.

1. Pierre Schneider, "*Ma longue marche* par Alberto Giacometti," *L'Express*, no. 521 (June 1961): 48–50; reprinted in Alberto Giacometti, *Écrits: Articles, notes et entretiens* (Paris: Hermann and Fondation Giacometti, 2007), 236.

2. Giacometti to Pierre Matisse, October 27(?), 1947, Pierre Matisse Gallery Archives, The Morgan Library & Museum, New York, box 11, folder 7, item 11.

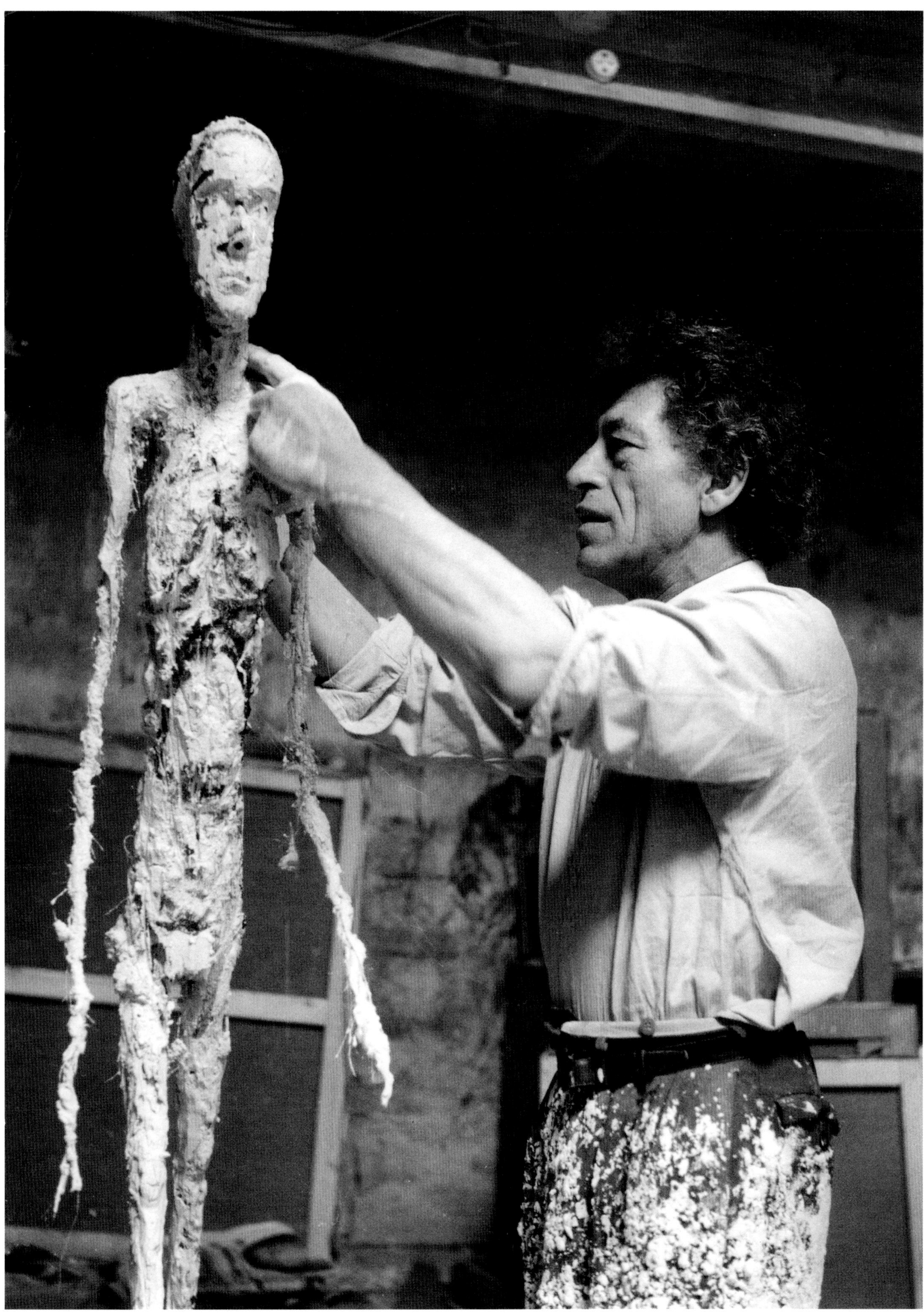

***Project for the Chase Manhattan Plaza*: Walking Man, Standing Woman, Head on a Base, 1959**
Bronze; *Walking Man*: 7.3 x 1.2 x 8.5 cm; *Standing Woman*: 10.5 x 3.9 x 2.6 cm; *Head on a Base*: 6.1 x 1.3 x 1.8 cm.
Fondation Giacometti

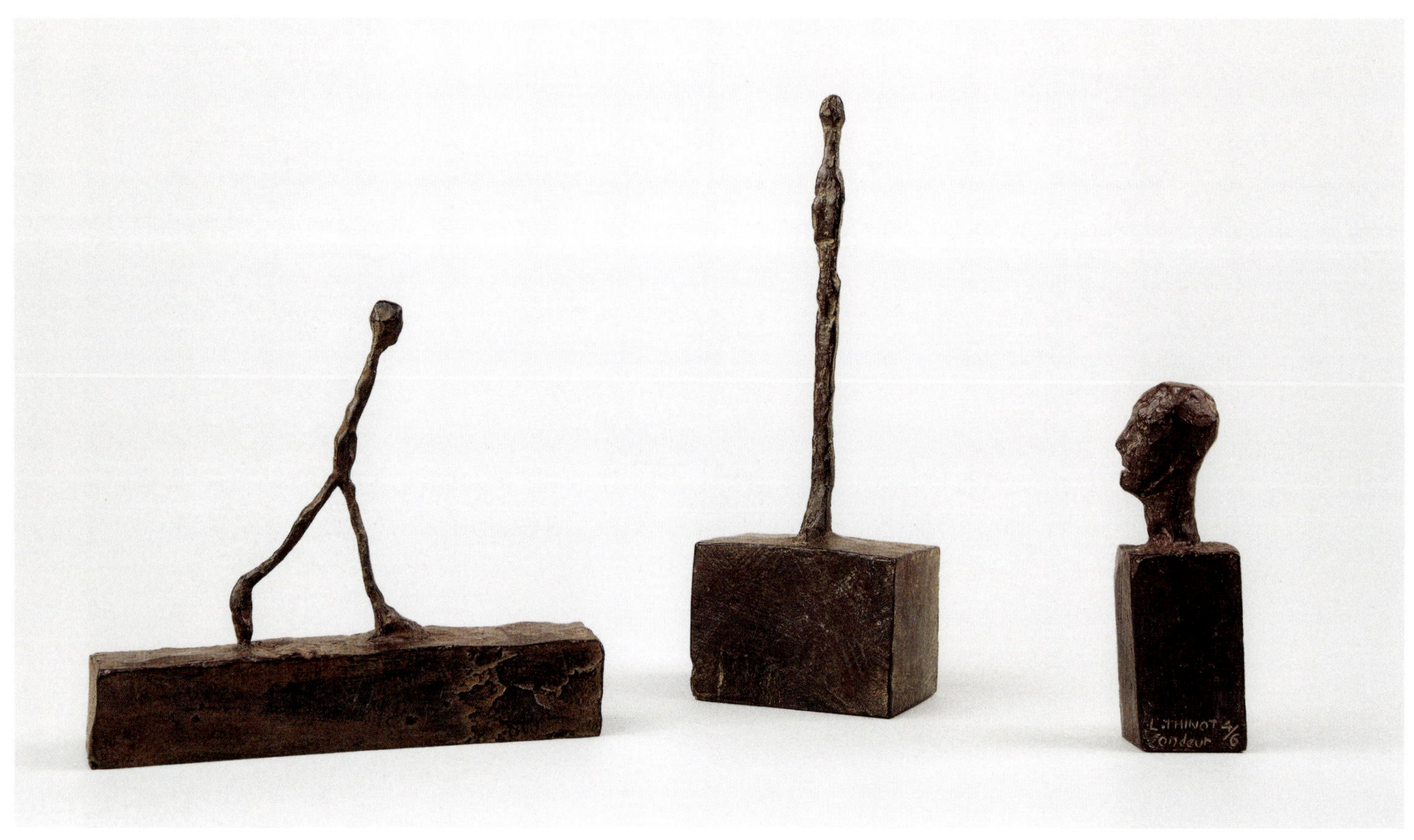

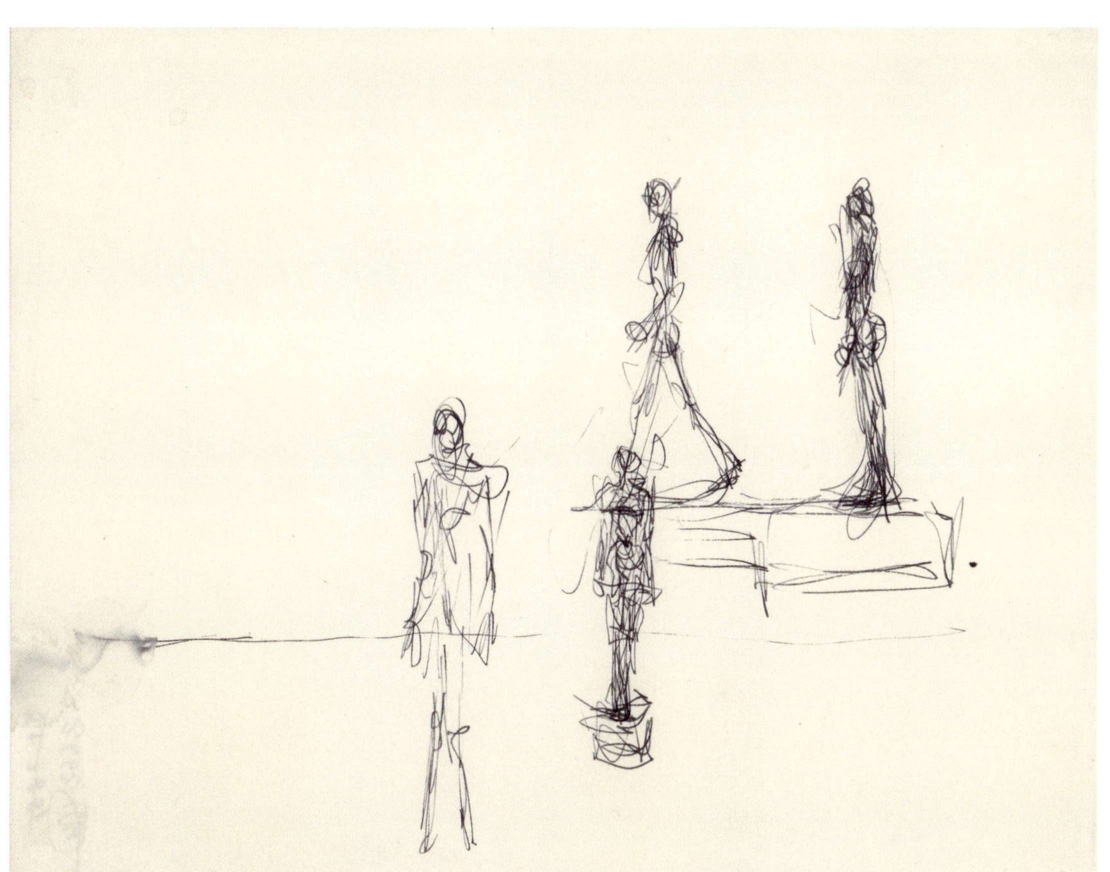

***Walking Men and Standing Figures*, 1959**
Blue ink on paper;
20.7 x 26.8 cm.
Fondation Giacometti

***Walking Man*, c. 1959**
Blue ballpoint pen on squared
paper; 17 x 11 cm.
Fondation Giacometti

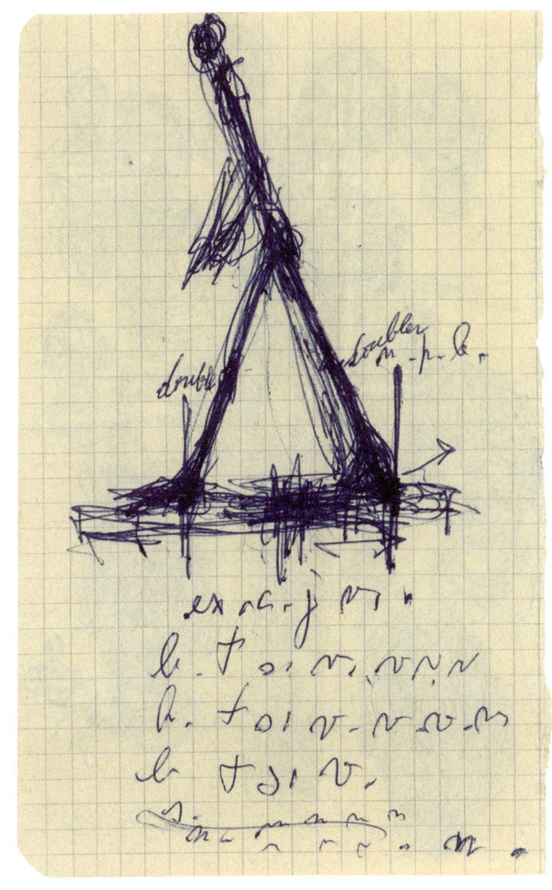

Standing Woman VII *and* Walking Man II, 1961–62
Printed by Les Presses de Maeght Editeur, Paris.
Lithograph; sheet: 32.5 x 50.4 cm.
Fondation Giacometti

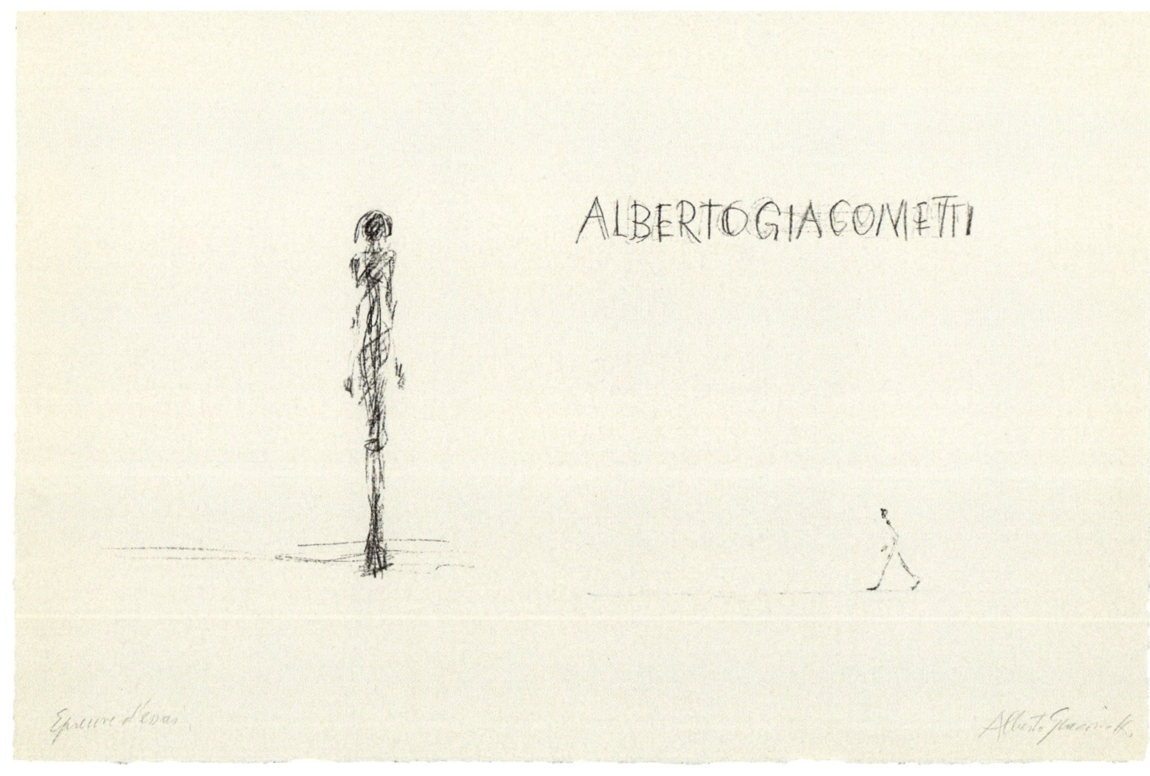

***Standing Woman, Figures, and Heads on the Invitation Card of the Exhibition* Hecq, *Galerie Raymond Creuze, April 1959*, c. April 1959**
Blue ballpoint pen on invitation card; 23 x 20.5 cm.
Fondation Giacometti

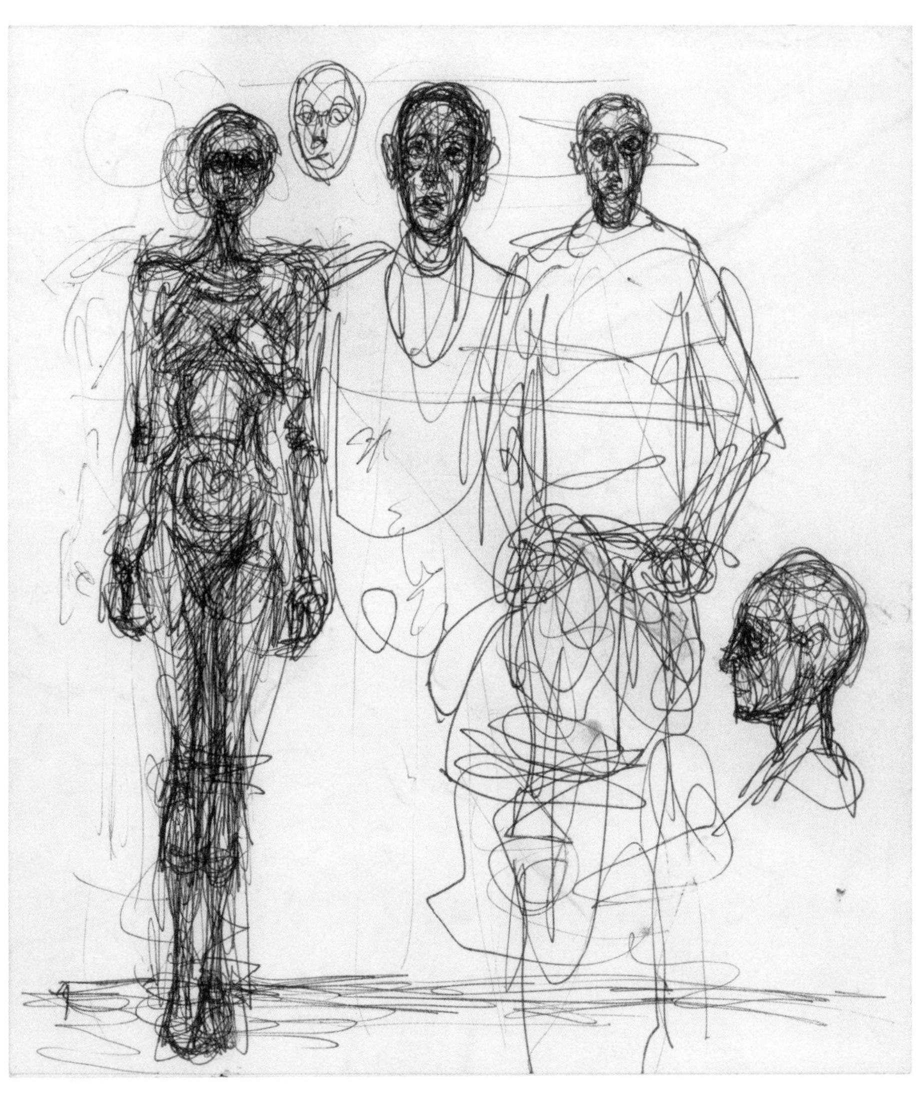

***Standing Nude*, c. 1935**
Pencil on paper; 49.1 x 31.5 cm.
Fondation Giacometti

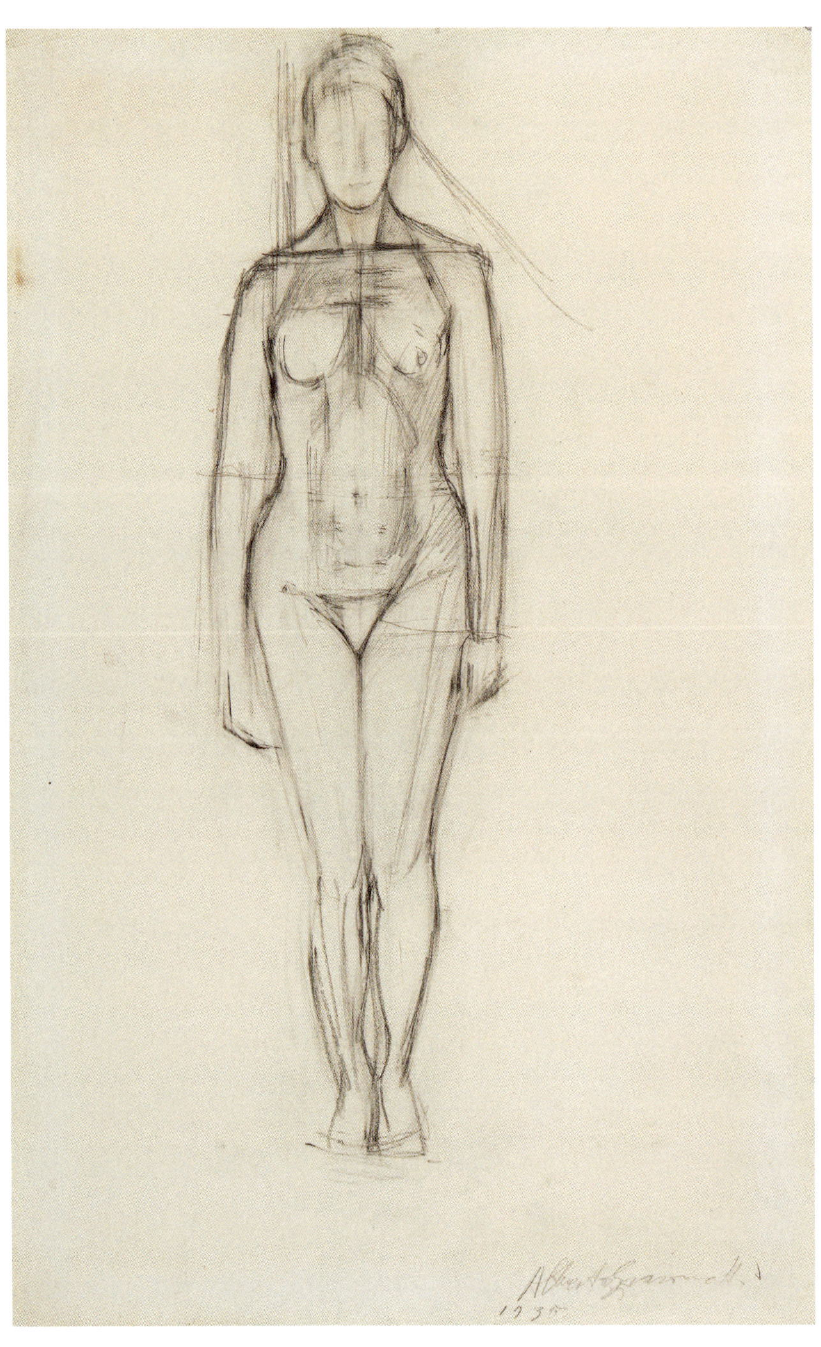

***Sketches for a Figure on a Base*, 1945–46**
Pencil on notebook;
notebook open: 12.5 x 15.8 cm.
Fondation Giacometti

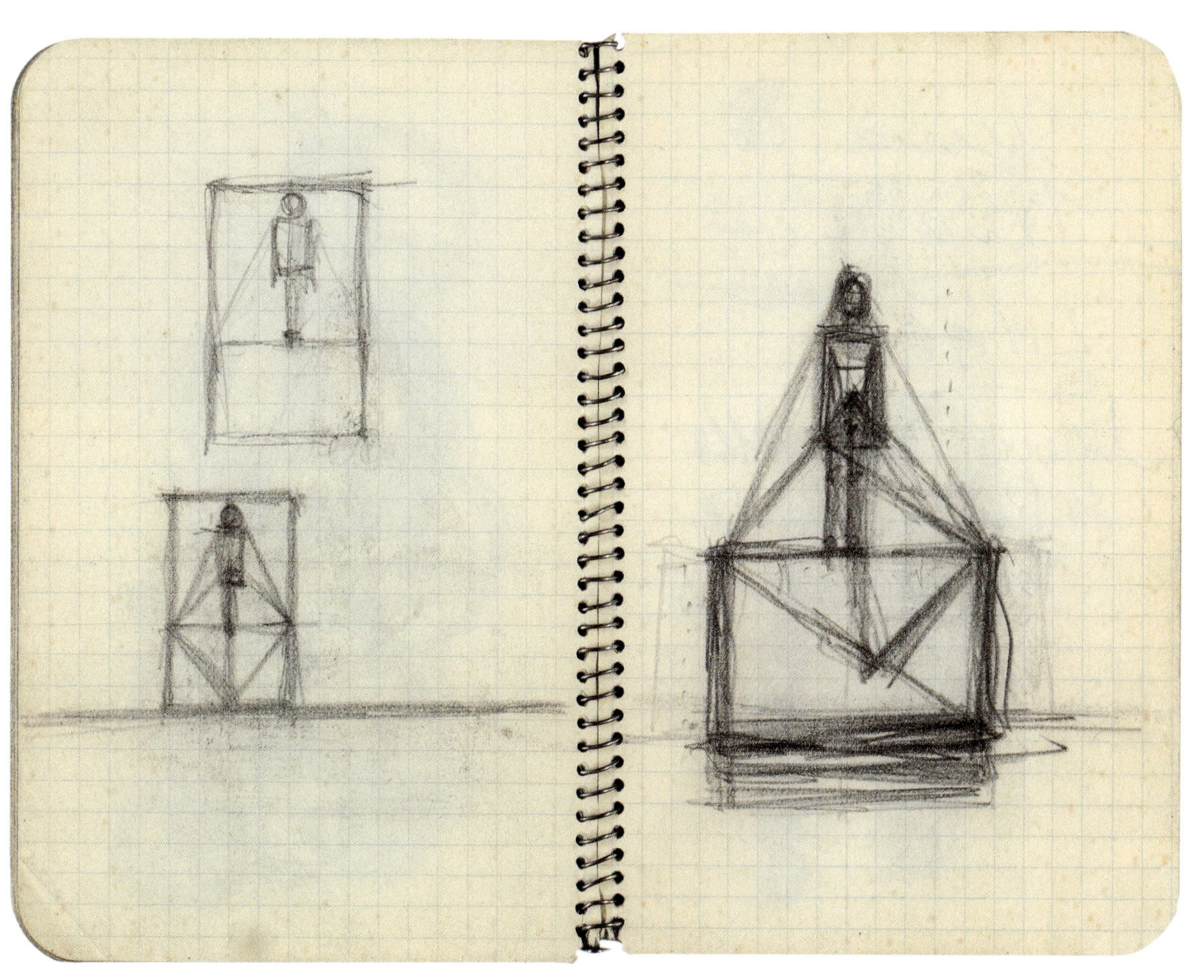

***Standing Nude*, 1949**
Pencil on paper; 50 x 32.5 cm.
Fondation Giacometti

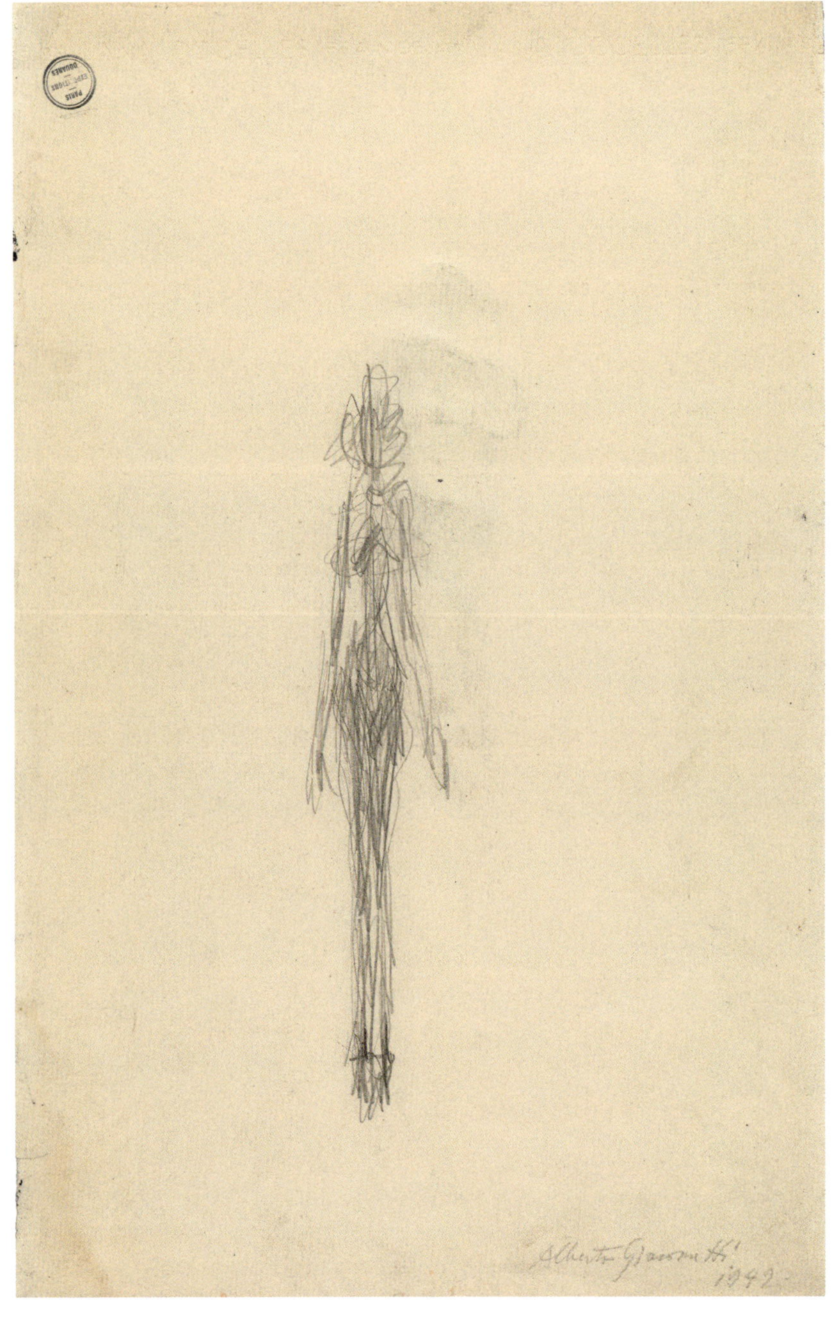

***Standing Nude II*, 1961**
Printed by Les Presses de Maeght.
Edited by Maeght éditeur, Paris.
Lithograph; 76.1 x 56.5 cm.
Fondation Giacometti

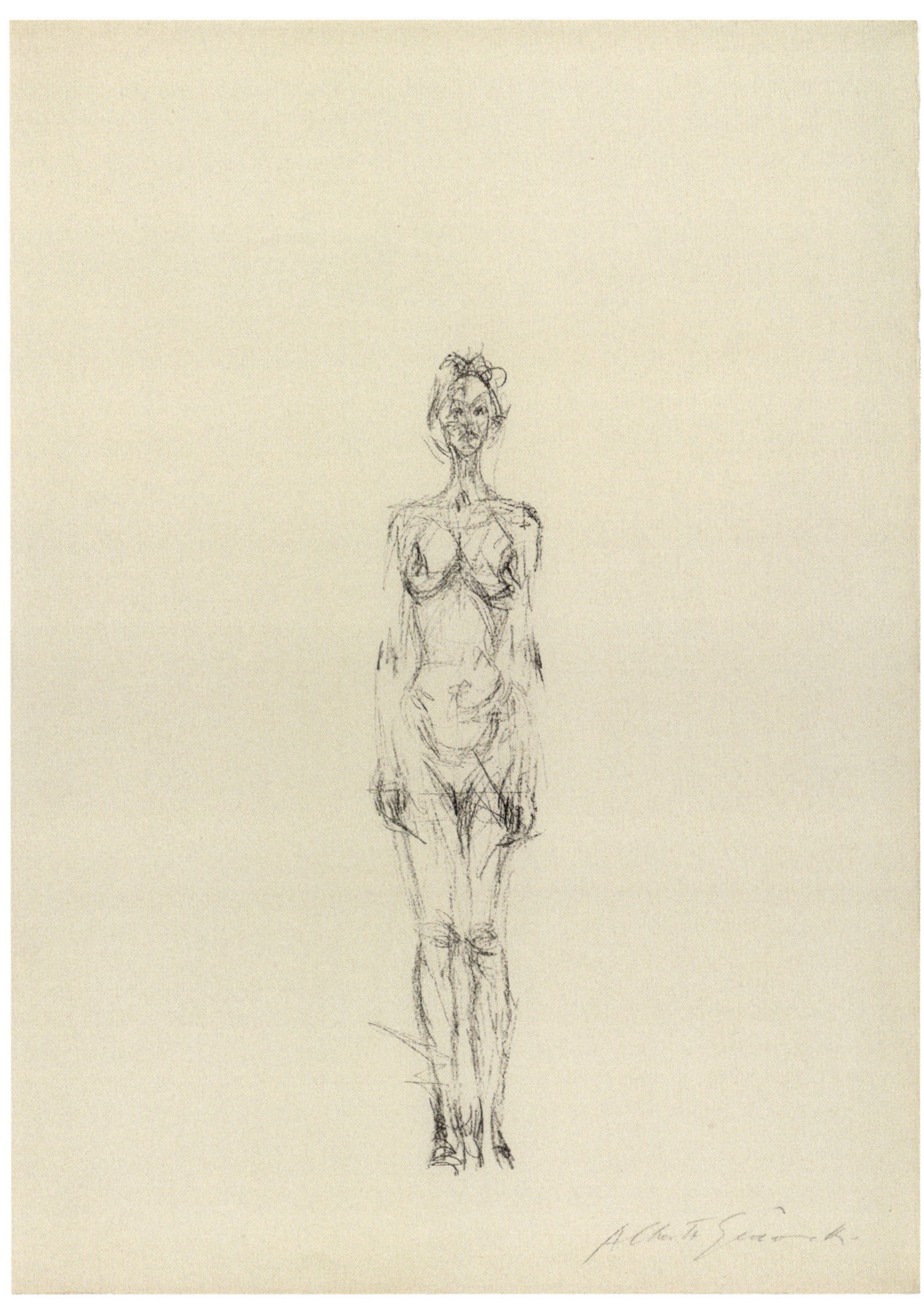

***Standing Nude in an Interior*,**
c. 1950
Pencil on paper; 50.4 x 32.7 cm.
Fondation Giacometti

***Standing Nudes on a Page of* Combat*, May 20, 1963*,**
c. May 1963
Ballpoint pen on a detached newspaper page; 52 x 37.6 cm.
Fondation Giacometti

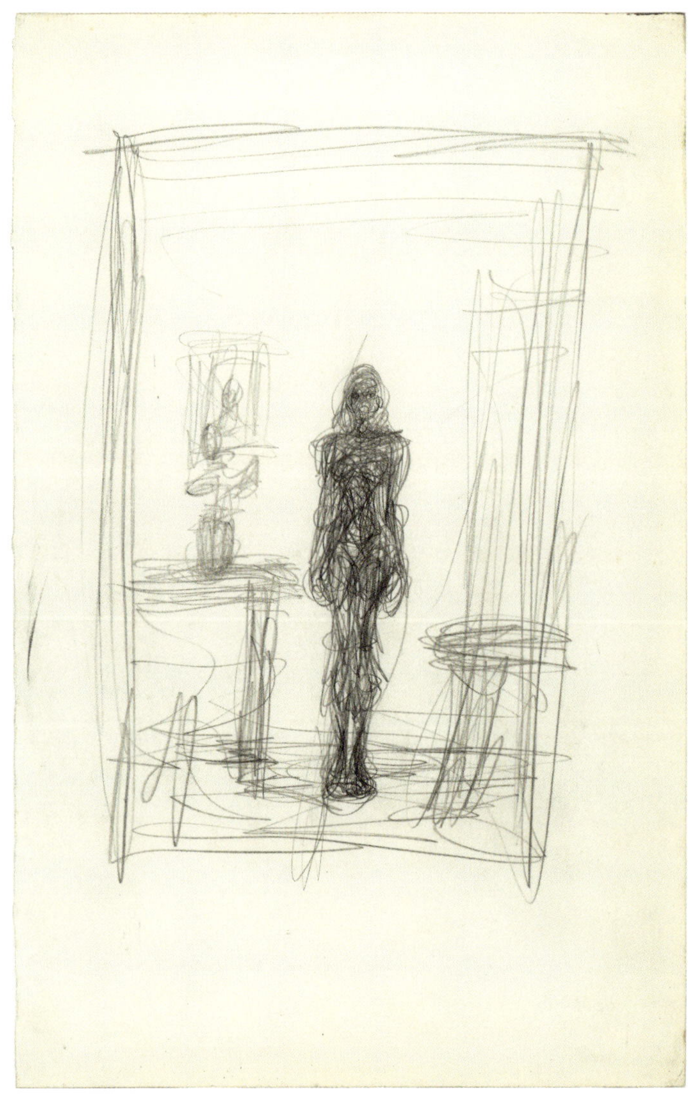

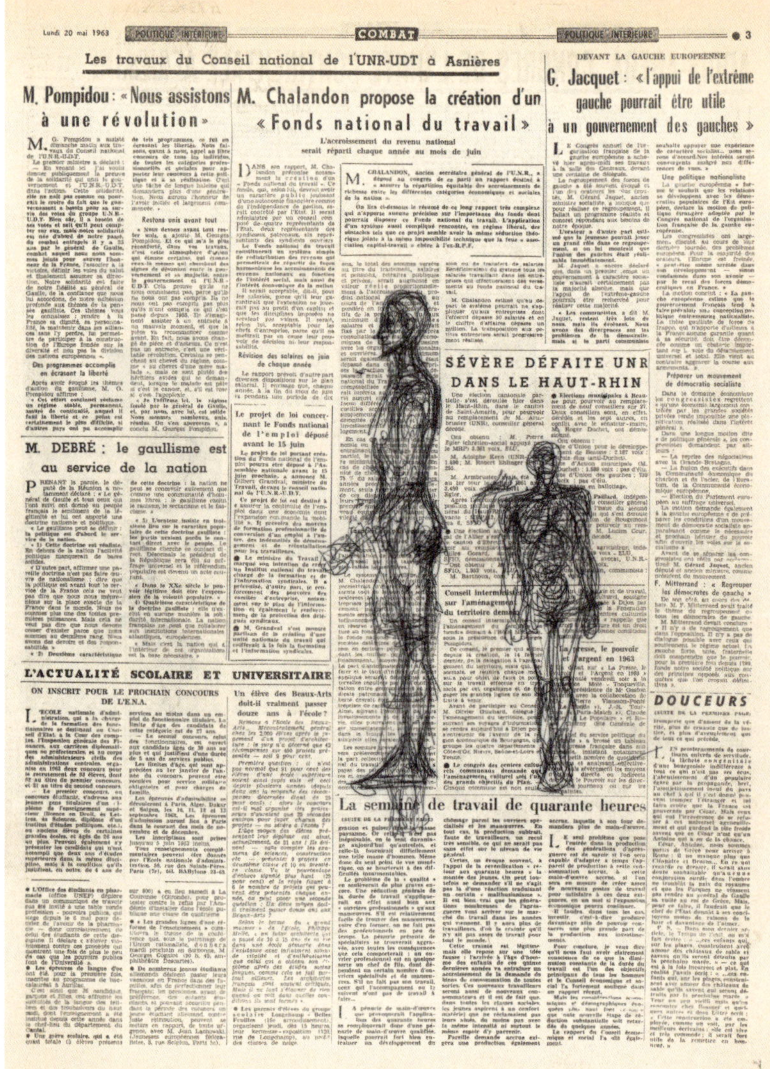

Lundi 20 mai 1963 POLITIQUE INTÉRIEURE COMBAT POLITIQUE INTÉRIEURE 3

Les travaux du Conseil national de l'UNR-UDT à Asnières

M. Pompidou : « Nous assistons à une révolution »

M. Chalandon propose la création d'un « Fonds national du travail »

L'accroissement du revenu national serait réparti chaque année au mois de juin

DEVANT LA GAUCHE EUROPEENNE

G. Jacquet : « l'appui de l'extrême gauche pourrait être utile à un gouvernement des gauches »

Une politique nationaliste

Restons unis avant tout

M. DEBRÉ : le gaullisme est au service de la nation

SÉVÈRE DÉFAITE UNR DANS LE HAUT-RHIN

L'ACTUALITÉ SCOLAIRE ET UNIVERSITAIRE

ON INSCRIT POUR LE PROCHAIN CONCOURS DE L'E.N.A.

Un élève des Beaux-Arts doit-il vraiment passer douze ans à l'école ?

La semaine de travail de quarante heures

DOUCEURS

***Standing Woman*,**
c. 1949–58
Oil on paper; 68.3 x 51.3 cm.
Fondation Giacometti

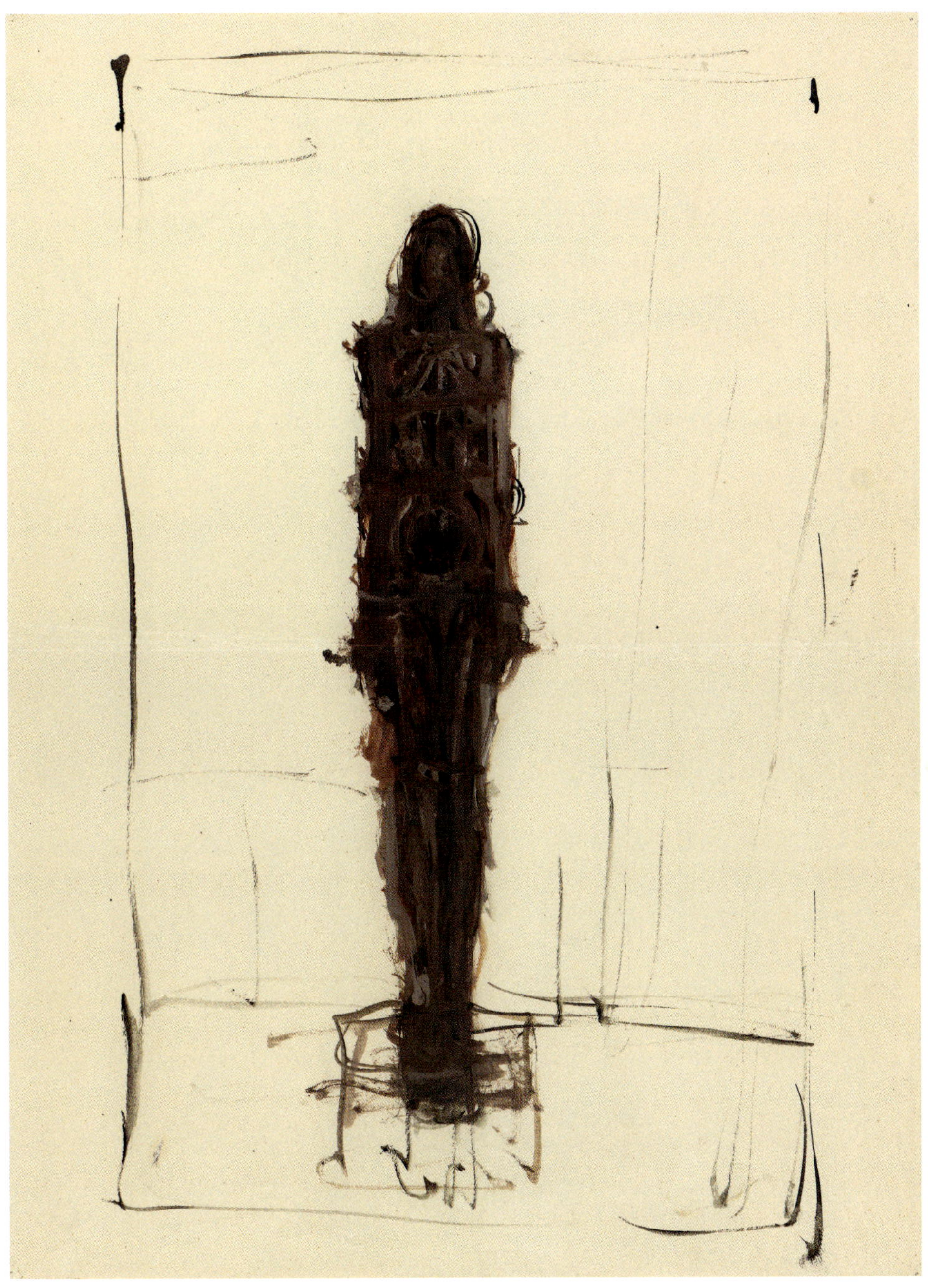

***Tall Woman IV*, 1960–61**
Bronze; 270 x 31.5 x 56.5 cm.
Fondation Giacometti

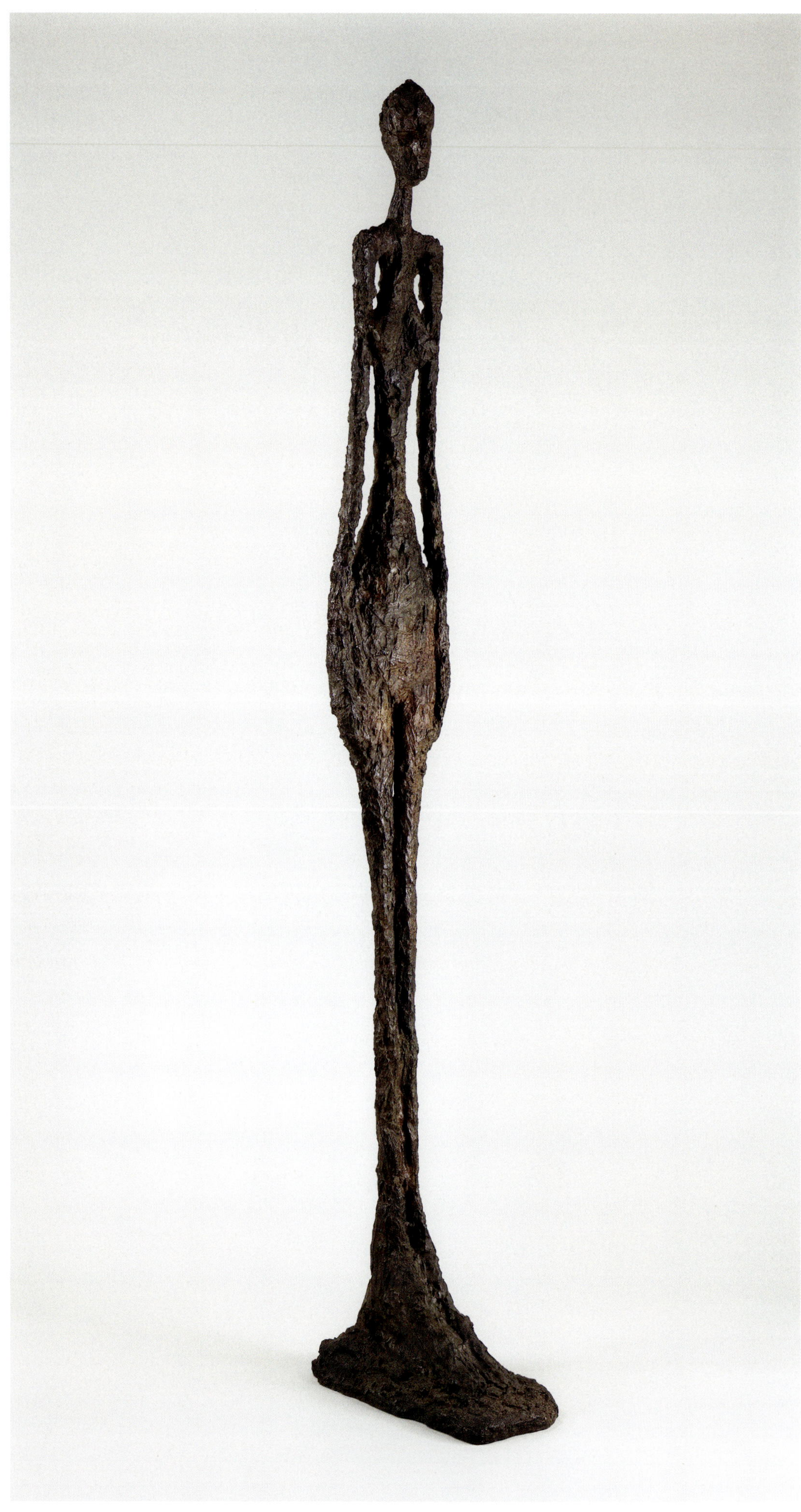

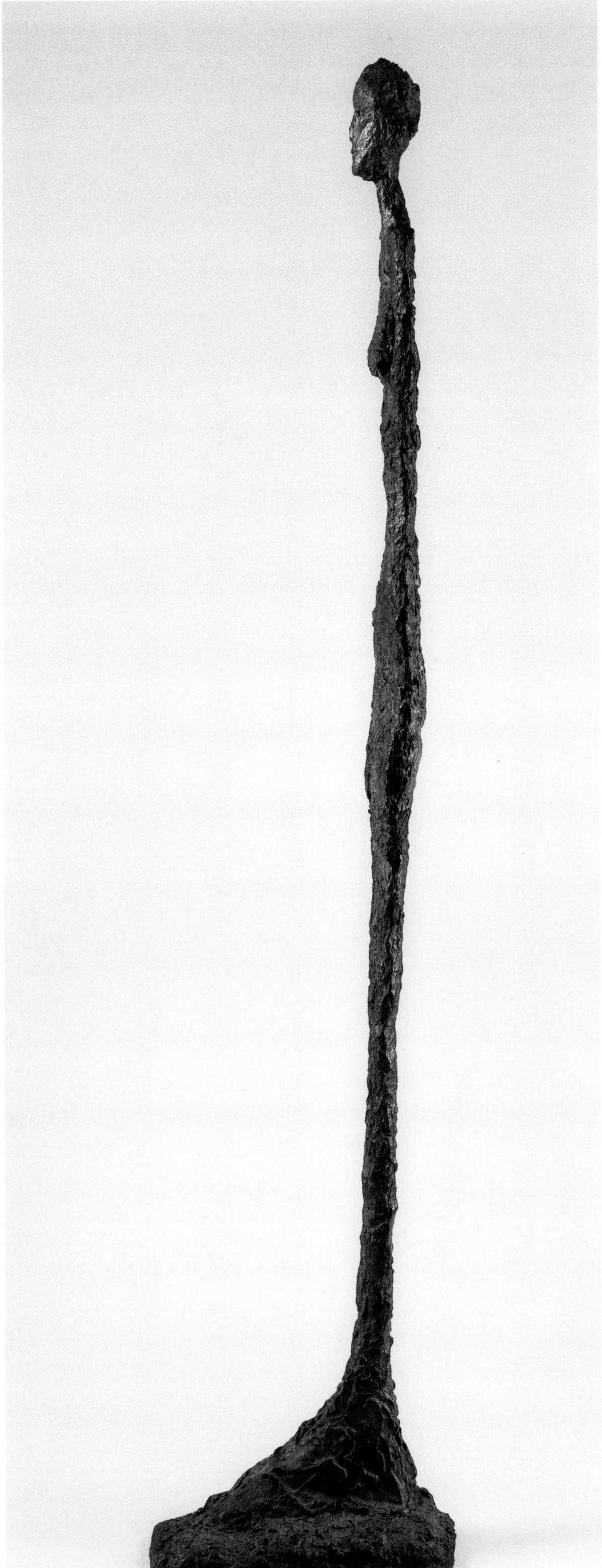

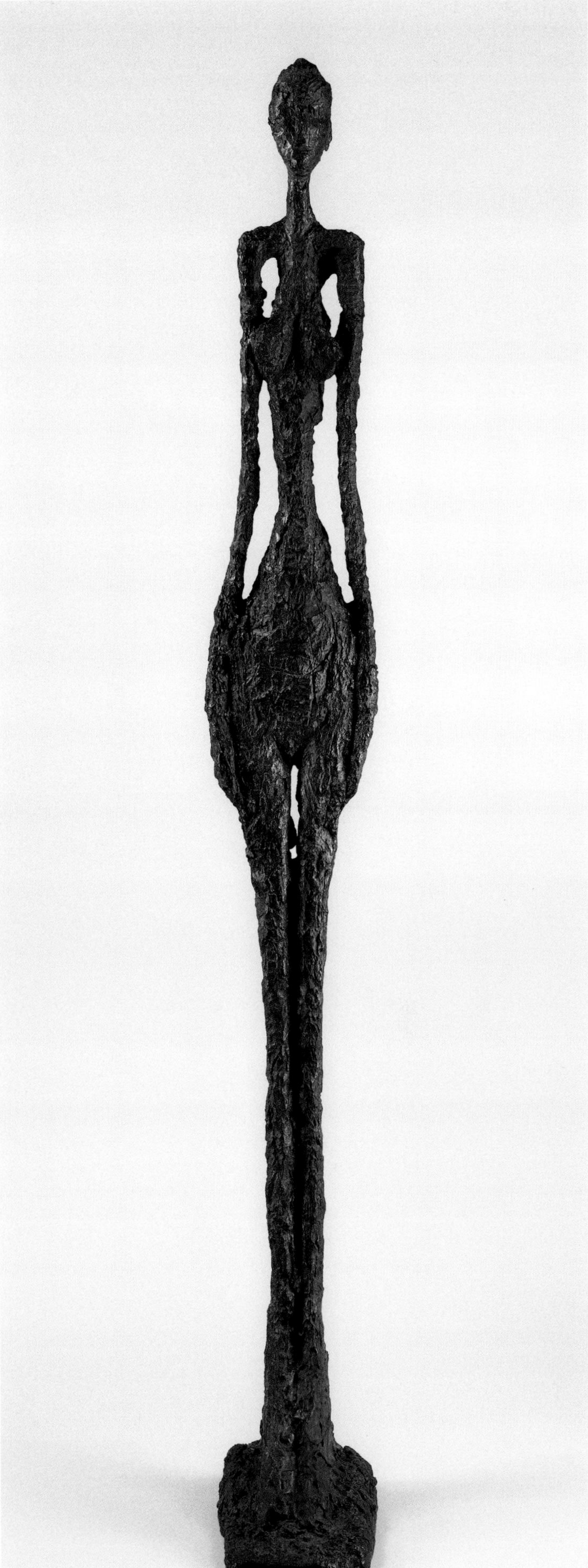

***Walking Man I*, 1960**
Bronze; 180.5 x 27 x 97 cm.
Fondation Giacometti

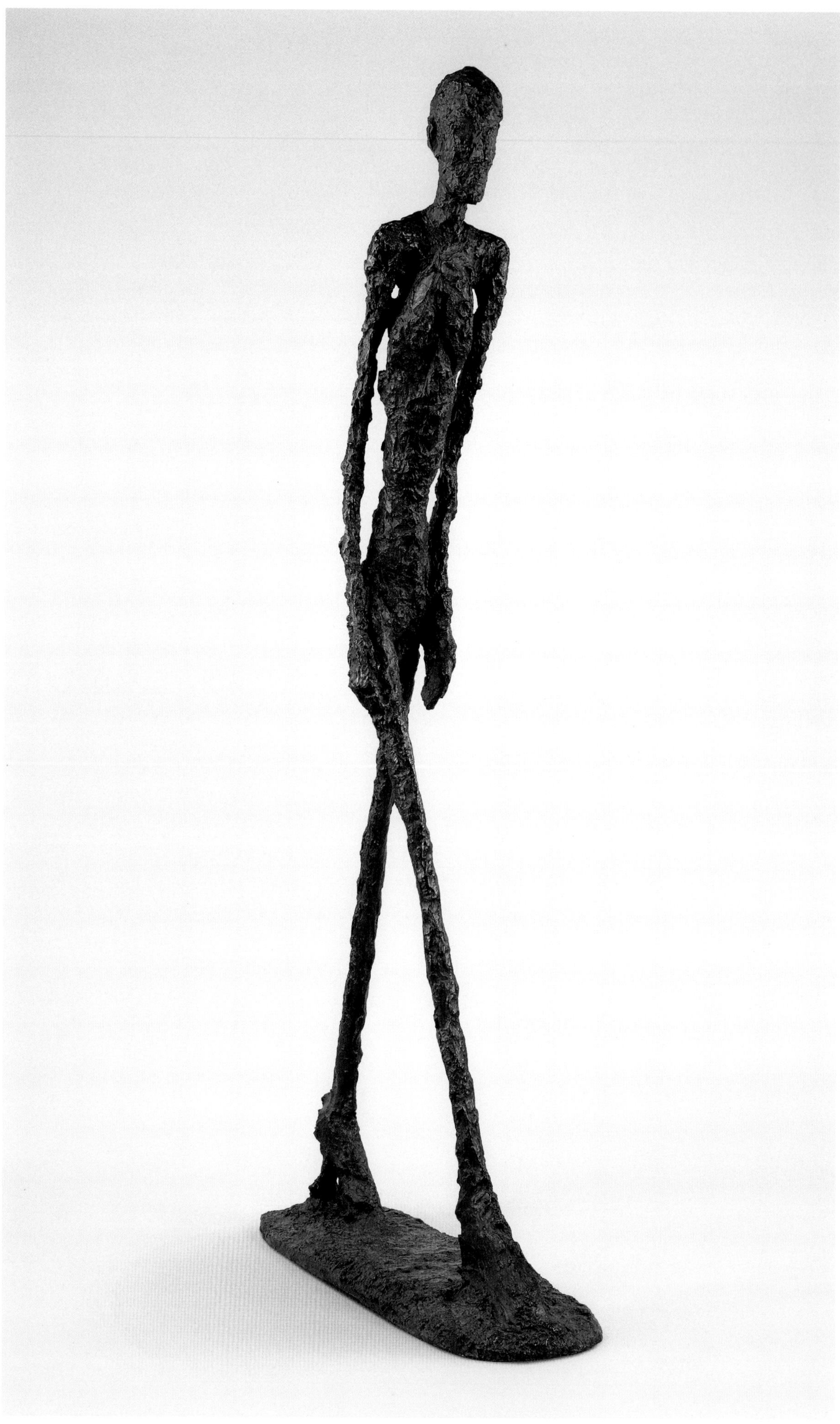

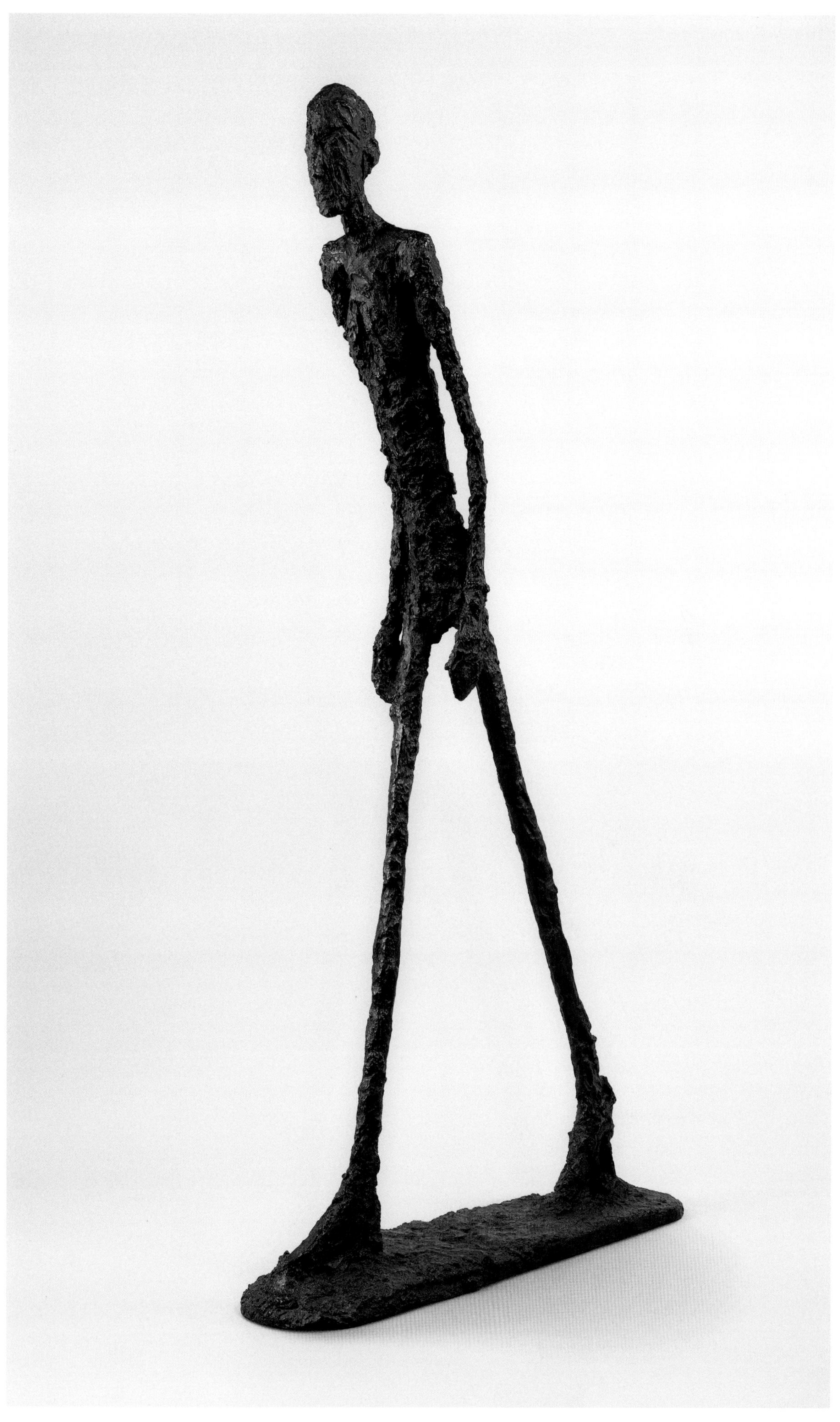

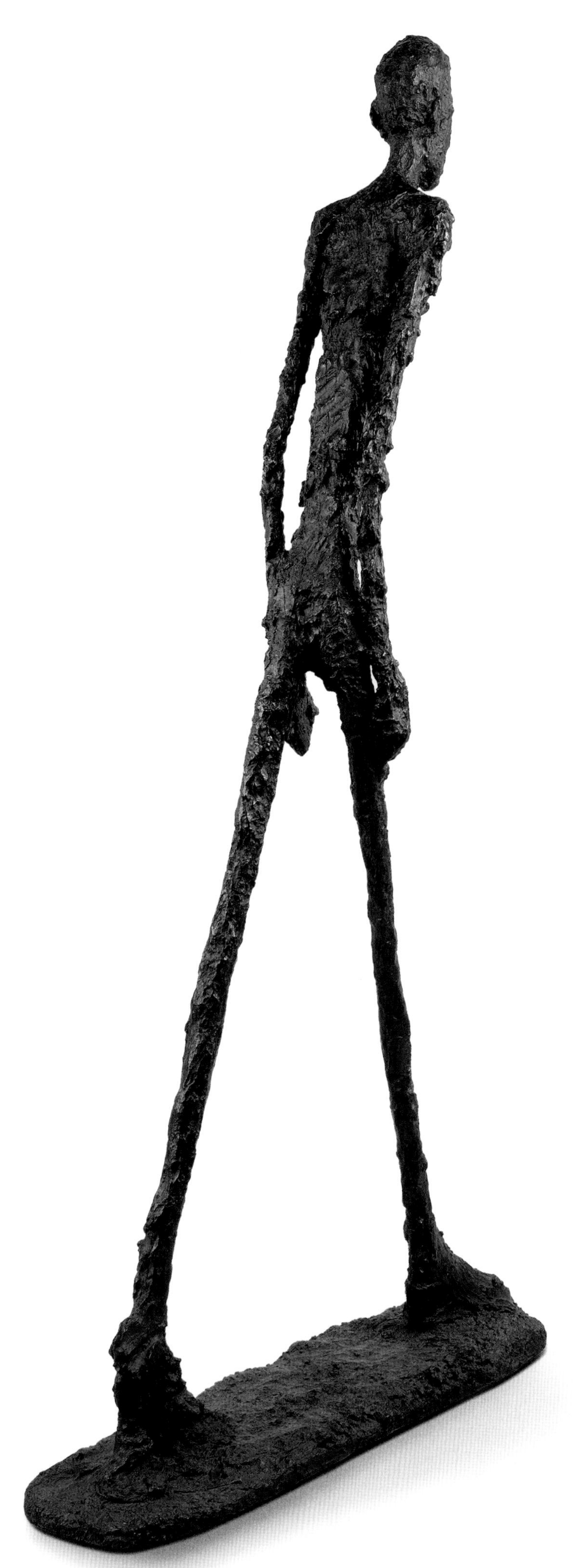

Chronology

Solo Exhibitions in the US
Major Group Exhibitions in the US

1901
OCTOBER 10: Birth of Alberto Giacometti in Borgonovo, a small village in Italian-speaking Switzerland. He is the first child of Swiss Post-Impressionist painter Giovanni Giacometti (1868–1933) and Annetta Stampa (1871–1964). After him came Diego (1902–1985), Ottilia (1904–1937), and Bruno (1907–2012).

1904
The family settled in Stampa, where Giovanni set up his studio.

1910
The Giacomettis bought a summer house in Maloja, on the bank of Lake Sils, where Giovanni set up a second studio.

Around 1914
First modeled portrait known, *Head of Diego as a Child*.

Around 1915
First oil painting known, *Still Life with Apples* (page 78 top).

1915–19
Studied at the Protestant secondary school of Schiers, near Chur, where he had access to a studio and made wood engravings.

1919
Abandoned his secondary education to enroll at the École des Beaux-Arts and the École des Arts et Métiers in Geneva, where he spent just one year.

1920–21
Traveled with his father to Venice, where he visited the contemporary art biennial and became enthusiastic about Venetian painting—namely, Tintoretto and Titian.

Embarked on a second trip to Italy, alone this time. Discovered Egyptian art in Florence. Lived in Rome from December 1920 to July 1921. Visited Assisi, Naples, and the sites of Pompeii and Paestum. Witnessed the death of Peter Van Meurs, a Dutch archivist with whom he had traveled in the Alps; this left a lasting impression on him.

1922
JANUARY: Settled in Paris to study sculpture. Lived in the studio of Alexander Archipenko, who had left for Berlin. Studied in Antoine Bourdelle's studio at the Académie de la Grande Chaumière until 1925, then occasionally until 1927; there he was taught drawing and sculpture from live models.

1924
Met Ossip Zadkine.

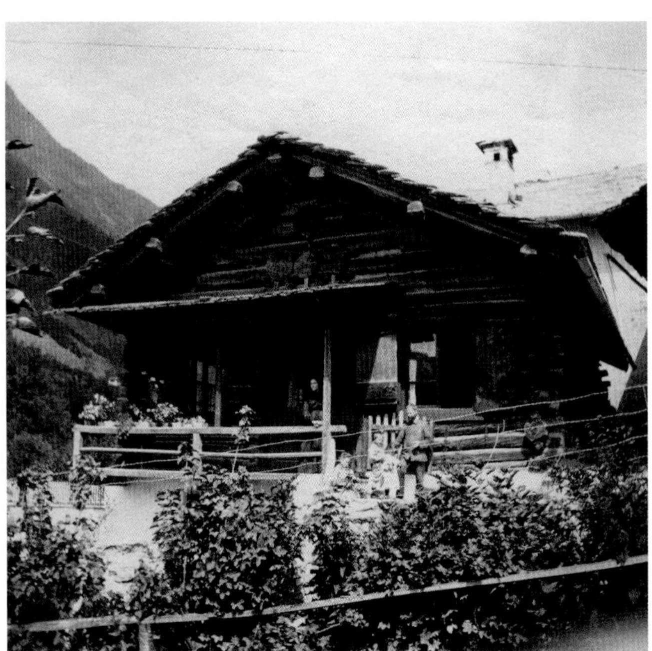

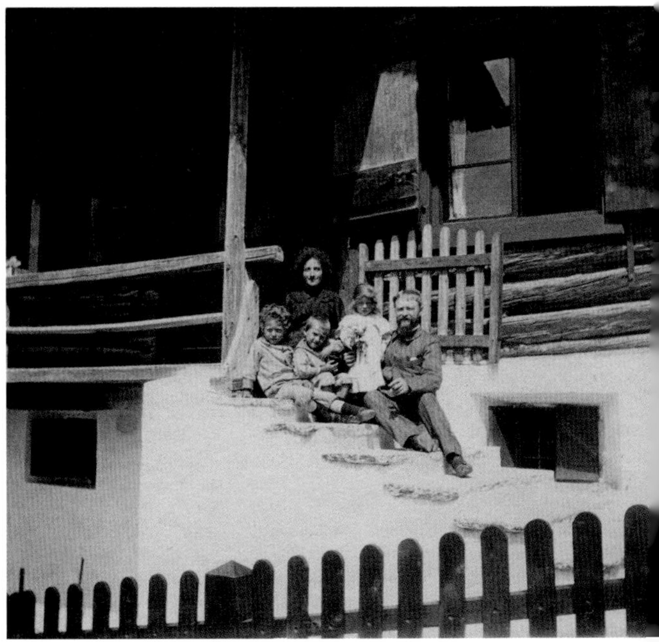

1925

Lived for one year in a studio at 37 rue Froidevaux, near Montparnasse Cemetery. His brother Diego joined him at the beginning of the year and became his occasional collaborator.

First participation in the Salon des Tuileries.

Began a relationship with American classmate Flora Mayo, whose portrait he made (*Head of a Woman*, 1926). Started "compositions" close to abstraction, in the wake of neo-Cubism.

1926

Met Jacques Lipchitz.

DECEMBER 1: Settled in the studio at 46 rue Hippolyte-Maindron, in the 14th arrondissement in Paris, which he kept until his death.

1927

Developed an interest in non-Western art and the arts of ancient antiquity. Often visited the Louvre and the Musée d'Ethnographie at the Trocadéro.

Made *Spoon Woman*, his first large sculpture.

Bought a Kota reliquary from his friend Serge Brignoni.

1928

Started to work on a series of *Flat Women* (page 89), among them *Gazing Head* (see fig. 10).

Became friends with Italian painter Massimo Campigli, who introduced him to the circle of "Italians in Paris," with whom he exhibited in February 1928 and April 1929.

1929

Met André Masson, who supported him and immersed him in the Surrealist milieu. Through Masson, he was offered a commission for a mural for the apartment of Pierre David-Weill.

Took part in the meetings of the Surrealist "dissidents" gathered around Georges Bataille, with Masson, Joan Miró, Robert Desnos, Raymond Queneau, Jacques Prévert, Michel Leiris, and Yves Tanguy, who remained his friends. Became friends with Hans Arp, Carl Einstein, Henri Laurens, and Louis Aragon.

Exhibited two sculptures at the Galerie Jeanne Bucher, one of which was bought by collectors Charles and Marie-Laure de Noailles.

Signed a one-year contract with the Galerie Pierre, directed by Pierre Loeb.

The material of his sculptures, which until then had been plaster, diversified (clay, bronze, and marble).

Became a high-profile young artist in the Parisian art milieu, close to the de Noailleses' circle.

OPPOSITE
Giovanni and Annetta Giacometti and their children in front of the studio in Stampa, c. 1907
Anonymous photographer. Archives, Fondation Giacometti

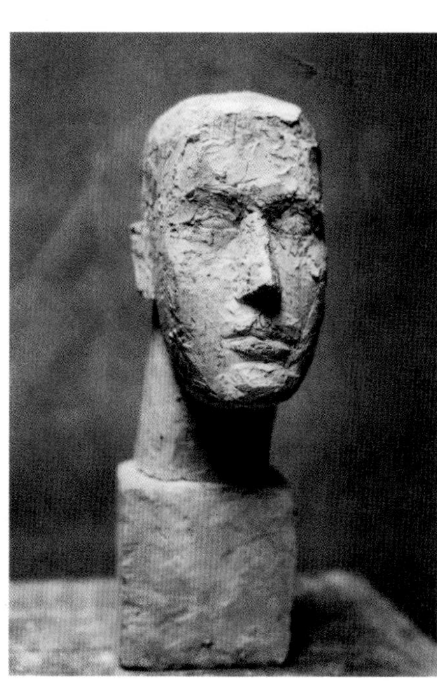

RIGHT
***Head of a Man on a Base*, c. 1925**
Anonymous photographer. Archives, Fondation Giacometti

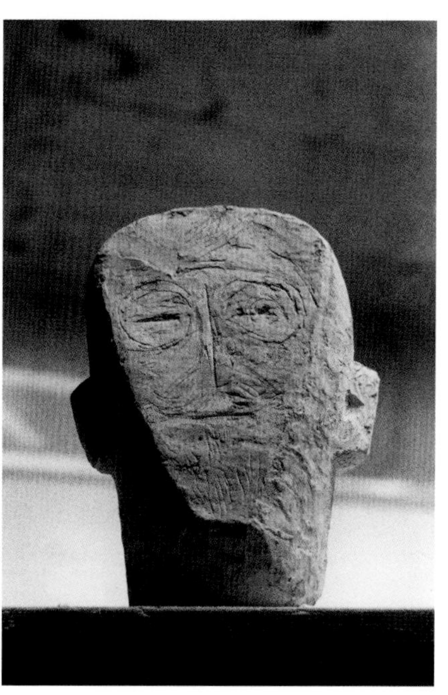

***Head of the Father, Flat I* (1927–30), in the studio in Maloja, 1959**
Ernst Scheidegger. Archives, Fondation Giacometti. © 2022 Artists Rights Society (ARS), New York / ProLitteris, Zurich

Presented his work in group exhibitions in the galleries of Georges Bernheim in Paris and Wolfensberger in Zurich.

Michel Leiris published "Alberto Giacometti" in the magazine *Documents*; it was the first article devoted to him.

The de Noailleses commissioned a sculpture for the garden of their villa in Hyères.

1930
His brother Diego joined him in Paris and became his technician and assistant.

Began collaborating with decorator Jean-Michel Frank, who became a close friend. Made nearly a hundred models for objects and light fixtures.

Participated in a group exhibition at the Galerie Pierre, with Joan Miró and Hans Arp. Among the works exhibited, *Suspended Ball* (see fig. 17) attracted the attention of Salvador Dalí and André Breton. Dalí saw the prototype there for the new Surrealist objects "with symbolic function."

Integrated into the Surrealist group and took an active part in its activities, exhibitions, and publications. For these, had his works photographed by Surrealist artists: Man Ray, Brassaï, and Dora Maar.

Began a tumultuous relationship with Denise Maisonneuve, which lasted until 1934.

1931
Created works with erotic and violent connotations, like *Disagreeable Object* (see fig. 33).

Published "Objets Mobiles et Muets" in the magazine *Le Surréalisme Au Service De La Révolution*.

1932
First solo exhibition in Paris, at the Galerie Pierre Colle.

Made *The Palace at 4 a.m.* (see fig. 15) and reproduced it in painting.

At Louis Aragon's request, created several political drawings, some of which were published in politically engaged magazines: *La Lutte anti-religieuse et prolétarienne*, *Commune*, and *La Ligue anti-impérialiste*.

1933
Made *Table*.

JUNE 25: Death of Giovanni Giacometti, which affected him deeply. Stayed for several long periods in Switzerland during the following months. Strengthened his friendship with André Breton, with whom he maintained an intense correspondence.

Albert Skira started the magazine *Minotaure*, to which Giacometti contributed.

1934
Made *Cube*.

Made *Head Skull* and *Invisible Object*.

Friend Max Ernst spent the summer in Maloja.

AUGUST 14: Was a witness at the wedding of André Breton and Jacqueline Lamba.

At Stanley William Hayter's Atelier 17, made Surrealist etchings, among them the illustrations for Breton's *L'air de l'eau*.

First solo exhibition in New York, at the Julien Levy Gallery.

> ***Abstract Sculpture by Alberto Giacometti*, Julien Levy Gallery, New York, December 1, 1934–January 1, 1935**

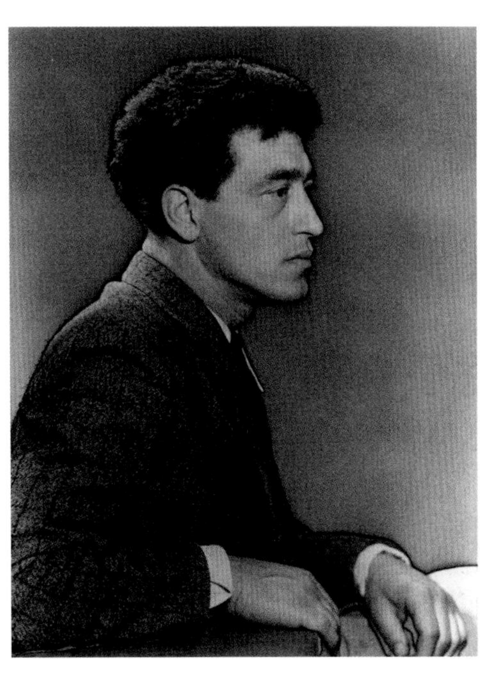

Alberto Giacometti in profile, 1932
Man Ray. Archives, Fondation Giacometti. © Man Ray 2015 Trust / Artists Rights Society (ARS), NY / ADAGP, Paris 2022

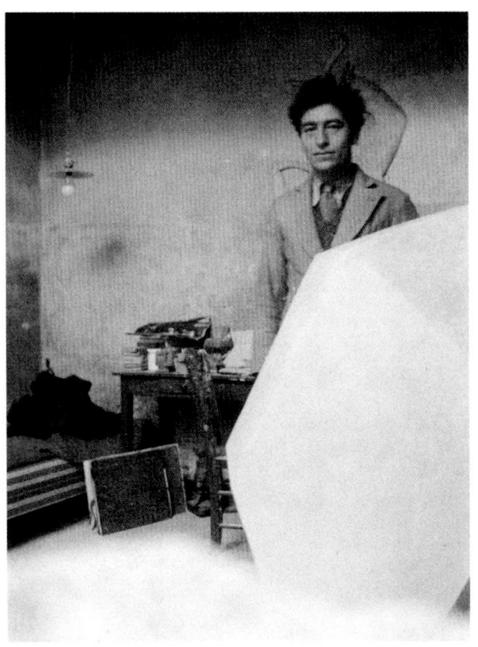

Alberto Giacometti in the studio with the *Cube*, c. 1933
Anonymous photographer. Archives, Fondation Giacometti

1935

Kept company with the abstract artists gravitating around the magazine *Abstraction-Création*, but refused to join their group.

Began new research with a series of heads modeled from life. His brother Diego and model Rita Gueyfier sat for him. This aesthetic turning point led him to distance himself from the Surrealist group, from which he was excluded on February 14. Kept contact with several artists from that movement, and continued to take part in some Surrealist exhibitions well into the postwar years, with works created before 1935.

Kept company with figurative painters Balthus and Francis Gruber, who became close friends.

Met Isabel Lambert Rawsthorne, an English artist, with whom he had an on-and-off relationship for several years.

Death of René Crevel, a close friend for whom he had made the frontispiece for *Les Pieds dans le plat* in 1933.

The AEAR (Association des écrivains et artistes révolutionnaires), to which he belonged since its creation in 1932, organized the exhibition *La Peinture en tournant*, at the Maison de la culture, where he exhibited two sculptures of heads.

1936

Took part in the *International Surrealist Exhibition* at the New Burlington Galleries in London.

The Museum of Modern Art in New York, directed by Alfred Barr, purchased *The Palace at 4 a.m.* and *Disagreeable Object to Be Thrown Away* (see figs. 15, 31).

Cubism and Abstract Art, The Museum of Modern Art, New York, March 2–April 19, 1936

Fantastic Art, Dada, Surrealism, The Museum of Modern Art, New York, December 7, 1936–January 17, 1937

1937

Exhibited with the abstract group *Circle* and kept company with artist Ben Nicholson.

Returned to painting, with a series of representations of apples and a portrait of his mother.

His sister, Ottilia, died giving birth to her first child, Silvio.

First exhibition at the Pierre Matisse Gallery, with *Walking Woman* (1932) on view.

Masterpieces of Modern Painting and Sculpture (Brancusi, De Chirico, Derain, Despiau, Giacometti, Gris, Maillol, Matisse, Miró, Modigliani, Picasso, Rouault), Pierre Matisse Gallery, New York, January 5–30, 1937

1938

Hit by a car in Place des Pyramides, an accident that left him with a limp; the event made a lasting impression on the artist, who interpreted it as a key moment in his existence.

Art in Our Time, 10th Anniversary Exhibition, The Museum of Modern Art, New York, May 10–September 30, 1938

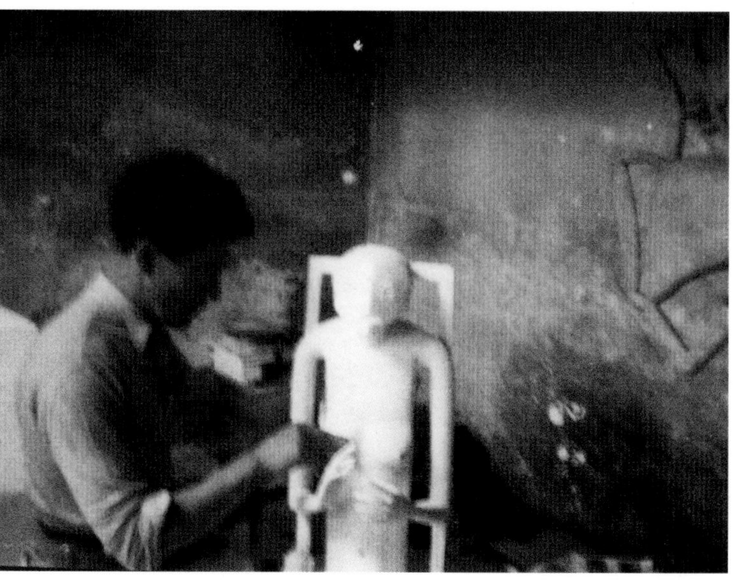

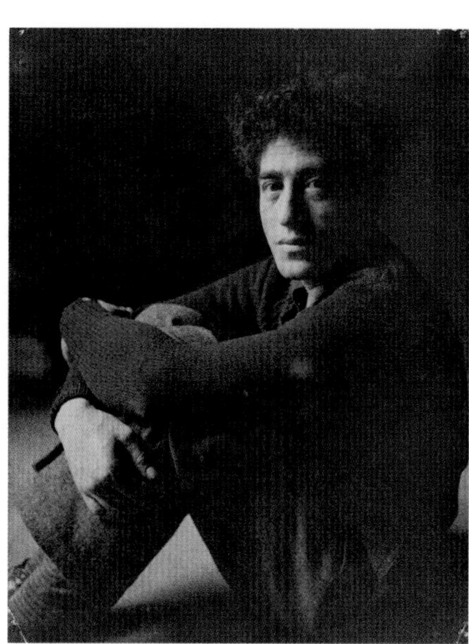

Alberto Giacometti with the *Invisible Object* in plaster and the wall relief for David-Weill, c. 1934
Anonymous photographer. Archives, Fondation Giacometti

Alberto Giacometti, c. 1935
Rogi André (French, b. Hungary, 1900–1970). Archives, Fondation Giacometti

1939
Invited to make an outdoor sculpture for the fashion pavilion at the Exposition Nationale Suisse; presented a very small sculpture set on a big base, which was turned down by the organizers.

1939–41
Spent much time with Pablo Picasso, as well as with Jean-Paul Sartre and Simone de Beauvoir.

DECEMBER 1941: Left France for Switzerland. His brother Diego stayed in Paris to look after the studio.

1942–45
Lived between Geneva, Stampa, and Maloja. Met Annette Arm (1923–1993), who would become his wife and model.

Made sculptures of a very small size, as well as *Woman with Chariot* (see fig. 41).

Took part in the discussions of the magazine *Labyrinthe* (with Albert Skira, Roger Montandon, Jean Starobinski, Balthus, and Brassaï) and published the texts "Un sculpteur vu par un sculpteur: Henri Laurens par Alberto Giacometti" (1945) and "À propos de Jacques Callot" (1945). The magazine published photographs of his works, shot by Eli Lotar.

> *Art of This Century: Objects-Drawings-Photographs-Paintings-Sculpture-Collages, 1910 to 1942*, Art of This Century Gallery, New York, October 1942

> *First Papers of Surrealism*, Coordinating Council of French Relief Societies, Inc., New York, October 14–November 7, 1942

1945
Returned to Paris. Became reacquainted with the Parisian art and literary milieu.

> *Alberto Giacometti*, Art of This Century Gallery, New York, February 10–March 10, 1945

1946
Spent time with Pablo Picasso, Balthus, Francis Gruber, Jean Hélion, and André Derain.

Annette Arm moved in at rue Hippolyte-Maindron.

Made a series of sculpted and drawn portraits of friends from the circles of arts and literature.

Received two commissions for public monuments, in homage to Jean Macé and Gabriel Péri, which did not come to fruition. At the request of Louis Aragon, worked on the portrait of Colonel Rol-Tanguy, probably for the *Art et Résistance* exhibition.

Painting and drawing became increasingly important in his practice. Pierre Matisse visited his studio, and offered to represent him in New York. Matisse also proposed to organize a solo exhibition, which stimulated the creation of new pieces. Went back to making decorative objects.

DECEMBER: Published "Le Rêve, le Sphinx et la mort de T." in Albert Skira's magazine *Labyrinthe*.

1947
First version of *Walking Man*. Made *Nose*, *Man Pointing*, and female figures that evoke ancient Egyptian and Greek statuary. His works are gradually characterized by stretching and thinning, which mark his postwar style.

Illustrated *Histoire de rats* for Georges Bataille, published by Éditions de Minuit.

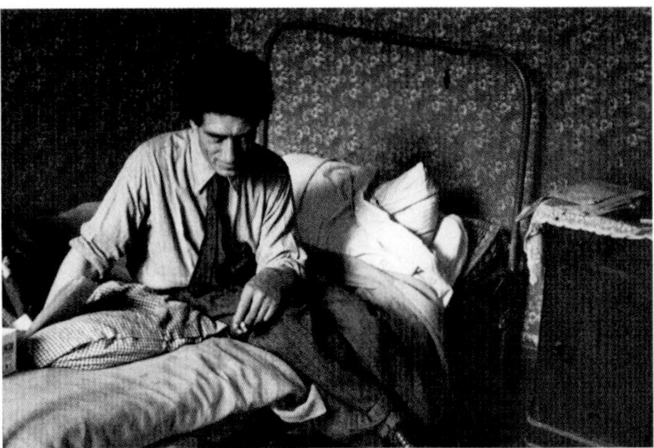

Alberto Giacometti in the room at the Hôtel de Rive in Geneva, c. October 1944
Eli Lotar (French, 1905–1969). Archives, Fondation Giacometti

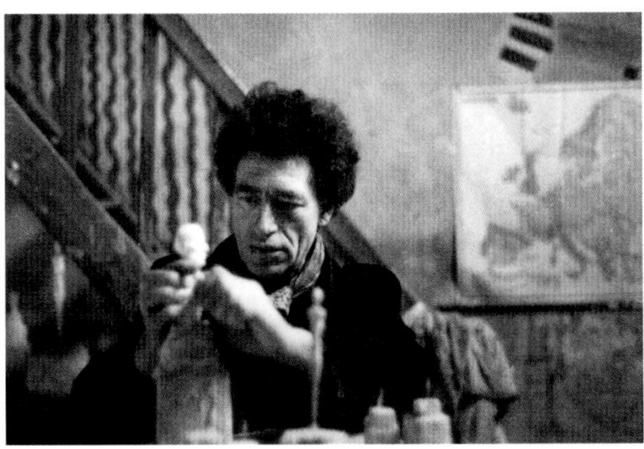

Alberto Giacometti in his studio, c. 1946
Henri Cartier-Bresson. Archives, Fondation Giacometti. © Fondation Henri Cartier-Bresson / Magnum Photos

1948

First solo exhibition at the Pierre Matisse Gallery, where plaster and bronze pieces were presented. Jean-Paul Sartre wrote the catalogue's preface, "The Search for the Absolute."

First group exhibition of the postwar years, at the Pierre Matisse Gallery. Other exhibitions followed annually.

> ***Alberto Giacometti*, Pierre Matisse Gallery, New York, January 19–February 14, 1948**

> *Carrington, Chagall, Dubuffet, Giacometti, Lam, MacIver, Matta, Miró, Tamayo, Tanguy*, Pierre Matisse Gallery, New York, May 18–June 5, 1948

1949

JULY 19: Married Annette Arm.

Discovered lithography with Fernand Mourlot; used the medium to make the frontispiece for Tristan Tzara's collection *Phases*.

1950

Made *The Chariot* (page 59), several sculptures called *The Cage* (pages 190, 191), and the series of "places," including *The Forest* and *The Glade* (pages 172, 173).

His brother Diego and his wife, Annette, sat for him. Began painting some of his bronzes. First drawings in biro. Also fulfilled commissions for decorative arts for private individuals.

First exhibition at the Sidney Janis Gallery. Other group exhibitions followed each year from 1954 to 1961 and in 1964.

> *Young Masters of the Twentieth Century*, Sidney Janis Gallery, New York, May 1950

> ***Alberto Giacometti*, Pierre Matisse Gallery, New York, December 12, 1950–January 6, 1951**

1951

First exhibition at the Galerie Maeght in Paris. Other exhibitions followed in 1954, 1957, and 1961.

Table (1933) is the first of Giacometti's works to enter the French national collections, thanks to a donation by the de Noailleses to the Musée national d'Art moderne.

Made *The Dog* and *The Cat*.

1952

Produced a series of *Dark Landscapes* representing the view he had from his studio in Stampa, made in gray and black tones.

> ***Alberto Giacometti: Lithograph Drawings of His Studio*, Wittenborn Gallery, New York, September 1952**

> *Sculpture of the Twentieth Century*, Philadelphia Museum of Art, October 11–December 7, 1952; Art Institute of Chicago, January 22–March 8, 1953; The Museum of Modern Art, New York, April 29–September 7, 1953

1953

> ***Sculpture and Painting by Giacometti*, Arts Club, Chicago, November 4–December 1, 1953**

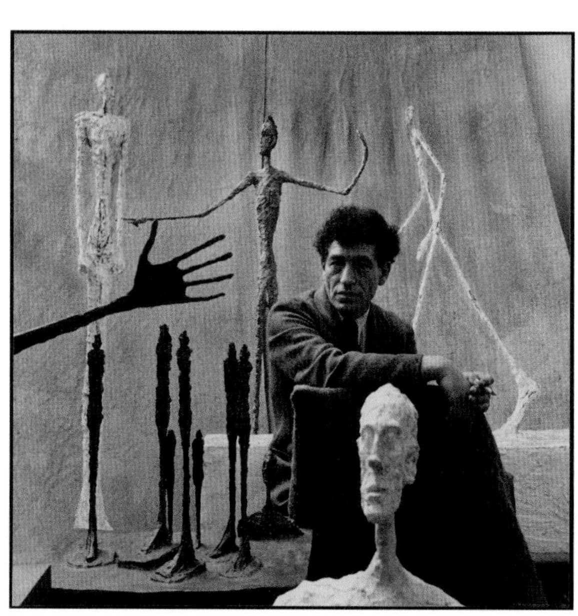

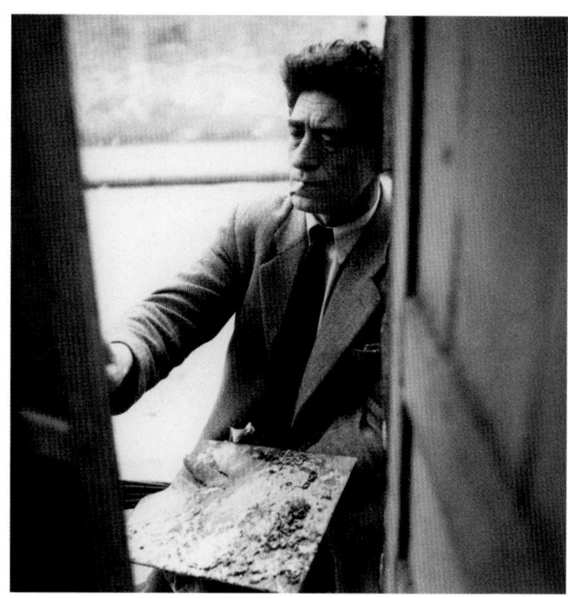

Alberto Giacometti in his studio, 1951
Gordon Parks (American, 1912–2006). Archives, Fondation Giacometti. © Gordon Parks Foundation

Alberto Giacometti painting the rue Hippolyte-Maindron from the studio's door, summer 1952
Roger Montandon (Swiss, 1918–2005). Archives, Fondation Giacometti. © 2022 Artists Rights Society (ARS), New York / ADAGP, Paris

1954

Met Jean Genet, who sat for paintings and drawings until 1957. Genet wrote about their conversations and the studio in the essay "L'Atelier d'Alberto Giacometti" published in the magazine *Derrière le miroir* in 1957.

Visited Henri Matisse, of whom he drew a series of portraits.

Created *Tall Thin Head* (pages 144–45) and several paintings.

> *Sculpture and Drawings by Alberto Giacometti*, Santa Barbara Museum of Art, July 13–August 15, 1954

> *Alberto Giacometti: Sculpture, Paintings, Drawings*, Perls Galleries, Los Angeles, August 21–September 18, 1954

1955

First museum retrospectives: at the Arts Council in London, at the Solomon R. Guggenheim Museum in New York, and in Germany.

> *Alberto Giacometti*, Solomon R. Guggenheim Museum, New York, June 8–July 17, 1955

1956

Exhibited in the French pavilion at the Venice Biennale an ensemble of female figures called *Women of Venice*, which were presented afterward at the Kunsthalle Bern.

Became friends with Isaku Yanaihara, a Japanese professor of philosophy visiting France, who modeled for him. Other sittings took place in 1957, 1959, 1960, and 1961, generating a series of sculptures, paintings, and drawings.

Made the doors for the family tombstone of American industrialist Edgar J. Kaufmann.

1958

Met Caroline Tamagno (1938–2015), who became his mistress; she posed for a series of paintings from 1960 to 1965.

Received an offer for a commission for the Chase Manhattan Plaza in New York (not completed). Chose for that project a *Large Head*, a *Tall Woman*, and a *Walking Man*, for which he made several attempts—producing three versions of *Walking Man*, four of *Tall Woman*, and two of *Large Head*. Abandoned the project in 1960, but later showed the pieces in various exhibitions.

> *Giacometti: Sculptures, Paintings, Drawings from 1956 to 1958*, Pierre Matisse Gallery, New York, May 6–31, 1958

1959

Started to work on a collection of lithographs, *Paris sans fin*, at Tériade's request, which would be published posthumously in 1969.

> *Sculpture of Our Time*, The Detroit Institute of Arts, May 5–August 23, 1959; Milwaukee Art Center, September 10–October 11, 1959; Walker Art Center, Minneapolis, October 25–December 6, 1959; William Rockhill Nelson Gallery of Art, Kansas City, December 20, 1959–January 31, 1960; The Museum of Fine Arts, Houston, March 4–27, 1960; Los Angeles County Museum of Art, April 11–May 15, 1960; M. H. de Young Memorial Museum, San Francisco, May 29–July 10, 1960; Colorado Springs Fine Arts Center, July 24–September 4, 1960; The Art Gallery of Toronto, September 30–October 31, 1960

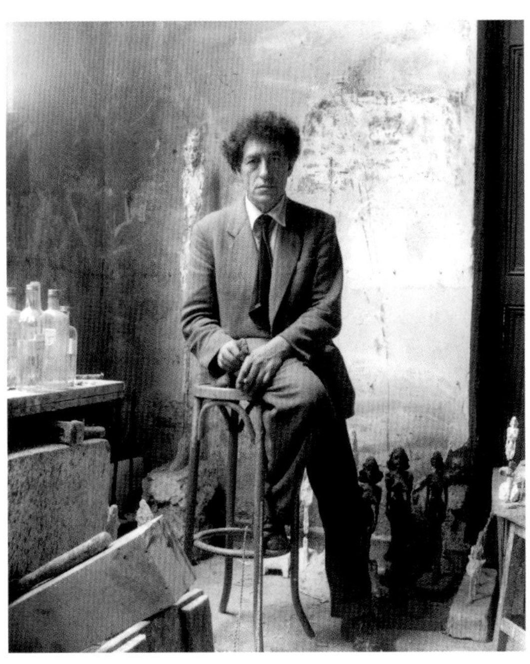

Alberto Giacometti in his studio, Paris, 1954
Denise Colomb. Archives, Fondation Giacometti

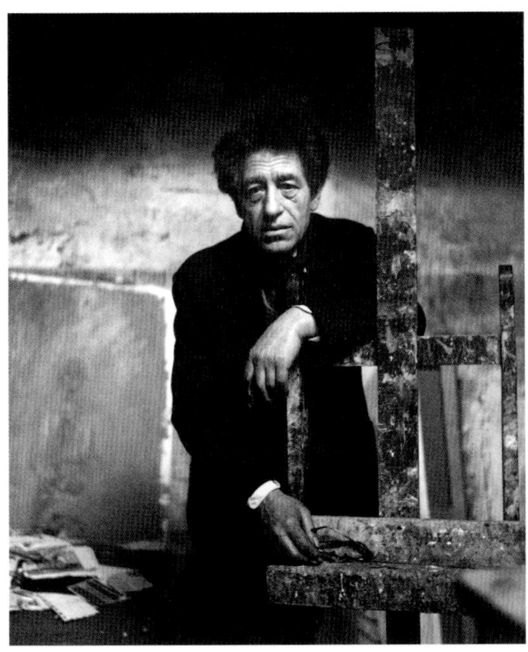

Alberto Giacometti in his studio, December 18 or 19, 1957
Robert Doisneau. Archives, Fondation Giacometti.
© Robert DOISNEAU / GAMMA RAPHO

New Images of Man, The Museum of Modern Art, New York, September 30–November 29, 1959; Baltimore Museum of Art, January 9–February 7, 1960

1960

***Giacometti*, New York, World House Galleries, January 12–February 6, 1960**

The Aldrich Collection (organized by the American Federation of Arts), October 1960–October 1962: Philbrook Art Center, Tulsa; Dallas Museum of Fine Arts; Municipal Gallery, Los Angeles; San Francisco Museum of Art; Seattle Art Museum; The Art Club of Chicago; The Baltimore Museum of Art; Albany Institute of History and Art; Allentown Art Museum; The Art Center, Tucson; City Art Museum of St. Louis

1961

Made the decor for Samuel Beckett's play *Waiting for Godot*.

Won the Carnegie Prize.

One Hundred Paintings from the G. David Thompson Collection, Solomon R. Guggenheim Museum, New York, May–August 1961

The 1961 Pittsburgh International Exhibition of Contemporary Paintings and Sculptures, Carnegie Institute, Department of Fine Arts, Pittsburgh, October 27, 1961–January 7, 1962. Also took part in the editions of 1955, 1958, and 1964.

***Giacometti*, New York, Pierre Matisse Gallery, December 12–30, 1961**

1962

Awarded the Sculpture Prize at the Venice Biennale.

First monograph, by Jacques Dupin.

Important retrospective at the Kunsthaus Zurich.

***Alberto Giacometti: A Loan Exhibition*, Phillips Collection, Washington, DC, February 2–March 4, 1962**

Modern Sculpture from the Joseph H. Hirshhorn Collection, Solomon R. Guggenheim Museum, New York, October 3–February 6, 1962

1963

Operated on for cancer, from which he recovered.

Drew Georges Braque on his deathbed.

Luigi Carluccio offered to edit a book on the copies the artist had made of historical artworks. The book, for which Giacometti wrote the preface, was published posthumously in 1967.

1964

JANUARY 25: Death of his mother, Annetta.

Opening of the Fondation Marguerite et Aimé Maeght in Saint-Paul-de-Vence, for which he donated several pieces and supervised their installation.

Photographer Eli Lotar became his assistant and model.

Received the International Award for Sculpture from the Solomon R. Guggenheim Museum.

***Guggenheim International Award 1964*, Solomon R. Guggenheim Museum, New York, January–March 1964**

***Alberto Giacometti: Drawings*, Pierre Matisse Gallery, New York, November 17–December 12, 1964**

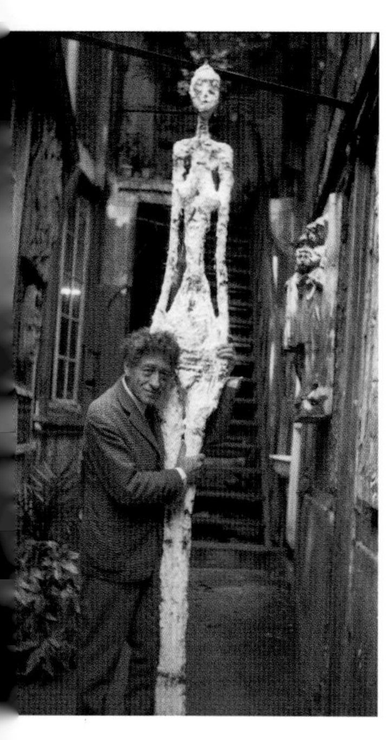

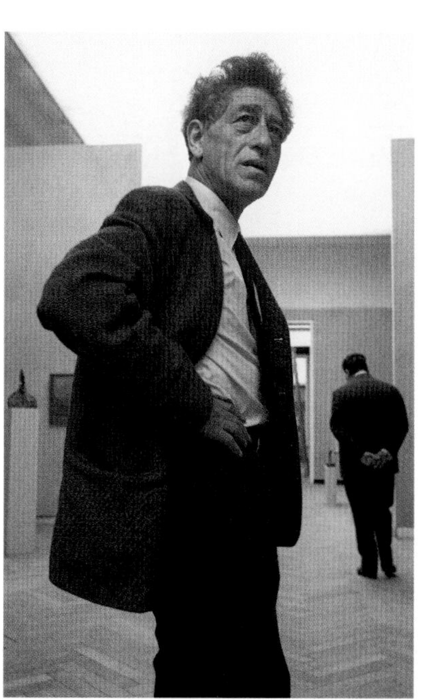

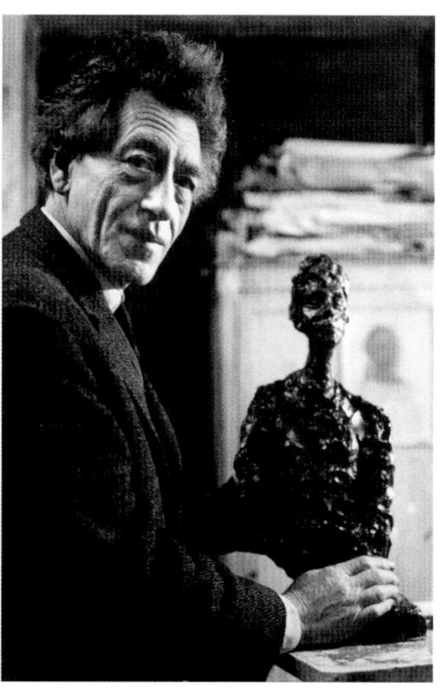

Alberto Giacometti with the plaster of the *Tall Woman IV* in the studio courtyard, Paris, 1960
Annette Giacometti (Swiss, 1923–1993). Archives, Fondation Giacometti

Alberto Giacometti, XXXI Biennial International Exhibition of Art, Venice, 1962
Ugo Mulas (Italian, 1928–1973). Archives, Fondation Giacometti. © Ugo Mulas Heirs. All rights reserved

Alberto Giacometti with the *Bust of a Woman with Crossed Arms (Francine Torrent)*, 1964
Gisèle Freund (French, b. Germany, 1908–2000). Archives, Fondation Giacometti

1965
Ernst Scheidegger made a documentary showing Giacometti in his studio being interviewed by Jacques Dupin.

Retrospectives held at the Tate Gallery, London; Museum of Modern Art, New York; and Louisiana Museum, Humlebaek.

Traveled to the United States for the first time.

Presented with the Grand Prix International des Arts by the French Ministry for Culture.

DECEMBER 16: Creation of the Alberto Giacometti-Stiftung, set up within the Kunsthaus Zurich, from the purchase of artworks belonging to American collector G. David Thompson.

> *Etchings and Lithographs by Alberto Giacometti*, Allan Frumkin Gallery, Chicago, April 1965
>
> *Alberto Giacometti*, The Museum of Modern Art, New York, June 9–October 10, 1965; The Art Institute of Chicago, November 5–December 12, 1965; Los Angeles County Museum of Art, January 11–February 20, 1966; San Francisco Museum of Art, March 10–April 24, 1966

1966
JANUARY 11: After being admitted for tests, Giacometti died at the hospital in Chur.

JANUARY 15: Buried in Borgonovo Cemetery.

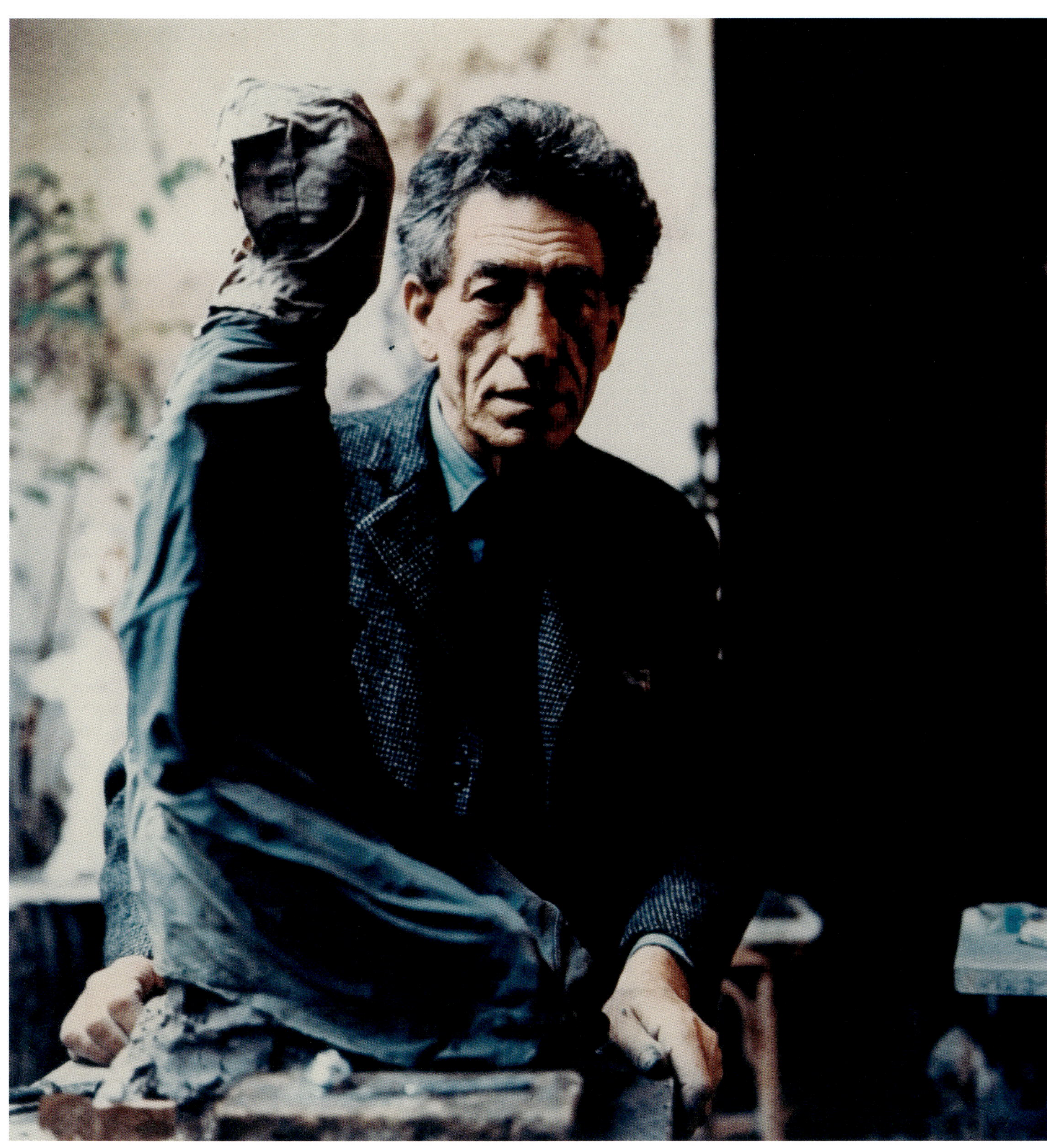

Alberto Giacometti in his studio, 1965
Milton H. Greene (American, 1922–1985). Archives, Fondation Giacometti. Photographed by Milton H. Greene. © 2022 Joshua Greene http://www.miltonhgreene.com

Checklist of the Exhibition

Still Life with Apples, c. 1915. Oil on cardboard; 36.2 x 36.6 cm. Fondation Giacometti
page 78 top

Street of Stampa in the Winter, c. 1917. Blue ink on paper; 34 x 21.7 cm. Fondation Giacometti
CLEVELAND, SEATTLE, AND HOUSTON ONLY
page 77 left

Mountain at Stampa, 1917–20. Oil on cardboard; 36.6 x 36.2 cm.
Fondation Giacometti
page 78 bottom

Bruno, c. 1918. Blue ink and graphite pencil on paper; 29 x 22.5 cm. Fondation Giacometti
NELSON-ATKINS ONLY
page 82 right

Diego in Profile and Copy after Cézanne's Self-Portrait, c. 1918. India ink and graphite pencil on paper; 34 x 25.7 cm. Fondation Giacometti
NELSON-ATKINS ONLY
page 82 left

Portrait of a Woman Seated on a Chair, Three-Quarter View, c. 1918. Black ink on paper; 48.1 x 35.1 cm.
Fondation Giacometti
NELSON-ATKINS ONLY
page 83 left

The Mountain Road, c. 1919. Watercolor and pencil on paper; 22 x 29 cm.
Fondation Giacometti
CLEVELAND, SEATTLE, AND HOUSTON ONLY
page 79

View of Stampa, c. 1919. Black ink on paper; 16 x 24 cm.
Fondation Giacometti
CLEVELAND, SEATTLE, AND HOUSTON ONLY
page 76

Landscape, c. 1920. Oil on cut canvas; 47.2 x 38.6 cm.
Fondation Giacometti
page 80 bottom

Mountain Landscape at Coltura, c. 1920. Oil on cut canvas; 30.4 x 30.2 cm.
Fondation Giacometti
page 80 top

Mountain Landscape, c. 1921. Oil on canvas; 60.3 x 50.1 cm.
Fondation Giacometti
page 81

Woman Sewing (Maria), c. 1925. Black ink on paper; 48.8 x 33.2 cm.
Fondation Giacometti
NELSON-ATKINS ONLY
page 83 right

Head of Woman (Flora Mayo), 1926. Bronze; 30.5 x 22.9 x 8.5 cm. Fondation Giacometti
page 108

Woman (Flat V), c. 1929. Bronze; 55.5 x 33.6 x 7.7 cm.
Fondation Giacometti
page 89

Head of Woman (Denise), c. 1932. Pencil and rubber on paper; 49 x 31.9 cm.
Fondation Giacometti
CLEVELAND, SEATTLE, AND HOUSTON ONLY
page 109 left

Head of Woman, c. 1935. Pencil on paper; 19.4 x 18.7 cm.
Fondation Giacometti
NELSON-ATKINS ONLY
page 109 right

Standing Nude, c. 1935. Pencil on paper; 49.1 x 31.5 cm.
Fondation Giacometti
NELSON-ATKINS ONLY
page 208

Head of Diego, c. 1936. Plaster; 23.5 x 14.6 x 21.2 cm.
Fondation Giacometti
page 112

Head of Woman (Rita), c. 1936. Bronze; 23.9 x 13.8 x 18.3 cm.
Fondation Giacometti
page 110

Head of Diego, c. 1937. Bronze; 19 x 11.6 x 16.9 cm.
Fondation Giacometti
page 114

Head of Isabel, 1937–38. Bronze; 21.3 x 16 x 17.2 cm.
Fondation Giacometti
page 113

Head of Woman (Rita), 1937–38. Bronze; 22 x 12 x 15.4 cm. Fondation Giacometti
page 115

Small Bust on a Double Base, 1940–41. Bronze; 11.6 x 6.2 x 5.4 cm. Fondation Giacometti
page 138 left

Small Bust of Silvio on a Double Base, 1943–44. Bronze; 18.3 x 12.8 x 11.5 cm.
Fondation Giacometti
page 139

Sketches for a Figure on a Base, 1945–46. Pencil on notebook; notebook open: 12.5 x 15.8 cm. Fondation Giacometti
NELSON-ATKINS ONLY
page 209

Head of Marie-Laure de Noailles on a Double Base, 1946. Bronze; 30.4 x 8.8 x 10.5 cm. Fondation Giacometti
page 116

Simone de Beauvoir, 1946. Bronze; 13.4 x 4 x 4.1 cm.
Fondation Giacometti
page 117

Self-Portrait with a Woman in a Mirror, c. 1946. Pencil and rubber on paper; 49.4 x 32.5 cm. Fondation Giacometti
NELSON-ATKINS ONLY
page 169

Small Bust of Annette, c. 1946. Bronze; 16 x 13.6 x 8.5 cm.
Fondation Giacometti
page 138 right

B Standing in a Cage II, 1946–47. Chisel and pen on paper; 28.1 x 22.5 cm.
Fondation Giacometti
NELSON-ATKINS ONLY
page 184

Apples in a Fruit Dish on the Table, 1947. Graphite pencil on notepaper; 29.7 x 21 cm.
Fondation Giacometti
NELSON-ATKINS ONLY
page 84

Heads of Men, 1947. Oil and pencil on cut canvas; 30.5 x 25.6 cm. Fondation Giacometti
page 119

Head of a Man and Figures on a Base on Critique, *no. 12, May 1947*, c. May 1947. Pencil on paper; book open: 22.3 x 28.6 x 1 cm. Fondation Giacometti
NELSON-ATKINS ONLY
page 118 top

Bust of a Man on a Base, c. 1947. Bronze; 54.5 x 11.4 x 10.1 cm. Fondation Giacometti
page 151

Diane Bataille, c. 1947. Bronze; 47.7 x 13.1 x 13 cm.
Fondation Giacometti
page 150

Figurine, c. 1947. Bronze; 28.4 x 9.3 x 10.4 cm.
Fondation Giacometti
page 140 left

The Nose, 1947–49. Bronze, painted metal, cotton rope; 80.9 x 70.5 x 40.6 cm.
Fondation Giacometti
pages 47–49

Three Men Walking, 1948. Bronze; 72 x 32.7 x 34.1 cm.
Fondation Giacometti
page 194

Bust of a Man on a Base, c. 1948. Bronze; 36.4 x 11.6 x 10.7 cm.
Fondation Giacometti
page 152

Standing Nude, 1949. Pencil on paper; 50 x 32.5 cm.
Fondation Giacometti
NELSON-ATKINS ONLY
page 210

Bust of a Man, The Chariot, Head on a Base, *Head of Pierre Loeb for* Regard sur la peinture, 1949–50. Pencil on paper; 21.7 x 17.5 cm.
Fondation Giacometti
NELSON-ATKINS ONLY
page 146

The Cage, First Version, 1949–50. Bronze; 90.5 x 36.5 x 34 cm. Fondation Giacometti
page 191

Sketch for The Cage, First Version, *Sketch for* Four Figurines on a Stand, *Sketches for* The Chariot *(Two Facing and One Profile)*, c. 1949–50. Painting on wall on canvas; 124.5 x 107.3 cm.
Fondation Giacometti
page 92

Standing Woman, c. 1949–58. Oil on paper; 68.3 x 51.3 cm.
Fondation Giacometti
page 213

The Cage, 1950. Bronze; 174 x 36 x 40.5 cm.
Fondation Giacometti
page 190

The Chariot, 1950. Painted bronze; 142.9 x 61.6 x 68.6 cm. The Nelson-Atkins Museum of Art, Kansas City, MO, Gift of the Hall Family Foundation, Acquired from the Patsy and Raymond Nasher Collection, F99-33/7
NELSON-ATKINS ONLY
page 159

The Forest, 1950. Bronze; 57 x 61 x 49.5 cm. Fondation Giacometti
page 173

Four Women on a Base, 1950. Bronze; 76 x 41.3 x 16.4 cm. Fondation Giacometti
page 143

Four Women on a Base, The Chariot, Bust of a Man on a Pedestal, Bust of a Man on a Plinth, Four Figurines on a Stand, Man Crossing a Square on a Sunny Morning, and *The Cage*, 1950. Pencil on a page of notebook; 29 x 22.4 cm. Fondation Giacometti
CLEVELAND, SEATTLE, AND HOUSTON ONLY
page 193

The Glade, 1950. Bronze; 61 x 66 x 53 cm. Fondation Giacometti
page 172

Bust of Annette, c. 1950. Painted plaster; 18 x 16.5 x 9 cm. Fondation Giacometti
page 95 left

Bust of a Man, c. 1950. Bronze; 56 x 15.5 x 16.7 cm. Fondation Giacometti
page 153

Figurine, c. 1950. Bronze; 15.5 x 4.5 x 5.7 cm. Fondation Giacometti
page 140 middle

Standing Nude in an Interior, c. 1950. Pencil on paper; 50.4 x 32.7 cm. Fondation Giacometti
NELSON-ATKINS ONLY
page 212 left

Four Figurines on a Stand (London Figurines), 1950–65. Bronze; 157.5 x 42 x 32 cm. Fondation Giacometti
page 192

Bust of Diego from Life, 1951. Bronze; 26.8 x 21.5 x 12.1 cm. Fondation Giacometti
page 97

Conifers, Houses, and Characters, c. 1951. Lithographic pencil on transfer paper; 49.8 x 32.6 cm. Fondation Giacometti
CLEVELAND, SEATTLE, AND HOUSTON ONLY
page 178 left

The Court of the Studio on the Rue Hippolyte-Maindron, c. 1951. Pencil on paper; 50 x 32.5 cm. Fondation Giacometti
CLEVELAND, SEATTLE, AND HOUSTON ONLY
page 178 right

Standing Man, c. 1951. Pencil on paper; 50 x 32.9 cm. Fondation Giacometti
CLEVELAND, SEATTLE, AND HOUSTON ONLY
page 120

Small Bust on a Stand, 1951–52. Bronze; 152.2 x 21.2 x 22.6 cm. Fondation Giacometti
page 157

Man with a Windbreaker, 1953. Bronze; 50 x 28.6 x 22.5 cm. Fondation Giacometti
page 177

Standing Nude on a Cubic Base, 1953. Bronze; 43.3 x 11.5 x 10.4 cm. Fondation Giacometti
page 154

Head of Diego, c. 1953. Aluminum alloy; 13.2 x 5.5 x 8.1 cm. Fondation Giacometti
page 121

Figurine, 1953–54. Bronze; 10.7 x 3.4 x 4.1 cm. Fondation Giacometti
page 140 right

Standing Woman (Poseuse I), 1954. Bronze; 56.1 x 13 x 18.2 cm. Fondation Giacometti
page 98

Tall Thin Head, 1954. Bronze; 64.5 x 38.1 x 24.4 cm. Fondation Giacometti
page 144

Annette Standing, c. 1954. Bronze; 47.5 x 10.5 x 20.3 cm. Fondation Giacometti
page 155

Bust of Diego, c. 1954. Bronze; 25.9 x 20.3 x 11.7 cm. Fondation Giacometti
page 162

Diego (Head with a Turtleneck), c. 1954. Bronze; 33.4 x 12.5 x 14 cm. Fondation Giacometti
page 163

Figurine, c. 1954. Bronze; 14.9 x 4.7 x 6.3 cm. Fondation Giacometti
page 141 far left

Heads of Annette and Diego, Eyes, and House, c. 1955. Blue ink on paper napkin; 29 x 51 cm. Fondation Giacometti
NELSON-ATKINS ONLY
page 128

Small Bust, c. 1955. Plaster; 20.8 x 17.5 x 7.8 cm. Fondation Giacometti
page 95 right

Seated Woman, 1956. Bronze; 51.3 x 15.6 x 23.7 cm. Fondation Giacometti
page 91

Woman of Venice III, 1956. Bronze; 118.5 x 17.8 x 35.1 cm. Fondation Giacometti
page 142

Figurine, c. 1956. Bronze; 23.4 x 7 x 10.3 cm. Fondation Giacometti
page 141 middle left

Figurine without Arms, c. 1956. Bronze; 14.1 x 6.2 x 7.1 cm. Fondation Giacometti
page 141 far right

Figurine without Arms, c. 1956. Bronze; 12.2 x 4.6 x 6.8 cm. Fondation Giacometti
page 141 middle right

Man Crossing a Square on a Sunny Morning and *The Chariot*, 1957. Blue ink on notepaper; 21 x 26.9 cm. Fondation Giacometti
CLEVELAND, SEATTLE, AND HOUSTON ONLY
page 147

Heads of Men on the Proof for the Exhibition Catalogue at Pierre Matisse Gallery, May 1958. Blue ballpoint pen on cardboard; 26.1 x 42 cm. Fondation Giacometti
CLEVELAND, SEATTLE, AND HOUSTON ONLY
page 122 top

Man, Tree, and Mountain, 1958. Oil on canvas; 60 x 80 cm. Fondation Giacometti
page 179

After Photographic Portraits of Jacques Duclos in L'Express, *no. 889, November 27, 1958*, c. November 1958. Blue and black ballpoint pen on newspaper; magazine open: 42.8 x 59.6 cm. Fondation Giacometti
NELSON-ATKINS ONLY
page 126

Copy after Cimabue, Santa Trinita Maestà, c. 1958. Blue ballpoint pen on paper; 32.4 x 25.6 cm. Fondation Giacometti
CLEVELAND, SEATTLE, AND HOUSTON ONLY
page 123

Head on a Base (known as *Head without Skull*), c. 1958. Bronze; 43.3 x 8.1 x 10.6 cm. Fondation Giacometti
page 156

Project for the Chase Manhattan Plaza: Walking Man, Standing Woman, Head on a Base, 1959. Bronze; *Walking Man*: 7.3 x 1.2 x 8.5 cm; *Standing Woman*: 10.5 x 3.9 x 2.6 cm; *Head on a Base*: 6.1 x 1.3 x 1.8 cm. Fondation Giacometti
page 204

Walking Men and Standing Figures, 1959. Blue ink on paper; 20.7 x 26.8 cm. Fondation Giacometti
CLEVELAND, SEATTLE, AND HOUSTON ONLY
page 205 top

Standing Woman, Figures, and Heads on the Invitation Card of the Exhibition Hecq, *Galerie Raymond Creuze, April 1959*, c. April 1959. Blue ballpoint pen on invitation card; 23 x 20.5 cm. Fondation Giacometti
CLEVELAND, SEATTLE, AND HOUSTON ONLY
page 207

Head of a Man in Profile, c. 1959. Blue ballpoint pen on paper; 65 x 19.3 cm. Fondation Giacometti
CLEVELAND, SEATTLE, AND HOUSTON ONLY
page 124

The Mother of the Artist in Stampa, c. 1959. Graphite pencil and rubber on paper; 50 x 32.8 cm. Fondation Giacometti
NELSON-ATKINS ONLY
page 85

Walking Man, c. 1959. Blue ballpoint pen on squared paper; 17 x 11 cm. Fondation Giacometti
CLEVELAND, SEATTLE, AND HOUSTON ONLY
page 205 bottom

Head of a Man, 1959–60. Blue ballpoint pen on squared paper; 17 x 10.5 cm. Fondation Giacometti
CLEVELAND, SEATTLE, AND HOUSTON ONLY
page 118 bottom

Walking Man I, 1960. Bronze; 180.5 x 27 x 97 cm. Fondation Giacometti
page 216

Head of a Man, Head of a Woman, and Female Figure Standing on a Letter from the Junior Council of the Museum of Modern Art, c. 1960. Blue ballpoint pen on paper letter; 27.9 x 21.6 cm. Fondation Giacometti
CLEVELAND, SEATTLE, AND HOUSTON ONLY
page 125

Heads of Men, Face and Profile, c. 1960. Blue ballpoint pen on envelope; 15.3 x 22 cm. Fondation Giacometti
NELSON-ATKINS ONLY
page 134 top

Tall Woman IV, 1960–61. Bronze; 270 x 31.5 x 56.5 cm. Fondation Giacometti
page 214

Figurine, 1961. Bronze; 44.4 x 8 x 16.1 cm. Fondation Giacometti
page 103

Illustrations for Pomme endormie *by Léna Leclercq*, 1961. Editions L'Arbalète 1958. Illustrated book with 24 lithographs on Japan paper; book open: 32 x 53 cm. Fondation Giacometti
pages 185–89

Standing Nude, 1961. Oil on canvas; 69 x 49.5 cm. Fondation Giacometti
page 201

Standing Nude II, 1961. Printed by Les Presses de Maeght. Edited by Maeght éditeur, Paris. Lithograph; 76.1 x 56.5 cm. Fondation Giacometti
NELSON-ATKINS ONLY
page 211

Standing Woman, c. 1961. Bronze; 45.4 x 8.1 x 11.2 cm. Fondation Giacometti
page 158

Standing Woman VII *and* Walking Man II, 1961–62. Printed by Les Presses de Maeght Editeur, Paris. Lithograph; sheet: 32.5 x 50.4 cm. Fondation Giacometti
CLEVELAND, SEATTLE, AND HOUSTON ONLY
page 206

Bust of Annette (known as *Venice*), 1962. Bronze; 46.2 x 26.5 x 16.2 cm. Fondation Giacometti
page 166

Bust of Annette VIII, 1962. Bronze; 59 x 28.7 x 22.8 cm. Fondation Giacometti
page 165

Heads and Nudes on the Invitation Card for the Exhibition Georges Braque, dessins, *Galerie Maeght, June 21, 1962*, 1962. Red ballpoint pen on invitation card; 12.5 x 16.1 cm. Fondation Giacometti
NELSON-ATKINS ONLY
page 129

Heads of Men, c. October 1962. Red ballpoint pen on paper; 28.5 x 22.6 cm. Fondation Giacometti
NELSON-ATKINS ONLY
page 130 right

Head of a Man in Masterpieces of Mexican Art, *1962*, c. 1962. Blue ballpoint pen on book; book open: 21 x 32.6 x 3.8 cm. Fondation Giacometti
NELSON-ATKINS ONLY
page 130 left

Heads of Men and a Small Figure, c. 1962. Blue ballpoint pen on envelope; 19.1 x 10.2 cm. Fondation Giacometti
NELSON-ATKINS ONLY
page 131 left

Portrait of a Man; Portrait of Annette, 1963. Blue and black ballpoint pen on notebook; notebook open: 18 x 24.6 cm. Fondation Giacometti
NELSON-ATKINS ONLY
page 132

Standing Nudes on a Page of Combat, *May 20, 1963*, c. May 1963. Ballpoint pen on a detached newspaper page; 52 x 37.6 cm. Fondation Giacometti
CLEVELAND, SEATTLE, AND HOUSTON ONLY
page 212 right

Heads of Men Front and Profile on the Catalogue of the Exhibition Sculptures de Duchamp-Villon, *Galerie Louis Carré, June–July 1963*, c. 1963. Blue and black ballpoint pen on paper; 27.5 x 23.9 cm. Fondation Giacometti
CLEVELAND, SEATTLE, AND HOUSTON ONLY
page 131 right

Heads and Busts on the Front Page of the Lettres Françaises, *no. 991, August 22–28, 1963*, c. August 1963. Blue ballpoint pen on detached newspaper page; 60.5 x 46 cm. Fondation Giacometti
NELSON-ATKINS ONLY
page 133

Heads and Bust of Men, c. 1963. Blue ballpoint pen on letter paper; 14.8 x 21 cm. Fondation Giacometti
CLEVELAND, SEATTLE, AND HOUSTON ONLY
page 122 bottom

Bust of a Man and Snail Shell, 1964. Blue ballpoint pen on envelope; 10.7 x 24.1 cm. Fondation Giacometti
NELSON-ATKINS ONLY
page 134 bottom

Head of a Man (Lotar I), 1964. Bronze; 25.5 x 28.2 x 13.2 cm. Fondation Giacometti
page 135

Bust of a Man (Lotar II), 1964–65. Bronze; 57.8 x 38.2 x 25 cm. Fondation Giacometti
page 174

Landscape in Stampa, 1964–65. Printed by Imprimeries de Maeght. Edited by Maeght éditeur, Paris. Lithograph; sheet: 65.4 x 48 cm. Fondation Giacometti
CLEVELAND, SEATTLE, AND HOUSTON ONLY
page 176

Bust of Annette X, 1965. Bronze; 43.9 x 18.8 x 13.7 cm. Fondation Giacometti
page 168

Bust of a Man (New York I), 1965. Bronze; 53.9 x 29.4 x 17.8 cm. Fondation Giacometti
page 198

Bust of a Man (New York II), 1965. Bronze; 46.9 x 24.5 x 15.9 cm. Fondation Giacometti
page 199

Figurine of London I, 1965. Bronze; 26.5 x 9 x 13.5 cm. Fondation Giacometti
page 159

Half-Length of a Man, 1965. Bronze; 59.1 x 19 x 32.1 cm. Fondation Giacometti
page 200

Head of Annette, 1965. Black ballpoint pen on notepaper; 27 x 21 cm. Fondation Giacometti
CLEVELAND, SEATTLE, AND HOUSTON ONLY
page 127

The Mountain (I), pl. 1, from *Retour Amont* by René Char, 1965. Printed by Atelier Crommelynck. Edited by Guy Levis Mano, Paris. Aquatint on paper; sheet: 38.2 x 28.3 cm. Fondation Giacometti
CLEVELAND, SEATTLE, AND HOUSTON ONLY
page 180

Man in the Rocks I, pl. 3, from *Retour Amont* by René Char, 1965. Printed by Atelier Crommelynck. Edited by Guy Levis Mano, Paris. Aquatint on paper; sheet: 38.2 x 28.3 cm. Fondation Giacometti
CLEVELAND, SEATTLE, AND HOUSTON ONLY
page 181 left

Man on the Precipice Looking into the Void, pl. 4, from *Retour Amont* by René Char, 1965. Printed by Atelier Crommelynck. Edited by Guy Levis Mano, Paris. Aquatint on paper; sheet: 38.2 x 28.3 cm. Fondation Giacometti
CLEVELAND, SEATTLE, AND HOUSTON ONLY
page 181 right

Sculptures in the Studio VII, pl. 28, from *Paris sans fin*, 1969. Printed by Mourlot. Edited by Tériade éditeur, Paris. Lithograph; sheet: 42.5 x 32.5 cm. Fondation Giacometti
page 90

Sculptures in the Studio VIII, pl. 29, from *Paris sans fin*, 1969. Printed by Mourlot. Edited by Tériade éditeur, Paris. Lithograph; sheet: 42.5 x 32.5 cm. Fondation Giacometti
page 99

Sculptures in the Studio IX, pl. 100, from *Paris sans fin*, 1969. Printed by Mourlot. Edited by Tériade éditeur, Paris. Lithograph; sheet: 42.5 x 32.5 cm. Fondation Giacometti
page 94

Sculptures in the Studio X, pl. 101, from *Paris sans fin*, 1969. Printed by Mourlot. Edited by Tériade éditeur, Paris. Lithograph; sheet: 42.5 x 32.5 cm. Fondation Giacometti
page 96

Sculptures in the Studio XI, pl. 128, from *Paris sans fin*, 1969. Printed by Mourlot. Edited by Tériade éditeur, Paris. Lithograph; sheet: 42.5 x 32.5 cm. Fondation Giacometti
page 102

Selected Bibliography

Books

Augais, Thomas. *Giacometti et les écrivains: l'atelier sans fin*. Paris: Classiques Garnier, 2017.

Bonnefoy, Yves. *Alberto Giacometti: biographie d'une œuvre*. Paris: Flammarion, 1991.

Clair, Jean. *Le Nez de Giacometti*. Paris: Gallimard, 2000.

Delmotte, Benjamin. *Le Visible et l'intouchable: la vision et son épreuve phénoménologique dans l'œuvre de Giacometti*. Paris: L'Âge d'Homme, 2016.

Didi-Huberman, Georges. *Le Cube et le visage: autour d'une sculpture d'Alberto Giacometti*. Paris: Macula, 1993.

Du Bouchet, André. *Alberto Giacometti: Dessin*. Paris: Maeght, 1991.

Dufrêne, Thierry. *Giacometti, "Portrait de Jean Genet": le scribe captif*. Paris: Adam Biro, 1991.

———. *Alberto Giacometti: Les Dimensions de la réalité*. Geneva: Skira, 1994.

Dupin, Jacques. *Alberto Giacometti*. Paris: Maeght, 1962.

———. *Alberto Giacometti, textes pour une approche*. Paris: Fourbis, 1991.

———. *Alberto Giacometti*. Tours: Farrago; Léo Scheer, 1999.

Dupin, Jacques, and Ernst Scheidegger. *Alberto Giacometti, éclats d'un portrait*. Marseille: André Dimanche, 2007.

Finck, Michèle. *Giacometti et les poètes: "si tu veux voir, écoute."* Paris: Hermann, 2012.

Fletcher, Valerie. *Alberto Giacometti: The Paintings*. New York: Columbia University, 1994.

Genet, Jean, and Ernst Scheidegger. *L'Atelier d'Alberto Giacometti*. Paris: L'Arbalète, 1963.

Giacometti, Alberto. *Écrits*. Presented by Michel Leiris and Jacques Dupin. Paris: Hermann, 1992.

———. *Écrits: Articles, notes et entretiens*. Paris: Hermann and Fondation Giacometti, 2007.

———. *Why I am a sculptor*. Paris: Hermann and Fondation Giacometti, 2017.

———. *Paris sans fin*. Preface by Mathilde Lecuyer-Maillé. Paris: Fondation Giacometti; Les Cahiers dessinés, 2018.

———. *The Dream, the Sphinx and the Death of T.* Paris: Hermann and Fondation Giacometti, 2021.

———. *I certainly practise painting*. Paris: Hermann and Fondation Giacometti, 2021.

———. *Notes on the copies*. Paris: Hermann and Fondation Giacometti, 2021.

Giacometti, Alberto, and Isabel Nicholas. *Correspondances*. Paris: Fondation Giacometti; Lyon: Fage, 2007.

Grenier, Catherine. *Alberto Giacometti: A Biography*. Paris: Flammarion, 2018.

Hohl, Reinhold. *Alberto Giacometti*. New York: Abrams, 1972.

Klemm, Christian. *Die Sammlung der Alberto Giacometti-Stiftung*. Zurich: Zürcher Kunstgesellschaft, 1990.

Lamarche-Vadel, Bernard. *Alberto Giacometti*. Paris: Nouvelles Éditions Françaises, 1984.

Leiris, Michel. *Pierres pour un Alberto Giacometti*. Paris: L'Échoppe, 1992.

Lord, James. *A Giacometti Portrait*. New York: Museum of Modern Art, 1965.

———. *Giacometti: A Biography*. New York: Farrar, Straus, Giroux, 1985.

Matter, Mercedes, and Herbert Matter. *Alberto Giacometti*. New York: Abrams, 1987.

Pleynet, Marcelin. *Les Modernes et la tradition*. Paris: Gallimard, 1990.

———. *Giacometti: "le jamais vu."* Paris: Dilecta, 2007.

Schneider, Pierre. *Alberto Giacometti: un pur exercice optique*. Paris: Hazan, 2007.

Soavi, Giorgio. *Giacometti: la ressemblance impossible*. Monaco: A. Sauvet, 1991.

Sylvester, David. *Looking at Giacometti*. New York: Henry Holt, 1994.

Wilson, Laurie. *Alberto Giacometti: Myth, Magic, and the Man*. New Haven, CT: Yale University Press, 2003.

Yanaihara, Isaku. *Avec Giacometti*. Paris: Allia, 2015.

Exhibition Catalogues

Giacometti. Text by Franz Meyer. Kunsthalle Basel, June 25–August 28, 1966. Basel: Kunsthalle Basel, 1966.

Alberto Giacometti. Texts by Jacques Dupin and Michel Leiris. Fondation Maeght, July 8–September 30, 1978. Saint-Paul-de-Vence: Fondation Maeght, 1978.

Giacometti's Paris. Arts Council of Great Britain, October 4–26, 1980. London: Arts Council of Great Britain, 1980.

Alberto Giacometti's Woman with Her Throat Cut, 1932. Edinburgh: Scottish National Gallery of Modern Art, 1980.

Giacometti: Sculptures, Paintings, Drawings. Serpentine Gallery, April 10–May 17, 1981. London: Arts Council of Great Britain, 1981.

Alberto Giacometti. Fondation Pierre Gianadda, May 16–November 2, 1986. Martigny: Fondation Pierre Gianadda, 1986.

Alberto Giacometti: retour à la figuration, 1933–1947. Texts by Christian Derouet, Hendel Teicher, and Marthe Ridart. Musée Rath, July 3–September 28, 1986; Musée national d'art moderne, October 15, 1986–January 5, 1987. Paris: Centre Georges Pompidou, 1986.

Alberto Giacometti: The Artist's Studio. Tate Gallery, March 20–December 29, 1991. London: Tate Gallery, 1991.

Alberto Giacometti: sculptures, peintures, dessins. Musée d'art moderne de la Ville de Paris, November 30, 1991–March 15, 1992. Paris: Paris Musées, 1991.

Bourdelle et ses élèves: Giacometti, Richier, Gutfreund. Musée Bourdelle, October 28, 1998–February 7, 1999. Paris: Paris Musées, 1998.

Alberto Giacometti: la collection du Centre Georges Pompidou, Musée national d'art moderne. Musée national d'art moderne, March 17–June 27, 1999. Paris: Centre Georges Pompidou–Réunion des musées nationaux, 1999.

Les Figures de la marche: un siècle d'arpenteurs. Texts by Maurice Fréchuret, Daniel Arasse, Patricia Falguières, et al. Musée national Picasso-Paris, July 1, 2000–January 14, 2001. Paris: Réunion des musées nationaux, 2000.

Alberto Giacometti: le dessin à l'œuvre. Centre Georges Pompidou, January 24–April 9, 2001. Paris: Gallimard; Centre Georges Pompidou, 2001.

Alberto Giacometti. Texts by Tobia Bezzola, Carolyn Lanchner, and Anne Umland. Museum of Modern Art, October 11, 2001–January 8, 2002. New York: Museum of Modern Art, 2001.

L'Atelier d'Alberto Giacometti: collection de la fondation Alberto et Annette Giacometti. Centre Georges Pompidou, October 17, 2007–February 11, 2008. Paris: Centre Georges Pompidou, 2007.

Giacometti: Der Ägypter. Texts by Christian Klemm and Dietrich Wildung. Staatliche Museen zu Berlin, October 29, 2008–February 15, 2009; Kunsthaus Zurich, February 27–May 24, 2009. Munich: Deutscher Kunstverlag, 2008.

Giacometti, Balthus, Skira: les années Labyrinthe, 1944–1946. Musée Rath, April 9–July 5, 2009. Geneva: Musées d'art et d'histoire, 2009.

Alberto Giacometti. Musée Rath, November 5, 2009–February 21, 2010. Zurich: JRP Ringier; Geneva: Musée d'art et d'histoire, 2009.

Giacometti & Maeght: 1946–1966. Fondation Maeght, June 27–October 31, 2010. Saint-Paul-de-Vence: Fondation Maeght, 2010.

Alberto Giacometti: espace, tête, figure. Texts by Richard Leydier, Hélène Vincent, and Véronique Wiesinger. Musée de Grenoble, March 9–June 9, 2013. Arles: Actes Sud, 2013.

Alberto Giacometti. Les Capucins, June 14–October 25, 2015. Landerneau: Fonds Hélène & Édouard Leclerc pour la culture; Paris: Fondation Giacometti, 2015.

Picasso–Giacometti. Musée national Picasso-Paris, October 4, 2016–February 5, 2017. Paris: Flammarion; Musée national Picasso-Paris, 2016.

Alberto Giacometti: Beyond Bronze; Masterworks in Plaster and Other Materials. Texts by Philippe Buttner, Casimiro Di Crescenzo, and Catherine Grenier. Kunsthaus Zurich, October 28, 2016–January 15, 2017. Zurich: Kunsthaus Zurich; Scheidegger & Spiess, 2016.

Giacometti. Texts by Lena Fritsch, Frances Morris, Catherine Grenier, and Mathilde Lécuyer. Tate Modern, May 10–September 10, 2017. London: Tate Publishing, 2017.

Derain, Balthus, Giacometti: une amitié artistique. Musée d'art moderne de la Ville de Paris, June 2–October 29, 2017. Paris: Paris Musées, 2017.

Giacometti, the Late Work. Galerie Lympia, June 23–October 15, 2017. Ghent: Editions Snoeck; Paris: Fondation Giacometti, 2017.

Bacon–Giacometti. Texts by Catherine Grenier, Ulf Küster, Michael Peppiatt, and Hugo Daniel. Fondation Beyeler, April 29–September 2, 2018. Berlin: Hatje Cantz, 2018.

Giacometti. Texts by Valerie Fletcher, Catherine Grenier, and Karole P. B. Vail. Solomon R. Guggenheim Museum, June 8–September 12, 2018. New York: Solomon R. Guggenheim Museum; Paris: Fondation Giacometti, 2018.

Giacometti–Genet: The Studio of Alberto Giacometti Seen by Jean Genet. Texts by Albert Dichy and Thierry Dufrêne. Institut Giacometti, June 21–September 16, 2018. Paris: Fondation Giacometti; Lyon: Fage, 2018.

Giacometti: entre tradition et avant-garde. Musée Maillol, September 14, 2018–January 20, 2019. Brussels: Fonds Mercator, 2018.

Alberto Giacometti, Annette Messager: nos Chambres. Texts by Christian Alandete, Catherine Grenier, and Marie Darrieussecq. Institut Giacometti, October 16, 2018–January 13, 2019. Paris: Fondation Giacometti; Lyon: Fage, 2018.

Alberto Giacometti—Teresa Hubbard / Alexander Birchler: Flora. Institut Giacometti, April 5–June 9, 2019. Paris: Fondation Giacometti; Lyon: Fage, 2019.

Rodin–Giacometti. Preface by Catherine Chevillot and Catherine Grenier. Fondation Pierre Gianadda, June 27–November 24, 2019. Martigny: Fondation Pierre Gianadda, 2019.

Giacometti–Sade: Cruel Objects of Desire. Institut Giacometti, November 21, 2019–February 9, 2020. Paris: Fondation Giacometti; Lyon: Fage, 2019.

Alberto Giacometti: The Walking Man. Institut Giacometti, July 4–November 29, 2020. Paris: Fondation Giacometti; Lyon: Fage, 2020.

Alberto Giacometti: Face to Face. Moderna Museet, October 10, 2020–May 30, 2021. Paris: Fondation Giacometti; Munich: Hirmer, 2020.

Alberto Giacometti, L'humanité absolue. La Cité Miroir, October 17, 2020–February 15, 2021. Liège: Mnema; La Cité Miroir, 2020.

Giacometti, Beckett: Rater encore; Rater mieux. Institut Giacometti, January 7–June 8, 2021. Paris: Fondation Giacometti; Lyon: Fage, 2021.

Giacometti and Ancient Egypt. Institut Giacometti, June 22–October 10, 2021. Paris: Fondation Giacometti; Lyon: Fage, 2021.

Alberto Giacometti, Marvellous Reality: A Retrospective. Grimaldi Forum, July 3–August 29, 2021. Paris: Fondation Giacometti and Skira; Monaco: Grimaldi Forum, 2021.

Alberto Giacometti / Barbara Chase-Riboud–Femmes Debout de Venise / Standing Women of Venice–Femme Noire Debout de Venise / Standing Black Woman of Venice. Institut Giacometti, October 20, 2021–January 9, 2022. Paris: Fondation Giacometti; Lyon: Fage, 2021.

Contributors

Émilie Bouvard
Director of Collections and Scientific Programme, Fondation Giacometti

Serena Bucalo-Mussely
Curator, Fondation Giacometti

Hugo Daniel
Head of the School of Modernities Programs and Associate Curator, Fondation Giacometti

Ann Dumas
Curator of European Art, Museum of Fine Arts, Houston

Catherine Grenier
Director of the Fondation Giacometti and President of the Giacometti Institute

Catharina Manchanda
Jon and Mary Shirley Curator of Modern and Contemporary Art, Seattle Art Museum

Romain Perrin
Associate Curator, Fondation Giacometti

William H. Robinson
Senior Curator of Modern Art, The Cleveland Museum of Art

William Keyse Rudolph
Deputy Director of Curatorial Affairs, The Nelson-Atkins Museum of Art, Kansas City

Fondation Giacometti

Direction

Catherine Grenier
Director of the Fondation Giacometti and President of the Giacometti Institute

Soizic Wattinne
Deputy Director

Céline Suer
Executive Assistant

Giacometti Institute

Christian Alandete
Artistic Director

Stéphanie Barbé-Sicouri
Administrator

Hugo Daniel
Head of the School of Modernities Programs and Associate Curator

Alice Martel
Manager of Public Programs and Mediation

Sandra Jouffroy
Operations Officer

Collection, Research, and Exhibitions

Émilie Bouvard
Director of Collections and Scientific Programme

Serena Bucalo-Mussely
Curator

Thierry Pautot
Head of Research
Associate Curator

Romain Perrin
Associate Curator

Collection and Exhibitions Management

Alban Chaine
Head of Registrars
Collection Manager

Clara Gibertoni
Registrar

Exhibitions Coordination and Publications

Philippe de Saint Martin Beyrie
Exhibition Coordination
Publication Officer

Legal Affairs

Émilie Le Mappian
Head of Legal Affairs

Communication

Anne-Marie Pereira
Press Officer

Administration Council

Didier Semin
President

Olivier Le Grand
Honorary President

Margit Rowell
Vice President

Thibault De Roquemaurel
Treasurer

Christian Klemm
Representative of the Alberto Giacometti-Stiftung

Estelle Guille Des Buttes
Representative of the Ministry of Culture

Dominique Dalmas
Representative of the Ministry of the Interior

Juliane Cosandier
Qualified Personality

Albert Lœb
Qualified Personality

Henri Loyrette
Qualified Personality

Jean-Louis Missika
Qualified Personality

Boards of Trustees

The Cleveland Museum of Art

Seattle Art Museum

The Museum of Fine Arts, Houston

Nelson-Atkins Museum of Art

Alberto Giacometti, sculptor, Paris, March 6, 1958
Richard Avedon (American, 1923–2004). Archives, Fondation Giacometti. © The Richard Avedon Foundation

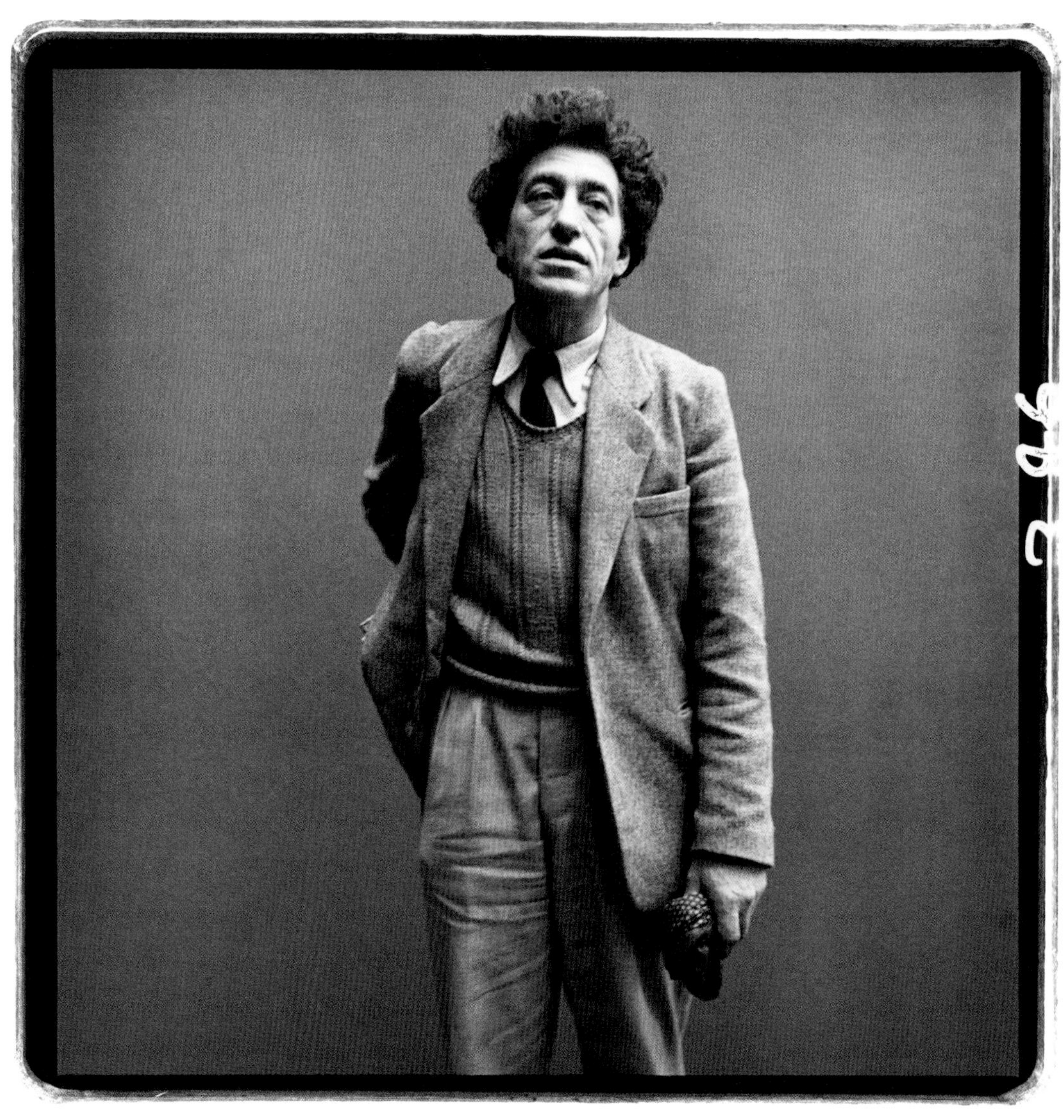